396-413
134-155
156-186

A COMPLETE

FOUNDATIONS

LIBRARY OF

FOR BIBLICAL

TOOLS AND RESOURCES

INTERPRETATION

A COMPLETE

FOUNDATIONS

LIBRARY OF

FOR BIBLICAL

TOOLS AND RESOURCES

INTERPRETATION

DAVID S. DOCKERY • KENNETH A. MATHEWS • ROBERT B. SLOAN

BROADMAN
& HOLMAN
PUBLISHERS

Nashville, Tennessee

4210-39
0-8054-1039-2

Dewey Decimal Classification: 220.07
Subject Heading: BIBLE—STUDY \ BIBLE—HISTORY
Library of Congress Card Catalog Number: 94-9693

Library of Congress Cataloging-in-Publication Data
Foundations for biblical interpretation / edited by David S. Dockery, Kenneth A. Mathews, Robert B. Sloan.
    p. cm.
Includes bibliographical references and index.
ISBN 0-8054-1039-2
    1. Bible—Hermeneutics.   I. Dockery, David. S.   II.
Mathews, K. A. III. Sloan, Robert Bryan, 1949– .
BS476.F67   1994
220.6'01.X—dc20   94-9693
                                           CIP

TO OUR TEACHERS WHO
TAUGHT US TO LOVE GOD'S WORD

CONTRIBUTORS

Linda L. Belleville, assistant professor of biblical literature, North Park Theological Seminary, Chicago, Ill.

David Alan Black, author and lecturer, LaMirada, Calif.

Craig L. Blomberg, associate professor of New Testament, Denver Theological Seminary, Denver, Colo.

Darrell L. Bock, professor of New Testament, Dallas Theological Seminary.

Chris Church, assistant professor of philosophy and religion, Union University, Baptist Memorial Hospital Campus, Memphis, Tenn.

E. Ray Clendenen, general editor, *New American Commentary*, Broadman & Holman Publishers, Nashville, Tenn.

Bruce Corley, dean of the School of Theology and professor of New Testament, Southwestern Baptist Theological Seminary, Fort Worth, Tex.

David S. Dockery, vice president for academic administration and dean of the School of Theology, Southern Baptist Theological Seminary, Louisville, Ky.

Millard J. Erickson, research professor of theology, Southwestern Baptist Theological Seminary, Fort Worth, Tex.

Donald L. Fowler, pastor, Harrison Center Church, Etna Green, Ind.

Duane A. Garrett, professor of Old Testament and Hebrew, Canadian Southern Baptist Seminary, Cochrane, Alberta.

Harold W. Hoehner, department chairman of New Testament, Dallas Theological Seminary.

Paul R. House, associate professor of biblical studies, Taylor University, Upland, Ind.

Walter C. Kaiser, Colman M. Mockler distinguished professor of Old Testament and director of the program in the biblical foundation for ethics, Gordon-Conwell Theological Seminary, South Hamilton, Mass.

Kenneth A. Mathews, professor of divinity, Beeson Divinity School, Samford University, Birmingham, Ala.

Richard R. Melick, Jr., president, Criswell College, Dallas.

John B. Polhill, James Buchanan Harrison professor of New Testament interpretation and associate dean of the School of Theology, Southern Baptist Theological Seminary, Louisville, Ky.

Leland Ryken, chairman of the English department and professor of English, Wheaton College, Wheaton, Ill.

Keith N. Schoville, professor of Hebrew and semitic studies, University of Wisconsin-Madison.

Mark A. Seifrid, assistant professor of New Testament interpretation, Southern Baptist Theological Seminary, Louisville, Ky.

Robert B. Sloan, dean, George W. Truett Theological Seminary, Baylor University, Waco, Tex.

Marsha A. Ellis Smith, associate vice-president for academic administration, Southern Baptist Theological Seminary, Louisville, Ky.

J. A. Thompson, retired, former director of the Australian Institute of Archaeology in Melbourne and lecturer in the former department of Middle Eastern studies at the University of Melbourne.

Bruce K. Waltke, professor of Old Testament studies, Regent College, Vancouver, British Columbia.

John H. Walton, professor of Bible theology, Moody Bible Institute, Chicago, Ill.

James Emery White, pastor, Mecklenburg Community Church, Charlotte, N.C.

Edwin M. Yamauchi, professor of history, Miami University, Oxford, Ohio.

CONTENTS

CONTENTS

ABBREVIATIONS

ABD	*Anchor Bible Dictionary*
ACNT	Augsburg Commentary on the New Testament
AEL	*Ancient Egyptian Literaure*, M. Lichtheim. 1971–80, 3 vols. Berkeley
AIR	*Ancient Israelite Religion: Essays in Honor of Frank Moore Cross*, ed. P. D. Miller, P. D. Hanson, and S. D. McBride. Philadelphia, 1987
ANET	*Ancient Near Eastern Texts Relating to the Old Testament*, 3d ed. with suppl., ed. J. B. Pritchard, Princeton, 1969
ANRW	*Aufstieg und Niedergang der römischen Welt*, ed. H. Temporini and W. Hause, Berlin, 1972–
ArOr	*Archiv orientální*
BA	*Biblical Archaeologist*
BAR	*Biblical Archaeologist Reader*
BARev	*Biblical Archaeology Review*
BASOR	*Bulletin of the America Schools of Oriental Research*
BBR	*Bulletin of Biblical Research*
Bib	*Biblica*
BJRL	*Bulletin of the John Rylands University Library of Manchester*
BSac	*Bibliotheca Sacra*
BT	*The Bible Translator*
BWDBA	*The Biblical World: A Dictionary of Biblical Archaeology*
BZAW	Beihefte zur ZAW
CAH	*Cambridge Ancient History*
CBQ	*Catholic Biblical Quarterly*
CBQMS	Catholic Biblical Quarterly Monograph Series
CHB	*The Cambridge History of the Bible*, 3 vols., ed. P. R. Ackroyd, G. W. M. Lampe, and S. L. Greenslade. Cambridge, 1963–70
CML	*Canaanite Myths and Legends*, J. C. L. Gibson. Edinburgh, 1977
CRINT	Compendia rerum iudaicarum ad novum testamentum
CTR	*Criswell Theological Review*
EAEHL	*Encyclopedia of Archeological Excavations in the Holy Land*, 4 vols., ed. M. Avi-Yonah, 1975 ed. C. F. Pfeiffer, Grand Rapids, 1966

EDNT   *Exegetical Dictionary of the New Testament*, ed. Horst Balz and Gerhad Schneider, Grand Rapids, 1990

EncJud   *Encyclopaedia Judaica* (1971)

EvQ   *Evangelical Quarterly*

ExpTim   *Expository Times*

GTJ   *Grace Theological Journal*

HAR   Hebrew Annual Review

HBBCMR   *The Holman Book of Biblical Charts, Maps, and Reconstructions*, ed. M. A. Ellis Smith, Nashville, 1993

HBD   *Harper's Bible Dictionary*, ed. P. J. Achtemeier, San Francisco, 1985

HBH   *The Holman Bible Handbook*, ed. D. S. Dockery, Nashville, 1992

HBT   *Horizons in Biblical Theology*

HDB   *Dictionary of the Bible*, 4 vols. ed. by J. Hastings et al. Dinburgh and New York, 1899–1904, Rev. by F. C. Grant and H. H. Rowley, 1963

HolBD   *Holman Bible Dictionary*, ed. T. C. Butler, Nashville, 1991

HSM   Harvard Semitic Monographs

HTS   Harvard Theological Series

HUCA   *Hebrew Union College Annual*

IBD   *The Illustrated Bible Dictionary*, 3 vols. Wheaton, 1980

IBHS   *An Introduction to Biblical Hebrew Syntax*, B. K. Waltke and M. O'Connor, Winona Lake, Ind.,1990

ICC   International Critical Commentary

IDB   *Interpreter's Dictionary of the Bible*, ed. G. A. Buttrick, 4 vols. Nashville, 1962

IDBSup   Interterpreter's Dictionary of the Bible Supplementary Volume, ed. K. Crim. Nashville, 1976

IEJ   *Israel Exploration Journal*

Int   *Interpretation*

IOS   *Israel Oriental Studies*

ISBE   *International Standard Bible Encyclopedia*, 2d ed., ed. G. W. Bromiley

JAAR   *Journal of the American Academy of Religion*

JANES   *Journal of the Ancient Near Eastern Society of Columbia University*

JBC   *The Jerome Biblical Commentary*, ed. R. E. Brown, J. A. Fitzmyer, and R. E. Murphy, 2 vols. in 1. Englewood, N.J., 1968.

JBL   *Journal of Biblical Literature*

JBR   *Journal of Bible and Religion*

JEA	*Journal of Egyptian Archaeology*
JETS	*Journal of the Evangelical Theological Society*
JJS	*Journal of Jewish Studies*
JLAS	*Journal of the Linguistic Association of the Southwest*
JNSL	*Journal of Northwest Semitic Languages*
JSJ	*Journal for the Study of Judaism*
JSNT	*Journal for the Study of the New Testament*
JSOTSup	Journal for the Study of the Old Testament Supplement Series
JSS	*Journal of Semitic Studies*
JTS	*Journal of Theological Studies*
JTSoA	*Journal of Theology for Southern Africa*
KB	*Lexicon in Veteris Testamenti libros*, L. Koehler and W. Baumgartner, 1953
MTS	Marburger Theologische Studien
NAC	New American Commentary
NDT	*New Dictionary of Theology*, ed. Sinclair B. Ferguson, D. F. Wright, J. I. Packer. Leiciester, England, 1988
NERT	*Near Eastern Religious Texts Relating to the Old Testament*, W. Beyerlin, ed., trans. John Bowden, Philadelphia, 1978
NICOT	New International Commentary on the Old Testament
NIDBA	*The New International Dictionary of Biblical Archaeology*, Grand Rapids, 1983
NovT	*Novum Testamentum*
NTS	*New Testament Studies*
OCD	*Oxford Classical Dictionary*
OrAnt	*Oriens antiquus*
OTL	Old Testament Library
PTR	*Princeton Theological Review*
QHBT	*Qumran and the History of the Biblical Text*, ed. F. M. Cross and S. Talmon, Cambridge, Mass., 1975
RevExp	*Review and Expositor*
SBLDS	Society of Biblical Literature Dissertation Series
SBLMS	Society of Biblical Literature Monograph Series
SBLRBS	Society of Biblical Literature: Resources for Biblical Study
SBT	*Studies in Biblical Theology*
SCS	*Septuagint and Cognate Studies*
Semeia	*Semeia*
SJT	*Scottish Journal of Theology*
SNTSMS	Society for New Testament Studies Monograph Series

TDNT	*Theological Dictionary of the New Testament*, 10 vols., ed. G. Kittel and G. Friedrich. Trans. G. W. Bromiley. Grand Rapids, 1964–76
TDOT	*Theological Dictionary of the Old Testament*, ed. G. J. Botterweck, H. Ringgren, and H. J. Fabry. Trans. J. T. Willis, G. W. Bromiley, and D. E. Green. Grand Rapids, 1974–
ThEd	*Theological Educator*
Them	*Themelios*
TJ	*Trinity Journal*
TOTC	Tyndale Old Testament Commentary
TWAT	*Theologisches Wörterbuch zum Alten Testament*, ed. G. J. Botterweck, H. Ringgren, and H. J. Fabry. Stuttgart, 1970–
TynBul	*Tyndale Bulletin*
VE	*Vox Evangilica*
VT	*Vetus Testamentum*
VTSup	Vetus Testamentum Supplements
WBC	World Biblical Commentary
WTJ	*Westminster Theological Journal*
WUNT	Wissenschaftliche Untersuchungen zum Neuen Testament
ZÄS	*Zeitschrift für Ägyptische Sprache und Altertumskunde*
ZAW	*Zeitschrift für die alttestamentliche Wissenschaft*, Berlin
ZPEB	*The Zondervan Pictorial Encyclopedia of the Bible*, 5 vols. ed. M. C. Tenney. Grand Rapids, 1975

PREFACE

The psalmist tells us that God's Word is a lamp to our feet and light to our path (Ps. 119:105). The contributors to this volume wholeheartedly affirm that testimony concerning the Holy Scriptures. It is because we believe the Bible is God's Word to His people that we have worked together to create this volume. All the contributors affirm the complete veracity and total authority of the Bible. Since this is the case, we believe it is important that the Bible be studied and applied properly. All of us, like the readers of this volume, face the challenge of what it means to hear and obey God's Word, to learn it, and to put it into practice. In order to interpret the Bible correctly we recognize the need to understand historical background material, cultural issues and contexts, ancient languages, hermeneutical practices, and the theological significance of the biblical text.

In the fall of 1990 we gathered to plan this volume to supplement other projects (*Holman Bible Handbook* and the *New American Commentary*) with which we were all involved at the time. Out of that meeting we assembled together a team of experts in various fields who could address the important issues related to biblical interpretation.

The volume is intended to be an introductory textbook for beginning students in college and seminary, but it can also serve as an update for ministers and Bible teachers as well. We also have attempted to make the book as user-friendly as possible so it can be used by laypersons and Sunday School teachers. We hope that we have put together a volume that can be employed in various areas of study.

It is our prayer that through the study of this book people will grow to love the Scriptures and seek to apply them more faithfully to their lives, to interpret them with greater clarity, and to teach and proclaim them more fervently.

We are each grateful to the people who have helped to bring this volume to its final form. We especially would like to offer thanks to Art Toalston and Amanda Sauer for their numerous hours of editorial work that have helped to bring coherence to the volume. We are indebted to the Broadman & Holman staff for their oversight of this project. The book would not have been possible without the capable editorial team of Frank Wm. White, Leslie Joslin, Lisa Parnell, Lee Ellis, Trina Hollister, Linda Scott, and Marc Jolly. As always, we are grateful to our families who sacrificed their time in order for us to work on this important project. We pray it will be used for the good of God's people and for His eternal glory.

Soli Deo Gloria,

The Editors

PART I

GENERAL ARTICLES

I

REVELATION

MILLARD J. ERICKSON

Revelation refers to God's action of making Himself known to humans. This action is necessary because humans, being limited, are unable to know God by their own ability of discovery. Just as dogs or cats cannot investigate their master, and if they could, would not really understand him, so humans do not have the capability of finding God by their own effort. Because God loves His human creatures and wants to have fellowship with them, He has therefore made Himself known.

This may not immediately seem to be true. Are there not, after all, persons who discover God simply by studying or at least observing nature, without any special revelatory action by Him? This, however, assumes that the discovery is really a human accomplishment, with God being simply passive in all of this. For even truth derived from nature is there because God has placed it there. This is known as general revelation.

GENERAL REVELATION

Revelation may be classified as general or special. General revelation is knowledge of God which He has made available to all persons at all times and places. It is general both in its universal availability and in the nature of its content. This general revelation is usually understood as having come through three avenues.

AVENUES OF GENERAL REVELATION

Nature. The first is God's self-manifestation in nature. There are abundant biblical references to this, especially the nature Psalms. Psalm 19, for example, says, "The heavens are telling the glory of God" (Ps. 19:1).* Paul referred to this revelation in Romans chapter 1; he spoke of the witness to God in the creation, which gives evidence of His power and deity (v. 19–20).

History. The second avenue of this general revelation is the events of general history. Here the providential hand of God can be seen by anyone who observes it. The remarkable preservation of the people of Israel in the face of concerted opposition over the years is the most striking form of this, of course. Some would see in the recent collapse of communism in Eastern Europe a similar indication of God's work. While any given event of history is not in actual practice available to everyone, there are actions of God in various segments of the world's society which witness to His reality and working. He, after all, is the God who gives victory and prosperity to one nation and defeat and obscurity to another (Dan. 2:21; Isa. 10:13).

Human Nature. The third avenue of general revelation lies in the nature of the human, all humans. All have been made in the image of God, and this apparently has not been destroyed by the fall, since humans are still referred to as being in the image of God in Genesis 9:6. Consequently, we should expect that there would be some basis for humans finding evidence of God within themselves. This is seen in the moral nature of humans.

Each human has a sense that there is such a thing as right and wrong. This is not a knowledge necessarily of what is right and what is wrong, but that there is such a distinction. This is the thrust of what Paul is saying in Romans 2:12–16 about the Gentiles who have the law written upon their hearts. He is not saying they have the entire code, so that they need not consult the special revelation, but that they know there is such a thing as right and wrong and there is a distinction between these two. This is a sense of oughtness, of obligation to God.

A number of theologians and philosophers have developed this concept into an argument. One of the first was Immanuel Kant, who, having rejected the idea of a theoretical knowledge of God, nonetheless said there

---

* Unless otherwise noted, Scripture quotations in this chapter are from the NASB.

were two things which impressed him: the starry heavens above and the moral law within. In more recent times, C. S. Lewis argued for this from a somewhat different perspective.[1]

THE POSSIBILITY OF NATURAL THEOLOGY

The Affirmative Position. One major theological issue concerning general revelation is whether it is possible to develop a natural theology from its data. There have been widely varied responses. Some have adopted the position that God's existence can be objectively proved, rationally, to anyone willing and able to examine the evidence. The major formulation of the position was made by Thomas Aquinas, the great theologian of the Catholic Church. Thomas formulated a fivefold proof for the existence of God, based upon the evidence of sensory experience. One was that everything must have a cause; therefore, the earth, or more correctly, the universe, must have a cause—a first cause—which is called God. Another was his argument for design, which says that within nature everything which shows adaptiveness to a purpose has had a designer; therefore, the world, which also shows signs of adaptiveness within it, must have had a designer, or God. Thomas and those who have followed him have accepted these arguments, thought to be demonstrably valid or that is, to be provable to any reasonable person willing to inspect the evidence.

The Negative Position. Others have come to exactly the opposite conclusion. Karl Barth argued that there can be no valid natural theology and that there is no valid general revelation, either. He held that knowledge of God, even His existence, is knowledge of His grace and mercy. If, therefore, humans could achieve some knowledge of God apart from the revelation in Christ, it would be a human accomplishment. It would be a human contribution, however small, to one's own salvation. If it were possible to know God outside the gracious revelation in Christ, there would be no need for Christ. It would, in other words, be a form of salvation by works.[2]

In addition to the theological objection raised by Barth and others like him to natural theology, numerous philosophical objections have been posed. One is that these are not purely objective or reasoned arguments. The seemingly certain premises, or first truths, upon which they rest are not undeniable. Upon closer examination, they appear to be assumptions, which some persons make but others do not.

Further, there are contrary data within the universe which the arguments fail to take into account. For example, the argument from design

1. C. S. Lewis, *Mere Christianity* (New York: Macmillan, 1960).
2. Karl Barth, "No!" *Natural Theology*, by Emil Brunner and Karl Barth (London: Bles Centenary, 1946).

draws upon features of the universe which obviously work for human benefit, thus arguing for the existence of a wise and beneficent designer. There are, however, also negative characteristics of the universe which count against this. There are natural evils, including disturbances of nature such as earthquakes, tornadoes, and hurricanes, as well as diseases which cause great human suffering, among them cancer, heart disease, and genetic disorders. There also are moral evils: the suffering, death, and oppression of human beings resulting from human cruelty, selfishness, and mistreatment by others. War, crime, and exploitation are rampant within our society and our world.

When these are taken into account, it is difficult to believe in the existence of a good God. One might have proved either the nonexistence of a good God, or the existence of an evil God. Perhaps this is actually a proof of the existence of the devil, rather than God.

In addition, the arguments seem able to prove only the existence of some sort of powerful being, but not necessarily the personal God of Christianity. How does one argue, for example, from the existence of a finite world, to the existence of an infinite God? An infinite creator is not necessary to account for a finite world. The only thing needed is a being sufficiently powerful to be able to create this world. Nor can we establish that the proof really refers to the same God. That is what Thomas believed he established, but perhaps he actually proved the existence of five different beings.

In light of these criticisms, the natural theology approach seems difficult to maintain. On the other hand, however, radical rejection of general revelation, as presented by Barth and others, also has numerous problems. Not the least of these is the fact that the passages noted above seem to teach rather clearly that there is a genuine witness to God in the creation. The interpretations of those passages rendered by Barth seem strained at best. How are these to be regarded?

A Mediating Position. A mediating position was presented by John Calvin and his theological followers. This position maintains there is a genuine and valid general revelation of God in nature. The Scriptures cited do teach that God has left a witness of Himself. Consequently, when believers see God's hand in nature and in history, they are not simply reading in the knowledge of God obtained from Scripture, doing eisegesis of nature, as it were. They are discovering what God has actually placed there.

Having said this, however, Calvin does not believe it is possible to construct a genuine natural theology from this general revelation. Humans as now constituted do not recognize God in the creation as it is now constituted. That is because of the destructive effects of sin and the fall. These effects are, at least in part, and most pertinently for our purposes here, upon the creation itself. Sin has marred its witness. The created universe came under a curse (Gen. 3:17–19) so that the ground would bring forth thorns and thistles and women would suffer anguish in childbirth. Paul also speaks of how the creation has been subjected to futility because of human sin, and groans and travails, awaiting its liberation (Rom. 8:18–25). Because of the effects upon it of human sin, creation only imperfectly reflects the glory of God, refracting it somewhat, and thus blurring it.

This blurring may not all be a direct result of the fall. It may be partly a result of humanity's continuing unwise and sinful actions. For example, our exploitation of nature has produced serious ecological dislocations. A severely polluted creation does not very clearly set forth God, and a creation, which because of our unwise treatment of it, presents hazards to human health also does not witness very effectively to God's goodness.

Beyond that, however, sin has affected human ability to know the truth. There is ample biblical testimony to this unfortunate fact. In Romans 1:21, Paul says that although men knew God they rejected this knowledge, and the result was spiritual blindness, or inability to recognize the truth. In 2 Corinthians 4:4, Paul attributes this blindness to the work of Satan, saying, "In their case the god of this world has blinded the minds of the unbelievers, to keep them from seeing the light of the gospel of the glory of Christ, who is the likeness of God"(NRSV). Although Paul is speaking in this passage of the ability to recognize and respond to the gospel, it appears appropriate to apply this as negatively affecting the ability to discern God in the creation, as well. Also pertinent are his statements in 1 Corinthians 1:18–29, about how the wisdom of God is foolishness to these persons.

Calvin's response to these two sets of data, namely the biblical witness to divine revelation in the creation and inability of sinful humans to recognize that revelation, is found in his concept of "the spectacles of faith." He draws an analogy between the condition of the sinner relative to the general revelation and the person who has a sight problem. When the latter person looks at an object, it is indistinct and blurry to him. When, however, that person puts on corrective lenses, the difficulty is removed. He can now see clearly what is actually there.

Similarly, says Calvin, when the sinner puts on the spectacles of faith, he can see clearly the general revelation.[3] When such a person is exposed to the special revelation found in the gospel and responds positively, spiritual perception improves. His mind is cleared through the effects of regeneration. He may now see clearly in the creation what was actually there all the while. This was the testimony of the psalmist for whom the heavens were indeed declaring the glory of God.

---

3. John Calvin, *Institutes of the Christian Religion*, book 1, chapter 6, section 1.

It is interesting that the fivefold proof for the existence of God was formulated by a Dominican priest, Thomas Aquinas. What these people were doing was not reading the knowledge of God from Scripture into the creation, but seeing what their faith now enabled them to recognize, the general revelation. All in all, Calvin's position seems to be the most adequate of the three we have examined, both in its ability to fit the biblical data and to fit human experience.

PRACTICAL ISSUES

Salvation Through General Revelation. What we have been considering here is the theological issue of the efficacy of the general revelation, the ability of theologians to discern truth about God from the general revelation. There is also, however, the religious issue, the question of whether persons can and do come to a faith in God through the general revelation that is sufficient to introduce them into a redemptive or saving relationship with Him. There has been a heightened interest in this issue in recent days among theologians.

Although those who do not have the benefit of the special revelation found in the Bible are not able to call upon the name of the Lord—an act Paul says which results in salvation (Rom. 10:13)—can they be saved? Is such conscious and definite or intentional trust in Christ the only way of coming to faith in Him? This is part of the question of the fate of the unevangelized.

Increasing attention has been given to the concept of implicit faith. This is the idea that while salvation rests upon the work of atonement done by Christ, the benefits of that atonement may be experienced by persons who do not know the basis of that salvation. Suppose that someone, under the influence of the witness to God in nature and the inner law that Paul speaks of, comes to believe there exists one good, all-powerful God. Suppose he also concludes that this God has very high standards of expectation of His human creatures. He recognizes that he falls short of what he believes God's standards of spirituality and morality to be, and that he can do nothing by his own effort to satisfy the demands of this supreme being. If, then, he throws himself upon the mercy of this being, offering nothing of his own righteousness but rather simply pleading for a gracious forgiveness, would not God save him? Such a person has an implicit, but not an explicit, faith in Christ. He has the form of the gospel, although lacking its content.[4]

---

4. David K. Clark, "Is Special Revelation Necessary for Salvation?" *Through No Fault of Their Own? The Fate of Those Who Have Never Heard,* ed.William V. Crockett and James G. Sigountos (Grand Rapids: Baker, 1991), 35–45.

Some who argue for this position maintain that the situation of such a person is for all practical purposes the same as that of the Jews prior to the time of Christ. They did not know about Jesus and the form which God's provision for forgiveness of sins would take in His person. They placed their trust immediately in the sacrificial system, which had no power in itself to save. Mediately, however, their faith was in Christ. If they could be saved, why cannot others who do not know of Christ but who have a faith similar to those Jews? These are people who live on this side of Christ's life and death, but who psychologically still live on the other side. They are therefore existentially in the same situation as were those Jews.

The major difference among those who allow for this possibility of salvation through implicit faith is the question of how many will actually come to a saving knowledge of God through this means. Some would question whether any at all actually do, citing passages like Romans 3, where Paul seems to say there are none who are pleasing to God. Others, however, are much more optimistic. One of their arguments is the "Melchizedek factor." This refers to persons, Melchizedek being foremost among them, who appear in the Bible, not being part of the covenant nation of Israel, but who seem to know the true and living God, Jehovah.

How shall this controversy be regarded? This is not simply an issue of what one hopes is the case. All true believers hope for all humans to be saved. The question, however, is what basis we have for this hope. Do we realistically have grounds for believing that many, perhaps very many, will be saved through the general revelation?

We should note that the Bible does not really address this issue very clearly. The impression is that there are few who find the way, even among those who hear the gospel (Matt. 7:14). We note also the scarcity of references to Melchizedek and those like him, and we are not told whether they came to know God from the general revelation or whether God specially revealed Himself to them.

When we examine the world religions, we find they do not include what we would call salvation by grace. They represent various forms of the human attempt to offer something to God on human behalf to obtain His favor. The principle of true salvation by grace seems far from the natural human tendency.

Common Ground Between Christians and Non-Christians. The fact of general revelation provides basis for belief that there is some common ground between nonbelievers on the one hand and believers of the gospel on the other. There is a common set of objective, observable data that can be looked at by both. And there is within the life and heart and experience of each person some basis for contact with God, some element of experience where the person is not totally cut off from sensitivity to divine or tran-

9

scendent things. The believer, in presenting the gospel, will want to look for those points of sensitivity as a place to which to relate the gospel.

Justification of Science. We should note there is incentive here for all forms of science, in the broadest sense of that word. Since the creation has been made by God and has been given its patterns of meaning by Him, all discovery of truth is actually uncovering God's truth. This explains how even unbelievers may have found truth in such areas as ethics, and thus are able to live to some extent, respectable lives. Even this, however, is a product of God's grace, His special grace.

Conflict Between Belief and Unbelief. Finally, we should note that because of the distortion of the general revelation and of the understanding of the persons who would know it, there will be some conflict between the biblical revelation and the understanding of the general revelation offered by unbelievers. We will therefore expect some antithesis between these two and approach the latter with a certain degree of skepticism. And, as Emil Brunner pointed out, as one becomes closer to God, the distortion becomes greater.[5]

General revelation serves an important purpose, but does not satisfy the most important need of humans, namely bringing them into contact with God in a saving relationship. Something more is required.

SPECIAL REVELATION

RELATIONSHIP TO GENERAL REVELATION

Special revelation is distinguished from general revelation in several ways. It is more specific in its content, dealing not only with general or theological truths, but also with particular historical events at specific times and places. It is also particular in the sense of coming to definite individuals or groups, and thus is unavailable to others, unless that revelation is in some way preserved and re-presented to them.

It is rather common to speak of general revelation as inferior to special revelation, in the sense of requiring special revelation for the fulfillment of general revelation. It should be noted, however, that special revelation is also dependent upon general revelation. The concepts involved in the special revelation must be somehow present in the understanding of the recipient of the revelation if it is to make any sense to him or her. The general concepts of God, of love, of trust come to one from the general revelation. While these concepts are relatively empty without the content supplied by the special revelation, it would be impossible to make sense of

---

5. H. Emil Brunner, *Revelation and Reason* (Philadelphia: Westminster, 1946), 383.

that special revelation without the structure or form which the general revelation gives.

CHARACTERISTICS OF SPECIAL REVELATION

Personal. It is helpful first to note the various characteristics of special revelation, or what we might term the style of special revelation. It is, first, personal in nature. This means that it comes to definite persons in time and space. It is not simply a document written by God "to whomever it may concern." Each writer had a definite audience in mind. While the author may not always identify that audience for us, the content of what is written is related to the recipients and their situation.

Anthropic. Further, it is anthropic. It comes to humans and thus bears certain human qualities. It is written in human language and utilizes common everyday terminology and concepts in many cases. At one time, many thought that Koine Greek was a special, heavenly language. We now know that it was simply the common or ordinary household Greek of that time. In this respect, revelation resembles incarnation. Whereas incarnation was the manifestation of the divine person or reality in human form, revelation was the manifestation of divine truth in human form.

Analogical. Third, it is analogical. In order to make divine or heavenly truth intelligible to human beings, God draws upon elements in human experience which resemble or bear an analogy to the divine nature of things being revealed. This analogical character means that our knowledge of God from the revelation is not an exact transcript of His nature, nor is it totally foreign or disparate from the nature of God.[6] This has several implications. One is that even though we are given absolute truth, we as humans do not know or understand it absolutely. There is always room for growth in our understanding of the revelation. A further implication is that language is more analogical when referring to objects we cannot experience, such as God. When the revelation deals with matters less transcendent and thus more overlapping with other disciplines, such as the nature of the human or of sin, more of the univocal element is present, and thus the concepts are less analogical.

MODALITIES OF SPECIAL REVELATION

Having seen something of the style or overall tone or mood of revelation, we next need to look at the modalities, or the different forms or means by which God reveals Himself. There are several of these.[7]

---

6. Bernard Ramm, *Special Revelation and the Word of God* (Grand Rapids: Eerdmans, 1961), 31–52.

7. Ibid., 53–122.

Historical Act. The first is what we may term historical act. This refers to the action of God in historical events which gives some indication of His nature. Sometimes this is large and conspicuous. An example of this would be the Exodus. Here God displayed His power, through the series of plagues by which He persuaded a reluctant Pharoah to release the people of Israel. Several other attributes of God also were displayed in this series of events, however. His faithfulness in delivering His people and maintaining the covenant which He had made with Abraham was one of these. Another was His mercy and care in protecting them from the plague of death which came upon the Egyptians. This is why the Passover is such an important event to the children of Abraham to this day. A less-inclusive event was the provision to Abraham of a sacrificial animal to offer in the place of his son Isaac. Here was a demonstration both of God's sovereignty in requiring the sacrifice of that which was most precious to Abraham and of His mercy in providing a substitute. He also demonstrated His dependability and faithfulness in maintaining His promise of an heir for Abraham.

Divine Speech. A second major modality of revelation is divine speech: the actual communication of truth from God to humans. This may take any one of several forms. It may come as actual audible speech, inaudible speech, or inward hearing. It may come in the form of a dream (a manifestation to the person while unconscious) or of a vision (a similar occurrence, but during the person's consciousness). Finally there is concursive inspiration, in which the Spirit of God guides the writer to record ideas arising within his consciousness, without awareness of the divine origin of the thoughts.

In many cases, this spoken word of God was the interpretation of an event. The "God who acts" emphasis of G. Ernest Wright and others stressed that the event was the locus of revelation and frequently regarded the biblical interpretation of the event as simply meditation upon that. The claim in Scripture, however, is that the interpretation was a divine revelation, not merely insight or reflection by the writer. In most cases the event being interpreted was in the past. In some cases, however, the event was in the future, and the interpretation is known as prophecy. This dimension of revelation as divine speech interpreting events is essential to those events functioning as revelation. Without it, they would be simply mute occurrences, admitting several possible interpretations. The death of Jesus, for example, could be thought of as simply the death of a martyr for his principles. When the meaning is unlocked through the word of interpretation, the opaque event becomes transparent for divine communication.

This occurrence of divine speech is witnessed throughout the Scriptures. Again and again, the writers say, "The word of the Lord came to me, saying, . . ." Examples of this are found in Jeremiah 18:1; Ezekiel 12:1; Hosea 1:1; Joel 1:1; and Amos 3:1. While addressing especially the revelatory role of Christ, the writer to the Hebrews nonetheless also affirms that God had spoken often in times past (Heb. 1:1–2).

Incarnation. The most complete modality of special revelation is incarnation. Here is a case of God's divine speech and divine act being united in one form. Jesus spoke words of divine truth from God. Beyond that, however, He was God actually functioning in the presence of human persons. He could say truly, as He did, "He who has seen Me has seen the Father" (John 14:9). John could write of that which they had seen and heard and their hands had handled (1 John 1:1). Whereas the prophets were men of God sent from the presence of God with a message from God, this was God having come and lived among persons in person. The writer to the Hebrews makes clear that this is a fuller revelation than that which had gone before (1:2).

Scripture. There is, however, one additional derived modality of revelation. This is Scripture as revelation. All of these other modalities involve the communication of truth from God to us. To the extent that the content of that revelation is preserved, we can speak of the resultant product as revelation as well.

This may seem to some to be inaccurate. The Bible reproduces and preserves for us the content of the message given by God; it is therefore God's revelation. If we distinguish revelation as process and revelation as product, then the Bible is genuinely revelation. It is revelation because inspiration is that activity and influence by God upon the Scripture writers such that what they wrote was genuinely the Word of God, preserving the divine revelation.

THEOLOGICAL ISSUES

Revelation, Inspiration, and the Bible. This understanding of special revelation leads to several theological issues. One of these is the relationship of revelation, inspiration, and Scripture. There was special revelation which was not preserved for us in the Bible. In other words, there was special revelation but no inspiration, and so the revelation has not been preserved or inscripturated (John 21:25).

Conversely, however, not all of what is in the Bible is necessarily special revelation. Presumably portions of material found within the Bible were simply matters of public knowledge, such as some of the Old Testament genealogies, which could be included without God having to specially reveal them. It is appropriate, in light of these two considerations, to say that the Bible is not simply coextensive with revelation.

Progressive. The reference to Christ's superiority to earlier revelations calls to mind the fact that revelation is progressive. The later revelation supplements and supercedes the earlier, so that it takes on a significance which the former did not have. It is important that we understand just what progressive revelation means.

Some persons of a more liberal persuasion have seen the earlier as untrue, so that the later displaces or disproves it. Closely tied with this is the idea that the earlier varieties of special revelation are more fully composed of human concepts, or myths, whereas the later are more divinely revealed or refined versions of truth. This assumption, however, is not supported by the Bible itself or by Jesus' statements. Jesus said of the law, "Do not think that I came to abolish the Law or the Prophets; I did not come to abolish, but to fulfil" (Matt. 5:17). An example of this was His references to earlier ethical and moral teachings (Matt. 5:21–22; 27–28). Jesus was not saying that what had been said before was incorrect or not binding, but that it was incomplete. It was true as far as it went, but it did not go far enough. He was telling them that He was taking them a step further in their understanding. With respect to the question of divorce, Moses' practice was indicated as not being the final word, but something of a concession (Matt. 19:7–9).

Correct understanding will keep us from setting up standards of teaching from Scripture without first asking at what point in the process of God's redemptive and revelatory work this teaching was given. We must, in other words, not simply level off all of Scripture and treat it alike. Such leveling leads to practices such as requiring the offering of sacrifices for salvation, or more mildly, worshiping on the seventh day of the week rather than the first. The opposite error is to discard earlier teachings in Scripture as simply outmoded or erroneous and therefore valueless, failing to realize that they, too, contain important truths, if seen within the correct perspective relative to the later writings.

Revelation: Personal and/or Propositional. One major issue which has concerned twentieth-century theology is the nature of revelation itself. Earlier thought had focused upon the question of where revelation is: Is it in the tradition (i.e., the church), in nature, in human experience, or in Scripture? To some extent this was the issue which separated Protestantism from Roman Catholicism and Fundamentalism from Modernism. In the twentieth century, however, the issue was, What is revelation? Specifically, the question became whether revelation is the presentation of information (frequently referred to as "propositional" revelation) or the real presence of the person of God in the experience of the person receiving revelation (or revelation as encounter). The former view was typical of traditional or orthodox theology, while the latter view was especially espoused by "neo-orthodox" theologians such as Karl Barth and Emil Brunner.

Although neo-orthodoxy has long since passed the peak of its popularity and influence, this underlying issue still remains. In part this is due to the renewal of interest in the thought of Barth. But to a greater extent it is a result of the generalized or diffused presence of a more subjective mood in our culture and also in the church and in theology. This particular view was never restricted merely to neo-orthodoxy. It was also found in the thought of such theologians as William Temple.

Actually underlying these two views of revelation are two different views of truth as their presuppositions. Soren Kierkegaard distinguished between objective truth and subjective truth. Objective truth is a quality of the proposition, according to which it corresponds to the state of affairs which it purports to describe. On this basis, a statement is true to the degree that it approximates the object. The less involvement of the subject (the knower), the better. Subjective truth is not a question of what is said, but of how it is said. It is a matter of the way in which the subject, or the knower, is affected by the object. It is therefore a matter of inwardness. To a large extent, the view of revelation espoused by Barth, Brunner, and others was a consequence of adopting the Kierkegaardian view of truth as subjectivity.

On this basis, revelation is not the communication of truths or information, even about God. It is the real personal presentation by God of Himself to us. What God reveals is God, not information about God. And, as a result, the Bible is not revelation. Revelation is the personal presence of God. That cannot be captured in words and ideas and cannot be committed to paper. The Bible is simply a report of the fact that revelation has occurred; it is not revelation and, strictly speaking, is not even a record of that revelation. When God in His sovereignty chooses to encounter the human through that writing, it can be said that in that moment the words of the Bible are the words of God. At other times, they are simply the words of the author or speaker of them. This means, of course, that the words of the Bible cannot simply be quoted to settle issues of true belief or correct action.

This view does not accord with Scripture's own claim, however. Note that in appealing to the Bible we are not assuming that it is a revelation. We are simply quoting it to ascertain the authors' beliefs and teachings. We see that Jesus quoted the Bible of His day as being God's message, and even rested His argument upon details of the text, and said that not even the smallest part of the Scripture could pass away (Matt. 5:18). He regarded Himself as being an objective presence of God, so that He could say, "He who has seen Me has seen the Father" (John 14:9). He could hold His hearers responsible for hearing, by saying, "He who has ears to hear, let him hear" (Matt. 11:15), as if the message was definitely there objectively, irrespective of whether one heard it or not. Peter and John referred to the Holy Spirit having spoken through the mouth of David (Acts 4:25).

There also are certain practical difficulties with this view of nonpropositional revelation. One is the problem of faith. If faith is placing one's trust in the person encountered in revelation, and if God does not reveal truths about Himself, how does one know that indeed it is God that one is encountering? May not one be encountering merely a psychological phenomenon? Although the analogy frequently used of human trust in another human person is helpful, it is limited. For in those situations in which we trust ourselves to our spouse or a friend, it is done only after an assessment, however brief and informal, of the person, to determine that this is indeed the person whom one believes him or her to be. In such intra-human experiences, there is sensory experience of the other person, which we do not have of God, and certainly the neo-orthodox do not claim that we have. The analogy therefore breaks down.

The other problem relates to the issue of theology. How do we get from nonpropositional encounter as revelation to the propositions of theology? This is of special importance to theologians like Barth and Brunner since they engaged in more than one debate over doctrinal issues like the empty tomb or the virgin birth. There is a paradox here, however, for given the view of revelation, it is not possible simply to quote the words of Scripture to settle the issue, as is done on the basis of the orthodox view of informational revelation. Presumably, the answer is that in the encounter with God which constitutes revelation, one knows that this is how God is. Consider, however, a doctrine such as the Trinity. How does one experience God as triune, rather than as simply individual unity? This and a number of other problems suggest the difficulty with the nonpropositional view of revelation.

A better way of formulating the doctrine is to observe that revelation is both personal and propositional. God does not simply reveal information for the purpose of informing. The knowledge of God is for the purpose of relationship. What God reveals is God. But the question must further be asked, How does He reveal Himself? The answer is, at least in part, through revealing information about Himself. He does not merely meet us; He introduces Himself to us and tells us about Himself.[8]

---

8. Edward John Carnell, *The Case for Orthodox Theology* (Philadelphia: Westminster, 1959), 33–35.

Extrabiblical Revelations. One further issue pertains to the question of extrabiblical revelations. As noted above, we do not know from the Bible the basis on which persons such as Melchizedek came into contact with God. Nothing in Scripture necessarily precludes that God may have revealed Himself to them or that He might do so to others today who do not have the possibility of contact with the special revelation as preserved in the Bible.

Prophecy Today. Another related but distinct issue is that of prophecy today. Here the various types of Pentecostal and charismatic Christianity have regarded God as giving special messages to believers having the gift of prophecy. This is often regarded as a "word from God," having equal value with the Bible, or, because it often is an interpretation of the Bible, superior to the Bible. In some cases, it is regarded as a "word of knowledge," sometimes quite specific in nature, indicating who has a particular need of healing or an individual's special spiritual need. It should be noted, however, that with the completion of the canon, we do have a common source of knowledge of God, available to inquiry by anyone. Any claimed knowledge of that should be consistent with it. And while God certainly does give guidance to individuals and groups, this should not be regarded as revelation in the sense of a message to be transferred to others as well.

While we as humans are unable to discover God by our effort, we have the sure Word of God (2 Pet. 1:19–21), revealed by Him and capable of making us wise unto salvation and building us up in the faith (2 Tim. 3:15–17). It will have the effect upon our lives to the extent that we read it, meditate upon it, and act upon its teachings.

FOR FURTHER READING

Baillie, John. *The Idea of Revelation in Recent Thought.* New York: Columbia University, 1956.

Berkouwer, G. C. *General Revelation.* Grand Rapids: Eerdmans, 1955.

Demarest, Bruce A. *General Revelation: Historical Views and Contemporary Issues.* Grand Rapids: Zondervan, 1982.

Dulles, Avery Robert. *Models of Revelation.* Garden City, N.Y.: Doubleday, 1983.

Erickson, Millard J. *Christian Theology,* Vol. 1. Grand Rapids: Baker, 1983

Helm, Paul. *Divine Revelation: The Basic Issues.* Westchester, Ill.: Crossway, 1982.

Henry, Carl F. H. *God, Revelation and Authority.* Vols. 1–4. Waco, Tex.: Word, 1976–79.

———, ed. *Revelation and the Bible.* Grand Rapids: Eerdmans, 1958.

McDonald, H. D. *Theories of Revelation: An Historical Study 1700–1960.* Grand Rapids: Baker, 1979.

Morris, Leon. *I Believe in Revelation: The Basic Issues.* Grand Rapids: Eerdmans, 1976.

Ramm, Bernard. *Special Revelation and the Word of God.* Grand Rapids: Eerdmans, 1961.

II

INSPIRATION AND AUTHORITY OF SCRIPTURE

JAMES EMERY WHITE

The Bible is the single most influential book in the history of civilization. It has been universally praised as a work of great literary achievement and value. Impressive as these accolades are, they fall far short of the greatest distinctive of the Bible—its inspiration by the living God. Because of the Bible's unique origin and nature, it is unlike any book in all of history, carrying unparalleled authority for our life.

INSPIRATION OF SCRIPTURE

The first chapter of this volume explored the concept of revelation. Revelation refers to the original event or word God used to communicate His mind and will. God has revealed Himself to His creation supremely in His Son, Jesus Christ, the Word incarnate. Inspiration is the process by which this original revelation is recorded and communicated to God's people through Holy Scripture.

19

BIBLICAL MATERIALS

The word "inspiration" is from the Greek word *theopneustos*, which literally means "God-breathed" (2 Tim. 3:16).* This is highly significant, for this intimates that the Scriptures are the result of God's creative activity and nature. Discussions of the biblical view of inspiration raise three issues for consideration: Scripture's view of itself, Jesus' view of Scripture, and the issue of New Testament (NT) inspiration.

Scripture's Self-Witness. One of the most consistent themes in the Bible is the idea that God communicates His truth and will to His people. "This is what the Lord, the God of Israel, says" (Ex. 5:1) is a continuing motif throughout the Old Testament (OT). "I have put my words in your mouth," God said to the prophet Jeremiah (Jer. 1:9; cf. Deut. 18:18).

The writers of the NT shared this understanding, viewing the OT as the very Word of God. When the apostle Peter quoted Psalm 2:1, he introduced God's relationship to the verse in the following way: "You spoke by the Holy Spirit through the mouth of your servant, our father David" (Acts 4:25). When Paul quoted Exodus 9:16 he said, "For the Scripture says to Pharoah" (Rom. 9:17). In Exodus 9:16 itself, however, God is the speaker. In Paul's mind, there was no difference between what God said and what Scripture said. When the author of Hebrews quoted Psalm 95:7, the writer said, "So, as the Holy Spirit says: 'Today, if you hear his voice, do not harden your hearts'" (Heb. 3:7).

Perhaps most noteworthy is the reference found in Paul's second letter to Timothy, where Paul writes that "all Scripture is God-breathed" (2 Tim. 3:16). This is highly significant, for it is a blanket endorsement for the inspiration of all of Scripture. In addition, Peter taught that "no prophecy of Scripture came about by the prophet's own interpretation. For prophecy never had its origin in the will of man, but men spoke from God as they were carried along by the Holy Spirit" (2 Pet. 1:20–21).

Jesus' View of Scripture. Jesus clearly held a high view of Scripture as the inspired Word of God. When tempted by Satan, Jesus used Scripture to repel Satan's attacks. Four times Jesus emphatically declared the truth of God over and against the lies of Satan with the words, "It is written" (Matt. 4:1–11). Jesus referred to the words of David in Psalm 110:1 as that which was spoken "by the Spirit" (Matt. 22:43). Jesus declared that the "Scripture cannot be broken" (John 10:35) and reprimanded His disciples following His resurrection for not believing "all that the prophets have spoken" (Luke 24:25). Jesus' high view of Scripture is perhaps best represented when He declared that "until heaven and earth disappear,

---

* Unless otherwise noted, Scripture quotations in this chapter are from NIV.

not the smallest letter, not the least stroke of a pen, will by any means disappear from the Law until everything is accomplished" (Matt. 5:18).[1]

New Testament Inspiration. While the passages in the Bible which refer to the "Scriptures" by and large refer to the OT, Jesus established the groundwork for the NT by bestowing His authority on His disciples. Jesus declared, "He who listens to you listens to me" (Luke 10:16). Further, Jesus said, "the Counselor, the Holy Spirit, whom the Father will send in my name, will teach you all things and will remind you of everything I have said to you" (John 14:26; cf. 15:26; 16:13, 15).

The writers of the NT seemed to understand the special nature of their role and of their writings. Paul wrote to the Corinthians of his conviction that "Christ is speaking through me" (2 Cor. 13:3) and that his teaching was based on the authority of the Holy Spirit (1 Cor. 2:13). When he wrote to the Thessalonians, Paul said he gave continual thanks that they "received the word of God" which they had heard from him "not as the word of men, but as it actually is, the word of God" (1 Thess. 2:13). The apostles were clearly the foundation of the NT church (Eph. 2:20). This was so much the case that by the time of the writing of 2 Peter, the writings of Paul were already noted as Scripture (2 Pet. 3:15–16).[2]

THEORIES OF INSPIRATION

There have been many suggestions as to how the Bible was inspired. The major views can be summarized as follows:

Ecstatic Theory. The ecstatic theory of inspiration suggests the writers of Scripture were like mystics overcome by ecstasy, or who found themselves in a trance, and thus their writing bypassed their rational faculties altogether. This view was present in Hellenistic Judaism and can be found in such early church writers as Philo, Athenagoras, and Tertullian. This view was so slanted toward the divine dimension of Scripture it never received a wide base of support in the church.

Dictation Theory. The theory of mechanical dictation contends the writers of Scripture were seized by the Holy Spirit in such a way that they

---

1. On Jesus and Scripture, see C.A. Evans, "Old Testament in the Gospels" in *Dictionary of Jesus and the Gospels*, ed. by Joel B. Green, Scot McKnight, and I. Howard Marshall (Downers Grove: InterVarsity Press, 1992), 579–90, as well as John W. Wenham's article, "Christ's View of Scripture" in *Inerrancy*, ed. by Norman L. Geisler (Grand Rapids: Academie/Zondervan, 1980), 3–36.

2. For a discussion of the many texts relevant to Scripture's self-attestation, see Wayne A. Grudem, "Scripture's Self-Attestation and the Problem of Formulating a Doctrine of Scripture" in *Scripture and Truth* (Grand Rapids: Academie/Zondervan, 1983), 19–59.

were mechanically controlled. In other words, they were mere stenographers. As a result, their human personalities and contexts were removed from the enterprise altogether. While there are portions of the Bible which may fall under this category, such as God's dictation of the Ten Commandments as recorded in Exodus, these passages are few and far between. In the early church, Chrysostom and Augustine used language which intimated some form of "dictation," but their use of such language was metaphorical. For many years the dictation view was erroneously attributed to evangelical understandings of inspiration, because evangelicals insisted the the biblical writers were completely controlled by the Holy Spirit. Yet, this is far from dictation, a theory of inspiration which has not been part of the evangelical tradition.[3]

Illumination Theory. An illumination view is that the inspiration of Scripture is little more than the inspiration any author has for any literary work. We talk of a novel as being inspired or a piece of music as being inspiring, but little more is meant by this than the manifestation of talent or insight. As a result, this view takes little notice of the divine dimension of God's Word.

Existential Encounter Theory. An existential encounter view of inspiration maintains that Scripture becomes the Word of God in a moment of personal encounter. Thus, the inspiration of Scripture is not tied to its words, but to the encounter with the living Jesus that Scripture points us toward. Popularized through the Swiss theologian Karl Barth, the emphasis is on the character of revelation as an event. This view overlooks the inseparable nature of event from interpretation. In other words, one cannot *experience* the revelation which the primary witness in Scripture points us toward without the *words* of the primary witness. To find "meaning" necessitates interpretation. The living Christ can only be encountered in faith *through* the text of the NT as interpretation of the Christ-event.

EVANGELICAL DEFINITION OF INSPIRATION

Few definitions of inspiration have improved upon that given by Charles Hodge, the great Princeton theologian, who defined inspiration as "the supernatural influence of the Holy Spirit on selected individuals which rendered them the instruments of God for the infallible communi-

---

3. This caricature of evangelical understandings is soundly engaged and refuted by J. I. Packer in *"Fundamentalism" and the Word of God* (Grand Rapids: Eerdmans, 1958), 78–79 and 178–79.

cation of his mind and will."[4] This definition maintains that inspiration is verbal and plenary and is simultaneously both human and divine in origin.

Verbal. That Scripture is verbally inspired means that inspiration involves the very words of Scripture, not simply the concepts or subjects of Scripture. In Paul's second letter to Timothy, it is the very *graphe* (word or Scripture) which is *theopneustos* (God-breathed).

Scripture itself supports this aspect of inspiration. Many arguments in Scripture rest on a *single word* (e.g., John 10:34–35; cf. Ps. 82:6). In other places, the very *tense* of a verb is decisive (Matt. 22:32). Paul builds a theological point on the OT's distinction between a singular and a plural noun (Gal. 3:16). The inspiration of the Bible clearly extends to the verbal level as the very Word of God.

Plenary. The Latin term *plenary* refers to that which is "full" or "complete." The idea here is that *all* of Scripture is equally inspired by God. The entire canon of Scripture is inspired by God, as opposed to partial inspiration, which attempts to isolate certain portions alone for inspiration.

Nevertheless, there is little doubt that certain parts of Scripture are more decisive for the church or the life of the believer than other parts. For example, most Christians find more nourishment for their spiritual life from the NT Gospel of Mark than from the OT Book of Numbers. But making this observation is far different from ascribing differing levels of inspiration to the various parts of Scripture. Instead, the various parts of the canon should be viewed as the instruments of a symphony orchestra. Some instruments may be more prominent than others, but each is essential to the harmony of the whole.[5]

Human and Divine. An evangelical view of inspiration balances the human and divine elements in Scripture. While representing and containing exactly what God intended, the biblical materials reflect the personality and style of each author. While there are some significant distinctions, the analogy of Christ has merit as a model for understanding this balance. Much as Jesus was both fully God and fully man, the Bible is completely God's Word even though it was written through the personalities and styles of human authors.

At this point a word should be said about bibliolatry. In other words, many have accused evangelical Christians of worshiping the Bible, as if holding to a high view of Scripture as the inspired Word of God means

---

4. Charles Hodge, *Systematic Theology*, vol. 1 (1863; reprint, Grand Rapids: Eerdmans, 1960), 154.

5. On this, see John Jefferson Davis, *Foundations of Evangelical Theology* (Grand Rapids: Baker, 1984), 175.

elevating it to a place of worship. This simply is not true. Rather, the Bible is seen by evangelicals as that which reveals the God whom we *do* worship.

INERRANCY OF SCRIPTURE

While there is general agreement regarding the meaning of the word *inspiration,* and that the Bible claims to be inspired, there is great debate surrounding the implications of inspiration for the biblical materials. The central term among evangelicals is "inerrancy," a word referring to the nature of the Bible's inspiration as being that which is "truth without error."

THE IMPORTANCE OF INERRANCY

Inerrancy is a decisive topic because it strikes at the heart of the Bible's inspiration and authority. If the Bible is not truth, then it cannot be authoritative. Inerrancy is a direct consequence of the Bible's inspiration. If the Bible is the result of an infinite, omniscient God who is the embodiment of truth, then Scripture itself is truth.

Inerrancy is of particular importance for our modern world. For centuries the inspiration and authority of Scripture did not need an elaborate articulation or defense in the Western world. Today's pluralistic milieu demands a careful and reasoned presentation of the truth of God's Word. As Carl Henry has written, no "movement can dramatically affect the course of the world while its own leaders undermine the integrity of its charter documents."[6]

REASONS FOR HOLDING TO BIBLICAL INERRANCY

There are three foundational and compelling reasons for holding to biblical inerrancy: Scripture's self-witness, the history of the Christian church, and inerrancy's importance to epistemology.

Scripture's Self-Witness. It has been noted that the Bible speaks to its own inspiration. But further, it can be posited that the Bible speaks also to its inerrancy. Though the term is never used in Scripture, thus sharing company with other important words not found in Scripture such as "trinity," it is strongly implied throughout the biblical materials.

In the OT, a test was given to determine between God's message and a message from a false prophet. The distinguishing characteristic of a message from God was that of complete truthfulness in the message (Deut. 13:1–5; 18:20–22).

---

6. Carl F. H. Henry in *Theologians in Transition: The Christian Century "How My Mind Has Changed" Series,* ed. James M. Wall (New York: Crossroad, 1981), 45.

In 2 Timothy 3:16 we read that "all Scripture is God-breathed." The same idea is presented in 2 Peter 1:20–21, where it clearly states that "no prophecy of Scripture came about by the propet's own interpretation . . . but men spoke from God as they were carried along by the Holy Spirit." As that which flows from the very being of God, Scripture's inerrancy is mandated.

It also should be noted that the Bible's claims to be authoritative depend on inerrancy. Jesus taught that heaven and earth would pass away before any aspect of the Law failed to be fulfilled and that Scripture *could not* be broken and thus demanded absolute allegiance (Matt. 5:17–20; John 10:34–35). For a text to embody such authority demands nothing short of complete truthfulness.

The very nature of God is that which is without error. Throughout Scripture there is an interchangeability in the phrases "God says" and "Scripture says" (cf. Gal. 3:8; Rom. 9:17; Matt. 19:4–5; Heb. 3:7; Acts 4:24–25). Where Scripture speaks, God speaks. God *cannot* lie (Num. 23:19; 1 Sam. 15:29; Titus 1:2; Heb. 6:18). As all of Scripture is a communication from God, all of Scripture is absolute truth. To hold to Scripture's inspiration implicitly demands an allegiance to biblical inerrancy. As the very breath of God, Scriptures must be fully truthful.

The History of the Christian Church. There is little doubt the Christian church historically has affirmed the idea of inerrancy. In the early years of Christendom, we find that Clement of Rome referred to Scripture as the "true utterances of the Holy Spirit" (*Epistles* 1.45). Irenaeus called Scripture "divine" and "perfect" (*Against Heresies* 2.41.1; 2.28.2). Augustine maintained that he believed "most firmly that no one of these authors has erred in any respect in writing" (*Epistles* 82.1.3). As J. N. D. Kelly has written, the general view of the early church was that "Scripture was not only exempt from error but contained nothing that was superfluous."[7]

The Reformation insistence on the truthfulness of Scripture is perhaps best revealed in the Lutheran Formula of Concord, which stated the Bible was God's "pure, infallible, and unalterable Word." As Calvin wrote, the Scriptures have "come down to us from the very mouth of God" (*Institutes* 1.vii,5).[8]

The position of contemporary American evangelicalism has been established by individuals such as Benjamin Breckinridge Warfield, who asserted the verbal, plenary inspiration of Scripture as truth without mix-

---

7. J. N. D. Kelly, *Early Christian Doctrines*, rev. ed. (San Francisco: Harper & Row, 1978), 61.

8. An excellent introduction to the Reformer's view of Scripture can be found in Timothy George, *Theology of the Reformers* (Nashville: Broadman, 1988).

ture of error.[9] Timothy Dwight, president of Yale, declared in the 1790s that the authors of Scripture were "absolutely preserved from errors."[10]

Kirsopp Lake was well known for conceding that church history was quite simply on the side of the conservative view in regard to the doctrine of biblical inspiration. He wrote:

> It is a mistake often made by educated persons who happen to have but little knowledge of historical theology to suppose that fundamentalism is a new and strange form of thought. . . . How many were there, for instance, in the Christian churches of the eighteenth century, who doubted the infallible inspiration of all Scripture? A few perhaps, but very few. No, the fundamentalist may be wrong; I think that he is. But it is we who have departed from the tradition, not he. . . . The Bible and the corpus theologicum of the church is on the fundamentalist side."[11]

From a sceptic!

Richard F. Smith concurs, writing that the idea that "scripture is inerrant is a constant element in Christian tradition."[12]

Epistemological Concerns. From an epistemological perspective, inerrancy is crucial. Epistemology is a word which designates the process of how we gain knowledge. In other words, the epistemological question is "How do we know?" If the Bible is not truth in all that it communicates, then any assertion it does communicate could be false. This does not mean that every claim *is* false, only that every claim *could* be false. With so much of the Bible beyond empirical verification, an errant Bible would be extremely weak in service as an epistemic base. Much of the theology of the Bible is based on the history of the Bible. If a historical error is theorized, then the theological claim is suspect.

THEORIES OF INERRANCY

There are three broad perspectives regarding inerrancy which can be enumerated: non-inerrantists, limited inerrantists, and complete inerrantists.[13]

---

9. Benjamin Breckinridge Warfield, *The Inspiration and Authority of the Bible* (Phillipsburg, N.J.: Presbyterian and Reformed, 1948).

10. Quoted in John D. Woodbridge, Mark A. Noll, and Nathan O. Hatch, *The Gospel in America* (Grand Rapids: Zondervan, 1979), 108.

11. Kirsopp Lake, *The Religion of Yesterday and Tomorrow* (Boston: Houghton Mifflin, 1925), 61.

12. Richard F. Smith, *JBC*, ed. Raymond E. Brown, et al. (Englewood Cliffs, N.J.: Prentice-Hall, 1969). This view has been challenged by Jack B. Rogers and Donald K. McKim in *The Authority and Interpretation of the Bible: An Historical Approach* (San Francisco: Harper & Row, 1979). Rogers and McKim have themselves been challenged in such volumes as *Scripture and Truth*.

13. A more detailed enumeration of various views related to biblical inerrancy can be found in David S. Dockery, *The Doctrine of the Bible* (Nashville: Convention Press, 1991), 86–88.

Non-Inerrantists. Those who do not embrace inerrancy are those who do not feel that the Bible's inspiration translates into an error-free transmission of God's Word to His people. Adherents to this view commonly point to alleged contradictions and inconsistencies in the biblical materials to support their stance. Many individuals who hold to this view claim they are simply being true to the Bible we have and that our Bible is simply not inerrant.[14]

Limited Inerrantists. Some evangelical Christians hold to what is perhaps best called a limited inerrancy, meaning that while they hold to the truth of Scripture, they do not understand that truth to apply equally to all of the biblical statements. What is commonly asserted is that the Bible is inerrant in matters of faith and practice, but not in matters of history or science. Thus, a "canon within the canon" becomes operative.[15]

Full Inerrantists. The position for this volume could be called "full" or "complete" inerrancy. That is, where the Bible speaks, it speaks without error. The Bible is inspired, "God-breathed," and the God of Christian faith cannot "breathe" error. Full inerrantists are convinced that all indicators point to the full truthfulness of God's Word.[16]

OBJECTIONS TO INERRANCY

The objections to inerrancy usually fall along the following lines: (1) we do not have a copy of the inerrant original, and the extant copies we do have in our possession contain "error"; (2) assuming the objective truth of Scripture as God's self-revelation does not address the question of subjective appropriation, thus making inerrancy irrelevant; (3) the Bible does not teach its own inerrancy; (4) the idea of biblical inerrancy is a philosophical category artificially imposed upon the biblical materials that is alien to its

---

14. One of the most persistent critics of biblical inerrancy has been James Barr; see his _Beyond Fundamentalism_ (Philadelphia: Westminster, 1984); _Holy Scripture: Canon, Authority, Criticism_ (Philadelphia: Westminster, 1983), _Fundamentalism_, 2d ed. (London: SCM Press, 1981); and _The Scope and Authority of the Bible_ (Philadelphia: Westminster, 1980). Barr's engagement has elicited many capable responses, the most focused being Paul Ronald Wells' _James Barr and the Bible: Critique of a New Liberalism_ (Phillipsburg, N.J.: Presbyterian and Reformed, 1980).

15. For a representative of limited inerrancy, see Stephen T. Davis, _The Debate About the Bible: Inerrancy versus Infallibility_ (Philadelphia: Westminster, 1977). Though there are some important distinctions, Clark Pinnock's recent writings also seem to fall into this category; see his _The Scripture Principle_ (San Francisco: Harper & Row, 1984).

16. A good introduction to biblical inerrancy can be found in Geisler's _Inerrancy_ which presents the fourteen papers presented at the International Conference on Biblical Inerrancy (ICBI), which in October 1978 formulated the nineteen-article "Chicago Statement" on biblical inerrancy.

nature and intent; (5) biblical inerrancy demands either an infallible hermeneutic or a literal hermeneutic, both of which are problematic; (6) inerrancy flows from the faulty understanding of revelation as text, as opposed to original witness to revelation.[17]

Inerrancy: The word itself

In regard to these arguments against biblical inerrancy, it must be asserted that the term "inerrant" is not a particularly good one, though what it intends to convey in regard to Scripture's truthfulness and trustworthiness is laudable and important. There are three primary reasons why the term "inerrant" is not a particularly good one: First, it is not taken from the biblical materials, such as the term "inspiration." Second, the term implies a mathematically precise, contemporary understanding of fact that is not always fair to the nature and context of the biblical narrative. Nonetheless, the term is now a part of theological dialogue and should therefore not be fought but rather carefully defined. Third, it takes attention away from what is decisive for evangelical theology, which is the authority of Scripture. This is not to say that inerrancy does not speak to the authority question, but rather that inerrancy is secondary to the authority question.

Evangelicals have written extensively regarding the subject of inerrancy and have defended the doctrine with great ability and care.[18] Evangelical responses to the many arguments lodged against biblical inerrancy include the following: (1) To claim that we do not have an inerrant original which can be produced to substantiate the claim to inerrancy, is responded to by stating that we do not have an errant original which can be produced to validate the alternate view. And as noted NT scholar F. F. Bruce stated, the Bible now in our possession is extraordinarily reliable.[19] (2) While there have been herculean attempts at forced harmonization in light of an alle-

---

17. Some of the more recent publications which have argued against biblical inerrancy have been generated by the controversy within the Southern Baptist Convention, which has found itself embroiled in division over this very subject. Such works include, but are not limited to, the following: Philip D. Wise, "Biblical Inerrancy: Pro or Con?," *ThEd*, 37 (spring 1988): 15–44; Gordon James, *Inerrancy and the Southern Baptist Convention* (Dallas: Southern Baptist Heritage Press, 1986); Robison James, ed. *The Unfettered Word: Southern Baptists Confront the Authority-Inerrancy Questions* (Waco: Word, 1987); *The Proceedings of the Conference on Biblical Inerrancy, 1987* (Nashville: Broadman, 1987); Clayton Sullivan, *Toward a Mature Faith: Does Biblical Inerrancy Make Sense?* (Decatur, Ga.: SBC Today, 1990).

18. A good introduction to evangelical interactions with opposing views can be found in *Challenges to Inerrancy: A Theological Response*, ed. Gordon R. Lewis and Bruce Demarest (Chicago: Moody, 1984); and Harvie M. Conn, ed., *Inerrancy and Hermeneutic: A Tradition, A Challenge, A Debate* (Grand Rapids: Baker, 1988).

19. F. F. Bruce, *The New Testament Documents*, 6th ed. (Grand Rapids: Eerdmans, 1984).

giance to biblical inerrancy, most evangelicals have addressed the textual difficulties with honesty, attempting to answer them from a scholarly viewpoint. An example of evangelical efforts to address the textual concerns of non-inerrantists can be found in such carefully constructed proposals as "The Chicago Statement on Biblical Inerrancy."[20] In regard to inerrancy being critiqued for mistakenly joining revelation and text, evangelicals insist the "event" of revelation cannot be separated from its biblical interpretation for the contemporary exegete. It is suggested that to separate the two in regard to truthfulness would lead to epistemological nihilism. (3) The critique that inerrancy demands an infallible hermeneutic is not held by any evangelical scholar of whom this writer is aware. What is maintained by evangelicals is that once a biblical teaching has been correctly identified, trust may be placed in that teaching without regard for falsity.

Three difficulties emerge with the non-inerrantist position: (1) the non-inerrantist position is more difficult to reconcile with the Bible's statements about the nature of its inspiration than the inerrantist position; (2) rejecting inerrancy is seemingly alien to the dynamics of how Jesus used the Bible during His earthly ministry; and (3) the non-inerrantist position is inconsistent with the early church's view of Scripture.

There are also many difficulties with the "limited" inerrancy view, not the least of which is that many statements in the Bible related to faith and practice are inextricably intertwined with historical narratives. The prime example is the resurrection; either it actually occurred in space and time as a historical event, or it did not. No "limited" inerrantist with whom I am familiar would deny the ultimate importance of the resurrection of Jesus Christ to orthodox Christianity, yet the resurrection is first and foremost a *historical* claim. Related to this is the enormous difficulty of how one determines what *is* true within the biblical materials. Nothing could be more intimidating—or impossible—than to approach the Bible with the task of separating fact from fiction.

---

20. See "The Chicago Statement on Biblical Inerrancy," in *Evangelicals and Inerrancy,* ed. Ronald Youngblood (Nashville: Thomas Nelson, 1984), 230–39. It could be proposed that the many qualifications in the "Chicago Statement," especially Article XIII, make the term "inerrancy" vacuous. In fairness, such an evaluation should take into account the definitional specificity such a term as "inerrancy" would necessarily demand for meaningful theological dialogue. It is to be noted that such rules of interpretation have accompanied Evangelicalism's understanding of biblical inerrancy long before the "Chicago Statement," evidenced by such careful treatments as Bernard Ramm's "The Problem of Inerrancy and Secular Science in Relation to Hermeneutics" in *Protestant Biblical Interpretation: A Textbook of Hermeneutics for Conservative Protestants* (Boston: W. A. Wilde, 1956), 182–95.

TOWARD A DEFINITION OF INERRANCY

The most fulsome definition of biblical inerrancy by evangelical Christians was put forth in a statement that has become known as "The Chicago Statement on Biblical Inerrancy." David S. Dockery has captured the essence of that carefully defined effort in the following concise statement:

> The idea that when all the facts are known, the Bible (in its autographs, that is, the original documents), properly interpreted in light of the culture and the means of communication that had developed by the time of its composition, is completely true in all that it affirms, to the degree of precision intended by the author's purpose, in all matters relating to God and His creation.[21]

There are several dynamics within this definition that bear exposition: (1) The idea that it depends on "all the facts being known." At present, we simply do not possess all of the information relevant to the Bible. (2) Inerrancy has always referred to the original autographs. Limiting inerrancy to the original manuscripts acknowledges that the transmission of the text has allowed minor discrepancies to manifest themselves. This does not reduce the importance of asserting the inerrancy of the original documents, however, for it makes a great difference to work from the basis of an inerrant original than an errant original. (3) Inerrancy should never be separated from the canons of sound biblical interpretation. Many seeming difficulties are nothing more than the result of a failure to exercise sound hermeneutical principles. (4) Inerrancy is tied to authorial intent. We must allow Scripture to establish its own standards of precision according to the purpose of the author and the literary genre being used.

In other words, inerrancy acknowledges what Anthony Thiselton calls the polymorphous character of truth, contending that no single concept of truth exists in relation to the biblical materials, but rather that the understanding of truth varies according to context.[22] This suggests that one must interact with a particular biblical text in light of the nature of truth it is *intending* to convey. Placher, putting it in terms of story, states that "the kind of claims you make depends on the particular story you use and the way you use it."[23]

---

21. Dockery, *Doctrine of the Bible*, 80. A similar definition can be found in Millard Erickson, *Christian Theology*, 1 vol. (Grand Rapids: Baker, 1983–85), 233–34.

22. Anthony C. Thiselton, *The Two Horizons: New Testament Hermeneutics and Philosophical Description* (Grand Rapids: Eerdmans, 1980), 408–15.

23. William C. Placher, *Unapologetic Theology: A Christian Voice in a Pluralistic Conversation* (Louisville: Westminster/John Knox Press, 1989), 130. Placher errs in concluding that the truth question regarding such issues as historicity can be bracketed off as inconsequential to the reading of the narrative.

The inerrantist maintains that one grants to Scripture the degree of truthfulness, historical or otherwise, to the degree the author of that biblical narrative intended. This truth might be poetic in nature, it might be propositional or didactive in nature, or it may be discussing truth in terms of personal response. This is in line with Article XIII of "The Chicago Statement on Biblical Inerrancy," which reads, "We deny that it is proper to evaluate Scripture according to standards of truth and error that are alien to its usage or purpose."[24]

Kevin J. Vanhoozer contends that what must be asserted is that diverse literary forms and truth are far from incompatible.[25] Scripture's literary forms should determine the hermeneutical approach. As a result, differing narratives should not be read similarly. This has much to say to the evangelical concept of truth in terms of the relationship between biblical inerrancy and epistemology, for Vanhoozer insists the literary form of the text should be allowed to determine the form of inerrancy that is maintained for the text. In other words, inerrancy must be interpreted in such a way as to encompass the truth expressed in Scripture's poetry, romances, proverbs, and parables—as well as its historical narratives.

Rather than leading to a radically subjective view of truth, this literary approach simply allows the text to determine the nature of truth being proposed. The diversity of literary forms does not imply that Scripture contains competing kinds of truth, but rather various kinds of fact, such as historical fact, metaphysical fact, moral fact, and so on. The nature of biblical truth is therefore determined by its literary form.[26]

AUTHORITY OF SCRIPTURE

Carl F. H. Henry, founding father of contemporary American evangelical theology, has written that the most important thing to be said about

---

24. See *Evangelicals and Inerrancy*, 230–39.

25. Kevin J. Vanhoozer, "The Semantics of Biblical Literature," in *Hermeneutics, Authority and Canon*, 53–104. A similar point is made by Feinberg in the same volume in his article titled "Truth: Relationship of Theories of Truth to Hermeneutics," 6. See also Vanhoozer's *Biblical Narrative in the Philosophy of Paul Ricoeur* (Cambridge: Cambridge University Press, 1990), particularly the chapter titled "A Literal Gospel?," 148–89.

26. For a fuller discussion of this subject, see James Emery White, *What Is Truth?* (Nashville: Broadman, 1994).

Scripture is its authority.[27] What Henry is saying is that the most correct understanding of biblical inspiration is meaningless unless individuals submit to its authority in life-changing commitment and obedience.

The Greek word for *authority* in Scripture is *exousia* which can also be translated "right" or "power." The Bible teaches that its own authority either can be bestowed or inherent. In other words, someone can give you authority or you can have authority inherent in who you are or the position you hold. The Bible has both bestowed and inherent authority. It carries bestowed authority as a result of its content as it points beyond itself to the living God. It has inherent authority through its inspiration and truthfulness. Because it is inspired and inerrant, it is authoritative.

Many individuals today challenge the Bible's authority. They refuse it any sense of inherent authority as the Word of God. At best the Bible is perceived to be a gathering of fallible writings upon which the Christian community has arbitrarily bestowed authority. To remain in the stream of orthodox Christianity, however, precludes any such denigration of the Bible's authority.

The Bible's authority is inextricably linked with God's authority, for all authority ultimately flows from God Himself. Authority rests in God's own being, and as the self-revelation of God the Bible shares that authority. God's authority is made known through His self-disclosure. Therefore, revelation and authority go together, for in revelation God makes His authority known.

Jesus proclaimed the absolute authority of the Scripture (Matt. 4:1–11; 5:18; John 10:35). The apostles claimed absolute authority for their writings as well, now contained in the NT (e.g., 2 Cor. 12:19; 1 Thess. 2:13).

---

27. Carl F. H. Henry, "The Concerns and Considerations of Carl F. H. Henry," *Christianity Today*, (March 13, 1981), 19; in this article Henry attempts to distance himself from H. Lindsell's *The Battle for the Bible* (Grand Rapids: Zondervan, 1976), which Henry felt made the following mistakes: (1) elevated inerrancy over authority and inspiration; (2) eclipsed the important issues of revelation and culture, hermeneutics, and propositional revelation; (3) wrongly created distrust over all but a small handful of conservative institutions, and (4) through overstatement made it easy for opponents of inerrancy to gain an undeserved sympathy for their views. Henry's perspective is that inerrancy should be viewed as a mark of evangelical consistency as opposed to evangelical authenticity. See *Evangelicals in Search of Identity* (Waco: Word, 1976), 48–56, where Henry notes that "the real question is whether, once scriptural inerrancy is affirmed, a consistent evangelical faith is maintained" (p. 55) and that the "duty of evangelical enterprise requires something higher than invalidating every contribution of evangelicals who halt short of that commitment" (p. 56); see also "Theology and Biblical Authority: A Review Article," *JETS* 19 (1976): 315–23.

The Bible also claims authority for itself, evidenced by the dominant claim of the OT: "Thus says the Lord." It is the Scripture of "truth" (*alethia*), and thus authoritative for every sphere of reality (Pss. 117:2; 119:89; Dan. 10:21). God is truthful, and as the Word of Truth, Scripture's authority is without question (John 3:3; 2 Cor. 6:7; Col. 1:5; Jas. 1:18; 1 John 5:20; Rom. 3:7).

As a result, interpretation tied to authorial intent is essential for biblical authority to be manifest. The farther we distance ourselves from the original, intended meaning of the Scriptures, the greater the "authority gap" widens. In other words, the application of the Bible's authority to an individual life must be wed to an interpretation that adheres closely to the thrust of the text.[28] Therefore, the joining of meaning and text is decisive for biblical authority.[29]

When one speaks of biblical authority, three areas emerge for consideration: the individual, contemporary culture, and the church.

BIBLICAL AUTHORITY AND THE INDIVIDUAL LIFE

The Bible's authority extends to the lives of people. The Bible speaks directly and has authority over all of the dimensions of human existence: the body, the mind, the emotions, and the soul (Josh. 1:7–8). Yet a radical subjectivism permeates many views of human life today. "What is true for you is true for you, and what is true for me is true for me" is the philosophy of the contemporary mind. The Bible as the authoritative Word of God does not allow this relativistic approach to life. What is true is God's truth; what is moral is God's morality (Heb. 4:12).

BIBLICAL AUTHORITY AND CULTURE.

Not only does the Bible have authority over the individual lives of people, but over the culture in which we live. Rather than having contemporary culture determine standards of morality, Scripture stands over and above culture as the great standard of unchanging truth. As a result, we work to impact our culture as "salt and light," bringing it closer to the biblical principles of God's absolutes.

---

28. On this, see Grant R. Osborne, *The Hermeneutical Spiral: A Comprehensive Introduction to Biblical Interpretation* (Downers Grove, Ill.: InterVarsity, 1991), 8.

29. See David F. Wells, "Word and World: Biblical Authority and the Quandary of Modernity" in *Evangelical Affirmations*, ed. Kenneth S. Kantzer and Carl F. H. Henry (Grand Rapids: Academie/Zondervan, 1990), 157.

BIBLICAL AUTHORITY AND THE CHURCH.

The "free church" tradition in Protestant Christianity is known for the slogan "No creed but the Bible." This was never meant to endorse a total lack of accountability in terms of biblical interpretation and application, but rather to say that the church's authority rests in Christ, and that our knowledge of Christ's teaching is found in the pages of the Bible.

The authority of the church today rests not in an ecclesiastical structure, a body of tradition, or in the person of a man or group of men. The authority of the church rests in God and His primary revelation, Jesus Christ, and His written revelation, the Bible. The nature of Scripture is of great importance, but it is reduced to meaninglessness unless it is allowed to function authoritatively in the life of the believer, culture, and church.

In summary, there is little disagreement that biblical inspiration has dominated theological and ecclesiastical dialogue for the past several decades. While this is an important issue that is far from settled, the crucial issue for the coming generation will not only be the inspiration and truthfulness of the Bible, but the biblical authority and interpretation. We must not "merely listen to the word, and so deceive" ourselves; we must "do what it says" (Jas. 1:22).

FOR FURTHER READING

Bruce, F. F. *The New Testament Documents: Are They Reliable?* 6th ed. Leicester, England: Inter-Varsity and Grand Rapids: Eerdmans, 1984.

Carson, D. A. and John D. Woodbridge, eds. *Scripture and Truth.* Grand Rapids: Academie Books/Zondervan, 1983.

Dilday, Russell H., Jr. *The Doctrine of Biblical Authority.* Nashville: Convention Press, 1982.

Dockery, David S. *The Doctrine of the Bible.* Nashville: Convention Press, 1991.

Erickson, Millard. *Christian Theology.* Vol. 1. Grand Rapids: Baker, 1983–85.

Garrett, Duane A. and Richard R. Melick, Jr., eds. *Authority and Interpretation: A Baptist Perspective.* Grand Rapids: Baker, 1987.

Geisler, Norman L. *Inerrancy.* Grand Rapids: Academie Books/Zondervan, 1980.

Henry, Carl F. H. *God, Revelation and Authority.* Vol. 4. Waco Tex.: Word, 1979.

Morris, Leon. *I Believe in Revelation.* Grand Rapids: Eerdmans, 1976.

Marshall, I. Howard. *Biblical Inspiration.* Grand Rapids: Eerdmans, 1982.

Packer, J. I. *"Fundamentalism" and the Word of God.* Grand Rapids: Eerdmans, 1958.

Warfield, Benjamin B. *The Inspiration and Authority of the Bible.* Phillipsburg, N.J.: Presbyterian and Reformed, 1948.

White, James Emery. *What Is Truth?* Nashville: Broadman/Holman, 1994.

III

STUDY AND INTERPRETATION OF THE BIBLE

David S. Dockery

The church has used the Bible in a variety of ways. Because of the multifaceted character of the Bible, its use and interpretation have taken a variety of forms. This chapter will briefly examine some of these uses, some basic principles of interpretation, an overview of the interpretation of the Bible throughout the history of the church, and some principles for applying the Bible in our modern context.

BIBLICAL INTERPRETATION: THE NEW TESTAMENT PATTERN

The writers of the NT adopted a Christological understanding of the OT. This pattern was based on the way Jesus Christ Himself read the OT. Following the current rabbinic practices, the apostles employed various approaches to the OT. Moral injunctions were generally interpreted literally. Other OT passages took on obvious Christological references, primarily through the use of typological interpretations. Yet no single image, pattern, motif, or theme can adequately express the apostles' interpretation of the OT. The NT emphasizes, however, that numerous themes, images, and motifs of revelation and response are fulfilled in Jesus Christ. The note of Philip's jubilant words, "We have found him" (John 1:45, RSV), was echoed by the NT writers as the way to interpret the OT events, pictures, and ideas. It was not so much one fulfillment idea but a harmony of notes presented in a variety of ways by different methods of interpretation.

Jesus became the direct and primary source for the church's understanding of the OT. The apostles, probably subconsciously rather than intentionally, practiced the procedures of interpretation followed by later Judaism. What the early church needed was an interpretive perspective, apart from the Jewish context, which could transform the Torah into the Messianic Torah. Jesus, through His example and through His exalted lordship via the Holy Spirit, provided the early church's ongoing approach to Scripture; therefore, at the heart of the apostles' interpretation a Christocentric perspective can be found.[1]

VARIOUS USES OF THE BIBLE

From the earliest days of Christian history, individual Christians and the church have used the Bible in various ways. This rich heritage influences today's Christians in the ways they use the Bible for individual and corporate purposes, such as (1) a text for preaching or teaching; (2) a source for information and understanding of life; (3) a guide for worship; (4) a wellspring to formulate Christian liturgy; (5) a primary source for the formulation of theology; (6) a guide for pastoral care; (7) the sustenance for spiritual formation in the Christian life; and (8) literature for aesthetic enjoyment. A survey of four primary uses of Scripture will help us understand the inestimable value of the Word of God.[2]

THE BIBLE AND WORSHIP

The procedure the earliest churches adopted to include Bible reading as a regular feature of worship is not known, but it is certain the first and primary use of the Bible was in the church's worship. It is imperative to remember that biblical interpretation was grounded in the church's use and understanding of the sacred text, not in the theoretical analysis of scholars. Following the pattern established in the Jewish synagogue, the

---

1. See R. T. France, *Jesus and the Old Testament: His Application of Old Testament Passages to Himself and His Message* (London: Tyndale, 1971).

2. William W. Klein, Craig L. Blomberg, and Robert L. Hubbard, Jr., *Introduction to Biblical Interpretation* (Dallas: Word, 1993), 377–99.

exposition of the sacred Word was of utmost importance in the church's worship. This pattern started with Jesus' exposition of Isaiah 61 at the beginning of His ministry, which He interpreted in light of His own messianic mission (Luke 4:16–22) and was continually practiced in the early church's worship (Acts 13:14–44; 14:1; 17:1; 19:8).

In 1 Timothy 4:13 Paul exhorted young Timothy to devote attention to the public reading of Scripture. Paul encouraged private study in 2 Timothy 2:15, but private study was not available to all. Public Scripture reading was therefore given a high priority. It was the apostles' conviction Scripture was given by the inspiration of God and was able to make the hearer wise unto salvation, which is in Jesus Christ (2 Tim. 3:15–17). Thus, the reading and exposition of Scripture in public worship were always central. The model Christian service, like the worship in the synagogue, was a Word-of-God service. The reference in 1 Timothy is the first historical allusion to the use of the Scriptures in the church's worship.

The NT letters were read in public meetings of the churches (Col. 4:16; Rev. 1:3). Apparently, each apostle expected his letter to be accepted as authoritative during his lifetime (2 Thess. 2:15; 2 Pet. 3:15–16). The letters were gradually accepted, circulated, and read aloud in public gatherings. In this way they became the objects of study and meditation.

The reading of Scripture was accompanied by its exposition. Almost all of the church's interpretation of Scripture and corresponding theologizing developed from the sermon. The apostle Paul explained the real meaning of preaching in 1 Corinthians 1:17–23. Paul claimed he came to preach the gospel, which he identified as the message of the cross—Christ crucified. This preaching attempted to demonstrate the Spirit's power so that faith would demonstrate God's power (1 Cor. 2:1–6). Paul built his theology of preaching on the elements of the *kerygma*: the incarnation, death, burial, resurrection, and exaltation of Christ. In this sense, preaching in the context of the worshiping community reenacted the event of Christ—the event that provided shape and meaning to worship and to the lives of worshipers.

The church's preaching interpreted the OT Scripture in terms of Christ's coming, as evidenced in the church's attitude toward the OT. First-century Christians regarded the Law and the Prophets, as well as the events and worship of Israel, as part of their heritage, because they believed these things testified to Jesus Christ. For example, in 1 Corinthians 15:3–4 Paul insisted everything concerning Christ took place "in accordance with the Scriptures." Soon, a typological interpretation of the OT became a standard way of expounding the Scriptures in the church's worship. Consequently, the early church's preaching initiated typological exegesis. The preaching of the early church was not a dispassionate recital of historical facts—a sort of nondescript presentation of certain truths, interesting enough but morally neutral. No, the facts were meant to become central in the lives of the worshipers, hence the constant offer of repentance, pardon, and a place in the new age inaugurated by the coming of God's Son.

The Holy Spirit dispensed to the church His gifts of pastors and teachers so the community of faith could be edified through reading, preaching, and teaching Holy Scripture to the measure of the stature of Christ in His fullness (Eph. 4:11–16;

Col. 1:28). The early church heavily emphasized scriptural instruction for Christians (Heb. 5:11–14) and charged Christian leaders to remain faithful to the tasks of interpreting and expounding the Bible (Col. 4:16–17; 1 Pet. 4:10–11). Thus, as in the synagogue, the church's worship was a Word-of-God worship, grounded in the Holy Scripture. This set the pattern for the church's use of Scripture throughout the ages.[3]

THE BIBLE AND PRIVATE READING

Because copies of the Bible were so expensive to produce in the time of the early church, and because many members of the early church were illiterate, most copies of the biblical text were owned by communities, not by individuals; therefore, the common people depended on public Scripture readings. Not until after the eighth century A.D. was a smaller, more affordable copy of the Bible available to a large number of people. Yet only wealthy individuals could purchase copies of the Bible or provide them for others. As a result, private Scripture reading and study were rare.

With the invention of the printing press and the development of the doctrine of the priesthood of believers in the Reformation, the private reading of Scripture increased. The practice of private study had been encouraged since Jerome (A.D. 341–420) and Augustine (A.D. 354–430), but the emphasis on believers' reading and interpreting Scripture is one of the mainstays of post-Reformation Protestantism. The strongest renewal movements have stressed the supreme importance of devotional Bible reading.

THE BIBLE AND THEOLOGY

In the early church theological construction was vitally related to, if not inseparable from, biblical interpretation. The basis of all true biblical theology in the history of the church is a sound exegetical understanding of Scripture. Most, if not all, theological deviations are caused by the neglect

---

3. See Ralph P. Martin, *Worship in the Early Church* (Grand Rapids: Eerdmans, 1964), 68–76.

of biblical truth or by a faulty interpretation of biblical texta. A theological interpretation of the Bible is mandatory.[4]

THE BIBLE AS LITERATURE

Although the Bible was never intended to be read solely as literature, it has undeniable literary and aesthetic qualities and has undoubtedly greatly influenced other literature, particularly in the English-speaking world. From a literary point of view, the Bible contains drama, poetry, narrative, and prose; it is worthy of literary study. The literary study of the Bible has increased greatly in the past decade,[5] but that is not the reason the Bible is the best-selling, most frequently read book in the world.

A HISTORY OF BIBLICAL INTERPRETATION: AN OVERVIEW

Since the beginning of the church, a dual heritage developed: (1) one maintains that Scripture's meaning is found only in its primary, historical sense and (2) another considers Scripture's ultimate meaning to rest in its plenary (full) sense. From these distinctions several models and combinations of models developed for interpreting Scripture in the early church.

THE EARLY CHURCH

The second-century apostolic fathers found the true understanding of the Bible in the teachings of Christ's apostles. The rise of false teachings (particularly Gnosticism) and challenges to accepted Orthodoxy created confusion in interpretation. To demonstrate the unity of Scripture and its message, theological frameworks were implemented by such scholars as Irenaeus (ca. A.D. 140–202) and Tertullian (ca. A.D. 155–225). These frameworks serve as guides for faith in the church. Continuing the christological emphasis of the first century, the rule of faith outlined the theological beliefs that found their focus in the incarnate Lord. Sometimes, however, the interpretation of Scripture through this theological grid forced the biblical text into a preconceived set of theological convictions. This approach resulted in a safeguard for the church's message but reduced the possibility of creativity among individual interpreters. It also tended to divorce the biblical text from its literary or historical context.[6]

---

4. See chapter 27, "Canonical Theology of the New Testament," by Robert Sloan.

5. See chapter 4, "The Bible as Literature, " by Leland Ryken.

6. See Robert M. Grant, *Greece Apologists of the Second Century* (Philadelphia: Westminster, 1988).

Creative biblical interpretation reached new levels with the rise of the Alexandrian school in the third century. The innovation of allegorical interpretation developed within this context. Allegorical interpretation assumes the Bible intends to say something more than what its literal wording suggests; it attempts to discover the deeper, mystical sense beyond the words themselves. The two great representatives of the Alexandrian school were Clement (ca. A.D. 150–215) and Origen (A.D. 185–254).

Those in the Alexandrian tradition understood biblical interpretation as a state of ecstatic possession; therefore, it was appropriate that biblical words imparted in this way should be interpreted mystically so their inner significance could be discovered. The Alexandrians did affirm the importance of the literal sense of Scripture, but the literal sense was not the primary meaning of Scripture. Origen, particularly, thought it absurd that a God-inspired Bible could not be interpreted spiritually. From this supposition followed Origen's threefold hermeneutical approach. He maintained the Bible had three different yet complementary meanings: (1) a literal or physical sense, (2) an allegorical or spiritual sense, and (3) a tropological or a moral sense. Yet in some instances the Alexandrians ignored the literal sense and found numerous spiritual meanings in a single passage, thus creating an entire scale of allegorical interpretation. Alexandrian interpretation was primarily practical, and the work of these allegorical interpreters cannot be understood until this is realized.[7]

The school of Antioch, which emphasized a literal and historical interpretation, challenged Origen's successors. The great Antiochene interpreters included John Chrysostom (ca. A.D. 347–407) and Theodore of Mopseustia (ca. A.D. 350–428). They believed biblical inspiration was a divinely given quickening of the writers' awareness and understanding in which their individuality was not impaired and their intellectual activity remained under conscious control. The Antiochenes focused on the biblical writers' aims, motivations, usages, and methods. They believed the literal-historical sense of Scripture was primary, and moral applications were made from it. The mature exegesis of Theodore and Chrysostom, while literal, was not a crude or wooden literalism that failed to recognize figures of speech in the biblical text. In continuity with the practices of Jesus and the early church, the Antiochenes read Scripture christologically through the application of typological interpretation.[8]

---

7. Joseph Wilson Trigg, *Origen: The Bible and Philosophy in the Third-Century Church* (Atlanta: John Knox, 1983), 31–75.

8. See Robert M. Grant with David Tracy, *A Short History of the Interpretation of the Bible*, rev. ed. (Philadelphia: Fortress, 1984), 63–72.

As the church moved into the fifth century, an eclectic and multifaceted approach to interpretation developed which rendered the literal, historical, allegorical, and always theological results. Augustine (A.D. 354–430) and Jerome (ca. A.D. 341–420) established the directions for this period. The biblical text was interpreted in its larger context and was understood as the biblical canon. The biblical canon established guidelines for validating both typological and allegorical interpretations; so the historical meaning remained primary, even though the deeper spiritual meaning was not ignored. Neither the allegorical practices of Alexandria nor the historical emphases of Antioch dominated. A balance emerged, influenced by pastoral and theological concerns. The Bible was viewed from the standpoint of faith, producing interpretations that emphasized the edification of the church, the love of neighbor, and primarily a knowledge of and love for God.[9]

THE MEDIEVAL AND REFORMATION PERIOD

From the time of Augustine, the church, following the lead of John Cassian (d. A.D. 433), subscribed to a theory of the fourfold sense of Scripture: (1) The literal sense of Scripture could, and usually did, nurture the virtues of faith, hope, and love. When it did not, the interpreter could appeal to three additional virtues, each sense corresponding to one of the virtues. (2) The allegorical sense referred to the church and its faith (what it was to believe). (3) The tropological or moral sense referred to individuals and how their actions should correspond to love. (4) The anagogical sense pointed to the church's expectation, corresponding to hope. For example, the city of Jerusalem, in all its appearances in Scripture, was understood literally as a Jewish city, allegorically as the church of Jesus Christ, topologically as the souls of men and women, and anagogically as the heavenly city. The fourfold sense characterized interpretation in the Middle Ages.[10]

Martin Luther (1483–1546), the great Reformer, began by using the allegorical method but later claimed to have abandoned it. It was Erasmus (1466–1536), however, more than Luther, who rediscovered the priority of the literal sense. John Calvin (1509–1564), the most consistent interpreter of the Reformation, developed the emphasis on the grammatical-historical method as the foundation for developing the spiritual message from the Bible. Luther's stress on a fuller sense found in the christological

---

9. See Gerald Bonner, "Augustine as Biblical Scholar" *CHB* 1: 541–63.

10. Beryl Smalley, *The Study of the Bible in the Middle Ages*, 2d ed. (Oxford: Blackwell, 1952), 26–36.

meaning of Scriptures linked the Reformers with Jesus, the apostles, and the early church.[11]

Some believe the followers of the Reformers shrank from the level of freedom in scriptural interpretation employed by Luther and Calvin. While this is an overstatement and an oversimplification, it is true they conducted their exposition along new theological boundaries, establishing a new Protestant scholasticism. This new form of scholasticism resulted in an authoritative and dogmatic interpretation. Almost simultaneously, enlightenment thought began to develop. This movement rejected both authoritative and dogmatic approaches, resulting in two reactions: (1) a newfound pietism associated with Philipp Jakob Spener (1635–1705) and August Herman Franke (1663–1727) and (2) a historical-critical method that stressed the importance of the historical over the theological interpretation of the Bible. The modern era has generally continued in one of three directions: the Reformation, the pietistic, or the historical-critical approach.

THE MODERN PERIOD

The "father of modern hermeneutics," F. D. E. Schleiermacher (1768–1834), argued that interpretation consisted of two categories: grammatical and psychological. Prior to Schleiermacher, hermeneutics was understood as special hermeneutics (hermeneutica sacra) and general hermeneutics (hermeneutica profana). Special hermeneutics was concerned with how the Bible ought to be interpreted, while general hermeneutics was for interpreting other kinds of literature. Schleiermacher, however, insisted the understanding of linguistic symbols, whether biblical, legal, or literary texts, should be derived from a consideration of how understanding in general takes place.[12]

THE PRIMACY OF THE AUTHOR

Schleiermacher saw that what was to be understood must in a sense already be known. Acknowledging this appeared circular; he nevertheless maintained this very account of understanding remained true to the facts of everyday experience. He stressed this by saying that every child arrives at the meaning of a word only through hermeneutics. The child must relate the new word to what is already known. If not, the word remains

---

11. David S. Dockery, "Martin Luther's Christological Hermeneutics" *GTJ* 2 (1983): 189–203.

12. See F. D. E. Schleiermacher, *Hermenuetics: The Handwritten Manuscripts*, ed. H. Kimmerle, trans. J. Duke and H. J. Forstman (Missoula, Mont.: Scholars, 1977).

meaningless. On the other side, the child must assimilate something alien or universal that always signifies a resistance for the original vitality. To that extent it is an accomplishment of hermeneutics. Schleiermacher added that since understanding new subject matter depended on positive relations to the interpreter's own known horizons, lack of understanding was never completely removed; therefore, interpretation or understanding constituted a progressive process, not simply an act that can be definitively completed. Schleiermacher contended a preunderstanding must occur before interpretation can happen.

For Schleiermacher, interpretation was related to the author's intention, and he articulated some of the most incisive statements found in all hermeneutical literature on the principles for grasping what an author willed to communicate. His grammatical hermeneutics were largely dependent upon the work of Ernesti's *Institute Interpret's Novi Testament* (1761). These were Ernesti's eleven rules:

1. Master the *usus loquendi* (the use which speakers/writers made of their words).

2. The sense of words is regulated by usage.

3. The sense is not totally determined by standard linguistic conventions, because each writer has personal style.

4. The interpreter needs to be immersed in the linguistic usage of the writer's place, time, and personal characteristics.

5. The aim is to establish the literal sense of the utterance, unless there are clear indications for non-literal understanding.

6. The interpreter must understand the verbal sense is often ambiguous and may have to appeal to indirect evidence such as (a) author's purpose, (b) analogies, or (c) common sense.

7. It should be remembered the author has freedom in usage of words but cannot stray too far from the conventional meaning or it becomes unintelligible.

8. The interpreter must never begin anywhere other than with words of the text and with the attempt to establish their sense. The hermeneutical task ends when the verbal sense has been discovered.

9. Scripture cannot be understood theologically until it has been understood grammatically.

10. There are two requisites of the competent interpreter: (a) The acuteness of understanding (*subtilitas intelugendi*) to discern the sense of a passage and (b) acuteness of skill (*subtilitas explicandi*) to exhibit that sense to the public.

11. Hermeneutics is the science which teaches us to find in an accurate and judicious manner the meaning of an author and appropriately to explain it to others.[13]

The grammatical meaning, however, was not enough for Schleiermacher. He argued the theme of an author's text was a product of the author's nature. The ultimate aim, therefore, involved getting through to an author's unique individuality (a psychological interpretation). Understanding required a knowledge of grammatical concerns and also a divinatory intuition through empathy with an imagination of the author's experience. The interpreter's goal focused on sharing a life relationship with the author. Understanding, then, involved more than rethinking what an author thought. It included reliving what was in the life of the author who generated the thought. Schleiermacher contended that if this reliving could take place, then the interpreter could understand the author's work as well as, or even better than, the author.

BIBLICAL INTERPRETATION IN THE TWENTIETH CENTURY

SCHLEIERMACHER'S AUTHOR-ORIENTED APPROACH

The prominent approach to biblical studies in both Protestant and Roman Catholic schools of interpretation until the middle of this century was an author-oriented approach in line with the Schleiermacher tradition, sometimes called the "literal-grammatical," "historical-contextual," or "historical-critical" method of interpretation. Advocates of this approach such as Krister Stendahl and John L. McKenzie, writing in the *Journal of Biblical Literature* (1958), defined interpretation as determining the meaning intended by the human author and understood by the original readers. Followers of this approach considered the meaning of biblical texts to be stable, univocal, and located in the historical situation. Stendahl defined the task of interpretation as furnishing the original meaning, reconstructing the transaction of the author to the original audience via the text.

---

13. Cited and discussed by Walter C. Kaiser, Jr., "Legitimate Hermenuetics," in *Inerrancy*, ed. N. Geisler (Grand Rapids: Zondervan, 1979), 117–47.

In an early edition of *A Short History of the Interpretation of the Bible* (1963), Robert M. Grant affirmed a very similar position.[14] He did this even while recognizing the shifts toward existential hermeneutics under the widespread influence of Martin Heidegger and Rudolf Bultmann. Grant maintained: "It would appear the primary task of the modern interpreter is historical, in the sense that what he is endeavoring to discover is what the texts and contexts he is interpreting meant to their authors in their relationships with their readers."[15]

HIRSCH'S APPROACH

In 1967, a University of Virginia literary scholar, E. D. Hirsch, Jr., published *Validity in Interpretation*; it advocated an author-oriented, normative hermeneutic. He followed this work in 1976 with *The Aims of Interpretation*.[16] Working within the Schleiermacher tradition of general hermeneutics, Hirsch called for a grammatical and historical interpretation that attempts to grasp the meaning an author intended to convey in what he wrote. His influence in biblical interpretation is praised by many scholars of diverse traditions.

Hirsch distanced himself from the Schleiermacher tradition, however, by maintaining it was not the task of the interpreter to have access to the mental process by which an author produced a work. He affirmed the author's verbal meanings can be grasped because the interpretation of texts is concerned with shareable meanings. Hirsch contended authors choose language conventions that will bring to readers' minds the things they are attempting to communicate, so the readers also can know what the authors wanted to share with their audience by words. Language is efficient in transmitting these meanings because it consists of conventions, elements the society using that language has agreed should stand for all its various aspects of common experience. Thus, "an author's verbal meaning is limited by linguistic possibilities, but is determined by his actualizing and specifying some of these possibilities."[17] The meaning of words is thus limited by a context determined by the author. Interpreters cannot therefore understand what writers meant except by what they actually wrote. With reference to biblical studies, G. B. Caird has summarized:

---

14. See Robert M. Grant, *A Short History of the Interpretation of the Bible* (New York: Macmillan, 1963).

15. Ibid., 186.

16. See E. D. Hirsch, Jr., *Validity in Interpretation* (New Haven: Yale University Press, 1967) and *The Aims of Interpretation* (Chicago: University of Chicago Press, 1976).

17. Hirsch, *Aims*, 47.

We have no access to the mind of Jeremiah or Paul except through their recorded words. A fortiori, we have no access to the word of God in the Bible except through the words and the minds of those who claimed to speak in his name. We may disbelieve them, that is our right; but if we try, without evidence, to penetrate to a meaning more ultimate than the one the writers intended, that is our meaning, not theirs or God's.[18]

Hirsch's position concerning an author-oriented interpretation said the task of the interpreter is to understand what an author meant at the time of the writing. This is possible because a text's meaning is controlled by language conventions that exist between the speaker and hearer or author and reader. Hirsch acknowledged interpretation takes the form of process, a process that takes the form of a guess, and there are no rules for making good guesses. There are, however, methods for validating guesses as Hirsch himself has elucidated: "The act of understanding is at first a genial (or a mistaken) guess and there are no methods for making guesses, no rules for generating insights; the methodological activity of interpretation commences when we begin to test and criticize our guesses."[19]

Paul Ricoeur, agreeing with Hirsch, has likewise observed:

As concerns of procedures of validation by which we test our guesses, I agree with Hirsch that they are closer to a logic of probability than a logic of empirical verification. To show that an interpretation is more probable in light of what is known is something other than showing that a conclusion is true. In this sense, validation is not verification. Validation is an argumentative discipline comparable to the judicial procedures of legal interpretation. It is a logic of uncertainty and of qualitative probability. . . . A text is a quasi-individual, the validation of an interpretation to it may be said, with complete legitimacy, to give a scientific knowledge of the text.[20]

The most important contribution Hirsch's theory has made to biblical studies is the distinction between meaning and significance. *Meaning* is what the writer intended to convey when addressing his original readers. However, Hirsch suggested the more important or meaningful a text is, the greater the possibility of deeper, fuller meanings. The *significance* of the text includes all the various ways a text can be read and applied beyond the author's intention.

Exegesis also focuses on the primary, normative meaning of the biblical text; exposition entails revealing the fuller meaning or significance of the

---

18. G. B. Caird, *The Language and Imagery of the Bible* (Philadelphia: Westminster, 1980), 61.

19. Hirsch, *Validity*, 19–20.

20. Paul Ricoeur, *Hermenuetics and the Human Sciences*, ed. and trans. J. B. Thompson (Cambridge: Cambridge University Press, 1986), 212.

biblical text in line with the way the early church read Scripture through the vehicles of typological and allegorical interpretation, plus the developments of *sensus plenior* (the fuller meaning of the text) and the analogy of faith since the second century.

The goal of interpretation, then, is not to psychologize an author but rather to determine the author's purpose as revealed in the linguistical structure of the text. In other words, the goal of interpretation concerns itself with what the author achieved. Ricoeur stressed that generally when one reads a text, the author is not present to be questioned about any ambiguous meaning. This is certainly true concerning the human authors of the biblical text.

Ricoeur, like Hirsch, maintains a text's meaning is intelligible across the historical and cultural distance. Because of the nature of writing, the text opens a possible world to the interpreter (the text world); the interpreter may enter into that world and appropriate the possibilities it offers. When that occurs, the meaning of the text is actualized in the interpreter's understanding. What is understood or appropriated, then, is the text itself, the result of the author's writing. Thus, the goal of biblical interpretation is to understand meaning from the standpoint of what the author actually wrote or to focus on the text as the result of the author's writing.[21]

TOWARD BIBLICAL INTERPRETATION

Before identifying steps involved in the process of biblical interpretation, certain issues need to be addressed. Each biblical document and each part of a biblical document must be studied in its context. This includes not only its historical context but its immediate literary context as well. An interpreter must therefore have an understanding of the following: biblical languages, types of literature employed in the Bible, historical and cultural backgrounds, geographical conditions, and life situations of biblical authors, readers, and hearers.

The meaning of some written material is seldom clearly self-evident. This is especially true for an ancient document like the Bible, which was written for people who lived in different cultural and historical settings. Exposing the issues identified requires asking several questions of the biblical text under consideration:

1. Who was the writer and to whom was he writing?

2. What was the cultural-historical setting of the writer?

---

21. I have discussed these matters in *Biblical Interpretation Then and Now* (Grand Rapids: Baker, 1992).

3. What did the words mean at the time of the writing?

4. What was the author's purpose for writing, and why did he write the way he did?

5. What does this mean for believers in the contemporary church?

Personal presuppositions also must be acknowledged before exegesis is attempted. All understanding requires an interpretive framework or context. The more knowledge the reader has about a text, the more likely it can be understood properly. If the Bible is God's revelation to His people, which is the presupposition and commitment of the contributors to this volume, then the essential qualification for a full understanding of the Bible is to know the revealing God. To know God we must have a relationship with Him. The Bible describes this relationship by using the term "faith." Only those who believe and trust in God can rightly understand what God has spoken in His Word. It is impossible to understand the biblical text if one denies there is a God or that the Bible is not from God.

A second commitment necessary is the willingness to submit to the text and obey what it says. Hermeneutics must not be limited to the grammatical-historical techniques that help explain the original meaning of the text. For those who accept the Bible as a sacred text—the church's book, God's unique self-revelation—its interpretation must rise above the fundamental level of grammatical-historical considerations; the theological level must not be ignored. The grammatical-historical level of interpretation may indicate the historical meaning in the Bible, but theological exegesis presupposes an overall unity for the Bible in the light of which a proper perspective of its diversity can be appreciated.[22]

Thus, to understand the Bible theologically and obey its teaching, the illuminating work of the Holy Spirit is required. The ministry of the Holy Spirit of God provides the resource for such obedient understanding of His truth. The illuminating work of the Holy Spirit utilizes hard work and proper principles of hermeneutics. The Spirit also enlivens the text so it can be properly understood and applied to the lives of believers, individually and corporately. This latter aspect must not be ignored. Interpreters of the biblical text must constantly be aware of the temptation of individualism and recognize their participation in the body of Christ—interpreting biblical texts for the good of others in the community of faith. The church is the instrument the Spirit uses to provide accountability for interpretation and protection against wrong-headed, individualistic approaches to the text; it also provides a check against self-serving conclu-

---

22. *Evangelical Dictionary of Theology*, s.v. "Interpretation of the Bible."

sions perhaps limited by individual circumstances. The church of Jesus Christ is a worldwide fellowship that crosses cultural boundaries. This means interpretation must make sense to others in Christ's worldwide body, as well as to those in a local setting.

A MODEL FOR CONTEMPORARY BIBLICAL INTERPRETATION

Interpreters must first recognize the foundational work of preceding interpreters. Scripture interpretation also must acknowledge our confessional setting which regards the Bible as the inspired and inerrant word of God.[23] Interpreters must affirm the possibility that the entire biblical text in its canonical context contains a theological meaning similar to what traditionally has been called *sensus plenior*. This term indicates a fuller meaning in the Scripture than what was possibly intended or known by the original human author. The more significant the text, the more this is true. Because of the canonical shape and divine nature of the biblical text, a passage may have a surplus of meaning or a full depth of meaning, which by its very nature can never be exhausted. The meaning of a text may actually exceed the conscious intention of the original authors or the understanding of the original readers.

GUIDELINES TO INTERPRETATION

How can these fuller meanings be determined? What guidelines exist to limit fanciful excesses? The guidelines are located within the text and the biblical canon. The fuller meanings must be consistent with the canonical message. Some guidelines help to develop a contemporary model. These include the following:

1. Approach the text with right presuppositions, which we have previously identified as biblical faith, accepting the Bible as fully truthful and authoritative.

2. Recognize that the historical and literal meaning of the Bible is the primary meaning but not the limit of meaning.

3. Acknowledge the possibility of deeper meanings in the prophetic-apostolic witness.

4. Affirm the human authorship of the text and its divine origin.

---

23. See David S. Dockery, *The Doctrine of the Bible* (Nashville: Convention, 1991).

5. Regard the biblical text as the place where meaning is concentrated more than primarily in the author's mind.

6. Understand that a text rests in its canonical context; thus, Scripture serves as the best commentary on Scripture.

7. Expect the Holy Spirit's illumination to assist in interpretation.

8. Expect the Bible to speak to the reader's contemporary concerns.

9. Interpret the Bible in light of the centrality of Jesus Christ.[24]

It is true that all reading is perspectival; that is, the reader participates in understanding the text and is not the determiner of meaning. There are contextual markers in the text itself, intentionally indicating an objective meaning. An objective meaning is thus mediated by the biblical text. A text's indicators limit the possibilities so the number of meanings available to the reader is *not* infinite. While stressing the historical meaning of the text, the concerns of the contemporary reader must not be neglected. The concept of the text's significance, in this way, is as important as its meaning, though not equated with it.[25]

Focusing meaning in the biblical text, rather than in the author or reader, acknowledges a text's verbal meaning can be construed only on the basis of its own linguistic possibilities. These are not given from some other realm but must be learned or approximated; this is a process which is entirely intrinsic to a particular social and linguistic system. According to Paul Ricoeur, appropriated textual understanding is nothing other than the disclosing power of the text itself, bridging the gulf between reader and author. A text is, indeed, historical in its origin but is also present in its power to communicate its sense and to open a world to its reader by its self-reference. It is in this sense that Ricoeur can suggest the letters to the Romans, Galatians, Corinthians, and Ephesians, as well as other books, are addressed to contemporary readers as much as to original readers. If that is true, then the seven following steps should help span the time gap between author and interpreter.

BRIDGING THE GAP BETWEEN AUTHOR AND INTERPRETER

Step 1: Introduction. The interpretive process begins with prayer. God's direction and enablement must be sought at each step; only then should

---

24. Ibid.

25. David M. Scholer, "Issues in Biblical Interpretation," *EvQ* 88 (1988): 5–22; cf. Grant Osborne, *The Hermeneutical Spiral* (Downers Grove, Ill.: InterVarsity, 1992).

textual inquiry begin. These three questions help introduce the issues: (1) What presuppositions do interpreters bring to the biblical text? Some already identified are faith, obedience, the expectation of the illuminating work of the Spirit, a commitment to the text, and a recognition of the contextual setting within the community of faith. (Our basic assumption is that the Scriptures are fully inspired and constitute a truthful, divine-human book.) (2) What is the author's historical situation? (3) What is the cultural context out of which the author wrote?

Step 2: Observation. When observing a text, an interpreter should look for keys, or structural signals, such as conjunctions, particles, etc. These signals, or text markers, help indicate the interpretive limits of a text. While the basic unit for consideration is the paragraph, individual sentences and words also must be considered. Credible interpretation is more than simple etymology, however, and an examination of the text's structure in paragraph units will help reveal the major idea communicated by the author.

Step 3: Translation. Through textual criticism and comparison of various translations, an interpreter can establish the text for investigation. It is likely that most interpreters will work from one basic, favorite translation and do minimal comparison with other translations. A thoughtful comparison and consideration of several good translations should precede the acceptance of one translation, however. Here the use of the original language is extremely helpful, if not mandatory.

Step 4: Basic Exegesis. The genre (kind) of the text must be considered next. It may be poetry, narrative, prophetic, parabolic, gospel, epistolary, or apocalyptic. Once the genre is determined, basic work with Bible dictionaries, concordances, and grammars can commence. Diagraming a sentence flow at this point can be extremely helpful for revealing the major emphases of the text. Gordon Fee's step-by-step instructions for analyzing the text with the use of sentence flow charts will be most helpful in this process.[26] For certain genres, discovering the plot or macrostructure of the text will be necessary at this point.

Step 5: Interpretation. This is the most important step in seeking the textual meaning from an author-oriented perspective. The question arises: What did the text mean in its historical setting to the initial readers? Here the question actually moves from *what* to *why*—Why was it written this way? An examination of commentaries helps trace the historical interpretation of the passage and helps reveal the meaning of the text in its literary and canonical context.

---

26. See Gordon D. Fee, *New Testament Exegesis* (Philadelphia: Westminster, 1983), 60–77.

Step 6: Theology. Determining the theological significance of the passage poses three questions: (1) What does the text mean to contemporary readers? (2) What cultural factors need to be contexualized or retranslated?[27] (3) How does the passage reflect the Bible's *sensus plenior?*

Step 7: Proclamation and Significance for the Church. Two more questions must be asked: How can the historical meaning and the contemporary significance be communicated to our contemporary world? How will the text be heard and understood today?[28] The final step of the process also includes application.

THE APPLICATION OF THE BIBLE

The Bible is God's authoritative Word to men and women. Guidelines for interpretation enable believers to hear and respond properly to God's Word in their cultural settings. Such contemporary issues as decision-making and ethical practices demand biblical answers and applications.

Some biblical teachings are specific, universal commands which speak directly to people in all cultures. Some general teachings have universal application. Some biblical principles have implicit authority. Finally, some matters can be addressed only by finding biblical guidelines that can be applied to a specific issue or question. The following examples can help apply the Scriptures to the contemporary world: (1) Passages such as prohibitions against stealing (Ex. 20:15; Eph. 4:28), are direct teachings that apply to all people in all times. (2) General teachings on love or justice can be applied to various situations in different settings. People in employee-employer relationships, family relationships, or broader societal situations must seek to apply principles of justice and/or love in these settings. (3) Teachings about drunkenness (Eph. 5:18) must be obeyed. Applications about abstinence from alcoholic beverages are implied rather than direct teachings; thus, the level of authority is different from the previous examples. (4) Some contemporary issues are not addressed specifically in Scripture. Where should we work? Whom should we marry? What church should we join? These are matters best resolved through the application of biblical principles. The answer to these issues must be dealt with differently and individually under the guidance of the Holy Spirit within the context of the believing community.[29]

---

27. See David Hesselgrave, *Communicating Christ Cross-Culturally* (Grand Rapids: Zondervan, 1978).

28. See John R. W. Stott, *Between Two Worlds: The Art of Preaching in the Twentieth Century* (Grand Rapids: Eerdmans, 1982).

29. See Roy B. Zuck, "The Role of the Holy Spirit in Hermeneutics," *BSac* 141 (1984): 120–30.

Because various levels of authority are in the Bible, a commitment to biblical authority is not out-of-date. The general teachings of Scripture reveal God's will in a variety of ways. The direct, implied, and applied principles of Scripture can cross the temporal, social, linguistic, and cultural barriers; thus, the Bible's adequacy, sufficiency, and authority for modern men and women can be affirmed. The Bible can speak at various levels to contemporary challenges and issues.[30]

The Bible is to be regarded as the ultimate standard of authority for God's people. The Bible derives its authority from the self-revealing and self-authenticating God. The Bible's authority can and does communicate across cultural, geographical, and temporal differences between biblical and contemporary settings. Scripture is authoritative and must be rightly and faithfully interpreted in its historical setting. The Holy Spirit's illumination helps communicate the biblical message. Likewise, the Spirit leads people to a recognition of the authority of Scripture and encourages Christians to respond and obey its message.

FOR FURTHER READING

Ackroyd, P. R., and C. F. Evans, eds. *CHB*. 3 vols. Cambridge: Cambridge University Press, 1970.

Black, David A. and David S. Dockery, eds. *New Testament Criticism and Interpretation*. Grand Rapids: Zondervan, 1991.

Dockery, David S. *Biblical Interpretation Then and Now*. Grand Rapids: Baker, 1992.

———. *The Doctrine of the Bible*. Nashville: Convention, 1991.

Grant, Robert M. and David Tracey. *A Short History of the Interpretation of the Bible*. Philadelphia: Fortress, 1984.

Klein, William W., Craig L. Blomberg, and Robert L. Hubbard, Jr. *Introduction to Biblical Interpretation*. Dallas: Word, 1993.

Kugel, James L. and Rowan A. Greer. *Early Biblical Interpretation*. Philadelphia: Westminster, 1986.

Osborne, Grant R. *The Hermeneutical Spiral*. Downers Grove, Ill.: Inter-Varsity, 1992.

Rogerson, John, Christopher Rowland, and Barnabas Lindars. *The Study and Use of the Bible*. Grand Rapids: Eerdmans, 1988.

Silva, Moises. *Has the Church Misread the Bible?* Grand Rapids: Zondervan, 1987.

Thiselton, Anthony. *Two Horizons: New Testament Hermeneutics and Philosophical Description*. Grand Rapids: Eerdmans, 1980.

---

30. Klein, Blomberg, and Hubbard, *Biblical Interpretation*, 401–26.

IV

BIBLE AS LITERATURE

LELAND RYKEN

The literary approach to the Bible is the dominant movement of the nineties. It represents the convergence of two streams of scholarship in our century—biblical scholarship and literary criticism. Biblical scholars have increasingly turned to literary methods as providing a better general approach than those favored earlier in this century (such as historical, theological, source, and redaction studies). Among literary critics, a subterranean stream kept alive in university courses in the Bible as literature came to the surface around 1970, and today the Bible is a fashionable part of the "canon" of literature that literary scholars teach in their courses and about which they write.

The current fashionableness of the movement raises important questions. Exactly what does it mean that the Bible is literature? How new or how old is the awareness that the Bible is literary? Among the multiple approaches to the Bible that claim to be literary, which ones deserve that designation? *Is* the Bible really like familiar English and American literature?

IS THE BIBLE LITERARY?

The question of how long people have viewed the Bible as literature is easily answered. Biblical writers themselves wrote with literary awareness, as we know from at least three pieces of evidence. One is the frequency with which biblical writers refer to their writings with technical precision as belonging to various literary genres, such as chronicle, saying, song, complaint, parable, gospel, apocalypse, epistle, and prophecy.

Second, the writing found in the Bible displays literary qualities. It regularly falls into familiar literary genres such as narrative and poetry. It shows signs of careful craftsmanship and conscious composition. Biblical storytellers realized that stories are structured on the principle of beginning-middle-end. They knew how to employ the resources of characterization, setting, irony, foreshadowing, and climax. Biblical poets were masters of poetic language. They wrote with an awareness that praise psalms have three main parts and lament psalms five.

Third, if we look beyond biblical writings to the context in which they were written, it becomes apparent that biblical writers often wrote with an awareness of the literature being produced in surrounding nations. To cite some specimen examples, the Ten Commandments are written in the form of the suzerainty treaties of Hittite kings; the Song of Solomon contains love poems that resemble Egyptian love poetry; biblical Proverbs were part of an international movement of wisdom literature; and the Book of Revelation reproduces some of the effects of Greek drama.

The early church fathers were the first to acknowledge the literary nature of the Bible, and because they were steeped in classical literature as well as the Bible, they wrestled with the precise nature of the relationship between the two. Was the Bible literary by classical standards? That was the question they could not resolve, and in many ways it remains the focus of attention in the current interest in the Bible as literature.

The response of Augustine in the fourth century can serve as an instructive paradigm. Augustine was trained as a classical rhetorician, and when he first studied the Bible, its "lowliness" seemed "unworthy to be compared to the stateliness of Tully."[1] But later Augustine came to regard the Bible as literary in the same ways that classical literature was. In fact, he conducted detailed analyses of biblical texts to show they possessed the same rhetorical eloquence that Greek and Roman writing did.[2]

---

1. Augustine, *Confessions* 3.5.
2. Augustine, *On Christian Doctrine* 4.6-7.

There is a familiar chronology to Augustine's encounter with the Bible. At first the Bible seems unliterary. Obviously the writers did not aspire to write literature the way Shakespeare or Dickens did. But when examined more closely, the Bible in many ways resembles familiar literature. Since this is how we tend to experience the matter, I have chosen to organize this chapter according to the same chronology. Before the Bible can be seen as a literary book, we need to acknowledge the ways in which the Bible is different from most literature. Of course these deviations from conventional patterns do not mean the Bible is not literary; they may simply mean it follows different literary conventions. After seeing what is distinctive about the Bible as literature, we will be in a position to see how it resembles familiar literature.

The most helpful framework within which to see what is familiar and unfamiliar about the Bible is to regard the Bible as an anthology—a collection of varied writings by diverse writers. Even the word "Bible" suggests this, since it means simply "little books." This anthology can be considered to have a national unity, with all but two books (Luke and Acts) having been written by Hebrew authors. Provisionally, the Bible is a literary anthology similar to *The Norton Anthology of English Literature*.

FIRST IMPRESSIONS: THE DISTINCTIVENESS OF THE BIBLE

The most apparent difference between the Bible and a typical anthology of British literature is the mingling of unexpected material. The historical or documentary impulse, for example, is highlighted. Side by side with stories is the bare recording of details associated with historical chronicles. A typical lead-in to a biblical story reads more like an entry in a diary or journal than what is expected of literary narrative.

In addition to this historical impulse to record the facts about events, there is a pervasive religious preoccupation. The Bible is a primarily didactic book (having the intention to teach), whereas most literature balance the desire to teach with the desire to entertain. Part of the overarching religious preoccupation of the Bible is the way in which God is the leading character in the stories and poems. The Bible is a God-centered anthology in a way no other literary collection is. It consistently places people and events into relationship to God.

The religious orientation of the Bible is reinforced by the sense of authority it claims for itself and Jewish and Christian religions have traditionally ascribed to it. Hebrew scholar Erich Auerbach noted in this regard that "the Bible's claim to truth is not only far more urgent than

Homer's, it is tyrannical—it excludes all other claims."[3] In a similar vein, literary critic C. S. Lewis, in an oft-quoted statement, wrote,

> Neither Aeschylus nor even Virgil tacitly prefaces his poetry with the formula, "Thus say the gods." But in most parts of the Bible everything is implicitly or explicitly introduced with "Thus saith the Lord." It is . . . not merely a sacred book but a book so remorselessly and continuously sacred that it does not invite, it excludes or repels, the merely aesthetic approach.[4]

This is not to say the Bible is not literary. Elsewhere Lewis observed there is a sense "in which the Bible, since it is after all literature, cannot properly be read except as literature; and the different parts of it as the different sorts of literature they are."[5] The Bible then combines three impulses that we do not expect to see combined in a literary anthology— the literary, the historical, and the religious. Usually one of these dominates a given passage, though not necessarily to the exclusion of the others. This means even if we view the Bible as literary, we are aware that it invites historical and theological approaches as well as a literary approach.

I have already implied the Bible seems relatively formless when judged by classical standards, where unity of content is the norm. The Bible is a cycle or collage or patchwork of relatively self-contained units, and this aspect is heightened by the preference biblical writers show for the brief unit. Long, sustained stories or poems like the Book of Job are almost absent from the Bible. Disjointedness is the normal procedure. Narrative books like Genesis and the Gospels are themselves anthologies of brief stories. Poetry takes the form of self-contained lyric poems. The Bible is a kaleidoscope of brief units.

The mixed-genre format of the Bible highlights this effect even more. Whereas a typical anthology is organized by genres such as narrative, poetry, and epistle, the Bible frequently mixes genres. Passages of poetry suddenly show up in stories and epistles. The prophetic books are usually written in poetic form and sometimes have interspersed narrative elements. The Bible, moreover, is a very aphoristic or proverbial book, with the result that memorable "sayings" appear on virtually every page.

In summary, there are good reasons for the hesitance that people have shown to see the Bible as literature. On the surface the Bible seems not to be governed by literary intentions. The material is too heterogeneous to resemble the usual literary anthology. Intermingled with the predomi-

---

3. Erich Auerbach, *Mimesis: The Representation of Reality in Western Literature* (Princeton: Princeton University Press, 1953), 14.

4. C. S. Lewis, *The Literary Impact of the Authorized Version* (Philadelphia: Fortress, 1963), 32-33.

5. Lewis, *Reflections on the Psalms* (New York: Harcourt, 1958), 3.

nantly literary material (itself very mixed) is expository (informational) writing that is not literary at all. And the writers seem more interested in conveying historical facts or religious teaching than in entertaining us with literary technique.

In addition, the nonpoetic parts of the Bible have a prevailing plainness that seems to be unliterary in effect or intention. The NT, for example, is written not in classical Greek but in the everyday Greek idiom known as *Koine*. Biblical narrative (as Erich Auerbach established in his landmark comparison of storytelling technique in Homer and the Book of Genesis) is normally written in a spare, unembellished style that seems initially to be artless.

A CLOSER LOOK: THE BIBLE AS LITERATURE

Once we have gotten past the obstacles to viewing the Bible as literature, we are in a position to see how thoroughly it resembles ordinary literature. What things, after all, make up an anthology of literature? We know that a collection of writings is literary if its subject matter is human experience, if its genres are those we regard as literary, if it displays artistry, if it employs special resources of language, and if it makes use of literary archetypes (recurrent images, plot motifs, and character types). By all of these criteria, the Bible is a thoroughly literary book.

In this section my purpose is to identify what things make the Bible a literary book. A later section will explore the methods of interpretation that flow from the literary nature of the Bible.

THE PRESENTATION OF HUMAN EXPERIENCE

We can profitably begin at the most basic level of all—the subject matter of literature. The subject of literature is human experience, as distinct from information, facts, or propositions. Literature is incarnational. Its aim is to re-create an experience in concrete rather than abstract form. Its characteristic method is to express truth through the imagination (our image-making and image-perceiving capacity).

A comparison of expository, narrative, and poetic passages on a common theme will clarify this literary impulse toward concrete presentation of human experience. For an expository description of the concept of godliness, we can take the following specimen from the NT Epistle to the Colossians (3:12–13):*

> Therefore, as God's chosen people, holy and dearly loved, clothe yourselves
> with compassion, kindness, humility, gentleness and patience. Bear with

---

* Unless otherwise noted, Scripture quotations in this chapter are from NIV.

each other and forgive whatever grievances you may have against one another. Forgive as the Lord forgave you.

Except for the metaphor of being clothed with virtues, the passage is direct and straightforward. The vocabulary is abstract. The appeal is to our intellect. The passage has no indirection that would require interpretation. All it asks us to do is grasp the commands with our mind and obey them with our actions.

Literary narrative does not *tell* us about godliness as the passage from the epistle does but instead *shows* us with the example of a godly person like Daniel. In the OT story of Daniel the quality of godliness is incarnated in the events that happened in the life of a character who performed actions in particular settings. Here the aim is to re-create a series of experiences with sufficient detail and concreteness that we can relive them in our imagination. In a story like this godliness is not an abstraction but consists of specific people engaged in action in identifiable settings. The storyteller does not tell us Daniel was a godly person, nor does he command us to be godly. The literary approach is thus more indirect than the expository, requiring a degree of interpretation on the reader's part.

The poetic version of godliness in Psalm 1 similarly avoids the abstract in deference to the concrete. Instead of incarnating godliness in character and event as narrative does, Psalm 1 relies on the images. Godliness is pictured as walking down a path and as a productive tree planted by streams of water. It is contrasted to wickedness, which is pictured as chaff driven by the wind or as a person condemned in a court of law. In short, the poet does not (like the expository writer) tell us to be godly but is content to suggest it by painting a heightened picture of the blessedness of the godly person, as contrasted to the misery of the wicked.

When measured by this literary criterion of the concrete presentation of human experience, how much of the Bible is literary? Eighty percent is not an exaggeration. The prevailing brevity of the stories and poems of the Bible should not be allowed to obscure how many appeals to our imagination these units typically possess. The Bible is much less interested in the exposition of theological, moral, or historical facts than it is in presenting human experience in the form of characters, actions, and images.

A related point is that the subject of literature is *universal* human experience. Although a story or poem is filled with particular images, paradoxically these particulars capture something universal—what is true for all people in all places at all times. While the newspaper and history book tell us what *happened*, literature tells us what *happens*. Even when a writer sticks to the facts of what actually happened, a piece of writing becomes literary to the degree to which we can recognize common human experience in it.

LITERARY GENRES IN THE BIBLE

In addition to its experiential content, literature is identifiable by its genres (literary types). Through the centuries, people have agreed that certain genres (such as story, poetry, and drama) are literary in nature. Other genres, such as historical chronicles, theological treatises, and moral commands, are expository. Still others can fall into one category or the other, depending on how a writer develops them. Letters, sermons, and orations, for example, can move in the direction of literature if they display the ordinary features of literature.

The Bible consists largely but not wholly of literary genres. The dominant one is narrative, which is the overarching framework of the Bible as a whole. More than anything else, the Bible tells a story of God's interaction with people. Its primary focus is a series of events, though of course many interspersed passages interpret the meaning of the events and give lyric expression to the human response to the events.

In terms of sheer space, poetry is no less central to the Bible than story is. Poetry is identifiable chiefly by the special language poets use. Above all, poets think in images. Next to that in importance is their inclination to compare one thing to another. If they use the specific formula "like" or "as," the statement is called a simile ("He is like a tree planted by streams of water."). In metaphor, the poet asserts that one thing *is* something else: "The Lord God is a sun and shield." Beyond the staples of image, simile, and metaphor, biblical poets draw from a larger repertoire of figures of speech—chiefly symbol, allusion, hyperbole, personification, and apostrophe (addressing someone absent as though present).

In addition to this poetic idiom, poetry uses verse form. In the Bible it does not consist of regular meter and rhyme, which is what we ordinarily mean by verse. It consists rather of thought couplets (or occasionally triplets), in which the poet states an idea more than once in different words but similar grammatical form. Synonymous parallelism uses similar grammatical form in successive lines:

Why do the nations conspire and the peoples plot in vain? (Ps. 2:1).

Antithetic parallelism introduces a contrast in the second statement:

A gentle answer turns away wrath, but a harsh word stirs up anger (Prov. 15:1).

In climactic parallelism the second line completes the first by repeating part of the first line and then adding to it:

Ascribe to the Lord, O mighty ones, ascribe to the Lord glory and strength (Ps. 29:1).

61

Synthetic (growing) parallelism is simply a two-line unit in which the second line completes the meaning of the first:

To the Lord I cry aloud, and he answers me from his holy hill (Ps. 3:4).

When we open a typical anthology of literature, we expect approximately half of the material to be poetry. The Bible meets our expectation. Whole books of the Bible are poetic—the Psalms, the Song of Solomon, the Book of Job (except for the prose prologue and epilogue), Proverbs, and others. Most of the OT prophetic books are in poetic form. Although the NT is mainly printed as prose, many of its passages are so replete with parallel construction they could be printed in verse form.

Narrative and poetry are the most common genres in the Bible, but the list expands beyond that. Visionary writing that portrays realities beyond the earthly or the present-day is quite extensive. The proverb or saying is conspicuous. Satire—the exposure of human vice or folly—is prevalent throughout the Bible. Considered in terms of space, the epistle is the genre that dominates the NT.

Another way to get a handle on the generic multiplicity—one might say the generic exuberance—of the anthology we know as the Bible is to list the subgenres that accumulate under the main headings. Under the umbrella "narrative," for example, we can list hero story, epic, tragedy, gospel, and parable. Within a single book like the Psalms, we find lyric, lament psalm, psalm of praise, encomium, royal psalm, nature psalm, worship psalm, and others.

To summarize, the Bible is literary in its reliance on literary genres. Any book that is governed so thoroughly by literary genres is a work of literature and must be approached accordingly.

ARTISTRY

Literature is more than the presentation of human experience in recognizable literary genres; it is also an art form. Whatever the genre, literature is characterized by craftsmanship, technique, and beauty. In literature, the "how" of an utterance is as important as the "what," and it is regarded as self-rewarding as well as something that intensifies the impact of an utterance.

All forms of literature share certain elements of artistic form, including unity or central focus, pattern or design, coherence, balance, contrast, symmetry, repetition or recurrence, variation, and unified progression. In addition, there is the subjective criterion of pleasure, delight, and artistic enrichment.

Once we train ourselves to look for such artistry in the Bible, we can find it in abundance. The sheer excellence and intricacy of technique in much of the Bible is enough to qualify it as a literary masterpiece. It is the literary nature of the Bible that partly makes it an interesting book rather than a dull one.

LITERARY RESOURCES OF LANGUAGE

Literature is also recognizable by its language. Literature manages to wring more meaning and beauty and affective power out of language than ordinary discourse does. It calls attention to its own eloquence and power and beauty in a way that ordinary discourse does not. It is not the mere presence of special linguistic resources that makes the Bible literature—it is their incidence. Literature defamiliarizes language with a view toward focusing our attention and finding the expression delightful in itself.

Literature gravitates toward concrete words, for example—not only in poetry, where it is the staple, but in other genres as well. The more concretely embellished a story is, for example, the further it moves from being a mere chronicle or plot summary to being fully literary. Similarly, Jesus' Sermon on the Mount is not a sermon in the ordinary sense: It is so filled with concrete pictures that it can be called poetic prose.

Literary language is also characterized by the presence of figurative language—metaphor, simile, allusion, pun, paradox, and irony. These are the very essence of poetry, but in the Bible they appear everywhere, not just in poetry. Figurative language abounds in the orations of Jesus and the NT Epistles. It is capable of showing up in the stories of the Bible, as when God tells Cain that his brother's blood "cries out to me from the ground" and that the ground has "opened its mouth to receive your brother's blood" (Gen. 4:10–11).

The presence of word play also can qualify a text as being literary, and the Bible is filled with it (as scholarly commentaries repeatedly show). The story of Ehud's assassination of Eglon (Judg. 3:15–25) serves as an illustration. The text tells us Ehud was "a left-handed man" and a "Benjamite." The name "Benjamin" means "son of my right hand." The juxtaposition of right and left strikes the keynote for this story of a crafty left-hander, since the whole plot turns on the ability of the left-handed hero to carry his sword on the unexpected right side, thereby escaping detection. The pagan king is named Eglon, which might be translated "fat calf," with associations of affluent complacency based on exploitation of an oppressed nation and of a sacrificial animal being prepared for the slaughter. Ehud gets Eglon to stand for the dagger thrust by claiming to have "a secret message for you, O king," and again we note the voltage that the language possesses, in this case stemming from dramatic irony.

In addition to these features of vocabulary, literature can gain its effects through the arrangement of clauses or other conspicuous elements of patterning. The parallel clauses of biblical poetry are an obvious example. So is the aphoristic conciseness and memorability of a biblical proverb. In the stories and poems of the Bible various elements of repetition are conspicuous. The NT Epistles feature such out-of-the-ordinary features as imaginary dialogues, repeated words or phrases, rhetorical questions, question-and-answer constructions, parallel clauses, and antithesis.

Literary language does more than language is ordinarily asked to do. Whenever a passage calls attention to the expression itself and gets more out of words than language ordinary discourse does, the resulting style lends a literary quality to the passage. Biblical writers consistently manipulate the literary resources of language, syntax, and rhetoric. Style is accordingly one of the things that makes the Bible literary.

ARCHETYPES

Archetypes are recurrent images (such as light, darkness, water, and crowns), plot motifs (such as journey, initiation, rescue, or transformation through ordeal), or character types (such as hero, villain, trickster, or innocent victim). Archetypes are the building blocks of the literary imagination. Their presence in a text is one of the things that allows us to consider a text literary.

The Bible is a book of archetypes.[6] In fact, the leading literary critic of our century called it "a grammar of literary archetypes"—the place where we can find the archetypes of the imagination in relatively complete and systematic form.[7]

Wherever we turn in the Bible, we are confronted with the master images of the literary imagination. For the most part, these are the archetypes of literature generally, partly because the Bible has been the single greatest influence on Western literature. Recognizing the link between familiar literature and the Bible is an important part of seeing the Bible as literature, for the simple reason that to speak of the Bible as literature at all depends on our giving ordinary meaning to the word "literature." An awareness of archetypes in the Bible also is an avenue to seeing that the

---

6. For more on the archetypes of the Bible, see Northrup Frye, *The Great Code: The Bible and Literature* (New York: Harcourt, 1982), 80; and Leland Ryken, *How to Read the Bible as Literature* (Grand Rapids: Zondervan, 1984), 187–93, and *Words of Delight: A Literary Introduction to the Bible* (Grand Rapids: Baker, 1987), 25–29.

7. Frye, *Anatomy of Criticism* (Princeton: Princeton University Press, 1957), 135.

Bible is a universal book and to seeing the Bible itself as a family of inter-locking material instead of a collection of unrelated fragments.

The Bible is literary by ordinary literary criteria. At the level of subject matter, it overwhelmingly presents aspects of human experience con-cretely instead of developing abstract concepts and logical arguments. At the level of form, the Bible is not primarily a collection of essays but an anthology of literary genres. The Bible repeatedly displays an abundance of artistry, and it exploits the resources of language and rhetoric in ways that go beyond ordinary discourse. It also presents the archetypes of the literary imagination on virtually every page.

HOW TO READ THE BIBLE AS LITERATURE

To acknowledge the Bible is in large part a work of literature is a neces-sary but insufficient starting point. The important corollary is to realize what methodology the literary nature of the Bible requires of us as we read and study and teach it. Bible commentaries in the traditional mold cannot be trusted to be of much help in this regard, inasmuch as their agenda of concerns is very different from what I am about to outline.

The umbrella under which to approach the Bible as literature can be summarized in the formula "meaning through form." The concept of "form" should be construed very broadly here to include anything that touches upon *how* a writer has expressed the content. Everything that a piece of writing communicates is communicated through a given medium, beginning with language.

While this is true for all forms of writing, it is especially crucial for lit-erature. Literature has its own forms and techniques. Before we can understand what a piece of literature says, we need to scrutinize the form in which it says it. If that form is a story, we need first to interact with characters, setting, and action. If it is a poem, we need to assimilate its images and figures of speech before we can understand its message.

The literary critic's preoccupation with the *how* of biblical writing is not frivolous. It is a quest for understanding as well as enjoyment. In a literary text, it is impossible to separate what is said from how it is said, content from form. A literary approach insists that reliving the text as a coherent whole is the first item on the agenda.

READING WITH THE RIGHT SIDE OF THE BRAIN

If the subject of literature is human experience, concretely presented, several corollaries follow. One is that we must read the Bible with our imagination and emotions as well as our intellect. In the terms popularized by recent brain research, we must read the literary parts of the Bible with the right side of the brain—that part of our being that experiences concrete images and feelings. As readers we must be active in re-creating experiences and sensations and events.

The literary parts of the Bible aim to convey a sense of reality, not only ideas. This, in turn, should affect how we regard the truth that the Bible communicates. By "truth" we ordinarily mean an idea that is true. But literature presents an additional type of truth—truthfulness to reality, to human experience, to the way things are in the world. To grasp this type of truth does not require us to formulate an abstract idea. When asked to define "neighbor," Jesus avoided an abstract definition and instead told a story. We do not have to translate His story into an idea before we have grasped the truth of His parable. All we have to do is *recognize* and *experience* the neighborly behavior of the Samaritan.

To read the Bible as literature, we need to develop the knack for recognizing human experience. Literature is a mirror in which we see ourselves, our experiences, and our world. Of course this requires that we meet it halfway and build bridges to familiar experience. The story of the fall (Gen. 3) tells us what various characters did in the garden on the fatal day. It is up to us to see in this story a picture not only of what happened but also of what happens—a picture of how the fall into sin happens in anybody's life, of how guilt operates in our lives as well as Adam and Eve's, of how the consequences of sin affect everyone at all times and in all places.

Traditional approaches to the Bible have been preoccupied with its theological and moral ideas, with the historicity of biblical events, and with the background or context of biblical passages. A literary approach asks us to supplement this agenda with an equally important but very different set of interests. In addition to expecting to encounter ideas as we read the Bible, we need to expect to encounter characters, events, settings, and images. This involves paying attention to matters that seem far removed from anything spiritual or edifying, but literary critics are unanimous in saying there is a sense in which the whole story or the whole poem is the meaning.

QUESTIONING THE TEXT

The importance of the presence of literary genres in the Bible is that every genre has its own rules of composition and implied methods of interpretation. We need to come to a given genre with the right expectations. If we do, we will see more than we would otherwise see, and we will be spared from misinterpretations. Literary genre is a "norm or expectation to guide the reader in his encounter with the text."[8] An awareness of genre will program our reading of a work, giving it a familiar shape and arranging the details into an identifiable pattern.

Much of what biblical scholars have been accustomed to calling the intention of the writer is actually a statement of how a given genre operates. Instead of speaking of the author's intention in these instances, we can more accurately say, with Northrop Frye, that the right interpretation of a biblical text is one "that conforms to the intentionality of the book itself and to the conventions it assumes and requires."[9]

To approach a biblical text in keeping with its generic expectations, we need to learn to ask the right questions of a text. What follows are specimens only; for a more thorough account, I refer readers to my book *How to Read the Bible as Literature*.

Stories consist of three basic ingredients—setting, characters, and plot or action—and we need to ask appropriate questions in all three areas. For setting, we need to ask first, What does the text tell me literally about the scene in which the action occurs? Then we need to move from observation to interpretation with such questions as these: How does the setting contribute to the action? What function does it serve in the story? What correspondence can I find between the setting and the characters and events that operate within it? What symbolic overtones (moral, affective, psychological) does the setting possess?

The goal of character analysis is to get to know characters as fully as possible. The questions that will help us to compose character portraits include the following: What do characters' actions or words tell me about them? What do I learn about them from the responses of other characters to them or from statements by the storyteller? What universal aspects of human nature are embodied in various characters? Do characters belong to a recognizable literary archetype?

The questions to ask about action spring from the nature of a story's plot. Conflict is the essence of a plot. In fact, a story is usually structured around the principle of a beginning (the set of circumstances that make the conflict possible), a middle (the unfolding progress of the conflict), and an end (the resolution or closure of the conflict). The central character in the conflict is the protagonist, and the forces arrayed against him or her are the antagonists. Characters in a story are typically put into situations that test them, and they are usually called to make significant

---

8. Jonathan Culler, *Structuralist Poetics* (Ithaca, N.Y.: Cornell University Press, 1975), 136.

9. Frye, *Great Code*, 80.

choices. It is also important to realize that stories are unified by a unifying *action*, not a unifying idea.

The corresponding list of questions to ask about plot are therefore these: What plot conflicts organize this story? How are these resolved? Who are the protagonists and antagonists in the story? What elements of testing and choice are important to the action? Does dramatic irony (the discrepancy between the superior knowledge of the reader and the ignorance of a character in a story) play a role in the story? What archetypal plot patterns (such as initiation or quest) give shape to the story? What is the unifying action (as distinct from unifying idea)?

Having relived the story, it is necessary to move from story to meaning. If novelist Flannery O'Connor was right in saying that storytellers speak *"with* character and action, not *about* character and action,"[10] we need to ask what the writer is telling us *about life* by means of the characters and events that have been presented. We must assume the storyteller was attracted to the story because it reveals the deep significance of life. So we can ask, What experiment in living do the characters (especially the protagonist) undertake? On the basis of the story's outcome, what verdict does the story offer about such an experiment in living? What is the story about, and what does it say about that thing?

Poetry requires a very different set of questions, though again the important principle is that the questions must be allowed to emerge from the nature of the genre. Knowing that poets think in images, we can begin with the literal, sensory level. Having experienced an image in a poem, we need to ask, What are the connotations of this image in this context? Are the connotations positive or negative? What more specific meanings emerge from the image? What is the logic of the poet using this image for this subject? Why, for example, would the poet compare God to a sun and shield?

Similes and metaphors likewise require a twofold process of interpretation. First, we need to determine the literal picture. If the godly person is like a tree planted by streams of water, we need to ask, What are the literal properties of this phenomenon of nature? Then we need to carry over the meanings to the other half of the comparison, as even the word metaphor implies (it comes from the Greek "to carry over"). If A is said to be like B, exactly what are the relevant points of similarity, given the context?

To round out our questioning of a biblical poem, we can ask, What further figures of speech are present in the poem? What meanings and feelings are communicated by means of these? What unifying idea, situation,

---

10. Flannery O'Connor, *Mystery and Manners* (New York: Farrar, Straus & Giroux), 76.

or feeling organizes the poem? What are the individual units within the poem, and how does each one of these constitute a variation on the unifying theme? What elements of contrast or repetition are important in the organization of the poem?

Other biblical genres require their appropriate questions. We know what questions to ask only as we develop our awareness of the conventions that underlie a genre. If we know that satire consists of four ingredients (an object of attack, a vehicle in which the attack is embodied, a standard by which the criticism is conducted, and a prevailing tone), we can formulate corresponding questions.

If we know that tragedy is constructed around a discernible sequence of events, we can formulate these questions: What characterizes the tragic hero, and in particular what constitutes his or her tragic flaw of character? What is the nature of the hero's tragic choice? What form do the hero's catastrophe and suffering take? Does the hero attain perception, and if so, what is its exact content?

A literary approach to the Bible is almost synonymous with a genre approach, especially if we include the notion that literature itself is a genre with identifiable traits. If we apply to the Bible what we know about literature generally and what literary handbooks tell us about various genres, we will handle the Bible competently.

ARTISTRY AND STYLE

After we have paid attention to the experiential subject matter and the literary genres of the Bible, we can move on to the finer points of artistry and style. The main activity this aspect of biblical literature requires is simply a sensitivity to it.

Unity is perhaps the most important aspect of artistry, and one of the things that has most consistently differentiated literary approaches to the Bible from other approaches has been the literary critic's preoccupation with the unity of passages. This begins with a belief that literature achieves its effects primarily through literary wholes, not through isolated parts. A concern for unity tends to generate awareness of other aspects of artistry—pattern and design, repetition, balance, symmetry, and coherence.

Artistry satisfies the human urge for beauty, delight, and enjoyment. A literary approach to the Bible is ready to value these purposes. It does not apologize for taking time to admire the craftsmanship of a biblical story or poem. That the Bible possesses such artistry is indisputable. The only question is whether we can develop the antennae by which to notice and enjoy the artistic side of the Bible.

Much the same is true of the linguistic nuances that I have claimed for the Bible. It is of course possible to get the big picture of a biblical passage without knowing about its smaller resources of language. But the literary nuances of language and rhetorical patterning often contribute to the meaning of a passage and offer additional reasons to admire it. At this level, as well as the level of human experience, the Bible is an inexhaustible book. It yields more and more as we enlarge the fund of experience and literary knowledge we are able to bring to it.

THE BIBLE AS AN
ANTHOLOGY: FINAL IMPRESSIONS

The implied thesis of my remarks has been that as a literary anthology the Bible is a mingling of the familiar and the unfamiliar. We find the familiar emphasis on human experience, the presence of familiar genres and archetypes, and the usual display of artistry and reliance on special resources of language. But along with these familiar features, much strikes us as distinctive (though not absolutely unique).

What impresses us most, perhaps, is the immense range of what is included. Every human experience is covered in some form in the Bible, the most comprehensive of all books. At the level of subject matter, the Bible is a book for all seasons and all temperaments. A similar range is found in the forms of the Bible. The list of genres and subgenres keeps expanding. In style the Bible ranges all the way from the prosaic and unliterary to the highly polished and embellished. The gallery of memorable characters exceeds anything we find in other anthologies. The Bible is the story of all things, embodied in a collection of all major literary genres.

The Bible is a paradoxical book. Because of its range and its truthfulness to human experience, it preserves the complexities and polarities of life to an unusual degree. The paradoxes of life are held in tension in what can be called the most balanced anthology ever compiled. Human responsibility and divine sovereignty, God's transcendence and immanence, humankind's potential for greatness and smallness, the importance of the earthly and yet its relative inferiority to the heavenly, the importance of the individual and yet the incompleteness of the individual apart from relationship, the literary impulse toward realism but also toward the more-than-earthly—these and other poles are simultaneously affirmed in the Bible. Even the style of the Bible is a paradox: It combines simplicity with majesty.

Despite its immense range of content and style, the Bible possesses more unity than other anthologies; it has a unifying plot. The central conflict is the great spiritual battle between good and evil. The protagonist is God, with every creature and event showing some movement, whether slight or momentous, toward God or away from Him.

This anthology tells a single story in a way other anthologies do not, beginning with the creation of the world, followed by the history of the human race and ending with the conclusion of human history and the beginning of eternity. A slightly more detailed chronology, with the accompanying literary form that dominates each part of the story, is this one: (1) the beginning of human history—creation, fall, and covenant (Genesis, or the story of origins); (2) Exodus (law); (3) Israelite monarchy (wisdom literature and poetry); (4) exile and return (prophecy); (5) the life of Christ (Gospels); (6) the beginnings of the Christian church (Acts and the Epistles); and (7) the consummation of history (apocalypse).

Despite stylistic and generic diversity, biblical writers generally share certain preferences. They prefer the brief unit to the long one, conciseness to prolixity, the realistic to the wholly idealized, the plain or simple style to the embellished style, the religious view of life to the secular, the historical to the fictional, dialogue and dramatization to summarized narrative, the happy ending to the tragic, the bare narration of what happened over an explanation of it. Biblical writers gravitate naturally to heightened contrasts, to master images like light and darkness and pilgrimage, to elemental human experience, to simplified virtues and vices, to a clear sense of the world and of what is right and wrong in that world, to the primacy of the spiritual as a basic assumption about life.

The literary approach to the Bible is incomplete in itself, but it is necessary. It enables us to understand what the Bible says and at the same time to enjoy how it is said. Reading the Bible as literature should constitute our initial reading of the biblical text. The literary approach allows us to relive the text. Having relived it, we can move on to other considerations, especially the theological and moral. Not to relive the text in a literary manner is to short-circuit the process of reading and interpretation.

FOR FURTHER READING

Auerbach, Erich. *Mimesis: The Representation of Reality in Western Literature.* Princeton: Princeton University Press, 1953. The opening chapter is especially noteworthy.

Alter, Robert. *The Art of Biblical Narrative* and *The Art of Biblical Poetry.* New York: Basic Books, 1981 and 1985.

Alter, Robert and Frank Kermode, eds. *The Literary Guide to the Bible.* Cambridge, Mass.: Harvard University Press, 1987.

Frye, Northrop. *The Great Code: The Bible and Literature*. New York: Harcourt, 1982.

Longman, Tremper. *Literary Approaches to Biblical Interpretation*. Grand Rapids: Zondervan, 1987.

Longman, Tremper and Leland Ryken, eds. *A Complete Literary Guide to the Bible*. Grand Rapids: Zondervan, 1993.

Preminger, Alex and Edward L. Greenstein, eds. *The Hebrew in Literary Criticism*. New York: Ungar, 1986.

Rhoads, David and Donald Michie. *Mark as Story*. Philadelphia: Fortress, 1982.

Ryken, Leland. *How to Read the Bible as Literature*. Grand Rapids: Zondervan, 1984.

———. *Words of Delight: A Literary Introduction to the Bible*. Grand Rapids: Baker, 1987.

———. *Words of Life: A Literary Introduction to the New Testament*. Grand Rapids: Baker, 1987.

———. ed. *The New Testament in Literary Criticism*. New York: Ungar, 1984.

V

GEOGRAPHY
OF THE BIBLE LANDS

KEITH N. SCHOVILLE

One can read the Bible without knowing anything about the geography of Bible lands, but a general knowledge of that geography is essential to attaining an informed understanding of the biblical text.

The lands of the Bible reach from Spain in the west to the borders of India in the east, from southern Europe (Italy and Greece) in the north to central Africa (Ethiopia and Sudan) in the south. Naturally, the geography in such a large area is quite varied.

Broadly speaking, geography itself is varied. Our word geography encompasses the physical nature of the earth's surface, but it also includes the features of climate, plants, animals, and natural resources.[1] Human geography is the study of the interaction between people and the geographic environment.

Because the Bible focuses on ancient Canaan, incorporating much of the area now occupied by the modern states of Lebanon, Syria, Israel, and Jordan, this region will receive our primary attention. The region forms the southern extension of arable land which curves north and east

---

1. *Webster's New World Dictionary*, 2d ed., s.v. "geography."

into the Mesopotamian Valley, or Fertile Crescent,[2] as it was named by Sir Henry Breasted. Beyond Syria-Palestine, as the region is often identified, the biblical world included Mesopotamia and Persia to the east and the Arabian peninsula and Egypt to the south. When we add the world of the NT to that of the OT, the entire Mediterranean Basin also comes into view.[3]

GEOLOGY AND GEOGRAPHY

Fundamental to geography is its underlying geological foundation. In the Genesis account of creation (1:1—2:3), the finished work was pronounced "good."* Inherent in that assessment, one may assume, is the continuing geological work of the earth in forming various types of rock.

Geologists have identified a series of geological eras during which the basic rock structures of the earth were formed. These have been named the Precambrian, the Paleozoic, the Mesozoic, and the Cenozoic eras.[4] The oldest rocks were formed in the Precambrian era when a crust formed on the molten earth. The wearing action of wind, rain, and dust eroded their surfaces, and natural forces carried the debris away to settle in seabeds. Under pressure, layers of sedimentary deposits hardened into limestone and sandstone. Tectonic forces pushed hot magma from the earth; it issued in volcanic eruptions or rose up into new mountains.

One of the major seams on the earth's surface is the geological fault that begins in northern Syria and extends down into central Africa. In the Holy Land it is called the Rift Valley, and within it flow the Jordan River, the Sea of Galilee, the Dead Sea, and to the south, the Arabah.[5] Such geological faults are prone to cause earthquakes and the uplifting and subsiding of the earth's surface. Variations in landscapes result from this action and from the continuous erosion of exposed rocks by water and wind. Different types of stone break down into varied soils. The type of stone found in a region will affect the construction of buildings, types of vegetation,

---

2. Charles F. Pfeiffer, ed., *The Biblical World* (Grand Rapids: Baker, 1966), 238–39.

3. Keith N. Schoville, *Biblical Archaeology in Focus* (Grand Rapids: Baker, 1978), 69.

4. Alice J. Hall, ed., *National Geographic Atlas of the World*, 5th ed. (Washington, D.C.: National Geographic Society, 1981), 22–23.

5. Carl G. Rasmussen, *Zondervan NIV Atlas of the Bible* (Grand Rapids: Zondervan, 1989), 19–22.

* Unless otherwise noted, Scripture quotations in this chapter are from NIV.

availability of water, and many other influences on human activity.[6] The Bible reader need not know the technical terminology of geology or even of geography to grasp the importance of these interrelationships: They provide the backdrop of the human and divine activities inscribed on the Bible's pages.

THE GEOGRAPHY OF CANAAN

Abraham was called to a land that is small. The land occupied on both sides of the Jordan by the tribes of Israel, his descendants, covers approximately 10,000 square miles. It is a narrow strip of habitable land between the Mediterranean Sea to the west and the Syrian Desert to the east. This strip at its widest does not exceed seventy-five miles. The mountains of Lebanon and Anti-Lebanon form a natural northern boundary. The length of the land in biblical tradition is "from Dan to Beer-sheba," (Judg. 20:1, NRSV) with Dan in the north at the base of lofty Mount Hermon (elevation 9,232 feet) and Beersheba in the arid southland (the Negeb). The distance between the two locations is approximately 150 miles.

The topography of this region also is diverse. The area divides naturally into five regions moving eastward from the Mediterranean: coastal plain, central highlands, Rift Valley, the hills of Transjordan, and the desert.[7]

COASTAL PLAIN

The coastal plain extends northward from the northern Sinai desert along the Mediterranean coast to the border of modern Lebanon. It narrows progressively from a twenty-mile width near Gaza on the Philistine Plain, to twelve miles near Joppa on the border of the Plain of Sharon, to less than two miles along the Plain of Dor south of Haifa. Sand dunes, especially along the coast of the Plain of Sharon, prevented water draining from the mountains to the east to flow easily into the sea. Swamps resulted, causing travelers through the area to swing eastward to the base of the mountains.

Mount Carmel, a northwesterly extension of the central highlands, interrupts the coastal plain where it meets the sea at the modern city of Haifa. North of Mount Carmel, the Plain of Acco (Acre), some five to seven miles in width, ends abruptly at the white limestone cliffs of Rosh Hanikra, the ancient "Ladder of Tyre." Beyond this point, narrow plains

---

6. Yohanan Aharoni, *The Land of the Bible, A Historical Geography*, rev. and enl., ed. and trans. A. F. Rainey (Philadelphia: Westminster, 1979), 11–13.

7. Schoville, *Biblical Archaeology*, 69.

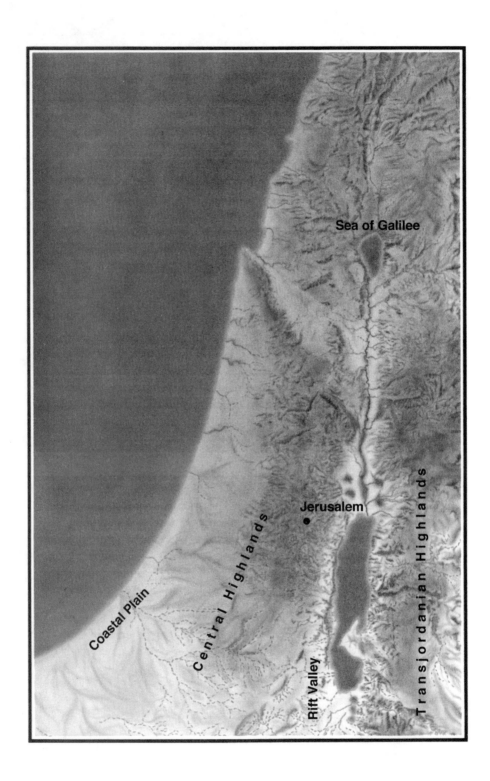

Sea of Galilee

Jerusalem

Coastal Plain

Central Highlands

Rift Valley

Transjordanian Highlands

occur irregularly along the coast between the mountains and the sea. Northward along this coast, the Phoenician cities of Tyre, Sidon, Beirut, and Byblus were built. Phoenicians also occupied the Plain of Acco in antiquity, and the area was a part of the land of Cabul given by Solomon to the Phoenician King Hiram in payment for services rendered (1 Kings 9:10–14).

An extension of the Plain of Acco in a southeasterly direction, parallel to and just north of the Carmel range, connects to the Jordan Valley. This plain in its several aspects is known as the Plain of Megiddo, the Valley of Jezreel, and the Plain of Beth-shan.[8] Galilee lies to the north, and the hill country of Ephraim (Samaria) stretches southward from this depression.

CENTRAL HIGHLANDS

The hills of Galilee comprise one of four main regions into which the central highlands may be conveniently divided. Upper Galilee has heights reaching to nearly 4,000 feet in the north and to about 2,700 feet farther south. Upper Galilee is a southern extension of the Lebanese mountains. Lower Galilee, in which Nazareth is nestled, does not exceed 2,000 feet in elevation. This area is separated from Upper Galilee by a slope rising from 1,500 to 2,000 feet.[9]

Farther south, beyond the Plain of Jezreel, the hill country of Ephraim rises to elevations between 2,500 and 3,000 feet, with the southern area higher than the northern. No clearly delineated geographical features separate the hill country of Ephraim from the hills of Judea to the south, but for convenience Jerusalem may be regarded as near the northern boundary of the latter region. These hills rise slightly as one goes south from Jerusalem to Hebron, which is situated at about 3,000 feet elevation. Continuing south from Hebron, the heights fall to about 2,000 feet in the eastern Negeb, but beyond the Negeb the mountains rise into the Sinai Peninsula to a height of almost 9,000 feet at Jebel Musa (the Mountain of Moses), the site of St. Catherine's Monastery.[10]

To the west of the Judean hills, before one reaches the coastal plain, lie the low hills of the Shephelah,[11] while to the east the land falls rapidly into the forbidding wilderness of Judea, the desolate area in which the Dead Sea Scrolls were discovered.[12] Here the terrain plunges into the Rift Val-

---

8. Aharoni, *Land of the Bible*, 22–23.
9. Ibid., 27–28.
10. Rasmussen, *Zondervan NIV Atlas*, 40–42.
11. Aharoni, *Land of the Bible*, 25–26.
12. Schoville, *Biblical Archaeology*, 72.

ley along the Dead Sea, 1,290 feet below sea level. Thus, a descent of more than 3,000 feet occurs within a distance of only ten to fifteen miles.

RIFT VALLEY

The awesome Rift Valley is actually a depression between two great parallel geological faults. This great cleft in the earth begins near the modern border between Syria and Turkey and continues south between the Lebanon and Anti-Lebanon Mountains. It carries northward the Orontes River on which Antioch was located (Acts 11:19). The valley extends southward through Palestine and the Gulf of Eilat (Aqaba) into Africa. The valley in Palestine averages ten miles in width and varies in altitude from about 300 feet above sea level in the north to 1,290 feet below sea level on the surface of the Dead Sea, the lowest point on the face of the earth apart from the oceanic depths.

Continuing southward, the valley floor rises to about 750 feet above sea level at the highest point in the Arabah, before it descends again to sea level at the mouth of the Gulf of Eilat, the site of biblical Ezion Geber (1 Kings 9:26). The Rift Valley can be divided conveniently into five areas from north to south: the Huleh Valley, the Sea of Galilee, the Jordan Valley, the Dead Sea, and the Arabah.[13]

Extending southward from the base of Mount Hermon, the Huleh Valley contained until recently an extensive body of water (Lake Huleh) along with surrounding swamps through which the upper Jordan River meandered. In modern times the river has been straightened and the swamps drained so that the present area of the lake is considerably reduced from its size in antiquity.[14] Farther south, the Jordan flows swiftly down into the basin of the Sea of Galilee, 630 feet below sea level. The descent from 210 feet above sea level at Lake Huleh is made in a distance of ten miles.

The Sea of Galilee, thirteen miles long and seven miles across at its widest point, reaches a depth of almost 200 feet along its eastern shore, where cliffs rise abruptly above it. The Jordan flows through it to make it the only natural freshwater lake in the region.

The Jordan Valley proper extends southward from the Sea of Galilee until it empties into the Dead Sea, approximately seventy miles farther south. The name *Jordan* means "that which goes down," and the swift descent of the waters is slowed only by the tortuous channel they have carved out of the valley floor; the actual course the waters follow is three times longer than the distance by air. A low, flat strip of dense jungle-like

---

13. J. Rogerson, *Atlas of the Bible* (New York: Facts on File, 1985), 58–60.

14. Efraim Orni and Elisha Efrat, *Geography of Israel* (Jerusalem: Israel Program for Scientific Translations, 1964), 73–74.

vegetation through which the river flows is called the Zor. The main part of the valley which stretches back to meet the hills on either side is called the Ghor.[15] In modern times, the environment has been changed by increased human habitation and irrigated agriculture, but in antiquity the Zor posed a formidable barrier, penetrated only at a few crossing points along the river.

As the waters of the Jordan empty into the Dead Sea, they bear a constant flow of dissolved minerals. Since the sea has no outlet and is subject to an extremely high rate of evaporation, a uniform water level is maintained. The high concentration of mineral salts prevents any form of marine life, hence the sea's name.[16] In the Bible it is most frequently called the Salt Sea (Gen. 14:3), but the Romans knew it as the Sea of Asphalt.

The Dead Sea, approximately forty-five miles long and ten miles across at its maximum width, is divided into two parts by the Lisan, a peninsula that extends into the sea from the eastern shore. North of the Lisan, the depth of the sea reaches about 1,200 feet, which, when added to the surface level of 1,292 feet below sea level, makes this one of the most astounding geological features on the face of the earth. South of the Lisan, the sea is only two to three miles across, and the depth is only thirty to thirty-five feet. The southern end has undergone dramatic shrinking due to modern exploitation of its mineral resources.[17]

The Arabah (Deut. 1:1) south of the Dead Sea to the Gulf of Eilat is 110 miles of valley floor between the mountains of the Negeb to the west and of Edom to the east.

TRANSJORDANIAN HIGHLANDS

The Transjordanian highlands, which rise sharply from the eastern floor of the Rift Valley, are broken into regions by deep canyons (wadis) which penetrated into the valley from the east.[18] These wadis are stream beds which are partially dry during the year but, during the winter rainy season, can become raging torrents. In the north, the Yarmuk enters the Rift slightly south of the Sea of Galilee. It provides a natural boundary between the present states of Syria and Jordan, while in biblical times north of the Yarmuk lay the areas of Geshur (the Golan Heights) and the Bashan (Num. 21:3). The Bashan, some 2,000 feet in elevation, lies in the midst of an area of basalt caused by now-extinct volcanoes. Similar volca-

---

15. Aharoni, *Land of the Bible*, 33–34.
16. Orni and Efrat, *Geography of Israel*, 85–86.
17. Both the State of Israel and the Hashemite Kingdom of Jordan have facilities at the south end of the sea to extract the valuable minerals.
18. Schoville, *Biblical Archaeology*, 74–75.

nic rock abounds on the west side of the Jordan River in the area north of the Sea of Galilee. The rich volcanic soil of the Bashan region provided pasture lands for the noted bulls of Bashan (Ps. 22:12).

Gilead, a tableland higher and more rugged than the Bashan, with heights approaching 3,000 feet, is cleft by the Jabbok River (Gen. 32:22), now known as the Nahr ez-Zarqa. It enters the Rift Valley about midway through the area of Gilead, a region jointly occupied in biblical times by the tribes of Gad and Manasseh. The Ammonites also inhabited a part of the area. Rabbath-Ammon, their ancient capital, is now the modern city of Amman, Jordan.

No distinctive natural boundary separated the region of Moab from that of Gilead, but the northern boundary of Moab was generally eastward from the north end of the Dead Sea. Moab proper was divided into two parts by the Arnon canyon (modern Wadi el-Mujib), which enters the Dead Sea midway along its eastern shore. Both areas consist of level table-lands with an elevation of 2,000 to 2,400 feet in the northern sector and occasionally exceeding 3,000 feet in the southern.

The Wadi el-Hasa, the biblical brook Zered, which enters the Dead Sea at its southeastern corner, provided a natural boundary between Moab and Edom to the south. The mountains of Edom rise in places to heights transcending 5,000 feet. The King's Highway of the Bible (Num. 20:17) coming from the east traversed Bashan, Gilead, Moab, and Edom before crossing the Sinai peninsula into Egypt. Other road systems branched off from it. One led southward into Arabia; another crossed the Arabah through the Negeb to the city of Gaza. Along the eastern fringes of the Transjordanian hills, the fertile land fades away into the forbidding deserts of Syria in the north and Arabia toward the south. Nomadic tribes from these desert regions often raided the settled areas, posing a continuing threat to Israelite village life (Judg. 6:3–5).

The diversity of terrain in the Holy Land fragmented the country, and this fragmentation affected social organization. Rather than establishing large, united kingdoms, the Canaanites developed small city-states with surrounding villages, pasture, and agricultural lands. The difficulty of travel through rugged mountains and valleys contributed to regional isola-tion. The intertribal conflicts detailed in the Book of Judges attest to the same effects of the land on the Israelite tribes, until the political power of David's and Solomon's kingdom brought a forced unification.[19]

WEATHER AND CLIMATE

A combination of factors affects the patterns of rainfall and the supply of water so essential to life in Palestine—the geographical location, the

---

19. Aharoni, *Land of the Bible*, 42.

prevailing winds, the landforms, and the geological substructures of the landforms. Underground aquifers and the surfacing of springs are determined by the composition and lay of the underlying bedrock.

The 30° north latitude crosses Palestine just north of the Gulf of Eilat and extends through Cairo, Egypt. In the United States, the same line crosses northern Florida.[20] The 32° line that crosses the hills of northern Galilee also crosses central Georgia. But unlike the southeastern United States, most of the Holy Land lies in a subtropical zone, modified by a Mediterranean climate, having a rainy season in the winter and a dry season in the summer (these are the "former and latter rains," Jer. 5:24; Hos. 6:3; Joel 2:23). In this respect, it is more similar to southern California. During the winter the prevailing winds blow out of the west-northwest across the Mediterranean, often producing violent thunderstorms, and then are forced upward by the mountains inland. At other times, easterly winds from the desert, the famous *khamsin*, flood the land with hot, dry air which scorches the countryside to a monotonous brown.[21] The forces of nature contend for dominion over this land, lying as it does between the desert and the sea.

The pattern of rainfall tends to decrease from the north to the south and from the sea inland, averaging some thirty inches annually at Safad, in Upper Galilee; twenty-three to twenty-five inches at Jerusalem; and eight to nine inches at Beersheba. Jericho, in the Jordan Valley, receives only four to six inches; the Tel Aviv-Jaffa area, eighteen to twenty inches; and Gaza, fifteen inches. These local variations in rainfall are compounded by differences in altitude. (For example, although Jericho is at approximately the same latitude as Jerusalem, its extremely low altitude makes it an oasis in the desert, a northern extension of the desert conditions of the Negeb into the Rift Valley. A few perennial springs in the area sustain life, for the rainfall is insufficient.) Marginal as well as rather severe fluctuations in annual rainfall combine to leave the Holy Land subject to droughts. During the long, rainless summers, heavy dew in the highlands provide some moisture to plant life. The value of the dew is implicit in David's lament upon the death of Jonathan and Saul (2 Sam. 1:21).

The precariousness of life among the peoples living along the desert fringes has produced throughout history a constant struggle for existence. The dependence upon rainfall for life-giving moisture influenced the religious ideas of the inhabitants as well. The chief god of the Canaanites was Baal-Hadad, lord of thunderstorms.[22] The Israelites also recognized Yah-

---

20. Rasmussen, *Zondervan NIV Atlas*, 16.
21. Aharoni, *Land of the Bible*, 8–9.
22. Helmer Ringgren, *Religions of the Ancient Near East*, trans. John Sturdy (Philadelphia: Westminster, 1973), 132.

weh, the Lord God, as the source of beneficial rain. Psalm 29 honors Him as Lord of the storm, and the drought was broken at His word in the time of King Ahab and the prophet Elijah (1 Kings 18).

NATURAL RESOURCES

The promised land is described as "a land whose stones are iron, and out of whose hills you can dig copper" (Deut. 8:9), yet the country is not blessed with mineral wealth. Some ancient sources of iron have been discovered in Transjordan, but the reference in Deuteronomy is more likely to iron-hard volcanic rock. Ancient slag dumps discovered in the Arabah testify to the smelting of both iron and copper, and copper was mined on both sides of the valley north of Eilat. The famous copper mines attributed to Solomon were already being exploited by Egyptians as early as the close of the Late Bronze Age (ca. 1200 B.C.). Nevertheless, the region is poor in metallic ores.

Apart from the basalt layers in the north and granite outcroppings in the south, most of the rocks are of limestone or sandstone. Various stones were quarried for the construction of homes, palaces, temples, and city walls. In NT times the basalt boulders in the Galilee and Golan regions were the basis of an industry that produced grinding mills from the hard stone. No doubt one of these was in the mind of Jesus when He warned His audience about the danger of causing a child to stumble, noting that it would be better for that person to have a millstone fastened around his neck and to be cast into the sea (Matt. 18:6). When stone was not available, mudbrick was employed in construction.

SOILS AND AGRICULTURE

The most abundant natural resource was the soil; thus, in Deuteronomy the description of the land primarily concerns agriculture. It is "a land of wheat and barley, of vines and fig trees and pomegranates, a land of olive oil and honey" (Deut. 8:8). While the honey produced by wild bees was known and collected, the reference here also may include a sweet date syrup. The richness of the soils depends on the rocky sources combined with sufficient moisture.

The hard limestone of the central highlands does not erode easily, but over time it slowly breaks down to form the fertile red soil known as *terra rossa*. This topsoil will soon wash away if not protected by vegetation and conservation. Some of the richness of the alluvial plains, such as the Plain of Jezreel, is the result of deposits of sediments washed down from the mountains. Although the Canaanites had begun to exploit the highlands in modest areas around Shechem, Gibeon, Bethel, Jerusalem, and Hebron, the Israelites were instructed by Joshua to clear the forests in the territory of Ephraim. Unfortunately, this vegetation was not commercially valuable like the famed cedars of Lebanon to the north, which were desired by rulers in Mesopotamia and Egypt alike.

To counteract the effects of deforestation, terraces were constructed on the mountain slopes to conserve the soil. Because few springs flow except at the base of mountains, village life in the highlands was made possible by transporting water in large ceramic jars on asses from a distant source or by collecting rainwater in rock-cut, plastered cisterns. Later, when the inhabitants were deported or they abandoned their villages, the terraces collapsed and the soil eroded, leaving some areas with bare rocky slopes where once intensive cultivation existed.

Along the Mediterranean coast, and particularly along the Plain of Sharon, extensive sand dunes and ridges of sandstone called *kurkar* were not conducive to agriculture, while inland the area was swampy. In modern times, however, agricultural engineering has made the Plain of Sharon a rich agricultural area. The gentle limestone hills of the Shephelah and its valleys were hospitable to agriculture, and the adjacent Plain of Philistia is covered with rich alluvial soils. The northern Negeb has a rich windblown soil (*loess*), but inadequate rainfall prevented widespread agriculture in antiquity. Patches of grain could be grown by nomadic inhabitants in the silty beds of wadis after the winter rains had passed, but such a practice was always a gamble. With irrigation the desert now blooms.

In the north, decomposed limestone or basalt provided fertile soils mixed with stones. Olive, fruit, and nut trees flourished in Galilee. And throughout the hill country, grapes and related products—raisins and wine—were produced. These, along with small grains, nuts, and fresh and dried fruits, comprised the bulk of the diet of biblical people.

Animal husbandry provided another avenue to sustenance. Shepherds from villages pastured flocks of sheep and goats in uncultivated areas, while a few cattle were kept in the villages. Over the centuries, the destructive feeding habits of the goat, willing to climb low shrubs and trees to devour the foliage, has contributed to the deforestation of much of the Mediterranean area. After the grain fields were harvested, the fodder remaining was used for pasture.

Meat was not a constant item in the diet of biblical peoples, but the fatted calf provided a special delicacy (Gen. 18:7; Luke 15:23). By-products of animal husbandry contributed to cottage industries in textiles and leather. A subsistence style of life meant that most products were locally made and consumed. The village potter provided an essential service, as did the carpenter and stone mason. Other skills included the making of jewelry and signet rings.

THE GEOGRAPHY OF ISRAEL'S NEIGHBORS

The small desert nations to the east, often referred to in the biblical accounts of wars and in the prophetic oracles (Amos 1:3—2:3) included Edom, Moab, and Ammon. They occupied an area near the desert that could not support large populations. The high mountains on the east side of the Rift Valley forced moisture-bearing winds to drop their precious load in the region occupied by the three peoples, leaving little or no precipitation for the desert to the east.

The Arabian peninsula is largely desolate desert, a vast space some 1,600 miles long by 1,400 miles wide. In antiquity, it was practically devoid of population except along the western and southern coasts, particularly toward Yemen in the southwest, and occasional oases. Along the western edge rise mountains 10,000 to 12,000 feet high. To the east beyond this range, the land begins to tilt toward the Persian Gulf and Gulf of Oman toward the northeast.

Yet mineral wealth, including the famous gold of Ophir, came from Arabia, and precious spices—myrrh and frankincense—coming from east Africa and western Arabia, were carried by caravan to the major population centers, with Syria-Palestine serving as outlets to the Mediterranean markets. Recent excavators at Caesarea believe that much of Herod the Great's wealth came from control of this lucrative trade, and he likely built the city and port as his commercial emporium.[23] According to 1 Kings 10, the Queen of Sheba was one of the most illustrious visitors to King Solomon's court. She was apparently ruler of the kingdom of the Sabeans. Archaeological evidence indicates that this kingdom was located in what is today Yemen.

More significant to biblical events, however, were the two great river valley civilizations of Egypt and Mesopotamia. The cultural, economic, and political superiority of these power centers always diminished the importance of events and achievements in Canaan—the relatively insignificant land which both joined and separated them. Because Canaan provided a bridge between the two, Egypt always sought to dominate the region and succeeded until the time of David and Solomon. Shortly after the division of the united kingdom into the two small states of Israel and Judah, the presence of the Assyrians from Mesopotamia began to be felt, and the Mesopotamian influence and domination continued for centuries thereafter. The Assyrians and Neo-Babylonians, in turn, were superseded by the Persians, who continued to dominate the promised land until the coming of the Greeks.

---

23. *ABD* s.v. "Caesarea."

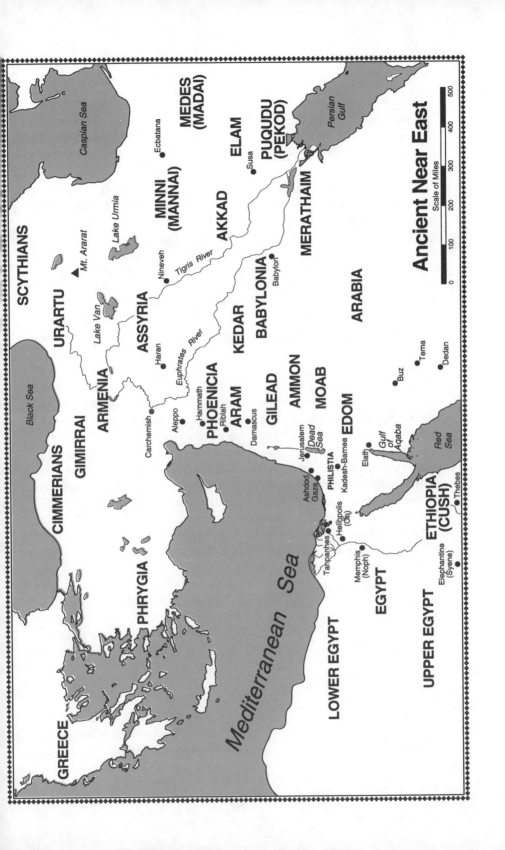

Ancient Near East

Scale of Miles

0 100 200 300 400 500

EGYPT

The Nile River was the source of life for Egypt and the reason for its existence, since it rarely rains there. In fact, Egypt can be considered a long oasis through the desert, for deserts lie on both sides of the river valley.

The biblical name for Egypt, *mizraim,* is a dual form, indicating two Egypts. In fact, Egypt was divided into Upper Egypt, from the head of the Delta up the valley to the south, and Lower Egypt, the delta proper. The two Egypts were united about 3100 B.C. by Menes (Narmer). Although thirty dynastic changes occurred through ensuing centuries, ancient Egypt existed under the rule of a series of pharaohs until the arrival of Alexander the Great, ca. 332 B.C. The boundaries of Egypt were the Mediterranean Sea in the north, the Gulf of Suez and Red Sea in the east, a series of oases about 120 miles west of the Nile, and to the south the first cataract (waterfall) at Aswan. Five additional cataracts farther south impeded the northward flow of the waters.

From Aswan to Cairo the river flows unimpeded approximately 575 miles, winding through a valley averaging about 12 miles in width. Near Aswan are granite quarries which provided stone for obelisks, statues, and sarcophagi (coffins). Farther north, the cliffs that hem the valley, particularly to the east, yield sandstone, limestone, and alabaster. The Sahara Desert lies west of the river. The Eastern Desert slopes upward to crest at 4,000- to 7,000-foot elevations before it descends to the Red Sea. Mineral wealth—copper, tin, and gold—was exploited in these mountains, and routes led from the Nile Valley to outlets on the Red Sea and trade connections with the Arabian peninsula, eastern Africa, and ultimately India. Egyptians also mined the Sinai for semi-precious stones—turquoise and lapis lazuli—and the Arabah for copper.

Near Cairo, the river divides into two main streams that empty into the Mediterranean through the Damietta mouth to the east and the Rosetta mouth to the west, the latter near Alexandria. From Cairo to the Mediterranean the river flows 100 miles across the delta. At its widest the delta measures approximately 150 miles. This 8,500-square-mile area produced bountiful crops, supplies of fish and wild fowl, and water creatures such as crocodiles and hippopotamuses. The eastern delta was the biblical land of Goshen, a region in which cattle were grazed and vines were grown, activities with which the Israelites were both familiar and expert.

The delta region receives six to seven inches of rain annually, which is barely sufficient to grow small grain. However, irrigation has always been available to water the crops, so canals crisscross its surface. The average annual rainfall at Cairo is about one inch, and practically no rain falls at Aswan.

The Nile, at 4,145 miles the longest river in the world, has two main sources: the White Nile, originating in the mountains of central Africa, and the Blue Nile, flowing out of the highlands of Ethiopia. Much of the silt borne by the Nile in its annual flooding comes from soil washed from the mountains into the Blue Nile. The rains are the result of the monsoon season in the East African Highlands. The two streams meet and join at Khartoum in the Sudan (biblical Cush). The annual floods of the Nile usually begin in July and last into January. The building of the high dam at Aswan has modified the effects of the annual inundation. Before its construction, at Thebes in Upper Egypt the river at full flood stage reached a height of thirty-six feet above normal. By the time the crest reached the head of the Delta it diminished to twenty-five feet above normal, and at the Mediterranean was further reduced to only four feet above normal. The inundation leaves a layer of fresh mud spread over the valley floor and into the delta, creating a rich fertile soil.

The predictability of the flooding and the climate no doubt contributed to the stability of early Egyptian civilization. Because the valley was surrounded by desert and sea, the rule of pharaohs was long-lasting and relatively peaceful. Dangers threatened mainly from Nubia (Sudan) to the south and Asia (Canaan) to the northeast. Egypt was protected from Canaan, however, by the natural barrier of a 100-mile-wide desert along the coast, separating the eastern Nile delta from Gaza, with the River of Egypt (Wadi el-Arish) south of Gaza as the southern border of Canaan. The Sinai peninsula provided another barrier against encroaching enemies. It was crossed by few routes and supplied little water to invading armies. Its vast emptiness served as an effective buffer against the threat of invasion from the east, and the small desert kingdoms of Edom, Moab, and Ammon to its east and north posed no danger. To Egypt's west, only Libya across the desert posed a threat, which only rarely materialized.

MESOPOTAMIA

The name Mesopotamia signifies "the land between the rivers." The two rivers, the Tigris and the Euphrates, lie east of Canaan and beyond the Arabian desert. They are among the four rivers named in the story of the garden of Eden (Gen. 2:14). Both rivers have sources high in the mountains of eastern Turkey (ancient Urartu, modern Armenia). However, the Euphrates has cut a channel to the west, making a wide swing toward the Mediterranean before turning southeasterly north of Carchemish near the modern Turkish-Syrian border. Two important tributaries of the Euphrates that flow through north-south valleys east of the big bend are the Balikh and the Habor. Biblical Haran (Gen. 11:31) and Gozan (2 Kings 17) both were situated in this region. Gozan was one of the cities to which the Israelites were carried into captivity by the Assyrians after the fall of Samaria in 722 B.C.

The Tigris follows a more direct route southward through the mountains and hills of ancient Assyria before drawing near the Euphrates in the plain near modern Baghdad. Most of the area of ancient Mesopotamia is now occupied by modern Iraq.

Like the Nile, these two rivers bring rich soil from the mountains into the wide, alluvial plain. However, the floods of Mesopotamia are more unpredictable and rampant than that of the Nile. Flooding often changes the course of the river completely, destroying irrigation canals, towns, and crops. Yet in the southern part of Mesopotamia, civilization began (4000–3500 B.C.) when a people not mentioned in the Bible, but whom we know from cuneiform documents as the Sumerians, settled in the south, in the area later known as Babylonia. Earlier the region was known as Sumer, and to the north of it developed a rival Semitic kingdom named Akkad.[24] By approximately 2400 B.C. the two were united by a powerful ruler, Sargon of Akkad.

Farther to the north along the Tigris another powerful group subsequently developed: the Assyrians. The plains in Assyria are semi-desert, and the terrain is less amenable to irrigation than the southern valley, but rainfall increases near the Zagros mountains to the east, where the soil was fertile enough to support Assyria's early population. Several tributaries flow westward through valleys to join the Tigris. Some of the earliest evidences of village life appeared in foothill regions in the north and east of Assyria.

The terrain of Assyria was conducive to an abundance of wild game, and bas-reliefs from the palaces of Assyia's monarchs testify to the popularity of the hunt. Depicted as quarry on the reliefs are wild asses, bulls, goats, and especially lions. Bird hunting, meanwhile, was more a commoners' sport than a sport of kings.

The environment of Assyria provided steppe lands, bush, and forests as habitat for wild game, but it lacked tall, straight trees important for constructing palaces and temples. To supply their need for such materials, the Assyrian rulers looked west to the forests on the well-watered slopes of the Lebanon mountains. Through commerce and conquest, Assyria obtained the famed cedars of Lebanon and pine for construction.

---

24. Schoville, *Biblical Archaeology*, 177–78.

From humble beginnings as tribesmen, Assyrians developed into a cosmopolitan nation, desiring and then requiring foreign products. They established commercial interests in the north, south, and east, but the desire to dominate resources gave rise to a powerful, highly trained military establishment. Assyrian monarchs from the time of Ashurnasirpal (883–859 B.C.) made regular forays of conquest. They ultimately brought much of the Middle East, including Babylonia, Syria-Palestine, and Egypt under Assyrian control at the height of the empire under Ashurbanipal (668–630 B.C.). This mightiest of Assyrian rulers is mentioned in Ezra 4:10 as "the great and noble Osnappar." After his death, a rapid decline followed. The end of the empire was marked by the fall of Nineveh in 612 B.C. at the hands of the Medes and the Babylonians. The destruction of Nineveh was prophesied in Zephaniah 2:13 and, most graphically, in Nahum.

PERSIA

The coalition of Medes and Babylonians that destroyed the Assyrian capital permitted the rise of the Neo-Babylonian (Chaldean) Empire under Nabopolasser and his famous son, Nebuchadnezzar. Yet their reign was short lived (626–539 B.C.) and was succeeded by the Persian (Achaemenian) Empire under Cyrus, who had conquered Media to unite the Medes and the Persians (550 B.C.). Babylon fell in 539 B.C., and by 525 B.C. Persia had conquered Egypt. The Persian Empire at its greatest extent reached from what is today eastern Afghanistan and Pakistan westward across Asia Minor and into Europe, including Macedonia. Greece, however, never capitulated to the Persians.

The original Persia, the land of the Medes and Persians, is today Iran. It is primarily a high, dry plateau extending between the Caspian Sea to the north and the Persian Gulf and Indian Ocean to the south. The Kurdistan and Zagros Mountains extend in a northwest-southeast line to the east of the Mesopotamian Valley. These mountains, containing peaks rising to the 12,000–14,000-foot range, comprise an area approximately 1,250 miles long and averaging over 1,250 miles in width. In the north the Alborz Mountains, south of the Caspian Sea and an easterly extension of the mountains of eastern Armenia, soar even higher. These mountains are rich in metallic ores, which were exploited by the inhabitants to be made into silver and gold jewelry, often adorned with semi-precious stones, and to be traded with the rich civilizations of Mesopotamia. One of the major sources of tin in antiquity was located in eastern Persia in the mountains of what is today Afghanistan, and as early as the Middle Bronze Age (ca. 2000–1550 B.C.), caravans transported the metal across Persia into Mesopotamia. This basic ingredient for making bronze was even shipped from Mari, on the Euphrates River in what is today Syria, to the Canaanite city of Laish (Hazor) north of the Sea of Galilee.

The mountains also forced moisture-bearing clouds to precipitate in the form of rains and snows, providing regions of fertility, particularly in western and northern Persia. South of the Caspian Sea a moist, mild climate prevails. The ancient Persians developed a system of underground canals called *kariz* (Arabic, *qanat aflaj*) to channel water from underground aquifers into otherwise dry lowlands. This system spread far and wide through Persian conquests and continues in use today. To the east, desert regions dominate the area to the borders of Pakistan. The southern fringe of the region along the Persian Gulf and the Gulf of Oman contains some modest coastal plains between the sea and the Makran mountain range, but historically they have attracted only modest populations.

The western foothills of the Zagros, east of Babylon, was a productive area that was once the home of the Elamites. When it came under Persian domination, the major city of the region, Susa, became one of the capitals. Ecbatana and Persepolis also served as governmental centers. Ezra and Nehemiah came to Jerusalem with the support of the Persian government. Esther and the apocryphal Book of Tobit also are set in Persia. Jews continued to live in Persia and Mesopotamia throughout the days of the empire and long afterward, maintaining vital connections with the religious center of Judaism in Jerusalem.

THE GEOGRAPHY OF THE NEW TESTAMENT WORLD

Following the life of Jesus and the origins of the early church in the environs of first-century A.D. Palestine, the NT traces the travels of the apostle Paul and his associates across both land and sea in the eastern and central Mediterranean world.

PHOENICIA

The Phoenicians were the remnant of the Canaanites who remained in the mountains and along the narrow coastal plains to the north of Israel. The rest of the Canaanites were either displaced, dispatched, or absorbed by Arameans, Israelites, and Philistines in the aftermath of the disruptions that occurred at the close of the Late Bronze Age (ca. 1200 B.C.). A long history of Canaanite maritime activity preceded the blossoming of the Phoenicians as the major commercial seafaring nation for many centuries, from the tenth century B.C. until their power waned with the arrival of the Greeks (ca. 330 B.C.) and then the Romans. They also established trading colonies throughout the Mediterranean, on Cyprus, Crete, Malta, Greece, Italy, Sardinia, Spain, and particularly in North Africa at Carthage. The traders also spread their alphabet, which was adopted and adapted by the Greeks and the Romans, providing the script for the recording and transmission of the NT. By the time of Paul, the colonies had become Romanized. Even Phoenicia proper had been ruled by the Romans for a century and was incorporated into the Roman province of Syria.

SYRIA

The gospel found receptive ears among the inhabitants of Antioch on the Orontes as it moved out of Jesus' homeland (Acts 11:20–21). The Orontes River rises in the northern extension of the Rift Valley between the Lebanon and Anti-Lebanon range. The river flows northward until it is forced by the rising terrain to turn westward to the sea. Antioch was located about sixteen miles inland from its mouth.

The city occupied an advantageous position on trade routes leading northward into Asia Minor, eastward into Mesopotamia, and southward to Damascus and Canaan. Founded by Seleucus I after the death of Alexander the Great and the dissolution of his empire, Antioch became a commercial center of note and the capital of Syria. Today its unimportant successor, Antakya, is located in Turkey a few miles north of the Syrian border.

Syria to the east of the Anti-Lebanon range is largely steppe land that fades into the desert. However, the eastern and northern regions receive adequate rainfall for agriculture and animal husbandry. Damascus is an oasis in the desert, owing its existence to the melting snows from the mountains to the west that feed the short Barada River. This valley also provides a route through the mountains into the Bekah Valley; the route continues through the Lebanon range to reach the coast at Beirut. Another route leads from Damascus to the northeast into the desert. The important oasis of Tadmor (Palmyra) flourished in apostolic times as a caravan stop on the trade route to Mesopotamia. East of Tadmor (Palmyra) on the Euphrates River, the Roman border-fortress city of Dura-Europus was situated. Excavations of its ruins have uncovered the earliest known Christian church structure, as well as a Jewish synagogue and pagan temples.

ASIA MINOR

North of Antioch on the Orontes, the Amanus Mountains press down to the Mediterranean until the coastal plain widens in the region where

Alexander the Great won the battle of Isis. Here the land mass of Asia Minor extends westward to form the southern coastline of modern Turkey. The Taurus Mountains allow a modest coastal plain, and at the base of the mountains stood Tarsus, the birthplace of Saul (Paul, Acts 21:39). Here Barnabas found Saul and returned with him to help with the work of the church in Antioch (Acts 11:25–26).

The region of modern Turkey has borne several names in history—Cappadocia, Asia Minor, and Anatolia. The plateau that forms the center of the region is ringed by mountains. Particularly in the east, the mountains of Armenia dominate the landscape, with Mount Ararat the highest peak at 16,915 feet. To the west, the mountains are lower, but still range from 9,000 to 12,000 feet. Large areas in the central plateau remain almost uninhabited due to the wide, sterile sheets of lava.

Asia Minor is largely bound by water, with the Black Sea to the north, the Aegean Sea to the west, and the Mediterranean Sea to the south. The central plateau and eastern mountains experience cold winters. The western region, where valleys carved by rivers flowing to the west soften the mountainous terrain, enjoys a Mediterranean climate. Rainfall ranges from approximately one hundred inches per year along the Black Sea to ten inches in the interior.

The apostle Paul penetrated the plateau region to Iconium in the Roman province of Galatia and other towns in the province—Lystra, Antioch in Pisidia, and Derbe (Acts 13:1—14:26), but much of his work was among the cities in the western part of Asia Minor and particularly at Ephesus. This western region was colonized by Greek settlers about 1000 B.C., and here were located the cities of the seven churches of the Apocalypse (Rev. 2—3).

The usual agricultural and grazing activities were carried on in Asia Minor, and maritime commerce and fishing were available to inhabitants of coastal cities. Especially advantageous for the inhabitants of the mountainous regions were the rich veins of gold, silver, copper, and semi-precious stones. The last king of Lydia, in which Sardis was located, was so wealthy that the saying "rich as Croesus" is still used.

GREECE

Paul's second missionary journey carried him by ship from Troas across the Hellespont (the modern Dardanelles), the narrow waterway separating Asia from Europe, to Macedonia (Acts 16:11–12). This region occupies the northern part of the Greek peninsula and was the homeland of Alexander the Great. Paul and his entourage traveled inland on the coastal plain to Philippi, named after Alexander's father, which was located on the famous Egnatian Way. This important Roman road ran from the Albanian coast in the west to the Dardanelles in the east, just across the strait from Byzantium (Istanbul), providing Rome with a connecting route to the eastern provinces of the empire. Paul continued westward on this highway to Thessalonica, a place named for the hot springs in the area, hinting at the underlying geological phenomena in an earthquake-prone zone.

Like much of the northern Mediterranean area, Greece is predominantly a mountainous region, interspersed by valleys and, near the sea, coastal plains. Mountains range up to 9,000 feet. Over time, the effects of goatherding and deforestation eroded the fragile soils on the mountain slopes but enriched the lower levels near stream beds and the alluvial plains at the base of mountains. Here the normal Mediterranean production of olives, fruits, small grains, and grapes were complemented by animal husbandry. The sea with its bountiful resources also made a significant contribution to Greek diets.

Paul apparently circumvented the difficult overland trip from Berea to Athens by sailing to Piraeus, the seaport of the famous Greek city. The Acropolis of Athens is built atop a small mountain with the Aeropagus at its base.

Paul left Athens and came to Corinth, forty miles to the west (Acts 18:1). Corinth was the Roman capital of southern Greece. It was located at the base of a 1,886-foot mountain just south of the four-mile-wide strip of land separating northern Greece from the southern Peloponnesus. All north-south land traffic passed through Corinth. Another economic advantage of Corinth was the practice of portaging passengers, cargo, and even smaller ships between the Saronic Gulf to the east and the Gulf of Corinth to the west. This was preferred to the alternative, a lengthy voyage around the Peloponnesus.

Paul's travels ultimately took him to Rome. En route the ship followed the coastline northward from Caesarea past Phoenicia and Syria, steering east of Cyprus to Myra in southern Asia Minor. A more direct route would have taken them west of Cyprus from Sidon, but contrary winds from the northwest prevented this (Acts 27:4). At Myra, Julius, the centurion, transferred his prisoners to a ship from Alexandria which was sailing for Italy. The more direct route westward past the Peloponnesus was impossible, due to the continuing contrary winds, so passing through the Sporades Islands, they came to the southern coast of Crete. Paul was well aware of the many islands that dot the Aegean Sea and islands of the Mediterranean including Cyprus, Crete, Malta, and Sicily. A terrain similar to that of the mainland is characteristic of these islands.

The ill-fated voyage of Paul to Rome clearly began in the fall, when the winter winds blowing from continental Europe to the west and north

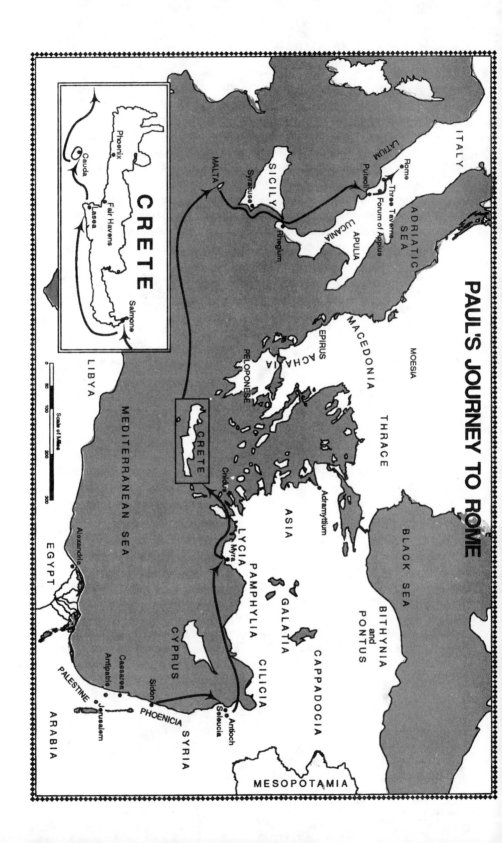

PAUL'S JOURNEY TO ROME

CRETE

Phoenix
Cauda
Fair Havens
Lasea
Salmone

Scale of Miles
0 50 100 200 300

MALTA
SICILY
Syracuse
Rhegium
ITALY
Rome
Three Taverns
Forum of Appius
Puteoli
ADRIATIC SEA
LATTIUM
LUCANIA
APULIA

MEDITERRANEAN SEA

LIBYA

EGYPT
Alexandria

CRETE
Cnidus

EPIRUS
MACEDONIA
ACHAIA
PELOPONESE
THRACE
MOESIA

ASIA
Adramyttium
LYCIA
Myra
PAMPHYLIA
GALATIA
CAPPADOCIA
BLACK SEA
BITHYNIA and PONTUS

CYPRUS
CILICIA
Sidon
Antioch
Seleucia
SYRIA
PHOENICIA
Caesarea
Antipatris
Jerusalem
PALESTINE
ARABIA
MESOPOTAMIA

sweep the moisture-bearing clouds of the "former rains" (Jer. 5:24) across the Mediterranean into Canaan. Maritime trade was restricted and risky during the stormy winter months.

With Crete on the right, they sailed with difficulty until they reached one of the few anchorages along the southern coast. Crete's mountains drop precipitously to the sea along the south coast, allowing little room for settlements or harbors. Wisdom would have dictated that they remain at Fair Havens, but the harbor was considered unsatisfactory as a wintering place (Acts 27:8, 12). Attempting to reach Phoenix fifty miles farther west, they were blown off course, and contrary winds ultimately shipwrecked them on the shores of Malta.

After three months on Malta, the centurion took his prisoners aboard another ship which had wintered there. Sixty miles north of Crete was the island of Sicily. The ship visited Syracuse on the east coast before passing over to Rhegium at the tip of the boot of Italy, then on through the Strait of Messina past Naples to Puteoli. Although Puteoli, on the north side of the Bay of Naples, lay 140 miles south of Rome, it was a favored harbor, and here Paul debarked (Acts 20:13). A good road led on to Rome, joining the Appian Way en route.

Italy has typical Mediterranean landscapes, dominated by the Appenine Mountains that form the backbone of the peninsula. These mountains, as do those of Greece, provide rich sources of fine limestone and marble as well as useful metals. The south of Italy is prone to earthquakes, and a number of active and latent volcanoes dot the region. Mount Etna in Sicily remains active. Mount Vesuvius, southeast of Naples, which Paul could have seen on his voyage, erupted savagely two decades later (A.D. 79). Its ash, mud, and lava buried the city of Pompeii at the base of the mountain near Naples.

The apostle Paul intended to extend his ministry to the Iberian Peninsula (Rom. 15:20). Whether he ultimately reached Spain remains unknown, since the Book of Acts closes with him in Rome. Tradition does allow this possibility before he was arrested a second time and martyred in Rome. Had he reached Spain, he would have found the typical Mediterranean environment with which he was familiar, with mountains, plains, and a climate south of the Pyrenees not too different from that in Italy south of the Alps. It was to be the challenge of later generations of Christians to carry the gospel northward across such mountain barriers into Europe.

FOR FURTHER READING

Aharoni, Yohanan. *The Land of the Bible: A Historical Geography.* Rev. and enl. Translated by A. F. Rainey. Philadelphia: Westminster, 1979.

Baines J., and J. Malek. *Atlas of Ancient Egypt*. New York: Facts on File, 1982.

Baley, Denis. *Geographical Companion to the Bible*. London: Lutterworth Press, 1963.

————. *The Geography of the Bible*. Rev. ed. New York: Harper & Row, 1974.

Beitzel, Barry J. *The Moody Atlas of Bible Lands*. Chicago: Moody, 1985.

May, Herbert G., ed. *Oxford Bible Atlas*. 3d ed. Rev. by J. Day. New York: Oxford University Press, 1984.

Pritchard, J. B., ed. *The Harper Atlas of the Bible*. New York: Harper & Row, 1987.

Rasmussen, Carl G. *Zondervan NIV Atlas of the Bible*. Grand Rapids: Zondervan, 1989.

Schoville, Keith N. *Biblical Archaeology in Focus* (Grand Rapids: Baker, 1978).

van der Woude, A. S., ed. *The World of the Bible. Bible Handbook*, vol. 1. Translated by S. Woudstra from the Dutch. Grand Rapids: Eerdmans, 1986.

VI

USE OF THE OLD TESTAMENT IN THE NEW

DARRELL L. BOCK

To think about the use of the Old Testament in the New is to enter one of the most fascinating and complex areas of biblical study. Yet even expressing the subject this way obscures a reality for the earliest Christians. Imagine someone walking up to the apostle Peter two millennia ago and asking him about Jesus' teaching on the use of the OT in the New. He would have looked back at the questioner puzzled. For him the issue would be understanding the promises of the Holy Writings of old: the Law, the Psalms, and the Prophets. It is hard for us to remember or appreciate that the NT did not exist while the books of the NT were being written. Their topic was simply the continuing fulfillment of God's promises. It is the exposition of those promises and what the revelation of Jesus Christ means in their context that brings about "the use of the Old Testament in the New."

Another key observation to make right at the start is the variety of ways in which the OT appears in the New. For example, in the United Bible Societies' first edition of the *Greek New Testament*, the editors note 401 OT quotations or allusions, which they put into bold print. Yet only about half (195) have some type of introduction in the biblical text to indicate that the OT is being cited.[1] Sometimes an author quotes the ancient text, sometimes he alludes to it, and sometimes he presents an OT idea without referring to a particular passage. The fulfillment of biblical prophecy also varies. Sometimes the OT text only looked to the future, but more often God made a promise and pictured it in contemporary history first, so that the promise presents a pattern of God's activity in history, which the fulfillment in Jesus only culminates. In other words, God's promises often work throughout history, rather than merely at a moment of time. Such fulfillment shows God's hand in all of history in a way that is more marvelous than merely seeing the Bible as making "crystal ball" promises.[2]

Our overview will begin by considering some historical factors of ancient exposition. Then we will consider six key theological presuppositions that influenced how the text was read. Next we will examine the unique issues raised by the text because it has dual authorship and addresses multiple settings at once. Next we will consider how the Bible can be read today, speaking of two ways of reading the text in light of progressive revelation. Finally, the variety of ways in which the NT uses the Old will be examined.

HISTORICAL FACTORS

LANGUAGE OF THE BIBLE

When we speak of the use of the Old Testament in the New, it is important to remember the OT was written in Hebrew and Aramaic, while the entire NT was written in Greek. This means the OT texts had to be translated. In addition, the dominant language used during many of the actual events described in the NT was Aramaic; so in discussions about the OT within these events, the OT would be cited in Aramaic, not Hebrew.[3] This means that using the OT involved a multilingual and multicultural setting (just as the use of our English Bibles also does). Fortunately, the Jews already had a process and a Bible for such purposes.

---

1. Klyne, Snodgrass, "The Use of the Old Testament in the New" in *New Testament Criticism and Interpretation*, ed. by David A. Black and David S. Dockery, (Grand Rapids: Zondervan, 1991), 409–34.

2. For a theological consideration of the area of biblical typology, see Francis Foulkes, *The Acts of God: A Study of the Basis of Typology in the Old Testament* (London: Tyndale, 1958), and Leonard Goppelt, *Typos: The Typological Interpretation of the Old Testament in the New*, trans. Donald H. Madvig (Grand Rapids, Eerdmans, 1982).

3. For the issue of what language Jesus spoke, see Joseph A. Fitzmyer, "The Languages of Palestine in the First Century A.D." in *A Wandering Aramean: Collected Aramaic Essays* (Missoula, Mont: Scholars, 1979), 29–56. Jesus probably spoke Aramaic and Greek, and possibly Hebrew as well, but most of His public conversation would have been in Aramaic.

The Bible was the Septuagint (LXX), a Greek version of the Hebrew OT. Different OT books were translated into Greek over a long period, starting in about 250 B.C. The entire OT was completed before the time of Christ. In some ways, it is better to think of the LXX as a collection of translations rather than one translation.[4] Still, most of the quotations in the NT reflect this OT version, although to differing degrees in different NT books.

The translation process was one of rendering the Bible into the language of the people for use in synagogue services, since books were not yet printed and collections of texts on papyri were rare. In the ancient world, the biblical text was most often heard, not read, except in the rabbinic centers. So the Jews had the targums, or Aramaic renderings of the OT, to be read in the synagogue. These renderings were sometimes literal. *Targum Onqelos*, for example, is a translation comparable to the KJV, NASB, NIV, or RSV in approach. At other times targums are interpretive; the *Neofiti* reminds one of the *Living Bible* in certain sections. The targums were an important part of Jewish religious involvement, since they put the text in language and wording the people could understand.[5] They made the Bible accessible. The versions that most NT writers would have been familiar with were these editions of the Bible.[6] Their wording was what people would recognize. The NT authors did not ignore this reality. They cited OT texts in these versions. Even Paul, who as a rabbi knew Hebrew and

---

4. On the issues associated with the nature of the Hebrew Scriptures in this period, including the issue of canon, see the article by D. Moody Smith, "The Use of the Old Testament in the New" in *The Use of the Old Testament in the New and Other Essays*, ed. James M. Efrid (Durham, N.C.: Duke University Press, 1972), 3–13.

5. On the nature of the targums and their function in ancient Judaism, see Daniel Patte, *Early Jewish Hermeneutic in Palestine*, SBLDS 22 (Missoula, Mont.: Scholars, 1975), 55–81; John Bowker, *The Targums and Rabbinic Literature* (Cambridge: Cambridge University Press, 1969), 3–28; Anthony D. York, "The Targum in the Synagogue and in the School," *JSJ* 10 (1979): 74–86.

6. On the diversity of usage within the NT, see Craig A. Evans, "The Function of the Old Testament in the New" in *Introducing New Testament Interpretation*, ed. Scot McKnight (Grand Rapids: Baker, 1989), 163–93; Richard Longenecker, *Biblical Exegesis in the Apostolic Period* (Grand Rapids; Eerdmans, 1975), and Donald A. Carson and H. G. M. Williamson, eds., *It Is Written: Scripture Citing Scripture* (Cambridge: Cambridge University Press, 1988). For Jesus' use of Scripture, see R. T. France, *Jesus and the Old Testament* (London: Tyndale, 1971). More historically critical oriented treatments of the NT are Barnabas Lindars, *New Testament Apologetic* (Philadelphia: Fortress, 1961) and Donald Juel, *Messianic Exegesis: Christological Interpretations of the Old Testament in Early Christianity* (Philadelphia: Fortress, 1988). These last two studies overplay the differences between the OT and the New. For an attempt to argue for certain central themes emerging from the use of the OT in the New, with their source going back to Jesus, see C. H. Dodd, *According to the Scriptures* (New York: Scribner's, 1952).

Aramaic, often chose to quote the version his audience knew (just as a pastor might know Greek and still be content to cite the English version today).[7]

MIDRASH EXPOSITION

Two other Jewish genres, "midrash" and "pesher," also may have relevance in how some OT texts are presented. Midrash refers to scriptural exposition.[8] It is a complex genre, since some Jewish expositions are straightforward, while others are rather speculative and fanciful (as sermons today can be). But attempts to "apply the Holy Writings of Old" had certain rules: the rules of Hillel, which reflect midrashic attempts to expound and apply the Scripture in new settings. Hillel was a Jewish rabbi of the first century B.C. He may not have invented the rules, but he received credit for codifying them and passing them along to later rabbis.[9] Some of these rules merely reflect logic, while others are arguments of a rhetorical type. Seven rules were dominant; three of these rules were most prominent, as noted below:

- *Qal Wahomer*, or "the light and the heavy," signified a meaning applied in a less important situation also applies in more important matter. NT texts that make a "how much more argument" reflect this style (Luke 11:9–13; Heb. 1:1–4).

- *Gezerah Shewa*, or "an equivalent regulation," meant that where the same words were present in two texts, those texts could be brought together for exposition. Mark 1:2–4 reflects such a textual combina-

---

7. The best-known study of Paul's OT interpretation is E. Earle Ellis, *Paul's Use of the Old Testament* (Grand Rapids: Eerdmans, 1957), while a more recent treatment of allusions in Paul is Richard B. Hays, *Echoes of Scripture in the Letters of Paul* (New Haven: Yale University Press, 1989). His study understates the value of Jewish backgrounds to this question and overstates the difference between the OT meaning and the NT sense.

8. The classic article on midrash is Renée Bloch, "Midrash" in *Approaches to Ancient Judaism: Theory and Practice*, ed. William Scott Green (Missoula, Mont.: Scholars, 1978), a translation of an article written in 1957. More recent treatments include John Bowker, *The Targums and Rabbinic Literature* and Gary Porton, *Understanding Rabbinic Midrash* (Hoboken, N.J.: KTAV, 1985). On ancient Jewish use of the Scripture, see Patte, *Early Jewish Hermeneutic*. For the wide variety of examples of midrash, see Jacob Neusner, *A Midrash Reader* (Minneapolis: Fortress Press, 1990). For a focused study on Palestinian Judaism and the NT, see Martin McNamara, *Palestianian Judaism and the New Testament* (Wilmington, Del.: Michael Glazier, 1983).

9. For a brief exposition of these rules, see Bowker, *The Targums and Rabbinic Literature*, 315–18; and Snodgrass, "The Use of the Old Testament in the New" 420–22.

tion in referring to John the Baptist. A similar combination appears in 1 Peter 2:2–8, around the concept of the stone.

- *Daber halamed me >inyano* is simply "explanation from the context." Numerous NT texts reflect citations that deal not only with the verse cited, but summarize arguments in the larger context. Luke 3:6, for example, has a reference to God's salvation that comes not from the verses cited from Isaiah 40, but from the later context of the same passage. Rather than citing the entire passage, which runs for several verses, the term is inserted to summarize the thrust of the larger passage.

Other rules of Hillel deal with how to relate different texts to one another. Such ways of relating the biblical text show how the text was read and understood at this time. To note this background is not to endorse Jewish technique, but the rules do reflect how texts were read and studied. A careful study of Jewish interpretation in this period shows they had a sense of which OT texts looked to the future and the end times. (At Qumran 4QFlor. is a clear example.) The rabbis just debated how to put those many pieces together. So many of the texts the NT uses were already well known in Judaism, though other texts the NT uses were not so well known.

PESHER EXPOSITION

Pesher is a special type of exposition.[10] It refers to exposition of texts that sees in them eschatological fulfillment in the current era. The Qumran community of the Dead Sea was known for reading the OT this way; they thought they were the end-time community of fulfillment. One of the aspects of this type of interpretation is the explanation of mysteries in the revelation. NT texts similar to such exposition in flavor include the mystery parables of Jesus' teaching, which expound the kingdom and often use and develop OT imagery in the process (Matt. 13), or the explanation of Paul's ministry to the Gentiles in Ephesians 3:4–6 where OT promise and the revelation of Christ to His apostles combine to help explain God's plan.

But if elements of Jewish interpretive technique are similar to that of the early church, then why did the Jews have such a hard time with NT exposition of the OT? To answer this question (and its contemporary equivalent), one has to examine the theological presuppositions about how

---

10. The major study is Maurya P. Horgan, *Pesharim: Qumran Interpretations of Biblical Books*, CBQMS 8 (1979).

these texts are read. Some Christian suppositions were shared with Judaism, but the issue of how the suppositions applied was debated.

THEOLOGICAL PRESUPPOSITIONS

Of the six suppositions we shall note, the first three were shared with Judaism, while the last three were not.[11]

SUPPOSTIONS SHARED WITH JUDAISM

The Bible Is God's Word. First, comes the belief that the Bible is God's Word. The implications of this first conviction are significant in three ways: (1) It meant the Bible should be read as a unit. The OT may be thirty-nine books, but it ultimately has one Author. This explains why some of Hillel's rules felt comfortable in associating texts that were historically distant from one another in time and setting. (2) It meant what God wrote then still has meaning now. This view of the Bible is crucial, because it meant that biblical promises expect fulfillment. This conclusion follows from the third implication: (3) The Bible is true. What it promises will eventually come to pass in full.

The One in the Many. The second conviction was the belief in the one in the many. This means a single member of a community can represent the whole. Biblical illustrations of this concept include how the figure of Adam is used by Paul as a representative of all humanity, just as Christ represents redeemed humanity (Rom. 5; 1 Cor. 15:20–23, 45–49). The OT contains this concept as well. The king or a priest would represent the entire nation. An animal sacrificed would bear sins representatively for all the people. A prophet like Hosea pictured a nation's fate as he carried out his call. This kind of representation is significant because what is said of one figure can then be applied to another who fits within the identity of the group or who serves as its representative.

Pattern in History (Correspondence or Typology). The third conviction is the concept of pattern in history (correspondence or typology). Here the idea is that God works in similar patterns so that one significant event will mirror or pattern another similar event. This would normally be called *analogy*, except that in biblical thinking the later fulfillment of the pattern usually exceeds the initial event in importance. In other words, it may

---

11. For a discussion of Christian suppositions, see E. Earle Ellis, "How the New Testament Uses the Old," in *New Testament Interpretation*, ed. I. H. Marshall (Grand Rapids: Eerdmans, 1978), 199–219. For a full survey of views about how the Testaments relate to one another, see D. L. Baker, *Two Testaments: One Bible* (Downers Grove, Ill.: InterVarsity, 1976).

escalate the pattern, so that the later fulfillment heightens the sense of realization in the promise.

The word *typology* for this phenomenon is used in a special way, not like popular discussion, which compares the tabernacle to Christ. *Types* in the sense we use refer to events or to office functions. The OT tends to apply this imagery to the concept of creation and re-creation or to the theme of exodus and new exodus. So when Isaiah spoke of a new exodus in Isaiah 40, he referred to the redemption of the nation out of exile, and yet his language also applies to what ultimate redemption will be like.

This idea of multiple referents ultimately fulfilled in a unique way is key to the study of the use of the OT in the New. The NT extends such creation and exodus imagery into other categories, such as promises made to righteous sufferers or promises made to the king, so that when these promises are realized in Jesus, they are realized in Him uniquely. In this way, He becomes the fulfillment of the pattern in a way that is true only of Him; so the NT points in terms of fulfillment expressed only in terms of Him (more on this below). This category is probably the least appreciated and yet one of the most significant suppositions for understanding the OT in the New. Here also is where Judaism and the church parted company. What the church saw fulfilled in Christ, Judaism thought was still awaited.

SUPPOSITIONS NOT SHARED WITH JUDAISM

These Are the Days of Fulfillment. The fourth conviction is that these are the days of fulfillment. No text declares this as loudly as Acts 2:17–21 (also Luke 4:16–20; Heb. 1:1–4). In fact, when Peter cited the text from Joel in Acts 2, he inserted (as one would in an explanatory targum) the phrase "in the last days" to make the point that the pouring out of the Spirit showed the fulfillment of last-days expectation had come. Paul's use of the idea of the coming of the New Covenant expounds and contrasts the Old Covenant of the Mosaic Law with the New Covenant (2 Cor. 3). The point in all of this is to say that the time of fulfillment had started in the early church. God's attestation of Jesus in the midst of His ministry (Luke 7:18–23) and the reality of Jesus' resurrection (Luke 24:43–47) gave ample basis to the mind of the earliest church to have this conviction.

Now and Not Yet. Yet in speaking of fulfillment, a fifth, corollary conviction also existed. It was that this fulfillment, though inaugurated, was both now and not yet. This meant God's promises, though initially fulfilled in Christ now, still had elements yet to be fulfilled. What Judaism expected to come all at once, Christians split into phases. Thus, in expounding the promise of the subjection of all things to Jesus in 1 Corinthians 15, Paul used Psalm 110:1 and Psalm 8:7 and affirmed both Christ's present rule and the future decisive subjection of all things to Him. In Philippians 2:11,

Paul used Isaiah 45:23 (LXX) to look forward to the eventual recognition of Jesus by all creation. In the Acts 2 example already noted, Peter pointed to the present fulfillment of the outpouring of the Spirit, while anticipating the yet-to-be-fulfilled arrival of the day of the Lord as the basis for his call to the audience to believe in Jesus and miss the judgment. What this conviction means is that some OT texts when cited as fulfilled may be only *initially* fulfilled, as opposed to fulfilled in a *consummative* sense. Fulfillment can be *inaugurated* without being *consummated*; in some cases it is partial, not exhaustive. The use of Joel in Acts is an example of this, since the decisive judgment of God is still awaited, though the outpouring of God's Spirit has come.

Jesus Is the Christ. These five convictions, which were framed by Scripture in union with events in Jesus' ministry, led to a final conviction and conclusion: *Jesus is the Christ and represents fulfillment par excellance of God's promises.* When the church says all of the Scriptures speak of Christ, this is what is meant. He is the goal and culmination of the promises of God. In saying this, it must be noted the OT's use in the New is not limited to affirming prophetic fulfillment, whether it be in pattern or direct prophecy. Other uses also exist. We shall look at these in our final section, but before getting there, we need to examine special issues.

UNIQUE ISSUES

Dual Authorship. The issue of dual authorship raises unique problems.[12] Although God inspired the authors who wrote the books, they did not understand all they had written. 1 Peter 1:10–12 indicates the human authors did not understand the time or circumstances of all they predicted. Daniel 12:5–13 makes it clear Daniel did not understand everything revealed and recorded in his visions. Some have espoused the concept of *sensus plenior* ("fuller sense") to explain the difference in understanding between the human author and the divine.[13] God knew the fuller sense of what He revealed, even if the prophet did not. God could have multiple referents in mind, even if the prophet may not have known all the

---

12. For a full discussion of the variations of approach to this question within evangelicalism, see Darrell L. Bock, "Evangelicals and the Use of the Old Testament in the New: Parts 1 and 2," *BSac* 142 (1985): 209–23, 306–19.

13. On an evangelical assessment of *sensus plenior*, see Douglas Moo, "The Problem of *Sensus Plenior*," in *Hermeneutics, Authority, and Canon*, ed. D. A. Carson and John Woodbridge (Grand Rapids: Zondervan, 1986), 179–211. For a Catholic treatment of this theme, see Raymond E. Brown, "Hermeneutics," *JBC* (Englewood Cliffs, N.J.: Prentice Hall, 1968), 605–23. For a vigorous argument against this approach, see Walter Kaiser, *The Uses of the Old Testament in the New* (Chicago: Moody, 1985), though aspects of this argument are overstated, as Moo's essay indicates.

constituent details. This concept is not a bad one, provided it is clear what the human author said and whatever more God says through him are related in sense. This concept raises two key related issues: language-referent issues and the concept of the progress of revelation.

Because of the presence of pattern in history, the possibility of addressing two or more events in the same utterance is possible. Language allows this as well, if descriptions are kept generic enough. To illustrate this point, some definition is needed about how words work. Those who study words often speak of a word having three elements which contribute to meaning (besides the context of the utterance, which is a crucial factor): symbols, sense, and referent.

Let us take the word *paraclete* in John 14 as an example. The *symbols* are the alphabetic signs which make up the word. In our example each letter of the word *p-a-r-a-c-l-e-t-e* comprises the symbols of what makes it up. (If the original Greek were used, the symbols would be the Greek letters for this word, Παράκλητος which is merely transliterated into English in our Bible to get the English word *paraclete*.) The *sense* is the dictionary definition of the word, its generic meaning in the context. Here that would be "comforter" or "encourager." This is likely the term one would see in a translation. But most important for specific interpretation is the specific thing, person, object, or concept referred to by the term in the context. This is the *referent*. (When preaching on a text is vague, often it is because the preacher has not made clear what the referent in the passage is.) In John 14, it is important to know that the referent is the Holy Spirit. Jesus has a specific one in mind when He discusses a comforter.

But what happens when a text discusses a pattern as opposed to one event only? The sense becomes key in the text and the referents in the passage become multiple as each context is addressed. We have already discussed how in Isaiah 40, a summary text introduces all the topics of Isaiah 40—66. Now it can refer both to the short-term situation and to the long-term one at one time. This is a simple example of the language-referent process. Salvation in the short-term setting merely refers in terms of its referent to "deliverance from exile"; but in the long-term view in the NT, the referent is "salvation in Christ" or "eternal life." Such a distinction reflects biblical typology, where the event escalates in its latter fulfillment, which also may mean that though the sense of a term is maintained at one level in all the fulfillments, it is heightened to a new realization on the other, because of the escalation in the new context.[14]

---

14. For a fuller treatment of this typological-prophetic category, along with numerous examples in Luke-Acts, see D. L. Bock, *Proclamation from Prophecy and Pattern: Lucan Old Testament Christology* (Sheffield: Sheffield Academic Press, 1987), 47–51.

Let me illustrate this possibility with a potentially more controversial example, Isaiah 7:14. For the sake of discussion and illustration, if this passage were read typologically, this is how the language-referent, multiple-context situation would work. In the short term, the referent must be one that Ahaz could appreciate about a sign child. So Isaiah points to a woman who is currently a virgin (referent: some unidentified woman in the court) to give birth to a child. That child represents "God with us." The child contextually would probably be Maher-Shalal-Hash-Baz, the short-term referent for the sign child (Isa. 8:1–4). But the text as a pattern text points to a "type" of sign child that has a second, escalated realization in Jesus. With the type's arrival in history comes the escalation to point to the unique culminating fulfillment. So now the woman (referent: Mary) who gives birth *is* a virgin *at the child's birth* (here is the escalation—the anticipated birth from a current virgin has escalated to become a virgin birth), and yet the child still represents (*and is*—a second escalation) "God with us." Note how the language of the text has not changed, but the referents and their force have shifted slightly (to reveal the escalation). Yet the relationship to the original pattern and its language is still clear. This is how language-referent and multiple settings can combine to allow God to develop the force of a text in the progress of revelation.

The mention of the progress of revelation introduces an idea that also is a special feature of the concept of dual authorship. It is that God gradually reveals His plan, so that the revelation of His plan progresses. This means that the force of earlier passages in God's plan as revealed in the OT become clearer or can be developed along fresh lines as more about the plan is revealed. This leads naturally into the question of two ways to read the Bible. It also raises the topic of the progress of revelation. But before turning to those topics, one illustration of referent expansion because of the progress of revelation is needed.

In Acts 4:25–27, the church prayed. They appealed to Psalm 2:1 as an example text for the nations raging and the peoples plotting against the anointed one of Israel. Every Jew reading that psalm in the OT would have assumed the enemies gathered against the Messiah and His Lord would be comprised only of the nations, of Gentiles (e.g., the *Midrash on Psalm 2*). Yet when the church prayed that prayer, the enemies opposed to Messiah included Jews who rejected Jesus. What produced this change in referent? It simply emerged as the psalm was read in a fresh context in light of the progress of divine events. The central idea, or sense, of the psalm was that many people stood opposed to God and His Messiah. So *whoever* opposed Messiah came under the heading of enemy in the psalm, whether that person was Jew or Gentile. Here is a wonderful example where the sense of a passage is fixed, but referents shift in surprising directions as a result of the progress of divine events.

Use of the Septuagint in the New Testament. Before discussing the progress of revelation in more detail, one other special feature of the use of the OT needs brief attention. We briefly alluded above to the issue of the use of the LXX in the NT. The significance of this observation is that when the OT is cited in the New, often the wording does not exactly match that of the Hebrew OT.[15] We already noted the issue exists because of the multilingual setting of these texts. This difference need not be significant, since concepts can be rendered in various ways. An examination of NT use of the Old shows this happens frequently. Some of these differences reflect the fact that the text is being rendered interpretively to bring out its full force according to targumic style (Isa. 61:1 in Luke 4:16–20). In other instances, summarizing larger context or other texts and concepts may be brought into the citation to compact the discussion (Ps. 68 in Eph. 4:7; Isa. 42:1 and Ps. 2:7 in Luke 3:21). At times pattern is invoked and the shift shows the escalation in the pattern (Ps. 40:7–9 in Heb. 10:5–16). Though what exactly is happening in particular cases often is hotly debated, the factors mentioned above usually enter into the wording of the text.

WAYS OF READING SCRIPTURE AND THE PROGRESS OF REVELATION

Much debate rages around the use of the OT in the New. Often, it is because the text is being read in two distinct ways and one is forced to make a choice between the readings. However, a recognition of the nature of dual authorship, the progress of revelation, and the use of pattern often makes this either/or choice unnecessary, since a both/and approach is appropriate.[16]

HISTORICAL-EXEGETICAL VS. THEOLOGICAL-CANONICAL

The two ways to read the text are the "historical-exegetical" reading and the "theological-canonical" reading. These terms are not altogether

---

15. For a work that lists such differences, but without reference to technical editions of the LXX and without a full discussion of the historical options, see G. Archer and G. C. Chirichigno, *Old Testament Quotations in the New Testament: A Complete Survey* (Chicago: Moody Press, 1983).

16. The categories of discussion raised in this section are a decidedly theologically conservative way to state the question. Many critics will simply pit the historical reading of a text in the OT against the reading of the NT without trying to probe the theological relationship between the two sets of text. For another, differently stated breakdown of this question attempting to deal with the same issue, see Vern Poythress, "Divine Meaning of Scripture," *WTJ* 48 (1986): 241–79.

adequate ones. Exegesis is theological, and theology should be exegetical. Still, they are chosen because they summarize the central concern in the reading. An historical-exegetical reading is primarily concerned with discussing a text in its original historical setting in terms of the human author's understanding and message for his original audience. A theological-canonical reading views the text in light of subsequent revelation and the full force the passage comes to have because of that additional revelation.[17] In such a reading the progress of revelation may "refract" on an earlier passage so that its force is clarified or developed beyond what the original author could grasp.

Again an illustration may suffice. Let us take a famous text, Genesis 3:15. Here is a promise that the serpent will bruise (i.e., "nip at") the heel of the child ("seed") of Eve, while the child will crush the serpent's head. In Christian circles, this is known as the *protoevangelium*, the first revelation of the gospel. This approach reads the text theologically-canonically, especially when it identifies the seed as Jesus Christ. When Genesis was written, the human author could not have named Jesus. That understanding is "refracted" onto the passage in light of the progress of revelation.

But is there more here? In the context of Genesis, one could argue the major thrust historically-exegetically is that enmity is introduced within the creation.[18] Nature and man are at odds with one another, where harmony had existed. Since the snake is condemned to the ground in Genesis 3:14, a battle between a man and a snake (enmity) now takes place (v. 15a) with the snake lunging at the man's most vulnerable target, the heel, while

---

17. One of the more debated aspects of this relationship between the Testaments is whether the NT usage of an OT text reflects only the original "literal" meaning of the OT, defines what the OT always meant, redefines (or resignifies) the OT hope, or serves to complement the older revelation by adding additional teaching to the area without negating what the OT originally taught. The differences in approach at this point serve as the major interpretive dividing point in the theological debate over eschatology among evangelicals. For a discussion of these issues, see Charles C. Ryrie, *Dispensationalism Today* (Chicago: Moody Press, 1965), 86–109, who defends "literal" interpretation; Hans K. LaRondelle, *The Israel of God in Prophecy: Principles of Prophetic Interpretation* (Berrien Springs, Mich.: Andrews University Press, 1983), 10–80, who challenges "literal" interpretation; John S. Feinberg, ed. *Continuity and Discontinuity: Perspectives on the Relationship Between the Old and New Testaments* (Westchester, N.Y.: Crossway, 1988), whose essays discuss both views side by side; Craig A. Blaising and D. L. Bock, *Dispensationalism, Israel and the Church: A Search for Definition* (Grand Rapids: Zondervan, 1992); and C. A. Blaising and D. L. Bock, *Progressive Dispensationalism* (Wheaton: Victor Books, 1993), who argue for a complementary relationship between the Testaments.

18. Josephus, *Biblical Antiquities* 1.1.4.40–51, reads the text this way. He is one of the earliest commentators on this text.

the man seeks to kill the lunging snake by crushing his head. In short, historically-exegetically the passage illustrates the devastating effects of the fall, as do the other parts of God's remarks in response to Adam's sin (3:14–19). The point in Genesis 3 alone is that after sin the creation becomes more hostile to man.

The issue is *not choosing* between the interpretations about Jesus as the seed of Eve and the introduction of hostility into the creation because of Adam's sin. Both are legitimate readings of the text, but it is a matter of which type of reading is being made. Subsequent revelation makes it clear Jesus is a son of Adam (Luke 3:38), meaning that Jesus is the Second Adam (Rom. 5:12–21). Subsequent revelation also compares Satan to a serpent who is crushed by God through Jesus (Rom. 16:20). The key in thinking through interpretations related to the use of the OT in the New is understanding *how* the NT text is reading the OT text. Which of the two levels of reading is being applied? The same goes for exposition of these passages in teaching the texts. Which consideration is being made? Is one interested in discussing a historical-exegetical reading or a theological canonical one, or both? In most cases where a Christological point is being made in the NT, a theological-canonical reading is being given, where the factors of additional OT revelation and the ministry of Christ have helped to clarify the existence of patterns and the presence of fulfillment through escalation.

Such readings are not limited to issues tied to Christology. When Isaiah 65—66 is related to the future, specifically with reference to either the new heavens and the new earth or the millennium, it is subsequent revelation (namely Rev. 20—22) and a theological-canonical reading which makes such specific identification possible. In the OT alone, one might sense one is discussing the kingdom to come, but to call it new heaven and new earth or millennium requires the specifics of Revelation. In fact, we often read the OT through such full revelatory glasses.

The benefit of understanding the possibility of a dual reading is that a text has a full range of meaning, depending on the contextual limits placed upon the reading. There usually is more in the text than we look for at any one level of reading. Some short-circuit the short-term message by leaping immediately to its larger canonical significance. Others cut short God's development of the imagery by limiting themselves only to the short-term historical context. The student of the Bible should be aware of the possibilities and know which is the concern of study. Of course, the student may want to be sensitive to both readings as the text is studied. The point is that the text can yield meaning at either level and the meaning of the two readings can be related, as our illustrations below shall seek to show.

TYPES OF USAGE

We have now laid sufficient background to turn our attention to specific types of usage.[19] The use of the OT extends beyond fulfillment about Jesus. The first few categories will deal with prophetic kinds of fulfillment, then we will move to more illustrative and explanatory categories.

Prophetic Fulfillment. Some texts reflect *directly prophetic* fulfillments. In such cases, the human author and the divine author share the expectation, and only one event or series of events is in view. The NT fulfillment of Daniel 7:13–14 is an example of such a fulfillment. Here the issue is the granting of authority to one like a Son of Man by the Ancient of Days (God). It pictures the vice-regent and representative authority which the Son of Man has for God's people. In this passage, the concept of the "one and the many" applies as well, since in Daniel 7:27 the Son of Man is associated with the vindication of the saints, the people of the Most High. Now the picture of the Son of Man is an image Jesus picked up and used for Himself. It was His favorite self-designation (Mark 14:62;Luke 22:69). He chose it because it beautifully weaves together His divinely bestowed authority with His representative role on behalf of God's people. In this case what the NT sees as fulfilled is all that was ever in view, the decisive vindication of God's people through a representative figure who receives total authority from God.

Typological-Prophetic. Other texts are *typological-prophetic* in their fulfillment. This means that pattern and promise are present, so that a short-term event pictures and mirrors (or "patterns") a long-term fulfillment. This category is frequently present, and it is debated whether it is prophetic in the strict sense of the term since often the pattern is not identifiable until the ultimate fulfillment is seen. In this category, it is best to distinguish two types of typological-prophetic fulfillment.

The first is *typological-PROPHETIC* fulfillment. In these texts, there is a short-term historical referent, and yet the promise's initial fulfillment is such that an expectation remains that more of the pattern needs "filling up" to be completely fulfilled. As such the passage begs for additional fulfillment and such expectation usually already existed among Jewish readers of these texts. A non-christological example is Isaiah 65—66, where the descriptions of victory over the enemies portrayed in terms of a new creation are so idyllic the expectation arose that the ultimate fulfillment of such a text must be in the total restoration of peace on earth, a type of "golden age." Although this is expressed most explicitly in Revelation

---

19. Moo, "The Problem of *Sensus Plenior*," is right to make the point that there are a variety of ways the NT uses the Old. His article contains numerous helpful references to periodical discussions on this theme.

21—22, the expectation was a part of Jewish thinking on the end times as well (1 Enoch 6—36; 90). Another way in which these passages might be fulfilled in this way is for a promise to be made, which is only partially realized in the short term, so that the expectation of its completion continues on into the future. A typical pattern image in the OT is the image of the "day of the Lord," which predicts catastrophic judgment. Although "day of the Lord imagery" is fulfilled in certain events within the OT (e.g., parts of Joel 2), the nature of that fulfillment looks forward to the decisive period of such fulfillment (the "day *par excellance*"). In all of these examples, the imagery is such that an aspect of the passage demands fulfillment beyond the short-term event and thus points to the presence of pattern. The prophetic character of the text resides in this "needs to be fulfilled" feature in the pattern.

Perhaps the best christological example of this category is the Servant figure of Isaiah (Isa. 42:1–9; 49:1–13; 50:4–11; 52:13—53:12). In Isaiah 49:3, this figure is explicitly called "Israel." Even Jewish hope saw a future for a glorified servant figure, viewed in terms of the nation; but they did not know how to integrate His suffering into the image or how to deal with the individuality of the expression in Isaiah 52—53. The issue of pattern and "one in the many" was not sufficiently taken into account. It is the decidedly individual nature of the language in Isaiah 52—53 which serves as the major clue that both pattern and "one in the many" are invoked. Interestingly, the NT application of the Servant image shows similar ambiguity. In Luke 1:54 Israel is called the Servant. But in Acts 13:47, servant imagery using Isaiah 49:6 is applied not to Jesus but to Paul and Barnabas. Other texts apply the image to Jesus (Acts 8:32–35). Thus, the image reflects a certain type of relationship to God in being His representative and experiencing suffering. Yet it is uniquely true of Jesus. But it also, according to the pattern, is true of others as well. Other OT texts which belong in this category include Psalms 110:1 and 118.

The second typological-prophetic category is better called *TYPOLOG-ICAL-prophetic*. Here the pattern is not anticipated by the language, but is seen once the decisive pattern occurs. Only then does the connection of design become clear. It is still a prophetic category because the issue is that God has designed the correspondence. But it is different from the previous category in that the pattern is not anticipated or looked for until the fulfillment comes.

Perhaps the outstanding illustration here is the use of Hosea 11:1 in Matthew 2:15. In Hosea, when the book is read historically-exegetically, this remark applies to Israel as she was called out in the exodus. Everything about the passage looks to the past. However, the *TYPOLOGICAL-prophetic* connection can be made when one recognizes that the exodus itself is a "pattern" image for salvation and that Jesus as King (and as the "one in the many") is able to represent (and thus recapitulate) the nation's history. Numerous righteous-sufferer psalms and other regal psalms applied to Jesus also fit here (Pss. 16, 22, 45, 69). These righteous-sufferer texts are used in the passion. In their historical-exegetical use, they described the plight of an innocent sufferer who is persecuted for identifying with God, usually an OT saint or king. But they are uniquely true of Jesus Christ. So when the NT points to their fulfillment in Him, they emphasize the uniqueness of the way He fulfills it. Psalm 45 is a beautiful illustration, since it is a wedding psalm, complete with reference to the queen who is marrying the king. Jesus never married a queen, but the "regal" tie allows the connection, so that what is said of the king in the psalm in terms of his position before God is also true of the subsequent and decisive king, Jesus. So the language of that portion of the psalm can be applied to Him as well in Hebrew 1:8–9, with the heightened sense that fits this category. Another possible example in this category is the use of Jeremiah 31:15 in Matthew 2:18, where the text and event are associated because of the pattern of suffering and the "one in the many" connection between Jesus and the nation.

Authoritative Illustration. A final category that appeals to pattern or analogy can be called *authoritative illustration* or simple *typology*. The title is reflected in the example of the exodus used by Paul in 1 Corinthians 10:1–13, where Paul explicitly spoke of exodus events as "types" (v. 6; in the NIV, the term is translated "examples"). Here the goal is *not* a prophetic use but one of exhortation. The Corinthians are to learn from past example about behavior to avoid, namely, associating closely with activities related to idolatry. The use simply points to the lessons of the past. Such illustrative and exhortative use of the OT is very common.

In a variation on such usage, the OT is appealed to because a *principle* of spiritual life is in view that is true. The text is cited because it states a truth to be applied for life or an event to contemplate its significance. Jesus' multiple use of Deuteronomy during His temptation is a good example of this. The use of Deuteronomy 5:16 in Ephesians 6:2–3 is another example, as is the appeal to Abraham and Rahab in James 2:20–26. Sometimes it is the analogy between the two situations that allows for the connection and calls for reflection.

Ideas or Summaries. Another use of the OT simply appeals to the use of *ideas* or *summaries*. Here a specific text is not cited, but the teaching of the OT is summarized and stated in fresh words in a proposition. Luke 24:43–47 is an example of such a summary, where the OT is said to teach about Christ's death, resurrection, and the promise that repentance shall be preached to all the nations in Jesus' name. No texts are cited explicitly, but one senses that all the texts Luke uses in Luke-Acts stand behind the remark. Another possible example is the debated sentence of James 4:5, which may be nothing more than a freshly worded summary of OT teaching that God is a jealous God.

A variation of this last use is the appeal to OT *language*, where no specific passage or context is in view, just the use of an OT image. Paul's remarks in 1 Corinthians 4:6 may appeal to the general tone of OT teaching about pride.

In conclusion, then, the use of the OT in the New has a variety of elements and is very complex. It is a rich area of study and reflection. The OT's use in the New also has a variety of functions; it points to God's design, reassures, instructs, and encourages. As the NT was being written, the ancient Scriptures of Genesis through Malachi served as the "Holy Book." That book was mined for information about God's promises, and the mine was full of gold. Different pieces emerged through different means, as authors used different kinds of "picks and shovels." Some tools used were old, drawn from study of the Scripture whose roots extended into Judaism; others were freshly made as a result of events in Jesus' life. Together they produced a set of convictions about how the Holy Writings of old should be read. With those convictions formed through Scripture and events, the church preached a Jesus of fulfillment. As the Christ and the Son of God, He fulfills God's promises and, in accordance with God's plan, reveals the way into everlasting relationship with the God of promise, the God of Abraham, Isaac, and Jacob.

FOR FURTHER READING

Baker, D. L. *Two Testaments: One Bible*. Downers Grove, Ill.: InterVarsity, 1976.

Bock, Darrell L. "Evangelicals and the Use of the Old Testament in the New: Parts 1 and 2," *BSac* 142 (1985): 209–23, 306–19.

———. *Proclamation from Prophecy and Pattern: Lucan Old Testament Christology*. Sheffield: Sheffield Academic Press, 1987.

Carson, D. A. and H. G. M. Williamson, eds. *It Is Written: Scripture Citing Scripture*. Cambridge: Cambridge University Press, 1988.

Dodd, C. H. *According to the Scriptures*. New York: Scribner's, 1952.

Efrid, James M., ed. *The Use of the Old Testament in the New and Other Essays*. Durham, N.C.: Duke University Press, 1972.

Ellis, E. Earle. "How the New Testament Uses the Old" in *New Testament Interpretation*. Edited by I. H. Marshall. Grand Rapids: Eerdmans, 1978.

———. *Paul's Use of the Old Testament*. Grand Rapids: Eerdmans, 1957.

Evans. C. A., "The Function of the Old Testament in the New" in *Introducing New Testament Interpretation*, edited by Scot McKnight. 163–93. Grand Rapids: Baker, 1989.

Foulkes, Francis. *The Acts of God: A Study of the Basis of Typology in the Old Testament*. London: Tyndale, 1958.

Feinberg, John S. *Continuity and Discontinuity: Perspectives on the Relationship Between the Old and New Testaments*. Westchester, N.Y.: Crossway, 1988.

France, R. T. *Jesus and the Old Testament*. London: Tyndale, 1971.

Goppelt, Leonard. *Typos: The Typological Interpretation of the Old Testament in the New*. Translated by Donald H. Madvig. Grand Rapids, Eerdmans, 1982.

Kaiser, Walter. *The Uses of the Old Testament in the New*. Chicago: Moody, 1985.

Juel, Donald. *Messianic Exegesis: Christological Interpretations of the Old Testament in Early Christianity*. Philadelphia: Fortress, 1988.

Lindars, Barnabas. *New Testament Apologetic*. Philadelphia: Fortress, 1961.

Longenecker, Richard. *Biblical Exegesis in the Apostolic Period*. Grand Rapids: Eerdmans, 1975.

Moo, Douglas. *The Old Testament in the Gospel Passion Narratives*. Sheffield: Almond Press, 1983.

_____. "The Problem of *Sensus Plenior*" in *Hermeneutics, Authority, and Canon*. Edited by D. A Carson and John Woodbridge, 179–211. Grand Rapids: Zondervan, 1986.

Poythress, Vern. "Divine Meaning of Scripture." *WTJ* 48 (1986): 241–79.

PART II

FOUNDATIONS FOR OLD TESTAMENT INTERPRETATION

VII

ARCHAEOLOGY AND THE OLD TESTAMENT

J. A. THOMPSON

The Old Testament makes contact with the world of the Ancient Near East (ANE) over a period covering thousands of years. The science of archaeology enables us today to gain a better understanding of the national and private lives of peoples who lived centuries before our own time. As a science, archaeology may be describe as the recovery and study of the material remains of human society that have survived the processes of decay and destruction. Archaeologists have devised techniques for finding as much durable remains of the past as possible in their original setting. Excavations are carried out using a technique called stratified excavation, the clearing of a particular site, locus by locus, during which distinctive soil layers or other features are kept separate. The archaeologist uses a very complex and detailed recording system, which in theory allows every item and locus exposed in an excavation to be preserved in, or returned to, its original position.

By using this detailed information and making cross references to ancient records like the Bible or the abundance of other written material from Egypt, Canaan, Babylon, Assyria, Persia, and other lands, we can make a possible interpretation of written and unwritten (archaeological) sources that are already available to us. Limitations to our knowledge will always remain because neither written nor archaeological material is ever complete. Only a limited amount of the material remains from any culture survives the destruction of time. Items of stone, baked clay, pottery, and sometimes items of metal survive; but items made of wood or fabric, except in rare cases, seldom do. Generally speaking, we are limited to accidentally durable remains.

Rarely is an ancient site excavated completely. Modern archaeological investigation only samples areas in a larger site in case later excavation using newer techniques reveals data that could modify earlier conclusions. In any case, results depend on the skill, integrity, and reliability of the excavator. For this reason, archaeological results are constantly changed and adapted. Even if these cautionary indications are enough to warn us against enthusiastic claims for the significance of archaeology in "proving the Bible to be true," we ought not adopt too readily the view that it holds little value for the Bible student. On the contrary, archaeology is a valuable adjunct to other tools for biblical research. Time and again the results of archaeological work illuminate, complement, and control historical texts.

Perhaps the most significant value of archaeological research for the Bible student lies in providing a wealth of information about ANE cultures from Sumer to Rome—and beyond. This provides substantial information about the life and culture of peoples referred to in the Bible—their architecture and building methods, art, technology, daily life, warfare, trade, religious beliefs, and practices. When the biblical narrative is set against this background, we find a broad picture of cultures referred to in the Bible. Very often this enables us to understand what a particular Bible writer is saying. Conversely the Bible sometimes provides a more exact understanding of something appearing in an excavation.

The subject of archaeology and the Bible is vast. At best we can only provide examples of several different areas where archaeological work has provided useful evidence in the study of the OT. Among these are:

1. The background to a variety of customs behind biblical narratives.

2. The physical appearance of important biblical towns with particular reference to important buildings.

3. Significant written records referring to biblical people and events found in excavations.

4. A variety of artifacts which provide visual evidence for many items referred to in the OT.[1]

CUSTOMS UNDERLYING BIBLICAL NARRATIVES

One of the most important contributions of modern archaeology to understanding the Bible is the information preserved by written records about laws and customs of biblical people. The excavator's spade has brought to light many incidental references to the customs of biblical people preserved in documents of everyday life. These include receipts, letters, contracts, licenses, etc.

LAW CODES

Further light is shed by various law codes, such as the Code of Hammurabi (preserved in stone), and those of King Lipit-Ishtar and of the town of Eshnunna.[2]

These codes, dating to the early part of the second millennium B.C. (1900–1700 B.C.), provide detailed information about life in Mesopotamia around the time of the patriarchal period. These three codes show a certain continuity in the customs of Mesopotamia during these centuries.

Information available from the great variety of baked clay tablets from such sites as Nuzi (Yorghan Tepe), Mari, Alalakh, Ebla, and others help us study the life of people in Mesopotamia, home of the patriarchs, in the centuries preceding and contemporary with the patriarchs. When the Nuzi documents were first published, many biblical scholars responded enthusiastically to insights the documents gave into the societies from which the patriarchs came. The documents seemed to portray a social milieu appearing to resemble the society of the patriarchs depicted in the Bible.[3] More mature reflection on the Nuzi material has led scholars to conclude that apparently unique parallels between the patriarchal narratives and the cuneiform texts from various parts of the ANE really indicate a parallel with a more general society over a considerable period of time. Conclusions from later research make it difficult to use these parallels as a guide for dating, although their value in helping us understand society in the second millennium B.C. is undoubted. The patriarchal customs are

---

1. A number of useful volumes on the background to biblical narratives is available, among which see J. A. Thompson, *Handbook of Life in Bible Times* (Downers Grove, Ill.: InterVarsity, 1986).

2. *ANET,* 159–77.

3. C. H. Gordon, "Biblical Customs and the Nuzi Tablets," *BA* (Feb. 1940); H. H. Rowley, "Recent Discovery and the Patriarchal Age," *BJRL* (Sept. 1949).

quite at home in the Mesopotamia of that period. We can infer that biblical traditions in Genesis 12—35 closely acquainted with a Mesopotamia way of life came with the original migrants to the Holy Land in the first half of the second millennium B.C.

IMPORTANCE OF INHERITANCE AND MARRIAGE

This point can be illustrated by referring to inheritance and marriage. In Mesopotamia, inheritance was of major importance. Property, theoretically at least, was inalienable and could not pass from the family. To overcome problems connected with transferring property in certain cases, the people used a fictitious system of adoption. A man was allowed to adopt any number of "sons" or "brothers" and pass property rights quite legally to them. Cases are known where there was a regular traffic in this kind of adoption. A property owner with no son would "adopt" an "heir" who might be a freeborn man, relative, or slave. A tablet of adoption was written on clay (and later baked) after proclamation at the city gate. When party A adopted party B, he willed to B the major portion of his lands, buildings, and other items in consideration. In return, B promised to serve A during A's lifetime and give him a decent burial upon his death. There was generally a provision that if A had no son, B would inherit the property outright. If, however, A subsequently had a natural son, the natural son would become the heir and take his father's "gods," the small baked-clay figurines used in family worship. These would assume a function akin to modern title deeds. The man who owned the property had possession of these "gods" and passed them to another in due course.

There was another possibility in the case of a man who had no son. His wife could take a slave woman for her husband, as a sort of secondary wife, in hopes that she might raise up a child for herself by this slave woman. In that case, the woman's son would become the heir if there were no other son. If, however, the true wife did give birth to a son, the true son would become the heir. Those familiar with the biblical record will readily make comparison with it (Gen. 16:1–4; 30:1–4, 9).[4]

Thus, as it grows apparent that ANE "tells"—hills covering the successive remains of ancient communities—still contain an untold wealth of tablet records that help us understand the society of biblical people, the potential for filling out the cultural background to the patriarchal age for the period 2000–1500 B.C. becomes enormous.

---

4. Mesopotamian texts for comparison are found in *ANET*, 219–20. See discussion in J. A. Thompson, *The Bible and Archaeology*, 3d ed. (Grand Rapids: Eerdmans, 1982), 29–40.

The background to other parts of the biblical story yields the same sort of investigation. For example, we can study the Egyptian background to the story of Joseph and the exodus through archaeological reports of excavations in Egypt. A wealth of Egyptian local color comes from bas-relief on Egyptian monuments and records written on other stone monuments and papyri.[5]

This section has given prominence to written records of one kind or another. There are other areas of archaeological discovery, however, that contribute equally to our knowledge of the Bible in its historical and cultural setting. One is the physical appearance of numerous biblical towns with some of their important structures.

EXCAVATIONS OF BIBLICAL CITIES

Many well-known biblical towns, not merely in the Holy Land but also in lands beyond, have now been archaeologically investigated in part.

JERUSALEM

Jerusalem has been a center of interest for archaeologists for well over a century.[6] The history of Jerusalem remains problematic since conclusions from its excavations have been subject to constant revision and dispute. In recent times opportunity has come to explore areas inside the confines of the walls. We can note only a few important facts that have come to light bearing on the OT. Until now, nothing of the temple of Solomon has been found. Along the eastern side of the old walled city, however, and along the eastern slopes and in areas to the south of the present wall, Kathleen Kenyon has been able to expose areas of the biblical city from the days of the kings of Judah. A series of terraces along this eastern slope supported houses and other structures. It has been proposed that the filling behind each terrace wall on which these structures rested is the "Millo" referred to in 2 Samuel 5:9; 1 Kings 9:15, 24; 11:27—a feature of the building program of David, Solomon, and later kings. The remains of houses from the seventh century B.C., from the last days of Jerusalem before it fell to Nebuchadnezzar, were clearly exposed by Kathleen Kenyon[7] and provide a good picture of the domestic structures of these times.

---

5. See *IBD*, s.v. "Joseph"; J. Vergote, *Joseph en Egypte* (Genèse 37—50, à la lumière des études égyptologique récentes. 1959).

6. See *ABD*, s.v. "Jerusalem."

7. Kathleen Kenyon, *Jerusalem, Excavating 300 Years of History* (1967), plates 47–48; see also her *Digging Up Jerusalem* (New York: Praeger, 1974).

A segment of the wall of Jerusalem from the late eighth or seventh century B.C. has come to light in the Jewish quarter.[8] Among other items found in recent excavations is a portion of the wall of Nehemiah.[9] Two important written documents from the days of the monarchy, the Siloam Inscription and the Babylonian Chronicle, also have been excavated in Jerusalem.

SAMARIA

The city of Samaria, once the capital of the Northern Kingdom, also has been extensively excavated. The royal quarter was traced in some detail. It was founded by Omri, king of Israel. Revealed by the excavation were the Israelite city wall with its distinctive masonry, its casemate wall, and the "ivory house," which yielded a superb collection of carved ivory pieces (1 Kings 10:18; 22:39; Amos 3:15; 6:4).[10] The ivory's designs show the strong influence of Phoenician and Syrian types. Pottery in the form of red burnished vessels recovered from this Israelite period was of superior quality. It is now known as "Samarian Ware."[11]

BETH-SHAN

An important town in the northern part of Israel was Beth-shan (Tell el Husn), marked today by a fine tell rising some eighty meters above the bed of the Harod River, which provided a perennial water supply. The town stood at the junction of the Valley of Jezreel and the Jordan Valley. Around the base of the tell there is evidence of settlement from the fourth millennium B.C. Before the Israelites occupied the site, it was an important Canaanite town with several temples on the tell. In the fifteenth century B.C. it was an Egyptian fortified outpost. During one period Philistine mercenaries occupied it. The town is mentioned in the Bible several times (e.g., Josh. 17:11,16; Judg. 1:27; 1 Sam. 31:10, 12; 2 Sam. 21:12; 1 Kings 4:12).

The central tell has preserved a number of Canaanite temples, which have added to our store of knowledge about the Canaanite cult. A temple in Level IX (fourteenth century B.C.) was dedicated to "Mekal, the Lord of Bethshan." In Level VIII (end of the fourteenth century B.C.) in the days of Pharaoh Seti I (ca. 1305–1290 B.C.), a stele was found which

---

8. *EAEHL*, s.v. "Jerusalem"; see N. Avigad, *Discovering Jerusalem* (Nashville: Abingdon, 1983).

9. Kenyon, *Jerusalem, Excavating*, plate 55.

10. A helpful comprehensive collection of samples of the Samaria ivories is in *EAEHL*, s.v. "Samaria."

11. *ABD*, s.v. "Samaria."

referred to a clash with some people, thought to be Hebrews (end of four-teenth century B.C., ca. 1300 B.C.). Levels VII (ca. thirteenth century B.C.) and VI (ca. twelfth century B.C.) also contained Canaanite temples. By that time the Israelites had arrived. Beth-shan was given to the tribe of Manasseh (Josh. 17:11), who were unable to capture it (Josh. 17:16; Judg. 1:27). After Saul was killed in battle by the Philistines, his body and the bodies of his sons were hung from the walls of Beth-shan and recovered by the men of Jabesh Gilead (1 Sam. 31:10, 12).

The two temples excavated in Level V (ca. eleventh century B.C.), one dedicated to the god Resheph and the other to the goddess Anti, are thought to be the temples of Dagon and Ashtaroth in which Saul's head and armor were displayed by the Philistines (1 Sam. 31:10; 1 Chron. 10:10). The city must have fallen to the Israelites in the time of David. It belonged to the fifth administrative district of Solomon (1 Kings 4:12). It was taken by Pharaoh Shishak in the days of Rehoboam (1 Kings 14:25). Its chief interest for biblical scholars, however, is as a source of important information about Canaanite religion. The area remains a significant center even today.

HAZOR

Another significant site in the northern part of the Holy Land is Hazor, excavated most extensively by Y. Yadin from 1955 to 1969. Located in the Jordan Valley between Lake Huleh and the sea of Galilee, it was once a large Canaanite town surrounded by a huge earth rampart. Passing centuries grew a large tell, the site for administrative buildings and a citadel. The lower city was occupied for a shorter period until it was destroyed by Israelite tribes in the thirteenth century B.C. The tell was founded in the twenty-seventh century B.C. and remained in use until the second century B.C., growing in height over the centuries. Excavation shows that in the tenth century the tell was occupied by Solomon after a period of limited Israelite settlement. Thereafter, there were several fine levels of Israelite occupation, namely Levels X to V that have yielded a wealth of architectural and cultural information. In Solomon's day (Level X), the tell was surrounded by a fine casemate wall, which preserved an excellent example of a typical Solomonic gate. That city was destroyed, probably by the invader Ben-Hadad I, but rebuilt in Omri's day in the ninth century B.C. as a fortified area with a large citadel covering practically the entire excavated area (Level VIII).[12]

---

12. A comprehensive view of excavations in part of Solomon's city and the later ninth century city of Omri is in *EAEHL*, s.v. "Hazor."

The excavation at Hazor revealed a splendid example of a typical water system. To reach the water table many feet below the surface, a shaft had to be dug through the accumulated debris of past centuries and then through solid rock. City residents could descend the shaft using a spiral staircase. This method of obtaining water was used by the Canaanites earlier and copied by the Israelites. Good examples can be seen at Jerusalem, Megiddo, and Beersheba, among other places. The example at Hazor was in use in the days of Omri. Hazor was destroyed by the Assyrian invader Tiglath-pileser III in 732 B.C.

Many fine examples of Israelite masonry have been preserved at Hazor. A monumental entrance to one area in Hazor can be seen today in the Israel Museum in Jerusalem.

MEGIDDO

Spectacular remains have been preserved at Megiddo, also an important Canaanite town. Excavations have identified twenty levels of occupation. A number of Canaanite shrines and small temples have come to light. The Israelite builders were active in the days from Solomon onwards. Their work is marked by important remains including a fine Solomonic gateway, a number of large buildings, a magnificent water system, and important structures at first identified as "Solomon's stables" (1 Kings 9:19) but subsequently as "Ahab's store houses." The water system consists of a vertical shaft with a spiral staircase leading to a nearly horizontal tunnel cut underground through rock to a cave containing a spring. It was a huge engineering achievement and guaranteed water to the town in a time of siege. It dates probably to the days of the Omride dynasty (876–843 B.C.).

Megiddo provides a good example of the way later research in archaeology sometimes refines and corrects earlier opinion. The so-called "stables" of Ahab's day were later found to be "store houses," when similar structures in Beersheba were found to contain large and small pottery vessels that seem to have been used for storing grain and other commodities. Beersheba was a center for the collection of commodities used by the king for the upkeep of his family and staff. They have represented taxation payments.

Megiddo failed to produce an archive where important written documents such as receipts and letters were stored. An important seal, however, bearing the name "Shema, the servant of Jeroboam" has become a commercial logo in modern times, for example on the cover of the *Journal for the Study of the Old Testament.*

LACHISH

Another town which had a long history is Lachish (Tell ed-Duweir).[13] Once a Canaanite royal city, it is mentioned in cuneiform letters found at Tell el-Amarna from the fourteenth century B.C. It appears in several places in the Bible. The town was captured by the Israelites (Josh. 10:5, 23, 32–33) and included in the territory of Judah. It became an important fortress for the defense of Judah's southwestern areas. In the days of Nebuchadnezzar, it was one of the last towns to fall to the Babylonian king (Jer. 34:7). Today it is represented by a large mound in the low hills west of Hebron.

In pre-Israelite times Lachish was a Canaanite political and religious center. Excavations have revealed an important temple complex used in the fifteenth and fourteenth centuries B.C. Three phases of its life were unveiled. Archaelogists have identifed important features of the structures, including an altar that changed its shape over the period (about 1430 to 1260 B.C.), cultic objects, figurines, the bones of sacrifices, libation vessels, etc. The archaeological finds from Lachish, combined with cultic information from other sites like Megiddo, Hazor, Arad, and even Jerusalem, offer a useful picture of Canaanite cultic practices.

Lachish was important for other reasons. Twenty-one letters written on pieces of broken pottery (ostraca) in the ancient Hebrew script were recovered.[14] Evidently, they belong in the days of Zedekiah, about 590 B.C., and were addressed mostly to "my lord Yaush," an army commander. The letters were dispatched to the garrison at Lachish by a subordinate officer at some outlying point where he could watch the signals of Lachish and Azekah. One letter opens with the date "in the ninth year," perhaps the year of the commencement of Nebuchadnezzar's siege of Jerusalem.

There was evidently a degree of medical skill in Lachish. Three trephined skulls were found in one area. The fact that the bone of one had begun to grow after an operation suggests that the patient survived at least for a time.

Lachish played an important role in the defense of the country. During the expedition of Sennacherib to the Holy Land in 701 B.C., Lachish was besieged (2 Kings 18; 2 Chron. 32; Isa. 36). The same campaign is mentioned in Assyrian records and bas-reliefs found in the king's palace in Nimrud. Excavations support the picture in the bas-reliefs. Two walls surrounded the town. The inner one, being erected on the crest of the tell, was six meters thick. The second wall was built down the slope. A three-

---

13. See *ABD*, s.v. "Lachish."
14. *ANET*, 321–22.

chambered gate in the inner wall led to a walled ramp that ran down the slope of the tell to a second gate. These defenses are portrayed on the reliefs from Nimrud. The excavation also uncovered arrowheads, scales of armor, sling stones, and an Assyrian helmet crest. Found near the gate, they testify to the siege of 701 B.C. The city was razed by the Assyrians, leaving an ash and destruction layer on the site. A reconstruction of the town may be seen in the British Museum in London.[15]

TELL ES-SABA'

Three miles east of the modern town of Beersheba lies a tell marking a well-planned and fortified town from the days of the Judahite monarchy. It is known today as Tell *es-Saba'*. There is good evidence of prehistoric occupation in the area, and archaeologists have defined a "Beersheba culture" there. The town itself was not occupied until the Israelite period in the time of the judges. It was unwalled at that time. In the tenth century B.C. a brick wall was built on stone foundations. It was a solid wall, four meters thick, resting on an artificial ramp six to seven meters high, made of layers of pebbles, earth, and ashes with a moat in front. It was covered with a glacis. This strong fortification was erected in the tenth century B.C. Later a casemate wall (a double wall, its inner wall being 1.6 meters thick and its outer wall 1.1 meters thick) was built in part on the foundations of the solid wall (ninth century B.C.). A new glacis was built over the older one. The new casemate wall remained in use until the end of the eighth century B.C. It would seem that already in David's time the casemate wall was coming into use (ca. 1000–960 B.C.). It was widely used in Solomon's day (ca. 961–922 B.C.) as we learn from several other Solomonic towns like Megiddo and Hazor. The city gate was discovered at the southern edge of the mound. In fact, two gates were uncovered, one on top of other, corresponding to the two town walls. The earlier one belonging to the solid wall (strata V and VI) is flanked on either side by two guard rooms and a tower and the later one (strata III and II) is contemporary with the casemate wall.

One impressive feature of the town was its careful planning. The gateway led into a ring-road that encircled the town. To the right of the gate lay a bank of three long rooms now recognized as storerooms. These yielded a fine collection of potting jars of various sizes. Each room contained a long hall separated by two rows of pillars similar to those in Megiddo and Hazor. The pottery vessels were of various types, suggesting they once held different contents.[16] An ostracon in one storeroom con-

---

15. *IBD*, 2.868.
16. *EAEHL*, s.v. "Beersheba, Tel."

tained the names Tolad (Josh. 15:30; 19:4) and Amam (Josh. 15:26), evidently the places from which the goods had been sent. Inside the gate was a large open space, perhaps the town square, twelve-by-twenty meters in size.

In the northeastern corner of the mound was a broad stairway, probably leading to the central water supply system. It has not been excavated. A number of domestic houses of standard shape (the four-room type) and several large "administrative buildings" were uncovered. A plastered pool, perhaps for ceremonial purposes, was discovered near the center of the town.[17]

Extending beyond the gate was a unique and excellently constructed network of drainage channels intended to collect rainwater into central cisterns.

Small cult objects such as figurines and miniature incense altars have been found in various parts of the town. One large vessel, a krater, carried the inscription q-d-$š$, which denotes the word $qōdeš$ or "holy."

The most astonishing discovery from the Israelite town was a collection of large stone blocks of a distinctive color found in the wall of one of the storehouses. The blocks came originally from a large altar, the horns of which were preserved on three corners. There were traces of a fourth, which had been broken off. A reconstruction of the altar appears on the covers of early numbers of *Tel Aviv*, the Journal of the Tel Aviv University Institute of Archaeology. No cultic building from which the altar had come was found in the excavation. The town was destroyed when it was sacked during Sennacherib's campaign in 701 B.C.

ARAD

In the same general area as Beersheba is the town of Arad. It was a large fortified town in early pre-Israelite times but fell into disuse for some 1,500 years after a new settlement was founded on the ridge in the southeast section of the old town, which was a small open village built around the rise. At its center was a sacred site with a square altar, probably a Kenite high place. In the tenth century B.C. the area became part of a strongly fortified royal citadel founded possibly by Solomon. During the monarchy, it was destroyed six times and burned, the first time by Pharaoh Shishak. Each time it was quickly rebuilt.

Arad was an administrative and defense center. It was also a religious center. These aspects of its significance clearly came to light as a result of the excavation.

---

17. For a good plan of the excavated sections of the city, see *IBD*, 1.181.

Almost two hundred inscribed potsherds were found, nearly half in Aramaic ca. 400 B.C. and the rest in Hebrew from the period of the monarchy.[18] This is the largest and most varied find of early written records from any Palestinian excavation. The Hebrew ostraca came from different strata in the excavation. Most are letters and dockets from royal archives. Some contain lists of private names, sometimes with numbers and an indication of commodities like wheat. A very significant group of ostraca was a series of letters from a certain Eliashib, son of Eshyahu, a high official, possibly the commander of the last citadel (ca. 600 B.C.).[19] The main contents of these letters were orders to provide rations of wine and bread to the Kittim, possibly mercenaries of Aegean stock in the service of Judah. One letter mentions Beersheba and "the house of Yahweh," perhaps the Jerusalem temple. Another letter calls for reinforcements of men from Arad and Kinah (Josh. 15:22) to Ramoth-negeb (Josh. 19:8; 1 Sam. 30:27) in anticipation of a threatening Edomite attack.

The other important feature emerging from this excavation was a discovery of the only Israelite temple unearthed by archaeology. Its orientation, ground plan, and contents were in basic agreement with the Solomonic temple. It had one main room and to the west of it a raised room (cella), the "holy of holies." Flanking the entrance to the "holy of holies" were two incense altars and inside was a small "high place" and a stone pillar. East of the building was a courtyard divided into a large outer part and a smaller inner part. Flanking the entrance to the large outer room were two stone slabs, perhaps the bases of pillars like the biblical Jachin and Boaz (2 Chron. 3:17). In the outer section was a large square altar for burnt offerings built of earth and unhewn stones five meters square and three meters high (Ex. 27:1). While the correspondence with the Jerusalem temple was not exact, there were several parallels.

The history of the temple at Arad corresponds with part of the development of worship in Israel. Built on a sanctified place in the days of the united monarchy, the altar went out of use at the end of the eighth century B.C. The temple was finally destroyed in the second half of the seventh century B.C. with the building of the last Israelite citadel. These two phases of its destruction correspond to the days of Hezekiah and Josiah. Both concentrated worship in Jerusalem.

There were six Israelite citadels in all. Tell 'Arad is generally identified with Israelite Arad because of an inscription on a bowl and references in the ostracon. The Canaanite Arad was located elsewhere. Numerous artifacts were discovered in the excavation, including potsherds of broken

---

18. Y. Aharoni, *Arad Inscriptions*, rev. and ed. by A. F. Rainey (Jerusalem, 1981).
19. *ANET*, 586–69.

pottery and shekel weights. The weights suggest a preoccupation with commerce.[20]

SHECHEM

The town of Shechem at the foot of Mounts Gerizim and Ebal is of some importance archaeologically and historically. The site dates back to the fourth millennium B.C. and is mentioned in early Egyptian documents. The sacred area has been discovered on the west side of the city and excavated. It was a center for Canaanite worship and is a rich source of information about Canaanite shrines and religious artifacts.

The town was included in the territory of Manasseh in Israelite times (Num. 26:31; Josh. 17:2, 7). In Solomon's day it seems to have been the center for the governor's headquarters. In the days of the united monarchy the town was a center for vigorous life. Pharaoh Shishak destroyed the town in 918 B.C. It was rebuilt and became a tax collection center in the eighth century B.C., as is attested by a large granary with a thick plastered floor built on the ruins of the Canaanite temple in the late ninth or early eighth century B.C. Shechem was the site of the assembly that rejected Rehoboam (1 Kings12). With the rise of Samaria at the time of the Omride dynasty, the town lost its central position. It was destroyed by the Assyrians in 724–722 B.C.

The town has proved archaeologically important for several reasons. It was surrounded by a massive wall with several gates from 1650 to 1550 B.C. in pre-Israelite times. Several important temples came to light during excavation. Among discoveries were the remains of sacred standing stones at the entrance to a "fortress-temple" and other broken stone pillars.[21]

RECOVERY OF WRITTEN RECORDS

ALPHABETIC WRITINGS

Passing reference has already been made to some written records discovered in Holy Land excavations. There is evidence that some form of alphabetic writing emerged in the general area of the Holy Land about 1700 B.C. Flinders Petrie, an English archaeologist, found material written on stone monuments at Serabit el-Khadem in the Sinai peninsula. It was associated with Egyptian material but was clearly alphabetic. In the following centuries it is evident that alphabetic (as distinct from cuneiform or hieratic writing) became widespread in the general area of the Holy

---

20. *ISBE*, s.v. "Arad"; *EAEHL*, s.v. "Arad."
21. *ISBE*, s.v. "Shechem."

Land. Ostraca used as receipts, ownership tags, and the like written on scraps of broken pottery have been recovered in excavations all over the Holy Land.

Alphabetic writing on potsherds from Gezer, Shechem, Tell el-Ajjul, Tell el-Hesy, Lachish, Beth Shemesh, Izbet Sartah, and several other sites attest to the widespread use of alphabetic writing in pre-Israelite and early Israelite times. The script underwent a moderate development over the centuries but remained easily recognizable. It was used regularly on seals, weights, receipts written on ostraca, stamps on jar handles, and in a variety of commercial situations. Sometimes the information helps in the identification of a site, as with some of the jar handles found at el-Jib that bore the name Gideon.

NON-ALPHABETIC WRITINGS

A remarkable non-alphabetic cuneiform tablet was found at Megiddo dating ca. 1479–1350 B.C. It records part of the Gilgamesh epic which refers to the flood story and shows this story was known in the Holy Land as early as the fourteenth or fifteenth century B.C. An important inscription from Mesopotamia written in cuneiform and preserved in the Babylonian Chronicle from ancient Jerusalem provides an exact date for the fall of Jerusalem to Nebuchadnezzar: July 587 B.C. (2 Kings 25:2f; Jer. 52:5f).

OTHER OSTRACA FINDINGS

A significant ostracon from the twelfth century B.C. was found at the small village of Izleet Sartah, three kilometers east of Aphek (Josh. 12:18; 1 Sam. 4:1; 29:1) It had five lines of writing on two matching pieces. The first four seem to have been random practice writing of an alphabet. The fifth was an alphabet written left to right. Though opposite the normal Semitic direction, the line consisted of a complete Hebrew abecedary (alphabet). It is the oldest and most complete one yet discovered. Its remarkable feature is that it was discovered in an Israelite agricultural settlement near the road to Shiloh in central Palestine, suggesting that already in the twelfth century B.C. the alphabet was in use in a village.

A tiny limestone tablet written in the ancient Hebrew script was discovered in the Gezer excavation dating from ca. 925 B.C.[22] It turned out to be an agricultural calendar. Very few inscriptions of any length have been found in Palestine, but they are not lacking altogether.

A longer inscription was discovered in 1880 on the wall of the underground tunnel that brought water into Jerusalem in the days of Hezekiah (ca. 715–687 B.C.; see 2 Kings 20:20; 2 Chron. 32:30). In six lines it

---

22. *ANET*, 321.

recounts the story of the day when the two parts of the tunnels drilled from two directions met, allowing the water to flow.[23]

The most important written material from ancient Israel comes from collections of ostraca to which we have referred already in passing. The collection of sixty-three ostraca found in Samaria proved to be records of oil and wine deliveries from the areas around Samaria to the royal household, probably as taxes of some kind. They date probably to the time of Jeroboam II (ca. 786–746 B.C.) or thereabouts.[24]

The Lachish ostraca came from the ancient Tell ed-Duweir. The main group came from a small room under the gate tower. Three others were found in other places in the town. Most letters found are addressed to a certain Yaush, the military commander of Lachish, from a subordinate outside Lachish. They provide insight into events during the last days before the town fell to Nebuchadnezzar, perhaps in the autumn of 589 or 588 B.C. when the prophet Jeremiah was still active in Jerusalem.[25] One letter mentions that the signals from Lachish can be seen, but those from Azekah were not visible for some reason (Jer. 34:7).

In addition to the Hebrew ostraca there were almost two hundred in Aramaic from about 400 B.C.

A third significant collection of ostraca came from Arad. We have already dealt briefly with these in our discussion about the town of Arad in the previous section.

The neighboring land of Moab has produced a long inscription commemorating the successful attempt of Mesha king of Moab to free his land from the yoke of Israel. The script is practically the same as the developed form of the old Hebrew script. The date of this inscription is roughly fixed by the reference in 2 Kings 3:4 to Mesha king of Moab. The contents of Mesha's stele suggest a date toward the end of his reign, perhaps about 830 B.C. The language, Moabite, is fairly close to Hebrew. No Hebrew inscription of this length has ever been found.[26]

SIGNIFICANT ARTIFACTS

Even a cursory reading of the OT will make it clear that many items of the domestic, commercial, religious, and cultural background of the OT are frequently mentioned. Through archaeology, actual examples of such items have been discovered that can be examined firsthand.

---

23. Ibid.
24. Ibid.
25. Ibid., 321–22.
26. Ibid., 320.

POTTERY

A good example is the wide range of pottery vessels discovered in excavations in the Holy Land, both in houses and other buildings in ruined towns and in graves of the people. An indispensable guide to the pottery of the Holy Land is a volume by Ruth Amiran[27] providing examples illustrated with photos and hand drawings of pottery vessels during each archaeological period from Neolithic to the Iron Age. She also includes a useful chapter on cult vessels. It is now possible to match the excavated items with the ceramic vocabulary of the OT.[28] Of particular interest for the study of OT is the pottery of the Late Bronze and Iron Age periods (1550–586 B.C.). Various items listed include bowls, goblets, chalices, cooking pots, plates, platters, kraters of various kinds from small vessels to large commercial jars, jugs, juglets, lamps, and large store jars. The major source of these vessels is naturally the Holy Land, where the presence of foreign pottery, too, indicates trade allows dating. Amiran links all of her pottery types to published archaeological reports, where they can be identified in particular excavated sites.

METAL OBJECTS

There is no volume like Amiran's pottery corpus to cover the wide range of metal objects in use in ancient times, although this has been done in part. It is clear that some pottery vessel were modeled on metal prototypes. Metal objects found in excavations are rarer than pottery. Because metal was important in manufacturing of weapons of war and tools for agriculture and building, it was eagerly taken as booty by conquering armies.

Sometimes metal weights have been found in excavations, although weights were more frequently made of stone.

There have been some metal objects found in excavations that were used as tools in various kinds of commercial, industrial, craft, or agricultural pursuits. These are made of copper, bronze, and iron. Corrosion and rusting naturally affect such items. They are normally listed in excavation reports and very often photographed or drawn. Limestone or pottery molds have been discovered for some of them. In earlier times stone tools were used but these gave way to copper, bronze, and finally iron. Copper and bronze remained in use even after iron was discovered. Adzes, axes, knives, saws, chisels, awls, and a range of agricultural tools such as hoes, mattocks, forks, etc. have been found.[29] Although the repertoire of tools found in excavations

---

27. Ruth Amiran, *Ancient Pottery of the Holy Land* (Jerusalem: Massada, 1969).

28. James L. Kelso, "The Ceramic Vocabulary of the Old Testament," *BASOR* (1948):Supp 5–6.

29. For tools found in excavations, see G. E. Wright, *BA* 6: 2/33–36, fig. 8.

is considerable, it is likely that many more await discovery in the numerous unexcavated sites in the Holy Land and elsewhere in the Near East.

RELIGIOUS MATERIALS

In the area of religious practice, valuable material found in excavations serves to explain and illustrate numerous aspects of Canaanite and other religions. A range of stone pillars (symbols of Baal) has been found at places like Shechem, Arad, and elsewhere. Evidence for sacred poles (symbols of the goddess Asherah) comes from the different soil colors caused by rotting wood. Excavations have uncovered a range of altars from various sites, in particular, a variety of cuboid stone altars including some with the horns of the altar still protruding from the top. The large stone altar found at Beersheba is a particularly fine example. Ruth Amiran's volume on ancient pottery provides photos of a variety of cult vessels, in particular, incense burners. Among other items used in the Canaanite cult were a range of pottery and metal figurines representing deities. All of these religious items serve to illustrate in tangible form a variety of items mentioned in Old Testament contexts.

FOR FURTHER READING

Aharoni, Y. *The Archaeology of the Land of Israel.* Translated by A. F. Rainey. Philadelphia: Westminster, 1982.

Avi-Yonah, M., ed. *EAEHL*, 4 vols. Englewood Cliffs, N.J.: Prentice-Hall, 1975–78.

Ben-Tor, A. *The Archaeology of Ancient Israel.* Translated by R. Greenberg. New Haven: Yale University Press, 1992.

Eakins, J. Kenneth and Jack P. Lewis. *HBD*, s.v. "Archaeology and Bible Study."

Freedman, D. N. "The Relationship of Archaeology to the Bible." *BARev* 11 (1985):6.

Millard, Alan. *Treasures from Bible Times.* Tring, England: Lion, 1985.

Schoville, K. N. *Biblical Archaeology in Focus.* Grand Rapids: Baker, 1978.

Shanks, H. and Dan P. Cole. *Archaeology and the Bible: The Best of BAR.* Washington, D.C.: Biblical Archaeology Society, 1990.

Thompson, J. A. *The Bible and Archaeology.* 3d. ed. Grand Rapids: Eerdmans, 1982.

Wright, G. E. *Biblical Archaeology.* Philadelphia: Westminster, 1962.

Yamauchi, Edwin. *The Stones and the Scriptures: An Introduction to Biblical Archaeology.* Philadelphia: J. B. Lippencott. Reprint. Grand Rapids: Baker, 1981.

VIII

CANON OF THE OLD TESTAMENT

PAUL R. HOUSE

Since the Reformation, Protestants, Greek Orthodox, and Roman Catholics have disagreed over what OT books are Scripture. All three traditions agree the identical lists of books found in Jewish and Protestant Bibles should be included. Yet Roman Catholics have added Tobit, Judith, Wisdom of Solomon, Ecclesiasticus (Sirach), Baruch, 1–2 Maccabees, Additions to Esther, and Additions to Daniel to their Bible. The Orthodox concur with the Roman Catholics, except that they omit Baruch. What books did NT writers consider sacred?

This article examines how OT books came to be accepted as Scripture by ancient Jewish and early Christian communities of faith. Various factors affected the process. Crucial historical events, such as the exile, the Maccabean revolt, and the fall of Jerusalem, provided the opportunity, even the necessity, of declaring what books were sacred. Theological issues also impacted selection of Scripture, since the prophets and writings cite the Pentateuch as an authoritative document and avoid doctrinal conflicts with it. Certain sociological matters also were vital. For example, priests and civic leaders like Ezra, Nehemiah, Judas Maccabeus, and the later rabbis led the canonizing movement, partly because they had the time and community esteem necessary to do so. Literary details also were vital, for designations like "Law" and "Prophets" have generic as well as historical and theological significance.

In order to examine these factors, four issues will be addressed. (1) A definition of canon will be suggested to demonstrate the topic's historical significance for the pre- and post-Jesus communities of faith. (2) OT texts that chart the canonization of the law and prophets will be noted. (3) The OT canon which the NT writers used will be examined. Key historical events that helped determine the selection of Scripture will be highlighted in this section, since the OT canon was closed by the time the NT was finished. (4) A proposed reconstruction of the canonical process will be offered to suggest how the OT may have come to its final form. No article this size can include an exhaustive treatment of these topics, but references to secondary literature will guide readers to more thorough sources of information.

DEFINITION OF CANON

The word "canon" comes from the Greek term *kanōn*, which R. H. Pfeiffer says originally meant

the stave of a shield, a weaver's rod, and ruler for drawing or measuring, a curtain rod, a bedpost (Jth. 13:6); and metaphorically a rule, a standard, a model, a paradigm, a chronological table, a boundary, a tax assessment, a tariff.[1]

By NT times, Pfeiffer adds, canon meant "'rule,' 'standard' (Phil. 3:16—textus receptus; Gal. 6:16), 'limit' (2 Cor. 10:13, 15–16)."[2] The word was first used as a designation for books considered Scripture "by Athanasius, bishop of Alexandria, in a letter circulated in A.D. 367."[3] Thus, the word *kanōn* itself was first used by the church to define its sacred literature.

Despite the term's Christian origins, it also is an appropriate word for describing how pre and post-Jesus Jewish interpreters selected Scripture. These persons had other phrases to mean "standard" or "rule," but their goals were the same as their Christian counterparts. For instance, rabbis in the second century A.D. spoke of holy books as those that "defile the hands."[4] Though such phrases do not necessarily refer to the canonizing

---

1. *IDB*, s.v. "Canon of the Old Testament."
2. Ibid.
3. F. F. Bruce, *The Canon of Scripture* (Downers Grove, Ill.: InterVarsity, 1988), 17.
4. David Kraemer, "The Formation of Rabbinic Canon: Authority and Boundaries," *JBL* 110, no.4 (1991): 615.

process,[5] they do imply that the rabbis considered some books of higher value than others. Therefore, the word "canon" is an adequate, even if imperfect, term to use for our study.

What does it mean to call a book canonical? To be part of the holy books means, first of all, that a book has particular binding authority for the community of faith. As S. Z. Leiman states, "A canonical book is a book accepted by Jews as authoritative for religious practice and/or doctrine, and whose authority is binding upon the Jewish people for all generations."[6] Second, and related to its authority, a canonical book is one considered inspired by God. Paul writes that "Scripture (*graphā*) is God-breathed (*theopneustos*)" and therefore "useful for teaching, rebuking, correcting and training in righteousness" (2 Tim 3:16).* The apostle clearly believed that Scripture's authority comes from its inspiration and that its inspiration is at least partly indicated by its appropriateness for instruction in godly living. Paul's conviction probably stemmed from OT texts that claim to be God's word mediated through human beings (e.g., Ex. 20:1; 24:4; 34:27; Isa. 1:2; Jer. 2:1).[7] W. H. Green observed that such passages were "believed to be from a divine source which the people and their rulers were bound to obey, and upon the faithful observance of which the prosperity of the nations and its continued existence were dependent."[8]

Canonical books, then, are God-given documents that people of faith feel constrained to obey. Such books differ from other religious texts for these reasons, rather than for any literary or historical brilliance they may display. Who wrote the texts, where they originated, and their doctrinal content helped decide their authority and inspiration, but were means to an end.

The Hebrew canon is divided into three sections: the Law, the Prophets, and the Writings (see chart). These divisions were first mentioned in a prologue to the apocryphal book Sirach (ca. 132 B.C.),[9] and are reflected in Luke 24:44 where Jesus states that "the Law of Moses, the Prophets and

---

5. Sid. Z. Leiman, *The Canonization of Hebrew Scripture: The Talmudic and Midrashic Evidence*, (Hamden, Conn.: Archon Books, 1976), 103.

6. Ibid., 14.

7. Pentateuchal texts claim that Moses wrote down what God spoke while the prophetic books state repeatedly the prophets spoke only what God commanded them to say.

8. W. H. Green, *General Introduction to the Old Testament: The Canon* (New York: Scribner's, 1898), 33.

9. This date is set by the author's comment that the prologue was written in "the thirty-eighth year of the late King Evergetes" (ca. 170–117 B.C.). Baba Bathra, a tractate from the Babylonian Talmud (3rd–4th centuries A.D.), also presents a three-part canon.

* Unless otherwise noted, Scripture quotations in this chapter are from NIV.

COMPARISON OF LISTS OF THE OLD TESTAMENT BOOKS

RABBINIC CANON 24 BOOKS	SEPTUAGINT 53 BOOKS	ROMAN CATHOLIC OLD TESTAMENT 46 BOOKS	PROTESTANT CANNON 39 BOOKS
The Law	*Law*	*Law*	*Law*
Genesis	Genesis	Genesis	Genesis
Exodus	Exodus	Exodus	Exodus
Leviticus	Leviticus	Leviticus	Leviticus
Numbers	Numbers	Numbers	Numbers
Deuteronomy	Deuteronomy	Deuteronomy	Deuteronomy
The Prophets	*History*	*History*	*History*
The Former Prophets			
Joshua		Joshua	Joshua
Judges	Judges	Judges	Judges
1-2 Samuel	Ruth	Ruth	Ruth
1-2 Kings	1 Kingdoms (1 Samuel)	1 Samuel (1 Kingdoms)	1 Samuel
The Latter Prophets	2 Kingdoms (2 Samuel)	2 Samuel (2 Kingdoms)	2 Samuel
Isaiah	3 Kingdoms (1 Kings)	1 Kings (3 Kingdoms)	1 Kings
Jeremiah	4 Kingdoms (2 Kings)	2 Kings (4 Kingdoms)	2 Kings
Ezekiel	1 Paralipomena (1 Chronicles)	1 Chronicles (1 Paralipomena)	1 Chronicles
The Twelve	2 Paralipomena (2 Chronicles)	2 Chronicles (2 Paralipomena)	2 Chronicles
Hosea	1 Esdras (Apocryphal Ezra)	Ezra (1 Esdras)	Ezra
Joel	2 Esdras (Ezra-Nehemiah)	Nehemiah (2 Esdras)	Nehemiah
Amos	Esther (with Apocryphal additions)	Tobit	Esther
Obadiah	Judith	Judith	
Jonah	Tobit	Esther	
Micah	1 Maccabees	1 Maccabees	
Nahum	2 Maccabees	2 Maccabees	
Habakkuk	3 Maccabees		
Zephaniah	4 Maccabees	*Poetry*	*Poetry*
Haggai		Job	Job
Zechariah	*Poetry*	Psalms	Psalms
Malachi	Psalms	Proverbs	Proverbs
	Odes (including the	Ecclesiastes	Ecclesiastes
	prayer of Manasseh)	Song of Songs	Song of Songs
The Writings	Proverbs	Wisdom of Solomon	
Poetry	Ecclesiastes	Ecclesiasticus (The Wisdom	
Psalms	Song of Songs	of Jesus the son of Sirach)	
Proverbs	Job		
Job	Wisdom (of Solomon)	*Prophecy*	*Major*
Prophets—	Sirach (Ecclesiasticus or The Wis-		
Rolls—	dom of Jesus the son of Sirach)	Isaiah	Isaiah
"the Festival Scrolls"	Psalms of Solomon	Jeremiah	Jeremiah
Song of Songs		Lamentations	Lamentations
Ruth	*Prophecy*	Baruch (including the Letter	Ezekiel
Lamentations	The Twelve Prophets	of Jeremiah)	Daniel
Ecclesiastes	Hosea	Ezekiel	
Esther	Amos	Hosea	
Others (History)	Micah	Daniel	*Minor*
Ezra-Nehemiah	Joel	Joel	Hosea
1–2 Chronicles	Obadiah	Amos	Joel
	Jonah	Obadiah	Amos
	Nahum	Jonah	Obadiah
	Habakkuk	Micah	Jonah
	Zephaniah	Nahum	Micah
	Haggai	Habakkuk	Nahum
	Zechariah	Zephaniah	Habakkuk
	Malachi	Haggai	Zephaniah
	Isaiah	Zechariah	Haggai
	Jeremiah	Malachi	Zechariah
	Baruch		Malachi
	Lamentations	*Appendix*	
	Letter of Jeremiah	The Prayer of Manasseh	
	Ezekiel	The two apocryphal	
	Daniel (with apocryphal additions,	books of Esdras	
	including the Prayer of Azariah and		
	the Song of the Three Children,		
	Susanna, and Bel and the Dragon)		

the Psalms" speak of His ministry. Various orders of the books within these categories existed in ancient times, yet the threefold pattern persisted.[10]

OLD TESTAMENT REFERENCES
TO THE CANONIZING PROCESS

Though there is obviously no individual OT text that speaks of a finished canon, there are several passages that explain how parts of Scripture were written, quoted, and eventually connected with other authoritative texts. These texts indicate that the Scriptures were considered special by people of faith soon after they were written. Dating passages and the times in which they were quoted is a task that evokes controversy, since traditional and non-traditional scholars disagree on these issues. Even with the disagreements, however, some generally acceptable dates can be ascertained. References to the canonizing process appear in each of the OT's three sections: the Law, Prophets, and Writings.

THE LAW

Several texts in the Pentateuch refer to the writing and established authority of both individual passages and larger sections of material. For instance, Exodus 17:14 says God commanded Moses to "write . . . on a scroll" the story of Amalek's defeat. Similarly, Exodus 24:4 states that Moses "wrote down everything the Lord had said," which refers to the Covenant Code that begins at Exodus 20:1 ("God spoke all these words. . . .") and ends at 24:3 ("Moses went and told the people"). Quite significantly, the nation accepted these words as binding (24:3). Further, Leviticus is presented as a series of laws that God delivered directly to Moses (e.g., 1:1; 4:1; 5:14; 6:1). Finally, Deuteronomy 31:9 states that after speaking the words contained in Deuteronomy, "Moses wrote down this law and gave it to the priests." He then ordered them to read the law to the people so they can "learn to fear the Lord" (31:13).

Clearly, the Pentateuch claims both inspiration and authority. Moses spoke and wrote God's own words, and Israel was expected to obey what Moses conveyed. Indeed punishment was threatened for all who refused to abide by these texts. It is true that each reference to God's revelation may refer to only a specific portion of the Pentateuch (e.g., Ex. 17:14), but the periodic references to God speaking directly to Moses and Moses'

---

10. Cf. Roger Beckwith, *The Old Testament Canon of the New Testament Church and Its Background in Early Judaism* (Grand Rapids: Eerdmans, 1985), 181–234, for a discussion of the historical development of the threefold canon.

subsequent writing indicate that, taken as a finished whole, the Pentateuch itself leads readers to conclude that all five are inspired and authoritative.

It is well known that commentators disagree about the date of the Pentateuch. Conservative scholars argue that Moses wrote the bulk of Genesis—Deuteronomy and thereby place the books in either the late fifteenth or mid-thirteenth century B.C., depending on when they date the exodus.[11] Non-traditional scholars claim that some segments of the Pentateuch are quite ancient, but that most of the material was written long after Moses' time.[12]

What is at stake for the canonical process in these disputes? Primarily, the earliest date for the first canonical books. If the Pentateuch was considered binding and inspired by 1250 B.C., the latest possible date for Moses' death, then more time was available for the canonization of the Prophets and Writings. A more leisurely process emerged. If the Pentateuch was not considered canonical until 450–400 B.C., as critical scholars argue, then the other books must have been accepted over a much shorter period of time.

On what points do all scholars agree? First, no one disputes that Ezra quotes the Pentateuch as Scripture (Neh. 8:1–18). Thus, by no later than ca. 450 B.C. Genesis—Deuteronomy became the first books in the canon. Second, all commentators concede the Pentateuch became the standard by which all subsequent additions to the canon were judged. Every biblical and extra-biblical reference to the canon begins by mentioning the law.[13]

THE PROPHETS

The former prophets (Joshua, Judges, Samuel, Kings) refer to Moses and Pentateuchal texts in several places. Joshua 1:1–18 mentions Moses, God's promises to him, and God's standards given through him. Israel was commanded to keep the Mosaic covenant (1:7; 8:34–35), divide the land according to Moses' plan (13:8), and to secure their future by adhering to Moses' commands (24:6). Judges and Samuel mention Moses infrequently, yet observe that Israel's disobedience to God's law led to their spiritual and political difficulties (cf. Judg. 2:1–15; 1 Sam. 12:6–15).

---

11. Note the survey of relevant opinions in R. K. Harrison, *Introduction to the Old Testament* (Grand Rapids: Eerdmans, 1969), 3–82, 495–541. See also, D. Garrett, *Rethinking Genesis* (Grand Rapids: Baker, 1991).

12. Cf. Otto Eissfeldt, *The Old Testament: An Introduction*, 3d ed., trans. Peter R. Ackroyd (New York: Harper and Row, 1966), 194–241, for an analysis of the Pentateuch from a source-critical perspective.

13. In this article, "Law" refers to the Pentateuch as a whole, while "law" or "laws" refer to individual parts of the Pentateuch, especially its legislative portions.

In Kings, David charged Solomon with keeping Moses' law (1 Kings 2:3), and Solomon referred to God's promises to Israel through Moses (1 Kings 8:56). Moses' name appears prominently in 2 Kings 18—25, where the author repeatedly condemned or praised monarchs based on their adherence to the Mosaic covenant.[14] As in Joshua, Judges, and Samuel, Moses and the Law are presented as canonical fixtures.

Probably the most-discussed canon-related text in the former prophets is 2 Kings 22:1—23:25, where priests working on the temple during Josiah's eighteenth year (622 B.C.) discovered "the Book of the Law" (22:8). Hilkiah, the high priest, had the book read to the king, who responded by initiating a national religious renewal (22:11—23:25). Conservative Jewish and Christian scholars argue this incident indicates the Law was a fixed authoritative entity by 622 B.C.[15] Other commentators maintain that this document was expanded into the present Book of Deuteronomy by priests who wished to encourage reform. Thus, the "Book" found is what critical scholars have termed the D-source portion of the Pentateuch.[16]

Given the regular references to Moses and the Law in 2 Kings 18—25, it appears the book's author intended to convey that a full body of legislation was discovered. The reforms included wide-ranging issues such as destroying idols, desecrating high places, and observing Passover (23:1–23). Clearly, then, a significant law code was canonical by the late seventh century B.C., though its actual length cannot be determined (cf. 23:1–3).

Martin Noth argues the former prophets themselves were written by one author, who wrote parts of Deuteronomy, and who collected and arranged relevant historical sources into a coherent theological account.[17] The author's primary aim was to show how Israel broke the standards set forth in Deuteronomy and consequently lost its homeland.[18] This history

---

14. See 2 Kings 18:6; 18:12; 21:8; 23:25.

15. Cf. Max L. Margolis, *The Hebrew Scriptures in the Making* (Philadelphia: Jewish Publication Society, 1922), 31–33; Leiman, *Canonization of Hebrew Scripture*, 20–26; and Green, *General Introduction*, 33–36. This article agrees with this opinion. For significant arguments in favor of Mosaic authorship of Deuteronomy, see M. G. Kline, *Treaty of the Great King: The Covenant Structure of Deuteronomy* (Grand Rapids: Eerdmans, 1963); P. C. Craigie, *The Book of Deuteronomy* in NICOT (Grand Rapids: Eerdmans, 1976), 24–69; and Harrison, *Introduction*, 495–541, 637–62.

16. Cf. S. R. Driver, *A Critical and Exegetical Commentary on Deuteronomy* in ICC (New York: Scribner's, 1895) xxxiv–lxxvii; and Gerhard von Rad, *Deuteronomy* in OTL, trans. Dorothea Barton (Philadelphia: Westminster, 1966), 23–30.

17. Martin Noth, "The Deuteronomistic History," trans. J. Douall et al., JSOT-Sup 15 (1981) 1957 reprint: 10.

18. Ibid., 79.

was completed "around the middle of the sixth century B.C. when the history of the Israelite people in the original sense was essentially at an end."[19] Though Noth's uncertainties about Mosaic authorship of Deuteronomy are unnecessary, if his other assertions are correct it is likely that the Pentateuch was canonical by as early as 622 B.C., but not later than 550 B.C. when the former prophets had been completed. Many scholars have modified Noth's influential thesis by locating a later editor,[20] but these variations still leave the Former Prophets complete by ca. 500 B.C., which is a minimum of fifty years before Ezra.

There are only five direct references to Moses in the Latter Prophets. Isaiah 63:11–12 mentions the miracles he performed, while Jeremiah 15:1 declares that God would not spare Israel even if Moses and Samuel prayed for them. Micah 6:4 reminds Israel that God redeemed them from slavery through Moses' ministry. Only Malachi 4:4 connects Moses to the Sinai covenant. If the Isaiah and Micah texts are dated in the eighth century,[21] then prophets from the eighth, seventh (Jeremiah), and fifth (Malachi) centuries knew Moses' work, yet only Malachi's reference relates to canonical issues. This fact supports the notion that Moses' writings were authoritative by at least 450 B.C.

Despite the infrequent use of Moses' name, the prophets use the words "law" and "covenant" repeatedly. These terms often refer to more than the Ten Commandments, since the law is said to come not only from Moses, but from Zion (Isa. 2:3) and the priests (Ezek. 7:26), which implies a body of tradition taught by professional cultic figures. The prophets denounced Israel for breaking what seems to be a well-known, clearly stated covenant (Isa. 24:5; Jer. 11:10; Ezek. 16:59; Hos. 6:7; Mal. 2:10). It seems likely, then, that the nation possessed a binding covenant that had authoritative, canonical force throughout the prophetic era. Whether or not this covenant was the Pentateuch itself or simply a major portion of it will continue to be debated. Still, it is proper to conclude that the canonical process began well before the former Prophets and Ezra were completed.

Two passages in Isaiah hint at the recognition of Scriptures beyond the Law. Isaiah 8:16, 20 state that Israel should look to the "law" and "testimony" for guidance, which may mean that the Law had been supplemented by other books or accounts. The term "testimony," however, appears only once in the OT, so it is impossible to argue strenuously for

---

19. Ibid., 12.

20. See Richard D. Nelson, "The Double Redaction of the Deuteronomistic History," JSOTSup 18 (1981).

21. Cf. John N. Oswalt, *The Book of Isaiah*, chapters 1—39 in NICOT (Grand Rapids: Eerdmans, 1986), 17–31.

this view. More significant, perhaps, is the virtual repetition of Isaiah 36:1—38:8 in 2 Kings 18:17—20:11. Some of the material is slightly different, but otherwise the texts are identical. If 2 Kings does indeed copy Isaiah, then the prophecy may have been canonical in the late sixth century B.C. At the very least, the similarity of the accounts show an "official" version of this important event was set well before Ezra's time.

Two other aspects of the prophetic books must be noted. First, the prophets viewed themselves as accurate, God-called preachers and interpreters of the covenant. Indeed, like Moses, they claimed they spoke for God, since they constantly punctuate their messages with "says the LORD," "a saying of the LORD," or other similar phrases. Thus, they claimed both inspiration and authority, and therefore demanded consideration when books in addition to the Pentateuch were considered binding by the community of faith.

Second, the prophets appear to influence one another. For example, Jeremiah 2:1–37 reflects Hosea's impact on the later prophet. Jeremiah 26:17–19 demonstrates that Micah's ministry remained influential decades after it ended. Similarly, Daniel 9:2 refers to Jeremiah's prediction of Israel's seventy-year exile. If the prophets quoted one another's ideas and phrases, it is possible they possessed and valued some body of writings.

THE WRITINGS

As has already been noted, the Writings speak often of Moses and the Law. Ezra 3:2 says that the altar erected (ca. 536 B.C.) for the second temple (ca. 515 B.C.) was fashioned according to what was "written in the Law of Moses." Further, Ezra 6:18 refers to the "Book" of Moses' laws, and Ezra 7:6 describes Ezra as a priest committed to teaching Moses' law. This commitment is evident in Nehemiah 8:1–14, where Ezra taught the people to obey "the Book of the Law of Moses" (8:1). Similarly, 1–2 Chronicles link Moses to commands (2 Chron. 8:13), general legislation (2 Chron. 23:18), and a distinct law book (2 Chron. 25:4). Because of their linguistic and thematic agreements, it is likely Ezra and 1–2 Chronicles were written by 450 B.C.[22] Even if 1–2 Chronicles emerged later, as some commentators contend,[23] their statements about Moses' book support Ezra and Nehemiah's comments about the Law.

Other texts in the Writings mention Moses, the Law, and the covenant (cf. Pss. 77:20; 90:1; 103:7; Dan. 9:11, 13), but these passages add nothing new to the discussion. They simply reinforce the obvious conclusion that by the time the last OT book was written the Law was already considered

---

22. Harrison, *Introduction*, 1153.
23. *IDB*, s.v. "Chronicles, I and II."

Scripture. They also imply this process began well before Ezra's era, and that the prophets urged Israel to obey the Mosaic covenant. This prophetic preaching demonstrates that the prophets claimed to be authoritative interpreters of the covenant, which opens the possibility that their own utterances and writings could eventually be considered canonical as well.

Besides the references to other scriptures, a few texts in the Writings indicate how those books were formed. For instance, Proverbs 1:1 states that what follows are "the proverbs of Solomon," who reigned in Israel ca. 970–930 B.C. A similar reference appears in Proverbs 10:1. In Proverbs 25:1, however, the text states that "the men of Hezekiah king of Judah" copied the Solomonic proverbs that follow. It appears, then, that during Hezekiah's reign (ca. 715–687 B.C.) Solomon's sayings were considered worthy of preservation and obedience, an attitude synonymous with canonization. Thus, Proverbs was probably considered Scripture by Hezekiah's time.

Psalm 72:20 may reflect the gradual collection of the Psalms. This text says it "concludes the prayers of David son of Jesse," yet psalms included after Psalm 72 have titles that attribute them to David. Though the titles are not original to the text, they do indicate that those who collected the Psalms attempted to state who wrote these passages and the situations that led to their writing.[24] This phenomenon, coupled with the fact Psalms is divided into five books in the Hebrew text, shows that over time these already cherished texts were united into a single, canonical text.

THE NEW TESTAMENT CHURCH'S CANON

From its inception, the church used the Scriptures inherited from its Jewish roots. Jesus says He came to fulfill, not abolish, the Law and the Prophets (Matt. 5:17). He also states that "the Law of Moses, the Prophets and the Psalms" speak of His life and work (Luke 24:44). Paul claims the Scriptures are inspired and authoritative (2 Tim. 3:16). Every OT book except Esther, Ecclesiastes, Song of Solomon, Ezra, Nehemiah, Obadiah, Nahum, and Zephaniah is quoted in the NT.[25] Obviously, the NT uses a canonical body of literature that approximates the OT.

---

24. Cf. Brevard Childs, "Psalms Titles and Midrashic Exegesis," *JSS* 16 (1971): 137–50. For a study of how the Book of Psalms was formed, see Gerald Wilson, *The Editing of the Hebrew Psalter* (Chico, Calif.: Scholars, 1985) and John H. Walton, "Psalms: A Cantata about the Davidic Covenant," *JETS* 34 (1991): 21–31.

25. G. Wildeboer, *The Origin of the Canon of the Old Testament: An Historico-Critical Enquiry*, trans. B. W. Bacon (London: Luzac, 1895), 51.

Given this acceptance, it is important to note how and when OT books became canonical in Jewish circles before the time of Christ. It is also necessary to decide whether the apocryphal books were excluded from the canon and to examine the NT's usage of those texts. When these issues have been addressed, the NT's position on the OT canon will be clearer.

In his monumental volume *The Old Testament Canon of the New Testament Church*, Roger Beckwith offers a comprehensive program for analyzing the contents of the NT authors' OT canon. He lists eleven sources that must be consulted, including the OT, the Apocrypha, the Pseudepigrapha, the Dead Sea Scrolls, Hellenistic fragments, Bible translations, Philo, first-century Christian literature, Josephus, the Early Church Fathers, and rabbinical literature.[26] Given the brevity of this article, this section will deal with the Apocrypha, the Dead Sea Scrolls, Bible translations, Jewish literature, and the NT itself. Once the evidence has been collected, a reconstruction of how the NT church received its OT can then be offered.

THE APOCRYPHA

After the OT was completed (ca. 300 B.C.),[27] other religious texts were written. These books vary in content. First and 2 Maccabees are historical in nature and focus on second-century B.C. events in Palestine. The Book of Wisdom and Sirach belong to Israel's Wisdom tradition, while Tobit and Judith parallel biographical works like Esther and Ruth, and Baruch supplements Jeremiah's prophecy. There is little evidence that these works were ever included in the Jewish community's list of Scripture, but they are accepted in later Christian circles. Their main value at this point in the discussion is the information they offer on when certain OT books were considered Scripture.

Sirach indicates that a threefold canon consisting of "the Law (*tou nómou*), and the Prophets (*tōn prophātōn*), and the others (*tōn állōn*) existed by 132 B.C.[28] The book's translator, the grandson of Ben Sirach, made this claim in an introduction to the book, in which he also said his grandfather had "devoted himself to the reading of the Law, the Prophets, and the other books of the Fathers" (NJB). Given this reference, H. B. Swete suggested "the original may have been composed some fifty

---

26. Beckwith, *Old Testament Canon*, 16–46.

27. This statement obviously implies early dates for the composition of Daniel and the Psalter.

28. Emil Schürer, *The History of the Jewish People in the Age of Jesus Christ* (175 B.C.–A.D. 135), rev. G. Vermes et al., 3 vols. (Edinburgh: T. and T. Clark, 1973–87), 2:316, n. 9.

years earlier."[29] Thus, the Law and at least some of the Prophets and Writings were canonical by ca. 180–130 B.C. Since little controversy about the Prophets ever emerged, it seems likely that the Law and Prophets as we know them were accepted by this time. It is also possible, though not certain, that all the Writings were also deemed sacred.

First and 2 Maccabees may reveal that the canon was set before 132 B.C. According to 1 Maccabees 1:54–56, Antioches Ephiphanes burned copies of the Law ca. 167 B.C. Because of this and other atrocities, Judas Maccabeus and his family led a revolt against Israel's Greek oppressor. One of Judas' religious acts was to make "a complete collection of the books dispersed in the late war" (2 Macc. 2:14, NJB). This gathering took place by 164 B.C. and paralleled an earlier collection made by Nehemiah (2 Macc. 2:13). Included in Judas' and Nehemiah's collections were "the books dealing with the kings and the prophets, the writings of David and the letters of the kings on the subject of offerings" (2 Macc. 2:13, NJB). Therefore, the Law, Former Prophets, Prophets, and Psalms were protected by Judas and valued by Nehemiah.

Scholars agree these passages from Sirach and Maccabees are quite significant. Though skeptical of some of the historical details in Maccabees, H. E. Ryle thought the revolt helped Israel's leaders set aside books "which had exerted the greatest influence over the spirit of the devout Jews during the time both of the great national rising and of the humiliation which preceded it."[30] Wildeboer believed the passages help prove that the "canonization of the prophetico-historical and other prophetic writings of the second section [of the canon] must, accordingly, be placed after Nehemiah and before the year 165 B.C.; probably about 200 B.C."[31] Beckwith goes even further. He claims that

> The fact that the third section of the canon had not yet received a name when the prologue to Ecclesiasticus was written, about 130 B.C., shows that it had not long been formed, and the date of its formation was probably the second great crisis in the history of the canon mentioned in 2 Maccabeus after the Antiochene persecution. In all likelihood, therefore, it was Judas Maccabeus and his associates who formed the Prophets and Hagiographa, by subdividing the miscellaneous non-Mosaic Scriptures, at a date around 164 B.C.[32]

29. H. B. Swete, *An Introduction to the Old Testament in Greek*, 2d ed. (Cambridge: Cambridge University Press, 1902), 270.

30. H. E. Ryle, *The Canon of the Old Testament: An Essay on the Gradual Growth and Formation of the Hebrew Canon of Scripture* (New York: Macmillan, 1892), 126.

31. Wildeboer, *Origin of the Canon*, 116.

32. Beckwith, *Old Testament Canon*, 165.

In other words, the entire canon was set in 164 B.C., a position Beckwith defends by charting the inclusion of all the Writings in virtually every later list of OT books.

Three conclusions emerge from this brief analysis of relevant apocryphal passages. (1) Sirach sets a date for the closing of the Law and Prophets segments of the canon and for at least the beginning of the selection of the Writings. Indeed, if Beckwith is correct, the entire canon was set by 132 B.C. (2) Maccabees demonstrates that canonical decisions may have been made three decades before the prologue to Sirach. (3) Maccabees reveals that crises often led to serious religious activity, including the selection of Scripture.

THE DEAD SEA SCROLLS

The Dead Sea Scrolls (DSS) are the most extraordinary archaeological finds of the twentieth century. They are valuable for historical, textual, and theological studies. Since the scrolls were copied at Qumran by the Essenes, a Jewish community of faith that "must have existed from the middle of the second century B.C. until A.D. 68,"[33] they may also provide vital information on the canonization process.

Unfortunately, the DSS evidence on the canon is not altogether clear. Since the Essenes were a sectarian group, the DSS may only reflect a small segment of Jewish thought. Further, all the OT books are represented except Esther, but so are Tobit, Ecclesiasticus, and some pseudepigraphical works.[34] As Leiman observes, "The scrolls and fragments published to date do not indicate the attitude of the sectarians to various types of literature."[35] Therefore, he concludes, it is only possible to say that "the Qumran library indicates which books were tolerated by the Dead Sea community."[36]

What can be learned about the canon, then, from the DSS? (1) It is important to note that thirty-eight of the thirty-nine OT books were included in these texts written two centuries before Christ. Even the Book of Esther's absence may be explained as accidental, since "only one copy of Ezra, Nehemiah and Chronicles has been discovered,"[37] or as the result of a dispute between the Essenes and the Maccabees.[38] (2) It is critical to remember that the fact that the Essenes *knew* non-canonical books does

---

33. *IDBSup*, s.v. "Essenes."

34. Cf. J. T. Milik, *Ten Years of Discovery in the Wilderness of Judaea* in SBT 26, trans. J. Strugnell (London: SCM, 1963), 31–37.

35. Leiman, *Canonization of Hebrew Scriptures*, 35.

36. Ibid.

37. Ibid.

38. Cf. Beckwith, *Old Testament Canon*, 291–94.

not mean they accepted them as Scripture.[39] The Law and the Prophets had special honor at Qumran, as did the Psalms. Still, it is impossible to say whether only the thirty-eight books were considered Scripture, or whether Jubilees and Sirach were as well.[40] (3) The DSS indicate that even if the canon remained open by 132 B.C. the books under consideration were not unlimited. Only two or three beyond the canonical texts were valued highly.

BIBLE TRANSLATIONS: THE SEPTUAGINT

Translations of the OT were made as Hebrew ceased to be a living language. For instance, Syriac and Aramaic translations appeared by the second century A.D. The most important translation, however, was the Greek, called the Septuagint (LXX). Though this translation's origins are shrouded in ancient lore,[41] it is quite possible parts of the OT were translated by the third century B.C.[42] Sirach certainly spoke as if all three sections of his canon had been translated by 132 B.C. Even Esther, the lone canonical book absent in the DSS, was translated by 114 B.C.[43] Therefore, the translation was attempted during the time period already established as the era when the Law, Prophets, and at least some of the Writings were canonized. Then, too, the very act of translation shows certain books were considered sacred above others.

LXX experts have long noted this version contains books outside the Hebrew canon,[44] and they have believed it originated among Jews living in Egypt. These notions led to the hypothesis that two canons existed simultaneously among the Jews: a smaller one in Palestine and a larger, more flexible one in Alexandria. This historical reconstruction was attractive to many because it helped explain why the post-NT church struggled to establish its own list of OT books.

Lately, though, several scholars have questioned this "Alexandria hypothesis." For example, A. C. Sundberg claims the Law and Prophets were complete in both Palestine and Alexandria by 132 B.C., but that "a wide religious literature without definite bounds circulated throughout Judaism" until A.D. 90, when the Jews closed their canon. The church was strong enough to ignore Judaism at this point, but it eventually settled on

---

39. Cf. Ibid., 7–8.

40. Cf. Leiman, *Canonization of Hebrew Scripture,* 35–36.

41. Swete, *Introduction to the Old Testament,* 10–12.

42. Ralph W. Klein, *Textual Criticism of the Old Testament: The Septuagint after Qumran* (Philadelphia: Fortress, 1974), 2–3.

43. L. B. Paton, *A Critical and Exegetical Commentary on the Book of Esther* in ICC (New York: Scribner's, 1908), 30.

44. Cf. Beckwith, *Old Testament Canon,* 382–85.

a canon similar to Judaism's.[45] Leiman also believes the Alexandrian and Palestinian canons agreed on the Law and Prophets, but he argues that the Writings also were identical. Why? Because he thinks most LXX texts are late and probably reflect Christian preference for including books the Hebrew canon rejects. Further, he says, Philo, an Alexandrian Jew (ca. 30 B.C.–A.D. 50) never cited apocryphal books as Scripture, nor does Sirach, Maccabees, or any of the later rabbis. It seems logical, then, to conclude the apocryphal books were regarded as valuable, but not as Scripture, by all Jewish groups. Therefore, later, post-Jesus LXX texts reflect popular Christian, not Jewish, canonical tradition.[46] Beckwith basically agrees with Leiman's perspective.[47]

Sundberg, Leiman, and Beckwith are certainly correct in their assertions about the Law and Prophets. Sirach and the DSS definitely support a common list of Mosaic and prophetic texts in Palestine and Egypt. Further, Leiman and Beckwith probably reflect the Writings' status more accurately than Sundberg. The apocryphal books are not listed as undisputably canonical in any Qumran, apocryphal, or rabbinical work. They are not quoted as Scripture in the NT (see next section). Thus, it is easier to explain the apocryphal books' existence in terms of valuable religious literature than as canonical Scripture.

THE NEW TESTAMENT

Regardless of one's viewpoint on its inspiration, the NT is a priceless resource for determining what books were considered Scripture by A.D. 50–100. George L. Robinson observes that by NT times there was a distinct, complete body of canonical writings known by various names, including

> "the scripture" (Jn 10:35; 19:36; 2 Pet 1:20), "the Scriptures" (Mt 22:29; Acts 18:24), "holy Scriptures" (Rom 1:2), "sacred writings" (2 Tim 3:15), "the law" (Jn 10:34; 12:34; 15:25;
>
> 1 Cor 14:21), "law and prophets" (Mt 5:17; 7:12; 22:40; Lk 16:16; 24:44; Acts 13:15; 28:23).[48]

In some instances, the term "the law" is even used as a designation for the OT in general, since the phrase refers to non-Pentateuchal writings in John 10:34, 12:34, 15:25, and in 1 Corinthians 14:21.[49] What deserves

---

45. A. C. Sundberg, *The Old Testament of the Early Church* in HTS 20 (Cambridge: Harvard University Press, 1964), 103.
46. Leiman, *Canonization of Hebrew Scripture*, 39–40.
47. Beckwith, *Old Testament Canon*, 338.
48. *ISBE*, s.v. "Canon of the Old Testament."
49. Ibid.

examination is whether such terminology ever applies to the Apocrypha, and whether any individual passages help reveal the extent of the OT canon of the NT writers.

Scholars differ over how extensively the NT uses the Apocrypha. Numerous possible allusions to the Apocrypha and pseudepigrapha are discernible in the NT,[50] yet direct "instances of apocryphal quotation in the NT prove to be very small, though one can hardly deny them altogether."[51] Robinson correctly asserts that no apocryphal text is quoted under the heading of the major canonical titles listed above.[52] Still, at least one NT passage, Jude 14–15, cites an apocryphal book (1 Enoch). How should allusions and direct references be treated?

Most of the allusions either reflect images or phrases from the Apocrypha, provide supporting information, or offer illustrative material in sermonic or teaching texts. An example of the first usage is Romans 1:20–32, which uses similar images as Wisdom 13–15.[53] The second case arises in texts like Hebrews 11:34–35, which supplements OT accounts by including material that perhaps comes from 2 Maccabees 6:18—7:42.[54] Examples of the third category appear in 2 Timothy 3:8, where Paul compared his opponents to Jannes and Jambres, two sorcerers who are not in any known apocryphal work, and, most likely, Jude 14–15, where Jude quoted from Enoch to warn of certain judgment. Though Jude quotes an apocryphal text, he does not equate it with Scripture, for he does not call it "law," "Scripture," etc. Beckwith concludes that

> the passages Jude borrows from the Assumption of Moses and 1 Enoch are being borrowed because they happen to be edifying and meet his present need. He is not implying that everything in those books is edifying, still less that the books have divine authority. He is treating the incidents he selects as pieces of narrative haggadah—edifying, but not necessarily historical.[55]

In other words, Jude uses the text to support his sermon without using it as canonical Scripture. Therefore, there are no NT texts that cite the Apocrypha as scriptural evidence the way canonical books are frequently quoted.

Two individual passages indicate the extent of the OT canon during NT times. In Luke 24:44, Jesus tells two disciples that "the Law of Moses,

---

50. Cf. the extensive list of possible usages in Sundberg, *Old Testament of the Early Church*, 54–55.
51. *TDNT*, s.v. "κρύπτω."
52. Robinson, "The Canon of the Old Testament," 558.
53. Wildeboer, *Origin of the Canon*, 52.
54. Ibid.
55. Beckwith, *Old Testament Canon*, 403.

the Prophets and the Psalms" all speak of His ministry. This verse does not specify the contents of the Prophets or any of the Writings except Psalms. It is likely, however, that "Psalms" represents other books, and "the Prophets" corresponds to that long-closed section of the canon. If so, Jesus' comment reflects terminology at least as old as Sirach.

Matthew 23:35 and its parallel text, Luke 11:51, also may indicate a canon that begins with Genesis and ends with Chronicles. Here Jesus condemned the religious leaders by saying:

> And so upon you will come all the righteous blood that has been shed on earth, from the blood of righteous Abel to the blood of Zechariah son of Berekiah, whom you murdered between the temple and the altar.

The designation of Zechariah as "son of Berekiah" has led to some confusion. Zechariah the prophet was Berekiah's son (Zech. 1:1) but was not slain in this fashion. A Zechariah "son of Jehoiada" was killed near the temple in 2 Chronicles 24:20. Luke 11:51 avoids the difficulty by not naming Zechariah's father, and at least one Greek manuscript also omits the phrase in Matthew.[56]

Since Jesus' description of Zechariah's death is so close to the story in 2 Chronicles, it is reasonable to assume that Jesus refers to that incident. The difficulty with Zechariah's father can be explained by a textual error, by the fact that Zechariah may have had an earlier ancestor Berechiah or by the possibility that Berechiah ("blessed of Yahweh") may have been a title given to Zechariah's father.[57] At any rate, linking Abel and Zechariah in a contrastive time frame probably means Jesus mentions the first (Gen. 4:8–12) and last (2 Chron. 24:20) murders recounted in the OT.[58] As W. C. Allen notes, these two events "represent the beginning and end of the OT Canon of Scripture, in which Chronicles is the last book."[59] Just as Jesus knew a three-part canon, so He also cited a canon that begins with Genesis and ends with Chronicles. It is likely, then, that Jesus was familiar with a canon that parallels the final Hebrew Bible very closely.

Given its direct references to the OT as authoritative Scripture, its quotations from the OT, and its allusions to a threefold, Genesis-to-Chronicles canon, it is unlikely the NT writers had a different body of Scripture than Judaism. No apocryphal book is cited as a scriptural

---

56. W. C. Allen, *A Critical and Exegetical Commentary on the Gospel According to St. Matthew* in *ICC*, 3d ed. (Edinburgh: T. and T. Clark, 1977), 250.

57. J. A. Broadus, *Commentary on the Gospel of Matthew* in *ACNT* (Philadelphia: American Baptist Publication Society, 1886), 477.

58. E. Schweizer, *The Good News According to Matthew*, trans. D. E. Green (Atlanta: John Knox, 1975), 444.

59. Allen, *Commentary on Matthew*, 250.

authority in the NT, so it also is unlikely its writers considered any apocryphal book canonical. Therefore, as far as the NT is concerned, the OT canon was closed and had probably been for some time.

JEWISH LITERATURE

Information gleaned from first-century Judaism and certain later rabbinical writings support the conclusion that the OT canon was set by NT times. This data comes from a treatise by Josephus, who lived ca. A.D. 37–107, from an evaluation of the council of Jamnia, supposedly held ca. A.D. 90, and from selected rabbinical disputes. These sources are valuable for assessing any proposed reconstruction of how the canonical books went from written documents to acknowledged Scripture.

Josephus commented on the books in the canon in a letter to Apion, an opponent of Judaism. Writing ca. A.D. 90, he claimed the Jews

> do not possess myriads of inconsistent books, conflicting with each other. Our books, those which are justly accredited, are but two and twenty, and contain the record of all time. Of these, five are the books of Moses ... the prophets subsequent to Moses wrote the history of the events of their own times in thirteen books. The remaining four books contain hymns to God and precepts for the conduct of human life.[60]

Clearly, Josephus knew a three-section canon. How long had these books been accepted? He added:

> We have given practical proof of our reverence for our own Scriptures. For, although such long ages have now passed, no one has ventured either to add, or to remove, or to alter a syllable; and it is an instinct with every Jew, from the day of his birth, to regard them as the decrees of God, to abide by them, and, if need be, cheerfully to die for them.[61]

His phrase "long ages have now passed" reveals Josephus' belief that the canon had been set for some time.

Are his 22 books the 24 books (39 in English) of the traditional Hebrew canon? Most likely so. Leiman claims, "Josephus' 22 books probably correspond to the 24 books of the talmudic canon, with the units Judges-Ruth and Jeremiah-Lamentations each counting as one book. Later Palestinian witnesses count 22 books precisely in this manner."[62] No recent canonical expert seriously disputes Leiman's conclusions.

Clearly, the evidence from the Apocrypha itself, the NT, and Josephus argues in favor of an OT canon closed by A.D. 50–100. How long it had

---

60. Cited in Leiman, *Canonization of Hebrew Scriptures*, 31–32.
61. Ibid., 32.
62. Ibid.

been closed is not certain, but Josephus spoke as if many years had passed. Philo, an Alexandrian Jew who died ca. A.D. 50, also used only the accepted books as Scripture. Before then, the Qumran community did not cite or quote explicitly any apocryphal text as authoritative in the same way they cited canonical books. Beckwith may be correct, then, to push the date back to Judas Maccabeus' time.

Many scholars believe the canon was closed by A.D. 90, near the time Josephus wrote his letter to Apion, because of a rabbinical council held at Jamnia. Jack P. Lewis notes that

> When R. Johanan b. Zakkai escaped from the siege of Jerusalem, he is said to have asked permission of the Roman general to reestablish his school at Jabneh. This college, without assuming the name of Sanhedrin, began to exercise legal functions, replacing the great law court in Jerusalem. It was ordained that certain privileges which previously had been peculiar to Jerusalem should be transferred to Jabneh.[63]

Between A.D. 80–117, the canon was discussed several times at Jamnia.[64] Several scholars have concluded that a "synod" of rabbis closed the canon ca. A.D. 90–100. For example, Frantz Buhl wrote, "At that synod the canonicity of the whole of the Sacred writings was acknowledged."[65] Ryle thought Jamnia at least "may symbolize the general attitude of the Jewish doctors, and their resolve to put an end to the doubts about the 'disputed' books of the Hagiography."[66] Indeed this date and place for the canon's closing has become almost canonical itself.[67]

Despite its prevalence, the Jamnia hypothesis has at least three flaws. (1) The deliberations had no binding authority, for debates about individual books continued.[68] (2) Only Ecclesiastes and Song of Solomon are discussed. There does not seem to be any major debates on the whole canon.[69] (3) The books "accepted" do not differ from those Josephus and the NT had already included. Thus, the discussions seem to be more an affirmation of an already-existing canon than a declaration of the canon. Given these facts, Lewis is correct to state "it would appear that the frequently made assertion that a binding decision was made at Jabneh covering all Scripture is conjectural at best."[70] In fact, Leiman may not overstate the case when he writes,

---

63. J. P. Lewis, "What Do We Mean by Jabneh?" *JBR* 32 (1964): 126.
64. Ibid.
65. F. Buhl, *Canon and Text of the Old Testament*, trans. John Macpherson (Edinburgh: T. and T. Clark, 1892), 24.
66. Ryle, *Canon of the Old Testament*, 172.
67. Cf. Lewis' survey in "What Do We Mean by Jabneh?," 125.
68. Beckwith, *Old Testament Canon*, 277.
69. Lewis, "What Do We Mean by Jabneh?," 130.
70. Ibid., 132.

"The widespread view that the Council of Jamnia closed the biblical canon, or that it canonized any books at all, is not supported by the evidence and need no longer be seriously maintained."[71] Again, it appears that the canon already existed by A.D. 100, and that the consultations held at Jamnia simply affirmed the authoritative Scriptures.

Wildeboer, Beckwith, Buhl, and Leiman surveyed and analyzed the large number of rabbinical statements on the canon. Though it is impossible to summarize the literature adequately in a few sentences, one conclusion stands out. The rabbis did discuss what texts were sacred, or "defiled the hands." With the possible, though not certain, exception of Sirach,[72] however, they did not debate *adding* books to the list of recognized texts. Instead, they questioned whether books like Esther and Song of Solomon, which do not mention God's name, or Ezekiel, which could be construed as difficult to harmonize with the Law, should be excluded from an already established list. In other words, after A.D. 100 the rabbis did not want their canon to have any unnecessary books. This attitude is quite different from any notion of an "open canon."

Though it remains impossible to determine the "OT canon of the NT church" with absolute certainty, some conclusions are appropriate. (1) Early Christians already possessed a body of canonical literature inherited from the Jews. NT writers knew and appreciated the same literature that was valued by Sirach, the Qumran community, and Philo. (2) The NT authors did not use any apocryphal book the same way they used the Law, Prophets, and Writings. They added no new books to the OT. (3) The lack of evidence concerning Jamnia, coupled with Josephus' direct statements, indicate that first-century Judaism and Christianity did not differ over the Hebrew canon. This agreement probably stems from a mutual acceptance of a canon that had existed for some time. If these conclusions are correct, the widespread belief, held by Buhl, Ryle, Wildeboer, Pfeiffer, and others that the canon was not set until A.D. 90 must be reassessed.

TENTATIVE RECONSTRUCTION
OF THE CANONICAL PROCESS

No one can legitimately claim to *know* how the OT canon was formed. The evidence is too ambiguous for certainty. Still, the data collected in this article does allow a tentative reconstruction of major dates and events in the process. Hopefully, future research will lead to certain conclusions.

---

71. Leiman, *Canonization of Hebrew Scriptures*, 124.
72. Ibid., 100.

In general, scholars agree on the latest possible date for the inclusion of the Law and Prophets into the canon.

Without question, the Pentateuch was the first section of Scripture to be canonized. By as early as 622 or 550 B.C., and by no later than 450 B.C., these books were quoted as binding authorities for faithful Israelites. In fact, the nation had a concept of a binding, law-based covenant from Moses onward. Every biblical or extra-biblical reference to the canon includes a statement about the Law.

The Prophets were all written by 400 B.C. and were deemed canonical by no later than 200 B.C. Their influence on one another indicates the prophets' writings were considered authoritative long before this time. Sirach's statements about the Law, Prophets, and other books are dated ca. 132 B.C. and probably reflect a situation spanning at least fifty years or more. Like the Pentateuch, the prophetic books claim divine inspiration and assert binding authority. Some of the Writings, such as Lamentations, may have been connected to the Prophets, which moves back the date of the acceptance of the attached texts.

Finally, the Writings were indeed complete by A.D. 90. But how long before A.D. 90 were they intact? Josephus says in A.D. 90 the books had been set for some time. Philo (d. A.D. 50) and Luke 24:44 seem to support Josephus' claim. The Qumran community knew at least twenty-three of the twenty-four Hebrew books, and Greek translations of the twenty-fourth book (Esther) were made by 114 B.C. Rabbinical sources imply discussions about an already-set canon. Therefore, it is probable the Writings were canonical between 180 and 114 B.C., which means the entire canon was fixed by ca. 150 B.C. or sooner, not in A.D. 90 as many authors have claimed.

Perhaps the Maccabean crisis led to the final decision about the books, as Beckwith claims.[73] This suggestion fits the general time frame the evidence suggests. Leiman's summary of the data is sound:

> Jewish sources such as the Apocrypha, Philo, and Josephus, as well as Christian sources reflecting Jewish practice, such as the NT and the church fathers, support the notion of a closed biblical canon in most Jewish circles throughout the first centuries before and after the Christian era. . . . Critical analysis of the book of Daniel, evidence from the Apocrypha, and newly discovered biblical texts in Hebrew and Greek (from Qumran, Nahal Hever, and elsewhere) suggest the possibility and likelihood that the biblical canon was closed in the Maccabean period. The talmudic and midrashic evidence is entirely consistent with a second century B.C. dating for the closing of the biblical canon.[74]

---

73. Beckwith, *Old Testament Canon*, 152.
74. Leiman, *Canonization of Hebrew Scripture*, 135.

In summary, canonical concerns have continued to surface from the early church period, through the Reformation, to the present day. For Protestants, however, who hold to the concept of *sola scriptura*, what the OT says about its own canonical process and what the NT says about the Hebrew Scriptures is vital. The "Bible" that Jesus, Paul, Luke, and John recognized as authoritative does matter to the Christian community. Later church traditions are not irrelevant; they simply do not have the same value as the Bible itself.

The church's OT has been handed down through much prayer, scholarship, and devotion. Christians can be confident of the OT's inspiration and its value for faith and practice. This article has sought to demonstrate that such beliefs are based on historical evidence. God has worked through faithful individuals, over many centuries, to produce Scriptures that have touched and continue to have impact on countless lives.

FOR FURTHER READING

Beckwith, Roger. *The Old Testament Canon of the New Testament Church and Its Background in Early Judaism.* Grand Rapids: Eerdmans, 1985.

Bruce, F. F. *The Canon of Scripture.* Downers Grove, Ill.: InterVarsity, 1988.

Green, W. H. *General Introduction to the Old Testament: The Canon.* New York: Scribner's, 1888.

Leiman, Sid Z. *The Canonization of Hebrew Scripture: The Talmudic and Midrashic Evidence.* Hamden, Conn.: Archon Books, 1976.

Ryle, H. E. *The Canon of the Old Testament: An Essay on the Gradual Growth and Formulation of the Hebrew Canon of Scripture.* New York: Macmillan, 1892.

Sundberg, A. C. *The Old Testament of the Early Church.* HTS 20. Cambridge: Harvard University Press, 1964.

IX

OLD TESTAMENT TEXTUAL CRITICISM

BRUCE K. WALTKE*

One of the exegete's first tasks is to determine the original text of the passage selected for exegesis. OT textual criticism therefore attempts to restore the original text, even the original edition of the OT. This involves investigating the OT's textual witnesses and their histories, defining the "original text," and evaluating variants in light of known scribal practices.

THE NEED FOR TEXTUAL CRITICISM

Before considering such matters successively, the need for textual criticism will be demonstrated by reflecting on its relation to the inspiration and authority of the Bible. Textual criticism is learned by an introduction to the discipline and by practical involvement with the textual witnesses, a lifetime of study.[1]

---

1. The best introduction to the textual criticism of the OT is Emanuel Tov, *Textual Criticism of the Hebrew Bible* (Minneapolis: Fortress, 1992). It supersedes all previous introductions. For other helpful introductions see "For Further Reading" at the conclusion.

* I would like to take this opportunity to thank Tyler F. Williams for his assistance in the writing, organization, and editing of this chapter.

NO ERROR-FREE OT MSS

Textual criticism is necessary because there are no error-free OT manuscripts (MSS). All OT textual witnesses result from a long process of transmission. The text was copied and recopied through many centuries by scribes of varying capabilities and philosophies of their trade. No matter how good a scribe may have been, errors inevitably crept into his work. Even in *Biblia Hebraica Stuttgartensia* (*BHS*), the most recent critical edition of the Hebrew Bible, printing errors can be found.

Errors in the printed editions sometimes reflect errors in the medieval MSS on which they are based.[2] Variants in the medieval MSS (ca. A.D. 1000–A.D. 1500) are small in comparison to those found in the Dead Sea Scrolls (DSS), which are more than a millennium older. In fact, the further back we go in the textual lineage the greater the textual differences.

In addition to these inevitable, accidental errors there are intentional errors; scribes occasionally changed the text for linguistic, exegetical, and, rarely, for theological reasons.

INSPIRATION, AUTHORITY, AND TEXTUAL CRITICISM

Students whose churches taught the biblical doctrines of Scripture's inspiration and authority find it troubling to discover no perfect MSS of the Bible exist. The following five points should dissuade any discouragement, however.

1. The Need for Proper Perspective. First, one needs to keep the data in perspective. A quick count of the textual variants in *BHS* shows that on average for every ten words there is a textual note—and many of these can be discounted. In sum, 90 percent of the text contain no variants. Textual criticism, however, focuses on the relatively few problem readings, not on the many uncontested readings, so a sense of proportion may be lost as the 10 percent variant garners much scholarly attention.

2. The Significance of the Variants. In gauging the importance of textual variants, most are insignificant, and hardly any affect doctrine. Most text critical work is boring because the differences are inconsequential. Douglas Stuart says: "It is fair to say that the verses, chapters, and books of the Bible would read largely the same, and would leave the same impression with the reader, even if one adopted virtually every possible *alternative* reading to those now serving as the basis for current English transla-

---

2. The variants in the medieval MSS were collected by B. Kennicott, *Vetus Testamentum hebraicum cum variis lectionibus*, Vols. 1–2 (Oxford 1776–80) and J. B. de Rossi, *Variae lectiones Veteris Testamenti*, 1–4 (Parma 1784–88; repr. Amsterdam 1969). The latter was meant to supplement the edition of Kennicott.

tions."[3] Out of the 10 percent of textual variations, only a few percent are significant and warrant scrutiny; 95 percent of the OT is therefore textually sound.

3. The Correctibility of the Text. An error in the transcriptional process is normally subject to human correction. In the same way we correct errors in a book or manuscript, we can correct biblical texts. That we can even mention intentional errors infers we can identify and correct them. Textual criticism reduces the ambiguity in the discipline of textual criticism to an even smaller percentage, enabling us to come even closer to the original text. Just as electrical engineers can remove unwanted static from a telecommunication signal, so text critics can remove scribal corruptions by a knowledge of typical scribal errors.

4. The Existence of Variants in the NT. The same kind of variants we find in the DSS also confronted our Lord and His apostles, yet they did not hesitate to rely on the authority of Scripture. Their citations agree with the varying text types found in the DSS. For example, in Stephen's speech before the Sanhedrin (Acts 7), he used a text known only in the pre-Samaritan. Textual differences did not trouble Jesus and His apostles. In spite of them, Jesus said Scripture (its message) cannot be broken (John 10:35).

5. Variant Text Types Affirm the Original Text. The variety of text types evident in the DSS actually underscores their relatively large consensus and close genetic relation to the original, not scribal collusion. Shemaryahu Talmon notes:

> The scope of variation within all these textual traditions is relatively restricted. Major divergences which intrinsically affect the sense are extremely rare. A collation of variants extant, based on the synoptic study of the material available, either by a comparison of parallel passages within one Version, or of the major Versions with each other, results in the conclusion that the ancient authors, compilers, tradents and scribes enjoyed what may be termed a controlled freedom of textual variation.[4]

Laird Harris provides this apt illustration for the reliability of the text, in spite of no perfect witness to it. He notes how the loss or destruction of the standard yard at the Smithsonian Institution would not enormously affect the practice of measurement in the United States, for a comparison of the multitudinous copies of that yard would lead us to something very

---

3. Douglas Stuart, "Inerrancy and Textual Criticism," in *Inerrancy and Common Sense*, ed. by Roger R. Nicole and J. Ramsey Michaels (Grand Rapids: Baker, 1980), 98.

4. Shemaryahu Talmon, "Textual Study of the Bible—A New Outlook," *QHBT*, 326.

close to the original standards.5 In sum, the relatively large percentage of agreement between MSS, their relative lack of theological and exegetical disagreement, their capability of being corrected, and their unabashed use in the NT shows an essentially reliable text exists for exegesis.

WITNESSES TO THE TEXT

Extant Hebrew MSS and the Hebrew *Vorlage* (the text "lying before" a scribe or translator) that can be retroverted from the extant MSS of the ancient versions bear witness to the abstract "text" of the Old Testament.[6]

THE HEBREW WITNESSES

Hebrew MSS are the most important witnesses to the OT text, for they bear direct witness to that text, whereas a retroverted *Vorlage* is more or less certain. There are four Hebrew witnesses to the OT text: (1) the Masoretic text (sometimes called the "received text"), (2) the Samaritan Pentateuch, (3) the scrolls from the Judean desert, and (4) a few, minor witnesses.

The Masoretic Text. The most important witness to the text of the OT is the Masoretic text (MT, also designated 𝔐). The Masoretes (A.D. 600–1000) were a group of Jewish scholars who developed a system of notes and signs to preserve the text and its reading. The oldest complete MS is Leningrad B19a (L), dated 1009; it served as the base of *BHS*.

The term *Masoretic text* is an abstract term for the distinctive kind of text the Masoretes produced. As a rule, the term is restricted to the final manuscript produced in the tenth century by Aaron Ben Asher; it is the primary base for hundreds of medieval MSS. Some of the oldest DSS reflect essentially the same text inherited by the Masoretes, hence the name proto-Masoretic text (proto-MT).

The sequence of books in the MT differs from that of the Septuagint codexes on which our English Bibles are based. The former's tripartite division is the Law, the Prophets, and the Hagiographa; the tripartite division of the latter is legal and historical books (starting with the Law), poetic and wisdom books, and prophetic books.

The activity of the Masoretes was fourfold. First, the Masoretes "hedged in" (surrounded) the consonantal text using a *Masorah*, scribal

---

5. R. Laird Harris, *Inspiration and Canonicity of the Bible* (Grand Rapids: Zondervan, 1957), 88–89.

6. By "text" we mean an abstract concept derived from extant data; by textual witnesses, the tangibly different forms of the text; and by MSS, scrolls, and codices, the uninterpreted, extant exhibitions of the text.

notes in the margins. Earlier scribes had settled on that text by the end of the first century A.D. Scribal precision in transmitting the consonants before the activities of the Masoretes is reflected in the Talmud. R. Ishmael said: "My son, be careful, because your work is the work of heaven; should you omit (even) one letter or add (even) one letter, the whole world would be destroyed" (*b. Soṭa* 20a).[7] Generations of Masoretes contributed an apparatus of instructions written in the margins around the text. By hedging the text with instructions in the margins, the Masoretes hoped to assure its precise transmission, even to its smallest details.

Second, above and below the inherited consonants the Masoretes added vocalization—vowel points to preserve the accompanying oral tradition. Prior to the Masoretes, scribes more or less sparingly represented important vowels by four Hebrew consonants, י (y), ו (w), ה (h), and א (ʾ), called *matres lectiones* ("mothers of reading"). Vowels, of course, can be decisive in meaning. Contrast the difference vowels made with the consonants "fr": "far," "fir," "fire," "for," "fore," "fur." A story told in the Talmud illustrates that the scribes recognized the importance of an accurate oral tradition. David reprimanded Joab when he killed only the men of Amalek and not the "remembrance" [Heb זֵכֶר, *zēker*] of Amalek. Joab defended himself, however, noting his teacher taught him to read: "to kill all their males" [Heb זָכָר, *zākār*]. Consequently, Joab later drew his sword against his poor teacher who taught him incorrectly (*b. B. Bathra* 21a-b).

Third, the Masoretes added a system of *accentuation* to the text. These diacritical accents that signify the melodious chant serve to beautify and to add dignity to the reading of the text, to denote the stress of the word, which can be as meaningful as the difference between English "pres´-ent" and "pre-sent´," and to denote the syntactical relation between words as either conjunctive or disjunctive. For instance, it makes some difference where one places the accents in Isaiah 40:3:

The voice of him that crieth in the wilderness, Prepare . . . (KJV).

A voice of one calling: "In the desert prepare . . ." (NIV).

Here, too, the Masoretes are preservers of an ancient tradition, not innovators, as seen in a Talmudic reference that Nehemiah taught the accents (*y. Meg.* 4.74d; cf. Neh. 8:8)

Fourth, the Masoretes also preserved various *para-textual elements*—the verse and paragraph divisions of the text found in the oldest MSS and ancient textual corrections. The numbering of the verses and division of the books into chapters, however, was done in the Latin Vulgate, not in Jewish sources. In addition, the Masoretes either preserved and/or added

---

7. Cited by Tov, *Textual Criticism*, 33.

corrections to the received text by marks within the text and within the margin. In the MT one finds inverted *nuns*, looking something like half-brackets, and extraordinary points, among other signals, to call attention to the received consonants in need of correction.

The most important corrections are the *Kethiv-Qere* [K-Q] variants. *Kethiv*, meaning "written," refers to the consonants in the text for which the reader must guess the vowels, and the *Qere* ("read") refers to consonants in the margin to which the reader must add the vowels found in the text. At first the Q readings were optional corrections of the consonantal text, but by the time of the Masoretes they became obligatory.

The Samaritan Pentateuch. The second major witness to the Hebrew text of the OT is the Samaritan Pentateuch (SP, also designated ‹‹‹). The Samaritans, once a very large sect, are now a small group still centered at modern Nablus, biblical Shechem/Sychar. Most Christians know this sect from Jesus' famous conversation with the Samaritan woman (John 4). As that story shows, the Samaritans distinguished themselves from Judaism by their worship on Mount Gerizim, not at Jerusalem. They restricted their Bible to the Torah because Moses only called for a central sanctuary without designating a specific location. In the Prophets, however, David selected Jerusalem, and the Hagiographa celebrates that city.

The SP began its own history in the last quarter of the second century B.C., though the sect itself may be centuries older. Waltke based himself on Gesenius, the first to classify the variants between SP and MT in a thorough and convincing way; he demonstrated from recent philological and textual research that the SP, which is written in a special version of the "early" Hebrew script, presents a secondarily modernized, smoothed-over, and expanded text.[8]

It is now known from the DSS that the Samaritans adapted a pre-Samaritan Jewish text to their idiosyncratic theology. For example, they were able to make the worship on Mount Gerizim the tenth commandment by combining the first two commandments into one and by inserting texts from Deuteronomy 11:29a; 27:2b–3a; 28:4–7; and 11:30 after Exodus 20:17, numbering the material from Deuteronomy 28:4–7 and 11:30 as the tenth commandment. In these roughly added interpolations from Deuteronomy into Exodus, it is instructive to note the change in divine names, doublets, style, and vocabulary; such are the criteria by which literary critics historically identified sources in the Pentateuch.[9]

---

8. B. K. Waltke, "The Samaritan Pentateuch and the Text of the Old Testament," *New Perspectives on the Old Testament*, ed. by J. B. Payne (Waco, Tex.: Word, 1970), 212–39.

9. By this observation we are not contending for the documentary hypothesis, but we are validating that the Pentateuch was composed from literary sources.

The Dead Sea Scrolls. The DSS are copied in Hebrew, Aramaic, and Greek.[10] By the techniques of paleography, numismatics, and archaeology, they are dated from the mid-third century B.C. to A.D. 135. Most MSS were found in the eleven mountain caves just west of Khirbet Qumran (an ancient city 15 km south of Jericho near the Dead Sea, which ceased to exist after A.D. 68). These caves yielded some 800 scrolls of all the books of the Bible, except Esther.[11] The other principal sites, Nahal Hever and Wadi Muraba'at, yielded texts that are somewhat later, all of which belong to the proto-MT. The scrolls found at Masada, which fell to the Romans in A.D. 70, are also proto-MT. E. Tov classifies these scrolls into five different text types.[12]

First, there are the *Proto-Masoretic* texts. As noted, the Masoretes finalized the proto-MT. The great number of Qumran scrolls belonging to this text type, about 60 percent of them, may reflect their authoritative status.[13]

Second, there are *Pre-Samaritan* texts. As previously mentioned, the Samaritans adopted and adapted an earlier Jewish text type attested at Qumran and in the Book of Chronicles. These scrolls have the characteristic features of the SP, aside from the thin layer of ideological and phonologial changes the Samaritans added. Because of this difference, however, Tov is right in calling this text pre-Samaritan rather than the customary proto-Samaritan text.

This text type is at least as old as Chronicles, for where the Chronicles (ca. 400 B.C.) are synoptic with Genesis they display a text type like these MSS, not like the MT. Since this text type was modernized by at least 400 B.C., the archaic proto-MT of the Pentateuch, and so the Pentateuch itself, must be much older.[14]

---

10. All texts are published in the official publication of these finds: *Discoveries in the Judeaean Desert (of Jordan),* I–(Oxford 1995–). For full bibliographical details see J. A. Fitzmyer, *The Dead Sea Scrolls, Major Publications and Tools for Study,* rev. in *SBLRBS* 20 (Atlanta: Scholars, 1990); L. Rosso Ubigli, "Indice italiano–inglese dei testi di Qumran—Italian–English Index of Qumran Texts," *Henoch* 11 (1989): 233–70; and E. Tov, "Groups of Biblical Texts Found at Qumran," in *The Dead Sea Scrolls—Qumran in Perspective,* ed. by G. Vermes, 2d ed. (London, 1992).

11. E. Ulrich, "The Biblical Scrolls from Qumran Cave 4—An Overview and a Progress Report on Their Publication," *The Texts of Qumran and the History of the Community,* ed. by F. Garcia Martinez = *RQ* 54 (1989), 207–28. Each scroll is designated successively by the locus in which it was found, its book, and the sequence of discovery. For example, 11QPs[a] means cave 11 at Qumran, the first scroll discovered of that book in that cave.

12. Tov, *Textual Criticism,* 114–17.

13. Ibid., 115.

14. See *ABD,* s.v. "Samaritan Pentateuch."

Third, there are *Septuagintal* texts among the DSS. The original Greek translations of certain books of the OT were based on a distinctive text type. Some Qumran scrolls, most notably Jeremiah (4QJer[b,d]), bear a strong resemblance to the Septuagint's *Vorlage*. Together with the preceding group, the Septuagintal text type comprises about 5 percent of the Qumran biblical texts.[15]

Fourth, many Qumran scrolls are not exclusively close to any one of the types mentioned above and therefore are classified as *non-aligned*. Tov explains: "they agree, sometimes insignificantly, with 𝔐 against the other texts, or with 𝔰 and/or 𝔊 against the other texts, but the non-aligned texts also disagree with the other texts to the same extent. They furthermore contain readings not known from one of the other texts."[16]

Fifth, there are texts among the DSS which are written in the *Qumran Practice*. Tov identifies a group of texts which reflect a distinctive orthography (i.e., spelling, similar to "favor" versus "favour"), morphology, and free approach to the biblical text visible in content adaptations, in frequent errors, in numerous corrections, and sometimes in negligent script. Tov thinks that only these scrolls were produced in Qumran.[17]

Additional Witnesses. The oldest evidence to the Hebrew Bible, found at Ketef Hinnom in Jerusalem, is two minute silver rolls about the size of cigarette butts that could be worn around the neck. They contain the priestly blessing (Num. 6:24–26) in a slightly different formulation than MT and are dated to the seventh or sixth century B.C.[18] Other witnesses are too insignificant to mention.[19]

EARLY VERSIONS OF THE HEBREW TEXT

Before the discovery of the DSS, the ancient versions were the primary sources for correcting the MT. In the light of the DSS, however, aside from the Greek translation, they are of lesser importance. Text critics, nevertheless, still compare variants in at least three early versions in addi-

---

15. Tov, *Textual Criticism*, 116.

16. Ibid.

17. Ibid., 114.

18. G. Barkay, "The Priestly Benediction on the Ketef Hinnom Plaques," *Cathedra* 52 (1989): 37–76.

19. The so–called Nash Papyrus (second century B.C.), containing a liturgical text of the Decalogue (Ex. 20 and Deut. 5) and the Shema (Deut. 6:4–5), helped date the Qumran scrolls. The many fragments of biblical texts contained in *mezuzot*, head–*tefillin*, and arm–*tefillin* (from ca. 200 B.C.–A.D. 200) often differ from the MT, possibly because they were written from memory as implied in the Talmud.

tion to the Septuagint: the Aramaic Targums, the Syriac Peshitta, and the Vulgate. These three normally agree with the MT, though their few differences can be important.[20]

1. The Greek Septuagint. The Septuagint (LXX or 𝕲) is the Greek translation of the Hebrew Scriptures made in Alexandria.[21] It is not a uniform translation, for numerous translators at different times and with varying capabilities and philosophies of translation rendered assorted portions of the OT. For example, the translation of the Torah is excellent, but the translation of the Minor Prophets scroll is second-rate. Nevertheless, the LXX is the most important tool for correcting MT because of its antiquity, its independence, and its completeness.[22]

According to the pseudepigraphal Letter of Aristeas (ca. 130 B.C.), the Pentateuch was translated at about 285 B.C. by seventy-two translators (hence its title, Septuagint). This tradition was later expanded to include all the translated books, including both the biblical books and other Jewish-Greek Scriptures. All the biblical books were translated into Greek in the third and second centuries B.C.

The name *Septuaginta* today includes all textual witnesses to the Greek text, including the later revisions of the original Greek translation. For this reason, scholars distinguish between the Old Greek (OG; i.e., the original translation) and the Septuagint (as represented in the extant Greek MSS).

Though fragments of the Greek text were discovered in Palestine and Egypt, some of them dating as early as the second century B.C., the uncial manuscripts of LXX, dating from the fourth to the tenth century A.D., constitute our main sources of knowledge.[23] During the more than fivehundred years that separate the OG from these MSS, the LXX was modified by the proto-MT, other texts, scribal idiosyncracies, and several

---

20. Tov notes: "Although there are thousands of differences between 𝔐 and the translations, only a fraction of them was created by a divergence between 𝔐 and the *Vorlage* of the translation. Most of the differences were created by other factors that are not related to the Hebrew *Vorlage*" (Tov, *Textual Criticism*, 123).

21. A handy English translation of the LXX is *The Septuagint Version of the Old Testament and Apocrypha with an English Translation* (Grand Rapids: Zondervan, 1977).

22. For a summary of biblical passages where the LXX is especially important, see Tov, *Textual Criticism*, 142.

23. The oldest uncials are Vaticanus (B), fourth century A.D.; Sinaiticus (S), fourth century A.D.; and Alexandrinus (A), fifth century A.D.

revisions. Therefore, before the Septuagint can be a useful tool in textual criticism, the OG must first be reconstructed.[24]

Scholars disagree, however, as to how the Septuagint developed. P. Lagarde asserts that the MSS which exhibit a distinct text type are recensions from an original text, and the critic who attempts to restore the OG must first classify the variants into several recensions. Basing himself on Jerome, Lagarde proposes essentially the following model:

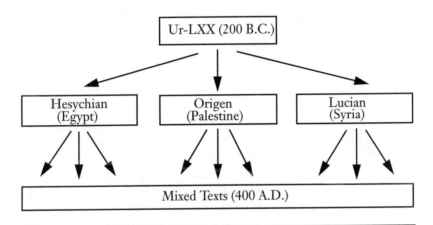

Figure 1. Lagarde's Model

According to this model, by classifying the variants according to their recensions, one can reconstruct for the OG an eclectic text. The Göttingen Septuagint series, named *Septuaginta, Vetus Testamentum graecum auctoritate societatis litteraum gottingensis editum,* essentially follows this model and method. An abridged version of this eclectic reconstruction was published by A. Rahlfs, *Septuagint, id est Vetus Testamentum graece iuxta LXX interpretes* (Stuttgart 1935).

P. Kahle, on the other hand, theorized there never was an original OG. According to him, the Christians in the second century A.D. standardized

---

24. The LXX is retroverted by use of the bilingual concordance, matching Greek words with the Hebrew and Aramaic equivalents, E. Hatch–H. A. Redpath, *A Concordance to the Septuagint and the Other Greek versions of the OT* (Oxford 1897–1906; repr. Graz 1954). Electronic concordances of all the equivalents of the MT and the LXX are J. R. Abercrombie and others, *Computer Assisted Tools for Septuagint Studies, Volume 1, Ruth* SCS 20 (Atlanta: Scholars, 1986); E. Tov, *A Computerized Data Base for Septuagint Studies, the Parallel Aligned Text of the Greek and Hebrew Bible, Vol. 2, JNSL,* Supplementary Series 1 (Stellenbosch, 1986).

numerous, earlier "vulgar" (i.e., texts to facilitate reading) translations, originally independent of each other. According to this view, one ought not attempt to reconstruct the OG, for such a text never existed. We can diagram his model thus:

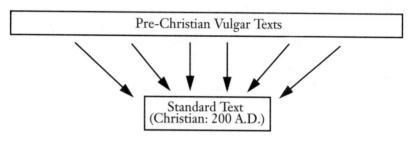

Figure 2. Kahle's Model

The edition by A. E. Brooke, N. McLean, and H. St. J. Tackeray, *The Old Testament in Greek* (Cambridge 1906–40), essentially follows this model. They chose Codex Vaticanus (B) as their base text, and where that manuscript was lacking, supplemented it from Codex Sinaiticus (S) and Codex Alexandrinus (A). As we shall see, Tov presents a mediating model.

Character of the LXX. In some portions of the OT, the LXX is significantly different from MT. For example, in the Book of Jeremiah it exhibits a different sequence of chapters and is one-sixth shorter than MT. Consider this from Jeremiah 28 (equivalent to Jeremiah 35 in the LXX). The additions in the MT are noted with italics, while additions in the LXX are boldfaced.

> And it came to pass *in that year, in the beginning of the reign of the reign* of Zedekiah king of Judah, in the fourth year, in the fifth month, Hananiah son of Azzur the **false** prophet, who was from Gibeon, said to me . . . : "This is what the LORD *Almighty, the God of Israel,* said to me: ' . . .Within two years I will bring back to this place *all* the articles of the house of the LORD *that Nebuchadnezzar king of Babylon removed from this place and took to Babylon,* and Jeconiah *son of Jehoiakim king of Judah* and *all* the exiles from Judah *who went to Babylon I am going to bring back to this place,'* declares the Lord" (Jer. 28:1–4a; 35:1–4a NIV).

Throughout Jeremiah, the MT consistently presents a more expanded version than LXX. Aside from the Pentateuch, the same is true of other units such as 1 Samuel 18—21 and Ezekiel. The LXX, in addition to other large-scale differences, also presents an entirely different text in Daniel and Esther. These differences raise serious questions about the nature of the original text and the goal of textual criticism to which we shall return.

Some scribes deliberately revised the OG according to the developing proto-MT. Prior to Origen (A.D. 200), who brought this process to completion in his famous Hexapla, revisers (editors) well known to history were Aquila (A.D. 125), Symmachus (A.D. 180), and Theodotion (A.D. 180). The French scholar Dominique Barthélemy recently recovered a fourth reviser from a Greek scroll of the Minor Prophets (middle of the first century B.C.). Barthelémy named it *Kaige* because of its distinctive translation of Hebrew םּ (*gam*). Later research showed that the translational units in the Septuagint which are ascribed to Theodotion actually belong to this revision, and so scholars now refer to it as *Kaige-Theodotion*. This recension became the text of the LXX in certain sections of the historical books and Daniel.

Lucian (A.D. 312) revised the text once again, this time in agreement with some texts known from Qumran. Some scholars think this is the OG itself, while others think it is close to it. Needless to say, it is a most important witness to the OG.

2. Aramaic Targums. Targum (Tg., also denoted by 𝕮) means specifically a translation into Aramaic.[25] When the knowledge of Hebrew decreased among the Jewish people, targums were created orally and later committed to writing. The targum fragments found at Qumran show that both free and literal targums were made. Later, these became standardized according to the proto-MT. The best-known targum of the Torah is *Tg. Onqelos* [Tg^O or 𝕮^O]. Scholars are divided about its date (first, third, or fifth century A.D.) and place of origin (Babylon or Palestine). There are also Palestinian targums of the Torah. The most important targum to the prophets is the *Tg. Jonathan*.

3. The Syriac Peshitta. The term *Peshitta* means, "the simple [translation]," and it refers to the Syriac Bible (Syr, also denoted by 𝕾).[26] Its Hebrew source is close to the MT, though it shows agreement and disagreement with the above versions, depending in part upon the book. P. Dirksen draws the conclusion: "No decisive arguments for either Christian or Jewish authorship have been advanced."[27] A critical edition is being prepared by the Peshitta Institute of the University of Leiden.[28]

---

25. The targums are now being translated into English in the series, *The Aramaic Bible: The Targums*, project director, Martin McNamara (Wilmington, Del.: Michael Glazier, 1987).

26. For a modern translation, though not precise, see G. M. Lamsa, *The Holy Bible from Ancient Eastern Manuscripts* (Nashville, 1933).

27. P. B. Dirksen, "The OT Peshitta," *Mikra, Text, Translation, Reading and Interpretation of the Hebrew Bible in Ancient Judaism and Early Christianity* (Compendia Rerum Iudaicarum as Novem testamentum, Section Two, 1; Assen/Maastricht/Philadelphia, 1988), 295.

28. *The Old Testament in Syriac according to the Peshitta Version* (Leiden, 1966–).

4. *The Latin Vulgate.* Recognizing the need for a uniform and reliable Latin Bible, Pope Damasus I commissioned Jerome (Hieronymous, A.D. 345-420) to produce such a work. Jerome's original translation of the Psalms (*Psalterium Romanum*) was a revision of the *Vetus Latina*, old Latin texts based largely on the LXX. Jerome's second translation of Psalms was based on the Hexapla (*Psalterium Gallicanum*). Dissatisfied with other translations, Jerome translated the Vulgate from the "original truth of the Hebrew text" with the help of Jewish scholars. The Vulgate translation, "the common one" (Vg or ひ), essentially agrees with the proto-MT. Apart from the Gallican Psalter, editions of the Vulgate include other books based on the *Hexapla*: Proverbs, Ecclesiastes, and Song of Songs.[29]

THE HISTORY OF THE TEXT

The fall of the second temple, the Jews' debate with Christians, and Hillel's rules of hermeneutics all called for a stablized text at about A.D. 100. The OT's textual history can be divided into five periods based on the evidence available and on the fortunes of the text: (1) from the time of composition to mid-third century B.C., for which no extant texts are available; (2) from mid-third century B.C. to end of first century A.D., when the five kinds of texts found at Qumran are attested; (3) from the end of the first century A.D. to the end of the tenth century, that is, from the survival of proto-MT alone to the work of Aaron Ben Asher; (4) from the end of the tenth century to the sixteenth century, attested by the hundreds of medieval Masoretic MSS; and (5) from sixteenth century to the present, the time of printed Hebrew editions of the Bible.[30] Having treated the last three periods sufficiently in the discussion of the MT, the following focus will be on the first two periods.

---

29. Two critical editions are available: *Biblia Sacra iuxta latinam Vlugatam versionem* (Rome, 1926–) and the *editio minor* of R. Weber, *Biblia Sacra iuxta Vulgatam versionem*, 2d ed. (Stuttgart, 1975).

30. Possibly the discovery of the DSS has so revolutionized our understanding of the text that it ought to be delineated as a new era. Harold Scanlin, United Bible Society translation advisor, says: "These changes in our understanding [of the history of the text] are at least as significant as the nineteenth century revolution in New Testament textual criticism, culminating in the work of Westcott and Hort" (Harold P. Scanlin, "The Presuppositions of HOTTP and the Translator," *BT* 43:1 (January 1992), 102.

THE EARLY PERIOD: FROM COMPOSITION TO MID-THIRD CENTURY B.C.

Though we are lacking extant MSS from this era, we can infer both from extra-biblical and biblical sources a tendency both to preserve and to revise the text.

1. The Tendency to Preserve the Text. There are three factors which demonstrate the early scribal tendency to preserve the text. First, that the biblical books persistently survived the most deleterious conditions throughout a more or less long history (until the extant MSS) demonstrates indefatigable scribes insisted on the text's preservation. The books were written on highly perishable papyrus and animal skins in the relatively damp, hostile climate of Palestine.[31] The prospects for their survival was most uncertain in a land that served as a bridge for armies in unceasing contention between the continents of Asia and Africa—a land whose people were the object of plunderers in their early history and of captors in their later history. That no other Israelite writings, such as the Book of Yashar (e.g., 2 Sam. 1:18) or the Diaries of the Kings (e.g., 2 Chron. 16:11), survive from this period indirectly suggests the determination of the scribes to preserve the biblical books.[32]

Second, the OT itself (cf. Deut. 4:2; 12:32; Josh. 1:7; 24:25–26; 1 Sam. 10:25; Ps. 18:30; Prov. 30:6–7; Eccl. 12:12) and relevant literature of the ancient Near East show that during the OT's composition, a mind-set favoring canonicity existed. For example, the famous Code of Hammurabi (ca. 1750 B.C.), and the Hittite treaties of the Late Bronze Age (ca. 1400–1200 B.C.), which closely resembles Deuteronomy, call down imprecations upon anyone who tampers with one word in them. This attitude must have fostered a deep concern for care and accuracy in transmitting the sacred writings.

Finally, scribal practices throughout the ancient Near East reflect a conservative attitude toward the text. W. F. Albright noted: "The prolonged and intimate study of the many scores of thousands of pertinent documents from the ancient Near East proves that sacred and profane documents were copied with greater care than is true of scribal copying in

---

31. See M. Haran, "Book-Scrolls in Israel in Pre-Exillic Times," *JJS* 33 (1982): 161–73.

32. Almost none of the extrabiblical finds are at all similar to the biblical materials; a notable exception is some prayers written on a cave wall ca. 600 B.C. See F. M. Cross, "The Cave Inscriptions from Khirbet Beit Lei," *Near Eastern Archaeology in the Twentieth Century: Essays in Honor of Nelson Glueck*, ed. by J. A. Sanders (Garden City, N.Y.: Doubleday, 1970), 299–306.

Graeco-Roman times."[33] To verify this statement one need only consider the care with which the Pyramid texts, the Coffin Texts, and the Book of the Dead were copied, even though they were never intended to be seen by other human eyes.

2. The Tendency to Revise the Text. On the other hand, both biblical and extra-biblical data show a tendency to revise the text during this period. This can be demonstrated by four strands of evidence. First, the post-exilic book, Ezra-Nehemiah, explicitly states that as Ezra read from the Book of the Law of God, he made it clear and gave the meaning so the people could understand what was being read (Neh. 8:8), implying he modernized and explained the earlier text.

Second, the many differences between synoptic portions of the Hebrew Bible strongly suggest that those entrusted with the responsibility of teaching the Bible felt free to revise the texts.[34] The differences between these synoptic portions resemble the same sort of variations found in the Qumran scrolls, suggesting that scribes, before the extant texts, felt free to revise the text within the same similar restraints as found in the Qumran scrolls as noted by Talmon.[35]

Third, Ezra's effort to clarify the text reflects textual practices in the ancient Near East. Albright said: "A principle which must never be lost sight of in dealing with documents of the ancient Near East is that instead of leaving obvious archaisms in spelling and grammar, the scribes generally revised ancient literary and other documents periodically."[36]

Finally, the Book of Chronicles in its synoptic parallels with the pre-Samaritan Torah and with the MT's Former Prophets exhibits the same kinds of revisions as found in the Qumran scrolls, reflecting the early revision of texts. In short, some biblical texts were being conserved and revised at the same time others were being composed.

3. Kinds of Revision. From ancient inscriptions and comparative Semitic grammar, we can plausibly trace the development of the biblical texts' script and grammar. From epigraphic evidence it appears that in its earliest stages the text was written in the proto-Canaanite alphabet, a pictographic alphabet. This script later developed into an angular, pre-exilic

33. W. F. Albright, *From the Stone Age to Christianity* (Garden City, N.Y.: Doubleday/Anchor, 1957), 78–79.

34. Cf. 2 Sam. 22 = Ps. 18; 2 Kings 18:13–20:19 = Isa. 36—39; 2 Kings 24:18–25:30 = Jer. 52; Isa. 2:2–4 = Mic. 4:1–3; Ps. 14 = 53; 40:14–18 = 70; 57:8–12 = 108:2–6; 60:7–14 = 107:14; Ps. 96 = 1 Chron. 16:23–33; Ps. 106:1, 47–48 = 1 Chron. 16:34–36; and the parallels between Samuel–Kings and Chronicles.

35. Talmon, "Textual Study of the Bible," 326.

36. Albright, *Stone Age*, 79.

Hebrew script, sometimes called Phoenecian.[37] During the same period. *matres lectiones* were gradually added to the text, and at about 1100 B.C. short vowels, indicating case and tense, were dropped.[38]

THE INTERMEDIATE PERIOD: FROM MID-THIRD CENTURY B.C. TO LATE FIRST CENTURY B.C.

From "the time prophecy ceased in Israel" (1 Macc. 9:27; i.e., ca. 400 B.C.) until the destruction of the second temple in A.D. 70, there also was a tendency to preserve and revise the text, as attested by the DSS and by contemporary Jewish literature.

1. The Tendency to Preserve the Text. Talmudic notices, calling for a careful preservation of the Hebrew Scriptures, are verified by discoveries in the Judean desert. The preservation of the archaic proto-MT of the Law reflects its antiquity and preservation. Furthermore, M. Martin's studies show that the DSS reveal a conservative scribal tendency to follow the exemplar both in text and form.[39] Finally, the para-textual scribal elements attested in the MT about the uncertainty of a few readings, such as inverted *nûns* and extraordinary points, probably hark back to this period and show an early concern for the text's preservation.

2. Tendency to Revise the Text. On the other hand, the five variant text types attested among the Qumran scrolls unambiguously show that the proto-MT, the pre-Samaritan, and the Septuagintal texts continued to be copied during this period and that those of the Qumran practice, and possibly of the non-aligned texts, arose at this time. These variants also find agreement in Jewish literature originating during the time in question, such as the Book of Jubilees (either late or early post-exilic) and the NT (ca. A.D. 50–90).

3. Kinds of Revisions. Sometime after the exile the Jews switched from the pre-exilic, angular script to the post-exilic, Aramaic script, also called square script because most of the letters are written within an imaginary square frame. In fact, some DSS of varying text types still bear the angular, paleo-Hebrew script. In addition, the pre-Samaritan text, for example, exhibits linguistic modernizations, expansions, interpolations, and exegetical smoothings.

---

37. W. F. Albright, *The Proto-Sinaitic Inscriptions and their Decipherment* (Cambridge/London: Harvard University Press/Oxford University Press, 1969).

38. See B. K. Waltke & M. P. O'Connor, *Introduction to Biblical Hebrew Syntax* (Winona Lake: Eisenbrauns, 1990), 8.1c,29.4j.

39. M. Martin, *The Scribal Character of the Dead Sea Scrolls* (Louvain: Publications Universitaires, 1958).

THE GOAL OF TEXTUAL CRITICISM

The concept of the *Urtext*, the assumed original, depends partially on how we understand the origins of the five text types found at Qumran and their relationships to the *Urtext*. Three models have been proposed to answer these questions.[40] In spite of the importance attached to this issue, no conclusive answer is possible because we still lack empirical evidence from the time of their origins.[41]

LAGARDE'S MODEL: AN ARCHETYPICAL *URTEXT*

Lagarde's model, historically embraced by the majority of text critics, presupposes one original text of a biblical book and that all textual witnesses derived from it. In practice the majority of critics first collect the texts into text types, the MT, the LXX, and the SP, and from them reconstruct the eclectic *Urtext*.

F. M. Cross refined this process by his widely influential theory of local texts. In his view the texts developed in geographical isolation: Babylon for the proto-MT of the Torah, Egypt for the Septuagintal, and Palestine for the pre-Samaritan Torah and for the proto-MT in the Prophets and Hagiographa (see fig. 3).[42] In Cross's view, furthermore, while the proto-MT preserved the Torah in a superb, pristine state, elsewhere it conserved the expansionistic Palestinian text type.[43]

Cross's local text theory, however, does not adequately account for the network of agreements and disagreements among the texts or for the non-aligned texts, and no compelling evidence exists for the proposed proviences of the developing text types. For example, the paleo-Hebrew script, which he thought secured the pre-Samaritan text in Palestine, was later found in other text types.[44] Talmon modified Cross's local text theory by pointing to sociological groups: Judaism (proto-MT), Samaritans (SP), and Christians (LXX).[45]

---

40. Cf. B. K. Waltke, "Aims of Textual Criticism," *WTJ* 51 (1989): 93–108.

41. Tov, *Textual Criticism*, 166.

42. This diagram is adapted from *QHBT*, 37.

43. Frank Moore Cross, "The Evolution of a Theory of Local Texts," *QHBT*, 307–8.

44. 11QpaleoLev is written in paleo-Hebrew and sometimes aligns itself with all three text types and other times stands apart. See K. Mathews, "The Leviticus Scrolls (11QpaleoLev) and the Text of the Hebrew Bible," *CBQ* 48 (1986):171–207.

45. Shemaryahu Talmon, "Aspects of the Textual Transmission of the Bible in Light of Qumran Manuscripts," in *The World of the Qumran from Within* (Jerusalem: Magnes, 1989), 71–116.

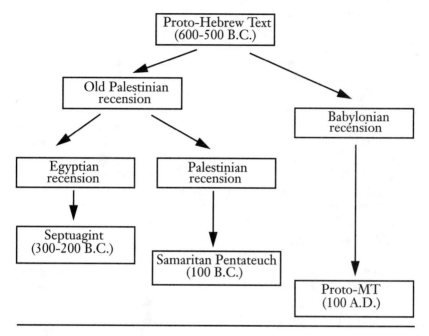

Figure 3. Cross's Model

KAHLE'S MODEL: FROM PLURALITY INTO UNITY

P. Kahle presupposed a multiplicity of texts from which a standard text emerged.[46] He presupposed the same development from independent, vulgar texts to the final forms of MT, LXX, SP, and to some portions of the biblical text as a whole.

Other scholars also hold to a number of pristine originals for biblical books: S. Talmon, on the basis of synonymous pairs of parallel readings; M. Greenberg, on the equally valid MT and LXX from an exegetical viewpoint; and W. Walters, on parallel stories in 1 Samuel.[47]

According to this view, the varying text types of certain books, such as Samuel, Jeremiah, Ezekiel, Daniel, Esther, call into question the notion of an original text and suggest instead a multiplicity of original, pristine texts.

---

46. Paul Kahle, *Cairo Geniza* (Oxford: Clarendon, 1951).

47. S. Talmon, "The OT Text," *CHB* 1 (1970): 1–41; M. Greenberg, "The Use of Ancient Versions for Interpreting the Hebrew Text," *Congress Volume:* Göttingen 1977 VTSup 29 (Leiden: E. J. Brill, 1978), 131–48; W. Walters, *The Text of the Septuagint. Its Corruptions and Their Emendation* (London: Cambridge University Press, 1973).

Text critics, therefore, should aim to re-create these original texts, not one eclectic, archetypical text that never existed. This view may find support in the parallel synoptic texts in the Bible.[48]

This theory, however, is vague about the origin and relationship of these independent texts. The theory also underestimates critics' ability to detect secondary readings within the textual witnesses. Moreover, because the text critic cannot decide the priority of one reading over another, it does not necessarily follow that both are an original; one may still be secondary. When the theory of independent texts of equal textual status is extended to the view that they also enjoy equal canonical status, the theory is unsatisfying from both a theologian's and historian's point of view.[49] A serious theologian will want to know whether or not the tenth commandment prescribes worship on Mount Gerizim, and a resolute historian needs to know whether the biblical historian recorded in Exodus 12:40 that Israel spent 430 years before the exodus in just Egypt (MT) or in Egypt and Canaan (LXX, SP). Both theology and history demand an original text in matters that impinge upon them. Finally, the evidence of synoptic texts does not prove the existence of parallel texts. The differences between these texts may be due to a linear development within the texts where they are now embedded.

TOV'S MODEL: ORIGINAL EDITIONS

According to E. Tov, certain biblical books such as Jeremiah and Ezekiel experienced more than one stage in their literary development, an early short edition and a later, expanded final edition. Before the later, final form was produced, the earlier forms were considered the original and copied. According to this argument, the Qumran scrolls and the versions preserve these earlier literary stages as well as the final edition behind the proto-MT. Other biblical material, such as the different edition of the LXX versus the MT, the Tgs., the Syr, the Vg of Proverbs and of Exodus 35—40, reflects different parallel editions. The date of the final stages differs from book to book and remains undetermined because it antedates the DSS. Tov explains his view: "Large-scale differences between the textual witnesses show that a few books and parts of books were once circulated in different formulations representing different literary stages, as a rule one after the other, but possibly also parallel to each other."[50]

In Tov's view, the text critic ought not necessarily reconstruct the earlier stages, such as the shorter Septuagintal text in the Prophets—that is

---

48. Talmon, *The World of the Qumran*, 71–116.
49. Waltke, "Aims," 101–2.
50. Tov, *Textual Criticism*, 177.

the task of literary criticism—but the final edition, such as the fully developed proto-MT in Jeremiah and Ezekiel. Tov further explains:

> This formulation thus gives a certain twist to the assumption of one original text as described in the scholarly literature. We do not refer to the original text in the usual sense of the word, since the copy with which our definition is concerned was actually preceded by written stages. Reconstructing elements of this copy (or tradition) is one of the aims of textual scholars, and usually they do not attempt to go beyond this stage.[51]

Tov's theory best explains the data. The final edited text is the end of the literary process and, at the same time, the starting point of the transmission of the text. Tov has put a new twist on the meaning of the "original" text. It now means "original edition," a view that mediates between Lagarde and Kahle.

Empirical evidence from the ancient Near East shows that indeed texts developed by supplementing earlier sources with later material.[52] As previously noted, scribes in the pre-Samaritan tradition added material from Deuteronomy into Exodus. Originally, portions of the Law were written on stone (Deut. 27:2–3; Josh. 8:32), and on that base the Pentateuch developed; likewise, a so-called Deuteronomist in the exile reworked earlier books of the Former Prophets by supplementing them with a distinctive theology. Plausibly, the process of literary development can be observed in the Qumran scrolls and in the ancient versions of certain biblical texts.

Tov wisely stops the process with the proto-MT for socio-religious and historical reasons.[53] That text, he argues, became the authoritative text within Judaism. For that reason he excludes the later midrashic literary compilations such as the Hebrew behind several sections in the LXX, namely, sections in 1 and 2 Kings, Esther, and Daniel. In short, text critics should aim to recover the original edition behind MT.

Ecclesiastics as well as rabbis accepted the edition behind the MT as authoritative. Both Origen and Jerome conformed the Septuagint and the Vulgate respectively to proto-MT, so that the MT essentially became the standard text of the OT within the church. Our English versions are based on the MT. That history should not be underestimated in deciding the question, "What is the original text?" The MT inherently commended itself to both the synagogue and the church. As the canon of the OT

---

51. Ibid., 171.

52. J. H. Tigay, ed., *Empirical Models for Biblical Criticism* (Philadelphia: Fortress, 1985).

53. Tov, *Textual Criticism*, 172.

emerged in the historical process, so also the MT surfaced as the best text of that canon.

THE PRACTICE OF TEXTUAL CRITICISM: EVALUATING THE VARIANTS

In the practice of textual criticism, critics traditionally distinguish between *external criticism* (i.e., the evaluation of the textual witnesses themselves), and *internal criticism* (i.e., the transcriptional and intrinsic probability of the readings themselves). For the former, the critics need to know the textual witnesses and their history; for the latter, critics must know the kinds of errors scribes made and have a sensitivity to the context and inner clarity of the text itself.

THE PRELIMINARY TASK: COLLECT THE VARIANTS

Before the variants can be evaluated, they need to be collected. Variants are first collected from the textual witnesses and then compared with the MT, more specifically with L (Leningrad Codex). Exegetes restricted to the English versions will find only the most significant variants in their text notes and may detect others in differences between the versions.[54] From the standpoint of OT textual criticism, the best English translations to use are NRSV, NIV, TEV, NAB, NEB, and NJB. These translations reflect careful consideration of available evidence concerning textual matters. Exegetes should avoid using paraphrases primarily based on other English translations, as well as old translations such as the KJV, which is about four centuries out of date when it comes to text critical matters.[55]

Exegetes using *BHS* will find significant variants in its apparatus, adequately and clearly explained in William R. Scott, *A Simplified Guide to BHS* (Berkeley, Calif.: Bibal Press), 16–22. Since the apparatus of *BHS*, however, contains errors of commissions and omissions with respect to the ancient versions and the DSS, the advanced exegete will appeal to the critical editions of the versions and to the DSS themselves.

---

54. For instance, Ps. 19:4 in the NIV reads "Their voice*[b]* goes out into all the earth." The superscript *b* leads the reader to the footnote which reads "b4 Septuagint, Jerome and Syriac; Hebrew *line.* " By this note the translators inform the reader the variant reading of the text, "voice," is found in the Septuagint, Jerome's *Juxta Hebraica*, and the Syriac Peshitta, while the MT variant is "line."

55. Cf. John Ellington, "Old Testament Textual Problems: A Pragmatic Approach for Nonscholars," *Notes on Translation* 3:2 (1989): 21–24.

EXTERNAL CRITICISM: EVALUATING TEXTUAL WITNESSES

Evaluate Relationship to "Original Edition." True variants are restricted to those that arose in the transmission of the "original edition" behind the MT. Before selecting any variant for further evaluation, the critic needs first to determine whether it is the product of a tendency within one of the five text types previously noted. For example, on the one hand, the shorter variants of Jeremiah should be passed over if they belong to the text's earlier literary development. On the other hand, the long variants in the Torah of the pre-Samaritan text, such as an interpolation of Deuteronomy into Exodus, should also be rejected because they represent a later stage of the text than the "original edition." When the critic has excluded variants that stand apart from that edition, he or she will then proceed to evaluate the variant by its internal criticism. Before presenting internal criticism, the traditional approach to external criticism must be rejected.

Reject Traditional External Criticism. Sometimes text critics evaluate variants on the basis of the textual witness in which it is found. For example, some critics prefer a variant in the MT over the SP, or a variant in the LXX over the Tgs., because normally the MT and the LXX are superior. For example, E. Würthwein notes, "The various witnesses to the text should be examined, beginning with 𝔐 and continuing with the rest in roughly the order of their significance for textual criticism, e.g., 𝔪, 𝔊, . . ."[56] Some critics think a variant in an early text has priority over a variant in a later one, or that a variant in the majority of texts should be preferred. Such external criteria should be ruled out, however, for four reasons:

1. Early corruptions obviously affected all textual witnesses, thus requiring conjectural emendations; this shows early errors could have corrupted numerous MSS.

2. The Qumran scrolls indicate an intricate web of relationships, so a critic cannot predict a corruption in any given MS.

3. Scribes tend to commit the same sort of errors, and therefore the same error could have arisen independently in several sources.

4. The Qumran scrolls, though a millennium earlier, do not necessarily contain better variants than the MT because the scribes in the later tradition tried harder to preserve the original than those at Qumran.

---

56. Ernst Würthwein, *The Text of the Old Testament* (Grand Rapids: Eerdmans, 1979), 112.

In summary, because the genetic relationship of any MS to the original edition is unknown, a variant in the MT and/or in many witnesses has no prior claim as the better variant; and a variant in an otherwise poor witness, or in only a few, cannot be ruled out.

INTERNAL CRITICISM: INTRINSIC AND TRANSCRIPTIONAL PROBABILITY

Having decided that a variant may stem from the original text, the critic should not evaluate it further on the basis of the textual witness but on its own merits. There are two facets to internal criticism: intrinsic probability and transcription probability.

The task of evaluating a reading on its intrinsic probability is both an objective science and a subjective art. The basic premise is "that reading is preferable which would have been more likely to give rise to the other." This premise inverted means "the variant that cannot be explained away is more probably the original." To explain away a variant, however, demands a firm grasp on scribal practices, extensive exegetical knowledge, and common sense.

There are no simple rules. A. E. Housman likened textual criticism to a dog catching fleas. A dog catches fleas not by following rules but by treating each flea individually, so also must the text critic investigate each variant individually, deftly, and reasonably.[57]

1. Intrinsic Probability. Evaluating a textual variant according to its intrinsic probability involves considering the author's style and the immediate context. Inasmuch as the inner clarity of the passage itself is the standard for evaluation, this is a subjective enterprise. It is sometimes difficult to determine what the author's style or particular vocabulary is as well as decide what fits the immediate context best; this quandary represents one of the major dificulties in OT textual criticism.

2. Transcriptional Probability. Here the text critic must remember that scribes committed several kinds of errors during the transmission of the text, both unintentional and intentional.

Unintentional Errors. Only the most common types of unintentional scribal errors will be cited.

a. Confusion of similar consonants. Sometimes scribes confused consonants that are similarly formed, depending on the script, or similarly sounded, such as the gutturals. For example, ד (*d*) and ר (*r*) are readily confused both in the Hebrew angular and square scripts. This is apparently what happened with the name of one of Javan's sons. Sometimes he

---

57. A. E. Housman, *The Proceedings of the Classical Association* 18 (1922): 67–84. Cited by McCarter, *Textual Criticism*, 18–19.

is called דדנים (*ddnym*), "Dodanim" (Gen. 10:4, MT), and other times רדנים (*rdnym*), "Rodanim" (1 Chron. 1:7, MT; Gen. 10:4, SP, LXX). Other consonants that often are confused are: כ/ב, מ/ב, נ/ב, ח/ג, ר/י, ח/ה, ר/ו, ו/י, נ/כ, ס/מ, and צ/ע.[58]

b. Haplography ("writing once"). Due to *homoioteleuton*, in words with similar endings, or, *homoiarcton*, words with similar beginnings, sometimes a letter or group of letters accidentally dropped out of the text. Compare the following readings of Genesis 47:16:

MT	ואתנה לכם במקניכם

"I will give you for your cattle" (cf. KJV).

SP, LXX	ואתנה לכם לחם במקניכם

"I will sell you *food* . . . for your livestock" (cf. NIV, NRSV).

"Food," לחם, *lhm*, comes after the similar sounding and appearing "you," לכם, *lkm*. The scribe skipped over "food" when copying the text.

c. Dittography ("writing twice"). Sometimes scribes accidentally repeated letters, words, or phrases. For example, Isaiah 30:30 in the MT, LXX, Tgs., Syr, and Vg all read: השמיע יהוה."The Lord shall make heard," while 1QIsa reads: השמיע השמיע יהוה "The Lord shall make heard, *shall make heard*." Apparently, the scribe inadvertently repeated השמיע, "make heard."

d. Doublets. This is the conflation of two or more readings, either consciously or unconsciously. For example, the LXX and 1QIsaa of Isa. 37:9 conflate the accounts of Hezekiah's consultation of Isaiah in the MT of Isaiah 37:9 and 2 Kings 19:9. Compare the following:

MT	וישב וישלח מלאכים
2 Kings 19:9	he again sent messengers

MT	וישמע וישלח מלאכים
Isa. 37:9	and when he heard it, he sent messengers

LXX, 1QIsa	וישמע וישב וישלח מלאכים
Isa. 37:9	and when he heard it, he again sent messengers

e. Metathesis. This is the accidental exchange or transposition of two adjacent letters within a word. For instance, Deuteronomy 31:1 reads:

---

58. McCarter, *Textual Criticism*, 43–49.

MT   וילך משה וידבר את־הדברים האלה

And Moses *went* [*wylk*] and spoke these words (cf. NIV).

4QDeut[n], LXX   ויכל משה וידבר את־הדברים האלה

And Moses *finished* [*wykl*] speaking these words (cf. NRSV).

The scribe evidently miscopied and reversed the order of ל and כ. The NRSV follows the reading in 4QDeut[n] and the LXX, while the NIV opted for the MT.

f. Different concepts of word and verse divisions. Sometimes scribes, for unknown reasons, divided words and verses differently. For example, a scribe evidently divided the words in Hosea 6:5 incorrectly:

MT   ומשפטיך אור יצא

And your judgments, light goes forth (cf. NASB, KJV).

LXX   καὶ τὸ κρίμα μου ὡς φῶς ἐξελεύσεται

ומשפטי כאור יצא =

And my judgment goes forth as light (cf. NIV, NRSV).

The copyist of the MT evidently attached the כ (*k*), of כאור (*kʾwr*), "as light," to the preceding word. Compare the following variants in Psalm 102:[101 LXX] :24–25a, involving different vocalization and misdivision of the verses:

MT   ענה בדרך כחו [Qere כחי] קצר ימי: אמר אלי

"He broke my strength on the way, he cut short my days. [25]I said, My God ...."

LXX   ἀπεκρίθη αὐτῷ ἐν ὁδῷ ἰσχύος αὐτοῦ

Τὴν ὀλιγότητα τῶν ἡμερῶν μου
ἀνάγγειλόν μοι

ענה]ו[בדרך כחו קצר ימי אמר אלי =

He answered him in the way of his strength:
The fewness of my days report to me.

The LXX is different from the MT in reading ענה (*ʿnh*),as (Qal) "to answer," rather than (Piel), "to humble"; taking בדרך כחו]י[(*bdrk khw/y*)

180

as a construct; and besides other vocalization changes, it also does not divide the verse in the same place.[59]

Intentional Errors. Sometimes the scribes deliberately changed the text. Four types of intentional changes can be noted.

a. Linguistic changes. Scribes often modernized archaic features of a verse, primarily in relation to spelling and grammar. For example, the SP replaces the old infinitive absolute construction of the MT with an imperative or finite verb form. In Numbers 15:35, the MT reads רָגוֹם: (*rāgôm*) but the SP reads רְגָמוּ (*rigmû*).

b. Contextual changes. Sometimes scribes changed the text to harmonize certain passages. For instance, in Genesis 2:2, according to the MT, the Tgs., and the Vg, God completed His work on the seventh day, but according to SP, LXX, and Syr (perhaps independently of each other), He finished on the sixth day. The scribe(s) evidently changed the text to avoid the possible inference that God worked on the Sabbath.

c. Euphemistic changes. Sometimes scribes changed the text for euphemistic reasons. In Genesis 50:23 the SP changes עַל־בִּרְכֵי יוֹסֵף (*ʿl-brky ywsp*), "upon the knees of Joseph," into עַל־בִּימֵי יוֹסֵף (*ʿl-bymy ywsp*), "in the days of Joseph," because it seemed improper that Joseph's grandchildren should be born upon his knees. In Deuteronomy 25:11 בִּמְבֻשָׁיו (*bmbšyw*), "his private parts," is changed to בִּבְשָׂרוֹ (*bbśrw*), "his flesh," because it seemed too obscene to mention that in a fight a woman would grab a man's private parts. Similarly, in Deuteronomy 28:30 שָׁגֵל (*šgl*), "lie with (?)," was deemed too obscene for public use and so it was changed to שָׁכַב (*škb*), "sleep," in both the SP and the MT=*Qere*.

d. Theological changes. We noted above how the Samaritans altered the pre-Samaritan text to defend Mount Gerizim as God's place of worhsip. Theological changes also occur in the MT. Compare the following renditions of Proverbs 14:32:

MT	וְחֹסֶה בְמוֹתוֹ צַדִּיק
	But a righteous man in his *death* finds a refuge (cf. NIV).
LXX	ὁ δὲ πεποιθὼς τῇ ἑαυτοῦ ὁσιότητι δίκαιος
	= וְחֹסֶה בְתוּמוֹ צַדִּיק
	But a righteous man in his *integrity* finds a refuge (cf. NRSV).

59. The Gallican psalter (Vg) has a similar reading at the LXX, while Jerome's final work on the psalms, the "Juxta Hebraeos," corresponds to the MT. See *IBHS*, 1.6.3k.

The change from בתומו (btwmw), "integrity," in the LXX to במותו (bmwtw), "death," in the MT could be a case of simple transposition of מ and ת. But some scholars think the change in the MT was intentional and reflects an anti-Sadducean point of view.[60] Better known are the changes of early names with the theophoric element בעל (Baʿal) by the derogatory element בשת (bōšet), "shame." For example, Esh-Baal, the name of Saul's fourth son in 1 Chronicles 8:33 is changed to Ish-Bosheth in 2 Samuel 2:8.

On the whole, however, theological changes are rare in the MT. G. R. Driver notes: "Theological glosses [in our terminology interpolations], are surprisingly few, and most are enshrined in the *tiqqune sopᵉrim*, which are corrections of the text aimed chiefly at softening anthropomorphisms and eliminating the attribution of any sort of impropriety to God."[61]

EMENDATIONS

Sometimes none of the transmitted variants satisfy exegetical expectations. In cases where all witnesses seem hopelessly corrupt, the text critic may find *emendation* (a conjectured variant based on the known variants) necessary. Qumran scrolls have now validated this procedure. F. M. Cross comments: "No headier feeling can be experienced by a humanistic scholar, perhaps, than that which comes when an original reading, won by his brilliant emendation, is subsequently confirmed in a newly-found MS."[62] Emendations must satisfy the same criteria by which known variants are evaluated. For example, there seems to have been a confusion of consonants in the angular script in Ezekiel 3:12.

All texts	ברוך כבוד־יהוה ממקומו
	May the glory of YHWH *be praised* in his dwelling place (cf. NIV).
Emendation	ברו[ם] כבוד־יהוה ממקומו
	As the glory of YHWH *arose* from its place (cf. NRSV).

---

60. A. Rofé, "The Onset of Sects in Postexillic Judaism: Neglected Evidences from the Septuagint, Trito–Isaiah, Ben Sira, and Malachi," *The Social World of Formative Christianity and Judaism*, ed. by J. Neusner et al. (Philadelphia: Fortress, 1988), 39–49.

61. G. R. Driver, "Glosses in the Hebrew Text of the OT," *l'AT et l'Orient* (Orientale et Biblica Lovaniensia 1: Louvain 197), 153.

62. F. M. Cross, "Problems of Method in the Textual Criticism of the Hebrew Bible," *The Critical Study of Sacred Texts*, ed. by W. D. O'Flaherty (Berkeley Religious Studies Series, Graduate Theological Union, 1979), 37.

The NIV's "be praised" is based on ברוך, *brwk*, "be praised," attested in all textual witnesses. The clause, however, is unique, awkward and contextless. Scholars salvage the line by emending ברוך (*brwk*) to ברו[ם] (*brwm*), "when [it] arose." In the angular script ך and ם are easily confounded.[63] The emendation nicely satisfies exegetical expectations, Hebrew syntax, and the context of the verse (cf. Ezek. 10:4, 15–18).

In summary, McCarter wisely counsels that a text critic should keep the image of a scribe clearly in mind, look first for conscious errors, know the personalities of the witnesses, treat each case as if it were unique, and beware of prejudices.[64]

TEXTUAL CRITICISM IN ACTION

Joshua 1:1 and Psalm 73:7 illustrate the practice of external and internal textual criticism, respectively.

EXTERNAL CRITICISM: JOSHUA 1:1

External criticism involves the evaluation of a variant in relation to the "original edition" of the MT. This means if a variant reflects an earlier stage in the literary development of a book, rather than a corruption during the course of its textual transmission, it should be disregarded by the text critic. Because these variants typically do not influence text/critical decisions, they are difficult to spot in English translations; therefore, this example comes directly from the Hebrew text. Compare the following readings of Joshua 1:1 in the MT and LXX:

MT	ויהי אחרי מות משה עבד יהוה
	And it was after the death of Moses *the servant of YHWH* . . . (cf. NIV, etc.).
LXX	Καὶ ἐγένετο μετὰ τὴν τελευτὴν Μωυσῆ
=	ויהי אחרי מות משה
	And it was after the death of Moses . . .

In this example the MT refers to Moses as עבד יהוה (*'bd yhwh*), "the servant of YHWH." This phrase is missing in the LXX. In fact, the MT of Joshua 1 has more than twelve additional words or phrases that are not found in the LXX; further, the LXX rendering of Joshua is about 4 to 5

---

63. See J. Kennedy, *An Aid to the Textual Amendment of the Old Testament* (Edinburgh: Clark, 1928), 83–84.

64. McCarter, *Textual Criticism*, 22–25.

percent shorter than the MT.[65] This evokes the conclusion that these differences in the LXX version of Joshua probably represent an earlier edition of that book; therefore, because this variant in the LXX stands apart from the "original edition" behind the MT, there is no need to evaluate it by internal criticism. It should be ignored.

INTERNAL CRITICISM: PSALM 73:7

The first example demonstrated the procedure involved when a variant is the result of a separate literary tradition. Psalm 73:7 provides a contrasting example of a variant which arose in the transmission of the original edition of the MT.

An examination of a few English versions of Psalm 73:7a reveals a significant textual problem. Compare the following translations:

NIV   From their callous hearts comes *iniquity* (cf. NAB).

NRSV   *Their eyes* swell out with fatness (cf. RSV, NEB, KJV).

In this verse there are two apparent divergences between the English translations, though only one of them reflects a textual difference. The NIV's reading "callous hearts," reflects an idiomatic translation of the word "fat" rather than a variant reading. "Fat," it is assumed, is a figure for stubbornness, and the translators took the liberty of interpreting the figure for the reader so that it makes sense, as modern readers do not think iniquity comes out of "fat."[66]

In this passage the textual variant pertains to "eyes" and "iniquity," as indicated by the footnote in the NIV, which shows that NIV followed the Syriac reading of the text. Conversely, the NRSV followed the MT reading.

With the textual problem discovered, the preliminary step is to collect the variants. While this can be done partially by referring to the notes in the English translations, exegetes should look to *BHS* to discover the exact nature of the textual problem. The verse in *BHS* reads:

BHS   יָצָא מֵחֵלֶב עֵינֵמוֹ[a]

Their eyes come forth from fat.

The superscript [a] leads to the second level of apparatus which reads:
7[a]frt עֵינָמוֹ cf 𝕲 𝕾 . This translates as: "perhaps (frt) we should read עֵינָמוֹ

---

65. Tov, *Textual Criticism*, 328.
66. Cf. "crassness" in the NAB.

(ʿăônāmô), 'their iniquity'" instead of the reading in the MT, and then it suggests a comparison with the LXX and the Syriac Peshitta.[67]

Now the variant can be evaluated on its transcriptional probability. The word in the MT for "eyes" is עֵין (ʿyn), while the variant suggested by *BHS*, and adopted by the NIV, is based on the LXX ἀδικία, retroverted to עֲוֹן (ʿwn), "iniquity." The difference between these Hebrew variants is very slight as in the square script ו and י are easily confused, especially in the DSS; therefore, the variant could be a result of the scribe confusing similar consonants.

In relation to intrinsic probability, the MT makes little sense. The truth is that "their eyes come out with fatness" is incoherent. The NRSV's "swell out" is an unattested extension of the meaning of יָצָא (yṣ').[68] In contrast, the idea of iniquity coming out of fatness, understood as a figure of speech for stubbornness, makes sense.

Therefore, in light of internal criticism, "their iniquity" is probably correct. First, the error in the MT can be easily explained away by the common scribal confusion of י and ו. Second, the MT is unintelligible: How do "eyes come out of fat"?, whereas "iniquity coming out of fat" is understandable once the metonymy of "fat" for "crassness" is understood.

FOR FURTHER READING

Albrektson, Basil. "Textual Criticism and the Textual Basis of a Translation of the Old Testament," *BT* 26 (1975): 314–24.

Barrick, William D. "Current Trends and Tensions in Old Testament Textual Criticism" *BT* 35 (1984): 301–8.

Brockington, L. H. *The Hebrew Text of the Old Testament: The Readings Adopted by the Translators of the New English Bible*. Oxford and Cambridge University Presses, 1973.

Cross, Frank M. and Shemaryahu Talmon, eds. *Qumran and the History of the Biblical Text*. Cambridge, Mass.: Harvard University Press, 1975.

Deist, F. E. *Towards the Text of the Old Testament*. Pretoria, 1978.

_____. *Witnesses to the Old Testament: Introducing Old Testament Textual Criticism*. Pretoria: N. G. Kerkboekhandel, 1988.

Ellington, John. "Old Testament Textual Problems: A Pragmatic Approach for Nonscholars," *Notes on Translation* 3.2 (1989): 4–29.

Eissfeldt, O. *The Old Testament: An Introduction*. New York: Harper & Row, 1965.

---

67. The LXX (= Ps. 72:7) reads: ἡ ἀδικία αὐτῶν, "their injustice."

68. Cf. KB, 393.

Goshen-Gottstein, M. H. "The Textual Criticism of the Old Testament. Rise, Decline, Rebirth," *JBL* 102–3 (1983): 365–99.

Klein, Ralph W. *Textual Criticism of the OT: From the Septuagint to Qumran.* Philadelphia: Fortress, 1974.

Millard, Alan. "In Praise of Ancient Scribes," *BA* 45 (1982): 143–53.

McCarter, P. Kyle. *Textual Criticism: Recovering the Text of the Hebrew Bible.* Philadelphia: Fortress, 1988.

Nicole, Roger. "The Nature of Inerrancy," *Inerrancy and Common Sense.* Edited by R. R. Nicole and J. Ramsey Michaels, 71-95. Grand Rapids: Baker, 1980. 71–95.

Roberts, R. B. *Old Testament Text and Versions.* Cardiff: University of Wales Press, 1951.

Sanders, J. A. "Text and Canon: Concepts and Methods," *JBL* 98: 5–39.

Stuart, Douglas. "Inerrancy and Textual Criticism," *Inerrancy and Common Sense,* 97–117.

Tov, Emanuel. *The Text-Critical Use of the Septuagint in Biblical Research.* Jerusalem: Simor, 1981.

———. "A Modern Textual Outlook Based on the Qumran Scrolls," *HUCA* 53 (1982): 11–27.

Waltke, Bruce K. "Aims of Textual Criticism," *WTJ* 51 (1989): 93–108.

Zeller, Hans. "A New Approach to the Critical Constitution of Literary Texts," *Studies in Bibliography.* Edited by Fredson Bowers. Vol. 28. Published for the Bibliographical Society of the University of Virginia by the University Press of Virginia, Charlottesville, 1975.

X

HISTORICAL CRITICISM OF THE OLD TESTAMENT

DUANE A. GARRETT

Historical criticism is a neutral term. That is, it does not imply that the document under scrutiny is either true or false. Many Christians, however, are uncomfortable with historical criticism of the Bible. The very idea sounds negative, and the last century of historical/critical scholarship reflects an outlook frequently hostile to assumptions Christians naturally make concerning the Bible's reliability.

Historical criticism is necessary and indeed universally practiced. Even a study Bible engages in historical/critical matters as it provides suggestions concerning the date, author, purpose, and setting for the Old and New Testament books. It is almost impossible for an adult reader to approach the Bible and not ask such questions. For the serious Bible student, the challenge is to understand what questions have been raised about a given book or biblical incident, how people have tried to answer those questions, and which of these answers is most probably valid.

THE WRITING OF THE BOOKS OF THE BIBLE

THE RISE OF CLASSIC LIBERALISM
IN OLD TESTAMENT SCHOLARSHIP

The Renaissance, Reformation, and Enlightenment together changed forever the history of biblical studies. The Renaissance opened the world of classical literary studies. Throwing off the constraints of medieval philosophy and theology, readers found a fresh and vital world in the words of the ancient poets and essayists. Classical writings initiated the rediscovery of the art of literary criticism and a renewed sense of history and historical judgment. The Reformation put the Bible into the hands of the people; no longer was it read and studied exclusively by an ecclesiastical hierarchy. During the Enlightenment, the Bible itself came under the scrutiny of historical criticism. For the first time, the Scriptures were subjected to methods of inquiry previously applied to secular writings only.

The first significant OT source critic was Jean Astruc (1684–1766). Although Astruc himself held to the Mosaic authorship of Genesis, he believed sources lying behind the Mosaic work could be detected primarily on the grounds of which divine name (Yahweh or Elohim) they used. J. G. Eichhorn (1752–87) seized upon the criterion of the divine names as a critical tool for investigating the Pentateuch. In his three-volume *Einleitung ins Alte Testament* (1780–83), Eichhorn showed little regard for the traditional Christian approach to the OT and dismissed much of it as spurious or unworthy of being regarded as sacred Scripture. In so doing, he blazed the trail higher criticism would follow.

W. M. L. De Wette (1780–1849), a prolific writer in biblical and theological studies, made his most enduring contribution in his doctoral dissertation wherein he asserted the legal core of Deuteronomy was "the book of the Law" published during the reign of Josiah after it was allegedly discovered in the temple (2 Kings 22). Thus arose the view that Deuteronomy was deemed a pious fraud, which claimed Mosaic authorship but was actually written by the reforming circles around Josiah. Subsequent scholars would focus on the Josianic reformation (621 B.C.) as the historical backdrop for Deuteronomy; Mosaic authorship for that book was then abandoned.

Herman Hupfeld (1796–1866), in a study of Genesis (1853), contended that four source documents lay behind the Pentateuch. These were (1) a source that used Elohim, (2) a second source that used Elohim, (3) a source that used Yahweh, and (4) the Deuteronomic material. Subsequently called P (Priestly Code), E (Elohist), J (Yahwist), and D (Deuteronomist), these four hypothetical source documents eventually dominated historical research in the Pentateuch. Hupfeld also asserted the source documents were combined by a "redactor" (editor) to create the present form of Genesis. This concept proved very influential.

Hupfeld had believed the Elohistic material subsequently called P was the *Grundschrift* (foundation document), that is, the earliest of the major sources. K. H. Graf (1815–69), however, convinced scholars that P was in fact the latest. He argued the historical books did not presuppose the priestly legislation of P. The order of appearance for these four hypothetical sources then changed from PEJD to the now familiar JEDP.

Julius Wellhausen (1844–1918) brought this tradition of German criticism to its climactic synthesis. His two great works are *Die Komposition des Hexateuchs* and the *Prolegomena zur Geschichte Israels*. Because of these works, the documentary hypothesis of Pentateuchal origins became forever associated with his name. His theory seemed complete and elegantly simple; it immediately drew wide support among OT scholars. It is important to recognize, moreover, that for Wellhausen, this was not merely a literary theory but was part of a program for reinterpreting the history and social institutions of Israel. It is not correct, therefore, to assume this is simply an obscure but harmless literary investigation. Rather, the whole story of Israel's history and faith was radically revised with very negative conclusions about the accuracy of the biblical account.

In the English-speaking world, the foremost spokesman for the newer higher criticism was S. R. Driver (1846–1914) of Oxford University, whose *Introduction to the Literature of the Old Testament* became the definitive English introduction to the OT for a generation of scholars. Notwithstanding a few spectacular heresy trials and forced resignations, such as that of C. A. Briggs (suspended from the Presbyterian ministry in 1893) and Crawford Toy (departed from the Southern Baptist Seminary in 1879), the progress of the documentary hypothesis and related theories continued unabated. The publication of the *International Critical Commentary* in 1910 was perhaps the greatest proof of how completely the leading English-speaking biblical scholars were persuaded by the new approach to Scripture.

Meanwhile, the other books of the OT did not escape critical attention. Eichorn argued that Isaiah 40—66, for example, was a later addition and not the work of the prophet himself. In 1892, Bernhard Duhm persuaded scholars that Isaiah 40—66 should further be divided into two separate works (chaps. 40—55 and chaps. 56—66). The Book of Isaiah was thus regarded as the work of three major authors: Isaiah ben Amoz (chaps. 1—39); Deutero-Isaiah (40—55, written during the Babylonian captivity); and Trito-Isaiah (56—66, written in the post-exilic community). Scholars also believed non-Isaianic interpolations were scattered throughout chapters 1—39 as well.

The authenticity of the Book of Daniel was questioned by the Neoplatonist Porphry (232–305) as early as the second century. He deemed it a Jewish fraud filled with legend and propaganda meant to support the Jews in their struggle with Hellenism. This viewpoint gained acceptance in critical circles by the early 1800s. James Montgomery's commentary on Daniel is a classic example of the higher critical approach to this book.[1]

Much the same could be said with regard to the wisdom literature, the poetic texts, and the other Prophets of the OT. Books were routinely regarded as having large-scale interpolations, or as extremely late (the Psalms and the wisdom literature were regarded as almost wholly post-exilic or even Maccabean in origin), or as filled with legend and non-historical accounts (e.g., various stories in Joshua and Jonah).[2]

THE RISE OF FORM: CRITICISM AND TRADITION CRITICISM

Hermann Gunkel (1862–1932) was intrigued by research in the composition and transmission of folk tales and suggested that the application of folk tale research to the OT could be fruitful. Gunkel distinguished between legend (which is based on oral tradition, concentrates on the story of a family, and is more poetic in form) and history (which is based on written documents, is political in orientation, and is prosaic in style). In his 1901 commentary on Genesis, Gunkel treated the patriarchal narratives as legend (folk tale) rather than as history. Gunkel further developed his views in *Das Märchen im Alten Testament* (*The Folktale in the Old Testament*). He argued that as Hebrew storytellers recounted ancestral legends to Israelites around the campfire, the stories underwent a long process of development through the generations until they were finally reduced to writing. Through application of the form-critical methods, moreover, it was possible to recover portions of the older oral legends behind the text.

The work of Axel Olrik (1864–1917) and Andre Jolles (1874–1946) supported Gunkel's methods. Olrik tried to show what were the distinc-

---

1. James M. Montgomery, *A Critical and Exegetical Commentary on the Book of Daniel*, in ICC (Edinburgh: T. and T. Clark, 1927).

2. For detailed surveys of the history of OT historical criticism from earliest attempts to about the middle of the twentieth century, see Otto Eissfeldt, *The Old Testament: An Introduction*, trans. Peter R. Ackroyd (New York: Harper and Row, 1965), 158–81; R. K. Harrison, *Introduction to the Old Testament* (Grand Rapids: Eerdmans, 1969), 3–82; Robert H. Pfeiffer, *Introduction to the Old Testament* (New York: Harper and Brothers, 1941), 41–49; and Georg Fohrer, *Introduction to the Old Testament*, trans. David Green (Nashville: Abingdon, 1965), 23–32.

tive characteristics of oral transmission over against written literature, and these characteristics have been called "Olrik's laws." Jolles argued the patriarchal stories were comparable to the Norse sagas which described heroic, tragic, and ancestral adventures, because both forms were of the same genre and were transformed through the evolutionary process of oral transmission. Armed with apparently scientific methods for analyzing the texts, OT scholars were able to contend that Genesis in particular had all the traits of oral folk tale and ought to be studied accordingly.

These conclusions bore fruit in the work of Albrecht Alt (1883–1956), Gerhard von Rad (1901–71), and Martin Noth (1902–68). Alt argued the tribal groups of Abraham, Isaac, and Jacob were originally independent of one another and that each group had its own traditions about its particular ancestor and the god he worshiped. As these tribes settled in Canaan, their gods became identified with the shrines of local deities (the god of Isaac, for example, became identified with the shrine of Beersheba). Eventually these groups melded and merged their traditions in a fictitious genealogy of Abraham, Isaac, and Jacob.[3]

In Noth's analysis, the early traditions of Israel consisted of five independent themes: (1) the deliverance from Egypt, (2) the guidance to the fertile land, (3) the promises to the patriarchs, (4) the protection in the wilderness, and (5) the revelation at Sinai. It is instructive to note that these five streams of tradition developed independently of one another and did not constitute a unified narrative in any sense until they were finally merged. Also, the process of oral transmission brought about major revisions in the stories. That is, the original events and stories may have been radically different from the accounts that finally emerged in the texts we possess.[4]

Von Rad's analysis emphasized the importance of a few, small, early creeds which apparently comprised the developmental core of Israel's traditions. For example, "A wandering Aramean was my father . . .," (Deut. 26:5b-9)* is thought to be a prime example of an early creed, and the whole complex of Israel's traditions reputedly evolved from this kind of primitive historical creed. In addition, von Rad contended it was the Yahwist who brought the diverse traditions of Israel into a unified, theological

---

3. Albrecht Alt, "The God of the Fathers," in *Essays on Old Testament History and Religion*, trans. and ed. R. A. Wilson (Oxford, 1966), 3–77.

4. Martin Noth, *A History of Pentateuchal Traditions*, trans. Bernhard W. Anderson (Englewood Cliffs, N.J.: Prentice-Hall, 1972).

* Unless otherwise stated, Scripture quotations in this chapter are from the RSV.

narrative. Followers of von Rad tend to attach great significance to the Yahwist as the formative theologian of the OT.[5]

RECENT DEVELOPMENTS

In more recent years, OT scholarship has lost any semblance of unity, particularly in studies of the Pentateuch. Although many critical scholars continue to pay lip service to the documentary hypothesis, and in particular to J and P, the older consensus is no more. Indeed, scholars on the leading edge of research have abandoned the documentary hypothesis in any but the most truncated form and eschew tradition criticism as hopelessly speculative.

R. N. Whybray, for example, devotes a large portion of his recent monograph on the Pentateuch to demonstrating that both the documentary hypothesis and tradition criticism are without merit and ought to be abandoned. He therefore argues the Pentateuch is a unified work from a single author writing around the time of the exile. He believes history as a literary form did not exist until around the sixth century and that the Israelites, contemporaneously with Herodotus, produced their histories at about that time.[6]

Rolf Rendtorff, on the other hand, identifies more with the traditional historical school of biblical criticism, but he has little use for the documentary hypothesis and, in particular, the importance scholars have attached to document J. Rendtorff's position is that the traditions about individual patriarchs grew up independently of one another, but the patriarchal promises first served the purpose of binding together stories about an individual patriarch and then drew the accounts of separate patriarchs to each other. He sees three different types of promises: promise of offspring, promise of land, and promise of guidance; he attaches great significance to the evidence he sees in the text for the developmental process of these themes.[7]

Yet another approach is advocated by Thomas Thompson. He argues that the *toledoth* texts ("these are the generations of . . ."; e.g., Gen. 2:4; 6:9; 10:1) provide the structure for the whole of Genesis and asserts Genesis 5:1 is the actual title of the book (Gen. 1—4 being a prologue). Behind the structure of the present book, he sees a five-stage development which occurred in the late monarchy. These stages are (1) smaller units and tales, (2) larger, compound tales, (3) complex-chain narratives, (4) the *toledoth*

---

5. See Gerhard von Rad, "The Form-Critical Problem of the Hexateuch," in *The Problem of the Hexateuch and Other Essays*, trans. E. W. Trueman Dicken (London: SCM, 1966), 178.

6. R. N. Whybray, *The Making of the Pentateuch* (Sheffield: JSOT, 1987).

7. Rolf Rendtorff, *The Problem of the Process of the Transmission of the Pentateuch*, trans. John J. Scullion, JSOTSup 89 (Sheffield: JSOT Press, 1989).

structure, and (5) a final redaction. Similar to earlier critics, Thompson extrapolates evidence for diverse sources in the text wherever he finds apparent contradiction, theological commentary, or the like. He maintains that all of Genesis and Exodus 1—23 constitute the origin tradition the Israelites developed about themselves.[8]

In summary, the last few centuries of OT historical criticism has been dominated by a skeptical outlook. Not only are the stories within the text generally regarded as historically unreliable, but the process through which the texts developed is generally at variance with the biblical accounts.

Several points stand out here. (1) The roles of the traditional authors are often rejected (e.g., Moses) or drastically reduced (e.g., Isaiah). (2) The text is said to have resulted from a long process of joining and editing material which was often contradictory. This process is often conceived in a dialectical fashion. (3) The stories in the Bible may therefore differ radically from the early material behind the text. (4) More recent scholarly work reflects a greater tendency to see biblical texts as unified works void of long redaction or tradition histories. These studies, however, tend to treat the texts as out-and-out fiction with little or no historical moorings.

THE CONSERVATIVE RESPONSE

In such an environment one should not be surprised that those who uphold the historicity of the Bible have shunned historical criticism or concentrated solely on answering its proponents. Indeed, the preponderance of conservative work has been strictly that: counterattacking the critics to show that Moses could have written the Pentateuch, that Isaiah could have written Isaiah 40—66, and that Daniel was a real historical figure from sixth-century Babylon.

These counterattackers do not overshadow the able attempts of conservative scholars to defend the Bible. Christians such as William Henry Green,[9] R. D. Wilson,[10] O. T. Allis,[11] and E. J. Young,[12] as well as Jewish

---

8. Thomas L. Thompson, *The Origin Tradition of Ancient Israel*, JSOTSup 55 (Sheffield: JSOT Press, 1987).

9. William Henry Green, *The Higher Criticism of the Pentateuch*. (Charles Scribner's Sons, 1895. Reprint. Grand Rapids: Baker, 1978).

10. See R. D. Wilson, "The Headings of the Psalms [part I]," *The Princeton Theological Review* 14.1 (1926):1–37 and "The Headings of the Psalms [part II]," *The Princeton Theological Review* 14.3 (1926): 353–95.

11. O. T. Allis, *The Five Books of Moses* (Nutley, N.J.: Presbyterian and Reformed, 1949).

12. E. J. Young, *An Introduction to the Old Testament* (Grand Rapids: Eerdmans, 1949).

scholars such as Umberto Cassuto,[13] cited many flaws in the critics' reasoning. Recent introductions to the OT, such as those by Gleason Archer[14] and R. K. Harrison,[15] have solidified the modern evangelical position.

Still, evangelicals have done little true historical criticism as it relates to how the books of the Bible were written. That is, they have not tried to answer questions about how, for example, Moses procured the material which enabled him to write the history of events that transpired hundreds of years earlier. Indeed, the failure of evangelical scholars to ponder and attempt to answer these questions has undoubtably been a factor behind the unchallenged dominance of more skeptical scholars and their ability to persuade evangelical scholars. An evangelical approach to source and form critical matters, however, is both possible and fruitful, as an examination of the problem of Genesis can demonstrate.

THE SOURCES OF GENESIS

In its classic form, the documentary hypothesis asserts the Pentateuch is comprised of four separate documents. One document, D, is primarily found in Deuteronomy and has little or no representation in Genesis. Document J is from the early monarchy, probably from Judah, and it was joined to document E, a somewhat later northern text by R^{JE} (Redactor JE). After the inclusion of D in the late seventh century, the post-exilic document P was created, and the whole Pentateuch was given its final shaping by R^{P} (Redactor P). Notwithstanding differences in terminology among documentary critics for various documents and sub-documents, and disagreements over the dating, origin, and even existence of some documents (e.g., whether there really was an E), the classic hypothesis is the starting point and basis for any meaningful discussion of whether the theory has any merit.

Five principal arguments bolster the hypothesis. (1) The divine names are said to distinguish a J from a PE document in Genesis since the former employs Yahweh and the latter, Elohim. It is argued that J believed the patriarchs knew the name Yahweh (Gen. 4:26), but P and E believed they did not (Ex. 3:13–15; 6:2–3). (2) Contradictions within the text (e.g., in the flood narrative) imply that at least two separate, and in some ways conflicting accounts, are behind the present Genesis version. (3) Parallel type stories (e.g., Gen. 12:10–20; 20:1–18; 26:7–17: three versions of a story in

13. Umberto Cassuto, *The Documentary Hypothesis and the Composition of the Pentateuch*, trans. Israel Abrahams (Jerusalem: Magnes, 1941).

14. Gleason Archer, Jr., *A Survey of Old Testament Introduction* (Chicago: Moody, 1973).

15. Harrison, *Introduction*.

which a patriarch passes off his wife as his sister) imply that a single story was told in different versions with variations of character names, locations, and so forth. (4) Each document has a distinctive style (J is a vivid story-teller, but P is more stilted and structured). (5) Each document has an evident unity and theological message.

None of these arguments bears examination. Use of parallelism and repetition, for example, is a trademark of ancient narrative technique. The existence of three stories in which a patriarch claims his wife is his sister is not strange, therefore, and does not imply that separate documents are behind the present text. So-called contradictions are generally more illusory than real. When examined carefully, the flood narrative is not self-contradictory but shows remarkable signs of unity.[16] Assertions that one can find diverse styles and theologies among the documents are now widely dismissed as artificial or exaggerated, even among adherents of the documentary hypothesis.[17]

The starting point for the whole hypothesis, the use of the divine names, has no value at all for source critical investigation. In a given text, Yahweh or Elohim might be chosen for stylistic or theological reasons (Yahweh being more personal and covenantal and Elohim being more universal and abstract). More than that, the above mentioned texts have been misinterpreted to mean that J and P operated under different assumptions as to when the name Yahweh was revealed. Exodus 6:2–3, for example, should be translated, "I am Yahweh / And I revealed myself to Abraham, to Isaac, and to Jacob as El Shaddai, / And my name is Yahweh, / Did I not make myself known to them?"[18] In short, it does not assert that the patriarchs did not know the name Yahweh.

Attempts to discover lengthy oral traditions underlying the text are groundless. Indeed, analyses such as those by Alt, Noth, and von Rad are hopelessly speculative. Most importantly, analogies from other cultures that oral tradition historians use to give their research a more scientific foundation are frequently misapplied, inappropriate, or based on out-of-date research in folk studies.[19] For example, parts of the patriarchal narra-

---

16. See Gordon J. Wenham, "The Coherence of the Flood Narrative," *VT* 28 (1978): 336–48.

17. Note the hesitation about the value of these criteria in Claus Westermann, *Genesis 1—11*, trans. John J. Scullion (Minneapolis: Augsburg, 1984), 584. See also Rendtorff, *Pentateuch*, 101–75.

18. See Francis I. Andersen, *The Sentence in Biblical Hebrew* (The Hague: Mouton, 1974), 102; and Duane A. Garrett, *Rethinking Genesis* (Grand Rapids: Baker, 1991), 18–22.

19. See Patricia G. Kirkpatrick, *The Old Testament and Folklore Study*, JSOTSup 62 (Sheffield: JSOT Press, 1988).

tive are often called family sagas, based on the analogy of the Icelandic sagas. It is not clear, however, the Icelandic material ever had a long oral history; at any rate, cultural and genre differences between this and the biblical material make any detailed comparison inappropriate.[20]

Each of the most recent efforts at Pentateuchal criticism (Whybray, Rendtorff, and others) has significant individual problems.[21] Certainly no effort from the more critical scholars has in any sense won a consensus of approval.[22] This lack of agreement indicates deep uncertainty among scholars concerning the origin of Genesis.

An evangelical solution to the problem of Genesis is possible. One must first recognize that although the message of Genesis is unique, its structure is not. As literature, Genesis participates in the literary standards of its world. The overall arrangement is prologue (1:1–11:26), Abraham (12:1— 25:11), Jacob (25:19—35:22b), Joseph (37:1—46:7), and conclusion (46:28—50:26). Genealogical material links these divisions, and each of the three central sections focuses on threats to the emerging people of Israel. This pattern is remarkably similar to the structure of the Mesopotamian story of Atrahasis, a creation myth. In addition, a similar pattern is found in several smaller units of Genesis (e.g., 1:1—11:32; also 25:21—35:22b).

Other passages in Genesis also have recognizable formal patterns. The structure or genre of these texts has parallels elsewhere in the Bible, in other ancient literature, or both. For example, Genesis 23:1–20, 24:1–67, and 34:1–31 structurally parallel each other as well as a part of the Ugaritic legend of Aqhat; consequently, in the Book of Genesis we see evidence of ancient literary patterns which are the key to the sources of Genesis. Contrary to the documentary hypothesis, these sources conform to ancient literary types and do not slash across the book in the way that J and P do. Also, these sources are not based on artificial lines of evidence (divine names or apparent contradictions), and they do not imply or rely on a lengthy process of oral transmission and transformation.

If anything, these sources imply the antiquity of the Book of Genesis. Beyond the fact that the literary patterns which Genesis and its sources follow are very ancient (Atrahasis, for example, dates to at least the Old Babylonian period [1600 B.C.]), the sources of Genesis discovered by this process better fit only one period of Israelite history: the Egyptian sojourn. This is because the material combines a sense of homelessness and alienation with an optimistic anticipation of entering the promised

---

20. See Bruce K. Waltke, "Oral Tradition," in *A Tribute to Gleason Archer*, ed. Walter C. Kaiser, Jr., and Ronald F. Youngblood (Chicago: Moody, 1986), 17–34; and John Van Seters, *In Search of History* (New Haven: Yale, 1983), 223–24.

21. See Garrett, *Rethinking Genesis*, 52–66, 243–51.

22. See Thompson, *Origin Tradition*, 200–1.

land. Space does not permit a complete review of all data here, but it suffices to say that no other time of Israelite history, including the Babylonian exile, can fill the role of the *sitz im leben* (situation in life) for these sources. The most reasonable conclusion is that the sources were maintained through the Egyptian period and then edited into the present Book of Genesis as a prologue to Exodus, by Moses.[23]

THE HISTORICAL INCIDENTS OF THE BIBLE

It should come as no surprise that scholars who held to the documentary hypothesis or other major critical theories were highly skeptical about the historical reliability of the OT. For Wellhausen, the documentary hypothesis was merely the starting place for a radically different vision of Israel's history. Tradition critics, such as Alt and Noth, were certainly no less critical. Noth, for example, considered Moses to have "had no historical connection with the event which took place on Sinai."[24]

A moderating influence came into OT scholarship with the biblical archaeology movement, particularly in the work of W. F. Albright. His student, John Bright, showed clearly the impact of this school of thought in his *A History of Israel*.[25] This book stands within the critical tradition and yet generally treats the OT as a credible source of history. A less conservative, European example of an archaeology-based Israelite historian from the same period is Roland de Vaux.[26]

Recent scholarly work, however, reflects a more critical approach. Two scholars who have mounted separate, major challenges to the historicity of Genesis are Thomas Thompson[27] and John Van Seters.[28] The historical research associated with John Hayes and J. Maxwell Miller asserts the place of the biblical text must be maintained in doing Israelite historical research but is generally skeptical about the credibility of the biblical accounts.[29] Another school, however, tends to ignore the Bible and base its findings on the allegedly more scientific tools of sociology and archaeology. A major work here is *The Tribes of Yahweh* by Norman

---

23. For a complete study of these issues, see Garrett, *Rethinking Genesis*.

24. Martin Noth, *The History of Israel* (London: SCM, 1960), 136.

25. John Bright, *A History of Israel*, 2d ed. (Philadelphia: Westminster, 1975).

26. See Roland de Vaux, *Ancient Israel* (New York: McGraw-Hill, 1965).

27. See Thomas L. Thompson, *The Historicity of the Patriarchal Narratives*, BZAW 133 (Berlin: de Gruyter, 1974).

28. See John Van Seters, *Abraham in History and Tradition* (New Haven: Yale, 1975).

29. See John H. Hayes and J. Maxwell Miller, eds., *Israelite and Judean History* (Philadelphia: Westminster Press, 1977).

Gottwald.[30] This approach radically reinterprets Israelite history and is driven by Marxist social analysis.

Conservative scholars, while again in the minority, have nevertheless done some significant work in OT history. Important works include those by K. A. Kitchen,[31] Edwin R. Thiele,[32] and more recently John Bimson[33] and Eugene Merrill.[34] Each of these investigations constructively addresses problems associated with reconstructing Israel's history. Ongoing work by conservatives, moreover, is forging the way for a deeper appreciation of the reliability of the biblical narrative, as the following example will illustrate.

THE DATE OF THE EXODUS AND THE FALL OF JERICHO

SURVEY OF CONTEMPORARY POSITIONS

The question of the date of the exodus and conquest is a fruitful area for historical critical investigation. Apart from being the premier historical event of the OT, it is the linchpin for the chronology of early Israelite history. Also, the study of this question involves a wide range of disciplines and issues.

The two major schools of thought regarding the nature and history of the exodus may be described as traditional and radical, and each of these may be subdivided into smaller camps. The traditional view is that the exodus was a massive movement of the Israelites out of slavery in Egypt. Moses was their leader, and all twelve tribes were involved in both the departure and subsequent invasion of Canaan. The traditional school divides into two major camps: those who hold to a mid-fifteenth-century B.C. (ca. 1450) exodus during the reign of Thutmose III (the "early date") and those who hold to an early thirteenth-century B.C. (ca. 1280) exodus in the reign of Rameses II (the "late date").

Radical interpreters maintain either that the exodus did not occur or that the actual events were altogether different from the biblical narrative.

---

30. Norman Gottwald, *The Tribes of Yahweh: A Sociology of the Religion of Liberated Israel, 1250–1050 B.C.E.* (Maryknoll, N.Y.: Orbis, 1979).

31. K. A. Kitchen, *Ancient Orient and Old Testament* (Chicago: InterVarsity, 1966).

32. Edwin R. Thiele, *The Mysterious Numbers of the Hebrew Kings,* rev. ed. (Grand Rapids: Zondervan, 1983).

33. John J. Bimson, *Redating the Exodus and Conquest,* JSOTSup 5 (Sheffield: Almond Press, 1981).

34. Eugene H. Merrill, *Kingdom of Priests: A History of Old Testament Israel* (Grand Rapids: Baker, 1987).

One such interpretation is the partial exodus theory; it says only a few tribes participated in the mid-thirteenth-century B.C. exodus and that other groups later wandered into Canaan from other places and joined the Israelites. Many scholars use the Greek amphictiony (a league of Greek city-states) as an analogy for the formation of Israel from separate, unrelated tribal groups. Another interpretation, the pastoral migration view, asserts the Israelites were pastoral nomads who gradually moved into and settled in Canaan; both the exodus and conquest narratives are therefore essentially fiction. A third position, the native revolt theory, states there was no exodus, migration, or invasion of Israel whatsoever, except perhaps for an exodus and migration of Levites. Instead, the Israelites were oppressed Canaanites who abandoned the cities and rallied to the Yahwistic ideal in the hill country, where they formed the Israelite nation. The exodus was thus an internal revolt of native Canaanites against their overlords.

Other idiosyncratic positions could be described also. For the purposes of this discussion, however, attention will focus on the two traditional interpretations. The radical positions claim little in the way of historical or archaeological evidence and claim nothing in the way of biblical confirmation except as reinterpreted by a tenuous tradition criticism.

BIBLICAL DATA ON THE DATE OF THE EXODUS

The Bible itself seems to give reasonably specific information regarding the date of the exodus in 1 Kings 6:1. According to this passage, the exodus occurred 480 years prior to the initial building of the temple in the fourth year of Solomon's reign. Allowing for rounded numbers and uncertainty in chronology, this places the exodus in approximately 1450 B.C. Judges similarly supports the early date. Jephthah, in Judges 11:26, said three hundred years had passed since the conquest. Also, Judges implies that Israel was in the land for an extended period of time before the Philistines became a menace. The Philistines arrived in Canaan about 1175 B.C., but they do not enter the narrative until one of the last judges, Samson. Thus, it appears that Israel inhabited the land long before the arrival of the Philistines.

None of this is easily reconciled with the late date. Some believe the figure 480 in 1 Kings 6:1 is an idealization of twelve generations (12 x 40) and not meant to be taken literally, but this is special pleading; the text implies none of this. The chronology of Judges is itself a problem, but it is impossible to correlate the Judges narrative to the narrow time frame demanded by a 1280 B.C. exodus and ca. 1240 invasion. It seems therefore reasonable to uphold the Bible's consistent assertion that the exodus occurred in the mid-fifteenth century B.C.

RATIONALE FOR THE LATE DATE

Several arguments are often advanced in favor of a late date exodus (ca. 1280 B.C.) in the reign of Ramesses II. First, Exodus 1:11 states the Israelites worked on two cities for the Egyptians, Pithom and Rameses. The city of Rameses was once identified with Tanis, a site at which a large quantity of Ramesside stonework was found. This reinforced the notion that the city was built by the Hebrews under Ramesses II. Similarly, some archaeologists locate Pithom at Tell el-Maskhouta, a site constructed by Ramesses II. All of this apparently indicates the Hebrews were in Egypt as late as Ramesses II.

Second, a number of cities associated with the conquest, such as Jericho, Bethel, Hazor, and Lachish, were reputedly destroyed in the late-thirteenth century B.C. Many contend that this destruction was wrought by the invading Israelites and correlate the destruction levels with an early thirteenth-century B.C. exodus.

Third, many contend it is impossible to correlate the early date of the exodus, which requires a conquest beginning ca. 1400 B.C., with available archaeological evidence. In particular, many scholars believe Jericho simply did not exist at this time and thus could not have been destroyed by the invading Israelites. Also, a number of scholars who follow the archaeological work of Nelson Glueck assert the Transjordan area was unoccupied at this time.[35]

Inadequate Arguments. As Bimson demonstrates, these and similar arguments do not bear scrutiny.[36] The identification of Rameses with Tanis is now clearly incorrect; the actual site of Rameses is Qantir. This site, Qantir, had a long history of building activity well before Ramesses II, and the construction occurring there, as described in Exodus 1:11, need not be dated as late as Ramesses II's reign. Pithom should be identified with either Tell er-Retebah or Heliopolis, not Tell el-Maskhouta. Both Tell er-Retebah and Heliopolis had long histories prior to Ramesses II. Israelites working at either site need not have been present as late as his reign.

Second, evidence for dating the destruction levels at Hazor, Bethel, Lachish, and other cities to the late-thirteenth century is ambiguous at best. Establishing firm dates for these destruction levels is especially diffi-

---

35. For a good statement of the "late date" approach to the exodus and conquest, see Bright, *History*, 105–39.

36. See Bimson, *Redating the Exodus*, for a full analysis of pertinent evidence which is only briefly summarized here.

cult. No evidence exists for a systematic Israelite sweep through the territory at this time. On the other hand, we know that the late thirteenth to early-twelfth century B.C. was a period of constant warfare and invasions (e.g., by the Egyptians under Merneptah, ca. 1227–1217, and by the Philistines a little later), and the destruction of various cities at various times in this era is to be expected.

Some of the Transjordan peoples who opposed Israel's migration to Canaan were semi-nomadic (Amalekites and Edomites) and would have left little evidence for modern archaeologists to find. Conversely, evidence for occupation of the Transjordan in the Middle and Late Bronze ages does exist, and a number of scholars reject Glueck's contention that this region was unoccupied. Jericho occupies a special place in the debate, and it is to that city we now turn.

The Fall of Jericho. One frequently reads that the city of Jericho was unoccupied ca. 1400 B.C. and it could not have been taken by Joshua's forces at that time. The archaeologist Bryant Wood offers compelling reasons for overturning this position.[37]

The archaeological eras in Palestine can be divided as in the following chart, although there is some variation among archaeologists in terminology.

Early Bronze (EB)	3000–2200
Intermediate Bronze (IB)	2200–1950
Middle Bronze (MB)	1950–1550
MB I	1950–1750
MB IIa	1750–1600
MB IIb-c	1600–1550
Late Bronze (LB)	1550–1200
LB I	1550–1400
LB IIa	1400–1300
LB IIb	1300–1200
Iron	1200–330

During the Second Intermediate Period of Egyptian history (ca. 1786–1575 B.C.), the power and prestige of the central Egyptian government declined until much of Egypt actually was under the control of foreigners—Asiatics—called the Hyksos. The last of the Hyksos were driven out

---

37. For a complete discussion of evidence summarized here, see Bryant G. Wood, "Did the Israelites Conquer Jericho?" *BARev* (March/April, 1990): 45–59, and "Dating Jericho's Destruction: Bienkowski Is Wrong on All Counts," *BARev* (September/October, 1990): 45–49, 68–69. The latter article is a response to Piotr Bienkowski, "Jericho Was Destroyed in the Middle Bronze Age, Not the Late Bronze Age," found in the same pages.

ca. 1567 B.C. by Amosis I and a new, vigorous Egyptian dynasty, the nineteenth, was created. Many scholars believe the Hyksos also had a series of fortifications in Canaan, and the Egyptians, after expelling the Hyksos from their homeland, systematically destroyed the Hyksos strongholds in Canaan.

In particular, there is a major destruction level in Jericho city IV, and many contend that this destruction happened at the end of MB IIb-c, ca. 1550 B.C. It is said that Jericho IV was a Hyksos-fortified city demolished by pursuing Egyptian forces and abandoned at least through LB I. So, if the Israelites arrived at Jericho ca. 1400 they would have found no city.

This entire reconstruction is in process of a major reexamination. First, there is no proof that the Hyksos had a series of fortifications in Canaan. A type of Middle Bronze Age fortification with sloping ramparts of beaten earth is classified as a distinctive Hyksos fortification, but no evidence exists to link this structure with the Hyksos. No such fortifications are found from Hyksos Egypt. Second, it is not clear the Egyptians attempted to obliterate a fortification system in Canaan at the end of MB IIb-c. The whole theory rests on reading a massive military campaign into two obscure references in two ancient texts from the reign of Pharaoh Amosis. While Amosis may have campaigned in Canaan during his latter reign, years after the expulsion of the Hyksos, there is no reason to think that he razed the countryside and even less that he destroyed so-called Hyksos cities. Indeed, a campaign by Amosis probably would have concentrated on the coastal trade routes, not the Jordan valley. Third, arguments for dating the fall of Jericho at ca. 1550 B.C. are weak.

In the 1930s, John Garstang conducted the first major excavation of Jericho and believed he found evidence of massive destruction (ca. 1400–1385 B.C.), which he regarded as Joshua's attack. In the 1950s, Kathleen Kenyon challenged Garstang's conclusions. She showed that what Garstang had thought was a double wall belonging to Joshua's Jericho was actually two separate walls from different times in Early Bronze Jericho. She also maintained the massive destruction of Jericho IV occurred at the end of MB IIb-c as part of the alleged Egyptian campaign against the Hyksos.[38]

While Kenyon indicated flaws in Garstang's work, her own conclusions are being challenged at several points by Wood. First, there is not a single piece of hard evidence in Jericho IV linking it to the Hyksos. Kenyon's

---

38. Kathleen M. Kenyon, *Digging Up Jericho* (London: Ernest Benn, 1957). Kenyon summarizes her position in "Palestine in the Middle Bronze Age," in *CAH*, ed. I. E. S. Edwards, C. J. Gadd, N. G. L. Hammond, and E. Sollberger, (Cambridge: Cambridge University Press, 1973), 2.1.77–116.

primary reason for rejecting an LB I date for the fall of Jericho IV was the absence of Cypriot ware, a type of pottery from Cyprus which is regarded as the distinctive pottery of LB I. Ironically, she could have found that Cypriot ware existed in Jericho IV if she had examined Garstang's reports. At the time of Garstang's work, scholars did not realize the importance of this pottery, and his findings lay ignored. Nevertheless, he did recover Cypriot ware from Jericho IV, and this is clear evidence that the city fell at the end of LB I, not MB IIb-c.

Many other lines of evidence support the view that Jericho IV fell ca. 1400 B.C. and that it was the city Joshua attacked. Jericho IV was heavily populated, but its destruction was total, and the city was burned (Josh. 6:24). Archaeological evidence also implies the walls were breached by seismic activity, as the Bible also indicates.

Interestingly, storage jars full of grain were found from Jericho IV. This indicates the attack came near harvest time, the city did not endure a long siege, and it was not plundered after its fall—all of which accords with the biblical account (Josh. 2:6; 5:10; 6:15–18).

In addition, a charcoal sample from Jericho IV was dated by carbon-14 to 1410 B.C. (plus or minus forty years). A small cemetery northwest of City IV contained several scarabs, small beetle-shaped amulets inscribed with the name of a pharaoh. These were of Hatshepsut, Thutmosis III, and Amenhotep III, whose reigns spanned the fifteenth century. This series of scarabs suggests the city was in continuous use through the end of LB I. Also, a significant amount of pottery distinctive to LB I was found in Jericho in addition to the Cypriot ware. For example, a type of rounded bowl with painted concentric circles on the inside is known to have existed only for a short duration in the latter fifteenth century. Similar pottery is found from LB I strata in Ashdod and Hazor.

All in all, evidence that Jericho IV fell in the late fifteenth century and that it was the very city that Joshua attacked is compelling. In addition, a strong case can be made that other cities of Joshua's campaign also fell at the end of LB I. These cities include Hazor, Lachish, Debir and Bethel. All of this implies the conquest began ca. 1410 B.C. and the exodus took place ca. 1450 B.C., at the end of the reign of Thutmoses III (MC).

The biblical account of the exodus and conquest should be read as historically accurate, although one must recognize that ancient narrative technique differs from modern historical accounts. Also, fixing these crucial events in a chronological framework allows for a reconstruction of the history of Israel in its ancient Near Eastern setting which, if not in every point verifiable, is at least not wildly speculative. Such cannot be said for many of the more radical re-readings of Israel's early history. A meaningful reconstruction must be based on collating primary literary sources (the biblical account) with other historical and archaeological evidence. Following such principles, a new historical criticism, which is both creative and faithful to the text of Scripture, may emerge out of the present chaos in Old Testament studies .

FOR FURTHER READING

Barton, John. *Reading the Old Testament*. Philadelphia: Westminster, 1984.

Bimson, J. J. *Redating the Exodus and Conquest*. JSOTSup 5. Sheffield: Almond Press, 1981.

Bright, John. *A History of Israel*. 2d ed. Philadelphia: Westminster, 1975.

Eissfeldt, Otto. *The Old Testament: An Introduction*. Translated by Peter Ackroyd. New York: Harper & Row, 1965.

Garrett, Duane. *Rethinking Genesis*. Grand Rapids: Baker, 1991.

Harrison, R. K. *Introduction to the Old Testament*. Grand Rapids: Eerdmans, 1969.

Kaiser, W. C., Jr. *Toward Rediscovering the Old Testament*. Grand Rapids: Zondervan, 1987.

Kitchen, K. A. *Ancient Orient and Old Testament*. Chicago: InterVarsity, 1966.

Longman, Tremper III. "Critical Methods and the Old Testament." In *HBH*, edited by D. Dockery. Nashville: Broadman, 1992.

Merrill, Eugene H. *Kingdom of Priests: A History of Old Testament Israel*. Grand Rapids: Baker, 1987.

O'Neill, J. C. *ABD* (1992), s.v. "Biblical Criticism."

Whybray, R. N. *The Making of the Pentateuch*. Sheffield: JSOT, 1987.

XI

LITERARY CRITICISM OF THE OLD TESTAMENT

KENNETH A. MATHEWS

Why do you read the Bible? What are you attempting to gain? Doctrinal instruction? Spiritual encouragement? Historical information? Enjoyment from good stories? Why the Bible is read determines *how* the Bible is read. While several purposes may be intended by the interpreter, different methods are employed to obtain each aim.[1]

Traditionally, the Old Testament was studied by the synagogue and church for worship and to derive religious instruction in doctrine, moral values, and ecclesiastical practices. The dawning of the Enlightenment, however, directed attention to historical questions concerning the Bible.

---

1. See R. Morgan and J. Barton, *Biblical Interpretation* (Oxford: Oxford University Press, 1988), 1–32; J. Barton, *Reading the Old Testament: Method in Biblical Study* (Philadelphia: Westminster, 1984), 1–19. Barton indicates that no single aim can claim sole validity; he calls for an integrative model for biblical interpretation. We differ with Barton since the Bible asserts for itself the purpose of Scripture is primarily for "instruction in righteousness" (2 Tim. 3:16).* Any pursuit inconsistent with the Scripture's own goals distracts the reader from the self-conscious purpose of the text.

The OT was read by the academy as a historical resource for reconstructing the institutional history of the Hebrews and the political history of the ancient Near East. The "Scriptures" of the seminary became the university's "Hebrew Bible" in the curriculum of its newly established department of religion.

Yet in the latter half of our century, skepticism concerning the success of historical readings opened the way for a reading of the Bible for the purpose of literary study. The university's literature department viewed the Bible as virgin soil for employing literary-critical theory, giving rise to the "Bible as literature" movement. Moreover, the discipline of semiotics (science of signs) and semantics (meaning) in the university's linguistics department provided additional models for a linguistic-based exegesis.

HISTORICAL AND LITERARY METHODS

The watershed event in the modern direction of biblical studies was the presidential address of James Muilenburg for the Society of Biblical Literature in 1968.[2] Muilenburg called for a study of Scripture that was holistic in character with an emphasis on the rhetorical features of the extant text. His rhetorical criticism invited experimentation in *synchronic* approaches to the Bible, that is, studies solely devoted to the existing form of the text.

Literary study of the Bible is not entirely new, however, and all methods of biblical study, in fact, are wedded principally to literary concerns, since the genesis of every study is the interpreter's encounter with the *text*. It is the text as the Word of God that motivates the religious reader to interpret theologically and ecclesiastically. It was, for example, the troublesome passages of the text, such as the civil laws of the Mosaic law, that encouraged the early church to interpret them christologically or allegorically. Although religious aims and the allegorical method of interpretation dominated the Middle Ages, there also was a growing regard for the literal level of the text. This factor coupled with the Enlightenment's enthrallment with institutional history, as opposed to traditional dogmatics, raised new questions generated by incongruities occurring at the literal level of the text. The historical-critical method in a mere century captured the academic centers of Europe and Britain; it became the new "traditionalism" by the 1880s and it continues its reign today among university and seminary scholars.

A very prominent example is Julius Wellhausen's *Prolegomena to the History of Israel*, which attempted to reconstruct the developmental history of

---

2. J. Muilenburg, "Form Criticism and Beyond," *JBL* (1969): 1–18.

Israel's religious institutions.[3] Yet Wellhausen's historical reconstruction was dependent on his prior literary judgments concerning the makeup of the Pentateuch (the "four source" theory). With good reason, therefore, this analytical approach to the Pentateuch's sources was known as "literary" criticism.[4] For Wellhausen, however, it must be kept in mind that his chief aim was not producing a new literary configuration for the Pentateuch but a rewriting of Israel's religious history.

The distinction between "historical" and "literary" criticism, then, is somewhat artificial, since even the historical methods are exploring the processes involved in the compositional history of the text. Such a distinction, however, is warranted because among the present literary approaches to the text are non-historical and ahistorical methods. Concerning the literary approaches to the Bible, D. Robertson comments ". . . the accuracy of historical assertions made in a work of literature is completely irrelevant to a literary discussion of it."[5] Most scholars have shown little enthusiasm for much of the new literary studies. Scholars who advocate literary-based approaches are responding to their critics by attempting to integrate diachronic and synchronic approaches for wider appeal among biblical scholars.[6]

In summary, the literary methods of this newer sort versus the traditional evangelical and historical-critical approaches are the subject of our essay. Our focus will be more descriptive, surveying the primary methods, than critical; however, we will include a response to the literary-critical methods with a brief critique. A special case is canon criticism, which we will address last. It is included because it shares with literary approaches a concentration on the final form of the text. We will conclude with a discussion of the flood account (Gen. 6—9) as an example of how literary studies have helped the interpretation of a specific passage.

---

3. J. Wellhausen, *Prolegomena to the History of Israel* (reprint 1888 edition; New York: Meridian Books, 1957).

4. Notice the title of N. Habel's treatment of source criticism: *Literary Criticism of the Old Testament* (Philadelphia: Fortress, 1971).

5. D. Robertson, *The Old Testament and the Literary Critic* (Philadelphia: Fortress, 1977), 12.

6. See J. D. Crossan, "'Ruth Amid the Alien Corn': Perspectives and Methods in Contemporary Biblical Criticism," in *The Biblical Mosaic*, ed. R. M. Polzin and E. Rothman (Philadelphia: Fortress, 1982), 199–210.

LITERARY APPROACHES TO THE BIBLE

We begin by responding at the outset to those expositors who may ask why a literary approach to the text is even warranted. A full(er) understanding of a passage involves a holistic approach to interpretation, which comprises both grammatical-historical studies and literary analysis. Holistic study is necessary because the Bible is literary, if not literature. By "literary," we mean that it is self-consciously conceived as literature.

We do not suggest by "literary" that the Bible is only literature whose value is just for good storytelling. On the other hand, neither is it a nonfictional, encyclopedic compendium of knowledge about Israel's religion. Its proclamation is expressed through the diverse literary genre of human discourse.

Discourse includes a complex of (1) content and (2) form, that is, the "packaging" of that content. The content of a message dictates the form, yet at the same time, the form contributes to the meaning of the passage. To drive a wedge between the content, whether it be historical or theological, conveyed by the text and the literary features of that conveyance distorts the "meaning complex." The evangelical scholar recognizes that the Bible is both the Word of God *and* the words of men.[7] To spurn the literary study of the Bible out of hand is to diminish the Bible's stature as the unique product of God and man.

Setting aside the question of literary study as a legitimate enterprise, we can turn now to the present scene. Contemporary literary approaches to the Bible were not created in a vacuum. They draw on a myriad of literary-critical theories and other disciplines, such as anthropology, psychology, linguistics, and political theory. One critic comments on the plethora of critical theories today:

> There is . . . no longer any such thing as a "working majority" in literary studies, and perhaps the time when there was such a thing was not such a very good time after all. Marxists, Freudians, Jungians, Semioticians, Structuralists, Formalists, myth critics, deconstructionalists, Lacanians, Foucauldians, Neo-Aristotelians, feminists, subjectivists, historical critics, rhetorical critics, old New Critics, and humanists of every kind and stripe, have laid before us a smorgasbord of interpretations and interpretive principles that if we are wise we can pick and choose from to reach *our own* critical method.[8]

---

7. See C. Armerding, *The Old Testament and Criticism* (Grand Rapids: Eerdmans, 1983).

8. R. Crosman, "Is There Such a Thing as Misreading?" in *Criticism and Critical Theory*, ed. J. Hawthorn (London: Edward Arnold, 1984), 11.

Lest we overindulge, we will limit our appetite to a cursory review of literary criticism's most salient approaches in its twentieth-century influence on biblical studies.

TRADITIONAL CRITICISM

Literary theorists have experienced a chain of evolving developments. These movements are best seen in contrast to traditional literary interpretation. The traditional task of the literary critic was to discover the authorial intent and historical circumstances of a composition's origins. Who is the author? the audience? the situation? The locus of meaning is in the author's intentions for writing as expressed through the text. In biblical studies, historical questions dominate both evangelical interpretation, with its grammatical-historical approach, and the historical-critical methods (source, form, redaction criticisms).

The leading spokesman of traditional criticism among secular literary critics is E. D. Hirsch, who has argued for an objective meaning of the text which is determined by the author's intention. He is responding directly to the contemporary modes of literary criticism which have "banished the author" from interpretation, such as new criticism, structuralism, and reader-response theories. The failure of contemporary criticism, he maintains, is its failure to distinguish between hermeneutics and criticism. What the text *meant* must be kept distinct from what the text *means*. The former is the author's intention which does not change; the latter is the significance of the original meaning. By "significance," Hirsch means there is "a relationship between that meaning and a person, or a conception, or a situation, or indeed anything imaginable."[9] The unchanging element in this relationship between text and interpreter is what the text originally meant.

Hirsch recognizes that authorial intent can only be discovered through a careful analysis of the author's product, the text itself, not by biography or psychoanalysis of the author. His argument is indebted in part to Edmund Husserl's intentional theory of human consciousness. Husserl contended humans approach the reality of the world through conscious intentions. Verbal meaning is the speaker's intentional object, which can be shared by the listener or reader under the appropriate conditions of literary convention. Hirsch admits any series of words can have potential meanings, but the determinative, objective meaning, he insists, is the author's conscious, intentional message. Our understanding of ancient

---

9. E. D. Hirsch, *Validity in Interpretation* (New Haven: Yale University Press, 1967), 8.

texts is possible because the author and reader as humans share sufficiently for communication to occur.[10]

We turn now to the literary methods themselves. In discussing the following approaches to the literary study of the Bible, it is not always easy to describe a clear and consistent typology for them. Their methods at times overlap either conceptually or in praxis. We have attempted to speak of each in terms of its distinctives.

ARCHETYPAL CRITICISM

One of the early influences on literary studies of the Bible was Northrop Frye's archetypal criticism. His *Anatomy of Criticism* explains that literature possesses an imaginative framework—"a mythological universe"—which gives the human portrayal of nature/reality. Frye views the structure of literary imagery as four archetypical (master) modes: the apocalyptic, romantic, realistic, and demonic. These logically are precursors to the literary genre of comedy, romance, tragedy, and irony/satire.[11] These four archetypes are expressed through conceptual oppositions. In his analysis of the Bible, Frye delineated its two essential archetypes: the apocalyptic (ideal world) and its opposite, the demonic model (unideal). For each master image are subcategories of experience: e.g., the divine, spiritual, paradisal, human, animal, vegetable, and mineral. The antithesis of the apocalyptic and demonic is expressed through opposing images: e.g., God/Satan, angels/demons, Eden/desert, Israel and Bride of Christ/cast-offs, sheep/wolf, harvest/harvest of wrath, and city/ruins.[12]

Leland Ryken, the leading evangelical literary critic, arranges biblical imagery similarly into the worlds of the ideal and unideal archetypes. He defines an archetype as "an image, character type, or plot motif that occurs throughout literature."[13] He recognizes in the Bible the imagery of archetypal characters and plot types, such as comedy, hero accounts, and tragedy.[14] However, Ryken does not reduce the Bible to a literary product alone. He affirms the value of the grammatical-historical approach to the

---

10. Ibid., 209–44, esp. 218–19; also see Hirsch, *The Aims of Interpretation* (Chicago: University of Chicago Press, 1976).

11. N. Frye, *Anatomy of Criticism: Four Essays* (Princeton: Princeton University Press, 1957), 131–42.

12. N. Frye, *The Great Code: The Bible and Literature* (New York: Harcourt Brace Jovanovich, 1981), 139–68, esp. 167.

13. L. Ryken, ed., *The New Testament in Literary Criticism* (New York: Frederick Ungar, 1984), 10.

14. See his article "The Bible as Literature" in this volume. See also *Words of Delight: A Literary Introduction to the Bible* (Grand Rapids: Baker, 1987).

text, answering historical and theological questions. He adds literary studies as a natural expansion of the process. While literary categories may be used in analysis, evangelical scholars affirm that the Bible is referential (relates reality) and conveys discursive information.

COMPOSITION CRITICISM

Composition criticism focuses on formal literary features of the text as clues of the narrator's message.[15] R. Alter defines this kind of literary analysis:

> . . . the manifold varieties of minutely discriminating attention to the artful use of language, to the shifting play of ideas, conventions, tone, sound, imagery, syntax, narrative viewpoint, compositional units, and much else; the kind of disciplined attention, in other words, which through a whole spectrum of critical approaches has illuminated, for example, the poetry of Dante, the plays of Shakespeare, the novels of Tolstoy.[16]

Since biblical narrative usually does not announce its intention overtly, it is necessary for the interpreter to derive it from the text by inference. For the most part, the reader is left to infer from rhetorical features of the text what the opinion of the narrator is.

Representative of compositional criticism are studies in the omniscience of the narrative's teller. M. Sternberg has explored in depth this feature of Hebrew narration. He concludes that the Hebrew use of omniscience gives the account a sense of authority which is derived from God. How does the narrator come by this privileged knowledge (even of God's own thoughts!)? Inspiration. The narration assumes inspiration. It serves as a "rule" of reading shared by the text and the reader.[17] Moreover, characterization is used by the composition to indicate its opinion. Alter's study devotes an extended investigation to characterization in bib-

---

15. Here we are using W. Kort's term; see his *Story, Text, and Scripture: Literary Interests in Biblical Narrative* (University Park: Pennsylvania University Press, 1988), 84–95. Also, for a review of how compositional features indicate authorial intention while maintaining historical integrity, see Kenneth Mathews, "Preaching Historical Narrative," in *Reclaiming the Prophetic Mantle: Preaching the Old Testament Faithfully*, ed. G. Klein (Nashville: Broadman, 1992), 19–50.

16. R. Alter, *The Art of Biblical Narrative* (New York: Basic Books, 1981), 12–13. For examples of composition criticism, see the collected essays in R. Alter and F. Kermode, eds., *The Literary Guide to the Bible* (Cambridge, Mass.: Harvard University Press, 1987) and A. Preminger and E. L. Greenstein, *The Hebrew Bible in Literary Criticism* (New York: Ungar, 1986).

17. M. Sternberg, *The Poetics of Biblical Narrative* (Bloomington: Indiana University Press, 1987), 33, 84–90.

lical narration. Seldom does the biblical narrator blatantly sum up a character. In particular, the author uses the dialogue of participants to indicate their character and thereby suggest the author's assessment. Ambiguity in biblical characters provides the reader with true-to-life portraits (e.g., Abram's lie, Moses' anger, David's adultery). By such ambiguities or contrasts, the author can show a development in the character of a protagonist.[18]

NEW CRITICISM

The origins of new criticism appeared in the 1940s and 1950s by secular literary critics such as T. S. Eliot, I. A. Richards, and William Empson. W. K. Wimsatt's and M. C. Beardsley's article "The Intentional Fallacy" articulated New Criticism's challenge to traditional criticism.[19] New Criticism distinguished literary history, which answers historical questions concerning author and composition, from the proper business of literary criticism, which is the study of the literary object itself.

J. Barton describes New Criticism as a reactionary movement to the ideals of Romantic criticism, which viewed the task of literary criticism as discovering the poet's experience of reality.[20] As a result, literary biography was an important component in traditional literary studies. New Critics contended, however, that the author's state of mind and feelings as well as the circumstances of the work were distractions. They did not believe that all historical questions concerning the text were irrelevant (e.g., what words meant in the author's day), but that a *valid* interpretation had to be based on the text alone. The literary object itself was determinative for meaning. This opinion opened the door for viewing texts as having lives of their own with many possible meanings as the text experienced new contexts. Since New Criticism perceived the text as an autonomous entity, it took an ahistorical stance toward the text, a position which significantly departed from traditional literary criticism.

---

18. Alter, *Art of Biblical Narrative*, 114–30. He also points to "key-wording" (*Leitwort*) as a compositional technique used to enhance thematic unity or highlight a motif. Key-wording is the repetition of a word or convergence of words (related in sound or form) occurring in strategic locations within a narrative (pp. 92–97).

19. W. K. Wimsatt and M. C. Beardsley, "The Intentional Fallacy," in *The Verbal Icon: Studies in the Meaning of Poetry* (reprint; Lexington: University of Kentucky, 1954). See also Wimsatt and C. Brooks, *Literary Criticism: A Short History* (New York: Knopf, 1957).

20. Barton, *Reading the Old Testament*, 149–50.

While this criticism had a short life among secular literary critics, superseded by structuralism and deconstructionism, it has had a stronger hold on biblical studies. Among these are the studies edited by literary critics K. R. R. Gros Louis, J. Ackerman, and T. Warshaw.[21] Gros Louis comments, "Our approach is essentially ahistorical; the text is taken as received, and the truth of an action or an idea or a motive, for literary criticism, depends on its rightness or appropriateness in context." In the same essay, he adds, "We know, as students of literature, that the author's intention, his goals in writing for his contemporary audience, and his religious convictions play a small role indeed in literary criticism and, more important, in the analysis of literary texts."[22] Biblical scholars who are text-focused do not always follow a strictly uniform theoretical approach. Their methods at times are eclectic, bridging composition and New Criticism with the more pragmatic features of structuralism.[23]

STRUCTURALISM

More impressive in secular literary circles was the emerging discipline of structuralism in the 1960s. By "structure," we are not referring merely to an internal plan or design of a composition; this is organizational structure and it describes the appearance (surface) level of the text which is consciously created and perceived. *Structuralism*, however, is a philosophy of reality; it is far more than a method of literary study.

Theoretical structuralism is applied to any entity that is a "system."[24] As a theory it cuts across diverse disciplines, such as anthropology, linguistics, mathematics, and literature. Literary structuralism is indebted to

---

21. K. R. R. Gros Louis, J. Ackerman, and T. Warshaw, eds., *Literary Interpretations of Biblical Narratives*, vol. 1 (Nashville: Abingdon, 1974) and Gros Louis and Ackerman, eds., vol. 2 (1982).

22. "Some Methodological Considerations," *Literary Interpretations*, 2:14, 16.

23. See M. Weiss, *The Bible from Within: The Method of Total Interpretation* (Jerusalem: Magnes, 1984); M. Fishbane, *Text and Texture: Close Readings of Selected Biblical Texts* (New York: Schocken Books, 1979); J. P. Fokkelman, *Narrative Art in Genesis: Specimens of Stylistic and Structual Analysis* (Assen/Amsterdam: Van Gorcum, 1975); D. M. Gunn, *The Story of King David: Genre and Interpretation* in *JSOT* (1978), *The Fate of King Saul: An Interpretation of a Biblical Story* in *JSOT* 14 (1980); A. Berlin, *Poetics and Interpretation of Biblical Narrative* (Sheffield: Almond, 1983); and J. Magonet, *Form and Meaning: Studies in the Literary Techniques in the Book of Jonah* (Bern: Lang, 1976).

24. J. Piaget, *Structualism*, trans. and ed. C. Maschler (New York: Harper & Row, 1970).

the structural linguistics of F. de Saussure. De Saussure's theory envisions language as *systems* of signification. He centered on defining the relational-effects in language systems, that is, the syntagmatic and the paradigmatic relationships, rather than on the origins and changes of language systems. E. McKnight illustrates these relationships by the sentence "James runs." The syntagmatic relationship is the linear sequence between "James" as the topic and the second word in the series "runs." Together they form an acceptable sentence, and the sequence helps define the relationship of the words. Paradigmatic, on the other hand, looks at each word in isolation. Each word bears "associative" meanings. Thus, "runs" has the related meanings "move," "flee," and "hasten," which also help define the word.[25]

A second feature of Saussure's theory is his understanding of how words convey meaning in a language system. Words are arbitrary signs. There is a gap between a language sign (signifier) and what that sign signifies (the signified). For example, there is no inherent conceptual relationship between the word "pencil" (sign) and the mental concept "pencil" (signified). This means that words have meaning only in terms of their contrast with other signs within a language system.[26]

Third, Saussure differentiates between language as a system (*langue*) and language as a speech act (*parole*). *Langue* is the structural network of language which is intuitively imposed on a speaker. *Parole* is the specific expression of language, a particular discourse. The structuralist seeks primarily to discover the underlying or "deep" structure which governs specific language acts. It is contended that the brain discerns meaning at the underlying structure by contrasts or oppositions. These opposites are known as binaries or pairs of opposites. In other words, to know what something is, the mind must know what it is not. Typical of binary pairs, for example, are life/death, wet/dry, and light/dark.

Since literature is conceived by structuralists as a language product, it is fertile ground for structuralist readings. Literature, it is contended, is a network of self-regulating operations. A specific text has many potential meanings (polyvalence) because it possesses several structures working at different levels.

Semiotic research focuses on the systems of signification which are the universals of language's network. For a structuralist the task is to discern the hidden, intuitive network of relationships; the deep level is the *determinative* meaning that gives rise to a derivative literary expression.

---

25. E. McKnight, *The Bible and the Reader: An Introduction to Literary Criticism* (Philadelphia: Fortress, 1985), 7.

26. See Kort, *Story, Text, and Scripture*, 61–62.

Meaning, it is assumed, is a relational-effect—"the effect produced by the relations among various elements which in and of themselves do not have meaning, but are merely poles between which the sparks of meaning flash."[27] Therefore, a specific text, while a textual system, is secondary to the semiotician's analysis, because universal meaning is discovered at the *langue* level. The quest is to describe *how* literature is created as opposed to *what* is created. Structural exegesis, on the other hand, acknowledges the universals of the semiotician's network of meaning and brings them to bear in the analysis of a specific literary expression. The exegete seeks to show how the universals take part in the meaning of a specific text.[28]

Related to structuralist theory is the recognition that the communication process includes conventions (rules) of reading that are unconsciously shared by the author/speaker and the audience. Conventions of communication function both at the cultural and language (oral/written) levels. We have already clarified that surface structure is a conscious exchange between author and reader whereas deep structure is an intuitive exchange. A reader who is competent at the surface level must know the rules of grammar and syntax to both process and generate text at the conscious level.

Structuralists believe that the deep level also has its "grammar." The conventions are public codes (accessible to all) that determine the meaning of the composition. Therefore, the "meaning" of the text resides not in the authorial intention or even at the surface level of the composition but in the conventions themselves. An analogy is a board game where a knowledge of the rules is required for the game to be executed meaningfully. A move on the board has meaning because the conventions *a priori* dictate the meaning. When a reader is not competent in recognizing the conventions of a particular genre (i.e., parable or law), then determinative meaning is lost.

With these features in mind, we can turn to structural narratology, the discipline which has had the greatest impact on biblical structuralism.[29] Structural narratology attempts to define the components of narrative as a system. Representative of this movement are V. Propp, C. Lévi-Strauss, and A. J. Gre-

---

27. D. Patte, "One Text. Several Structures," *Semeia* 18 (1980): 5.

28. See the discussions of Patte, "One Text," 3–24; Polzin, *Biblical Structuralism*, 5; S. A. Geller, "Through Windows and Mirrors into the Bible," in *A Sense of Text: The Art of Language in the Study of Biblical Literature* (Winona Lake: Eisenbrauns for Dropsie College, 1983), 28.

29. A helpful analysis of the leading theoreticians and biblical applications is D. C. Greenwood, *Structuralism and the Biblical Text* (Berlin: Mouton, 1985).

imas.[30] Propp, the Russian formalist, defined the "grammar" of folktale by defining its form. By analyzing one hundred examples of Russian folktales, he identified the possible number of plots and character roles that make up "folktale."

The structure of folktale consists of any combination of seven character "spheres of action" (e.g., villain, donor, hero) and thirty-one plot functions (e.g., a family member leaving home, hero marries and ascends the throne). Moreover, there are six kinds of possible plot "moves" that occur within a tale. In other words, folktale has a fixed range, or set of "recipes," which determine what constitutes folktale. His approach was syntagmatic since he described the organization of the folktale in terms of its chronological (linear) sequence or narrative plot development.

Structural reading of OT texts was pioneered by French structuralists, particularly R. Barthes whose studies in narrative drew largely on the theories of Greimas and Propp. His analysis of Jacob's struggle with the angel (Gen. 32:23–33) has become a signal example of structural readings among biblical texts.[31] Appealing to Greimas' model of *actants*,[32] he recognizes that the narrative structure of the account expresses an unexpected and ambiguous picture for the roles of "Sender" and "Opponent"—both are filled by God. Clearly, Jacob is the "Subject" and the crossing of the Jabbok is the "Object," but God who sends Jacob on this "Quest" proves to be the very "Opponent" who guards the river. Moreover, Barthes points

---

30. Originally published in 1928 (Russian), Propp's work was translated in 1958 and revised in this second edition: *Morphology of the Folktale*, rev. and ed. L. A. Wagner (Austin: University of Texas Press, 1968); C. Lévi-Strauss, "The Structural Study of Myth," in *Structural Anthropology*, trans. C. Jacobson and B. G. Schoepf (New York: Basis Books, 1963), 206–31; A. J. Greimas, *Structural Semantics: An Attempt at a Method*, trans. D. McDowell et al. (Lincoln: University of Nebraska Press, 1984). Greimas' model has been described by J. Calloud, *Structural Analysis of Narrative*, trans. D. Patte (Philadelphia: Fortress/Missoula: Scholars, 1976). See also R. C. Culley, "Exploring New Directions," in *The Hebrew Bible and Its Modern Interpreters*, ed. D. Knight and G. Tucker (Philadelphia: Fortress/Chico, Calif.: Scholars, 1985), 175–77.

31. R. Barthes, "The Struggle with the Angel: Textual Analysis of Genesis 32: 23–33," in *Structural Analysis and Biblical Exegesis*, ed. R. Barthes et al., trans. A. M. Johnson (Pittsburgh: Pickwick, 1974), 21–33.

32. Greimas' model has six sets of relationships which determine the character roles and their interactions at the surface level of the narrative. The Subject *actant* desires someone or something, which is the Object *actant*. The source of the Object, that which makes it desirable, is the Sender *actant*. The Object is passed on to a Receiver *actant*. The Subject in the process of obtaining the Object is caught up in a power play between Helper and Opponent *actants*.

out the structural oddity of the struggle itself where the angel delivers the "deathblow," disabling the patriarch. Yet, rather than victor, the angel himself, surprisingly, cannot wrench free from Jacob until he concedes to the patriarch's wishes. This kind of analysis, Barthes points out, exposes the discontinuities layered in the text at the unconscious level.[33]

Propp's model of structural narratology has made its impact on Hebrew narrative studies through, among others, J. M. Sasson and R. C. Culley. Sasson applied Propp's model to the Book of Ruth. He identified the character roles of the story in terms of Propp's folktale roles: "Dispatcher" (Naomi), "Hero on a Quest" (Ruth), "Sought-for Person" (Obed), and both "Donor" and "Helper" (Boaz). On the basis of the story's agreement with Propp's model, Sasson concludes that the appropriate genre for Ruth is "folktale."[34] Culley, who modified Propp's theory, organized a group of fourteen biblical narratives around a series of linear sequences or actions. His goal was to define what makes up Hebrew narrative plot. He describes the patterns for particular story prototypes, such as deception stories and miracle stories, and offers a typology.[35]

Finally, the field of biblical studies has shown an indebtedness to Lévi-Strauss' model for understanding myth.[36] Edmund Leach, the British anthropologist,[37] by using Lévi-Strauss' paradigmatic model analyzes Genesis 1—4 as comprising three "myths": the seven-day creation, the

---

33. Barton, *Reading the Old Testament*, 117, suggests at the conscious level readers have always been troubled and, at the same time, fascinated by the account, which may be explained by what Barthes' structural analysis shows at the unconscious level of "folktale." See also, the interesting contrast between Gunkel's source explanation for the account and Barthes' structural analysis in Greenwood, *Structuralism*, 41–61.

34. J. M. Sasson, *Ruth: A New Translation with a Philological Commentary and a Formalist-Folklorist Interpretation* (Baltimore: John Hopkins University, 1979).

35. R. C. Culley, *Studies in the Structure of Hebrew Narrative* (Philadelphia: Fortress/Missoula: Scholars, 1976).

36. Whereas Propp followed a syntagmatic model of analysis, Lévi-Strauss proposed a paradigmatic model for the study of myth. When the events (plot lines) of variant tellings of a homogeneous corpus are compared, the underlying structure of "myth" can be known. The syntagmatic events are only a manifestation of the underlying schema of what actually constitutes "myth." See R. M. Polzin's analysis of Job, which depends heavily on Lévi-Strauss' structural study of myth (*Biblical Structuralism: Method and Subjectivity in the Study of Ancient Texts*, in Semeia Supplements [Philadelphia: Fortress/Missoula, Mont.: Scholars, 1977], 54–125).

37. E. Leach, "Anthropological Approaches to the Study of the Bible during the Twentieth Century," in *Humanizing America's Iconic Book*, ed. G. Tucker and D. A. Knight (Chico, Calif.: Scholars/Society of Biblical Literature, 1982), 73–94.

Garden of Eden story, and the Cain and Abel story.[38] He explains that myths contain the same recurrent patterns, regardless of their outer trappings, which can be recognized when each tale is superimposed upon another paradigmatically. These mythic structures are best interpreted where they are expressed as contradictions or binary oppositions in a series of paradoxes, such as death/life, static world/moving world, God/man, man/woman. The Genesis myths taken together therefore tell the same story.

There is a flood of structuralist studies in Hebrew narrative. In particular, the experimental journal *Semeia* has devoted several issues to this subject. Among them, for example, is a collection of essays on Genesis 2 and 3, which shows different structuralist approaches to the same passage.[39]

DISCOURSE ANALYSIS

From the 1950s to the 1970s, a holistic method of analysis for conversation (oral text) and written text was developed and continues to be refined today.[40] Discourse analysis as a sub-field of textlinguistics gives attention to the "grammar" of discourse above the sentence level. Just as the syntax of the grammatical sentence has its rules of compositional constraints, whole discourses, at the paragraph level and above, also have their rules. A discourse typology was developed, including hortatory discourse, narrative (story), and exposition discourse, for example. Each discourse has its constituent "grammar." Discursive text involves a hierarchy of components, from the sound, word, phrase, clause, and sentence levels to the discourse level made up of paragraphs. Discourse analysis views texts in terms of their inner-relationships as parts to wholes. It explains how the parts combine to form a stretch of discourse. This enables the analyst to recognize the building blocks of a given discourse.

---

38. E. Leach, *Genesis as Myth and Other Essays* (London: Jonathan Cape, 1969). See also Leach and D. Alan Aycock, *Structuralist Interpretations of Biblical Myth* (Cambridge: Cambridge University Press, 1983).

39. "Genesis 2 and 3: Kaleidoscopic Structural Readings," *Semeia* 18 (1980), which includes articles by Patte, Culley, Jobling, and White. See also "Classical Hebrew Narrative," *Semeia* 3 (1975) and "Perspectives on Old Testament Narrative," *Semeia* 15 (1979). Additionally, see VTSup 22 (1972) and *Int* 28 (1974) for discussion of structuralism and structural exegesis.

40. K. L. Pike, *Language in Relation to a Unified Theory of the Structure of Human Behavior* (reprint; The Hague: Mouton, 1964); T. A. van Dijk, *Some Aspects of Text Grammars* (The Hague: Mouton, 1972); R. A. de Beaugrande and W. Dressler, *Introduction to Text Linguistics* (London: Longman, 1981); R. E. Longacre, *The Grammar of Discourse* (New York: Plenum, 1983).

R. E. Longacre, linguist and literary critic, explains that every discourse, oral or written, has a macrostructure which *drives* the discourse.[41] The macrostructure controls the linear development of a text which provides cohesion and coherence by structural surface devices. Making up the macrostructure are its various constituent parts, such as embedded discourses, paragraphs, clauses, and so forth. But each discourse also has vertical strands running down the discourse which contribute to the cohesion and coherence of the text. These vertical strands are (1) the mainline development of the text, according to its discourse type, and (2) its participant/thematic reference.

The development of a discourse can be traced by recognizing certain junctures where particular grammatical-lexical features at the surface level mark its stages of growth. These surface markers may be, for example, shifts in verbal tenses, incidence of repetition, change in participants, dialogue length, and others. The macrostructure has a structural *"peak(s)"* which is indicated by the surface markers where a "zone of turbulence" occurs. When the peak(s) is plotted with the story's event-line, a profile of the discourse's rise and fall of tension(s) can be drawn.

Longacre has applied his approach to the flood account, to which we give more attention later. His textlinguistic study of the Joseph account is the fullest treatment of his theory to a biblical passage. His results are a complex morphology of paragraphs that provides a diagram of the story's discursive profile. His analysis concludes that the peak climax of the story occurs at Genesis 41 where Joseph ascended the throne in Egypt. The peak denouement is marked at chapters 43—45 where the brothers' confession of sin and Joseph's self-revelation reach the story's resolution.

READER-RESPONSE CRITICISM

Whereas traditional criticism focuses *behind* the text and composition criticism and structuralism *in* the text, reader-response criticism may be said to discover meaning in *front* of the text. For the reader-response critic, reading the Bible "as literature is to retrieve it from the museum, to relate it to the life of contemporary readers."[42] The actualization of literature is

---

41. For an overview of Longacre's method, see his *Joseph: A Story of Divine Providence. A Text Theoretical and Textlinguistic Analysis of Genesis 37 and 39—48* (Winona Lake: Eisenbrauns, 1989). See also "Verb Ranking and the Constituency Structure of Discourse," *JLAS* 4 (1982): 177–202 and "Discourse Peak as Zone of Turbulence," in *Beyond the Sentence*, ed. J. Wirth (Ann Arbor: Karona, 1985), 81–92.

42. E. McKnight, *Post-Modern Use of the Bible: The Emergence of Reader-Oriented Criticism* (Nashville: Abingdon, 1988), 123. McKnight prefers the term "reader-oriented" to describe his approach.

dictated by the interaction between the text and reader. All other readings, such as historical or theological ones, are valid but not complete. Full(er) meaning is possible only when the Bible is read as literature, where the Bible is reimaged by the reader in the sense of the reader's own world.

Reader-response criticism assumes that knowledge is grounded in life. Meaningful knowledge is discovered when the reader's social experience impacts the text so as to make it meaningful to that person. As McKnight contends, "readers make sense" of texts, the world, and themselves.[43] Since the interpretive process includes the reader's own worldview as well as that presupposed by the text, the text becomes infinite in its potentialities for meaning. Paul Ricoeur's hermeneutics of symbolism and phenomenology acknowledges that the text had a meaning for the author and original audience, but once that was experienced, the sense of the text lies beyond it and resides in us as readers "in front of" the text.[44]

All other aspects of literary analysis, such as historical and text-centered readings, are incomplete and subject to the reader-significance reading. McKnight, however, cautions not every reading is valid. There are controls of interpretation in the process, "for systems of interpretation involve components that must be correlated with each other and with the reader—components that are dynamic in themselves as well as parts of a dynamic system."[45] These include an interpretation that is possible, consistent, and satisfying to the reader and his worldview.

Radical reader-response criticism, whose heart is the reader's eyes, invites readers to bring to the text their own ideological nuances. Marxist, feminist, materialist, and liberation readings are among these sociological approaches to the Bible.[46] Exemplary of ideological readings is feminist criticism which reads a biblical account through the lens of gender.[47] E. Schüssler Fiorenza explains the shift from androcentric readings to a feminist hermeneutic: "A feminist critical interpretation of the Bible cannot take as its point of departure the normative authority of the biblical archetype, but must begin with women's experience in their struggle for liberation."[48] The means, then, is to deconstruct the male voice that dominates

---

43. McKnight, *Bible and the Reader*, 12, 133; *Post-Modern*, 176–77.

44. P. Ricoeur, *Essays on Biblical Interpretation*, ed. L. S. Mudge (Philadelphia: Fortress, 1980); see especially Mudge's "Introduction," 16, 25–27.

45. McKnight, *Bible and the Reader*, 133.

46. See N. K. Gottwald, ed., *The Bible and Liberation: Political and Social Hermeneutics* (Maryknoll, N.Y.: Orbis Books, 1983).

47. See A. Bach, ed., *The Pleasure of Her Text: Feminist Readings of Biblical and Historical Texts* (Philadelphia: Trinity Press International, 1990).

48. E. Schüssler Fiorenza, *Bread Not Stone: The Challenge of Feminist Biblical Interpretation* (Boston: Beacon, 1984), 13.

the story and its chauvinist ideology and construct the feminist voice by a retelling of the story.[49]

P. Trible combines her feminist readings with structural exegesis to critique the role of women and men in the Bible.[50] In the account of Ruth, for instance, Naomi and Ruth are engaged in the on-going struggle of women to obtain security in a male-dominated society. Trible concludes, "Ruth and the females of Bethlehem work as paradigms for radicality. All together they are women in culture, women against culture, and women transforming culture. What they reflect, they challenge. And that challenge is a legacy of faith to this day for all who have ears to hear the stories of women in a man's world."[51]

DECONSTRUCTIONISM

Also known as "poststructuralism," this literary analysis has its roots in the philosophy of Jacques Derrida whose theory has resulted in extreme skepticism about the possibility of meaning.[52] The publication of Derrida's *De la grammatologie* in 1967 inaugurated the movement. It has become an important force in literary criticism since the 1980s, but it has had little impact on biblical studies. To understand Derrida's theory, we must recall the long-held opinions of Western society concerning how meaning is achieved in communication.

First, it has been assumed that meaning is grounded in an objective reality which can serve as a basis for communication. This reality is referred to as the "metaphysics of presence." Derrida terms this assumption "logocentric": Original truth is attributed to the *logos*, that is, a word, reason or the Word of God. In logocentricism, *being* is always determined in terms of an entity's *presence*. It is this ontological presence (being) or center that gives the elements of a system its balance and coherence.

Second, Western civilization has accepted that speech (word) is more reliable for discovering and relating meaning than writing since the

---

49. See J. Cherly Exum, "Murder She Wrote: Ideology and the Manipulation of Female Presence in Biblical Narrative," in *The Pleasure of Her Text*, 45–67.

50. See *God and the Rhetoric of Sexuality* (Philadelphia: Fortress, 1978) and *Texts of Terror: Literary Feminist Reading of Biblical Narratives* (Philadelphia: Fortress, 1984).

51. P. Trible, "A Human Comedy: The Book of Ruth," in *Literary Interpretations* 2: 161–90, quote from 190.

52. For this discussion, see V. B. Leitch, *Deconstructive Criticism: An Advanced Introduction* (New York: Columbia University Press, 1983), 24–45, esp. 41–45; McKnight, *Bible and the Reader*, 84–86; Selden, *Contemporary Literary Theory*, 84–89; and Longman, *Literary Approaches*, 41–43.

speaker can exercise greater control. There is created an opposition between the origin (speech) and the manifestation (writing). Logocentricism assumes that these oppositions occur between an origin and its fall, with the first having priority; for example: presence/absence, voice/writing, sound/silence, being/nonbeing, conscious/unconscious, truth/lie, transcendental/empirical, meaning/form, literal/metaphorical, signifier/signified, and so forth.

All literary-critical methods assume this logocentricism, but Derrida challenges the tradition. He argues there is no absolute ground or origin. Every term is itself a product. Derrida exposes the weakness of Saussure's proposition of a gap between the signifier and what is signified in a language system (see structuralism above). Derrida contends that the gap is far less stable than Saussure's system permits. Derrida holds that meaning is not an original presence, rather an *absence* which distinguishes a word. Moreover, a sign always has a dependence on a prior context or differentiation in a speech act. Writing, Derrida argues, is prior to speech. Thus, there is no original *logos*, and there is left a perpetual instability or distancing between the signifier and the signified. The oppositions created in this system are inverted, e.g., absence/presence, nonbeing/being, signified/signifier, metaphor/literal.

Derrida invents the term *différance* as a concept to reveal the slippage between signifier and the signified. *Différance* has three significations: (1) to differ (to be unlike, dissimilar); (2) *differre* from Latin (to scatter, disperse) and (3) to defer (delay, postpone). In French the *a* in *différance* (to defer) is silent; the word sounds like *différence* (to differ). This distinction is perceived only in writing. "Differ" is spatial distinction and indicates the sign arises in terms of its differences or spaces (absence!) within the system. The "defer" is a temporal distinction, and the sign perpetually postpones *presence*. *Différance* for Derrida is not just a word or concept, a force or event; it can be conceptualized as "the structured and differing 'origin' of difference."[53] An example is the sign "chair" which brings to mind (consciousness) the idea of a chair (signified), but the real chair is not actually present. The sign is employed, but we delay or postpone producing the actual referent. In other words, the sign "chair" marks an "absent present." Both *différance* (delay) and difference between sign and referent disrupt logocentricism's center of *presence*. It is not actual presence but metaphor or delusion.

When applied to literary analysis, deconstructionists explain how the text subverts or deconstructs itself. J. Culler comments,

---

53. Leitch, *Deconstructive Criticism*, 43.

... to deconstruct a discourse is to show how it undermines the philosophy it asserts, or the hierarchical oppositions on which it relies, by identifying in the text the rhetorical operations that produce the supposed ground of argument, the key concept or promise.[54]

The text does not have a meaning as a reference to something that is signified; the text is an infinite "play of signifiers" that is brought about by the contingencies of language. For the deconstructionist, meaning is not in the author, the textual artifact, the deep structure, or the reader. There can be no determinative judge or arbiter of meaning, for that, too, is subject to deconstruction; the text is metaphor or pun. The critic "plays with the text" as an exercise of criticism for its own aesthetic sake.[55]

This kind of radical skepticism has hindered deconstructionism's influence among biblical scholars. P. D. Miscall is an Old Testament scholar who has read Genesis 12 and 1 Samuel 16—22 from a deconstructionist perspective. His "close reading" of the text exposes what he believes are the ambiguities, ambivalences, and gaps of the narrative. He concludes that no consistent reading is possible for the characters Abraham or David. He reads the text as "decidedly undecidable," which means there is no determinative meaning, whether it be authorial, phenomenological, structuralist, or existentialist. The indeterminateness of the text prevents a definitive reading and a coherent one; there can be no historical or theological or ideological meaning.[56]

CANON CRITICISM

We turn now to a criticism which is better known among biblical scholars because it was introduced by one of its own members and is uniquely suited to biblical studies. Canon criticism can be better apprehended by the student in light of what we have discovered up to this point since it shares features of the literary approaches.

The seminal work of canon criticism is B. S. Childs' *Biblical Theology in Crisis*, which outlined a new direction in biblical interpretation.[57] His contention was that the development of historical-critical methods had created a crisis in the possibility of doing biblical theology. He set forth a new

---

54. J. Culler, *On Deconstruction: Theory and Criticism After Structuralism* (London: Routledge and Kegan, Paul, 1982), 86.

55. See P. D. Jubl, "Playing with Texts: Can Deconstruction Account for Critical Practice?" in *Criticism and Critical Theory*, 59–72.

56. P. D. Miscall, *The Working of Old Testament Narrative* (Philadelphia: Fortress/Chico, Calif.: Scholars, 1983), 140; See also, his *1 Samuel: A Literary Reading* (Bloomington: Indiana University Press, 1986).

57. B. S. Childs, *Biblical Theology in Crisis* (Philadelphia: Fortress, 1970).

agenda to save the discipline of biblical theology by giving it a new basis. This new beginning point is the extant canon which functions as the normative expression of religious faith by the believing communities of Judaism and Christianity. The proper stance of the critic toward the Bible, contends Childs, is a person of faith within the community who views the text as "Scripture." Thus, Childs' *Introduction* focuses on the text in its final form as a fixed religious canon.[58] As "religious" texts they are only properly interpreted when related to the fuller affirmations espoused by synagogue and church. In other words, the present canonical shape provides the interpretive framework for the expositor's reading.

Childs acknowledges his criticism shares with the synchronic literary approaches whose emphasis is the integrity of the text. Yet he insists canon criticism differs from such studies by its relating the text to a community of faith. Canon criticism is driven by theology, he says, not literary categories for their own sake. Approaching the text as "Scripture" gives the text its referential orientation in the roots of historic Israel whereas synchronic studies view the Bible as non-referential. Nevertheless, Childs speaks of canonical context in the sense of its literary context, not its historical.

Childs distances his analysis from historical-critical methods by insisting that only the canon, that is, the final form and arrangement of the biblical texts, can serve functionally as a hermeneutical norm. He opposes the fragmentation of the text as typically achieved by historical criticism. Childs does not deny the efficacy of historical-critical methods when it comes to answering historical questions, but he believes such methods cannot provide an adequate basis for doing theology. In his opinion, the failure of historical criticism is its restriction of textual meaning to the past.[59]

A rival voice within this movement is J. A. Sanders whose work has much in common with Childs but which differs at significant points.[60] Sanders agrees that historical criticism effectively cut the Bible off from the very communities that revered it. He comments, "For some the Bible has become a sort of archaeological tell which only experts can dig."[61] He

---

58. B. S. Childs, *Introduction to the Old Testament as Scripture* (Philadelphia: Fortress, 1979).

59. Childs, *Introduction*, 73–83. The practical outworking of Childs' canon approach is illustrated in his *The Book of Exodus: A Critical, Theological Commentary* in OTL (Philadelphia: Westminster, 1974).

60. See his review of Childs in "Canonical Context and Canonical Criticism," *HBT* 2 (1980): 173–97; reprinted in *From Sacred Story to Sacred Text* (Philadelphia: Fortress, 1987), 153–74. See also his *Torah and Canon* (Philadelphia: Fortress, 1972).

61. J. A. Sanders, *Canon and Community: A Guide to Canonical Criticism* (Philadelphia: Fortress, 1984), 5.

adds that the old criticism assumed that the original meaning of the text alone had a valid meaning worthy of "scientific" study. Consequently, such interpreters gave the original context, as reconstructed by form criticism, the only authoritative meaning. This false notion of authority encouraged a deconstruction of the canon where the layers of canonical shaping given by the faith communities were systematically stripped away. Sanders also agrees with Childs that an adequate hermeneutic requires relating the literature to the historic communities of faith. Thus, they concur that the concept of canon is not merely the closure of a sacred list but how the canon functioned within community.

Sanders, unlike Childs, sees canon criticism as a natural extension of the historical-critical methods. Canon as a process for Childs is limited to the period once the text was stabilized. Sanders believes that the proper canonical context is not solely the final form of the text but also includes the prior successive stages of the canonical process in its historical development. Sanders disagrees with Childs that there is one canon, but rather he contends for many canons.

Historical tools, therefore, are needed to isolate the various stages of canonical development, tracing the function of those traditions that finally reside in the extant canon. For this reason Sanders insists on the terminology "canonical" criticism, as opposed to canon criticism, because he believes that the canonical process is a continuum operating along the same dynamics whether in the past (intrabiblical) or among the Jewish and Christian community life settings today. He sees canonical shaping reaching beyond the stabilization of the text, for he believes that the on-going history of hermeneutics continues along the same basic tenets as the canonical processes in antiquity.

Both Childs and Sanders make it clear their call for canon or canonical criticism is not a return to precritical traditionalism. Their work presupposes the advances of historical-critical studies, particularly the work of Sanders. Canon criticism does not provide solace for "fundamentalism." Childs does not encourage the precritical practices of allegory or harmonization practiced by the church fathers and reformers. Unlike evangelical scholarship, he admits the canon possesses theological and historical disagreements, but unlike historical critics he seeks to discover a coherent meaning within the parameters of the community's vision of the whole. He shows how the church successfully read the Bible despite its incongruities.[62]

Evangelical scholars can applaud some consequences of Childs' and Sanders' efforts. (1) The correction of historical criticism, that is, its "decan-

---

62. See Barton, *Reading the Old Testament*, 85–86.

onizing" of the text, is long overdue. (2) Childs' affirmation that the text is Scripture which can be and should be read as a cohesive whole is refreshing among critical scholars. (3) Childs acknowledges that the extant text provides the normative reading for understanding the text as opposed to the historical critic's specious "original" meaning. (4) The canonical method encourages evangelical scholars to look at passages in their whole biblical context, permitting them to impact and be impacted by the whole. The evangelical approach to canon understands the Hebrew Bible as "Old Testament," which affirms the genetic relationship between the Old and New.

Where canon criticism fails is its continued dependence on historical-critical conclusions, though it curbs its excesses. Also, the opinion that the original meaning of a passage has been significantly altered in the development of the canon is unfounded. Rather, the canonical shaping of a passage unveils the already-present meaning (latent) which is clarified and deepened by the intrabiblical commentary.[63]

QUESTIONING MODERN LITERARY THEORIES

Like any movement among biblical scholars, the expositor must carefully weigh the role of literary studies to discover those elements that might be helpful while discarding those approaches that are detrimental.[64] Our evaluation at this point will address those problems that the modern movement of literary theory pose for the biblical expositor.

QUESTION OF THEORY

Literary studies of the Bible are tied to literary-critical theories that may not be appropriate for ancient Hebrew literature. These theories are derived from continental studies based on modern literature. A clear example of this is the work by Sasson who applies Propp's structuralism to the story of Ruth. What relationship does Russian folktale have for a Hebrew account of the first millennium?

QUESTION OF HISTORY

The most damaging feature of modern literary approaches is their neglect, if not rejection, of history. As indicated earlier, some practitioners

---

63. See B. K. Waltke, "A Canonical Approach to the Psalms," in *Tradition and Testament: Essays in Honor of Charles Lee Feinberg*, ed. J. S. Feinberg and P. D. Feinberg (Chicago: Moody, 1981), 3–18.

64. For an assessment of the literary approaches from an evangelical perspective, see Longman, *Literary Approaches*, 47–64; for a traditional historical-critical scholar's critique, see also Geller, "Through Windows and Mirrors," 3–40.

are responding to this criticism by calling for a hermeneutic in which both diachronic and synchronic models are used. Since the biblical message and claim are anchored in historical event, it is inappropriate to study the text exclusively from a synchronic view.

This distancing between the author and text has redefined what communication is and how meaning can be obtained. While it is true much of the Old Testament is anonymous, there remain substantial portions of the Bible rooted in the experience of its authors, such as Moses for the Pentateuch, David for the Psalms, and the whole prophetic corpus.

Also, much of today's literary criticism is reader-response interpretations whose ideological readings are at odds with the biblical tradition. The locus of meaning shifts away from an authoritative text to the authority of the reader. Polyvalence invites relativism and leaves us with a Bible without an authoritative reading and one that is cut off from history's moorings. Instead of being judged by the text, ideological readings sit in judgment over the text. Moreover, the biblical authors have an ideological agenda of their own and require the interpreter to accept their ideological point of view as authoritative.

QUESTION OF REALITY

It is the contention of much literary criticism that the literature itself is sufficient for study. As an autonomous entity, it is viewed as unrelated to an objective base of reality. Thus, it is not perceived as relating historical realities and therefore is only a representation of reality. As an outcome of this, the text becomes no more than an extended metaphor or pun. It is not a source of discursive information. Therefore, the Bible has no value for discovering God and His work in history. The extreme skepticism of deconstructionists, for example, results in the Bible becoming the critic's playbox of ideas.

USING LITERARY ANALYSIS FOR HOLISTIC EXPOSITION

We have made it clear there are dangers in an uncritical use of modern literary models; however, cautious and thoughtful appropriation of certain features of literary analyses may be helpful to the expositor's work. The positive helps of literary approaches in general are stated here:

First, literary criticism reminds the biblical expositor that the Bible has a literary aspect which must be respected if Scripture is to be interpreted fully. Biblical interpreters must permit the text not only to say what it wants to impart but also how it wants to convey it. Understanding the formal features of biblical literature gives the expositor additional tools for controlling the message of the text.

Second, literary criticism places the proper emphasis on Scripture in its extant, final form. Too much interpretation, whether it is the precritical allegory of Origen or the form criticism of Gunkel, has sought to rewrite the biblical text. Many of the excesses of historical criticism have been rightly called into question, particularly the splintering of the text.

Third, biblical scholars are respecting the text in terms of its holistic configuration and as a cohesive unity. The renewed appreciation for the integrity of the text has been one important consequence of literary studies. At the exegetical level, students are studying the text beyond the word and phrase levels to the paragraph and discourse levels. Particularly helpful has been the work of structural exegesis, such as narratology and discourse analysis, which gives the expositor an added tool which is based on linguistic advances.

Fourth, literary theorists have reminded expositors that no one reads the Bible free from contextualization. For communication to occur, there must be sufficient analogy between the text and the experience of the reader for understanding. While meaning is not located foremostly in the reader's experience, the text is impacted by the reader. At least, awareness of this influence forewarns the expositor to guard against reader-influenced excesses.

LITERARY APPROACHES AND THE FLOOD NARRATIVE (GEN. 6—9)

To illustrate the positive effects of literary theory on biblical exegesis, we will see how literary studies have influenced recent views of the flood account (Gen. 6—9). This passage is a celebrative example of the source-critical method. Almost universally, the passage is dissected into two roughly parallel accounts which underlie the present form of the text: the J(ehovah) account of the tenth century B.C. and the later exilic version, known as the P(riestly). As it stands, the passage is deemed by source critics as a hodgepodge of duplicate and contradictory viewpoints.

J. Skinner in the *International Critical Commentary* on Genesis, a commentary series methodologically based on the source-critical approach, remarked that the flood narrative "is justly reckoned amongst the most brilliant achievements of purely literary criticism, and affords a particularly instructive lesson in the art of documentary analysis."[65] Skinner, typical of the approach, reviews the four criteria for discerning the two accounts: (1) the linguistic (e.g., J has "Yahweh" and P has "Elohim"); (2)

---

65. J. Skinner, *Genesis*, in ICC (Edinburgh: T. & T. Clark, 1910), 147–48.

diversity of representation (e.g., J has clean [seven pair] and unclean [one pair] animals, while P has only pairs without distinction); (3) duplicates (e.g., the occasion for the flood, 6:6–8 and 6:11–13); and (4) theological perspective (J is picturesque and has anthropomorphisms, and P is formal and abstract). After distinguishing the literary pieces, he proceeds to his exegesis where he treats the J and P accounts independently so as to create two different portraits of the event, each having a different message for its different religious times.

Recent studies using literary approaches, however, have challenged the source opinion while at the same time opening the passage to greater exegetical precision.[66] Working independently and employing different literary techniques, G. Wenham and B. W. Anderson concurred that, as it stands, the flood account is a literary whole arranged chiastically. Both also agreed that the literary center of the narrative is 8:1.[67] Anderson charts the chiastic unity:

Transitional introduction (6:9–10)

  1.Violence in God's creation (6:11–12)

    2.First divine address: resolution to destroy (6:13–22)

      3.Second divine address: command to enter the ark (7:1–10)

        4.Beginning of the flood (7:11–16)

          5.The rising flood waters (7:17–24)

          GOD'S REMEMBRANCE OF NOAH

        6.The receding flood waters (8:1–5)

        7.The drying of the earth (8:6–14)

      8.Third divine address: command to leave the ark (8:15–19)

    9.God's resolution to preserve order (8:20–22)

  10.Fourth divine address: covenant blessing and peace (9:1–17)

Transitional conclusion (9:18–19)

---

66. For an example of how rhetorical studies of the flood account are now used to contest the two-source explanation, see I. Kikawada and A. Quinn, *Before Abraham Was* (Nashville: Abingdon, 1985) and D. Garrett, *Rethinking Genesis: The Sources and Authorship of the First Book of the Pentateuch* (Grand Rapids: Baker, 1991), 13–33.

67. G. Wenham, "The Coherence of the Flood Narrative," *VT* 28 (1978): 336–48; B. W. Anderson, "From Analysis to Synthesis: The Interpretation of Genesis 1—11," *JBL* 97 (1978): 234–39.

Anderson, although still working within the old paradigm of two literary traditions, admits this alternative analysis (synchronic) reveals Genesis 6—9 to be a unified literary art, not a mere patchwork of sources.[68] Wenham's examination further demonstrates the balance of the structure by listing parallel terms in the first and second halves; this is particularly well illustrated by the references to the number of days.[69]

7 days of waiting for flood (7:4)

    7 days of waiting for flood (7:10)

        40 days of flood (7:17a)

            150 days of water triumphing (7:24)

            150 days of water waning (8:3)

        40 days' wait (8:6)

    7 days' wait (8:10)

7 days' wait (8:12)

The effect of the chiastic arrangement of the narrative is that it reinforces the content of the account, which describes the floodwaters rising and then receding. At the same time the chiasm marks out the "hinge" verse of 8:1, which explains the turn of events. Wenham concludes that though the unity and coherence of the account can be attributed to a late redaction of two sources, he opts for the simpler hypothesis of one account that has been supplemented by a later hand.[70]

The linguistic-based analysis of R. E. Longacre takes a different tack.[71] He demonstrates through his discourse analysis that the macrostructure of the narrative is triple. For him this explains the numerous peculiarities of the text, such as its repetitions. The trifold structure is (1) God's instructions to Noah to embark in an ark to preserve his life, (2) a destructive flood, and (3) God's covenant with Noah and the other survivors. Longacre's approach isolates the event-line narrative, the "backbone" of the story, from the supportive narrative. His study of the discourse's stylistics leads him to the "peak" of the account by discerning its peculiar rhetorical features. The peak, according to Longacre, is 7:17–24, which gives the story's climax. This passage describes the waters reach-

---

68. Anderson, "From Analysis to Synthesis," 38.

69. G. Wenham, *Genesis 1—15* in WBC 1 (Waco, Tex.: Word, 1987), 156–57.

70. Wenham, "Coherence," 347–48.

71. R. E. Longacre, "The Discourse Structure of the Flood Narrative," *JAAR* (1979): Supp. B:89–133.

ing their height and prevailing over the earth. The peak's denouement or resolution is 9:1–17 in which God promises never again to send another destructive flood. He comments, "The application of contemporary discourse analysis to this portion of Genesis reveals a story elegantly structured with marked cohesion and highlighting in its various parts."[72] Longacre concludes that such a carefully crafted piece commends the view that it is an originally unified work whose sources cannot be recovered by modern efforts.

FOR FURTHER READING

Abrams, M. H. *A Glossary of Literary Terms*. 4th ed. New York: Holt, Rinehart, and Winston, 1981.

Alter, Robert. *The Art of Biblical Narrative* and *The Art of Biblical Poetry*. New York: Basic Books, 1981 and 1985.

Barton, John. *Reading the Old Testament: Method in Biblical Study*. Philadelphia: Westminster, 1984.

Berlin, A. *Poetics and Interpretation of Biblical Narrative*. Sheffield: Almond, 1983.

Culley, R. C. "Exploring New Directions." In *The Hebrew Bible and Its Modern Interpreters*, edited by D. Knight and G. Tucker. Philadelphia: Fortress/Chico, Calif.: Scholars, 1985.

Greenwood, D. C. *Structuralism and the Biblical Text*. Berlin: Mouton, 1985.

Longacre, R. E. *Joseph, A Story of Divine Providence: A Text Theoretical and Textlinguistic Analysis of Genesis 37 and 39—48*. Winona Lake: Eisenbrauns, 1989.

Longman, Tremper. *Literary Approaches to Biblical Interpretation*. Grand Rapids: Zondervan/Academie, 1987.

Powell, Mark A. *The Bible and Modern Literary Criticism: A Critical Assessment and Annotated Bibliography*. New York: Greenwood Press, 1992.

Ryken, Leland. *Words of Delight: A Literary Introduction to the Bible*. Grand Rapids: Baker, 1987.

---

72. Ibid., 129.

XII

HISTORY AND CHRONOLOGY
OF THE OLD TESTAMENT

Read on
4 May 02

DONALD L. FOWLER

The words "history" and "chronology" initially prompt thoughts of dates and numbers and their intercalation of calendar placement. Those who are interested in OT history and chronology, identifying the date for creation, the birth of Abraham, the dates of the exodus and conquest, or precise integration of the monarchical period with its world (who was the Pharaoh who gave his daughter in marriage to Solomon?) will likely be dissatisfied with the biblical text's ability to answer such questions. For example, "Pharaoh" appears some 180 times in the Pentateuch without any specific identification. While a servant of Pharaoh, Potiphar, is named, the Egyptian princess who rescued Moses from the river is simply called "Pharaoh's daughter." This kind of ambiguity in areas that are vital to our way of doing history is, however, typical of the biblical text.

Failing to recognize ambiguity of Hebrew historiography led Bishop Ussher to arrive at a fixed date for the creation—the evening of October 22, 4004 B.C. At the other extreme, a contemporary response to these historical omissions has been, all too often, doubt and skepticism—the story is not factual or historical. This is unfortunate since much of the misunderstanding centers around the failure to understand the "way" history is done in the OT.

MATHEMATICS AND METHOD

UNDERSTANDING HISTORIOGRAPHY

Western history is characterized by impartiality on the part of the writer and an exhaustive and chronological presentation of the data. Such an approach to biblical history is methodologically unworkable.

A primary feature of OT history is that it is theological history. Consequently, the meaning of the event supersedes the need to explain the event in complete detail. In short, it is an interpretation of the events of the OT from God's perspective and for His purposes. Since the interpretation is from the One who guides all events, it is characteristically partial. The goal of the text is to show what God is doing in the events of history. For this reason, it is characteristic that evaluating a king as good or bad was more important than chronicling all the events of his reign. Thus, only a few verses recorded the means by which David conquered his empire, but seven chapters (2 Sam. 13—19) described the tragic events of David and Absalom. Similarly, despite the fact Ahab was a major player in the ancient world, the text ignored those events completely and focused on his struggle with Elijah and the ramifications of his marriage to Jezebel.

This unique view of history resulted in a text that recorded not only what history meant but also where history was going. At all times, the text moved the reader to see the specific direction of events shaped by the sovereign God. Since the OT basically is a book of promise, the historical events are to be understood as lessons from God demonstrating either His blessing or judgment. This idea may be seen clearly in the terms of the covenant where God set forth His stipulations in Deuteronomy 27—28 to the members of the covenant. But this is not a static, endless record of blessings and curses. Rather, there is a specific goal (*telos*) to the OT story. God's faithfulness is framed with Israel's failure to show the nature of His judgment (exile) and His mercy (return) and the complete fulfillment of His promises to Israel through His Messiah. Israel's history is, therefore, a study of God's movement in the events of the OT toward a great climactic day, the day of the Lord, when God would judge both His covenant people (Amos 5:18–20) and the nations (Zeph. 3:8) and pour out His blessings on both (Zeph. 3:9).[1] In this sense, the entire OT story could be con-

---

1. Simon John DeVries, *Yesterday, Today and Tomorrow: Time and History in the Old Testament* (Grand Rapids: Eerdmans, 1975).

233

> God's answers are often not what we expected, but always better.

densed to the formula "now . . . not yet . . . but near." "Now" is the study of what God has done is history. "Not yet" captures the idea of coming judgment and blessing. "Near" is a reminder to the reader of any era that God acted decisively in the past and He is acting in the "tomorrows" of human experience.

INTERFACING CHRONOLOGY

In light of this unique kind of historiography, it is not surprising that the study of OT chronology has resulted in widely varying conclusions. Such diversity is not because the text is inaccurate; rather, it is incomplete. If the exodus was the most important demonstration of God's deliverance in the OT, it would seem crucial to modern readers to approach the event from an integrative historical perspective. When did it occur and who were the participants and how are those answers to be used to write a history of Israel?

The heart of the discussion centers around interpreting 1 Kings 6:1 where the text says that Solomon's fourth year of rule was the 480th since the Israelites had left Egypt.[2] If Solomon took the throne about 970 B.C. and 480 years is added to his fourth year (966 B.C.), the date for the Exodus should have been 1446 B.C. This important reference is buttressed with Jepthah's claim (Judg. 11:26) in his dispute with the Ammonites that Israel had already been in Canaan for three hundred years. This reference would also seem to indicate a fifteenth-century date.

Against this, however, many have said that the 480 years of 1 Kings 6:1 is not a purely mathematical number but is representative or symbolic. The idea is that it represented twelve generations, thus 12 x 40 = 480. Since a generation more likely equalled twenty-five years the mathematical value would have been more like three hundred years, that is, in the middle of the thirteenth century B.C.

At first glance, the reader might be surprised to see numbers used symbolically. Indeed, such an understanding awaited the arrival of nineteenth-century biblical scholars. Symbolic interpretation is the result of the need to integrate the archaeological materials unearthed in recent history with ancient biblical text. Simply put, while there is very little archaeological evidence of Israel's entry to Canaan that supports the fifteenth century B.C. early date view, there is abundant evidence of massive destruction in the thirteenth century B.C. that supports the late date view. There are, of course, arguments for the thirteenth century late date of the exodus such as Exodus 1:11, which mentions the Israelites building the store cities of

---

2. Andrew E. Hill and John H. Walton, *A Survey of the Old Testament* (Grand Rapids: Zondervan, 1991), 107–9.

Pithom and Rameses (Rameses II of the nineteenth dynasty). At its core, however, the issue boils down to text versus archaeology. It is unsettling to the serious interpreter to make conclusions on inclusive data. When 1 Kings 6:1 and Judges 11:26 are seen together, however, they may tip the scale in favor of a literal 480 years.

Even if a decisive date for the exodus could be determined, there still would be difficulty with chronology. There is some debate, for example, over the time period of the bondage. This question seems to center around the Septuagint's (LXX) rendering of Exodus 12:40, as opposed to that of the Massoretic Text (MT). The following graph illustrates how the dates diverge.

	Massoretic Text *966 B.C.	Septuagint Text *966 B.C.
1 Kings 6:1	480 years	480 years
The exodus	1446 B.C.	1446 B.C.
Bondage	430 years	215 years
Exodus 12:40		
	1877 B.C.	1662 B.C.
Abraham came to the land	215 years	215 years
	2092 B.C.	1877 B.C.

966 B.C. was the fourth year of Solomon's rule

It would seem unnecessary to take the prediction of Genesis 15:13 about enslavement for four hundred years as a period (as LXX does) including the years in Palestine. Thus, if the Massoretic Text is correct in its use of numbers, Abraham would have been born in 2166 B.C. and come to Palestine about 2092 B.C. His descendants would have gone to Egypt about 1877 B.C., where they were in bondage until 1446 B.C.

To integrate biblical history precisely into its world, go to the period of the monarchy. The mention of Ahab as a participant of the great battle of Qarqar in 853 B.C. by Shalmaneser III provides an important date for beginning intercalation of biblical events and the surrounding countries. Therefore, chronological accuracy is generally attainable throughout the period of the monarchy. Because of the phenomena of co-regencies, differing calendars and calculating systems, internal adjustments in the years of some kings are necessary.[3] For the most part, however, the chronology of the monarchical period can be brought under control.

CREATION AND COVENANT

The Book of Genesis is the masterpiece of Hebrew narrative with its tightly bound structure and linear movement of story made possible by subtle interweaving of theme development and carefully devised literary techniques. It may be thought of as the introduction to the rest of Scripture. Two subjects, creation and covenant, structure the contents of the book itself (chaps. 1—11 and 12—50) and provide a theological matrix for unfolding the divine plan.

CREATION

The point of the text will be, in some ways, missed if Genesis 1—11 are not seen as a unit. While the creation account in 1—2 should be studied in its own right, it will be helpful to understand it as it fits the larger literary unit.

In the present debate over creationism and alternate theories, it is easy to lose the perspective of what the text might have been emphasizing. The New International Version is correct in arranging the text of Genesis 1 as poetry or elevated prose. This poetic format actually emphasizes the fact that Israel's Creator God is Lord over all the earth and its peoples. It is this universalism that dominates chapters 1—11 and contrasts with the particularism of 12—50. God's statement at the end of creation week, "it was very good,"* is a commentary on the Creator as well as creation. In characteristic narrative style, chapter 2 repeated the basic idea of creation while emphasizing the Garden, the creation of Eve and the ominous warning about the "tree of the knowledge of good and evil" (v. 17). The description that Adam and Eve were naked (ʿărûmmîm, 2:25) but not ashamed connects this chapter to 3:1 where the serpent was craftier (ʿārûm) than all other creatures. Utilizing this word play, the author drew attention to two themes of the fall: the deadly knowledge (craftiness) of Satan and Adam and Eve's loss of nakedness (innocence). The curses aptly

---

3. Edwin R. Thiele, *The Mysterious Numbers of the Hebrew Kings* (Grand Rapids: Zondervan, 1983). His dates are followed throughout this article.

* Unless otherwise stated, Scripture quotations in this chapter are from the NIV.

depicted the present condition of humankind, Satan, and the earth which flowed naturally from the idea of covenant.

The twice-repeated command, "be fruitful and increase in number," provides the theme of chapter 4 as the couple conceives three times. Again, the divine plan was seemingly thwarted as first Cain and then Lamech took life. Violence and marital excess (Gen. 4:19; 6:2) struck at the heart of God's plan so that the divine response was "de-creation," the destruction of the earth and all on it. Solidarity between humankind (ʿādām) and earth (ʿădāmâ) was an important theme represented repeatedly in following covenants. Most importantly, opposition to the divine plan, whether by Satan or fallen humans, became the paradigm for all subsequent history. Similarly, though the whole world rage against God and His plan, He works through His chosen, be that Noah or "the remnant."

A partial explanation for the great detail in which the flood account was narrated was to draw attention to the absolute control of this Creator God over His creation. The escalating violence of Lamech's boast in his poem found its dramatic counterpart in the promise "never again" (8:21) by the One who alone has the power to wreck violence on a global scale.

God's re-creational command to Noah and his sons, "Be fruitful and increase in number and fill the earth" (9:1), was identical to that given to Adam and Eve. The new pair was now a new family through whom the Creator God worked His plan. A new kind of nakedness seemed to thwart the family when Canaan "saw" (the same verb in 3:6 where Eve saw the fruit) his father naked. Again, sin brought a curse, but this time from Noah against his own son (9:25).

The genealogical passages are strategically located. Chapter 5 was situated to show the reader that while God had blessed and people had multiplied, instead the earth was "full of violence" (6:11). Then, in chapter 10, the whole earth was repopulated through the three sons of Noah whose son, Shem, and his line (from whom Abraham came) closed the chapter (10:21–31). This line was then expanded in 11:10–32 to include Abraham's father, Terah, and to introduce the new, divinely chosen couple, Abraham and Sarah.

Humanity's attempt to build a tower that "reaches to the heavens, so that we make a name for ourselves and not be scattered over the face of the whole earth" (11:4) was open rebellion against divine rule. God explicitly told Adam and Eve "to fill the earth" (1:28) and repeated it to Noah (9:1, 7). Thus, the sin was not just the tower but also the intent behind its construction, namely, to fortify so as to oppose God's command. This resulted in the scattering of the people "over all the earth" (11:8) and the abandonment of the city named Babel (a pun on the name Babylon, symbol of evil in both testaments).

Thus, in this compact and incredibly powerful unit is concentrated the stuff of all subsequent history. Perhaps the idea can be grasped by thinking of the word "authority." It is in these early chapters (1—11) that authority was established because God created and commanded. Authority was vested as God told Adam and Eve to rule the earth and its creatures. Authority was abused, first by Adam and Eve and then in escalating fashion by Cain, Lamech, and all humankind (chap. 6). Even after the Flood, initial abuse of power was seen in Canaan's behavior in his father's tent and then climaxed in the open rebellion of all humankind in the city (chap. 11). The consistent message of the abuse of authority was that God would certainly judge those who (being made in His image) violated this divinely instituted order.

COVENANT

While the emphasis in Genesis 1—11 was to show God acting on a global scale, the remainder of the book emphasized God's covenant acts within a particular setting: among Abraham and his descendants. The idea of covenant had been stated explicitly in Genesis 9 with Noah and was implied in God's initial relationship with Adam and Eve: granting land, giving commands, and setting forth stipulations.

While the etymology of "covenant" continues to be debated, it can be defined in its simplest form as "a general obligation concerning two parties."[4] A covenant could be secular (between two people) or sacred (between God and the person He chose). It could be confirmed by an oath (Gen. 21:22–24), a solemn meal (Ex. 24:11), sacrifices (Ex. 24:4–8), or some other act such as dividing an animal in two and passing between its parts (Gen. 15:9–21).

Attempts to compare the form of OT covenants with ancient Near Eastern contracts, suzerainty treaties, or Babylonian boundary stone inscriptions have failed to win a consensus view. There now seems to be a return to the liberal-critical view of nineteenth-century biblical scholars who perceived the idea of covenant as something invented in the period of the exile. If the form of covenant cannot be successfully interfaced with ancient Near Eastern examples, the idea of covenant is nonetheless a primary vehicle for expressing religious thought in both testaments.

The Abrahamic covenant is characterized by four important features: (1) it was sovereignly instituted (chap. 12); (2) promissory in character (land and progeny); (3) confirmed with a sacred oath (chap. 15); and (4) sealed with a sign (circumcision, 17:9–14). The remainder of the book was modeled upon Abraham and his descendants' response to these features.

---

4. *EncJud* 5, s.v. "covenant."

"Abram believed the LORD, and he credited it to him as righteousness" (15:6).

The remaining patriarchal stories, on the surface, read as if they were simply registering the familial vagaries of Abraham's immediate descendants. The drama surrounding the heir apparent (primogeniture) that dominated the subsequent chapters belies vagary. Abraham's God was blessing and leading the family of seventy to the land where they would reside for the next four centuries (15:13–14). It was no accident, therefore, that the book ended with the death of Joseph in Egypt. So certain was the theme of divine control (45:4–8) that it comforted Joseph before his death and climaxed the book in 50:20: "You intended to harm me, but God intended it for good to accomplish what is now being done, the saving of many lives." That Joseph's last concern was that he would be reinterred in the promised land serves as a fit commentary on his faith in the God of the covenant.

THE COVENANT/PROMISE IS KEPT: EXODUS—JOSHUA

There are numerous ways to approach the text legitimately. This section of Scripture brings together the two great promises to Abraham: progeny and land. Since the promise was made in the form of a covenant, this will be the organizing theme for this section.

EXODUS

While the events described in the Book of Exodus are among the best known to Bible students, the meaning of the events is less transparent. The book's first words, "These are the names . . ." effectively set the stage for the fulfillment of the promise to Abraham about progeny (Gen. 15:4). For example, in Exodus 1:7 three of the verbs are the same as those in God's command in Genesis 1:28. Furthermore, God's order to "fill up the land" was completed in the phrase, "the land was filled with them." It was precisely this fulfillment that resulted in a new, unique claimant to power: Pharaoh, god incarnate (in Egyptian theology).Chapters 1—19 reflect the central theme of power as claimed by Israel's God through Moses and the opposition of the gods of Egypt as embodied in the head of the pantheon, Pharaoh, the incarnate Amun-Re.

Israel's God was obliged by covenant to hear their cries (2:23–25; 3:7–8) and bring them to the land He promised. The resultant ten plagues were artfully arranged in groups of three so that the tenth was highlighted. The first struck at the very lifeblood of Egypt, the Nile, which also was the deity Nun, god of the primeval water. The last, falling of the firstborn, demonstrated that just as God gave the firstborn throughout Genesis, so He could take the firstborn of the disobedient in Egypt.

Perhaps the main theme of Exodus is that Israel's God was now present with them. This is seen in the revelation of the name Yahweh (I AM = I will be with you, as in 3:12), the descent to Mount Sinai in chapter 19 and the threat to withdraw presence after the golden calf (see chaps. 33—34). Thus, when Yahweh is present (chap. 19), Law is given (chaps. 20—24), and He orders a tabernacle built (25:8–9) so that "I will dwell among them." From 25:10—31:18 instructions about the tabernacle religious rites and civil laws were given and were immediately followed (chap. 32) by the violation of the first commandment, "You shall have no other gods before me." Following the punishment and Moses' remarkable intercession, Yahweh reveals Himself to Moses in a stunning display of glory (34:4–8). The remainder of Exodus centered on the giving of Law, primarily highlighting the tabernacle.

It would be difficult to exaggerate the importance of the Law (Torah) in the history of Israel. If Covenant was the vehicle for God's movement in history, Torah was the engine. It was the evidence of His grace and the standard to which all must conform.

LEVITICUS — relationship w/ God

Seen in this light, the laws in Leviticus centered around explaining how this new relationship between God and His people was to function. While the book appeared to be concerned with priestly functions ("priest" occurs 730 times and "Levite/Levites" 290 times), it is the relationship with Yahweh that was at the heart of Leviticus's message. This is captured in the first command to Moses in 1:1–3 where the Israelite is told to bring his offering "to the LORD," that is, into the presence of the Lord. As a "kingdom of priests" (Ex. 19:6), each worshiper had direct access to the presence of the God of the covenant. This great privilege was made possible by a divinely ordered program that was to be kept meticulously.

NUMBERS

The Hebrew title of Numbers, "In the wilderness of Sinai," better captures its contents. Its primary historical contribution is that it tells about the thirty-eight-year and nine-month period from leaving Sinai to the start of the Book of Deuteronomy. While its contents are somewhat miscellaneous, Numbers gives the reason why the Israelites had to die in the wilderness (chap. 14): because they proposed returning to Egypt, thereby rejecting Yahweh and His authority vested in Moses.

The pervasive theme of divine presence is demonstrated when the tabernacle was covered with a cloud during the day and a burning light during the night (9:15–23). When the people refused the report of Caleb and sought to stone Moses (chap. 14), they were refused entry to Canaan. In great disobedience, they went into battle but were defeated because Yahweh was not with them (14:41–45). The mumbling of disbelief was silenced by the grave in the trackless wilderness of Sinai.

DEUTERONOMY

It is fitting that the Pentateuch should close with a book so centralized around law (Torah). The Israelites by this time had journeyed as far as the land of Moab and the Amorites, but Moses was allowed only a mountaintop gaze (32:48–52; 34:1–4) because of his sin at Meribah's waters (Num. 20:12).

In many respects, Deuteronomy contributed to the history of the OT more than any other book. Its sermonic style provided the framework for much of the following historical books (Joshua—Kings) as well as the shape for the following prophetic exhortations.

JOSHUA

It is significant that the campaign to conquer the land depended on Joshua's obedience to the law (1:7–8). In dramatic fashion the Jordan was parted and the ark led the Israelites across the river (3:14–17) where they were to obey the sign of the covenant and be circumcised (chap. 5). The incredible, miraculous victory over Jericho was tempered by the tragic defeats at Ai for disobeying the law of *herem* (everything is devoted to Yahweh) (chaps. 7—8). If the text is in chronological order, it was strategic that Joshua's next act was to take the Israelites to Mount Ebal in the center of the hill country where "There was not a word of all that Moses commanded that Joshua did not read to the whole assembly of Israel" (8:30–35). The theological point of this passage simply was that Joshua's subsequent victories were the product of faithfulness to the law.

It does not seem likely the primary purpose of the book was to provide a description of how the Israelites conquered the land. Apart from Jericho and Ai, Joshua only led a southern campaign that was opposed by the Amorite coalition (10:1–27) and a northern campaign against Jabin, king of Hazor. It is significant the text states that only Hazor (11:13) and Ai (8:28) were burned. It would seem Joshua's campaigns were field victories rather than conclusive and conflict-ending triumphs (note the frank admission of Israelite failure to take the land in Judg. 1). The account of campaigning was clearly given in religious terms: It is Yahweh the Warrior who gives these great victories.

THE KINGDOM PERIOD: THE COVENANT IS ABUSED

The following lengthy discussion covering Judges to the end of the twin kingdoms can be summarized in a principle constant in both testaments: Abuse of the covenant has inevitable consequences. The long record that comprises the OT historical books demonstrates a failure to obey the covenant at every level of responsibility. God's people were responsible to keep the covenant; the institution of kingship meant the king was responsible in seeing the Torah (framing the covenant requirements) was obeyed. Since the land was God's gift for entering into covenant with Him (Deut. 6:10), the appropriate punishment for the breaking of the covenant by the Israelites was they were taken from their land (Lev. 26:27–33).

PRELUDE TO KINGDOM—CHAOS

One of the great mysteries of OT history is that there was no successor to Joshua. It would be inconceivable to think of the Israelites leaving Egypt and going to Palestine without Moses or conquering the land independent of Joshua's leadership. Still, Joshua's parting words, "be careful to obey all that is written in the Book of the Law of Moses" (Josh. 23:6) and the covenant renewal ceremony (chap. 24) where Israel repeatedly swore obedience to the law, explained the chaos of Judges. The reason for military failure was presented as purely theological—the Israelites failed to be obedient (Judg 2:1–4).

The chronology of Judges depends solely on how 1 Kings 6:1 and Judges 11:26 are interpreted. If the numbers are taken literally, the period began soon after the Israelites entered the land of Canaan in the beginning of the fourteenth century and lasted until approximately 1050 B.C. when Saul was chosen by God to be king.

The most striking characteristic of Judges is its "deuteronomistic" (sermon-like) style demonstrated in the recurring cycle: Israel committed apostasy, Yahweh sent an oppressor, Israel cried out and Yahweh raised up a deliverer (judge). This style is so dominant that some interpreters argue that Judges' primary purpose was to serve as an apologetic on behalf of kingship. Certainly the formula, "In those days Israel had no king . . . " (17:6; 18:1; 19:1; 21:25) is positioned to highlight the tragic and gross behavior of Israel without a vested authority. The paradigm proposed in the section "Joshua" above was given an ironic twist in this book. God already established authority in giving the law and acting as the Divine Warrior. The twist was Yahweh now vested authority in response to the Israelites' sin. It was their abuse of Yahweh's authority that resulted in Yahweh raising an oppressor and then a deliverer. The oppressors, however, (Mesopotamians, Moabites, Philistines, Canaanites, Midianites, Ammonites, and Philistines) were all small neighboring powers. The unique way in which each deliverer succeeded was meant to remind the reader it really was Israel's Warrior God who gave the victory.

Sadly, this was a time period dominated by apostasy and atrocity. In a book covering nearly four centuries (or two hundred plus for those who hold to the late date for the exodus), there is only one mention of a prophet (6:8), one prophetess (Deborah, chaps. 4—5), no orthodox priests (note the apostate priest in chaps. 17—18), one mention of the ark (20:27), and no mention of the tabernacle. The last two stories (chaps. 17—21) must have occurred at the beginning of the period (20:27) but were appended for theological purposes. The Danite migration (chaps. 17—18) explained why Dan came to be an apostate religious center (1 Kings 12:29). The horrifying story of the Levite and his concubine and the resultant civil war (Judg. 19—21) prepared the reader for impending kingship as well as the tribe from which the king was to be chosen. Nonetheless, Israel's stupefying behavior was reassuringly matched by God's faithfulness to His covenant. This faithfulness is seen in His righteousness (judging sin) and His mercy (perpetuating the covenant).

While the archaeological evidences of the Israelites in this period are meager, two important events need to be mentioned. Merneptah, Pharaoh of Egypt (1224–1204 B.C.) provided the first extrabiblical mention of Israel in an inscription in which he claimed he defeated Israel. Second, early in the twelfth century, the "sea peoples" were defeated at the gates of Egypt by Ramses III. Some of these Aegean peoples settled in the coastal area of Israel and became Israel's chief adversary at the end of Judges and during the early years of the monarchy. Ironically, these Aegean peoples, called Philistines in the OT, provided for this land, previously called Canaan, the name Palestine.

PREREQUISITE TO KINGDOM—UNITY

From the time of Moses through the period of Judges, it should be obvious to readers, the Israelites had no clear national ethos. As early as Joshua 22, the tribes were nearly at war with one another. There was a discernible consistency to their national unwillingness to follow a leader. It was this startling social centrifugalism that brought the Israelites to the place where they were nearly overwhelmed by the Philistines, a lesser opponent.

The demand for a king "such as all the other nations have" (1 Sam. 8:5, 20) was an absolute crux for the Israelites. Consequently, the idea of kingship has been variously interpreted by scholars of every theological stripe. The primary reason for the confusion is texts can be marshalled to show that the Israelites' request was evil (1 Sam. 8:6–9; 10:17–27) and that only Yahweh should rule as king (Judg. 8:22–23). On the other hand, Yahweh agreed to the request. He carefully chose and divinely enabled Saul to be king (1 Sam. 9; 10:9–12). These seemingly contradictory passages are further complicated by some external factors. The first-century A.D. Jewish historian, Josephus, coined the word "theocracy," the rule of God, to argue the ideal rule was that of Moses when only God was king, and that the institution of kingship was undesirable. When this New Testament-era concept is coupled with the deep antimonarchicalism in some modern Western traditions, it is understandable why the OT materials can be so easily misread.

The answers to the king question can be most readily seen in the Pentateuch. The Law of the King (Deut. 17:14–20) anticipated the legitimate issues of kingship: divine election (v. 15); antimilitarism (v. 16); anti-internationalism—multiplication of wives (v. 17); centralization of wealth (v. 17); and responsibility to keep the Torah (vv. 18–20). It would seem clear, therefore, that the question was not the office of kingship but the manner of rule.

A study of Moses reveals that Yahweh was actually acting as King through Moses, the chosen king of His people. In the prologue of ancient Near Eastern law codes, a number of similarities with the law of Moses may be seen. In the code of Lipit-Ishtar, king of Isin (ca. 1934–1924 B.C.), the prologue reveals five themes characteristic of both biblical law and ancient Near Eastern law.

1. There is a great god (here Enlil) who is king.

2. The gods have "given" kingship to Sumer (as a gift).

3. They have "called" Lipit-Ishtar to be king.

4. As "wise shepherd" he has "established justice" and as "humble shepherd" he established justice in accordance with the word" of Enlil.

5. The law themes that make up the prologue are primarily familial and social (slaves, etc.).[5]

First, while Yahweh was rarely addressed as "king" in the Pentateuch (Ex. 15:18 and possibly Deut. 33:5), His rule was clearly seen in His con-

---

5. *ANET*, 159.

test with Egypt's king, Pharaoh, who was named more than one hundred times from Exodus through Deuteronomy. Second, the vesting of power in Moses (Ex. 7:1; 19:9; 33:7–11, 17; Deut. 34:10–12) was a gift that was specifically transferred to his successor, Joshua (Deut. 34:9). Third, Moses was divinely and dramatically called by God to lead (Ex. 1—6). Fourth, Moses was specifically called a lawgiver (Deut. 33:4–5) and was the central person responsible for writing down and implementing the law (Deut. 31:9–13). This same responsibility toward the law may be seen in Joshua's call and commission (see also Deut. 17:18–20). Fifth, while there is no discernible prologue to OT law, themes such as family and society compare favorably with ancient Near Eastern law. It may be concluded that the picture of Moses painted by the text revealed the major components of kingship demonstrated in Moses' rule (note Deut. 33:5a which may be interpreted to say Moses was a king).

The problem of kingship, therefore, was not theocracy versus monarchy but the manner of how a king would rule. The sin of the Israelites' request was captured in their words "like all the other nations" (1 Sam. 8:5). Not only were the powers of the king specifically demarcated (1 Sam. 10:25, i.e., the regulations of kingship as in Deut. 17:14–20), but the length and success of his rule depended specifically on obedience to the Torah (1 Sam. 12:14–15; 20—25). This new constitution was deposited "before the LORD" (1 Sam. 10:25) and, in effect, placed this office within the domain of the covenant.

The customary understanding of the period of the United Monarchy suggests a homogeneity among its three kings that is unsupported by fact. While the exact year of Saul's ascension is not clear (1 Sam. 13:1 lacks "thirty" and "forty" in the Massoretic Text in describing his age and the length of his rule), the possession of the title "king" brought with it none of the trappings of kingship. Those would be earned over the course of his rule and began with Saul's successful defeat of Nahash the Ammonite and deliverance of Jabesh in Gilead (1 Sam. 11). Saul had no throne, palace, capital city, army, or tax-generating capability; indeed, in his first conflict with the Philistines, because of the Philistine monopoly of iron (1 Sam. 13:19–22), only Saul and Jonathan were armed. The amazing Israelite victory (1 Sam.14) is positioned between two chapters that chronicle in tendentious language the twofold rejection of Saul—"You have rejected the word of the LORD, and the LORD has rejected you as king over Israel!" (15:26).

The jarring suddenness of Saul's rejection over comparatively minor offenses has long troubled interpreters. A careful reading of David's life reveals behavior that would seem to be far worse than Saul's. The answer, of course, is theological: "Man looks at the outward appearance, but the

LORD looks at the heart" (1 Sam. 16:7) and David was the "man after his own heart" (13:14). Beyond this, however, there was a new structuring of authority as a result of the establishment of the monarchy. The emergence of dynastic rule was mirrored in the emergence of the office of prophet (9:9). The king, possessing vested authority, was unlike Moses who possessed both royal and prophetic gifts. The king was thus dependent upon the prophet who knew the will of the heavenly King. Saul's rule was a paradigm for the entire monarchy. He violated the revealed law, disobeyed the guardian of the law (the prophet Samuel), and failed to meet the spirit of the law. This latter point is painfully clear when it is remembered that the man who selfishly failed to exterminate the Amalekites (chap. 15) did exterminate eighty-five innocent priests and their families (22:6–20)—a darkly mocking commentary on Saul's inner man.

The unparalleled transparency of leading authority figures in the biblical text is best seen in David's life. His personal failures and their consequences dominated the story of his life. His awesome success in kingdom building was marred by his tragic personal choices. From the ashes of despair, his reign was a paradigm as well: "The sacrifices of God are a broken spirit; a broken and contrite heart, O God, you will not despise" (Ps. 51:17)

Even with the death of Saul, the unification of the nation was achieved only with difficulty (2 Sam. 2—4). It is important to note that when David was finally anointed king over all Israel (2 Sam. 5:1–5), the next event in the text was the capture of Jerusalem (5:6–13). Juxtaposition of the royal court with the national religious center in the same city was perhaps the most important contribution of David. It is significant that after David ordered the ark of God brought to Jerusalem (chap. 6), the Davidic covenant (chap. 7) was instituted.

Much of Saul's concern centered around his desire for his son to follow him as king (1 Sam. 20:30–31; 22:8; 23:15–18; 24:16–22; 25:44; 26:21–25). Though Yahweh forbade David from building the temple, He promised that unlike Saul, David's son would be king. In one sense, this covenant needs to be thought of within the framework of the Abrahamic covenant. God made David a great name (2 Sam. 7:9) and gave him land through conquest (7:9–10). Furthermore, dynastic privilege can be considered as similar to primogeniture in Genesis. While the debate concerning the conditionality and unconditionality of the covenant is legitimate, the fact remains that as long as there was a throne in Jerusalem, a descendant of David occupied it. This demonstration of God's grace is characteristic of all of His covenants: "I will give one tribe to his son so that David my servant may always have a lamp before me in Jerusalem, the city where I chose to put my Name" (1 Kings 11:36).

Solomon's reign (ca. 970–930 B.C.) featured the last harvest of the glorious blessing of God and the deadly seeds of apostasy that brought God's judgment. It has always been difficult to comprehend how this man, uniquely gifted with wisdom and empowered to build God's house, could have come to violate every regulation of kingship (Deut. 17:14–20). It may be theorized that some type of deep-seated cynicism led to wholesale abandonment of the Torah. This resulted in four major abuses that Deuteronomy 17 had addressed: 1) unchecked centralization; 2) internationalism; 3) religious syncretism; and 4) militarism.

The first violation may be seen as the nearly inevitable result of centralizing the political and religious in one place. By breaking up the old tribal boundaries and setting up twelve new districts (1 Kings 4:7–19), Solomon sought to weaken the former power wielders (elders). The description of the lavish, daily, royal requirement (1 Kings 4:21–28) and the garish display of ivory and gold (the latter mentioned six times in the reign of David but thirty-four times in 1 Kings 6—10) demonstrated both God's blessings and Solomon's excesses. The divine commentary on such wealth is laconically stated in 1 Kings 14:26 when, after Solomon's death, Shishak, king of Egypt, "took everything, including all the gold shields Solomon had made."

Solomon's internationalistic policies are best seen in his unprecedented employment of diplomatic marriages (1 Kings 11:1–8). These resulted in the syncretism of multiple religious systems, since the tolerance of the foreign deities of each wife made it difficult to resist tolerating the religions of those over whom Solomon ruled (12:33).

Power that is usurped is power that must be defended. For this reason Solomon committed the great sin of relying on military might (9:15–23, 26–28; 10:26–29). God's response to this usurping of power was to raise up three adversaries: Hadad the Edomite (11:14), Rezon of Damascus (11:23–25), and Jeroboam (11:26–40). The destruction of the house of Solomon was the direct result of Solomon's violation of the four major responsibilities of the power God had vested in him.

POSTSCRIPT TO KINGDOM—DIVISION

Up to this point, the covenant's promise of nation, land, and vested leader drove the historical record with expectancy of the continued blessing of God. Significantly, it was the prophet Ahijah who set the tone for the Divided Monarchy by warning Jeroboam (and thus all later kings) to expect judgment if Solomonic practices continued (1 Kings 11:29–39). This judgment was to fall specifically on the nation, its land, and its leader.

RULERS OF THE DIVIDED KINGDOM

RULERS OF ISRAEL		RULERS OF JUDAH	
Jeroboam I	931–910	Rehoboam	931–913
		Abijah	913–911
		(Abijam)	
Nadab	910–909	Asa	911–870
Baasha	909–886		
Elah	886–885		
Zimri	885		
Omri	885–874		
Ahab	874–853	Jehoshaphat	872–848
Ahaziah	853–852	Jehoram	853–841
Jehoram	852–841	Ahaziah	841
(Joram)			
Jehu	841–814	Athaliah	841–835
Jehoahaz	814–798	Joash	835–796
Jehoash	798–782	Amaziah	796–767
(Joash)			
Jeroboam II	793–753	Azariah	792–740
		(Uzziah)	
Zechariah	753–752		
Shallum	752	Jotham	750–732
Menahem	752–742	Ahaz	735–716
Pekahiah	742–740	(Jehoahaz)	
Pekah	752–732		
		Hezekiah	716–687
Hoshea	732–722	Manasseh	697–643
		Amon	643–641
		Josiah	641–609
		Jehoahaz II	609
		(Shallum)	
		Jehoiakim	609–598
		(Eliakim)	
		Jehoiachin	598–597
		(Jeconiah)	
		Zedekiah	597–586
		(Mattaniah)	

The Northern Kingdom, Israel, (931–722 B.C.) consisted of nine dynasties, eight of which were established by a violent act. Only the first (Jeroboam), fourth (Omride), and fifth (Jehu) were of any consequence.

Jeroboam's scandalous rejection of the Levites and the Jerusalem temple resulted in a new syncretistic religion that led to the demise of the United Monarchy after 930 B.C. Indeed, the paradigm for evil for all succeeding kings in the North was that they "walked in the ways of Jeroboam" (1 Kings 16:2). Since the supreme demonstration of God's power was redemption from Egypt, it is likely that the invasion of Shishak, who devastated both Israel and Judah within six years of their formation, was meant to make a theological point: Behind ill-gotten gains will be gains unable to be sustained, or, in NT thought, "a man reaps what he sows" (Gal. 6:7). God's faithfulness to the Abrahamic covenant brought the Israelites out of Egypt, and the covenant curse brought Egypt out to Israel. Jeroboam lost battles with Aram of Damascus, Philistia, Moab, and Judah; his son Nadab also was defeated by Philistia. Baasha finally assassinated Nadab and exterminated all the male heirs of Jeroboam (1 Kings 15:29–30).

The assassination of Baasha's son, Elah, by Zimri and the death of Zimri in battle with Omri within the space of a year echoes the sad litany of a nation bound for destruction. However, just when the reader of history comes to expect destruction, Israel's fortunes experienced a dramatic reversal. The exclusively theological description of Omri's reign (16:21–28) was interrupted with the ominous note that he made Samaria his royal capital.

Toward the end of the tenth century a new and disturbing page of history was turned. Assyria, during the reign of Adad-Nirari II (911–891 B.C.), began an imperial march that did not halt until the entire fertile crescent, Elam to the East, Urartu to the North, and Egypt to the Southwest all experienced the unique terror of Assyrian brutality. Ahab (and perhaps Omri) was quick to recognize the impending danger. When Shalmaneser III (858–824 B.C.) overcame the greatest of the Aramean kingdoms, Bit-Adini (Amos 1:5; 2 Kings 19:12; Isa. 37:12), the West responded forcefully. A coalition of twelve Aramean kings, including Ahab, fielded an army of nearly 4,000 chariots and 60,000 infantry and met the Assyrians at Qarqar on the Orontes. Ahab's military might may be seen in his contribution of half the chariots and 10,000 soldiers. The result seems to have been a great victory for the coalition.

Ahab's understanding of the era led him to follow the identical policies of Solomon: internationalism (diplomatic marriage to the Phoenician, Jezebel, and political alliances), religious syncretism (1 Kings 16:29–34), and militarism, including the great battle of Qarqar in 853 B.C. The biblical record of Ahab centers around two subjects: his conflict with Elijah and three wars with Aram of Damascus. In the first two battles, Ahab was promised victory by a prophet (20:13) and a man of God (20:28) so that "you will know that I am the Lord" (20:13, 28). Ahab's unwillingness to abandon his policies brought about one of the most dramatic examples of divine intervention in the OT. Concerning the third battle with Damascus, Ahab was warned by the prophet Micaiah that he was to be killed—and he was, in a powerful expression of God's sovereignty. In the same year of Ahab's dramatic triumph at Qarqar (not mentioned in the OT), he also campaigned for Ramoth-Gilead where "someone drew his bow at random and hit the king of Israel between the sections of his armor" (22:34).

The death of Ahab in battle was also the death of militarism. Jehu (841–814 B.C.) eradicated the entire line of Ahab, the prophets of Baal, and the King of Judah (2 Kings 9—10). By 841 B.C., Shalmaneser had smashed the western wall and received tribute from five regions on Mount Baalirasi (probably Mount Carmel), including Jehu, who is pictured on the famous Black Obelisk, prostrate before the Assyrian.

Following the death of Shalmaneser there was a great civil war that resulted in a dramatic halt in the Assyrian march. The halt was, however, ephemeral, for in 743 B.C. the mighty Tiglath-pileser III (744–727 B.C.) came west and received 1,000 talents of silver from Menahem (2 Kings 15:16–22). In 733 B.C. he marched again into Israel at the request of Ahaz, king of Judah, who had been besieged by Pekah, king of Israel. Tiglath-Pileser III deported the Israelites of the Transjordan and the area north of the Carmel range. Israel was left with only the central hill country until the final blow in 722 B.C., when Samaria's fall to Shalmaneser V (726–722 B.C.) was anticlimactic. The point of the history of the Northern Kingdom was summarized after the fall by the text, "All this took place because the Israelites had sinned against the LORD their God, who had brought them up out of Egypt" (2 Kings 17:7).

JUDAH

With notable exceptions, few of David's twenty descendants have captured the attention of Christian readers. During the period of Assyrian weakness (ca. 823–745 B.C.), both Israel and Judah under Jeroboam II (793–753 B.C.) and Uzziah (also spelled Azariah, 792–740 B.C.) experienced a dramatic resurgence of power and prosperity. This seems, however, only to have blinded both kingdoms to the message of the prophets Hosea and Amos. Isaiah's grand vision (Isa. 6), commissioning him as a prophet, is framed around a subtle, but effective, polemic against pompous and blasphemous kingship, specifically against Uzziah's attempt to usurp priestly functions (2 Chron 26:16–21 with Isa. 6:1–5). Judah's experience in this time period was only marginally different from that of Israel's.

Hezekiah (716–687 B.C.) unwisely took the path of alliance and militarism when he chose to rebel against Sennacherib (704–681 B.C.). In a remarkable demonstration of theological history, the Assyrian field commander's blasphemous words (Isa. 36:4–20) provided the reason for divine intervention (37:4, 14-17) which resulted in the destruction of the entire Assyrian army (37:36–37). Because "the king of Assyria with all his pomp" (Isa. 8:7) actually was God's rod (10:5), the God who wielded the rod (v. 15) brought Assyria down with a mighty blow.

An alliance of Babylon, Medes and Persians and Scythians, managed to strike during a weak moment in Assyrian history. In less than a decade (617–609 B.C.), Assyria was permanently obliterated, a perpetual reminder of the hatred it engendered and the God who engineered its destruction.

The godly Hezekiah was followed by the godless Manasseh whose reign (697–643 B.C.) of fifty-five years was both the longest and worst of Judean kings. "Manasseh led them astray, so that they did more evil than the nations the LORD had destroyed before the Israelites" (2 Kings 21:9). This demanded the judgment of God precisely because of the covenant. The destruction of Jerusalem and exile of Judah was the only appropriate punishment (2 Kings 21:10–15). The late repentance of Manasseh and the remarkable zeal of Josiah (2 Kings 22:1—23:30 and 2 Chron. 34—35) could not arrest the inevitable consequence of covenant.

Jehoiakim (609–598 B.C.) was placed on the throne by Pharoah Neco (2 Kings 23:34–35) but wisely accepted the sovereignty of Nebuchadnezzar when Judah encountered Babylonian power (2 Kings 24:1). He later foolishly sought an international solution by listening to the Egyptians and refusing tribute to the Babylonians. This, not surprisingly, brought Nebuchadnezzar west with his army (24:10–13), but Jehoiakim died before the army arrived. He was followed by his son, Jehoiachin, who promptly surrendered (24:11–16) to Nebuchadnezzar. The treasures of the temple, the nobility and skilled workers, as well as 10,000 inhabitants were deported to Babylon.

Nebuchadnezzar then named Mattaniah, Jehoiachin's uncle, as king and changed his throne name to Zedekiah (24:17). Those in the West continued to resent domination by Babylon (Jer. 27) and plotted rebellion. Zedekiah finally declared independence, probably with the support of Hophra, king of Egypt. If Jehoiakim's revolt was futile ten years earlier, this one was downright suicidal. The city fell in July of 586 B.C. and much of the territory was devastated (2 Kings 25:1–21; 2 Chron. 36:17–20; Jer. 39:1–20). The Lachish Letters (potsherds ca. 588 B.C.), discovered in the mid-1930s, provided a poignant contemporary commentary to the fall of nearby Azekah.[6] While it has been calculated that the Assyrians exiled some 4.5 million people, the Babylonians continued to deport on a smaller scale. Consequently, Israel and Judah had become "like all the nations" as they followed their king into exile.

LANDLESS BUT NOT LOST:
EXILE AND RETURN

Perhaps there is no greater example of God's faithulness to the covenant He made with Abraham than His graciousness in bringing His people, Abraham's descendants, back to the land and enabling them to rebuild their homes as well as the temple. Since the OT essentially is a book of promise, it is appropriate that the historical period closes with God lovingly keeping all His promises made to Abraham in Genesis 15. It is that faithfulness to God's OT covenant that illuminates for the Christian reader the certainty of Scripture concerning His commitment to the new covenant, which was promised (Jer. 31:31) and kept (Luke 22:20). The utter faithfulness of Israel's God now is revealed in the incarnate Son of David: "Jesus Christ is the same yesterday and today and forever" (Heb. 13:8).

CAPTIVITY

Jeremiah predicted the Judahites would be in captivity for seventy years (Jer. 25:11–12; 29:10; 2 Chron. 36:21) while Isaiah predicted earlier that Cyrus would issue the decree to rebuild Jerusalem and its temple (Isa. 44:28). The Chronicler added the point that the seventy years was to give the land its Sabbath rest and then repeated Isaiah's prediction about Cyrus (2 Chron. 36:20–23). Consequently, the captivity itself was addressed in covenant shape—punishment through the land and firm promise to return. Ironically, most Jews chose to stay in exile, but most of the biblical record deals with those who returned.

RETURN

Around 538 B.C., Sheshbazzar, assisted by Zerubbabel and Joshua, the High Priest (Ezra 3:8), led some 50,000 Jews to a homeland filled with uncertainties. A bewildering mixture of peoples awaited them: Jews who had never been exiled; foreign settlers from Ammon, Edom, Sidon, and Tyre; and Samaritans, people settled in Samaria by the Assyrians. The lat-

---

6. Ibid., 321–22.

ter bitterly opposed the reestablishment of Jerusalem as the religious center of the province now called Yahud (Judah). When the returning Jews rejected the local inhabitants' offer of help in reconstructing the temple, the local inhabitants managed to halt the project completely (Ezra 4:1–5). The prophets Haggai and Zechariah sixteen years later challenged the people to build the temple and it was completed in March of 515 B.C. (Ezra 5:3—6:14).

While the date for Ezra's return is debated, the majority view places it in 458 B.C. (Ezra 8) when he led some 1,500 Jews and 38 Levites to Judah. Ezra also led the reform aimed at Jews who had intermarried. He challenged them to divorce (Ezra 9—10).

Around 445 B.C. Nehemiah received permission from Artaxerxes I to return to Jerusalem and oversee the building of the city walls. Despite serious opposition, the task was completed (Neh. 2:11—6:19) and Nehemiah served as governor of the province for twelve years (chaps. 7—12). After a brief return to Persia, Nehemiah came back to Judah for a second governance, insisting that specific mosaic laws assiduously be kept (chap. 13).

CONTINUITY

As the OT story closes, it is striking to observe that the age-old issues of the Torah, land, and temple continued to dominate the biblical record. Faithful obedience to the Torah was at the heart of the ministries of Ezra and Nehemiah. The last of the OT prophets, Malachi, who called for ritual purity, ended the prophetic literature with a command from the covenant: "Remember the law of my servant Moses, the decrees and laws I gave him at Horeb for all Israel" (Mal. 4:4). The "either. . .or" of the covenant led Malachi to warn Judah that God had promised, ". . . or else I will come and strike the land with a curse" (4:6).

Because God was faithful to His promise to Abraham, the covenant continued. The Great King returned His people to the land and shaped events to result in the successful rebuilding of the temple. The believing community now eagerly awaited the promised son of David (Ezek. 34:11–31; 37:15–28) or as Malachi put it, "But for you who revere my name, the sun of righteousness will rise with healings in its wings" (4:2).

FOR FURTHER READING

Ben-Sasson, H. H. ed. *A History of the Jewish People*. Cambridge: Harvard University, 1976.

Bright, John. *A History of Israel*. 3d rev. ed. Philadelphia: Westminster, 1981.

Harrison, R. K. *Old Testament Times*. Grand Rapids: Eerdmans, 1970.

Hayes, John H. and J. Maxwell Miller, eds. *Israelite and Judaean History*. In OTL. Philadelphia: Westminster, 1977.

Hill, Andrew E. and John H. Walton. *A Survey of the Old Testament*. Grand Rapids: Zondervan, 1991.

LaSor, William Sanford, David Allan Hubbard and Frederic William Bush. *Old Testament Survey: The Message, Form and Background of the Old Testament*. Grand Rapids: Eerdmans, 1982.

Merrill, Eugene H. *Kingdom of Priests: A History of Old Testament Israel*. Grand Rapids: Baker, 1987.

Payne, David F. *Kingdoms of the Lord: A History of the Hebrew Kingdoms from Saul to the Fall of Jerusalem*. Grand Rapids: Eerdmans, 1981.

de Vaux, Roland. *Ancient Israel*. 2 Vols. New York: McGraw-Hill, 1965.

Wood, Leon. *A Survey of Israel's History*. Rev. ed. Grand Rapids: Zondervan, 1986.

XIII

CULTURAL BACKGROUND OF THE OLD TESTAMENT

JOHN H. WALTON

"Your father was an Amorite and your mother a Hittite." So recites Ezekiel as he begins his treatise on Israel's history of unfaithfulness (Ezek. 16:3).* Israel's culture, like her ancestry, was a patchwork quilt, pieced together with remnants taken from here and there, but woven together with the thread of divine revelation.

For centuries our ignorance of the culture, language, and history of the ancient Near East contributed to a view that Israel was somehow an entity unto itself, sequestered in holy isolation by virtue of its divine election. As this perspective became entrenched, then canonized, our ability to understand the Israel of the OT diminished and rendered ever more probable a distorted exegesis of their literature. When the great discoveries of the late nineteenth and early twentieth centuries began to unfurl the tapestry that was the ancient Near East, the similarities between, for example, Israel and Babylon, especially as exploited by those critics who sought to discredit the Bible, disarmed us and often led to reactionary disavowal of any basis of comparison despite the evidence to the contrary.

---

* Unless otherwise stated, Scritpure quotations in this chapter are from the NIV.

But finally the dust has settled somewhat and we are in a position to undertake a balanced investigation of the cultural background of Israel by means of what has come to be known as the "contextual" approach.

THE CONTEXTUAL APPROACH

GUIDELINES

Some of the guidelines for this approach to the OT are as follows:

1. Both similarities and differences must be considered.

2. All elements must be understood in their own context as accurately as possible before comparisons are made.

3. Proximity in time, geography, and spheres of cultural contact all increase the possibility of interaction leading to influence.

4. The significance of differences between two pieces of literature is minimized if the works are not of the same genre.

5. Similar functions may be performed by different genres from one culture to another.

6. Just as in comparative Semitics where a word may be borrowed, but then assume a vastly different semantic range, so, too, when literary or cultural elements are borrowed they may in turn be transformed into something quite different.

7. A single culture will rarely be monolithic, either in a contemporary cross-section or in consideration of the passage of time.[1]

COMPARISON

With these cautions in mind the task of comparison can begin. The areas in which comparison can take place are many and varied.

Language. The field of comparative Semitics has been greatly enhanced by the decipherment of the languages and translation of the texts from Mesopotamia, Syria-Palestine, Egypt, and Anatolia. Similarities of gram-

---

1. For discussion of these points of theory and others, see Tremper Longman III, *Fictional Akkadian Autobiography* (Winona Lake, Ind.: Eisenbrauns, 1991), 30–36; K. van der Toorn, *Sin and Sanction in Israel and Mesopotamia* (Assen: Van Gorcum, 1985), 1–9; and William W. Hallo, "Compare and Contrast: The Contextual Approach to Biblical Literature" in *The Bible in Light of Cuneiform Literature, Scripture in Context* 3, ed. W. W. Hallo, B. W. Jones, and G. L. Mattingly (Lewiston, N.Y.: Edwin Mellen, 1990), 1–30.

mar, vocabulary, and syntax have all been enormously helpful in working out some of the obscure details of Hebrew.

Topoi. Cultural institutions such as sacrifice, priesthood, temples, prophecy, kingship, and family structures can each be studied comparing what is found in the ancient Near East at large to what is attested in Israel. Similarities can help us to appreciate areas of continuity and influence, while differences are often traceable to theology.

Philosophy. Concepts and beliefs such as the afterlife, retribution principle, the structure of the cosmos, the existence of evil, the origin of civilization, and the origin and role of mankind all have a basis for comparison.

Literature. Each of the categories listed above depends on analyses of the pertinent literature. Nevertheless, the literature itself is yet another area in which similarities and differences occur. Various genres were common to a number of Near Eastern cultures (e.g., wisdom, hymns, history, law, etc.). Often the very forms of the literature can be profitably compared (e.g., proverbs, treaties/covenants, casuistic law). Even literary devices may be shared by cultures (e.g., certain metaphors, word pairs). In this category the analyst must also address the issue of literary dependence: i.e., to what extent may a piece of literature in one culture have been dependent on a specific piece of literature of another culture.

In the remainder of this chapter we will survey the various types of literature in the OT, highlighting some of the specific contributions the contextual approach has made to our understanding of the OT's cultural background.

COSMOLOGY

There is no particular genre that is used consistently to convey cosmological information. In the ancient Near East, mythological texts often contain cosmological information, but hymns (*Enuma Elish*), epics (*Gilgamesh*), and incantations are just a few of the other genres that contribute to our understanding of cosmology. In the OT the early chapters of Genesis contain much cosmology, but Psalms and Job also add information to the profile. The main issues for comparison are (1) creation of the cosmos; (2) creation of people; and (3) the flood.

CREATION OF THE COSMOS

Aside from scattered remarks in Sumerian myths, the main information concerning ideas about creation in Mesopotamia come from the work entitled *Enuma Elish*. Though the genre and form of *Enuma Elish* differ considerably from Genesis, comparison of their respective philosophies can be profitably explored. In actuality, what similarities exist are superficial and could well be incidental. The differences, on the other hand, are significant.[2]

The first is there is nothing lasting that is created by the deity (Marduk) in *Enuma Elish*. Instead, his exercise of dominion involves the organization of the cosmos. In contrast, Genesis portrays Yahweh as Creator as well as organizer.

The second key difference is that elements of the cosmos are seen as coming into being in *Enuma Elish* by means of the birth of the god who is associated with that element of the cosmos (e.g., fresh water, sky). In this sense cosmogony (origin of the cosmos) is expressed in terms of theogony (origin of the gods). This philosophy is countered quickly in Genesis with the words "In the beginning God." There is no hint of theogonic mythology in the straightforward biblical narrative.

A final key distinction is that creation (organization) in Mesopotamian (and Canaanite) texts takes place by means of, or in the aftermath of, conflict. Defeat of rebel forces or overcoming chaos opens the way for the deity to impose his order on the cosmos. While some interpreters have seen such a motif in Psalms, the serenity of the Genesis account is indisputable.[3]

Egyptian creation accounts appear in several different versions featuring different gods. While the intermixing of theogony with cosmogony is again prominent, the Memphite theology portrays a creator god (Ptah) creating by means of the spoken word, as in Genesis.[4] In this sense, the Egyptian material provides for closer parallels than the Mesopotamian literature, though the differences remain substantial.

CREATION OF PEOPLE

Similarities exist in the creation of human beings to the extent that clay or dust is used by the deity as the molding material with an additional divine ingredient provided as a catalyst. In the Mesopotamian accounts it is most often the blood of a slain rebel deity that is mixed with the clay, as well as spit in Atrahasis. In the Egyptian Hermopolitan account the tears

2. For a helpful summary, see W. G. Lambert, "A New Look at the Babylonian Background of Genesis" *JTS* 16 (1965): 287–300.

3. See J. Day, *God's Conflict with the Dragon and the Sea: Echoes of a Canaanite Myth in the Old Testament* (Cambridge: 1985); and Carola Kloos, *Yhwh's Combat with the Sea: A Canaanite Tradition in the Religion of Ancient Israel* (Leiden: Brill, 1986).

4. For further discussion, see J. Hoffmeier, "Some Thoughts on Genesis 1 and 2 and Egyptian Cosmology" *JANES* 15 (1983): 1–11.

of the creator-god are the active ingredient. The biblical account does not mix anything in, but it is the breath of life from Yahweh that animates the new creation. This breath of life also may be referred to in Egyptian wisdom in the *Instruction of Merikare*.[5]

The Genesis account portrays people as having been created in the image of God. Though differences of opinion continue to exist regarding the meaning of that claim, it has been asked whether other cultures made a similar claim. Again, it is the Egyptian *Instruction of Merikare* that offers the closest parallel. There, people are stated to be the likenesses of Re and as having come forth from his body.[6] The suggestions of similarity on this point in Akkadian texts are much more problematic and have not been convincing.[7]

The principal difference in the area of cosmology concerns the purpose and function of humanity. In Mesopotamian literature people were created to provide relief for the gods. The work of maintaining the civilization the gods had created had become too strenuous and led to social stratification in the divine realm. To resolve the problems, people were created as slave labor to do the work the gods had previously been obligated to and, thus, to provide the needs of the gods. It was the latter function from which humankind derived its dignity—the gods needed them—rather than from some high purpose for which they were destined. On that count they had been only an afterthought for convenience sake.

In contrast, the Israelites viewed people as central to the eternal plan of God. Everything else that had been created had been created with them in mind and to suit the specification that would benefit them most. God entrusted to them the care of His creation, but He Himself was beyond needs they could provide. The life of toil and hardship was not what they were created for; they had brought it upon themselves by their disobedience. Inherent dignity is to be found in their lost estate and in the surviving image of God—in what they were created to be instead of what they were driven to do.

An additional difference could be found in the biblical claim that God initially created one pair from whom all others were descended. It is this factor that serves the theological purpose of transmitting the sin of the first couple to all of their descendants. In Mesopotamia, on the other hand, there is never an indication that only one or two were created. In

---

5. For discussion, see J. M. Plumley, "The Cosmology of Ancient Egypt" in *Ancient Cosmologies*, ed. C. Blacker and M. Loewe (London: 1975), 36.

6. See Hoffmeier, *JANES* 15: 9–10.

7. Edward M. Curtis, "Images in Mesopotamia and the Bible" in *The Bible in Light of Cuneiform Literature*, 33–34.

some contexts seven pairs are mentioned, but usually it appears to be creation *en masse*.

THE FLOOD

While Egyptian and Canaanite sources are virtually silent regarding a massive flood in antiquity, Mesopotamian literature preserves accounts for us in a number of different (though probably interdependent) pieces of literature. Similarities include a decision by deity to ravage the earth by means of flood, the warning of a particular individual and instructions to build a boat to provide for the deliverance of some, a flood of vast extent, grounding of the boat on a mountaintop, the sending of birds to determine whether rehabitation is possible, the offering of a sacrifice by the survivors, and a subsequent blessing on the survivors bequeathed by the gods.

Differences would include the type of boat, the length of the flood, the people who were saved, the outcome for the hero, the reason for the flood, and the role of the gods. The latter is particularly noticeable as the gods are in constant tension with one another in the Mesopotamian accounts. As a matter of fact, the intention of the divine council was that none would survive the flood. It was only an act of treachery on the part of the god Ea/Enki that let the information slip out to the one who was eventually saved.

Though the similarities between the respective literatures are striking, the case for literary borrowing is hard to make. Many of the similarities are of the sort that could occur coincidentally, i.e., any story of a flood might be expected to have them. Likewise, in some places where differences occur, there is no easy explanation for how the differences would have arisen if there indeed was literary dependence. In the end, it is the sending out of the birds that is the most suggestive of literary interrelationships, but more missing links would have to be located for the case to be made with conviction.

PERSONAL ARCHIVES

The personal archives found in Mesopotamia (primarily at Nuzi) are not pieces of literature per se, but are rather like family records: contracts, receipts, etc. As a result they cannot be compared literarily with the patriarchal narratives in Genesis, but they nevertheless provide information by which comparisons of cultural practices can be made. From these it can be determined that the culture of the patriarchs was not dramatically different from that found throughout the ancient Near East during the Middle Bronze Age (first half of the second millennium B.C.). The specific parallels that have been recognized as legitimate provide some supplementary details for understanding some of the actions of the patriarchs (e.g., Abraham producing an heir through Hagar), as well as giving additional examples of some of the practices found in Genesis.

LAW

There are several levels of comparison that can be undertaken within this general category. On the literary level, the form and content of individual laws as well as the form, content, structure, and function of legal collections can be compared and contrasted. Second, there are a number of topoi that find their focal points in the legal literature. These would include cultic practices such as sacrifice and ethical issues such as the status of women. Finally, on the philosophical level, the concept of law itself and its function within society can provide for productive comparisons.

PHILOSOPHICAL COMPARISON

In this category one of the key differences concerns the source of law. The numerous legal collections found in the ancient Near East often include prologues or epilogues that give us some perspective about the collection. From these we discover that many of the legal collections (e.g., Hammurabi's Code), were compiled by the king as a report to the gods (particularly Shamash, the god of justice) regarding his success in carrying out his duties as king. The cases presented were designed to show the gods what a just administration the king had established. Consequently, the law was not seen as having its source in the divine realm. The gods had not instructed the people or the king how they ought to run society. The gods were the guardians of justice and had entrusted the king with the task of maintaining justice. Law was society's attempt to carry out that responsibility. As a result the goal of the law was justice. There was no absolute standard by which justice could be measured, for the gods had not communicated any such criteria, and no one ever made the mistake of thinking the gods intended their own behavior to be emulated.

In contrast, law in ancient Israel was understood to have been revealed by Yahweh and to represent the standard by which He judged the conduct of His people. Moreover, that revelation was in total harmony with the character of God, for the revelation was primarily of his nature: "Be holy because I, the LORD your God, am holy" (Lev. 19:2). God was the source of the law and the goal of the law was to produce an understanding of what God was like and thereby to provide a model for individual and national conduct.

LITERARY COMPARISON

With regard to individual laws, one would find a great deal of similarity both in the general content of the laws as well as in the casuistic style of formulation (i.e., "If someone does x, then the punishment will be y"). There also would be areas of difference. Besides the casuistic style formulation, the biblical law codes offer a considerable amount of apodictic legislation ("Thou shalt not . . ."). Such formulation is extremely rare in ancient Near Eastern collections. Likewise, in its overall content the biblical collections go well beyond what is typical for the Mesopotamian material. The Mesopotamian collections contain various categories of civil and criminal legislation, but no cultic legislation (e.g., rules about ritual cleanness or instructions for sacrifice). The OT, conversely, not only mixes in a large amount of cultic legislation but could even be said to focus on it. In Mesopotamia offense is ultimately viewed in relation to society, while in Israel all offense is ultimately against God.

An important possible explanation for some of these observed differences comes to light when we explore the issue of genre. It must be recognized that much of biblical law is in the context of the covenant between the Lord and Israel. As a result the genre is not really comparable to the legal collections of the ancient Near East, which had little more than a propagandistic function. Mesopotamian legal collections were an attempt by the king to reveal what he was like. Like a politician giving a campaign speech, the king wanted to put the best possible face on his reign. In Israel the laws were intended to show what God was like, not so He could be vindicated or gain approval, but so people would know what His expectations were and could try to conform to the model of behavior He offered. In genre they are comparable to the stipulations of a treaty (see the section "Treaties and Covenants" below). In fact, the treaty stipulations frequently feature apodictic formulation, as is found in the laws of Israel. The covenantal function of Israelite law differs then from the royal apologetic function of Mesopotamian legal collections. They are distinct genres in terms of function, though they use the same form. The Israelite laws address what is right or wrong in accordance with their covenant agreement with God. The Mesopotamian legal collections are more interested in creating order in society in place of chaos, and the king is attempting to convince the gods and his people that he has done so.

TOPOS: SACRIFICE

One of the central institutions of Israelite life and worship was sacrifice. Their laws had much to say about how the sacrificial system was to be operated and what its function was. The details of ritual slaughter, of blood expiation, and of the resulting forgiveness of individual and corporate offenses are well known to anyone familiar with the OT or even with Christian theology as explained in the NT by the author of Hebrews and others.

It should not be surprising that the other cultures of the ancient Near East also practiced sacrifice. Many of the types of sacrifice from Leviticus also are referred to in Ugaritic literature documenting Canaanite religious practices. The Mesopotamian rituals have recently been studied contextually by M. Katz.[8] While similarities exist in the fact that slaughter of animals is used as a ritual procedure for maintaining purity and right relationship with deity and is related to the consumption of meat, even these basic ideas are construed in very different ways in each culture.

The differences surface in the concept and function of sacrifice. In Mesopotamia, sacrifice (along with upkeep of the temple) served as a principal part of the care and feeding of the gods. Sacrifices were to provide for the needs of deity and preserve access to the deity and the sanctity of his dwelling. If the deity's needs were not met, he would become angry and withhold favor, thus necessitating appeasement. These sacrifices had no relation to the conduct of the worshiper. There was little emphasis on the blood, and there was no concept of atonement or sacrifice for sin. This contrast is summarized well by Katz: "The Israelite system, in tracing contamination to human misdeeds rather than to devils and spirits, 'devitalizes' the notion of evil and thus represents a revision of the Mesopotamian concept of impurity."[9]

There is no question that some of the laws and practices in Israel were very much like the laws and practices in Mesopotamia. Likewise, there is no reason to doubt that Israel's laws, whether as practiced in society or as written in their literature, are heavily indebted to Mesopotamia. Such commonality, however, is largely superficial in light of the striking differences observable in the concept and function of law and in the transformation of institutions such as the sacrificial system.

TREATIES AND COVENANTS

The similarity between the format used for treaties in the ancient Near East and that used for covenants in the Bible has become one of the showcase examples of comparative studies. It has also become a testing ground for determining how much the comparative method can prove.

---

8. M. A. Katz, "Problems of Sacrifice in Ancient Cultures" in *The Bible in Light of Cuneiform Literature*, 89–201.

9. Ibid., 120.

In the early part of the twentieth century the documents from the Hittite Empire began to be published, among them about three dozen treaties. It was not until the middle of the twentieth century that scholars began to recognize the structural similarities between them and Deuteronomy. Besides the Hittite corpus, a Neo-Assyrian corpus from the seventh century now is available for comparison, as well as more than a dozen other assorted treaties.

The basic elements characteristic of treaties as a genre include the following:

1. Introduction of the speaker

2. Historical prologue

3. Stipulations

4. Statement concerning the document

5. Divine witnesses

6. Curses and blessings

The historical prologue is the focus of much of the interest because the Hittite treaties consistently include it while treaties from other times or areas attest that section sparsely if at all. Also of interest is the section of curses. Here the Neo-Assyrians were much more prolific and detailed, while their Hittite counterparts were somewhat brief and formulaic. A final disparity between the Hittite and Neo-Assyrian treaties is in the order of the elements. The Neo-Assyrian treaties, along with other first-millennium treaties, typically place the witnesses section prior to the stipulations.

Having identified the basic differences between the second-millennium Hittite treaties and the first-millennium treaties from Syria and Assyria, scholars then began to suggest which set the biblical treaties more closely approximated. At stake is the dating of the Pentateuch—a sensitive issue between the various camps of interpreters.

In this matter there can be no doubt the biblical format more closely resembles the second-millennium (Hittite) format than it does the first-millennium (Assyrian) format. Before we declare the early date of the Pentateuch "proven," however, it must be recognized that the first millennium data are very limited. We cannot be certain the so-called Hittite form did not continue in use in some areas during the first millennium even though changes are evident in the Assyrian and Syrian adaptations.

While matters of date may not be concluded, the comparative materials in this category have helped us to understand some of the perspective of the OT in the presentation of the covenant. Among other things, the covenant is to be viewed as a treaty between God, the Suzerain, and His vassals, His chosen people, Israel. This is a case where a literary comparison has led to a conceptual understanding not previously recognized.

HISTORIOGRAPHY

While there is a limited extent to which comparisons may be made on a literary level, of more interest is the way in which each society carried out the task of historiography, utilizing, at times, vastly disparate literary forms. Primarily, this is a case of philosophical comparison. How was history viewed and what were the goals and methods of recording history? What was the role of deity in events and what was the importance of achieving objective truth in historical reports? How were historical documents used? What relationship existed between events in history and events in the natural world? What constants or assumptions dictated the understanding of cause and effect? These are all philosophical questions a study of the historical documents of a culture can help to answer. It is presumptuous for us to assume the biblical view of history and historiography must be the same as ours if it is to be considered credible and correct. We must formulate our expectations based on our understanding of their culture rather than dictate requirements based on our philosophical principles.

PURPOSE OF HISTORIOGRAPHY

History is always someone's propaganda, not necessarily by design but always by nature. It always makes someone look good, whether it has that intention or not. Likewise, history is always someone's revelation in that it offers a portrayal of some individual or some entity. Despite these truisms, historiographical analysis revolves around intent. On one end of the spectrum, historical presentations may include both favorable and unfavorable revelation, leaving propagandistic values to lie where they fall. Here the intent could be identified as revelation. The revelation may be of the character of an individual or entity, of trends, of instruction, or simply of a course of events. On the other end of the spectrum, historical presentations may include only favorable revelations with the data being manipulated to maximize propagandistic values. Here the intent is propaganda. There are times, at least in theory, when revelation is so favorable by nature it cannot be distinguished from propaganda. In this case some outside control is necessary to determine which is intended.

The historiography of the ancient Near East, whether represented in royal inscriptions or chronicles, king lists or annals, has by all accounts a propagandistic agenda. Much like the campaign speeches of our day, truth can be useful, but it is not the prime objective. Propaganda is greatly enhanced when it has truth in its favor, but if it only has facts, it must make do. The perspective on truth these texts have will always seek to present the king in the best light. Many of the sources function as revelation of the king; but since they are highly controlled revelation, they qualify as propaganda.

In the OT the revelations given about individuals invariably contain favorable as well as unfavorable information. The same is true for the corporate people of Israel. As a result, this material would be very ineffective propaganda, though undoubtedly some parts could serve propagandistic purposes for some individuals. The Bible also makes it clear throughout that its purpose is not to offer revelation of any particular person or group, but to serve as Yahweh's revelation of Himself. That is its historiographical purpose.

Since the revelation of Yahweh is all favorable, one might claim this is propaganda devised by Israel on behalf of their God. This propaganda would indirectly work to their advantage, for it would substantiate their claims of election. The objection to this is that it stretches our credulity to suppose such a long-lasting practice of self-effacement could be sustained to support the effort. Such altruism runs counter to the nature of propaganda.

A real difference between the historiographies of the ancient Near East and Israel is that the historiographic genres of Mesopotamia generally have a propagandistic purpose, while the historiographic literature of Israel is viewed as God's revelation of Himself to His people. Neither seeks to present a comprehensive, objective account of what happened. Mesopotamian sources manipulate the information to present the king in a favorable light. Biblical literature selects the information that concerns Yahweh's covenant program. A further key difference is there is nothing in Mesopotamia to match the scope and range of the biblical material, which itself transcends boundaries of reign, dynasty, and era.

ROLE OF DEITY

In light of the conclusions drawn in the previous section, we would expect the role of Yahweh in biblical historiography would be more pronounced than the role of deity in other ancient historiographies. On the other hand, similarities can be seen in that intervention by deity in history is assumed by all. In Mesopotamia, however, intervention is usually intended to preserve the status quo, whereas in Israel Yahweh's intervention is designed to further His plan. It promotes a sovereign scheme for all of history that could never be claimed by the gods of Mesopotamia.

CONCEPT OF HISTORY

The omen literature of Mesopotamia demonstrates the perception of a close relationship between the events of history and occurrences in the natural world. As the activities of the gods had ripple effects through history, in the same way they had ripple effects through nature. The theory of omens assumed if the effects in nature could be recorded in minute detail and catalogued in reference to the concurrent historical events, then similar future historical events could be anticipated when the catalogued natural effects occurred. This omen mentality is the constant in their view of the flow of history. They sought to identify possibilities for recurrence and, if the events were undesirable, to avoid recurrence through the use of incantations.

For Israel, Yahweh is the cause of all events and His attributes and program are the constants by which all history is driven. Instead of looking to omens to figure out what God was going to do, they looked to conformity or lack of conformity to the revealed law of God for an understanding of the events of history. Our Western historiography sees human nature as the key to understanding cause and effect. Israel considered knowing Yahweh to be the key to understanding cause and effect.

HYMNS AND PRAYERS

All of the peoples of the ancient Near East, like Israel, offered hymns and prayers to their gods. As might be expected, the attributes that deities are praised for and the complaints and petitions that are poured out vary little from one society to another. Additionally, there is some similarity in genre and structure. There are, however, a number of very distinct differences that can be observed.

PRAISE PSALMS

Praise psalms of the Bible are categorized either as descriptive praise (in which God is praised for His attributes) or declarative praise (in which God is praised for specific acts of intervention in the individual's experience). The descriptive praise of Israel features an imperative call to praise, unlike the Mesopotamian hymns, which typically enumerate epithets and attributes, and the Egyptian hymns, which focus more on the physical attributes of deity and depict the process of praise in action. Unlike descriptive praise, which is common to each of the cultures, declarative praise is only preserved in Israelite literature. This could be explained by the corporate nature of the extant ancient Near Eastern hymns, but alternatively it could be a reflection of differences concerning divine intervention on behalf of the individual.

PRAYERS

The lament psalms of the OT offer petitions for deliverance from oppression. In the Book of Psalms these generally constitute a separate genre from that of praise. In contrast the hymnic literature of Mesopotamia typically begins with descriptive praise and then moves into complaint and petition for deliverance.

With only a few exceptions, the Israelite authors of the lament psalms considered themselves innocent of any wrongdoing capable of bringing on their oppression. They therefore sought vindication from a just God. The Mesopotamians, on the other hand, had little criteria by which to determine whether they had committed an offense. Consequently, they concluded they had offended a god in some way and were attempting to appease an inscrutable god. Because of the nature of the Babylonian religion, the offense often was assumed to be ritual in nature, so ritual appeasement was the solution. The laments of Mesopotamia most often were accompanied by magical rites, ritual enactments, and incantations that were thought to exert power over the spiritual forces causing the oppression. None of this magical aspect is evident in the Israelite prayers.

WISDOM LITERATURE

PROVERBS

Kenneth Kitchen has done a thorough study of the formal characteristics of ancient Near Eastern instructional literature.[10] He not only found consistent formal similarity, but considered the details of conformity to be such that the unity of the Book of Proverbs, as well as the early date of the book, could be defended on the basis of form analysis. Michael Fox included Proverbs in his conclusion that there was a wisdom genre in the ancient world that transcended cultural boundaries.

---

10. K. Kitchen, "Proverbs and Wisdom Books of the Ancient Near East" *TynBul* 28 (1977): 69–114; see also his "The Basic Literary Forms and Formulations of Ancient Instructional Writings in Egypt and Western Asia" in *Studien zu Altägyptischen Lebenslehren*, ed. E. Hornung and O. Keel (Göttingen: Universitätsverlag Freiburg, Schweiz, Vandenhoeck and Ruprecht, 1979), 235–82.

The similarities in form and content between Israelite and Egyptian didactic wisdom literature have been so well established that there can be no doubt that Israelite wisdom is part of an international genre (which includes Mesopotamian wisdom) and cannot be studied in isolation.[11]

Likewise, the content of the instructional literature is strikingly similar in its scope and message. What distinguishes Israelite instruction is the orientation toward deity rather than toward society. This is a reflection of the biblical author's contention that the fear of Yahweh is the beginning of wisdom.

One of the closest relationships between a biblical text and a piece of ancient literature is found in comparison of Proverbs 22:17—24:22 with the Egyptian *Instruction of Amenemope*.[12] Though parallels are identified in areas of structure and imagery, it is in the area of content that the most sweeping claims are made. While the subject matter shows great similarity, it may be argued the similarity is no more or less than that shared with ancient wisdom literature in general. Furthermore, one must observe there is much subject matter in each that is not shared with the other. Concerning view of deity, the inclusion at the beginning and end of this section of Proverbs emphasizes the importance of the "fear of Yahweh," but otherwise little theological difference can be discerned. Likewise, both share a high ethical tone. In the end, however, though there is no reason to doubt the overall influence of Egyptian wisdom on Solomon and his colleagues in Israel, the evidence is insufficient to build a firm case for literary dependence of Proverbs on *Amenemope*.

JOB

While the depth and variety found in Job is unique in ancient literature, the subject matter and basic dialogue form is not. The issue of theodicy (the justice of God) and the philosophy known as the retribution principle (the righteous will prosper and the wicked will suffer) are common topics of discussion in the various genres of wisdom literature. The solutions offered in the Mesopotamian literature affirm the truth of the retribution principle, but since the criteria by which the gods determined righteousness was unknown, the justice of the gods was considered inscrutable and the ability of any man to claim righteousness was seriously ques-

---

11. Michael V. Fox, "Two Decades of Research in Egyptian Wisdom Literature" *ZÄS* 107 (1980): 120.

12. See Glendon Bryce, *Legacy of Wisdom* (Cranbury, N.J.: Bucknell University Press, 1979); John Ruffle, "The Teaching of Amenemope and Its Connection with the Book of Proverbs," *TynBul* 28 (1977): 29–68.

tioned. Vindication was out of the question; appeasement was always necessary.

In contrast, the Mesopotamian view is represented in the advice of Job's friends and is soundly rejected as insufficient. It is assumed from the beginning of the book that Job has a rightful claim to righteousness. Job's integrity is maintained in his unwillingness to accept the Mesopotamian solution (27:3–6). The solution the book offers comes in the speeches by God: that God's justice is vindicated by His wisdom. Justice is not easily proven, but wisdom is clearly demonstrated. Just as His wisdom is real, yet infinite and unfathomable, so His justice is real, infinite, and unfathomable. This is a far more sophisticated philosophy than the easy agnosticism of the Babylonians.

LOVE POETRY

The exquisite love song found in the Song of Solomon is paralleled by a number of similar pieces from Egyptian literature of the twelfth and thirteenth centuries B.C. (contemporary to the Judges period in Israel). Some fifty-four songs have been identified and reflect the same literary categories as Song of Solomon.[13] Whereas in other genres the theological concepts served as the primary basis for differences between biblical and ancient Near Eastern literatures, in this genre the near absence of theological influence on the Israelite literature results in minimal differences. This is not the same as suggesting the Israelites borrowed their literature from Egypt. Rather, it recognizes that Israel's literary application of the genre varied little from the use found in the wider international realm.

PROPHECY

There is a growing corpus of prophetic texts from the ancient Near East. The texts from Mari (eighteenth century B.C.) now number about fifty and about a dozen additional texts are known from seventh-century Assyria. These texts portray a prophetic institution very similar to what is called pre-classical prophecy in Israel (i.e., preceding the writing prophets of the eighth century; e.g., Elijah, Elisha, Nathan, etc.). In these texts the prophecies were addressed primarily to the king and offered military advice or cultic instruction. There is nothing to parallel the wide-ranging eschatological or covenantal aspects found in Israel's classical prophets, where instead of oracles that suggest this battle or that battle will be won

---

13. Translations and full discussion of both the Egyptian and biblical material can conveniently be found in M. V. Fox, *The Song of Songs and Ancient Egyptian Love Songs* (Madison: University of Wisconsin Press, 1985).

or lost, we discover messages concerning the long-range political destiny, not only of Israel, but of many nations of the ancient Near East. These messages reflect belief in a God who is totally sovereign and carrying out a plan in history rather than belief in the ancient Near Eastern gods who intervene arbitrarily.

CONCEPT OF DEITY

The one philosophical concept that transformed Israelite culture and literature into something unique in its world was the concept of deity. It was not just Israel's monotheism that was revolutionary, for if all of the gods of Babylonia were rolled into one deity that was the sum of all the parts, it would still be no match for Yahweh, the God of Israel. There are several ways in which these differences are manifested.

ULTIMATE POWER

There is no question but that the existence of many gods constituted a limitation on the sovereignty or jurisdiction of any one god. Beyond the issue of numbers, however, the sphere in which the pagan gods operated had built-in limitations. The realm of deity was not independent and was not absolute. This is identified by Y. Kaufmann as the distinguishing feature of paganism.

All these embodiments involve one idea which is the distinguishing mark of pagan thought: the idea that there exists a realm of being prior to the gods and above them, upon which the gods depend, and whose decrees they must obey. Deity belongs to, and is derived from, a primordial realm. This realm is conceived of variously—as darkness, water, spirit, earth, sky, and so forth—but always as the womb in which the seeds of all being are contained. Alternatively, this idea appears as a belief in a primordial realm beside the gods, as independent and primary as the gods themselves. Not being subject to the gods, it necessarily limits them. The first conception, however, is the fundamental one. This is to say that in the pagan view, the gods are not the source of all that is, nor do they transcend the universe. They are, rather, part of a realm precedent to and independent of them. They are rooted in this realm, are bound by its nature, are subservient to its laws. To be sure, paganism has personal gods who create and govern the world of men. But a divine will, sovereign and absolute, which governs all and is the cause of all being—such a conception is unknown. There are heads of pantheons, there are creators and maintainers of the cosmos; but transcending them is the primordial realm, with its pre-existent, autonomous forces. This is the radical dichotomy of paganism; from it spring both mythology and magic.[14]

---

14. Y. Kaufmann, *The Religion of Israel* (New York: Schocken, 1972), 21–22.

It is this difference that serves as the foundation for all of the others.

RELATIONSHIP BETWEEN GODS AND PEOPLE

The gods of the ancient Near East were not obliged to be ethical, moral, or even fair. There was no code to which they were bound. People were not expected to imitate the gods. Neither had the gods revealed anything about themselves or their expectations. Even their past actions could not be used to gauge their reactions or conduct, for they were not consistent. The result of this was that people had no behavioral guidelines to live by, other than those society laid down. Their responses to the gods were generally ritual in nature. It was believed that rituals either met needs that the gods had or magically bound the gods in some way. In both cases, appeasement and coercion were the main features. Nonetheless, there were often occasions when these approaches appeared to be futile. The frustration is evident in the words of this worshiper whose cultic acts have not brought relief from his trouble:

> I wish I knew that these things were pleasing to one's god! What is proper to oneself is an offence to one's god; What in one's own heart seems despicable is proper to one's god. Who knows the will of the gods in heaven? Who understands the plans of the underworld gods? Where have mortals learnt the way of a god?[15]

Thus, the Israelites enjoyed a relationship with their God that was not possible for their neighbors—a relationship built on revelation and on the consistent, benevolent, and sovereign attributes of Yahweh.

FOR FURTHER READING

Finkelstein, J. J. "Bible and Babel," *Commentary* 26 (1958): 431–44.

———. *The Ox That Gored.* Transactions of the American Philosophical Society 71:2. Philadelphia, 1981, 8–13.

Frankfort, Henri, et al. *Before Philosophy.* Harmondsworth: Penguin, 1949.

Kitchen, Kenneth. *The Bible in Its World.* Downers Grove, Ill.: InterVarsity, 1978.

Millard, Alan and D. J. Wiseman. *Essays on the Patriarchal Narratives.* Winona Lake, Ind: Eisenbrauns, 1983.

Saggs, H. W. F. *The Encounter with the Divine in Mesopotamia and Israel.* London: Athlone, 1978.

---

15. W. G. Lambert, "Ludlul Bel Nemeqi" in *Babylonian Wisdom Literature,* (Oxford: Oxford University at Clarendon Press,1960), 41: 33–38.

van der Toorn, K. *Sin and Sanction in Israel and Mesopotamia*. Assen: Van Gorcum, 1986.

Walton, John. *Ancient Israelite Literature in Its Cultural Context*. Grand Rapids: Zondervan, 1989.

XIV

RELIGIOUS BACKGROUND OF THE OLD TESTAMENT

E. RAY CLENDENEN

The Bible is God's self-revelation and the account of His retrieval of a world enslaved by sin and ignorance with a liberating and life-changing power called the righteousness of God (Rom. 1:16–17). A better understanding of that world of darkness into which the gospel came will help us to appreciate more fully the power of the gospel and its significance for our world.

The stark contrast between the world and the gospel is highlighted by Joshua in his demand for commitment in Joshua 24:15. The conditional nature of Joshua's exhortation to choose is often missed, thereby misunderstanding Joshua's message as an invitation to choose the Lord. Joshua is, in fact, not issuing an invitation but a demand. He has already commanded in the previous verse that in response to the grace of God (vv. 2–13) Israel must commit itself to follow Him fully. The point of verse 15, then, is that if Israel should refuse to respond reasonably to the Lord's grace and serve Him wholeheartedly (cf. Rom. 12:1, 2), they will face a plethora of gods from which to choose. The situation is similar today for an individual in our pluralistic society.

The world is filled with various value systems and worship systems which direct our lives. To refuse to follow the clear and certain wisdom of the Lord of Truth is to be lost in a maze of conflicting and uncertain voices. In the ancient world these voices were personified in gods and goddesses of various cultures. It is within the context of these gods of Mesopotamia, Egypt, and Canaan that God began to demonstrate the power of His righteousness.

Religion in general may be defined rather simply as that aspect of human culture constituting the response of individuals to the prevailing concepts of the supernatural. This includes what people believe about the supernatural and how their beliefs directly affect their actions. The Bible accounts for world religions as a perversion of the truth about God (Rom. 1:18–25).

Religion can take many forms, such as animism, polytheism, henotheism, and monotheism. The nations which were the backdrop for the biblical account were polytheistic. This means they viewed the supernatural as embodied in many individual deities, i. e., beings possessing some type of immortality and supernatural ability. Each of these was associated with a certain astral body, like the sun or moon, with a part or force of nature such as the sea or the trees, or with certain objects or activities of human experience like the hoe, craftsmanship, childbirth, or war.

Since there were many gods, however, none could possess unlimited wisdom or power. The activities of one god could often be counteracted by the activities, opposition, or deceit of another. In the Babylonian flood story, for example, the god Enlil's plan to destroy humankind in a flood was thwarted by Ea-Enki who secretly revealed the plan to the human hero, with instructions to build a great boat. In one version the hero Atrahasis declares to the elders, "My god is no longer in accord with yours, Enki and Enlil are at war with one another" (*NERT,* 92). The divine will was thus fragmented so that a person could never be safe and secure from divine displeasure and punishment, since the will of one god may very well conflict with that of another. In the Sumerian "Lament for Urnammu of Ur" the goddess Inanna accuses An and Enlil of uttering false promises to Urnammu the king and altering "all the determinations of fate" and changing their word (*NERT,* 142–45). Thus, the revolutionary nature of Deuteronomy 6:4–5 is striking, which summons Israel to the monotheistic worship of Yahweh. Since there is only one God, we can be wholehearted in our devotion to Him.[1]

---

1. See P. C. Craigie, *The Book of Deuteronomy* in NICOT (Grand Rapids: Eerdmans, 1976), 169. In their pursuit of idols Israel failed to obey this command. Thus, the new covenant provision in Ezek. 11:19 included an "undivided" heart (lit. "one heart").* See the discussion in L. E. Cooper, *Ezekiel,* NAC (Nashville: Broadman & Holman, 1994), 139.

* Unless otherwise noted, Scripture quotations in this chapter are from the NIV.

Although the religions of the peoples of the ancient Near East had much in common, their considerable differences make it necessary to examine the main regions separately. We will follow the biblical account of redemption and begin in Mesopotamia, then proceed to Egypt, and finally to Canaan.

MESOPOTAMIA

Although it is impossible to place Abraham with certainty in an exact historical and cultural context, it is known that before the Lord called him, Abraham and his family worshiped the gods of Mesopotamia (Josh. 24:2). The earliest known religious system in Mesopotamia (third millennium B.C.) was that of the non-Semitic Sumerians in the southern region. Their society was organized into city-states, each viewed as the domain of a patron god and his divine family. All these divine families were under the direction of the patriarchal god *Enlil*, god of the religious capital Nippur. Sumer and the rest of Mesopotamia was ruled by various Semitic peoples throughout most of its history beginning at the end of the third millenium. Nevertheless, Sumerian culture so strongly influenced the later Babylonians and Assyrians that Sumerian, Babylonian, and Assyrian religions can be described as a whole. Most of the Sumerian gods were worshiped by the Semites, although usually by different names. Scribes even compiled god lists that identified Semitic and Sumerian equivalent deities.[2]

Inhabitants of Mesopotamia had names for more than three thousand gods, but many of these are different names for the same god, others only designate servants to the gods, old local gods; good spirits, and demi-gods. H. Ringgren suggests that the list of about twenty in the prologue to Hammurabi's code is probably closer to the number of significant deities.[3] They were understood to be responsible for order and well-being—cosmic, political, socio-economic, and personal. Many had rather complex and sometimes seemingly contradictory functions. This results from differences in the way certain gods were viewed in different places, by different social groups, and at different times. Growing political unity in Mesopotamia resulted in growing cultural unity and the need to explain the various forms and functions of individual gods and the relationships between the gods. Eventually the "pantheon" was conceived, a scheme by

---

2. J. Finegan, *Myth and Mystery* (Grand Rapids: Baker, 1989), 25. Gods with both Sumerian and Semitic names are given here in hyphenated form with the earlier Sumerian name followed by the Semitic name, as in Nanna-Sin.

3. H. Ringgren, *Religions of the Ancient Near East*, trans. J. Sturdy (Philadelphia: Westminster, 1973), 53-54. See *ANET*, 164-65.

which various gods are listed in an organized fashion and ranked either by the prominence of the cosmic phenomena they controlled or by family groupings.

In the first millennium, however, political rivalry between cities, especially between the north and the south, expressed itself in the religious sphere as well. In myths, An and Enlil suffered at the hands of Marduk and Ninurta. Rituals also sometimes portrayed political realities in cultic terms, with statues of the gods playing the parts. And military incursions within and outside Mesopotamia usually included plundering the temples of one's enemies and capturing the statues of their gods (*ANET*, 283–84, 291, 302).

THE GODS

Anu-An. The creative deities were *An, Enlil, Ninhursag,* and *Enki.* Father of the gods (including evil spirits), An presided over the divine assembly and was viewed as the ultimate source of all authority. He also was god of the heavens, and kings paid him homage to assure the proper operation of the seasons. He was sometimes described as a bull whose bellowing was the thunder and whose semen impregnated the earth (*Ki,* his spouse, known later as *Ninhursag,* "midwife of the gods") in the form of rain. The end of the spring rains was sometimes explained by his death and descent to the netherworld.

Enlil. The son of An, Enlil was also referred to as father and king of the gods and was actually the most prominent god of the Sumerian pantheon. He is sometimes referred to as *Bel,* the East Semitic equivalent of West Semitic *Baal.* His authority was represented by his possession of the "tablets of destiny." Kingship was understood to have derived from both An and Enlil. Enlil was viewed as lord of the air and ruler over the earth. Both destructive storms and spring rains originated with him and he was described as "the lord who determines destinies" (*NERT,* 108, 118). In the Sumerian epic "Gilgamesh, Enkidu and the Underworld," on the day of creation when he separated heaven and earth (cf. Gen. 1:6–8), Enlil is said to have chosen the earth as his domain as An chose the heavens and *Ereshkigal* the underworld (*NERT,* 74). He is also said to have created the human race by striking the earth with his hoe (*NERT,* 75). But according to the *Atrahasis* epic, he decreed human destruction in a flood because their excessive noise disturbed his sleep (*NERT,* 91).

Enki-Ea. As the god of the subterranean fresh waters, Enki was thought responsible for agricultural productivity, the art of incantation and purification from evil, and for the skills of artisans and craftsmen (for which water was an important tool). According to the myth "Enki and the

Ordering of the World," he was the originator of human civilization, assigning gods to govern the various elements of creation and human culture (*NERT*, 78–80). Civilization and cities are viewed much more positively in Mesopotamian literature than in Genesis, where they are the product of Cain (Gen. 4:17), the Hamites (Gen. 10:6–12), and the rebellious builders of Babel (Gen. 11:1–9).[4] G. Wenham, in fact, argues that Genesis "is flatly contradicting" the Mesopotamian optimistic viewpoint of civilization's progress under divine guidance.[5]

In the creation epic *Enuma Elish*, "Ea the wise" is said to have created humankind from the blood of the rebellious god *Kingu* and then assigned humans the task of serving the gods, thus freeing the gods from unpleasant labor (*ANET*, 68; *NERT*, 77, 84). Humans were understood, then, to possess a divine spark, although a troublesome one. Jacobsen notes that Enki was known not as a god of power but of cunning. He "persuades, tricks, or evades to gain his ends. He is the cleverest of the gods, the one who can plan and organize and think of ways out when no one else can."[6] In the flood stories he was the one who revealed the divine plan of human destruction to the human hero, who then built a boat and saved humanity. Thus, Enki-Ea played an important role in Mesopotamia by protecting the people from the demons of illness and misfortune.

Nanna-Sin. Considered the firstborn son of Enlil, Nanna was the moon god who traversed the night sky in a boat lighting the night, marking the months, and ensuring fertility. His worship was considered especially important at the beginning of a new year, during a lunar eclipse (the result of a demon attack), and at the moon's monthly disappearance to serve as judge in the netherworld. Special rites were performed when the moon disappeared to ensure that Nanna-Sin would return. The chief city of his worship was Ur, where a royal princess served as his high priestess representing his divine spouse *Ningal*. Haran was another center of his worship (cf. Gen. 11:31).

Utu-Shamash. Apparently not as significant among the Sumerians as among the later Semites, Utu-Shamash was the sun god, the offspring of the moon god. As sun god he is variously described as crossing the sky on

---

4. In the "Eridu Genesis" account Ninhursag/Nintur gives city building to humankind to deliver them from a life of wandering (T. Jacobsen, "The Eridu Genesis," *JBL* 100 (1981): 515).

5. G. Wenham, "The Perplexing Pentateuch," *VE* 17 (1987): 13. Gen 1–11, he says, "is a tract for the times challenging ancient assumptions about the nature of God, the world and man," 12. See also G. Hasel, "The Polemic Nature of the Genesis Cosmology," *EvQ* 46 (1974): 81-102.

6. T. Jacobsen, *The Treasures of Darkness: A History of Mesopotamian Religion* (New Haven: Yale University Press, 1976), 116.

a horse or in a chariot or boat, dispersing darkness and dispensing light and life.[7] His power over darkness caused him to be associated with the art of divination. He was also god of justice, noted for protecting the oppressed. He is pictured on the stele of Hammurabi commissioning the king to promulgate the laws.

Marduk. Son of Enki-Ea, he was god of thunderstorms and the city-god of Babylon where he was worshiped at the great temple called *Esagila.* Increasing royal power and prestige accompanying the development of city-states into great empires resulted in an increase in the influence of national gods. Religious and political perceptions were intertwined. The Babylonian creation epic *Enuma Elish* (dating to the late second millennium) celebrated Marduk's defeat of evil *Tiamat,* goddess of the sea, his organizing the world, and his receiving from the gods (notably Enlil) the "tablets of destiny." His consequent attainment of lordship was expressed by attributing to him fifty names climaxing in "Lord of the Lands" (*ANET,* 6072). He is frequently referred to as *Bel,* earlier used of Enlil. A first-millennium text even figuratively identifies the various high gods (Ninurta, Nergal, Enlil, Sin, etc) as aspects of the one god Marduk. His major festival was the eleven-day New Year *akītu* festival when *Enuma Elish* was read and his defeat of Tiamat was celebrated. He appears in the Bible in Isaiah 46:1 (as *bēl*)[8] and Jeremiah 50:2 (as *mĕrōdāk* and *bēl*).

Inanna-Ishtar. Daughter of Nanna-Sin (or sometimes An or Enlil) and mistress of the shepherd god *Dumuzi-Tammuz,* she is usually depicted either as a young bride or as "a rather willful, high-handed, young aristocratic girl of marriageable age."[9] Jacobsen calls her "the most intriguing of all the members in the pantheon."[10] In her various facets (probably resulting from the syncretism of several gods and goddesses) she was associated with the date harvest, spring thundershowers, fertility, war, the morning

---

7. In Ps 19:4-6 Yahweh declares His glory in the sun, which is said to rise in the morning like a bridegroom/warrior emerging full of vigor from his tent. P. C. Craigie says, "The Babylonian hymns to Shamash, the Egyptian hymns to various sun-gods, even the glorious hymn to Aten, differ in one remarkable respect from Ps 19. In those psalms, nature itself is deified; the gods are praised in nature. Yet in Ps 19, nature is personified, not deified, and personified nature raises the chorus of praise to the only Creator and only deity, the one true God" (*Psalms 1–50,* WBC [Waco: Word, 1983], 181).

8. Marduk's firstborn *Nabu* or *Nebo,* god of nearby Borsippa and scribe of the gods, was also very prominent in the first millennium, as can be seen in the names Nebuchadnezzar and Nebuzaradan, (cf. 2 Kgs 25; Jer 39, etc.). He also appears with Marduk in Isa 46:1. See *ABD,* s.v. "Nebo."

9. T. Jacobsen, "Mesopotamian Religions," in *Religions in Antiquity,* ed. R. M. Seltzer (New York: Macmillan, 1989), 21.

10. Jacobsen, *Treasures of Darkness* 135.

and evening star (the planet Venus), and harlotry. Particularly among the Assyrians she was known as the goddess of war and appears often in the royal annals. She was called "mistress of heaven" and her temple in Uruk was called *Eana* ("house of heaven"). She eventually displaced the spouse of An and became "queen of heaven" (cf. Jer. 7:18; 44:17–19, 25).[11] In the most famous of her myths, "Inanna's Descent to the Nether World," her characteristic lust for power leads her to attempt to usurp power in the realm of the dead from her sister *Ereshkigal* (Akkadian *Allatu*; cf. *ANET*, 52–57, 106–9). Although she dies there, spelling barrenness on the earth, Enki saves her by his cunning. As goddess of fertility, especially at Uruk, her cult involved the use of cult prostitutes whose activity was thought to promote fertility in the land.[12] Her cult was widespread, and in Babylon, where she was worshiped as Marduk's mistress, the most impressive of the nine city gates was named for her. A beautifully decorated procession way enhanced the thousand-yard path to Marduk's temple.

Dumuzi-Tammuz. Although not one of the gods mentioned in Hammurabi's prologue, Dumuzi (Akkadian *Duʾūzu*, Hebrew *Tammûz*) functioned as a minor vegetation god in Mesopotamia and was known as the shepherd god. He was especially important, however, as Inanna's lover. In some versions of the Inanna myth, Dumuzi (the main character in these versions) must descend to serve as her substitute in the underworld but is freed and replaced in the netherworld by his sister six months of the year (*ANET*, 5257). The relationship between Inanna and Dumuzi was celebrated annually in a sacred marriage ceremony in which the king represented Dumuzi and the priestess of Inanna represented the goddess (*ANET*, 640–41). The ceremony was intended to secure success for the king and fertility for the land in the coming year. Associated with it were hymns and offerings to Inanna and a ritual union between the king and the goddess on a special bed covered with greenery. After the end of the Old Babylonian period (ca. 1800 B.C.) and the decline of divine kingship, the role of Dumuzi-Tammuz in religion was reduced to Inanna-Ishtar's unfortunate husband, remembered with wailing during the hot summer month that bore his name (cf. Ezek. 8:14; *ANET*, 84). Among the Assyrians and Babylonians a sacred marriage ceremony continued to be

---

11. The "queen of heaven" in Jeremiah may also be either the Canaanite goddess *Anat* (B. Porten, *Archives from Elephantine* [Berkeley, 1968], 165, 176–78) or *Asherah* (W. J. Fulco, *The Canaanite God Rešep* [New Haven: American Oriental Society, 1976], 23–28).

12. Cf. Ringgren, *Religions of the Ancient Near East*, 59–61; J. Bottéro, *Mesopotamia: Writing, Reasoning, and the Gods*, trans. Z. Bahrani and M. van de Mieroop (Chicago/London: The University of Chicago, 1992), 189–98.

observed symbolically in which a statue of the city god would be brought into Ishtar's temple.[13]

Nergal. City-god of Kutha, he was worshiped as god of war, plagues, sudden death, and ruler of the realm of the dead (cf. Jer. 39:3, 13). The Babylonians identified him with *Erra*, their god of riots and slaughter. Ereshkigal, Ishtar's sister, was his consort. The netherworld, also called the "Land of No Return," the "Wasteland," and the "dark house," was viewed as a city surrounded by seven walls and entered through seven gates. It was a dark dusty place full of frightening creatures, where the inhabitants ate dust and wore feathers like birds (*ANET,* 55, 98–99, 107–10). Life was full of uncertainty, and when someone died, "his emasculated spirit descended to the dark, dreary nether world where life was but a dismal and wretched reflection of its earthly counterpart."[14]

Nergal or Ereshkigal usually headed an assembly of gods who judged departed spirits, although it was headed at times (i.e., at night) by the sun god Utu-Shamash or by Nanna the moon god (when the moon was not visible). The gates served especially to protect the world of the living from the departed spirits who were also propitiated from evil in mortuary cults involving food offerings and who were wooed to do good by divination involving incantations and mediums.[15]

---

13. *ABD,* s.v. "sacred marriage." He cautions against the idea of "a common fertility cult in the ancient Near East" of a mother goddess and a dying and rising god of vegetation. "Ancient cultures and religions do not follow a common pattern, as it was formerly assumed but greatly differ from each other . . . . Accordingly, careful distinction should be drawn between Mesopotamian fertility cult on the one hand, and seemingly similar cultic phenomena in other ancient Near East cultures" (p. 869).

14. S. N. Kramer, *The Sumerians* (Chicago/London: University of Chicago, 1963), 123. See also pp. 134–35.

15. Cf. M. Bayliss, "The Cult of Dead Kin in Assyria and Babylonia," *Iraq* 35 (1973): 115-25. E. Yamauchi has suggested that the myth of Inanna/Ishtar's descent, in which she is accompanied in her return by several demons, was associated with mortuary practices ("Tammuz and the Bible," *JBL* 84 [1965]: 288). For evidence of the cult of the dead in Israel, in addition to the prohibitions in Lev. 26:30; Deut. 14:1; 26:14, see Isa. 65:3–5; Jer. 16:5; Ezek. 43:7–9; Amos 6:7; Pss. 16:3-4; 106:28; 2 Chron. 16:12, and the discussion in D. Block, "Ezekiel's Vision of Death and Afterlife," *BBR* 2 (1992): 129–31. Block notes (pp. 117–18), "The doctrine of malevolent spirits remains remarkably undeveloped in the Old Testament. . . . If the Old Testament writers recognized demons at all, they remain faint and indefinite figures, and the influence of malevolent spirits has been almost if not totally expunged. Yahweh has assumed all power over life and death, health and illness, fortune and misfortune."

RESPONSE TO THE GODS

The temple in Mesopotamia was considered the home of a god and his family and was designed much like a royal throne room. Part of the temple complex was the well-known beautifully colored ziggurat, probably intended as an intermediary between heaven and earth, with a stairway leading to the top (cf. Gen. 11:3–5; 28:12). The Babylonian temple consisted of a central court surrounded by rooms, one of which housed the fully dressed image in which the god dwelt. The image was positioned so that it could barely be seen from the court. Whereas the Assyrian king was to minister before the image daily, the Babylonian king only appeared there once a year at the New Year festival.[16]

Images were made of gold-plated wood, almost always in human form, with jewels for eyes (cf. Isa. 44:9–20; Jer. 10:1–16). After construction, they were consecrated in a nightime ritual thought to "open" their eyes, ears, and mouth and to fill them with the god.[17] Each day the image would be cleaned, dressed, and fed meat, fruit, and drink (wine and beer) by the priests. The god's "leftovers" were consumed by the king and the temple personnel. Unlike offerings in Israel, neither the sacrificial blood nor the smoke played a significant role.

Typical of the ancient Near East, ordinary people had little contact with official religion except at festivals. During the Babylonian era of the second millennium, the most important festival in Mesopotamia was the New Year festival, celebrated annually in the fall at Babylon. Its climax was the procession of the divine images to the *akitu* temple, accompanied by the king, who would grasp the hand of Marduk after humbly declaring his innocence (*ANET*, 331–34, 429–52). The festival also included prayers and hymns to Marduk and the recitation of the *Enuma Elish* along with a cultic drama. The point of the festival seems to have been primarily the renewal of kingship and order in the land with divine blessings for success and abundance. After Sennacherib's destruction of Babylon in 684 B.C., a similar festival was conducted yearly in Ashur, celebrating their patron god in the place of Marduk.[18]

There were various types of priests responsible for administration, sacrifices, or purification. For example, the *ašipu* administered purification in

---

16. A. L. Oppenheim, "The Mesopotamian Temple," in *BAR*, ed. G. E. Wright and D. N. Freedman (Garden City, N.Y.: Doubleday, 1961), 158–69. See also *ABD*, s.v. "temples and sanctuaries: Mesopotamia."

17. See E. H. Merrill, "The Unfading Word: Isaiah and the Incomparability of Israel's God," in *The Church at the Dawn of the 21st Century*, ed. P. Patterson et al. (Dallas: Criswell Publications, 1989), 138–41.

18. See *ABD*, s.v. "Akitu," ; K. A. Kitchen, *Ancient Orient and the OT* (Chicago: Inter-Varsity, 1966), 102–106.

homes through incantations designed to protect the homes from demons. The *kalu* priest was to appease the gods through music. Divination was the responsibility of the *baru* and others. There were also prophets who received divine words through ecstasy.[19] Some priests were eunuchs, especially in the cult of Ishtar, which included cult prostitutes as well.

As early as the second millennium there is evidence of belief in personal deities who dwelt in individuals. Any of the gods of the pantheon could be one's personal god, which was received at birth from one's parents, hence the Assyrian expression "god of my fathers." This personal god was thought responsible for success in life (especially in acquiring a son) and in protection from demons which caused sickness and other misfortunes. Sickness, misfortune, or lack of success, then, resulted from offending one's personal god.[20] Solutions consisted of ritual acts, incantations, and the wearing of amulets. The discovery of past offenses and how to remove them and of future difficulties and how to avoid them came through various kinds of divination, some public and official, others private and personal. Means included the interpretation of dreams and the observation of entrails of sacrificial animals, the movement of incense smoke, oil poured on water, astrology, etc. There were handbooks listing symptoms and omens of the past that form "the largest single category of Akkadian literature in terms of sheer numbers of texts."[21]

EGYPT

Many have experienced the allure of ancient Egypt's impressive and beautiful artifacts and have been romanced by its history. But for the Bible student, the importance of a study of Egypt is suggested by more than six hundred biblical references to it. Most important, Egypt functioned as the womb in which God created the nation of Israel (Gen. 46:3). Egyptian religion is of special interest to the study of the book of Exodus, since the plagues (Ex. 7—12) amounted to a demonstration of the Lord's supremacy over and judgment upon the gods of Egypt (Ex. 5:2; 7:5; 9:14–16; 12:12; Num. 33:4; cf. Josh. 9:9; 1 Sam. 4:7–9), whom some in Israel had begun to

---

19. See H. Ringgren, "Prophecy in the Ancient Near East," in *Israel's Prophetic Tradition*, ed. R. Coggins, et al. (Cambridge: Cambridge University, 1982), 1–11.

20. Jacobsen, *Treasures of Darkness*, 152–61. There is also literature showing that suffering sometimes came as a result of basic human sinfulness. See *ANET*, 438–40; W. G. Lambert, *Babylonian Wisdom Literature* (London: Oxford University, 1960), 21–62, 86. On personal gods in Mesopotamia see H. W. F. Saggs, *The Encounter with the Divine in Mesopotamia and Israel* (London: Athlone, 1978), 93–105.

21. W. W. Hallo and W. K. Simpson, *The Ancient Near East: A History* (N. Y.: Harcourt Brace Jovanovich, 1971), 158. See also *ABD*, s.v. "Astrology in the Ancient Near East"; Bottéro, *Mesopotamia: Writing, Reasoning, and the Gods*, 105–37.

worship (Josh. 24:14; Ezek. 20:7). These gods would also prove to be a stumbling block to the Egyptian exiles in the sixth century B.C. (Jer. 44:8, 15) and would again be the object of the Lord's judgment (Jer. 43:8–13; 46:25; Ezek. 30:13).

THE GODS

The names of about forty gods and goddesses from ancient Egypt are known, many by more than one name. The more than three thousand years of Egyptians' history and their lack of interest in a consistent system of religious beliefs have resulted in a very complex picture of Egyptian deities. As E. Hornung describes, "In their constantly changing nature and manifestations, the Egyptian gods resemble the country's temples, which were never finished and complete, but always 'under construction.'"[22] There were about forty districts (nomes) in Egypt, each of which had its own cult for its favorite god or gods. Some of these became national gods as well, operating within the system of deities in a more limited sphere such as war (Sekhmet and Neith) or craftsmanship (Ptah). Politics frequently played a part in the ascendancy of one god over another or the syncretism or identification of one god with another. There were several major religious centers in ancient Egypt, such as Thebes, Hermopolis, Heliopolis, Abydos, and Memphis, and their explanations of the gods and the universe conflict in many places. Few of the gods are known to have had only one area of involvement or persona, and both aspects of many gods overlapped or conflicted. For example, creation is credited in various myths to Atum, Aten, Khnum, Thoth, Amun, or Ptah. Many of the deities were pictured as animals or part animals. Khnum was a man with a ram's head. Both Re and Osiris could appear in the form of a mythical phoenix; but they often could be represented in human form as well. Hathor appears sometimes as a woman, sometimes a cow, and is pictured on the Narmer Palette with a woman's head and the horns and ears of a cow. She could even be represented by a falcon, which also depicts Re, Horus, and Montu. Horus also appears as a falcon-headed man. Thoth could be an ibis, a baboon, or an ibis-headed human.[23]

According to D. P. Silverman, the way the gods were depicted did not represent their "actual forms" but were intended to convey characteristics

---

22. E. Hornung, *Conceptions of God in Ancient Egypt*, trans. J. Baines (Ithaca, N.Y.: Cornell University, 1982), 256.

23. S. Morenz, *Egyptian Religion*, trans. A. E. Keep (Ithaca/London: Cornell University, 1973), 20; D. P. Silverman, "Divinity and Deities in Ancient Egypt," in *Religion in Ancient Egypt*, ed. B. E. Shafer (Ithaca/London: Cornell University, 1991), 20. A human or human-animal form of several gods is pictured in G. Steindorff and K. C. Seele, *When Egypt Ruled the East*, rev. ed. (Chicago: University of Chicago, 1957), 133.

which they shared with these "concretizations." He attempts to explain this in a way that perhaps sheds light on why the God of Israel does not want to be worshiped with images of any kind (Deut. 4:15–20): "At first the supreme force would seem awesome and mysterious, but once it could be comprehended as an entity, it could be recognized, understood, and then reinterpreted in a familiar and recurrent form. In a way, the force could be harnessed."[24]

The sense that one could harness the power of the gods also came from knowing their names. The name of an individual, whether human or divine, was thought to be an aspect of and link to the person. One important key to continuing existence after death was having one's name written on his tomb; removing the name ended that existence.[25] There are texts which offer rewards for uttering someone's name after their death. In one tale used as a charm against the bite of a scorpion, the goddess Isis uses a scorpion to obtain power from Re by discovering his hidden name (*ANET*, 1214). The tale, however, never reveals the name. At least during the Middle Kingdom (ca. 1970–1640 B.C.) it was the practice to write the names of one's enemies on a tablet, bowl, or clay figurine, then smash it, thus breaking their power. The fragments were then buried near one's tomb for protection in the next world. Discovered collections of the remaining fragments are known as "Execration Texts" (*ANET*, 328–29).

Nature. As in other polytheistic cultures, several deities were thought to be the forces behind various cosmic entities; but in several cases, explanations conflict. Several gods could be considered sun gods. The most common, especially in early periods, was *Re*, often combined with other gods into Re-Horakhty, Re-Atum, Amun-Re (the major deity of the New Kingdom, known as "king of the gods"), Sobek-Re, Khnum-Re, etc.[26] The morning sun was called Harakhti, the midday sun was Re or Khepri, and Atum was especially the setting sun (*AEL*, 2.89). Aten, which Pharaoh

---

24. Silverman, "Divinity and Deities in Ancient Egypt," 18. See also V. A. Tobin, *Theological Principles of Egyptian Religion* (New York: Peter Lang, 1989), 36, 38.

25. J. A. Wilson, *The Culture of Ancient Egypt* (Chicago/London: University of Chicago, 1951), 225. Cf. Job 18:17; Prov. 10:7; Isa. 14:22; 48:19; 56:5; Dan. 12:1; Nah. 1:14; Zeph. 1:4; Zech. 13:2. In the Old Testament Yahweh's name often represented His presence and power (cf. Ezra 6:12; Neh. 1:9; Prov. 18:10; Isa. 18:7; 30:27; 50:10; Jer. 7:12).

26. On syncretism in Egyptian religion see Morenz, *Egyptian Religion*, 139–42; Tobin, *Theological Principles of Egyptian Religion*, 14–17. Tobin points out that Amun-Re was not a true syncretism since both gods retained their separate identities. The same was true of Re-Horakhty. This capacity of the gods to be combined in this way, he says, shows their "symbolic nature."

Akhenaten (fourteenth century) briefly elevated to supreme and all-encompassing god, was the sun disk.[27]

Heaven could be conceived as the cow *Hathor* ("mansion of Horus") standing over the earth and giving birth to the sun each day, or as the goddess *Nut* bending over *Geb*, the earth god, touching the western horizon with her hands and the eastern horizon with her feet. She reputedly gave birth to the sun every morning and swallowed him every night. According to the Book of the Dead, Re was "the one who illumines the earth at his birth each day." In the same way, but at opposite times, Nut was also responsible for the stars.[28] The sky god *Shu* is pictured supporting Nut with raised arms. *Tefnut*, the goddess of moisture, was Shu's consort.

The sun could also be described as the sun god Re traveling the sky in a boat, making the journey back through the underworld at night. His emergence from the darkness in the morning involved battling the serpent god *Apopis*.

The moon god was *Khonsu* ("the one who travels across"), worshiped at Thebes as the offspring of Amun and Nut. The main temple at Karnak was also dedicated to him. Also associated with the moon was *Thoth*, the divine scribe and patron of scribes whose cult center was at Hermopolis. He was described as the pilot of the sun god's boat and sometimes as the one who slew Apopis (*AEL*, 2.100–103). Other gods connected with the moon were Osiris, Min, Shu, and Khnum.

There were several gods associated with the Nile, especially its annual inundation upon which the productivity of Egypt's crops depended. The main one, responsible for the inundation, was *Hapy*, depicted as an obese man. The crocodile god *Sobek* was lord of the fish. *Khnum* was god of the first cataract of the Nile, from which the inundation was thought to originate.[29]

---

27. Although Amenhotep IV/Akhenaten led a religious revolution toward monotheism that removed many other divine names and images from monuments, it was not a true monotheism, much less the world's first (Moses preceding Akhenaten by a century). It was still a solar religion, it retained the importance of *ma'at*, and it even promoted the deity of the king and his family, who served as the Aten's only images. It also failed to capture the allegiance of the people. See Silverman, "Divinities and Deities in Ancient Egypt," 74–87, whose helpful discussion nevertheless contains the view that "Akhenaten's religion went further toward monotheism than any of the world's religions had previously attempted" (p. 82).

28. Tobin, *Theological Principles of Egyptian Religion*, 49; Finegan, *Myth and Mystery*, 46. See the discussion of the "heavenly cow" motif in relation to other conceptions of the heavens in R. Anthes, "Mythology in Ancient Egypt," in *Mythologies of the Ancient World*, ed. S. N. Kramer (Garden City, N.Y.: Doubleday, 1961), 17–22. He points out that competing conceptions of the heavens are found in the same royal tombs.

29. Silverman, "Divinity and Deities in Ancient Egypt," 21, 25; Hornung, *Conceptions of God in Ancient Egypt*, 77–79; Morenz, 78, 264

Ma'at and *Seth* represent the duality of balance, order, and stability on the one hand (Ma'at), and chaos, disorder, and death on the other (Seth). Seth's realm was the desert (also foreign nations), which constantly threatened to overwhelm the stability of life in Egypt. As the mythological slayer of his brother Osiris, he represented the evil that threatened Egypt, especially during the transfer of rulership when the king died. Related to him as a threat to stability and life was the eternal serpent Apopis, who had to be defeated and driven out in the process of creation. He also daily opposed the sun god in his journey through the sky.[30]

The concept of Ma'at, variously viewed as symbol, principle, and goddess, was fundamental to Egyptian religion. Ma'at was "the cosmic force of harmony, order, stability, and security, coming down from the first creation as the organizing quality of created phenomena and reaffirmed at the accession of each god-king of Egypt."[31] According to V. A. Tobin, it was "the basis for the unity of all things, the basis of cosmic order, of political order, of morality, of life itself, of art and science, and even of good etiquette in normal everyday affairs." He also claims, "No other culture of the ancient world has evolved a single concept which is so totally all-inclusive as was the Egyptian concept of Ma'at."[32] Identified at Heliopolis with the cosmogonic deity Tefnut, daughter of Atum, Ma'at was viewed as foundational to divine as well as human existence, an eternal and always benevolent order that could be disturbed but never destroyed. The human and cosmic order were considered perfect from their inception, needing only to be maintained and periodically restored by the pharaoh and the cult. It was thus both a gift and a duty. History then was understood cyclically rather than teleologically, with no need for a concept of an eschatological goal.

Afterlife. Gods in Egypt were frequently depicted holding in their hand the Egyptian hieroglyph for life. It is usually shown being presented to a king. Until the First Intermediate Period, ca. 2135–2040 B.C., immortality was considered primarily the prerogative of the king and his nobles. Elaborate tombs with inscriptions exist from the Old Kingdom (ca. 2650–2135 B.C.) in the royal pyramids and for high government officials. But the time of political disorder between the Old and Middle Kingdoms resulted in a broadening to include any who venerated *Osiris* and could

---

30. Hornung, *Conceptions of God in Ancient Egypt,* 158–59,275; Morenz, *Egyptian Religion,* 168. Cf. Gen. 49:17; Ex. 4:3–5; Job 26:12–13; Isa. 27:1; Rev. 12:9; 20:2.

31. Wilson, *The Culture of Ancient Egypt,* 48.

32. Tobin, *Theological Principles of Egyptian Religion,* 77. See also Hornung, *Conceptions of God in Ancient Egypt,* 213–16. The biblical concept of "wisdom" has many of the features of ma'at. See the discussion of ma'at in the context of Egyptian ethics in Morenz, *Egyptian Religion,* 113–30.

perform the necessary rituals and burial procedures. Ordinary people began providing tombs for themselves with brief inscriptions on stelae consisting of a moral epitaph showing their worthiness for life in the next world and also prayers for offerings to sustain that life (*AEL*, 1.8). If finances allowed, before burial one's mummy would be carried to Abydos where Osiris was thought to have been buried. Sometimes a memorial stele was set up there, or at least a boat was included in the tomb furnishings to provide transport to Abydos after death.[33] This "democratization of heaven" carried with it the increasing popularity of the god Osiris and an increasing focus of Egyptian religion generally on the attainment of life after death. The wealthy anticipated an eternal life of luxury in their well furnished tombs, their daily tasks performed by *ushabtis*, figurines placed in the tomb to serve. Commoners hoped for a plot of land in the "field of reeds," the world of Osiris thought to lie just below the western horizon, where they would farm in continuous springtime amid lush vegetation.

The myth of Osiris's murder by his brother Seth and his vindication by his son *Horus* was concerned with both fertility and with life after death. Like Dumuzi-Tammuz in Mesopotamia and Baal in Canaan, Osiris was a type of dying and rising god.[34] But unlike other gods, he rose only in the next world, while his son Horus continued in his place on earth. The living pharaoh was identified with Horus, but when he died he became Osiris, judge and lord of the dead, and lived forever in the underworld. The language of identification with Osiris found in the Old Kingdom Pyramid Texts was later used by people from all levels of society. As Osiris imparted his power to defeat evil and restore fertility to the land each year, he also was thought to restore life beyond the grave. It became customary when writing the name of the deceased to precede it with the name "Osiris" and to follow it with the words "true of voice" or "justified," indicating acceptance by this underworld court.

Entrance into eternity was attained by a combination of devotion to Osiris, morality, and magic. The Pyramid Texts from the Old Kingdom, then the Coffin Texts from the Middle Kingdom (ca. 2040–1650 B.C.),

33. A. R. David, *The Ancient Egyptians: Religious Beliefs and Practices* (London/ N.Y.: Routledge, 1982), 105–12. See also L. H. Lesko, "Egyptian Religion," in Seltzer, *Religions in Antiquity*, 51; Baines, "Society, Morality, and Religious Practice," 156–58.

34. Tobin, *Theological Principles of Egyptian Religion*, 105; David, *The Ancient Egyptians*, 107–11. The most complete version of the myth is in an eighteenth dynasty (ca. 1550–1305 B.C.) hymn to Osiris (*AEL*, 2.81–86). But it was thought inappropriate to describe directly the actual slaying of Osiris. Silverman explains that "an event narrated in detail would be rendered eternal" ("Divinity and Deities in Ancient Egypt," 29).

and finally the Book of the Dead (papyrus texts collected from tombs in later periods) contain spells and instructions for the trip into the netherworld. In addition, one had to pass the test of having one's soul weighed in the balance by the divine scribe Thoth, who recorded the verdict. One's life had to have exemplified the principles of Ma'at, represented on the opposite balance by her symbol, a feather. Failing the test or lacking the proper spells and rituals would lead to torture and destruction.[35]

The dead were not thought to have departed completely, however, but were still part of Egyptian society. There was a regular Festival of the Wadi in which visits were made to the dead in their tombs, including communal meals. They could afflict the living if offended and were consequently propitiated by offerings. They could also assist the living, evidenced by letters found asking the dead for help.[36]

Kingship. Egyptian religion was not an aspect of Egyptian culture but rather its binding framework. It operated around the dual foci of myth and ritual and was the expression of basic concerns for the maintenance of order, stability, and life. The myths as they were perpetuated through the rituals of the cults expressed the values of Egyptian culture and the Egyptians' trust in the divine. The cycles of nature, represented especially by the daily rising of the sun and the yearly flooding of the Nile, symbolized these values. The myths made them more comprehensible and manageable and the rituals gave the Egyptians a means to express their dependence upon divine forces and to contribute to their continuing operation. The myths spoke of a continuing struggle of light and darkness, order, and chaos upon which the Egyptians' lives depended.

The preeminent symbol of continuity and order was the throne. The coronation of a new pharaoh was a reenactment of Re's daily victory over Apopis and of the myth of Horus and Osiris. As the dead king had become identified with Osiris and begun to receive worship as fully divine, so the new king became the new "Horus in the palace." From the fourth dynasty kings were called "son of Re," and in the Middle Kingdom "image of Re." In fact, as E. Hornung explained, there was "a comprehensive and fundamental kinship that links the king with all deities."[37] As the gods were thought to be manifest in certain heavenly bodies, in sacred animals, or in cult statues, the creator god dwelt in the human king. As the Egyptians

---

35. Hornung, *Conceptions of God in Ancient Egypt,* 205–206. Magic, also a tool of the gods, had a wider role in Egyptian religion than providing entrance into the underworld (cf. pp. 207–10; see also Baines, "Society, Morality, and Religious Practice," 164–72).

36. Baines, "Society, Morality, and Religious Practice," 147–55.

37. Hornung, *Conceptions of God in Ancient Egypt,* 139. See also Morenz, *Egyptian Religion,* 168.

were dependent upon Re to maintain the cosmos by defeating the powers of darkness each day, they also were dependent upon the king to maintain order and stability on earth. Ramesses II, from the New Kingdom, is even described as "likeness of Re, illuminating this world like the sun disk." During his lifetime his statues were worshiped.[38]

The king was understood to have divine powers; nevertheless, his human origin was not overlooked. He usually had been one of the sons of his father's main wife and was understood to possess both divine and human attributes. Besides having a human origin, he had to attain immortality, his accomplishments were with the help of the gods, and he could have faults. Silverman describes the position of the king as being in both human and divine realms. "Without him neither realm could function, and the universe would end."[39] Insofar as his office of kingship was concerned, Silverman explains that the pharaoh was the identification of Horus and the son of Re, a divine king. When he ascended the throne, he is pictured as presenting Ma'at to the gods. "He, like them, had set the world aright."[40] Nevertheless, coronation did not completely transform a human into a god. There were limits to his divine powers.

RESPONSE TO THE GODS

The rituals in the temples were the means by which the Egyptians contributed to holding the forces of chaos at bay. The temple itself is generally thought to have symbolized the primeval hill from which the gods and all life originated. Thus, in addition to being the "house of god," it represented the divine power that maintained order and life. There was at least one temple in each district and major town dedicated to the local deities. In addition, the main religious centers had temples to the national gods. As portrayed in temple wall scenes, the king was the official high priest of all the cults and symbolically represented the people before the deity. But his actual functions were performed by professional priests, except perhaps at the main temple to the major deity, where he had daily ritual responsibilities.

Temples were of two types—mortuary temples dedicated to deceased kings and cult temples dedicated to the other deities. The ritual varied little between them. Each morning the officiating priest would bring the statue representation of the god out of the darkness of its shrine into a

---

38. Hornung, *Conceptions of God in Ancient Egypt*, 140.

39. Silverman, "Divinity and Deities in Ancient Egypt," 67.

40. Ibid., 70. Morenz calls this dual nature of kinship the "doctrine of the king's two bodies." He notes a consistent distinction in the use of different terms for the king as person and as office bearer. The living king existed as both man and god and thus served as intermediary between the two spheres. When he died, however, he died as man, but he continued his existence as god (*Egyptian Religion*, 37–41).

special chamber to be served in fear. There the image would be cleaned, perfumed, dressed, beautified with cosmetics, and fed in order to make it a fit dwelling place for the god. Gods, like people, were given three meals a day, after which the food offerings would be given to the priests as their daily portions. At the end of the day the statue was returned to its shrine to rest until the following day.

While a chief priest would have been permanently attached to each temple, most priests only served at the sanctuary for three months of every year. They were usually highly educated laymen such as physicians, lawyers, and scribes, who served gods related to their professions. Chief priests of the major cults often came from the royal court and were very powerful men. The priesthood was usually inherited and limited to males, although ritual singers and dancers could be female. While serving at the temple, purity was a requirement, maintained by such behavior as the avoidance of sexual intercourse, wearing only linen garments, daily shaving of head and body, and bathing several times daily in the "sacred lake."[41]

In addition to priestly offerings that were considered necessary duties in order to maintain Ma'at, additional offerings were brought. These came from individuals of every level in society as gifts to the gods in return for the life and love that the deity had bestowed. Offerings also accompanied appeals for aid or relief from affliction. Many were votive offerings, often statues associated with women's fertility. Devotion to a god and protection from harm also were signified by amulets, often devoted to one of the household deities such as *Bes*, god of love, and his consort *Tauert*, a hippopotamus goddess of fertility and childbirth.[42] One New Kingdom text says, "He has made a shrine to protect them, and when they weep there, he hears them" (*AEL*, 2.197–99; *NERT*, 8–11). The gods had two sides, one unpredictable and terrifying to which the appropriate response was fear, and the other benevolent and productive.

> Cult actions do not coerce but they do encourage the gods to show their gracious side—for the converse of a god's love of mankind is his violent aspect, which is always present beneath the surface and must be assuaged by means of appropriate cult services. . . . Thus the cult is not only mankind's response to the god but also protection against the god's threatening side.[43]

---

41. David, *The Ancient Egyptians*, 126–34; Morenz, *Egyptian Religion*, 87–88.

42. Hornung, *Conceptions of God in Ancient Egypt*, 201-203; Baines, "Society, Morality, and Religious Practice," 180–83; David, *The Ancient Egyptians*, 143.

43. Hornung, *Conceptions of God in Ancient Egypt*, 205. See also "The Destruction of Mankind" and allusions in "The Teachings of Merikare" (*NERT*, 44–47).

On certain special holy days, which varied from temple to temple as special days in the "life" of the god, the deity's statue would be brought out of its "house" in procession before the people. It was sometimes even carried on a visit to another deity to participate together in a festival (the Egyptian term for which was related to a term meaning "appear"). At that time it would be borne in a boat on the shoulders of priests, although probably still in an enclosure, protected from the eyes of the people. The major festivals of the most popular deities drew crowds from all over Egypt and included singing, dancing, eating, and drinking. Each year, during the last month of the inundation of the Nile, the most popular festival in Egypt was held at Abydos to assure and celebrate Osiris's resurrection. Festivals also were opportunities for individuals to receive personal benefits through prayers and oracles. The behavior of the images in procession could provide answers to inquiries.

Temples also offered other opportunities for contact with the divine. Some temples had special sections where prayers could be offered. Questions could be brought to the temple at various times for oracular responses from priests. Such questions might involve what field to cultivate or crop to plant, auspicious days for certain activities, what remedy to apply to an affliction (medicine and magic were interrelated), whether a child would survive an illness, whom to appoint to a position, etc.[44] Dignitaries also erected intermediary statues in outer courts of the temple that promised to intercede with the god of the temple on behalf of an individual. Dreams offered another medium through which contact with the gods were sought.[45]

CANAAN

The most immediate religious context for the study of ancient Israel and the OT is that of Canaan and Syria, usually studied simply as Canaanite religion. Although also used more narrowly, the term *Canaanites* (Gen. 12:6; 24:3; Ex. 13:11; Judg. 1:1, 27–33; Neh. 9:24; Ezek. 16:3) alternates with *Amorites* (Gen. 15:16; Josh. 24:15–18; Judg. 6:10; 1 Sam. 7:14; 1 Kings 21:26; 2 Kings 21:11; Amos 2:10) in the OT to describe

---

44. There was a large number of gods and goddesses connected with medicine, healing, and childbirth. See Silverman, "Divinity and Deities in Ancient Egypt," 53–54.

45. Morenz, *Egyptian Religion*, 101–104; Baines, "Society, Morality, and Religious Practice," 169–72, 183–86. Baines (176–78) also finds evidence for individual piety in names, which he says are "meaningful utterances, most of them relating to gods."

the many tribes occupying Palestine and Syria when the Israelites arrived.[46]

Archaeology has revealed a striking continuity of ancient Semitic culture from Palestine north through Phoenicia to ancient Ugarit, where a corpus of ancient documents was discovered that greatly illuminates that culture. Nevertheless, cultural differences certainly existed, especially after the introduction of Hurrians, Philistines, and Arameans into the area.[47]

The main sources for Canaanite religion are (1) religious texts including myths, god lists, and sacrificial lists from Ras Shamra, ancient Ugarit (texts dating from LBIII, 1365–1185 B.C.), and from Tell Mardikh, ancient Ebla of the third millennium; (2) polemical allusions in the OT; (3) classical sources, especially (a) Eusebius (fourth century A.D.) who quotes from a translation by Philo of Byblos (ca. 100 B.C.) of a Phoenician history by a Phoenician priest named Sanchuniathon of Beirut, and (b) Lucian of Samasota, *On the Syrian Goddess*, a second-century A.D. work describing the cult of Astarte in Hieropolis; (4) Phoenician and Punic inscriptions; (5) Egyptian texts such as those from Amarna; and (6) archaeological remains of ancient temples, shrines, and cult objects.

Although caution must be exercised in assuming similarites when evidence is insufficient, Canaanite religion shared much with that of Mesopotamia.[48]

THE GODS

According to A. M. Cooper, "a central feature of Ugaritic religion was the veneration of two divine pairs." El and Athirat symbolized "kingly and

---

46. "Canaanites" was also used for the peoples occupying the plains and the Jordan valley, over against the "Amorites" who occupied the hills and Transjordan north of Edom and Moab (cf. Num. 13:29; 14:25; 21:13f.; Deut. 1:7f.; 3:8; Josh. 10:5; 11:3; 24:8). Both terms appear also to have been used even more narrowly (Gen. 15:21; Ex. 3:8; 13:5; 23:23; 33:2; 34:11; Deut. 7:1; 20:17; Josh. 3:10; 9:1; 12:8; 24:11; Ezra 9:1;Neh. 9:8). R. de Vaux (*The Early History of Israel* [Philadelphia: Westminster, 1978], 133) suggests that "Amorite" was applied first to tribes in Transjordan and the western hill country, then to those of the whole region. "Canaanite," on the other hand, was used first of all of the inhabitants of the Egyptian province of Canaan, then more specifically of those of the plain and the Jordan valley, and finally of the Phoenicians.

47. de Vaux, *Early History of Israel*, 140. Some, in fact, would prefer to limit the term "Canaanite religion" to that of second millennium Ugarit and to discuss separately its successors, Phoenician religion and the syncretism of first millennium Israel. See A. M. Cooper, "Canaanite Religion," in *Religions in Antiquity*, ed. R. M. Seltzer (New York: Macmillan, 1989), 80, 94.

48. G. E. Wright, *The Old Testament Against Its Environment* (Naperville, Ill.: Alec R. Allenson, 1957), 16–19.

queenly sovereignty over the world," and Baal and Anat "represented brother and sister, caught in the flux and turmoil of the world, engaged in constant struggle for survival and supremacy."[49]

El was the high god, the patriarch who ruled over the "assembly of the gods," begetter of the gods (known as "sons of El") and creator of the world and of humanity. He was noted for his wisdom and benevolence (called *Latipan*, "kindly one"), but like the Mesopotamian god An, he was not considered particularly active in worldly affairs. He is sometimes called "the bull El," but "he is omnipotence at a distance, interfering only on certain decisive occasions."[50] He is said to have dwelt "at the source of the rivers, amid the springs of the two oceans."[51] The Ugaritic text most likely to have been used in a "sacred marriage" rite concerns El, who after destroying the god of death impregnates two women identified as *Athirat* and *Rahmay* (perhaps *Anat*).[52]

His chief wife was *Athirat*, mother of the gods (called the "seventy sons of Athirat"), also called *Elat* ("goddess"), "lady Athirat of the sea," and "the Holy one" (*qdš*, literally, "holiness"). Figurines commonly identified as *Athirat/Qdš* (perhaps *Qadesh* or *Qudshu*) have been found in second-millennium Syria-Palestine which picture her as a nude goddess holding plants or animals, apparently signifying fertility.[53] She appears in the OT apparently as Baal's consort *Asherah* (1 Kings 18:19; 2 Kings 23:4, 7). Her symbol, a pole probably representing a tree, is referred to often either in the singular form *ʾAsherah* or the plural *ʾAsherim* (masculine) or *ʾAsherot*

---

49. Cooper, "Canaanite Religion," 85.

50. Ringgren, *Religions of the Ancient Near East*, 129.

51. This is found in "The Palace of Baal," in J. C. L. Gibson, *Canaanite Myths and Legends [CML]* (Edinburgh: T. & T. Clark, 1977), 53. This is the most accessible scholarly edition of the major texts. Gibson cites as related Old Testament passages Gen 2:6,10ff.; Job 28:11; 38:16–17; Ezek. 28:2; 47:1ff.; Joel 4:18; Zech. 14:8.

52. See the study of *El* in *TDOT*, s.v. "אֵל/ēl," by F. M. Cross, especially pp. 246–48. Gibson argues for a cosmogonic interpretation, however, rather than a fertility ritual (*CML*, 29–30).

53. See *ANEP*, 160–65. At least some of these may represent Anat or Ashtart or an assimilation of mother goddesses. But see O. Margalith, "A New Type of Asherah-Figurine?" *VT* 44 (1994): 109–15. He identifies as Athirat some figurines recently found at Aphek and Ekron of "a goddess suckling twins and pointing at her vagina." He suggests they represent the Asherah of Jezebel (1 Kings 16:33; 2 Kings 13:6) introduced to Jerusalem by Manasseh (2 Kings 21:3). Recent excavations at Ekron, he says, uncovered ostraca with the words *qdš, qdš lʾšrh,* and *lʾšrh.*

(feminine).[54] According to the Bible, her worship included the practice of sacred prostitution. There is also inscriptional evidence that a syncretistic form of Yahwism may have existed in ancient Israel that considered Asherah to be Yahweh's consort.[55]

Baal was the most popular male deity among the Canaanites, appointed king of the gods by El. He was a fertility god, the provider of rain and responsible for lightning and thunder, often called "rider on the clouds" (cf. Ps. 68:4). The term *ba'al*, which meant "lord" or "husband," was probably first simply an epithet for the personal name *Hadad*, "thunderer," known among eastern and western Semites as god of storm, war, fertility, and divination (also known variously as Haddu, Adad, and Hada).[56] Baal is often called "mightiest" (*'aliyan*), "prince" (*zbl*),[57] and sometimes "the name" (*CML*, 42, 44, 46). Among the Phoenicians he was known as *Baal-shamem*, "Baal of the heavens." In the OT, the name always appears with the article and is usually plural, probably referring to local manifestations of the deity. This is supported by place names such as Baal Peor (Deut. 4:3), Baal Gad

---

54. Ugaritic *th* is the linguistic equivalent of Hebrew *sh*, and the Ugaritic feminine ending *t* is in Hebrew *h*. Thus, *Asherah* is the Hebrew equivalent of Ugaritic *Athirat*. It is singular in Deut. 16:21; Judg. 6:25–30; 1 Kings 15:13; 16:33; 2 Kings 13:6; 17:16; 18:4; 21:3,7; 23:6,15. The masculine plural occurs in Ex. 34:13; Deut. 7:5; 12:3; 1 Kings 14:15,23; 2 Kings 17:10; 23:14; 2 Chron. 14:2; 17:6; 24:18; 31:1; 33:19; 34:3–7; Isa. 17:8; 27:9; Jer. 17:2; Mic. 5:13. It is feminine plural in Judg. 3:7; 2 Chron. 19:3; 33:3. For possible distinctions between singular and plural see M. S. Smith, *The Early History of God* (San Francisco: Harper & Row, 1990), 81. Gibson, however, claims, "Contrary to the generally accepted opinion she probably does not appear in the Bible, where the term *'ăšērāh* 'sacred pole, tree' means simply and more exactly '(holy) place' or 'shrine' (*CML*, 4, n. 1)." See also P. D. Miller, "The Absence of the Goddess in Israelite Religion," *Hebrew Annual Review* 10 (1986): 239–48.

55. Z. Meshel, "Did Yahweh Have a Consort?" *BAR* 5.2 (1979): 24–35; J. A. Emerton, "New Light on Israelite Religion: the Implications of the Inscriptions from Kuntillet 'Ajrud," *ZAW* 94 (1982): 2–20; W. A. Maier, *'Ašerah: Extrabiblical Evidence*, HSM (Atlanta: Scholars, 1986); Smith, *Early History of God*, 80–114; J. Day, "Asherah in the Hebrew Bible and Northwest Semitic Literature," *JBL* 105 (1986): 385–408; S. A. Olyan, *Asherah and the Cult of Yahweh in Israel*, SBLMS 34 (Atlanta: Scholars, 1988); R. J. Pettey, *Asherah: Goddess of Israel* (N.Y.: Peter Lang, 1990).

56. Hadad was the main deity of the Arameans, worshiped at Damascus as *Hadad-Rimmōn /Rammān* (cf. 2 Kings 5:18; Zech. 12:11). The name "Hadad" is common in the Bible in names of kings of Damascus. See also J. C. Greenfield, "The Aramaean God *Rammān /Rimmōn*," *IEJ* 26 (1976): 195–98; idem, "Aspects of Aramean Religion," in *Ancient Israelite Religion*, ed. P. D. Miller, et al. (Philadelphia: Fortress, 1987), 67–78. On the Eblaite deity Hada, see G. Pettinato, *The Archives of Ebla* (Garden City, N.Y.: Doubleday, 1981), 246.

57. The title Baal Zebul, "Baal the prince," is intentionally corrupted to Baal Zebub, "lord of flies," in 2 Kings 1:2f. (cf. Matt. 10:25).

(Josh. 11:17), and Baal Zaphon (Ex. 14:2). In eighth-century B.C. Israel, many apparently had identified Baal with Yahweh (Hos. 2:18–19).

The major myths about Baal involve his defeat of *Yam* ("sea," also called *Nahar*, "river"; *CML*, 37–45; cf. Ps. 74:13), the building of his palace (temple; *CML*, 46–67), and his conflict with *Mot* ("death") in which he dies and rises again (*CML*, 68–81, especially 74–78). This latter myth was associated with fertility/sterility cycles caused by seasonal changes or by periods of famine or plenty. Baal's defeat of Yam in a primeval battle may be compared to Marduk's defeat of Tiamat in the *Enuma Elish*. Associated foes or other names for Yam were *Leviathan* (*ltn*), the seven-headed serpent (*btn*), and the "dragon" (*tnn*; *CML*, 7, 50, 68).[58] He was thought to dwell on Mount Zephon (*spn*), modern Jebel el-Aqraᶜ, the highest peak in Syria.[59]

In Ugarit, Baal's chief consort was his sister *Anat*, a fierce warrior goddess who defeated and dismembered Mot, thus rescuing Baal from the underworld, thereby ensuring the restoration of fertility. She also helped Baal defeat Leviathan. She is described in "The Palace of Baal" as slaying the inhabitants of two cities, tying their heads and hands to her garments, and wading through blood up to her knees, as "her liver swelled with laughter" (*CML*, 47–48). She is often called "the Virgin Anat," a title perhaps explained by an Egyptian text that characterizes her as conceiving but never bearing.[60]

The worship of Anat was evidently not as popular among the Canaanites in direct contact with Israel, as her name only appears in the OT in place names (Anatoth in Josh. 21:18 and Jer. 1:1; Beth-anath in Josh. 19:38 and Judg. 1:33; and Beth-anoth in Josh. 15:59) and in the designation of Shamgar, the minor judge who fought the Philistines, as "son of Anat" (Judg. 3:31; 5:6).[61]

Another of Baal's consort's, appearing frequently in the OT and in Phoenician inscriptions but less prominent in the Ugaritic texts, was known at Ugarit as *Athtart* (*CML*, 42, 86; Phoenician *Ashtart*, Greek *Astarte*). She is called *Ashtoret* (or *Ashtarot*, plural) in the OT, usually understood to be a derogatory term derived by combining her name (*Ash-*

---

58. Cf. Job 3:8; 7:12; 41:1; Pss. 74:13–14; 104:26; Isa. 27:1; 51:9.

59. Baal Zephon, meaning "Baal of the north," was a site in Egypt of unknown location apparently named for him (Ex. 14:2; Num. 33:7). The worship of Baal and other Canaanite gods was popular in Egypt, especially in the north. The term *ṣāpôn* in Hebrew means "north," but in Ps. 48:2[3] it is a mythological allusion.

60. *ABD*, s.v. "Baal."

61. This is understood by P. C. Craigie to be a reference to his military status ("A Reconsideration of Shamgar ben Anath [Judg. 3:31 and 5:6]," *JBL* 91 [1972]: 239–40). F. M. Cross, on the other hand, suggested that Ben Anath was the name of Shamgar's father, named for the goddess ("Newly Found Inscriptions in Old Canaanite and Early Phoenician Scripts," *BASOR* 238 [1980]: 1–20).

trt) with the vowels from *bōšet,* "shame."[62] It seems the role played by Anat at Ugarit was played by Ashtart in Canaan.

Like the other polytheistic peoples of the ancient Near East, the Canaanites had many minor deities as well. Although El is sometimes designated Baal's father, his father is usually said to be *Dagon* (or Dagan), whose name suggests he was a corn god. He also is known from the Middle Euphrates (Mari and Terqa) and was the main god at Ebla.[63] One of the two temples on the acropolis at Ugarit was dedicated to Dagan, suggesting to some an identification with El (*CML,* 10). According to the OT he was the main god of the Philistines (Judg. 16:23; 1 Sam. 5:2), who, being latecomers to Palestine, apparently adopted him from the Canaanites.

The sun was worshiped at Ugarit as the goddess *Shapash,* who scorches the earth while Baal is in the underworld (*CML,* 53).[64] She was thought to travel through the underworld at night (similar to Mesopotamian Shamash; cf. *CML,* 81), where the shades, or deified dead, dwelt. She sometimes served as El's messenger. There was also a moon god, *Yarikh,* apparently the patron deity of Canaanite Jericho. His marriage to the moon goddess Nikkal and the subsequent birth of a son is celebrated in a myth that may have been used in incantations for blessing and protection in childbirth (*CML,* 30–31, 128–29).

Apparently escorting Shapash through the underworld was the underworld's doorkeeper *Resheph,* known also at Ebla (as *Rasap*), Mari, Egypt (Amarna), and from Punic inscriptions. The god of pestilence, he was sometimes called "Lord of the arrow," that is, the arrow of pestilence.[65] A god list identifies him as the equivalent of the Mesopotamian Nergal. He may have been the god referred to by the name *Rapiu* "healer," patron god of the deified dead (*rpʾum;* cf. Heb. *rĕpāʾîm,* "shades" and *rāpāʾ* "to heal").[66]

---

62. See Jer. 3:24; 11:13; Hos. 9:10 and comment in F. B. Huey, *Jeremiah, Lamentations,* NAC (Nashville: Broadman & Holman, 1993), 78. The name is clearly related to Babylonia's astral deity Ishtar.

63. Hallo and Simpson, *The Ancient Near East,* 96; Pettinato, *Archives of Ebla,* 246–48. Pettinato understands the meaning of the name as "cloud, rain."

64. At Ebla the sun was worshiped as the male deity *Sipiš* (Pettinato, *Archives of Ebla,* 246). King Josiah removed from the temple horses and chariots previously given as votive offerings "to the sun" (*laššemeš*) according to 2 Kings 23:11.

65. Ringgren, *Religions of the Ancient Near East,* 137; Gibson, *CML,* 82. The Hebrew word *rešep* "flame" is sometimes associated with arrows (see Ps. 76:4[3]), lightning (Ps. 78:48), or pestilence (Deut. 32:24; Hab. 3:5). See J. C. Greenfield, "Smitten by Famine, Battered by Plague (Deuteronomy 32:24)," in *Love and Death in the Ancient Near East,* J. H. Marks and R. M. Good (Guilford, CT: Four Quarters, 1986), 151–52. For a detailed study of the god, see Fulco, *The Canaanite God Rešep.*

66. Cooper, "Canaanite Religion," 86; A. Caquot and M. Sznycer, *Ugaritic Religion* (Leiden: Brill, 1980), 15.

Many other deities were important in certain regions and were often regarded as local manifestations of common deities. Inscriptions identify the primary deity of Byblos as the goddess *Ba'alat*. There was also a god there apparently called *Adon* ("lord"), probably an epithet applied to various gods, including Baal, Eshmun of Sidon, Melqart of Tyre, and others. He is known primarily from Greek sources as *Adonis*. A fertility god, he was said to have been killed by a boar while hunting, but Aphrodite managed his release from Hades for half the year.[67]

The chief god of Edom, not mentioned in the Bible (cf. 2 Chron. 25:20), seems to have been known as *Qaus*.[68] The national god of the Moabites was *Chemosh* (*kāmôš*) according to the OT and the Moabite stone.[69] He is another god sometimes associated with Nergal. The god of the Ammonites is known from the Bible as *Milcom* (Hebrew *milkōm* or *malkām*, both rendered by NIV as "Molech"). A Canaanite deity whose worship was connected to a cult of the dead involving divination and to some extent child sacrifice was *Molek*.[70] Both names are based on the root *mlk* "king" (Hebrew *melek*), suggesting to some that the biblical terms are only epithets for another deity—Baal, Melqart, Athtar, etc.[71] The identification of Chemosh as god of the Ammonites in Judges 11:24, as well as Chemosh's association with child sacrifice (cf. 2 Kings 3:26–27), has led to

---

67. *ABD*, s.v. "Canaan, religion of," by J. Day. The first clear and explicit reference to an Adonis cult is from Theocritus (*Idyll* 15; third century B.C.). It describes a festival at Alexandria that celebrates a sacred marriage using statues of Adonis and Aphrodite, followed by laments for Adonis' death. Direct reference to an Adonis cult at Byblos comes from Lucian (*De Dea Syria* 6,8; second century A.D.). See A. S. F. Gow, *Theocritus*, 2 vols. (Cambridge: Cambridge University, 1950), 264; M. H. Pope and W. Röllig, "Syrien. Die Mythologie der Ugariten und Phönizier," in *Wörterbuch der Mythologie*, ed. H. W. Haussig (Stuttgart: Ernst Klett, 1962), 234.

68. D. I. Block, *The Gods of the Nations* (Jackson, Miss.: Evangelical Theological Society, 1988): 33–35.

69. Num. 21:29; Judg. 11:24; 1 Kings 11:7,33; 2 Kings 23:13; Jer. 48:7,13,46; *ANET*, 320. There was a god *Kamiš* at Ebla (Pettinato, *Archives of Ebla*, 247).

70. First Kings 11:7 gives the Ammonite god as *mōlek*, but this is regarded by many as a scribal error. In the NIV "Molech" renders *mōlek* in Lev. 18:21; 20:2–5; 1 Kings 11:7; 2 Kings 23:10; Jer. 32:35. It is also used for *milkōm* in 1 Kings 11:5,33; 2 Kings 23:13, and *malkām* in Jer. 49:1,3; Zeph. 1:5.

71. Melqart, whose name is derived from *mlk* "king" and *qrt* "city," in fact may have been Molek, as Albright argued, noting that *qrt* may have refered to the underworld rather than to Tyre (*Archaeology and the Religion of Israel*, 3d ed. [Baltimore: Johns Hopkins, 1953], 81, 196 n. 29). Cf. G. C. Heider, *The Cult of Molek: A Reassessment*, JSOTSup 43 (Sheffield: JSOT, 1985), 175–79,181; Block, *The Gods of the Nations*, 49.

the further suggestion that he also was only a local manifestation of the same god.[72]

RESPONSE TO THE GODS

Scholarly objections are becoming more frequent to the views that Canaanite religion in the second millennium B.C. was primarily a fertility cult and that the myths from Ugarit should be interpreted seasonally, recited at festivals, or served as librettos in sacred drama. It is certain, however, that agricultural productivity was a major concern to peoples throughout the ancient Near East and that they relied on the gods in this regard. There must have been rituals, then, that involved fertility; furthermore, the theme does permeate myths from Ugarit. Nevertheless, there are other themes as well. Perhaps the overriding theme is order versus chaos in both divine and human spheres, which included themes of kingship, fertility, suffering, and death.

The only ritual from Ugarit for which a detailed description exists involved the king, who was the cultic head, and his queen. The king purified himself and made offerings to various deities over the course of several days. Offerings consisted primarily of sheep and included one called *shlm*, "peace" (cf. Hebrew *šālôm*). It was a gift to the gods that was burned entirely on the altar. Offerings also included precious metals. Another aspect of the ritual was divination by the analysis of livers from sacrificial

---

72. P. C. Craigie followed Fohrer and Gray in identifying both Chemosh and Milcom with the Ugaritic god Athtar/Ashtar (cf. the name "Ashtar-Chemosh" in the Mesha inscription, *ANET*, 320). See *ISBE*, s.v. "religions of the biblical world: Canaanite," by P. C. Craigie and G. H. Wilson; G. Fohrer, *History of Israelite Religion* (Nashville: Abingdon, 1972), 50–52; J. Gray, *The Legacy of Canaan*, VTSup 5, 2d ed. (Leiden: Brill, 1965), 171–73. Many have disputed even the identification of Molek as a god in favor of the view that *mlk* originally referred to a type of sacrifice (*molk*). This is the "Eissfeldt hypothesis" summarized by Heider (*Cult of Molek*, 34–39) and most recently defended by P. Mosca (*Child Sacrifice in Canaanite and Israelite Religion: A Study in 'Mulk' and 'mlk'* [Ph. D. diss., Harvard University, 1975]). It is refuted by Heider and others. Another view, no longer widely held, was that *mōlek* was the result of a revocalization of *melek* with the vowels of *bōšet* (like Ashtart/Ashtoret discussed above). See R. de Vaux, *Ancient Israel* (N.Y.: McGraw-Hill, 1965), 446; Mosca, 123–34; Heider, *Cult of Molek*, 4,9–10, 224. Heider notes, however, that in 2 Kings 23:10 Josiah desecrated the "Topheth" ("furnace") in the Valley of Ben Hinnom where *Molech* had been worshiped with child sacrifice, and according to verse 13 in a separate act he desecrated the high place dedicated to *Milcom*, "the detestable god of the people of Ammon" (see Freedman, ed., *ABD*, s.v. "Molech," by G. C. Heider). Furthermore, he has shown that there was a west Semitic god worshiped in a cult of the dead who was variously known at Ebla, Mari, Ugarit, and in Mesopotamia as Malik, Milku/i, and Muluk (*Cult of Molek*, 94–168). Akkadian god lists equated him with Nergal.

animals. Concluding the ritual was a prayer, probably recited by the queen, which called upon Baal to "chase the strong enemy from our gates." The prayer also mentions the consecration of a firstborn and the offering of a tithe. The only public festival for which we have clear evidence called for the assembly of the entire populace at Ugarit for the purpose of purification. Everyone offered sacrifices, sang, and prayed to El and the other gods for protection from enemies.[73]

The only Ugaritic myth containing clear evidence of ritual performance is called "Shachar and Shalim and the Gracious Gods." Here the king and queen again took part along with other cult officials. The ritual included offerings, a banquet, singing, and a sacred drama about the destruction of death, El's seduction of Athirat and Rahmay, and the birth of the two gods Shachar (dawn) and Shalim (dusk). There is no indication when or how often the ritual occurred, nor what was its purpose, although it is usually associated with fertility.

A cult of the dead also was practiced at Ugarit in which the dead were summoned to a drunken orgy (perhaps at a family tomb) called a *marzih* and invoked for help and protection. It is described in a ritual text called the "Document of the Feast of the Protective Ancestral Spirits." The dead were called *rpʾum* (see above) and the elite group among them (*mlkm*) comprised past kings of Ugarit. The head or patron deity of the *rpʾum* was the god *Rapiu*, perhaps identified with El, Resheph (see above), Malik/Molek, Baal, or "the personification of the *rpʾum*."[74]

A seasonal association for at least some of the Ugaritic myths is difficult to deny (cf. the agricultural motifs in "Baal and Mot"), and their use in festivals of harvest celebration and appeal seems probable. The dependence of merchant seamen on good weather also would expand the importance of the regular observance of such cultic festivals. Although evidence for an extensive "fertility cult" among the Canaanites involving male and female prostitutes is being reevaluated, biblical evidence for it is strong. The bib-

---

73. Cooper, "Canaanite Religion," 88–89. See also Caquot and Sznycer, *Ugaritic Religion*, 17–18.

74. Caquot and Sznycer, *Ugaritic Religion*, 19. A brief description of the feast may be found in Cooper, "Canaanite Religion," 90. See also C. E. L'Heureux, *Rank among the Canaanite Gods: El, Baʿal and the Repha'im*, HSM 21 (Missoula, MT: Scholars, 1979), 169–72; M. Pope, "The Cult of the Dead at Ugarit," in *Ugarit in Retrospect*, ed. G. D. Young (Winona Lake, IN: Eisenbrauns, 1981), 159–79; idem, "Notes on the Rephaim Texts from Ugarit," in *Essays on the Ancient Near East*, ed. M. Ellis (Hamden, CT: Archon, 1977); T. J. Lewis, *Cults of the Dead in Ancient Israel and Ugarit*, HSM (Atlanta: Scholars, 1989). On the cult in Judah see E. M. Bloch-Smith, "The Cult of the Dead in Judah: Interpreting the Material Remains," *JBL* 111 (1992): 213–24. On similar practices in Mesopotamia see above. For a discussion of other views on the *mlkm* see Heider, *Cult of Molek*, 128–33.

lical terms *qādēš* and *qĕdēšâ* seem to refer to male and female cult prostitutes (respectively).[75] They were frequently associated with local
sanctuaries called "high places" (Hebrew *bāmôt*) that in Israel came to be
centers of a syncretized Baal/Yahweh worship; this included the use of
Asherah poles symbolizing the female deity, standing stones (*maṣṣēbôt*)
symbolizing the male deity, incense altars, and sometimes human sacrifice.[76] There was a class of temple personnel at Ugarit called *qdšm* who
are mentioned alongside the *khnm* ("priests"; cf. Hebrew *kōhănîm*), but
their function is not specified.[77] P. C. Craigie's conclusion was that a
Canaanite fertility cult was widespread, confirmed archaeologically by
"temples with chambers where sexual activity took place" and the many
fertility goddess statuettes. Such cultic sexual activity, he said, amounted
to "'stockpiling' fertility energy, which ensured the continuing stability of
agricultural as well as human and animal productivity."[78]

THE UNIQUENESS OF
BIBLICAL RELIGION

The worship of Yahweh and the religions of the surrounding peoples of
the ancient Near East shared many of the same forms. They all had multi-
chambered temples and various kinds of offerings, priests, and other temple personnel. Words for "god" were often quite similar as were also those
for priests and other elements of the cult. They all assumed a close connection between divine favor and individual human lives, seeking divine
help through prayers and offerings, and celebrating divine blessings with
more offerings and songs of thanksgiving and praise.

---

75. Gen. 38:15–18, 21–22; Deut. 23:17–18; 1 Kings 14:23-24; 2 Kings 23:4–7;
Jer. 2:20; Ezek. 16:31; Hos. 4:13–14. See the argument by E. A. Goodfriend, however, that biblical *qĕdēšâ* and *zônâ* referred to a common prostitute and *qādēš* and
keleb (lit., "dog") referred to pagan cult officials (*ABD*, s.v. "prostitution [Old Testa-
ment]." See also *TWAT*, s.v. "קדש *qdš*," by H. Ringgren (who notes that while evidence is strong for cult prostitution in Mesopotamia connected to the cult of Ishtar,
such evidence at Ugarit is ambiguous); *ABD*, s.v. "Canaan, Religion of."
76. Cf. Lev. 26:30; Num. 33:52; 1 Kings 14:23–24; 2 Kings 16:4;17:8–17; 23:15;
Isa. 16:12; Jer. 7:31; 19:5; 32:35; Ezek. 6:3–6; 16:16–25; 20:26–32.
77. K. van der Toorn describes them as "all the nonpriestly temple personnel,
who had been dedicated to a deity" (*ABD*, s.v. "prostitution [cultic]." While she
denies that biblical *qĕdēšîm* were necessarily prostitutes, she admits that a practice
that could be called "cultic prostitution" did exist in Israel. She defines it, however,
as the payment of vows to the temple by means of prostitution. See also K. van der
Toorn, "Female Prostitution in Payment of Vows in Ancient Israel," *JBL* 108
(1989): 193–205.
78. Craigie and Wilson, "Religions of the Biblical World: Canaanite," 100.

For those who acknowledge the faith of Yahweh to be derived from direct revelation, such similarity may be surprising. One might expect greater divergence between religions that were the products of human imagination and desires and one that was revealed by God. It should be remembered, however, that the worship of Yahweh was not a late development, despite critical assumptions to the contrary. According to the Bible, other religions began as corruptions of an original faith in the one true God (Rom. 1:21–23). Furthermore, the other nations, peoples, and cultures are not independent of divine supervision. They have developed or deteriorated within divinely decreed limits to suit God's purposes. Therefore, the world in which the nation of Israel and its religion were born was in a sense divinely prepared for His purpose. The forms that Israel shared with other nations were creations of His common grace.

Even if such were not the case, God would have revealed to His people a faith and a worship they could comprehend, that is, one which fit the forms with which they were familiar, insofar as they were salvageable for His use. Although such forms should not be treated as trivial or expendable, it was as they were united to the substance or heart of Israel's faith that they became meaningful and functionally distinctive, since the heart of Israel's faith diverged drastically from that of their neighbors.[79]

First and foremost, the worship of Yahweh was to be monotheistic and exclusivistic. Cities in the ancient Near East often were filled with temples to various gods. Each of Babylon's nine city gates was dedicated to a different god. Furthermore, the practitioners of the other religions often expended great effort either identifying their gods with the gods of other nations (hence the frequently discovered god lists) or demonstrating the subordination of other gods to their patron deity. Such god lists or stories of how Yahweh had assumed the powers or duties of other deities would have been inconceivable to orthodox worhipers of Yahweh. Israel's God demanded more than a special place in their pantheons and hearts; He demanded their entire hearts, souls, and strength (Deut. 6:5). As E. Smick expressed it, "Their God was the unique and cosmic deity who demanded exclusive allegiance. Such a concept ran against the grain of all the religions of the day."[80]

---

79. See Wright, *The Old Testament against Its Environment*, 9–41; J. N. Oswalt, "Golden Calves and the 'Bull of Jacob': The Impact on Israel of Its Religious Environment," in *Israel's Apostasy and Restoration*, ed. A. Gileadi (Grand Rapids: Baker, 1988): 9–18.

80. E. B. Smick, "Israel's Struggle with the Religions of Canaan," in *Through Christ's Word*, ed. W. R. Godfrey and J. L. Boyd III (Phillipsburg, N.J.: Presbyterian and Reformed, 1985), 108; Block, *The Gods of the Nations*, 67-68.

Second, the God of Israel was not the personification of forces of nature and did not need the assistance of other gods or the participation of a king and his subjects in a divine struggle to maintain order in the universe, nor did He need to be tended or fed in temples. He is the transcendant one who created an inanimate universe of nature out of nothing and who continually maintains and controls it for His glory. J. N. Oswalt declares, "In many ways this is the profoundest insight of Hebrew religion. Whatever God is, he is not the world around us."[81] Furthermore, "Moses understood fully that unless the link between Creator and creation was broken, it would become impossible in any ultimate sense to maintain God's unity and exclusiveness, and his immunity to magic, all of which were central to the new faith."[82]

Third, existing above and apart from nature, God has not kept His character and His will hidden. The gods of the other peoples did not reveal their will in clear and certain terms. As T. Jacobsen describes Enlil, "Man can never be fully at ease with Enlil, can never know what he has in mind. . . . In his wild moods of destructiveness he is unreachable, deaf to all appeals."[83] As S. N. Kramer explains, "The proper course for a Sumerian Job to pursue was not to argue and complain in face of seemingly unjustifiable misfortune, but to plead and wail, lament and confess, his inevitable sins and failings. But will the gods give heed to him, a lone and not very effective mortal, even if he prostrates and humbles himself in heartfelt prayer? Probably not."[84] Revolutionary, then, was Deuteronomy 4:6–8 in praise of the Mosaic Law as "your wisdom and your understanding in the sight of the peoples" and of Israel's secure relationship to the Lord. Unlike Enlil, our God is characteristically one who has revealed "what he Has in mind" and who hears our appeals. The other nations needed divination through household deities, departed ancestors, etc., to discover (usually only after the fact) how to deal with situations in their lives. Furthermore, such supernatural assistance often demanded great human agony and physical pain, even bodily mutilation (cf. Deut. 14:1; 1 Kings 18:26–29).

The basis for differences in gaining divine access or attention is yet another area of divergence of Israel's faith from that of her neighbors: the

---

81. Oswalt, "Golden Calves and the 'Bull of Jacob,'" 13.

82. Ibid., 15. The one exception to God's separation from His creation is the incarnation, hinted at in the Old Testament and expounded in the New. Stories of humans becoming gods and periodically dying and rising gods were not uncommon, but the concept of God becoming human is a radical departure and a radical solution to the problem of sin.

83. Jacobsen, *Treasures of Darkness*, 101–102.

84. Kramer, *The Sumerians*, 125–26.

nature of the relationship between the people and their god/gods. The gods of the nations were said to have created the world for themselves; humankind was an afterthought, a necessary nuisance whose function was only to serve the gods. Aside from irritation, about the only emotional response we find from the gods toward their human creatures is an occasional sense of pity or remorse for their grievous situation. The Bible, on the other hand, presents humankind as the "crown of creation" and the natural world as theirs to oversee and enjoy.

Also, D. Block has shown that the gods of the nations were primarily gods of the land and only secondarily gods of the people of the land. They had a kind of feudal relationship in which the gods were lords of the estate and the people were their serfs whose sole purpose was to tend the land. The religion of Israel was unique in understanding God's relationship to His people as primary, formed before He provided them a land, and continuing after their sin resulted in the loss of that land (cf. Deut. 32:9; 2 Kings 17:26; Ezek. 11:16).[85] Yahweh had formed a people, bound them to each other and to Himself by covenant, and pledged to shepherd them faithfully forever by His grace and to guard jealously their relationship to Him. As J. Baldwin explains, "Nowhere in the Old Testament is God portayed as impassive, aloof, uninvolved with our world. The utter holiness of His love only intensifies the suffering involved when that love is rejected, and His desire to save men from the death towards which they are heading is something we only dimly appreciate (Ezek. 18:23, 31,32)."[86] Biblical religion gives at the same time a higher view of humanity and a higher view of God—omnipotent, undivided, purposive, merciful, and uniformly righteous.

Finally, while the worship of Yahweh included ritual as an expression of dependent faith, loyalty, and obedience, that ritual was never to be an end in itself (cf. 1 Sam. 15:22; Pss. 40:6; 50:8–15; 51:16–17; Hos. 6:4–6). There was to be an internal quality to the faith of Israel that was not found in the other religions. The other religions aimed at manipulating the gods into granting favors. Thus, they were driven by ritual. But Yahweh looked on the heart, and He abhorred ritual that did not arise from righteous devotion. From the beginning Israel was enjoined not only to love the Lord but also to "rejoice before the Lord your God" (Deut. 12:12, 18; cf. 14:26; 16:11, 14—15; 26:11; 27:7,) and they would be judged because they

---

85. Block, *The Gods of the Nations*, 7–23, 28, 60, 96–97.

86. J. G. Baldwin, *Haggai, Zechariah, Malachi*, TOTC (London: Inter-Varsity, 1972), 98–99. See also J. A. Thompson, *Deuteronomy*, TOTC (Leicester, England: Inter-Varsity, 1974), 70.

did not "serve the Lord your God joyfully and gladly in the time of prosperity" (Deut. 28:47).

Thus, Israel was to be a kingdom of priests, singing to the Lord and declaring His glory among the nations day after day. "For all the gods of the nations are idols, but the Lord made the heavens" (1 Chron. 16:26).

FOR FURTHER READING

Block, D. I. *The Gods of the Nations.* Jackson, Miss.: Evangelical Theological Society, 1988.

Cooper, A. M. "Canaanite Religion." In *Religions in Antiquity*, edited by R. M. Seltzer. New York: Macmillan, 1989.

Finegan, J. *Myth and Mystery.* Grand Rapids: Baker, 1989.

Heider, G. C. *The Cult of Molek: A Reassessment*, JSOTSup 43. Sheffield: JSOT, 1985.

Jacobsen, T. *The Treasures of Darkness: A History of Mesopotamian Religion.* New Haven: Yale University Press, 1976.

Morenz, S. *Egyptian Religion.* Translated by A. E. Keep. Ithaca/London: Cornell University, 1973.

Ringgren, H. *Religions of the Ancient Near East.* Translated by J. Sturdy. Philadelphia: Westminster, 1973.

Shafer, B. E., ed. *Religion in Ancient Egypt.* Ithaca/London: Cornell University, 1991.

XV

POLITICAL BACKGROUND OF THE OLD TESTAMENT

EDWIN M. YAMAUCHI

The revelations recorded in the Old Testament came to Abraham and his descendants over a period of two millennia and centered in Palestine, a tiny land which served as a land bridge between Egypt to the west and Syria/Mesopotamia/Persia to the east. Palestine's geo-political significance far surpassed its geographical area. The distance from Dan to Beersheba measures just 150 miles; it is only 45 miles from Joppa (modern Jaffa) on the coast to Jericho. The area includes a little more than 6,000 square miles. The highway between Egypt and points northeast ran long the coast, cut through the Megiddo Pass, and then went inland around the Sea of Galilee to Damascus. Because it served primarily as a corridor between larger empires on either side of her, Palestine was overwhelmed by its powerful neighbors for most of its history. The descendants of Abraham eventually were scattered outside of Palestine to Egypt, Mesopotamia, and Persia.

ANCIENT MESOPOTAMIA (3000–1100 B.C.)

SUMERIAN AND AKKADIAN ERAS

The earliest chapters of Genesis center on Mesopotamia, the land between the Euphrates and Tigris Rivers (Gen. 2:14). Genesis 10:10 refers to the cities of Nimrod as Babel (Babylon), Erech (Uruk), and Akkad (Agade) in Shinar, that is, in Babylonia. Abraham came from Ur (Gen. 11:28–31), a major city-state in lower Mesopotamia. Chronological indications would place Abraham about the twenty-first or twentieth century, or what archaeologists would call the early Middle Bronze Age.[1]

The Sumerians of lower Mesopotamia were the earliest literate civilization in the world.[2] Earlier pre-literate civilizations are known by their pottery types and cultures as the Hassuna (5800–5500), Samarra (5600–5000), Halaf (5500–4500), Ubaid (5000–3750), Uruk (3750–3150), and Jemdat Nasr (3150–2900) periods. It is possible that clay tokens used for counting during these epochs developed into the earliest pictographic signs for writing. The earliest tablets recovered from Uruk are lists of animals. The vast majority of over 500,000 cuneiform tablets recovered were inscribed for accounting purposes.

The Sumerians, whose origins are still uncertain, developed a series of important city-states in the Early Dynastic Era (2700–2500). The Sumerian King List, which was composed ca. 1900 B.C., traces the succession of kingship at a series of cities one after the other, though we know that they flourished at the same time. These cities included Eridu, Badtibira, Larag, Sippar, and Shuruppak before the flood, and Kish after the flood. The eight kings who are listed are said to have reigned for a total of 241,000 years![3] Uruk was the home to Gilgamesh, who interviewed Utnapishtim, the survivor of the flood according to Babylonian tradition. We have reason to believe that Gilgamesh was a historic king, who reigned ca. 2700 B.C.

The *Lu-Gal* ("Big Man") was the king, who ruled over various subordinates called *En* ("lord") or *Ensi* ("governor"). Each city had its tutelary deity, its main temple, and other temples. Lagash had twenty temples. The chief god of Ur was the moon god (Sumerian *Nanna*; Akkadian *Sin*), a deity also honored at Haran. (Abraham's father's name, Terah, Gen. 11:31, has been associated with a lunar deity.) Uruk was the largest of the Sumer-

---

1. A. R. Millard and D. J. Wiseman, eds., *Essays on the Patriarchal Narratives* (Leicester: InterVarsity, 1980).

2. S. N. Kramer, *The Sumerians* (Chicago: University of Chicago Press, 1963).

3. T. Jacobsen, *The Sumerian King List* (Chicago: University of Chicago Press, 1939); J. Walton, "The Antediluvian Section of the Sumerian King List and Genesis 5," *BA* 44 (1981): 207–8.

ian cities, with 1,110 acres. Its circuit of walls had nearly a thousand semi-circular towers.

At Ur, C. L. Woolley uncovered a series of royal tombs from the Early Dynastic Era. Among the objects recovered were remains of harps, gaming boards, and magnificent gold jewelry. Most startling was the discovery that when the kings and queens were buried, they were accompanied by their servants. In one pit were found the remains of six menservants and sixty-eight women.[4]

The Vulture Stele of Eannatum (2400 B.C.), ruler of Lagash, illustrates the conflicts between city-states. This celebrates the victory of Lagash, under its tutelary deity, Ningirsu, over its neighbor, Umma, in a war which erupted over the breaking of a previous treaty. In the top register Eannatum and his phalanx of heavy infantry march over the prostrate enemy. In the next register the king in a war chariot leads his light infantry. Some 3,600 casualties were inflicted.

In the midst of Sumerian dominance during the third millennium B.C., there was a brief Semitic interlude with the Akkadian rulers of Agade, an unidentified site near Babylon. The founder of the first Mesopotamian Empire was Sargon (2371–2316), whose name represents *sharru(m)-ken(u)* ("The King Is Legitimate"). Later legends describe his obscure birth and his extensive conquests as far as Anatolia, and trade to remote areas such a Dilmun (Bahrein), Magan (Makran in southern Iran), and Meluhha (India). Though Sargon appointed Semites to key posts, he also respected Sumerian tradition by having his daughter serve as the priestess of the moon god Nanna at Ur.

Sargon's grandson, Naram-Sin, was a notable ruler who engaged in extensive trade and conquests. His famous stele, now in the Louvre Museum, depicts him as a conqueror over his enemies in a mountainous region. He wears a horned helmet, which is the emblem of deity; he also prefixed the dingir (god) sign before his name. As a rule, Mesopotamian kings did not claim to be divine, but some later Sumerian rulers also followed Naram-Sin's example. It was more customary for the king simply to claim to be the representative of the gods.

Naram-Sin destroyed the kingdom of Ebla, a site which has been identified with Tell Mardikh in northern Syria.[5] Excavated since 1964 by Italian archaeologists, Ebla has yielded nearly 20,000 tablets, including those in Sumerian and others in a new Semitic language called Eblaite. Adminis-

---

4. C. L. Woolley, *Ur of the Chaldees* (New York: W. W. Norton, 1965).

5. C. Bermant and M. Weitzman, *Ebla: An Archaeological Enigma* (London: Weidenfeld & Nicolson, 1979); P. Matthiae, *Ebla: An Empire Rediscovered* (Garden City, N.Y.: Doubleday, 1981); G. Pettinato, *The Archives of Ebla* (Garden City, N.Y.: Doubleday, 1981).

trative tablets reveal the population of greater Ebla totaled 260,000, overseen by a bureaucracy of 4,700 officials. Although initial claims that Sodom and Gomorrah are mentioned in the texts have proved unfounded, Ebla had numerous trade contacts with Palestinian cities, including Hazor and Megiddo.

After the Gutians from the Zagros Mountains to the east had destroyed Agade, the Sumerians enjoyed a brilliant renaissance. The acme of Sumerian art and language is represented by the numerous inscribed statues of Gudea, a governor of the city of Lagash. The outstanding Ur III Dynasty was established by Ur-Nammu (2113–2096), who built the great ziggurat (staged temple tower) and who also issued the earliest known law code. This indicates that the king made sure "the orphan did not fall a prey to the wealthy." From the period we have three hundred court records, mostly from Lagash.

Shulgi (2095–2048) reformed the calendar and standardized measures. He claimed the authorship of several hymns and served as the patron of literature. He built a defensive wall to the west and arranged diplomatic marriages of his daughters to governors in Elam (southwest Iran) to the east. Amar-Sin (2047–2039) built temples and conducted wars in the northeast. Shu-Sin's reign (2038–2030) was peaceful and prosperous. Foreign trade, which was a royal monopoly, involved imports of metal, exotic foods, plants, and woods. The 100,000 Ur III cuneiform tablets are primarily economic. Shu-Sin had a thousand men a year working for seven years to erect a temple at Shara which required 26 million bricks.

Ibbi-Sin's reign (2029–2006), however, was beset by increased attacks from the Amorite bedouin from the northwest. They simply bypassed the fortress built to control them. As a result inflation and famine became rampant, so that prices rose sixtyfold. Less than a quart of grain now cost a shekel of silver or a month's wage (cf. 2 Kings 6:25). In spite of previous marriage alliances, the Elamites from the east took advantage of Sumer's weakness to sweep down and devastate the hapless Ur, an event commemorated in the poignant "Lamentation for Ur."

THE AMORITE DYNASTIES

Ishbi-Erra, a subordinate of Ibbi-Sin, proclaimed himself king in Isin, inaugurating the so-called Isin-Larsa Era, during which the Sumerian hegemony was ended by waves of Semitic Amorites, who took control over major cities including Mari, Ashur, and Babylon. Though the Sumerians lost political power, their culture continued to exercise influence. A major law code, written in Sumerian, is attributed to Lipit-Ishtar (1932–1906 B.C.) from the Isin-Larsa period.

The early second millennium B.C. was the period of both the Old Assyrian and the Old Babylonian Dynasties. The nomadic origin of the former kings is acknowledged in the Assyrian King List which begins with "17 kings, tent dwellers." Shamshi-Adad (1813–1781), the king of Ashur, left us three hundred letters in which he berates his younger son and compares him unfavorably with his older brother.[6] The Old Assyrian era is also notable for the Assyrian merchants who established colonies in Cappadocia in eastern Turkey. Some of their letters indicate they paid taxes to the local rulers. It has been suggested that Abraham may have functioned like one of these *tamkarum* (merchants).

Of great significance for the background of the biblical patriarchs is the palatial city of Mari on the Middle Euphrates.[7] The palace of its last king, Zimrilim, which was destroyed by Hammurabi (1757 B.C.), covered eight acres. Its archive contained 25,000 tablets, including many texts on diplomacy, the movement of bedouin tribes, customs duties, and prophecy. Names similar to those borne by the biblical patriarchs and their ancestors have been found in these texts. Abraham would have passed nearby on his way from Ur to Haran, to the north of Mari.

At the beginning of his reign Hammurabi (1792–1750 B.C.) of Babylon was but one among a number of similar rulers. An emissary reported to Zimrilim, "There is no king who is mighty by himself. Ten or fifteen kings follow Hammurabi, the man of Babylon, a like number Rim-Sin of Larsa, a like number Ibalpiel of Eshnunna, a like number Amutpiel of Qatana, and 20 follow Yarimlim of Yamkhad."[8] This may be similar to the political background of the coalition of kings who attacked Palestine and took Lot captive (Gen. 14). But then Hammurabi defeated one rival after another, including Larsa, Mari, Subartu, and Eshnunna. The archives of letters from Larsa indicate the king often overruled his governor Sin-Iddinam in response to complaints from his subjects. The king periodically delivered *misharum*, decrees for economic reforms, inviting injured citizens to appear before him. Hammurabi's famed law code depicts him before Shamash, the sun god, and the deity of justice. This contains 282 case laws, which reveal there were three levels of society: (1) *awilum* "citizen," (2) *mushkenum* "client of the palace or temple," and (3) *wardum* "slave."[9]

---

6. J. Laessøe, *People of Ancient Assyria* (New York: Barnes & Noble, 1963).

7. G. Young, ed., *Mari in Retrospect* (Winona Lake, Ind: Eisenbrauns, 1992).

8. G. Dossin, "Akkadian Letters," *ANET*, 628.

9. G. R. Driver and J. C. Miles, *The Babylonian Laws*, 2 vols. (Oxford: Clarendon, 1955–56); W. F. Leemans, "King Hammurapi as Judge," in *Symbolae Iuridicae et Historicae Nartino David Dedicatae*, ed. J. A. Ankum et al. (Leiden: Brill, 1968), 107–29. On comparisons between Babylonian and biblical laws, see: A. Van Selms, "The Goring Ox in Babylonian and Biblical Law, *ArOr* 18 (1950): 321–30; N. Greenberg, "Some Postulates of Biblical Criminal Law," in *Yehezkel Kaufmann Jubilee Volume*, ed. N. Haran, (Jerusalem: Magnes, 1960), 5–27.

THE KASSITES

After the Hittites from distant Turkey made a lightning raid upon Babylon in 1595 B.C., the Kassites from the Zagros Mountains descended to the plain and established a long-lived dynasty which controlled Mesopotamia for four centuries until 1160 B.C.[10] We have a Kassite king list with thirty-six names, some inscriptions, and administrative documents. Among the most interesting documents of this period are the letters sent to the Egyptian pharaohs, asking for gold from Egypt, and Kassite seals which were found at Thebes in Greece. The Babylonian kings asked the Egyptians not to correspond with the Assyrians, whom they considered their vassals. The Kassites built a new capital at Dur Kurigalzu (Aqar Quf), thirty miles west of Baghdad, which today contains the tallest standing ziggurat (170 feet high).

ANCIENT EGYPT (3100–1100 B.C.)

The history of Egypt is divided according to the various dynasties of rulers as provided by Manetho, an Egyptian priest (third century B.C.) who wrote in Greek. This is supplemented by various Egyptian sources such as the Palermo Stone. Herodotus (fifth century B.C.) offers few reliable data from the earlier periods but is quite important for the two centuries prior to his writing. The task of correlating these sources is complicated by the fact that the Egyptian kings had up to five different names (Horus name, Nebty name, Golden Horus name, Prenomen, and Nomen).

Egypt had an abundance of predynastic phases, such as the Badarian, Amratian, and Gerzean phases. Earlier scholars had sought the stimulus for the new dynastic civilization of Egypt either by an influx of a "ruling race" or in contacts with Mesopotamia. Recently scholars have traced prototypes of kingship at Qustual, a site in Nubia (Sudan).

Egypt, as Herodotus observed, was "the gift of the Nile," the sole major river which flows south to north. It rises deep in Africa with the joining of the White Nile, rising out of Lake Victoria, and the Blue Nile, from the highlands of Ethiopia. Its course between Khartoum and Aswan is intercepted by six major cataracts, granite outcroppings which make navigation difficult if not impossible. The natural boundary between Egypt and Nubia was at the First Cataract near Aswan; later Egyptian kings would extend their frontiers to the Second Cataract at Buhen. On either side of the Nile were forbidding deserts. The area of Lower (north-

---

10. *NIDBA*, s.v. "Kassites."

ern) Egypt included the fertile Delta area where the Nile reached the Mediterranean.

ARCHAIC ERA (3100–2700 B.C.)

All of our sources report that the founder of Dynasty I was Menes, who first united Upper and Lower Egypt ca. 3100 B.C., establishing the capital city of Lower Egypt at Memphis. Most scholars identify Menes with Narmer, whose slate palette shows him with the white crown of Upper Egypt on the obverse and with the red crown of Lower Egypt on the reverse. Narmer's name has been found at several sites in Palestine. Other scholars prefer to connect Menes with either Scorpion or Hor-Aha. Several of the kings of Dynasty I were buried with sacrificed servants. These kings have tombs at Saqqarah in the north and cenotaphs (empty tombs) at Abydos in the south. They are known as *mastaba* ("bench" in Arabic) tombs because of their shape.

OLD KINGDOM (2700–2200 B.C.)

Imhotep, an architect, designed the Step Pyramid at Saqqarah for Djoser of the Third Dynasty (2700 B.C.).[11] This was the world's first large monumental stone structure. It rose in six stages to a height of two hundred feet. Sneferu, the first king of the Fourth Dynasty (2615 B.C.), built the first true pyramid after considerable experimentation; he had three pyramids built before he was satisfied. The famous pyramids at Giza were built by Cheops (Khufu), Chephren (Khafre), and Mycerinus (Menkaure). Cheops' structure was the largest; it is the only one of the Seven Wonders of the World which still survives. Chephren was also responsible for the carving of the sphinx, the man-headed lion. Two dismantled ceremonial boats, originally over one hundred feet long, were discovered at Giza. It is in the pyramid of Wenis (Unas) of the Fifth Dynasty that we have the first pyramid texts, magico-religious inscriptions which ensured the immortality of the royal family. Also necessary for the afterlife was the preservation of the body by mummification and the provision of food, either by endowments that funded priests who offered daily sacrifices of bread and beer or by magico-symbolical depictions of food in the tombs.

The kings of Egypt, later called *pharaohs* ("big house" in Egyptian), were always considered divine, the incarnation of Horus while alive, who were transformed into Osiris upon death. There was no question about

---

11. For early Egypt, see C. Aldred, *Egypt to the End of the Old Kingdom* (New York: McGraw Hill, 1965). For Egypt and the Bible, see P. Montet, *Egypt and the Bible* (Philadelphia: Fortress, 1968) and C. F. Aling, *Egypt and Bible History* (Grand Rapids: Baker, 1981).

the exalted status of the king. When people came into his presence, they kissed his foot or the ground. "The Tale of the Eloquent Peasant" recounts the story of an aggrieved peasant whose gifted speech won him an audience with the king. Some have explained the lack of law codes from Egypt by the divine status of the pharaohs. However, as we do have texts which refer to laws, the fact that we have not yet discovered collections of laws may best be explained by the accidents of survival and of discovery. The demands of administering affairs required a host of scribes educated in the intricacies of writing hieroglyphic signs. A scribe, for example, would have to learn the names of ninety-six cities. Commoners with ability could attend classes with princes and achieve notable careers. Temples with their bevies of priests controlled vast properties and riches. They were, however, subject to royal approval.

THE FIRST INTERMEDIATE ERA (2200–2100 B.C.)

As the pharaohs entrusted more and more powers to local governors known as monarchs, who passed on their power to their heirs, central authority was weakened toward the end of the Old Kingdom. This led to a period of disorder known as the First Intermediate Era (2200–2100), during which there were no less than four dynasties, VII–XI, centered at Heracleopolis. Despite or because of the political instability, a number of notable literary works such as the *Instruction for Merikare* came from this period.

MIDDLE KINGDOM (2100–1700 B.C.)

The Eleventh Dynasty shifted power south to Thebes. Vigorous kings such as Mentuhotep II (2060–2010) pushed Egyptian borders south into Nubia. One of the few Middle Kingdom monuments which still survives is this king's temple at Deir el-Bahri, west of Thebes. The founder of the Twelfth Dynasty (1991–1786 B.C.), Amenemhet I, established a new capital to the north at It-Tawi, just south of Memphis. He continued expansion into Nubia, the main source of gold for Egypt. It was the assassination of this king which served as the background for the famous story of Sinuhe, who fled to Palestine. Much like David, Sinuhe lived as a refugee and fought a single-handed combat with the enemy's champion.[12]

Sesostris II's tomb at Beni Hasan has a famous scene which depicts colorfully clad Semites bearing gifts and products to Egypt. This recalls the visit of Abraham and his descendants to Egypt, particularly in times of famine. The greatest king of the Twelfth Dynasty, Sesostris III (1887–

---

12. A. F. Rainey, "The World of Sinuhe," *IOS* 2 (1972): 369–408; J. Baines, "Interpreting *Sinuhe*," *JEA* 68 (1982): 31–44.

1850 B.C.), established numerous forts and garrisons in Nubia. He was eventually worshipped as a god there. He also conducted one campaign into Palestine; its report refers to the city of Shechem. Important execration texts, written either on bowls or on pottery figurines, provide valuable lists of Palestinian cities upon whom curses were uttered. These texts reflect the changes in Palestine during the twentieth–nineteenth centuries from a tribal to a more urban society.

SECOND INTERMEDIATE ERA (1700–1570 B.C.)

The unity and serenity of Egypt was shattered during the Second Intermediate Period by the invasion of the Hyksos, Semitic invaders from Palestine. After about 1700 B.C. Egypt was divided among the Fifteenth Hyksos Dynasty in control of Lower Egypt, the Fourteenth Dynasty in control of the western Delta, and the Thirteenth Dynasty at Thebes. Many scholars have been inclined to place Joseph in the Hyksos era, but a case can be made for placing him earlier in the Middle Kingdom, as there is evidence of Semites in high positions in this period. The Wilbour Papyrus (1740 B.C.) lists a number of "Asiatic" (i.e., Semitic) slaves from Palestine.

Joseph may have obtained the office of vizier, which included the duties of chief of treasury, chief of police, chief judge, chief of war, and chief of agriculture. Egyptian officials and courtiers were fond of titles, which they reproduced in their tombs. Joseph may have acquired honors corresponding to the following titles: "Royal Seal-bearer" (Gen. 41:42), "Overseer of the Granaries of Upper and Lower Egypt" (Gen. 41:35), "Great Steward of the Lord of the Two Lands" (Gen. 41:40), "Chief of the Entire Land (Gen. 45:8), "Foremost Among His Courtiers" (Gen. 41:40), and "Father to Pharaoh" (Gen. 45:8). The latter may represent the Egyptian "God's Father," meaning an adviser to the king, who was considered a god.[13]

NEW KINGDOM (1570–1200 B.C.)

The expulsion of the Hyksos under the leadership of the Theban Seventeenth Dynasty ca. 1570 B.C. led to the most glorious period of Egyptian power. During this imperial period the Egyptians extended their power eastward into Palestine and Syria. Tuthmosis III (1457–1425) even reached the Euphrates. The predecessor of Tuthmosis III was his stepmother Hatshepsut (1479–1457), who served as his regent and then

---

13. D. B. Redford, *A Study of the Biblical Story of Joseph* (Leiden: Brill, 1970), is quite skeptical of the historicity of this story because of the late attestation of Egyptian names in the narrative. But see the review of Redford's work by K. A. Kitchen in *OrAnt* 12 (1973): 233–42.

refused to relinquish power when he came of age. During the New Kingdom the Egyptians continued to maintain their control over Nubia and received ambassadors from the Minoans on Crete and the Mycenaeans in Greece.

The fourteenth century cuneiform tablets found at Amarna illustrate the extensive international contacts of Amenhotep III (1394–1356) and his successor, as they include letters from rulers in Anatolia, Mitanni, Assyria, Babylonia, Syria, and Palestine. These letters also record the political marriages between these pharaohs and the princesses of Mitanni.

Amenhotep IV (1356–1340) changed his name to Akhenaton and promoted a monotheistic worship of Aton. He set up a new capital on the Middle Nile at Amarna to establish his independence from the dominance of the priests of Amun at Thebes. The Amarna letters indicate that Akhenaton was so preoccupied with his religion that he failed to send the troops requested by the kings of various Palestinian cities against marauding Habiru. His religious reformation was short lived, as his successor Tutankhamon, as his name indicates, reverted to the worship of Amon.[14]

The Nineteenth Dynasty was dominated by the long reign of Ramesses II (1279–1213). In his fifth year a major battle was fought between the Egyptians and the Hittites at the Syrian site of Qadesh. Though Ramesses boasted of a great victory, the results were more of a stalemate. Later in his reign Ramesses concluded a diplomatic marriage with a Hittite princess. Ramesses II was the most prodigious builder in Egypt and in Nubia, erecting colossal statues at Abu Simbel and the monumental hypostyle hall at Karnak.

The "early date" of the exodus (ca. 1440 B.C.) would mean that Tuthmosis III was the pharaoh of the exodus; the "late date" of the exodus (ca. 1270 B.C.) would indicate that Ramesses II was that pharaoh. From the reign of Merenptah (1213–1204) we have the only reference to Israel in Egyptian texts. During the reign of this king and of Rameses III, Egypt was battered by invasions of Sea Peoples. Among the defeated groups were the Philistines, who occupied the Palestinian coast and fought with the Israelites over the Shephelah or foothills. The Philistine pentapolis of five cities—Gaza, Ashkelon, Ashdod, Ekron, and Gath—was ruled by *serenim* or "lords."

---

14. See C. Aldred, *Akhenaten Pharaoh of Egypt* (New York: McGraw-Hill, 1968); D. B. Redford, *Akhenaten, The Heretic King* (Princeton: Princeton University Press, 1984); E. Yamauchi, "Akhenaten, Moses, and Monotheism," in *Tell el-Amarna, 1887–1987*, ed. B. Beitzel and G. Young (Winona Lake, Ind.; Eisenbrauns, forthcoming).

THE EARLY HEBREWS (1150–850 B.C.)

THE UNITED MONARCHY

The earliest Hebrews were semi-nomadic clans. The twelve tribes, descended from the sons of Jacob, were united under the covenant God gave Moses. Led by Joshua, they partially conquered the TransJordan and Palestine from the Canaanites. They were protected from invading tribes by charismatic military leaders called *shophtim*, the so-called "Judges." An early request that he establish a hereditary rule was refused by Gideon (Judg. 8:22–28). Despite the warnings of Samuel, the people clamored for a king to be "like other nations" (1 Sam. 8:5, NRSV).

The Israelites in the period of the United Monarchy (eleventh-tenth centuries B.C.) were ruled by three kings. First was Saul, who won some victories over the Philistines. But he was upstaged by the young David, who become a popular hero by his exploit of slaying the Philistine champion, Goliath. After the death of Saul and his son Jonathan, David succeeded to the throne (2 Sam. 2:4). David, who was supported by foreign mercenaries, seized Jerusalem which became his new capital. David's conquests extended Israel's rule over the Philistines, Aramaeans, Ammonites, Moabites, and Edomites (2 Sam. 8:1–14). He sometimes allowed their kings to rule as vassals (2 Sam. 8:2; 10:19; 1 Kings 2:39) and sometimes appointed governors over these groups (2 Sam. 8:6, 14).

Solomon, who was the second son of Bathsheba, succeeded to the throne (971–931).[15] He made a drastic reorganization of his kingdom into twelve administrative districts, which were with some exceptions not based upon the old tribal areas (1 Kings 4:1–19). Solomon's administration may have owed much to Egyptian prototypes, as the titles of his various officers seem to be the Hebrew equivalents of Egyptian titles. Solomon at first drew from the alien populations for his burden bearers and stonecutters (1 Kings 5:15–18; 1 Chron. 2:2, 17–18; 1 Kings 9:20–22). But he then used Israelites in the corvée, or forced labor system (1 Kings 5:13–14). He introduced a fundamental change in Israel's military organization—a reliance upon chariotry. His father David had disabled the horses which he had captured from the king of Zobah in Syria (2 Sam. 8:4).

Solomon was able to ally himself with King Hiram of Tyre, a Phoenician city to the north. The Phoenicians, who occupied the coast north of Palestine, were the outstanding seamen and traders of the Mediterranean. They were blessed with excellent harbors and with great stands of timber for shipbuilding. The Tarshish ships (1 Kings 10:22), which were

---

15. *NIDBA*, s.v. "Solomon."

employed by Solomon in cooperation with Hiram, were originally vessels which went to Tarshish, perhaps to the distant Phoenician colony of Tartessus in southern Spain. Solomon imported horses from Que (i.e., Cilicia in southeastern Turkey). His fame attracted the visit of a queen from Sheba in southwestern Arabia (1 Kings 10:1–3). The joint Red Sea fleet of Solomon and Hiram made voyages every three years to a distant port called Ophir (1 Kings 10:11–22), from which were brought back a variety of objects including fine gold. Ophir has been variously located in south Arabia, east Africa, and northwest India.

Solomon's great international prestige is demonstrated by the fact that he was given a pharaoh's daughter in marriage (1 Kings 3:1). This is one of the few instances in which a king of Egypt deigned to give his daughter in marriage to an alien. This pharaoh was probably a king of the Twenty-first Dynasty, probably Siamun (978–960). This pharaoh captured Gezer (1 Kings 9:16) and presented it to Solomon as a dowry for his daughter. According to 1 Kings 11:3 Solomon had seven hundred wives and three hundred concubines, among whom were Moabite, Ammonite, Edomite, Sidonian (i.e. Phoenician), and Hittite women (1 Kings 11:1).

THE DIVIDED KINGDOMS

After the death of Solomon, the twelve tribes of Israel were divided into two kingdoms, by the rebellion of Jeroboam I, a rebel who had found refuge in Egypt (931 B.C.). Solomon's son, Rehoboam, presided over the two southern tribes, Benjamin and Judah. Though ruled at times by apostate kings, Judah continued under kings who were all descendants of the House of David for three centuries. In Rehoboam's fifth year (1 Kings 14:25–26) Shishak, the founder of the Twenty-second Libyan Dynasty, who had harbored Jeroboam, invaded Judah. The account in 2 Chronicles 12:2–10 is expanded by Shishak's own monument at Karnak, which lists over 150 sites conquered in Palestine.[16]

The Northern Kingdom was wracked by constant assassinations and coups d'état. It was also menaced by the growing power of Assyria to the northeast. Israel established a new capital at Samaria under Omri in the ninth century B.C. One of the most noteworthy kings of the Northern Kingdom was Ahab (869–850), son of Omri. Ahab married the notorious Jezebel, a Phoenician princess, who promoted the worship of Baal. A fascinating light is shed on the activities of Omri and his successors in Transjordan by the famous Moabite Stone of Mesha, king of Moab.[17] It is one

---

16. K. A. Kitchen, *The Third Intermediate Period in Egypt, 1100–650 B.C.* (Warminster, England: Aris and Phillips, 1973); *NIDBA*, s.v. "Shishak."

17. A. Dearman, ed., *Studies in the Mesha Inscription and Moab* (Atlanta: Scholars, 1989).

of the few royal texts which comes from the area of Israel/Jordan. Mesha rebelled against the Israelites and, in a desperate battle against them, sacrificed his own son.

THE ASSYRIANS (900–612 B.C.)

The Assyrians developed an overpowering military juggernaut which moved steadily westward through the northern Aramean states. Ashurnasirpal II (883-859) built a major new capital at Calah (modern Nimrud) and celebrated by hosting a ten-day banquet for 69,574 guests. It was this king who expanded Assyrian power to the Mediterranean. This posed a threat to many Aramean states in northern Mesopotamia and Syria.

A key confrontation took place at Qarqar on the Orontes River in Syria in 853 B.C.[18] Shalmaneser III (858–824) was faced with an anti-Assyrian coalition of about dozen states. Damascus served as the head of the Aramean states. Its king, Hadad-ezer, supplied 1,200 chariots, 1,200 cavalry, and 20,000 soldiers. Ahab of Israel supplied no less than 2,000 chariots and 10,000 men. Though the Assyrians claimed a victory, they faced continual opposition from this coalition. In 841 B.C. Shalmanesser III invaded Israel itself (Hos. 10:14–15).

The Omrides were replaced by the usurper, Jehu (842–815). In 841 B.C. Jehu offered tribute to Shalmaneser III, as depicted in the latter's famous Black Obelisk. Jehu may also have been interested in gaining Assyrian aid against Hazael, king of Damascus, who was beginning to attack Israel (2 Kings 10:32).

Adad-nirari III (810–783) was confronted again by a coalition led by Damascus. His advance against Damascus in 805 B.C. may have provided relief to Israel (2 Kings 13:4–5). A newly discovered stele from Rimah records the tribute the Assyrians received from Joash of Israel. A period of Assyrian weakness which followed allowed Israel to enjoy the long and prosperous reign of Jeroboam II (786–746).

Tiglath-pileser III (745–727) became the first Assyrian king in five centuries to rule directly over Babylonia.[19] He also occupied the Phoenician and Philistine coast in 734 B.C. When Rezin of Damascus and Pekah of Israel tried in vain to get Ahaz of Judah to join their anti-Assyrian coalition (2 Kings 16:5), Ahaz appealed to Tiglath-pileser (2 Kings 16:7–9), who swooped down and destroyed Damascus in 732 B.C. Menahem of Israel had paid tribute to the king (2 Kings 15:19–20) early in Tiglath-pileser's reign. However, in conjunction with his campaigns against Dam-

---

18. *NIDBA*, s.v. "Qarqar."
19. *NIDBA*, s.v. "Tiglath-pileser."

ascus in 733–732, the Assyrian armies ravaged Gilead and Galilee and destroyed Hazor and Megiddo (2 Kings 15:29). Tiglath-pileser boasted that he deposed Pekah and placed Hoshea in his stead over the throne of Israel.

When Hoshea failed to pay tribute, Shalmaneser V (727–722) besieged Samaria for three years. The Bible (2 Kings 17:3–6) rightly assigns the capture for Samaria to this king, though his successor, Sargon II (721–705), claimed credit for this. The Assyrians practiced the policy of deporting people from one area and importing others to weaken the possibility of local opposition. Sargon deported 27,000 from the Northern Kingdom who ultimately became the "Ten Lost Tribes" as they became assimilated with the populations of Mesopotamia.

After the fall of the Northern Kingdom in 722 B.C., Judah maintained its uneasy independence by paying tribute to the Assyrians. However, when Hezekiah, inspired by the prophet Isaiah, rebelled against the Assyrians, Sennacherib (705–682) launched a massive invasion in 701 B.C.[20] The Assyrians were momentarily distracted by a force led by Tirhakah, who later became king of the Twenty-fifth Cushite Dynasty of Egypt (2 Kings 19:9; Isa. 37:9). One Judean city after another, including the great southern fortress of Lachish, fell to the Assyrians. The Lord intervened to frustrate the capture of Jerusalem (2 Kings 18—19; Isa. 36—37). Sennacherib boasted, however, that he received tribute from Hezekiah, acquired much booty, and removed many captives. One of his texts speaks about the deportation of 200,150, which some scholars believe is an error for 2,150.

After his deliverance from the Assyrians, Hezekiah fell ill. During this illness he received messengers and a present from Merodach-Baladan, king of Babylon (2 Kings 20:12–18; Isa. 39:1–8). This Chaldean king was acting not out of solicitude for the Hebrew king's health but was seeking allies against his Assyrian overlords. Both Sargon II and Sennacherib tried repeatedly to suppress Merodach-Baladan, who seized Babylon in 721 B.C.

Esarhaddon (680–669) conquered Egypt in 675 B.C. by defeating Tirhakah, the Nubian pharaoh. He returned to Egypt in 669 B.C. to crush a rebellion there. Esarhaddon's role in settling foreigners in Palestine is mentioned in Ezra 4:2. Esarhaddon summoned Manasseh, king of Judah, to Nineveh (cf. 2 Chron. 33:10–33) with other kings to provide building materials. Ashurbanipal (669–627), the last great Assyrian king, is best known for the great library he developed at Nineveh.

---

20. On Sennacherib's siege of Lachish, see D. Ussishkin, "Answers at Lachish," *BAR* 5.6 (1979): 16–39.

Late in the seventh century B.C. the Chaldeans of southern Mesopotamia, in alliance with the Medes of western Iran, attacked the Assyrians.[21] Nineveh fell in 612 B.C., just as the prophet Nahum had predicted.[22] An Assyrian remnant tried to hold out in Haran until 610 B.C. It was in a futile attempt to block Egyptian aid to the embattled Assyrians that Josiah, king of Judah, met his death at Megiddo in 609 B.C. (2 Kings 23:29).

THE NEO-BABYLONIANS (626–539 B.C.)

The Chaldean, Nabopolassar (626–605), was the founder of the brilliant but brief Neo-Babylonian Empire.[23] After gaining control of Babylon, Nabopolassar allied himself with the Median king, Cyaxares. The greatest of the Neo-Babylonian kings was Nabopolassar's son, Nebuchadnezzar (605-562).[24] In 605 B.C. Nebuchadnezzar fought a battle against the Egyptians at Carchemish (Jer. 46:2). This involved Greek mercenaries on both sides. In his first year (Dan. 1:1) Nebuchadnezzar advanced against Palestine and deported a number of young Jewish captives, including Daniel and his three companions (Shadrach, Meshech, and Abednego) to Babylon, his splendid capital.[25]

The Chaldean Chronicles reveal that in 601 B.C. the Babylonians and Egyptians mauled each other.[26] This may have encouraged Jehoiakim to rebel against the Babylonians in spite of the warnings of Jeremiah (27:9–11). Late in 598 B.C. Nebuchadnezzar led the Babylonian army against Judah. Just before the invaders' arrival, Jehoiakim died and his eighteen-year-old son, Jehoiachin, came to the throne. He was to rule a little over three months (2 Chron. 36:9) before Jerusalem fell in 597 B.C. Nebuchadnezzar sent back to Babylon great treasures and 10,000 captives (2 Kings 24:14), including Jehoiachin and members of his family. Their presence in Babylon is attested by ration tablets discovered there. It is estimated that 5,000 or 10,000 others also may have been deported. An important difference between the deportations by the Assyrians and the Babylonians was that the latter did not replace the deportees with pagan

---

21. *NIDBA*, s.v. "Chaldea, Chaldeans."

22. *HolBD*, s.v. "Nineveh."

23. *NIDBA*, s.v. "Nabopolassar."

24. D. J. Wiseman, *Nebuchadrezzar and Babylon* (Oxford: Oxford University Press, 1991).

25. E. Yamauchi, "Babylon," in *Major Cities of the Biblical World*, ed. R. K. Harrison (Nashville: Nelson, 1985), 32–48.

26. D. J. Wiseman, *Chronicles of Chaldaean Kings in the British Museum* (London: British Museum, 1956).

newcomers. Thus Judah, though devastated, was not contaminated with polytheism to the same degree as was the northern area.

Psammetichus II, who had won a signal victory over the Nubians, made a triumphal tour of Palestine in 593 B.C. This may have encouraged the Jews to lean on the "broken reed" of the Egyptians against the Babylonians. In any case, Zedekiah, Jehoiachin's uncle, who had been appointed king over Judah, chose to rebel. This brought back Nebuchadnezzar's forces, who sacked Jerusalem and destroyed Solomon's temple in 586 B.C. Nebuchadnezzar was succeeded by a series of ephemeral kings including Evil-Merodach (562–560). Evil-Merodach released Jehoiachin from imprisonment after thirty-six years of captivity and treated him kindly (2 Kings 25:27–30; Jer. 52:31–34).

The last Neo-Babylonian king was Nabonidus (555–539), who was devoted to the god Sin of his native Haran.[27] But his devotion to this god led him to neglect the god Marduk of Babylon. This alienated the king from the Babylonians and led him to a ten-year exile at Tema, a city in Arabia, which was five hundred miles away from Babylonia. In his absence his son, Belshazzar, became the de facto king in Babylon, a situation reflected in the Book of Daniel. Nabonidus returned sometime between 542 and 540 B.C. to mount opposition against the advancing Persians. But Babylon fell to Cyrus with little opposition in October 539 B.C., as the Persians entered the city by diverting the Euphrates River, which bisected the city.

THE MEDES AND THE PERSIANS (850–331 B.C.)

The Medes and Persians were closely related Indo-European peoples who had migrated into the Iranian plateau in the late second millennium B.C. They were first mentioned in the ninth-century texts of Shalmaneser III. Tiglath-pileser III and Sargon II invaded Media to acquire horses. The Assyrians deported Medians to Palestine and settled some of the displaced Israelites in Media (i.e., in the Zagros Mountains [2 Kings 17:6]).

According to Herodotus the Medes were united by Deioces sometime after 700 B.C. The development of the Median state was interrupted by a twenty-eight-year (645–617) interregnum of Scythians, nomadic archers from the steppes of Russia. It is possible that references to the threat of foes from the northern frontier in Jeremiah and in Zephaniah may refer to these horsemen-archers. The Scythians, who reached the borders of Egypt, readily served as mercenaries for various groups. After they were

---

27. *ISBE*, s.v. "Nabonidus."

expelled from Media, the Scythians settled in the Ukraine, north of the Black Sea.[28]

When the Scythians originally crossed over the Caucasus at the beginning of the seventh century B.C. they were in pursuit of another group from Russia, the Cimmerians (biblical Gomer). The Cimmerians, however, went westward into Anatolia, where they attacked the legendary king of the Phrygians (biblical Meshech), Midas, and his capital at Gordium. They even reached some of the Greek cities on the western coast of Anatolia before disappearing as a distinct entity. The collapse of the Phrygian kingdom in the center of Anatolia allowed for the rise of the Lydian kingdom to the west.

The Median king Cyaxares fought with Alyattes of Lydia in western Asia Minor before a truce was arranged in 585 B.C. The last Median king was Astyages (585–550). His grandson Cyrus, who was part Persian, defeated him in 550 B.C. and established Persian supremacy over the Medes. Cyrus was aided in his victory by the defection of some of the Medes to his side. Cyrus next turned his forces against the Lydians. After an indecisive battle, the Lydian king Croesus retired to his capital at Sardis under the mistaken belief that Cyrus would not pursue, as winter was approaching. Croesus sent messengers asking for aid in the following spring from his three allies, Egypt, Babylonia, and Sparta. Cyrus, however, pursued and captured not only Lydia in 546 B.C. but also the Ionian Greek cities on the coast.

Upon his capture of Babylon in 539 B.C., Cyrus issued an edict permitting the Jews in captivity to return to the Holy Land. We have a Hebrew copy of his edict in Ezra 1:1–4 and an Aramaic memorandum of the same in Ezra 6:3–5. Cyrus' generosity to the Jews was not unique but was paralleled by his benevolence to the Babylonians and to others. According to the lists in Ezra 2 and Nehemiah 7, about 50,000 Jews took advantage of the opportunity to return. Many others must have stayed behind, however, as we have evidence from the Murashu texts of a prosperous Jewish community in Mesopotamia under the Persians. Among 2,500 individuals named in these texts, about 70 have Jewish names. Jews were to be found in 28 of 200 settlements around Nippur in southern Mesopotamia.[29]

Cyrus' successor, Cambyses (529–522), is not named in the Old Testament. His major achievement was the conquest of Egypt in 525 B.C. It is possible that Cambyses, in the course of his expedition south of Nubia, recruited the Jewish mercenaries who had been first established on Ele-

---

28. E. Yamauchi, *Foes from the Northern Frontier* (Grand Rapids: Baker, 1982).

29. M. W. Stolper, *Entrepreneurs and Empire* (Leiden: Nederlands Historisch-Archaeologisch Instituut te Istanbul, 1985).

phantine Island near Aswan by Psammetichus II. According to Herodotus, both the Nubian expedition and an attempt to reach the oracular shrine at Siwa in the Libyan desert were failures. Herodotus' account that Cambyses stabbed the Apis bull is directly contradicted by evidence that the Persian king dedicated a sarcophagus to this incarnation of the god Ptah. While Cambyses was away in Egypt, he learned of a coup de état at home. In hurrying home the luckless king accidentally stabbed himself and died.

Darius (522–486) and six nobles overthrew the usurper, Gaumata, after he had ruled for seven months. It was Darius' trilingual (Old Persian, Akkadian, Elamite) Behistun Inscription, which tells of Darius' triumph in nineteen battles, that led to the decipherment of cuneiform. The Jews who had returned under Cyrus had laid the foundation of a second temple. But work was soon halted in the face of opposition (Ezra 4:1–5). In the reign of Darius, the Jews, under the leadership of Zerubbabel and Jeshua the high priest, stirred by the prophets Haggai and Zechariah, renewed efforts to complete the work. Enemies of the Jews challenged their right to do this and complained to the Persian authorities. After the futile search at Babylon, the documentation of Cyrus' decree was discovered at Ecbatana. Darius then solemnly warned the enemies of the Jews against interfering in the rebuilding of the temple (Ezra 6:11). The temple was then finished in 515 B.C. (Ezra 6:14–15), a little over seventy years after its destruction.

Darius was responsible for the organization of the Persian Empire into districts governed by satraps. Royal inspectors, called by the Greeks "the King's Eyes" and "the King's Ears," checked up on the satraps periodically. Darius standardized weights and measures and began the minting of coins: silver coins known as *sigloi* and his famous gold *darics*. He also established the "pony express" courier system on the royal road which linked Susa in southwestern Persia to Sardis in western Anatolia.

The Ionians rebelled against the Persians from 499 to 494 B.C. After suppressing the revolt, Darius in 490 B.C. sent a punitive expedition to punish the two cities which had sent aid to the Ionians, Eretria and Athens. Some of the Eretrians were transported to Mesopotamia, but the Persians were defeated at Marathon by ten thousand Athenians, led by Miltiades. When Miltiades fell into disgrace through his inflated pride, Themistocles rose to prominence. It was his foresight which enabled the Athenians to develop a fleet of two hundred triremes in anticipation of a renewed Persian attack.

Xerxes (485–465) succeeded his father Darius. His name was transliterated as "Ahasuerus" in the Book of Esther. Before Darius died a rebellion had broken out in Egypt. Xerxes went in person to suppress this revolt in 485 B.C. Two short-lived uprisings in Babylon were harshly repressed. As a punishment the Persians destroyed the great ziggurat and the temple of Marduk in Babylon, according to classical sources.

After the suppression of these revolts, Xerxes was ready for this massive invasion of Greece. As his huge army and navy advanced into northern Greece, many key Greek states such as Thessaly and Thebes went over to the Persian side. The gallant stand of the Spartans under Leonidas at the Thermopylae pass (480 B.C.) slowed but did not stop the Persian advance. Panicked, the Athenians abandoned their city. Under the brilliant leadership of Themistocles, the Greeks were able to lure the Persian fleet into the narrow waters of the Bay of Salamis for a decisive victory. Concerned for his safety, Xerxes fled to Asia Minor, but still left behind a substantial force. The final battle on the Greek mainland was fought in 479 B.C. at Plataea. The Spartans under the leadership of Pausanias won a great victory, but hostilities between the Greeks and the Persians continued for another thirty years.

According to Herodotus, Xerxes' queen was a very powerful woman named Amestris; according to the Book of Esther, she was Vashti. Some scholars have suggested that Vashti is a variant of Amestris. The gap between the third year (Esth. 1:3) and the seventh year (Esth. 2:16) of Ahasuerus can be synchronized with Xerxes' absence in Greece in 480–479 B.C.

Esther's guardian was named Mordecai, a name which is attested among the roster of Persian officials in the Elamite tablets of Persepolis, which come from the reigns of Darius and Xerxes. Mordecai sat "in the gate" at Susa as an indication of his official status (Esth. 2:19). French excavators have, after many year of searching, recently discovered the gate of the Achaemenid palace at Susa.[30]

Upon his return from the west, Xerxes was mainly preoccupied with completing the work of his father at the magnificent site of Persepolis. After reigning for twenty years, Xerxes was killed in a palace plot in 465 B.C. by Artabanus, the captain of his bodyguard.

Artaxerxes I began his long reign (464–424) by killing Artabanus. It was under Artaxerxes I that Ezra in 458 B.C. (Ezra 7:6) and then Nehemiah in 445 B.C. (Neh. 2:11) came to the Holy Land to serve there, the former as a teacher of the Torah and the latter as the governor of Judah. The fact that Artaxerxes I commissioned Ezra the Scribe to administer the Law to his people fits in perfectly with Persian policy. A close parallel is the simi-

---

30. E. Yamauchi, "Mordecai, the Persepolis Tablets, and the Susa Excavations," *VT* 42 (1992): 272–75; see also E. Yamauchi, *Persia and the Bible* (Grand Rapids: Baker, 1990).

lar commission given by Darius to Udjahorresnet, an Egyptian priest and scholar.[31]

Nehemiah had occupied the prestigious position of cupbearer before Artaxerxes I (Neh. 1:11), which meant he had to taste the wine to make certain there was no poison in it. The province which Nehemiah came to govern had been greatly reduced in size. The archaeological evidence of Yehud (Judah) coins and seals confirms the biblical boundaries. Recently recovered bullae (clay seal impressions) and coin inscriptions have been use to develop a list of the governors who preceded Nehemiah. Inscriptional evidence is available to confirm the historicity of Nehemiah's various opponents including Sanballat the Samarian governor, Tobiah the Ammonite, and Geshem the Arab. Archaeologists have been able to trace the line of Jerusalem's walls in Nehemiah's day. The diminished circuit of the walls helps to explain the rapidity with which the reconstruction was accomplished, once Nehemiah had aroused the people with his inspired leadership.

The economic distress of the people of Judah, including inflation and indebtedness, was caused by Persian taxation (Neh. 5). Though taxation did not produce a scarcity of cash, it did concentrate wealth in the hands of entrepreneurs like Murashu and Sons, who could take advantage of the situation. Many of the poor had to pledge themselves and were then sold into slavery when they could not pay their loans and the accumulated interest.[32]

Aramaic papyri from Elephantine, dated to the fifth century B.C., illuminate the linguistic, political, and cultural background of the Jews in Egypt under the Persians. The Jews had built a temple of Yaho (Yahweh), which was destroyed in 411 B.C. by fanatical Egyptians. The Jews then asked the Persian governor for permission to rebuild the temple. The papyri reveal the incidence of mixed marriages, which led to syncretistic practices—a problem faced also by both Ezra and Nehemiah. Letters of Arsames, the satrap of Egypt, reveal him as an all-too-typical governor, greedy for wealth and power—a striking contrast to the selflessness of Nehemiah.

The last Persian monarch was Darius III Codomannus (336–331), whose armies fell to Alexander the Great (Dan. 8). "Darius the Persian" (Neh. 12:22) may be Codomannus or a predecessor, Darius II Nothus (423–404).

---

31. J. Blenkinsopp, "The Mission of Udjahorresnet and Those of Ezra and Nehemiah," *JBL* 106 (1987): 409–21.

32. E. Yamauchi, "Two Reformers Compared: Solon of Athens and Nehemiah of Jerusalem," in *The Bible World: Essays in Honor of Cyrus H. Gordon*, ed. B. Rendsburg et al. (New York: KTAV, 1980), 269–92.

THE GREEKS (1500–165 B.C.)

The Old Testament contains some sporadic references to the Aegean world, which lay on the outer fringes of the Hebrews' known world. In the second millennium B.C. the brilliant Minoan civilization flourished on Crete, to be supplanted by the Greek Mycenaean culture after 1500 B.C. The Minoans had splendid palaces at Knossos, Phaistos, Mallia, and Zakro. Mycenaean palaces have been uncovered at Mycenae, Tiryns, and Pylos. The Mycenaean kings, celebrated in the Homeric poems, ruled as warrior kings but not as absolute monarchs.

The Minoans traded with Egypt, as did the Mycenaeans. Mycenaean pottery has been found at many Palestinian sites, and Canaanite ware was imported into Greece. Amos (9:7) was aware of the tradition that the Philistines came from Caphtor (Crete). Goliath, the Philistine champion, wore typically Aegean-type armor, including greaves (shin guards). David employed Cherethites (Cretans) in his bodyguard (1 Sam. 30:14).[33]

The brilliant civilization of the Mycenaeans was ended by the Dorian invasions ca. 1200 B.C., which may be linked to the massive migrations of people in the Mediterranean, including the assault of the Sea Peoples against Egypt at this time. These developments led to the collapse of the Hittite Empire in Anatolia and the destruction of Ugarit in Syria. In the Aegean a Dark Age began in which literacy apparently disappeared, and culture was greatly diminished.

As Greece emerged from the Dark Age in the eighth century, it established trading outposts in the eastern Mediterranean such as Al Mina on the Orontes River in Syria. The Archaic Age (800–500) also saw development of the *polis* or "city state," the establishment of many colonies, and the borrowing of the Phoenician alphabet. The Hebrew word for the Greeks, (*Yawan*; modern, Javan), indicates they first made contact with the Greeks of Ionia on the west coast of Turkey. Genesis 10:4, which lists the sons of Javan as Elishah, Tarshish, the Kittim, and the Rodanim, betrays knowledge of Greek settlements on Rhodes and Cyprus which date back to before 1000 B.C.[34]

Ezekiel (27:13) speaks of Tyre's trade with Greece. The Hebrews were accused of selling their kinsmen as slaves to the Greeks in Joel 3:6. The word *Kittim*, which comes from the Greek settlement of Kition on Cyprus, appears in several passages. An abundance of Greek pottery has

---

33. E. Yamauchi, *Greece and Babylon* (Grand Rapids: Baker, 1967).

34. E. Yamauchi, "The Archaeological Background of Daniel," *BSac* 137 (1980): 3–16; idem, "Hermeneutical Issues in the Book of Daniel," *JETS* 23 (1980): 132–42; idem, "Daniel and Contacts between the Aegean and the Near East before Alexander," *EvQ* 53 (1981): 37–47.

been found in Palestine from the Archaic Era. East Greek wares in large quantities at Mesad Hashavyahu on the coast probably came from a Greek mercenary camp serving the Egyptians. Farther inland at Arad, ostraca listing payments to Kittim probably represent Greek mercenaries in the employ of the last kings of Judah before Nebuchadnezzar's conquest.

From the classical era (fifth century B.C.), when Athens had become preeminent in its defense of the Greek homeland against the Persian invasion, we have the interesting inclusion of the Palestinian seaport for Dor in the Athenian tribute lists. After the signing of the Peace of Callias (449 B.C.), Pericles used the surplus from the Delian League and the manpower from his demobilized sailors to rebuild many splendid buildings on the Acropolis, including the famed Parthenon.

While there is an abundance of evidence for the presence of Greeks and Greek objects in the Near East prior to the fourth century B.C., it was the wide-ranging campaign of Alexander the Great which radically changed the situation (prophesied in Dan. 8:5–8). After his death in 323 B.C., Alexander's generals carved up the vast territories he had conquered among themselves. Ptolemy seized Egypt, and Seleucus acquired vast territories in Persia, Mesopotamia, and Syria. Palestine was a vital land corridor coveted by both the Ptolemies and the Seleucids. Their incessant wars also divided the Jews into pro-Ptolemaic and pro-Seleucid factions (Dan. 11). When the Seleucids gained the upper hand, Antiochus Epiphanes attempted to force them to abandon their Judaism and adopt the Greek religion—the abomination of desolation foretold by Daniel (9:27), which provoked the Maccabean Revolt of 165 B.C.

FOR FURTHER READING

Aldred, C. *The Egyptians.* Rev. ed. London: Thames & Hudson, 1984.

Hallo, W. W. and W. K. Simpson. *The Ancient Near East: A History.* New York: Harcourt, Brace, Jovanovich, 1971.

Knapp, A. B. *The History and Culture of Ancient Western Asia and Egypt.* Chicago: Dorsey, 1988.

Kramer, S. N. *The Sumerians.* Chicago: University of Chicago Press, 1963.

Saggs, H. W. F. *The Greatness That Was Babylon.* Rev. ed. London: Sidgwick & Jackson, 1988.

———. *The Might That Was Assyria.* London: Sidgwick & Jackson, 1984.

Wiseman, D. J., ed. *Peoples of Old Testament Times.* Oxford: Clarendon, 1973.

Yamauchi, E. M. *Greece and Babylon.* Grand Rapids: Baker, 1967.

———. *Foes from the Northern Frontier.* Grand Rapids: Baker 1982.

———. *Persia and the Bible.* Grand Rapids: Baker, 1990.

XVI

BIBLICAL THEOLOGY OF
THE OLD TESTAMENT

WALTER C. KAISER, JR.

For more than two hundred years, "biblical theology" has been a programmatic term for a new and independent method of approaching the Bible in theological research. Ever since Johann Philip Gabler's inaugural address, "An Oration on the Proper Distinction Between Biblical and Dogmatic Theology and the Specific Objectives of Each,"[1] at the University of Altdorf on March 30, 1787, this new biblical discipline has flourished.

---

1. The Latin title was "Oratio de justo discrimine theologiae biblicae et dogmaticae regundisque recte utriusgue finibus," in *Kleinere theologische Schriften 2*, ed. T.A. Gabler and J.G. Gabler (Ulm: Verlag der Stettinischen Buchhandlung, 1831), 179–98. An English translation is now available in J. Sandys-Wunsch and L. Eldredge, "J.P. Gabler and the Distinction Between Biblical and Dogmatic Theology: Translation, Commentary and Discussion of His Originality," *SJT* 33(1980): 133–58. It is also repeated, in part, in Ben C. Ollenburger, Elmer J. Martens and Gerhard F. Hasel, eds., *The Flowering of Old Testament Theology: A Reader in Twentieth-Century Old Testament Theology, 1930–1990* (Winona Lake, Ind.: Eisenbrauns, 1992), 492–502.

However, in spite of a prodigious amount of scholarship in this relatively recent discipline, this fledgling study of the Scriptures has produced few, if any, final answers in most of the Biblical Theologies. OT theology, like NT theology, is a discipline in search of a definition, an agreed upon methodology, an organizing center or motif, and a permanent berth in the curriculum of divinity.

OLD TESTAMENT THEOLOGY: A PROBLEM OR A POSSIBILITY?

Few will contest the fact that there is a need for a theology of the OT: that is the only fact that most biblical scholars seem to agree on. The hope is that this discipline will halt the growing fragmentation that has come with recent biblical exegesis of the OT. There also is a strong plea for this discipline to outline some of the major lines of biblical faith.

But along with the agreed upon needs and hopes that most contemporary biblical scholars have for this discipline, there is no agreement on what the formulation of a biblical theology would look like! It is not that there is an unwillingness to attempt to recover the theological dimensions of the text as fully as we can. Instead, it is the complaint that the OT contains such a plurality of theologies that any attempt to find a theology (note: the word is singular and not plural) for the OT is declared dead from the very start! What can hold together so rich a diversity of themes, ideas, and theologies?—many of which are said by critical scholarship to be plainly in contradiction one with another!

The problems briefly traced thus far are all too frequently self-induced. Biblical scholarship may only be reaping the whirlwind of some of its own deeds. For example, the declaration that there are many theologies in the Hebrew Bible is mainly the product of several hundred years of critical scholarship that has insisted on starting from the assumption that the claims of the text as to unity of authorship are extremely suspect and probably to be rejected. What would happen if we began our study of the text from the opposite point of view: namely, that the claims of the Bible are to be taken on their own terms unless proven otherwise? This latter approach seems fairer to the text, its claims, and to the discipline of biblical theology itself.

Another reason why this discipline that has such a great potential is in such deep trouble presently is because it has attempted to make biblical theology more scientific than systematic/dogmatic theology. In order to do this, many accepted the mandate of Krister Stendahl to limit biblical theology to a descriptive discipline, not a normative one, which only seeks to portray what the text "meant," not what it "means" today.[2] But the separation of these two tasks was artificial; it leaned too heavily toward the side of placating the historical-critical agenda while hoping that at least a minimum of theology could also be objectively validated from the OT.

But one of the primary goals for OT biblical theology has been the OT must be understood as a whole. This is because theology by definition has to do with the ordering of thought into some kind of wholeness. OT theology is systematic simply because it is OT *theology*. But that is where the rub comes for modern scholars: Unity, a theological center, and systematic endeavors are older formulations that must now give way to pluralism, diversity, and competing perspectives.

Is it any wonder that this discipline has been pronounced dead, moribund, "in crisis," and generally declared to be deficient? There is a problem with biblical theology; however, its problem is not in the text, in some insoluble methodological problems, or even in some perceived plurality of theologies found in the OT. Its problem, as A. K. M. Adam so wisely pointed out, is the problem of "modernity."[3] Adam explains that modernity "in this context does not refer to the quality of being particularly recent." Instead:

> "Modernity" designates a specific interpretation of what is to be done in a given discipline; it is a label for a set of assumptions which underlie and regulate an enterprise. There are admittedly as many different kinds of "modernity" as there are people who think about modernity. . . .
>
> Lacking an authoritative definition of "modernity," I will stipulate the following characteristics: first, a proclivity for the adjective "scientific"; second, a pattern of citing newer sources as most authoritative; and third, a reluctance to admit that current biblical interpretations stand in continuity with biblical interpretation through the centuries. There is a fourth mark of modernity, namely the assumption that any interpretation which does not exercise historical criticism is "uncritical" or "precritical" as though historical interpretation provides the only legitimate criteria for judgment. . . .[4]

This diagnosis of the alleged problem with OT theology is right on target. These scholars have wedded biblical theology with historical criticism

---

2. This thesis was first set forth by *IDB*, s.v. "Biblical Theology, Contemporary." It is now reprinted as "Biblical Theology: A Program," in *Meanings: The Bible as Document and as Guide* (Philadelphia: Fortress, 1984), 11–44. For the best critique of this view, see Ben C. Ollenburger, "What Krister Stendahl 'Meant'—A Normative Critique of 'Descriptive Biblical Theology,'" *HBT* 8 (1986): 61–98.

3. A. K. M. Adam, "Biblical Theology and the Problem of Modernity: *Von Wredestrasse zu Sackgasse*," *HBT* 12 (1990): 1–18.

4. Ibid., 1–2.

and divorced it from dogmatic/systematic theology. The result has been a "critical OT theology." Furthermore, in defending the "principle of criticism" within the historical-critical method, its adherents had to admit such historical research "produces only probabilities, a conclusion which raises questions about the certainty of faith and its object in theology." [5]

Many of these same problems could be avoided if this discipline were more closely aligned with a canonical approach instead of a critical or a historical one. Surely the claims of the text ought to be taken on their own terms unless, or until, it can be shown that they cannot be verified. Initially approaching any text in the humanities on any other bases would be preemptive and represent contemporary imperialism of the worse sorts.

The real problem, therefore, is this: Does a key exist for an orderly and progressive arrangement of subjects, themes, and theological teachings of the OT? And even more important: Were the OT writers consciously aware of such a key as they continued to add to the historical stream of revelation?

The answer to both of these questions is yes. There is a unifying center to the OT that is to be found in the text itself. If such a unifying center were to be drawn up from such external sources as philosophy and creedal statements of the church, then were dropped over the OT as a type of grid through which the text was to be interpreted, it would be as artificial and unjustified as the critical theologies that have already been rejected by many in this century. But there is a unified plan of God that is continually disclosed by the succession of OT writers over the centuries. And they show they were conscious of its existence both in their overt didactic statements as well as in the multiplicity of literary formats and situations found in the OT.

OLD TESTAMENT THEOLOGY DEFINED

In spite of all the pessimism about the possibility of finding a center or any kind of integration for the whole of OT theology, the OT itself openly espouses just such a plan and demonstrates conscious use of it throughout the entire canon. To say the center is Yahweh is only to state the subject; it leaves unstated the predicate: Yahweh is and does what? To say it is Israel is to focus only on its main object, but that leaves the subject and the action of any verbs unstated. A proper statement of the center of OT theology must satisfy four conditions simultaneously: (1) the subject of that unity must be everywhere in evidence throughout the whole OT corpus; (2) the object(s) to whom the action, plan, or ideas pertain also

---

5. Edgar Krentz, as cited by Gerhard F. Hasel, "The Future of Old Testament Theology: Prospects and Trends," in *The Flowering of Old Testament Theology*, 375.

must be clearly in the limelight; (3) a predicate that links the subject and the object must be clearly stated in key teaching passages that act as *sedes doctrinae* (i.e., chair passages) and that set the grand goals and objectives for everything the subject is going to be and do for the object(s) specified in the text; and (4) the linking of the previous three conditions must be set forth explicitly in the OT rather than brought in from external sources, such as philosophical grounds, historical considerations, theological preferences, or critical allegiances.

THE PROMISE-PLAN OF GOD

One such candidate for the center of OT theology does exist. It is the *promise-plan of God*. The promise-plan of God meets all four conditions: (1) its subject is Yahweh; (2) its object is primarily Israel, and then, secondarily, all the nations of the earth; (3) its predicate involves both who and what God will "be" (ontology) and what He will "do" (in His verbal declarations and in His mighty saving acts in the history of Israel); and (4) it is strategically placed numerous times in the OT in large blocks of teaching texts, but best epitomized in Genesis 12:1–3.

The promise-plan of God is His declaration to be and to do something for Israel, and thereby, to be and to do something for all the nations of the earth. It is a plan that is at once singular, simple, and focused on the Messiah who is to come; yet its single promise spreads out into a multiplicity of specifications that is continually being fulfilled, continually expanded, and continually enlarged.

Interestingly enough, there is no one single term that the OT uses to refer to this plan; instead, it uses a whole constellation of terms to refer to the promise: word, oath, covenant, house, kingdom, and many more such terms. But by NT times the biblical writers had settled on the term *epangelia*, "promise." They identified this promise as the one God had made with Abraham, Isaac, Jacob, and the whole nation of Israel (Heb. 6:13–15, 17; 11:9, 39–40; Rom. 4:13–14, 16–17a, 20). For these NT writers, it was all *one* promise, as Paul announced before Agrippa, "And now it is because of the promise of God made to our fathers that I am on trial today. This is the promise our twelve-tribe nation is hoping to see fulfilled as they earnestly serve God day and night. O king, it is because of this hope that the Jews are accusing me" (Acts 26:6–7). Even though this promise was one, it had many specifications, including the themes of present and future rest, the kingdom of God, the Messiah, the salvation of the Gentiles, the resurrection of the body, the ministry of the Holy Spirit, a present and coming peace, and the gospel itself. Moreover, this promise was continually being fulfilled, yet it was always moving on to a larger fulfillment (Acts 7:2, 17–18; 13:22–23; Luke 1:69–70, 72–73).

The high point of the promise's fulfillment culminated in Jesus Christ, so that when the apostles of the early church preached Christ, they were actually preaching the OT promise as well (Acts 2:38–39; 3:25–26; 13:23, 32–33; Gal. 3:22). On one point the NT writers were most insistent: God's promise to Abraham also was a promise for the Gentiles and the nations at large (Gal. 3:8, 14, 29; Eph. 1:13; 2:12; 3:6–7; 4:23, 28). In fact, they connected the doctrine of the promise with the doctrine of redemption from sin and its consequences (Rom. 4:2–5, 9–10; Jas. 2:21–23). As further evidence of the extreme importance that the NT writers attached to this theme of the promise as their fair summary of the theology of the OT, it can be noted that the noun "promise" appears fifty-two times in the NT (twenty-six times in Paul, fourteen times in Hebrews, nine times in Luke, twice in 2 Peter, and once in 1 John), the verb appears fifteen more times (five in Paul, four in Hebrews, twice in James, and once each in Mark, Acts, 2 Peter and 1 John), with only two of the twenty-seven NT books (Matthew and Jude) making no reference to this summary theme of the OT.

All of this NT evidence may leave the wrong impression: The promise theme should be adopted as the proper center for OT theology because the NT has pronounced it to be so. However, the NT evidence is secondary (in order of appearance and thus in our order of considering it) and only functions in a support role. Our case, on the contrary, is that this theme is announced first in the OT and self-consciously developed in that portion of the canon even though it was not known under this rubric of the "promise."

However, even when the word "promise" was not present in the OT, the substance and content of the divine declaration that would become the centerpiece in all of revelation was. That centerpiece was to be found in the divine decision to elect one man, Abraham, to be the object of God's special blessing so that through him all the nations of the earth might receive the good news of the gospel (Gen. 12:3, repeated in Gen. 18:18 and 28:14 and commented on in Gal. 3:8 by the apostle Paul). So crucial was the passive form of the verb "be blessed" (often incorrectly rendered as a reflexive, "bless themselves")[6] that Bertil Albrecktson acknowledged if the Hebrew Niphal form of the verb is to be translated in the passive

---

6. The most definitive discussion of this rendering as a passive form of the verb "to bless" is found in O.T. Allis' "The Blessing of Abraham," *PTR* 25(1927): 263–98. This essay has never been answered as far as we have been able to determine.

voice, and not the reflexive voice as he and many modern translations of the Bible had concluded, then there was a clear reference to a divine plan in this text.[7] The center of the theology of the OT would be that God had picked Abraham as His chosen instrument to reach all the nations of the earth with the good news that through his offspring God would grant blessing to all the world.

Here, then, was divine intentionality, divine planning, divine revelation, divine election, and divine prediction. What is more, with almost routine regularity, the disputed verb "to bless" was treated in Samaritan, Septuagint (Greek), and Vulgate (Latin) versions as a passive. Likewise, the Targums (Babylonian [Onkelos] and Jerusalem [Pseudo-Jonathan]) also uniformly treated this verbal form as a passive. Once again, the problem rested more with our contemporaries who espoused modernity while concluding that prediction and knowledge of the divine mind were highly unlikely features—especially for such an early period as the text claims for itself. But there is no break in our evidence for the passive form of this verb until we find polemical pressures emerging late in the history of interpretation.

The promise is not a magic wand waved over the text, nor is it an abstract divining rod used to yield a message slanted in favor of one type of theology over against another. The biblical text itself places the concept of the promise in its most prominent position. This can be determined by the sheer number of times it is directly, or indirectly, raised throughout the canon. It also can be seen from the universality of its scope: It features all the nations as recipients of its gifts. It embodies the person around whom the whole story of theology will revolve—Christ the Messiah—both in His person and work, but known at that time as "the seed." The theology and story of the OT cannot be reduced solely and exclusively to the doctrine of the Messiah, but neither can the Messiah be taken out of the center of that story and theology either. Christ remains the goal toward which all the OT was headed (Rom. 10:4).

AN OUTLINE FOR OT THEOLOGY

How, then, shall we organize OT theology? Will a collection of all the doctrines of the OT after the manner and style of systematic theology be adequate? If so, of what use would such a truncated collection of doctrines serve since it would not include the NT? Why not simply go on to include the NT in this collection and make the whole project into a dogmatic or sys-

7. Bertil Albrektson, *History and the Gods* (Lund, Sweden: C. W. K. Gleerup Fund, 1967), 79. See our brief review of Albrektson's line of reasoning and his evidence in *Toward an Old Testament Theology* (Grand Rapids: Zondervan, 1978), 13, 29–32.

tematic theology? This partial listing of just the OT doctrines would hardly seem to be worth all our effort. The discipline of biblical theology would be redundant and merely duplicate what was available elsewhere in systematics.

The role OT theology should have is altogether distinctive and separate from the aims, methods, and structuring systematic theology traditionally has used. Biblical theology, from its inception, has had strong ties with the historical development of doctrine and with the progress of revelation in space and time. Therefore, a distinctive contribution OT theology should make to the study of the Scriptures is one that must take some note of the general state of theology in each epoch of revelation, moving diachronically, i.e. "through [each epoch of] time"—generally conceived into broad centuries in the OT (with a narrowing into single decades in the NT's only century of revelation, the first century A.D.).

This is not to claim contemporary readers and scholars can and ought to date each revelatory event or section of a book or the canon with precision. But that type of precision is usually not needed, even though it might be available on a few rare occasions in the OT. It will usually be adequate to group the OT materials into their proper centuries without demanding a precise date for each book or section of a book when some of the longer books appear to stretch over several decades.

Thus, it can be proposed that approximately eleven periods of time covering at least fifteen hundred years of writing activity with a minimum of several more millennia of divine activity that was prior to this fifteen hundred years of God's divine revelation to those who claimed to be the recorders of what He revealed to all mortals.

All of this means that the real motivation for doing biblical theology is to add the very essential theological advantage to our exegesis and interpretation of biblical texts. Whereas most have proclaimed in the past that biblical theology was a handmaiden to systematic theology, this proposal changes all of that and announces a new agenda for this two-and-a-half-century-old discipline.

Biblical theology is the twin discipline to exegetical theology rather than to systematic theology. Its role is so distinctive that without it the task of interpreting falls into a mere descriptive analysis that talks *about* the text and all too often leaves it locked up in the historicism of a B.C. or first-century A.D. *then* perspective, with little or no carryover to the *now* of the proclamation or application for the contemporary listener. The message of every pericope in the OT must be related to the center and core of the canon. When this distinctive pattern, plan, or center is kept in the interpreter's view, the results of the exegesis are fairer to the perspective of the writer and it is now possible to enter into discussions about what in the text is *normative*, rather than being merely reduced to making *descriptive* statements on the text.

Depending on where the exegete is working in the OT, he or she will use the theology of the center and the theology of the preceding periods as a measure against which to judge analogous or identical topics, key words, similar theological interests, and shared references to persons and events that have now become bywords for succeeding generations. It is this progress of revelation that "informs" the new text being exegeted and supplies the background and available message against which this new message now being interpreted in the text was given.[8] Therefore, instead of using the NT, or even any subsequent OT texts and ideas, to interpret or reinterpret the old material, OT theology will provide the interpreter with a set of accumulating terms, key theological concepts, and designations of significant interpretive moments in the history of God's plan in accordance with the announced center and pivotal fulcrum for the entire OT. Only by using biblical theology in this way will contemporary interpreters be delivered from mere historicism and be enabled instead to ground their understanding on the abiding message and the normative aspects of the OT.

The resulting outline that emerges for OT theology, with its "long-cut" diachronic base moving through history and its normative implications for the exegete, is as follows:

- Prolegomena to the Promise: Prepatriarchal Era

- Provisions in the Promise: Patriarchal Era

- People of the Promise: Mosaic Era

- Place of the Promise: Premonarchical Era

- King of the Promise: Davidic Era

- Life in the Promise: Wisdom Era

- Day of the Promise: Ninth-century Prophets

- Servant of the Promise: Eighth-century Prophets

- Renewal of the Promise: Seventh-century Prophets

- Kingdom of the Promise: Exilic Era Prophets

- Triumph of the Promise: Post-exilic Era Prophets [9]

---

8. This term was first used by John Bright in *Authority of the Old Testament* (Nashville: Abingdon, 1967), 143, 170. For my own development of this same concept, with a contrast between what I call "The Analogy of Antecedent Scripture" and "The Analogy of Faith," see "Hermeneutics and the Theological Task," *TJ* 12NS (1990): 3–14.

9. This outline is only a slightly revised outline that appears in my book, *Toward an Old Testament Theology* (Grand Rapids: Zondervan, 1978).

This outline, though in some ways arbitrary, is a suitable anchor around which to gather the distinctive concepts, revelatory moments, and periodic advances in the progress of the promise-plan of God in the OT.

A DIACHRONIC PRESENTATION OF OLD TESTAMENT BIBLICAL THEOLOGY

Since the two hallmarks of biblical theology are a theological center and a regard for the development of that theological center's progress through the epochs or eras of time, our presentation will roughly follow eleven of these generally large periods of time. Our designations will group the materials with a double concern for both the historical as well as the canonical flow of the materials. The reason for this arrangement, again, is to be as helpful as possible to the exegete who wishes to have some general sense of what came before the text he or she is interpreting and what came after.

There can be little doubt that the key theme of the creation narratives, that marks the commencement of the OT canon, was the "blessing" of God over all His creatures in the sea and air (Gen. 1:22) and on man and woman (Gen. 1:28). But the "blessing" theme does not end at that point; it is the dominant theme throughout the whole prepatriarchal era found in Genesis 1—11. For instance, it can be found in Genesis 5:2 before the flood and in Genesis 9:1 after the flood.

But the blessing of God was to be found even where the appearance of the word "bless" or even the formula of blessing —"And God blessed them saying, 'Be fruitful and multiply and fill the earth'"—was not explicitly stated. This same blessing of God was also found in three momentous divine announcements in response to three world crises brought on by the sinfulness of mortals: the fall, the flood, and the flop of the tower of Babel. The three blessings that formed the grounds for the promise-plan of God were Genesis 3:15; 9:27; and 12:1–3.

The OT canon began with the blessing of creation. It, like God's promise, began with the divine word. One of the most frequently stated expressions in the creation narrative of Genesis 1 is "And God said" (vv. 3, 6, 9, 11, 14, 20, 24, 26, 29). Therefore, everything that exists, must be traced to the creative power of God's word: That is the method by which the world was created. Later theologies will celebrate this same fact (Ps. 33:6, 9; John 1:1–4; Heb. 11:3). God concluded the whole creative process by blessing the seventh day and sanctifying it since it was on that day He stopped (the root of the word for the Sabbath) from all His work of creation (Gen. 2:3), thereby drawing a dividing line between His work in creation past and His continuing work of providence.

Even though God placed His image in the man and woman He created, disappointingly they failed the single test placed before them: They ate of the tree of the knowledge of good and evil. It was not that this tree had any special kinds of enzymes or magical powers in it; it merely stood for the possibility of these mortals' rebellion against the word of God.

But there was another factor in the fall of humanity into sin: "the serpent." This created being "was subtle above [and beyond] the beasts of the field" (Gen. 3:1). There can be little doubt that this being was the one who would later be known as Satan, the great dragon, that ancient serpent (Rev. 12:9; Rom. 16:20; 2 Cor. 11:3, 14). Consistently he spoke on his own; he was not a surrogate for someone else, and he knew alternative results as he worked his deception on the woman.

As a result, Satan was condemned to defeat, not that he would literally live on a diet of dirt and be reduced to the form of locomotion of crawling on his belly (Gen. 3:14–15). These expressions of defeat of one's enemies were too well known and too frequently used to be missed by any in that day just as some shout at a football game to let the visiting team "bite the dust." As a result of this sad fiasco, not only was Satan condemned, but so was the woman (Gen 3:16), the man (v. 17), and even the ground (vv. 18–19).

The Blessing of Genesis 3:15. But in the midst of all this tragedy, God had a surprise (Gen. 3:15). A male descendant from the woman would at some unspecified time in the future crush the head of "the serpent." This coming male person would be among the "seed" or "offspring" of the woman. What could such an enigmatic promise mean? Did Eve understand it to refer to anyone of significance?

There may be a very important clue in Genesis 4:1 where Eve says in response to her giving birth to Cain, "I have gotten a man, even the LORD." Most translations cannot believe what they are reading in the Hebrew text, so they render it, while also adding some words, by saying "with the help of the LORD" (RSV). But there is little to justify that rendering. Eve may be telling us she thought the birth of Cain was God's immediate answer to His promise of a male descendant whom she also somehow believed would be none less than the Lord! If so, her instincts about the basic meaning were correct, but her identification and her timing were all off. [10] Here, then, is the earliest promise of the Messiah in the

---

10. For those who suspect the equation of the "seed" in Gen. 3:15 might be a later Christian retrojection back to this text, note that three centuries before the Christian era, the Greek translation of the OT, the Septuagint, broke the rules of grammatical agreement only this once in Gen. 3:15, refusing to make the masculine pronoun "he" agree with the neuter word (in Greek) "seed," after forcing the

canon. This promise of the doctrine of the "seed" will be one of the central but growing themes of OT theology.

The Blessing of Genesis 9:27. A second promise came in another divine word as an aftermath to the flood brought on once again by the sin of mankind. Genesis 9:27 states, "And he shall dwell in the tents of Shem." Who was the "he" spoken of here? Since the subject in the first part of this verse was "God," grammar demands (even though the translators incorrectly insist on pulling the object of the previous line, "Japheth," forward) that the antecedent of the pronoun "he" and the subject of the line be the same. Therefore, the promise was that God would come and "dwell" in the tents of the Semitic (our way of bringing over into English the word Shem) peoples. But which one of the Semites? Only after the call of Abraham would it be clear God had chosen the Hebrew line of the Semitic peoples. Even more startling was the promise that God would come and make His abode among mere mortals. The mighty, omnipotent God would camp, or tabernacle, in our kind of world? This would be evidenced in the theology of the shekinah ("dwelling") glory of God in the pillar of fire and cloud by day as Israel would go through the wilderness. It would be evidenced in the Christophonies, i.e., the appearance of Christ in preincarnate form as "the Angel of the LORD" throughout the OT. But it would reach a high point in John 1:14 where "The Word became flesh and dwelt [or 'tabernacled'] among us" in the incarnation of Jesus Christ.

The Blessing of Genesis 12:1–3. The third and final declaration of God came in response to another failure: the flop of the tower of Babel. Just as mortals had that insatiable desire for a "name" in Genesis 6:4, so here, once again, human hubris quested for a "name," a "reputation," and a mark of human success.

But God rejected this early experimentation in humanism and human pride. Instead, he called one man, Abraham, and promised to bless him by making his "name great" (Gen. 12:2). But God would do this for a special reason: It was so that He might be the means of blessing "all the peoples of the earth" (Gen. 12:3). A list of seventy nations had just been given in Genesis 10: These were to be the beneficiaries of the blessing that had come to Abraham. In fact, the word "bless," "blessing," or "blessed" appears five times in Genesis 12:2–3, thereby tying together Genesis 1—11 with the patriarchal era of Genesis 12—50.

---

agreement in 103 other instances in its translation of the Book of Genesis. This was pointed out by R. A. Martin, "The Earliest Messianic Interpretation of Genesis 3:15," *JBL* 84 (1965): 427.

PROVISIONS IN THE PROMISE: PATRIARCHAL ERA

A radically new departure commenced with the declarations of God's blessing in Genesis 12:1–3. From now on, God intended to make His blessings available to all mortals on planet earth, but He would use mortals from the line of one known as Abraham.

The contents of God's blessings could be summarized in three oft-repeated provisions: an heir, known as the "*seed*" (Gen. 12:7; 15:4; 17:16, 19; 21:12; 22:16–18; 26:3–4, 24; 28:13–14; 35:11–12); an inheritance of the *land* (Gen. 12:1, 7; 13:17; 15:18; 17:8; 24:7; 26:3–5; 28:13, 15; 35:12; 48:4; 50:24); and a heritage of the good news of the *gospel* (Gal. 3:8) that "in your seed all the people of the earth will be blessed" (Gen. 12:3; 18:18; 22:18; 26:4; 28:14).

To demonstrate the eternality and the one-sidedness of these gracious provisions from our God, only the Lord passed between the pieces as the covenant promising these blessings was concluded in Genesis 15:9–21. Thus, God obligated Himself to fulfill all these promises without simultaneously making any of them conditional on Abraham or the subsequent beneficiaries of such wonderful benefits.

During this same patriarchal period, there was an increased prominence given to the *word* of God. Thus, the three fathers of Israel—Abraham, Isaac, and Jacob—were called "prophets" in Genesis 20:7 and Psalm 105:15. Eight times Abraham is the recipient of revelation, besides having the Lord Himself come to him as the Angel of the Lord (Gen. 16:7; 19:1, 21). God's "promise" was first and foremost His word, His declaration of blessing to a man, and His line of descendants for the set purpose they might be the means of bringing blessing to all the peoples of the earth. Surely this is a theology of missions long before most traditionally even think that missions appeared in the canon!

PEOPLE OF THE PROMISE: MOSAIC ERA

Four hundred years of revelatory silence intrude between Genesis and Exodus, just as a similar four hundred years of silence reemerge between the last book of the OT, Malachi, and the NT. But the text of Exodus opens without missing a beat in the promise-plan of God: Exodus 1:6–7 uses seven words (in Hebrew) to stress the fact God is still blessing His people with the promised increase He had given in the preceding eras. Moreover, God remembered the promise He had made with Abraham, Isaac, and Jacob, even though they had generally forgotten both the Maker of the promise and the mission assigned to them as a result of that promise (Ex. 2:24).

The promise moved on relentlessly, in spite of everything. Here God would now form this "seed" into a "people" (Ex. 5:1; 7:14; 8:1, 20; 9:1; 10:3) and call them His "firstborn son" (Ex. 4:22–23); a "nation" (Ex. 19:6), His "treasured possession" (Ex. 19:5), a "holy nation" and a "kingdom of priests" (or "kingly priests" Ex. 19:6). All of these titles not only stressed the privilege of their calling and election, but their responsibilities to be a light to the nations and mediators of God's blessing to the world.

Since Israel was called to be a "holy nation," they were expected to be different from the rest of the nations. The promise of God was not conditioned on their holiness or obedience, but their participation in the fullness of the life God had intended for them certainly was. Accordingly, God gave the gracious gift of His law. But in no case was eternal life or the maintenance of the promise itself dependent on a law of obedience. Leviticus 18:5 had said, "Do this and you shall live in them," but this was addressed to those who already believed as the beginning and end of the chapter demonstrate: "I am the LORD your God" (vv. 2,20). And the things that Israel was to do were the Lord's statutes and commands, which in this context were sharply contrasted with the idolatrous customs and ordinances of the Egyptians and Canaanites. The law of God must not be thought of as a fence, or as sets of strictures one must rigidly adhere to; instead, the word *torah* came from the root that meant to point out the direction or the path that persons were to take. At the heart of the Torah stood the character and nature of God. It urged, "Be holy because I, the LORD your God, am holy" (Lev. 19:2). Therefore, even though the law exhibits a unity, the Bible itself makes the point that what is based on the character of God (e.g., the Ten Commandments of Ex. 20:2–17 and the holiness law of Lev. 18—20) is more basic and logically prior to those examples of moral principles found in the civil law (e.g., the covenant code of Ex. 21—23) or the typological ceremonies of Exodus 25—40 through Leviticus 1—17.

The ceremonial law had a built-in obsolescence in that it acknowledged what had been revealed in the mountain of Sinai to Moses was only a "model" or "copy" of the real (e.g., Ex. 25:40). That meant when the real [Jesus], which was in heaven, came, all the tabernacle, its services, its ministers, sacrifices, and rules for what was clean and unclean would be rendered outmoded and suddenly replaced by the real. But in the meantime, all of these ceremonies and rituals pointed away from themselves to a fulfillment that would complete all God had implied in these promised types and shadows of the future.

PLACE OF THE PROMISE:
PREMONARCHIAL ERA

The promise of God would also take on spatial relationships, for God would put His name in a *place* He would choose (Deut. 12:5, 11, 21; 14:23–24; 15:20; 16:2, 6, 11; 26:2; Josh. 9:27). This would be a further fulfillment of the promise that God would "dwell" in the midst of His people.

The emphasis of making His "name" "dwell" in this place did not mean, as some have taught, that this "name-theology" replaced the older "glory-theology." The "name" of God stood for His total being, character and nature. It meant He intended to take up His abode on earth among mortals even though His permanent abode was in heaven (Ex. 25:8; 29:45; Lev. 26:11; Num. 16:3). Thus, while God was "enthroned" and "sat" in heaven, He also tabernacled on earth.

The theme of "place" was, of course, nothing more than a further revelation of the promise of the inheritance of the land. Now God would put His sanctuary in that land. Accordingly, the parallel promise of the "rest" for Israel developed during this time. So special was this rest that Yahweh would call it "his rest" later on (Ps. 95:11; Isa. 66:1). There would be the messianic "Man of rest" (1 Chron. 22:9) who would finally be given respite from all His enemies in the Messianic era (Ps. 132:14; cf. 2 Chron. 14:6). Thus, both the physical and spiritual aspects of the doctrine of rest grew up together. The land of Canaan was a present fulfillment to this promise, but one day God would extend His hand a "second time" to recover the remnant of Israel from all over the world. Then would come the millennial rest celebrated in the Psalms such as Psalms 93—100. Every other rest, whether it was the occupation of the land in Joshua's day or the Sabbath day of rest, were only earnests and partial downpayments on God's final sabbath rest that would come after the second coming of Messiah. [11]

The promise of the "seed" also received further development during this era, for that promised male descendant who was to come would be "a prophet" "like [Moses]" "from the midst of [the Jewish] brethren" (Deut. 18:15–19). When Messiah came, He would have a prophetic office.

KING OF THE PROMISE: DAVIDIC ERA

Second only to the Abrahamic promise in Genesis 12:1–3 is the amazing Davidic promise of 2 Samuel 7. Here, in response to David's proposal

---

11. For further development of this important theme, see Walter C. Kaiser, Jr., "The Promise Theme and the Theology of Rest," *BSac* 130 (1973): 135–50.

to build a house for God to replace the aging tabernacle, the prophet Nathan is commissioned by God to announce that God instead has decided to make a "house" (i.e., a dynasty) out of David, and to give him a "throne" and a "kingdom" that will have no termination point forever (2 Sam. 7:16).

So staggered is David by this bold declaration, which obviously picked up themes from the antecedent theology and promises of God, that he went into the house of God in 2 Samuel 7:19 and prayed in a flabbergasted exclamation: "This is your charter for humanity, O LORD!" He could not believe God had designated his house to the one through which he would continue the promise of the seed made to Eve, Abraham, Isaac, and Jacob. Nor could he fathom it would be through one of his descendants that all humanity would receive the blessing that first had been extended through Abraham.[12]

Even though the word "seed" is only used once in 2 Samuel 7:12, the promise of a line of offspring that would eventuate in a king who would be claimed as God's own Son (2 Sam. 7:14) amazed David. Naturally, the word "seed" had a collective meaning here just as it did in Genesis 3:15; 12:7; 13:15. But the seed simultaneously pointed to the one person who represented the whole group and who was the earnest in that generation of the ultimate one who would eventually come in a climactic fulfillment.

This phenomenon of speaking simultaneously of the one representative and the whole group under one term is fairly common in the OT world. In our own day, the only illustration that comes to mind is that of a corporation such as General Motors Corporation. If one of us were to sue GMC, for legal purposes the suit would read our individual name versus GMC, which in this case would be treated as if it were a single individual. Nevertheless, at the same time GMC also would stand for its management, stockholders, and all employees. In the same manner the OT used some of these terms that evidenced the same kind of corporate solidarity so that in one and the same term, the whole group as well as the single representative could be brought together in one word such as "seed." In Hebrew, "seed" is neither a singular or plural word, but it is what gram-

---

12. It is sad to witness how poorly both ancient and modern texts render this fairly straightforward Hebrew clause in 2 Sam. 7:19. Why this text has been so abused is hard to say unless its presentation of the heart of the gospel has been the special object of the evil one for blinding the minds and eyes of so many. For the full argumentation here, see W. C. Kaiser, Jr., "The Blessing of David: A Charter for Humanity," in *The Law and the Prophets*, ed. John Skilton (Philadelphia: Presbyterian and Reformed, 1974), 298–318.

marians call a collective singular, just as we say in English four "deer," not four "deers."

In this Davidic era, the doctrine of the kingdom of God began to receive prominence. There had been previous hints it would be God's intention to set up a kingdom, for God had promised "kings" would come out of Abraham's seed (Gen. 17:6, 16; cf. 35:11; 36:31), and God had inaugurated a "kingdom" during the Mosaic era (Ex. 19:6; Num. 24:7) and a "dominion" (Num. 24:19). God then enlarged on His promise as He assigned this kingship and its rule and reign over to David and his line (2 Sam. 7:23–27). The throne David and his son Solomon would sit on would be "the throne of the kingdom of the LORD" (2 Chron. 13:8; cf. 9:8). As such, they were called the "LORD'S anointed" (1 Sam. 24:6; 2 Sam. 19:21). The verb "anoint" was the same root from which the word "Messiah" came. Thus, the die was cast for the Christ to come from the line of David. This theme received greater development in the royal psalms (Pss. 2, 18, 20, 21, 45, 72, 89, 101, 110, 132, and 144). Six times David's kingdom was declared to be "eternal" or "everlasting" in Nathan's prophecy (2 Sam. 7:13, 16, 24, 26, 29). Therefore, just as the promises made in the Abrahamic covenant were declared to be irrevocable, so David's covenant promises were likewise proclaimed to be without conditions of any sort, for God would assure its fulfillment.

LIFE IN THE PROMISE: WISDOM ERA

It has become almost a trivial commonplace to complain that OT biblical theologies have been unable to integrate the wisdom materials found in Proverbs, Ecclesiastes, Song of Songs and the wisdom psalms (such as Pss. 1; 19; 32; 34; 37; 49; 78; 111—112; 119; 127—128; and 133) into any theological center. But all such talk usually comes from those who have never written an OT theology. Furthermore, the problem generally lies in the fact that these same complainers have not been able to relate law to grace; thus, it is no wonder the problem carries over into the wisdom materials, since wisdom is mostly a popular form of much of the same content as is found in the law. Check any marginal reference Bible and note how many times, for example, the references in the Book of Proverbs are linked to the informing theology and the antecedent Scriptures found in Exodus, Numbers, and Deuteronomy. Proverbs is filled with citations and allusions to the Law of Moses. Consequently, to solve the problem of the relationship of law to promise is to solve the relationship of wisdom to promise: The issues and the solutions are identical.

More than any other phrase, "the fear of the LORD/God" links together the Patriarchal/Davidic promise with law and wisdom. The goal of fearing the Lord, found so frequently in the wisdom literature of the OT, is the same goal that God had set for Abraham, Isaac, Jacob, and the nation of Israel under Moses. Trust in God's promise was to produce attitudes and acts of obedience that were summarized under the term "fear of the LORD." Thus, whether it was the response of Abraham seen in his willingness to offer his son Isaac (Gen. 22:12), Joseph's believing response (Gen. 42:18), Job's quality of life (Job 1:1, 8–9; 2:3), the midwives' refusal to take life (Ex. 1:17), or Israel's response at the exodus (Ex. 14:31) and afterward (Ex. 20:20), promise and law/wisdom were intimately connected. To live the life of faith in the promise meant to "fear God" (Lev. 19:14, 32; 25:17, 36, 43).

In fact, the last book of the Law of Moses, Deuteronomy, made the fear of the Lord one of its focal points (Deut. 4:10; 5:26; 6:2, 13, 24; 8:6; 10:12, 20; 13:4; 14:23; 17:19; 28:58; 31:12–13). To fear God was to commit oneself in faith as some of the Egyptians did (Ex. 9:20, 30) when a "mixed multitude" left Egypt with the Israelites (Ex. 12:38). This indeed had been the prayer of Solomon that "all the peoples of the earth" would come to "know [His] name and fear [Him]" (1 Kings 8:43).

Accordingly, when Proverbs 1:7 announces "the fear of the LORD" as the motto for the whole book and Ecclesiastes 12:13–14 summarizes the argument of its whole book as "fear the LORD," the linkage between promise and wisdom is not as remote, strange, and unrealizable as most have suggested. Proverbs will refer to the "fear of the LORD" thirteen more times (beside its motto verse and the additional verbal forms "to fear").

The result of fearing God is not eternal life, but abundant life. Repeatedly, the connection is drawn between the fear of the Lord and life lived in the joy of the Lord (Prov. 10:27; 14:27; 19:23; 22:4). The path to such spiritual life and joy was to be found in the attitude of trust and belief (called here the fear of the Lord) that resulted in a willing obedience. That was the same type of obedience Moses had spoken about in Deuteronomy 8:1.

Ecclesiastes made the same point: Six times the fear of God appeared in the book (Eccles. 3:14; 5:7; 7:18; 8:12–13). The central verse in the whole book, Ecclesiastes 3:11, wrapped up the whole case for fearing God. "[God] has made everything beautiful in its time: also He has set eternity [Hebrew *hāʿōlām*] in their heart so that no man can find out the work that God does from beginning to the end." Thus, try as we may, no one has been able to piece together the puzzle of life. We cannot make heads or tails of any of it until we come to know Him. That is what it means to fear God! Only for those who fear Him will the wholeness of truth, living, learning, and a world-life view begin to come together. This text almost sounds as if St. Augustine parodied it when he said, "Thou hast made us for thyself and our hearts are restless until we rest in Thee."

Wisdom takes the promise of God and applies it down in the everyday secular world where the "rubber meets the road." Even the sanctity of dating and marriage receives its treatment as another sphere where marital fidelity and commitment are lauded in the Song of Songs. Solomon, writing under the inspiration of God, told how he loved, attempted to woo yet one more beauty for his harem, and lost to a shepherd boy back home to whom the Shulamite maiden had been pledged. He recorded his lesson in Ecclesiastes 8:6–7 for all to observe who would live in the promise and wish to exemplify the fear of the Lord. Wisdom is God's great school of everyday practical living for those who are members of the promise seed.

DAY OF THE PROMISE:
NINTH-CENTURY PROPHETS

Now that David's "house" and Solomon's temple had both been established, the promise of God had reached a provisional plateau. The sixteen writing prophets could now focus their attention on the worldwide aspects of the promise-plan of God first broached in Genesis 12:3—"In your seed all the peoples of the earth will be blessed." As such, the promise doctrine exhibited under the prophets' ministry a twofold character as Willis J. Beecher noted: "It was a standing prediction of the time to come, and it was an available religious doctrine for the time being." [13] Thus, the hallmarks of the prophets' message could be stated as (1) "turn" to the Lord (Zech. 1:4); and (2) "Behold the man whose name is the Branch [i.e., the 'seed,' the 'Messiah']" (Zech. 6:12).

Joel and Obadiah may well have ministered as early as the ninth century B.C. If so, they were the earliest of the prophets. Twenty-seven of Joel's seventy-three verses (in part or in whole) are found in his colleagues' books. While this does not establish which came first, there is a presumption of favor of Joel being the first until firm evidence establishes it otherwise.

Both Joel and Obadiah preach "the day of the LORD" as being "at hand" and a time of awful judgment and wrath from God against all wickedness and unrighteousness. That future day will be a time when the whole world will come under God's judgment (Joel 2:11; 3:14–15; Obad. 15). However, some will be delivered during that time, for there will be a

---

13. The thesis of the promise-plan of God traced in this chapter owes much to Willis J. Beecher, *The Prophets and the Promise* (Grand Rapids: Baker, 1975, reprint of 1905 Princeton Stone Lectures), 242.

discrimination between the righteous and the unrighteous, between Israel and the nations (Joel 3:16; Obad. 15–21).

But like many prophecies in the OT, there was a *now* and a *not yet* aspect to these predictions. For Joel, the impetus for preaching on the "day of the Lord" came with a mighty locust plague. This became the occasion for Joel to twice call for the people to "turn" back to the Lord in repentance (Joel 1:13–14; 2:12–14). And the people did (Joel 2:18; note the past tense is the only possible translation of the Hebrew narrative tenses here). Therefore, God sent immediate relief (Joel 2:19–27) while promising distant salvation and unprecedented judgment (Joel 2:28—3:21).

The occasion for Obadiah's call for the nation of Edom (the nation that came from Jacob's twin brother) to repent was that time when they refused to get involved and rescue their brother Israel. Therefore, God rebuked the pride of their hearts and warned of the awfulness of the coming day of the Lord.

SERVANT OF THE PROMISE: EIGHTH-CENTURY PROPHETS

Prior to the fall of Damascus in 732 B.C. and the fall of Israel's northern capital Samaria in 722 B.C., God sent a whole bevy of prophets to head off the threatened judgment: Amos, Hosea, Micah, Isaiah, and Jonah. Unfortunately, except for the small pockets of occasional response, such as that given to the preaching of Micah (Jer. 26:18–19) verified a century later, the northern ten tribes plunged headlong into the threatened judgment.

One aspect of the promise doctrine that received development during this period was the issue of the inclusion of the Gentiles in the promise and the kingdom of God. Genesis 1—11 had a universalist scope to its message, and so had the purpose of the Abrahamic promise in Genesis 12:3. But in Amos 9:11–12, it became even more apparent that the "house" of David (here called a "booth" or a "hut"), because of its dilapidated and collapsing condition, was a firm decision to have the Gentiles as part of its beneficiaries. The decrepit condition of David's kingdom would be remedied by the Lord Himself in that day. And God would remedy this situation so that Edom along with the other nations might be brought under the reign of that coming future Davidic King. The emphasis placed on the appositional clause, "even all the Gentiles who are called by your name" (v. 12) made it clear that the rule, reign, and realm of God extended beyond national Israel to include a spiritual seed from the Gentiles.

The prophecy of Jonah only reinforced this conclusion that God's kingdom included the Gentiles. Even though Jonah was reluctant to go to

Israel's cruelest enemy, he was somewhat drawn into the task through the gracious provision of God, undeserving though he was. Clearly, God wished Gentiles to repent and turn from their sins just as much as He wanted the Hebrews to do so; however, this displeased Jonah. In his view, sinners who were such brutal and bitter enemies should get what they deserve: death and everlasting destruction! He wanted no part of any offer of mercy and grace to such vile people.

The portrayal of the servant of the Lord in the prophet Hosea, however, took on a softer presentation. Nowhere in the Bible is the love and grace depicted any more graphically and in any more compelling terms. After Hosea had married Gomer and had three children by her, she left him to enter into a life of prostitution. But in spite of her treacherous act, Hosea remained faithful and resolved to win her back as his wife again, just as Yahweh announced through this same prophet He would graciously take back Israel even though she had forsaken her covenant with the Lord by means of her spiritual adultery. After many days, God would regather His people back in the land and the bond that had once existed would be restored again.

Micah develops the picture of that future day by announcing a "ruler" would come out of Bethlehem, David's hometown, whose origins and beginnings could be traced back to eternity (Mic. 5:2)! The scope of this ruler's government would be worldwide (5:5–15). Best of all, he would "pardon sin and forgive transgression . . . and hurl all our iniquities into the depths of the sea" (7:18–19). No wonder Micah cried out: "Who is a God like you?" (7:18a).

The promise theologian, par excellence, is Isaiah. For him, God was "the Holy One of Israel" (twenty-six times repeated evenly through both alleged divisions of Isaiah: twelve times in 1—39 and fourteen times in 40—66). God revealed Himself as the Holy One in the call He gave to Isaiah (6:1), but there He also set forth His glory as well.

But the character that stands out above all in Isaiah is the servant of the Lord. The "servant" appears twenty times, always in the singular form, in Isaiah 40—53 and eleven more times in Isaiah 54—66, but here it is always in the plural form. At the heart of all these references stand the four great servant songs of Isaiah 42:1–7; 49:1–6; 50:4–9 and 52:13—53:12 wherein the servant is presented as an individual who ministers to the whole nation of Israel. Therein lies one of the greatest puzzles: How can the servant simultaneously be the whole nation of Israel, the prophet, and the Messiah who is to come?

Once again the answer lies in the concept of corporate solidarity in which the one can represent the many, just as we illustrated above with the notion of GMC treated for purposes of law as a single individual, yet also as the whole company, its leaders, employees, and stockholders. The servant is the whole nation in Isaiah 41:8–9; 42:6; 43:1; and 44:2, 21, 24; but in Isaiah 42:1; 49:1, 3, 6, he is an individual whose work and ministry (especially in 52:13—53:12) has an effect on the whole nation.

It is difficult to avoid the conclusion the servant is anyone other than the Messiah who will come first to suffer (Isa. 52:13–14) and again a second time with such glory He will take away the breath of even kings, monarchs and presidents (52:15). His vicarious suffering will effect reconciliation between God and man (53:4–6). He will suffer a death with common criminals (53:9a), yet be buried with the rich (53:9b). Yet He will live again (the resurrection) to see the seed (all his spiritual offspring) and live forever (53:10). No wonder Isaiah (52:13a) announced, "Behold, my Servant shall have success!"

Isaiah relates the teaching about the "servant" with the earlier canonical teaching about the "seed" (41:8; 43:5; 44:3; 45:19, 25; 48:19; 53:10; 54:3; 59:21; 61:9; 65:9, 23; 66:22); the "covenant" that also had been given earlier (42:6; 49:8; 54:10; 55:3; 56:4, 6; 59:21; 61:8); and with "Abraham" (41:8; 51:2; 63:16), "Jacob" (41:21; 44:5; 49:26; 60:16), and "David" and the "everlasting covenant" (55:3; 61:8). In fact, the whole of Isaiah 40—66 could well serve as a magnificent shorter theology of the OT. His dependence on the antecedent theology can be seen at almost every turn. It is little wonder Isaiah's theology has so profoundly affected mortals over the centuries.

RENEWAL OF THE PROMISE:
SEVENTH-CENTURY PROPHETS

The great additions to the promise-plan of God that came from this century were found in two marvelous texts: Habakkuk 2:4, "The just shall live by faith" and Jeremiah 31:31–34, the new covenant.

Just or righteous people are enabled to live even in the face of the collapse of the Davidic kingdom, its temple, and everything surrounding both of these institutions—but it must only be by faith. Faith was simply an unwavering trust in the promise of God. In contrast to the overbearing disposition of the haughty despisers of God and His truth, believers were to anchor their hope with an immovable confidence in the word of the One who had promised He would fulfill all He had promised.

At the bedrock of this faith came a new announcement of the old promise: God's new covenant.[14] While this is the only place in the OT where

---

14. For more details, see W. C. Kaiser, Jr., "The Old Promise and the New Covenant: Jeremiah 31:31–34," *JETS* 15 (1972): 11–23, now reprinted in *The Bible and Its Literary Milieu: Contemporary Essays*, ed. Vincent L. Tollers and John R. Maier (Grand Rapids: Eerdmans, 1979), 106–20.

the name "new covenant" is used, the concept appears under such additional titles as "the everlasting covenant" (Isa. 24:5; 55:3; 61:8; Jer. 32:40; 50:5; Ezek. 16:60; 37:26); "covenant" or "My covenant" (Isa. 42:6; 49:8; 59:21; Hos. 2:18–20); a "new heart and a new spirit" (Jer. 32:39 [LXX]; Ezek. 11:19; 18:31; 36:26); and a "covenant of peace" (Isa. 54:10; Ezek. 34:25; 37:26). So important was this text that it became the basis for the church father Origen to name the last twenty-seven books of the Bible "The New Testament."

Actually, this was not a brand new covenant, but a renewal of the Abrahamic-Davidic provisions in the accumulating promise-plan of God. This is seen from the fact it contained (1) the same covenant-making God; (2) the same law of Moses; (3) the same divine fellowship; (4) the same "seed"; and (5) the same forgiveness.

But there were brand new features as well: (1) the universal knowledge of God; (2) universal peace; (3) universal material prosperity; (4) a sanctuary in the midst of Israel lasting forever; and (5) universal possession of the Spirit of God.

Why then was this new covenant contrasted with the old covenant made with Israel when God took them out of Egypt? Because the fault with that earlier covenant was not with the covenant-maker or with the contents of that covenant, but rather with the fact that "they broke my covenant" (Jer. 31:32; cf. Heb. 8:8—"God found fault with the people"). Furthermore, the word for "new" could just as well be translated "renewed," since there are not two separate words in Hebrew for these two concepts as there exists in Greek or English.

The new covenant was addressed to a revived national Israel for the future, but its linkage with the Abrahamic and Davidic promises made it proper to speak of a Gentile participation in its benefits as well. Thus, Gentiles drink the blood of the new covenant at the communion table of the Lord and some are ministers of that same new covenant even now!

KINGDOM OF THE PROMISE:
EXILIC ERA PROPHETS

The worst had happened! Jerusalem fell in 587 B.C. With it came not only the collapse of the temple with all its services and the collapse of the Davidic kingdom, but the nation went into captivity to Babylon for seventy years.

The promise of God was not dead, however. For it was during this same seventy-year period God sent Daniel and Ezekiel to set forth the further details on the coming new Davidic kingdom. The rightful king would be installed (Ezek. 21:26–27; cf. Gen. 49:10), and he would set up a kingdom in the days of the four last great empires on earth that would never have an end (Dan. 2:44). The dried-up bones of the nation of Israel would be collected by the word of the Lord, and the nation would be resurrected and given both the breath and the power of God (Ezek. 37:1–14).

In Daniel's startling prophecy of Daniel 7:9–14, God the Father, here called "the Ancient of Days," handed over to another, called here "the Son of Man," all authority, glory, sovereign power, and dominion. He it is who will then set up that kingdom, so frequently mentioned in the earlier promises made to the "seed" that would never perish.

The promise-plan of God had now reached one of its zeniths: The one previously known as the seed, the servant, the branch, and the Anointed One (Messiah) is now given the rights to all rule, all realms, and all dominions. The colossal attempts of humanity to immortalize their own achievements by brutalizing the rest of humanity will now have ended for good and for a kingdom wherein righteousness, peace, and blessing were the norms for all.

THE TRIUMPH OF THE PROMISE: POST-EXILIC ERA PROPHETS

As some of the people returned after the seventy years of captivity in Babylon, God sent three more prophets to remind them once again of His promise-declaration: Haggai, Zechariah, and Malachi.

Haggai announced the reigning Davidic governor, Zerubbabel, was God's "signet ring" (Hag. 2:23) and continuing assurance that God had not renounced His promise made with David. Indeed, the "mercies of David" (Isa. 55:3) were "sure" and "unchangeable." He was "My servant," the current place-holder and reminder of the fact that God would one day send His own Son to be the final fulfillment of the ancient promise.

Zechariah viewed the climax to history in one decisive battle that will be fought by Yahweh Himself (Zech. 14). All the nations of the earth will be gathered to fight this battle, but they will suffer their most humiliating defeat ever as the Lord Himself suddenly enters the battle and concludes the historic process. Only then will holiness be the order of the day throughout all realms, including even the lowliest of instruments such as the pots and pans themselves. What a magnificent Lord!

Malachi adds that God will send a forerunner who will announce His coming (Mal. 3:1a). However, the "messenger of the covenant" (Mal. 3:1b), who was the owner of the temple, would suddenly appear to judge all sorcerers, adulterers, perjurers, defrauders of wages, oppressors of widows, orphans, and aliens (Mal. 3:1–5). But for those who loved this messenger of the covenant (yet another name for the one now successively known as the seed, the servant, My son, My firstborn, Branch, Son of

Man, Messiah), He shall reappear a second time with healing for all who have longed for His coming (Mal. 4:2).

No less insistent on this theme on the triumph of the kingdom were the post-exilic writers of Chronicles, Ezra, Nehemiah, and Esther. For them, it was clear that the kingdom belonged to the Lord; thus, they saw in the events of history past and present a model of what things would be like when the King of kings finally arrived.

By now it should be clear that it is not only possible, but actually desirable to read the theology of the OT from the perspective that God did have a unifying center and a plan whereby He was directing all events, revelation and disclosures of Himself to mortals on earth! That plan is the same one first stated in principal form by Eve, formalized to Abraham, Isaac, and Jacob, but given final shape in the promise made to David and in the reiteration and enlargement of the same made in the new covenant.

FOR FURTHER READING

Bock, Darrell L. and Craig Blaising, eds. *Israel and the Church*. Grand Rapids: Zondervan, 1992.

Hasel, Gerhard. *Old Testament Theology: Basic Issues in the Current Debate*, 3d ed. Grand Rapids: Eerdmans, 1982.

Kaiser, Walter C., Jr. *Toward an Old Testament Theology*. Grand Rapids: Zondervan, 1978.

———. "Old Testament Biblical Theology." In EBC. Vol. 1, edited by F. Gaebelein. Grand Rapids: Zondervan, 1979.

———. "Kingdom Promises as Spiritual and National." In *Continuity and Discontinuity: Perspectives on the Relationship Between the Old and New Testaments*, edited by J. Feinberg. Wheaton, Ill.: Crossway Books, 1987.

———. *NDT*, s.v. "Old Testament theology."

Martins, E. A. *God's Design: A Focus on Old Testament Theology*. Grand Rapids: Baker, 1981.

Ollenburger, B. C., E. J. Martens, and G. Hasel, eds. *The Flowering of Old Testament Theology: A Reader in Twentieth-Century Old Testament Theology, 1930–1990*. Winona Lake, Ind.: Eisenbrauns, 1992.

Robertson, O. P. *The Christ of the Covenants*. Philadelphia: Presbyterian and Reformed, 1981.

Waltke, B. K. "Kingdom Promises as Spiritual." In *Continuity and Discontinuity: Perspectives on the Relationship Between the Old and New Testaments*, edited by J. Feinberg. Wheaton, Ill.: Crossway Books, 1987.

PART III

FOUNDATIONS FOR NEW TESTAMENT INTERPRETATION

XVII

ARCHAEOLOGY AND THE NEW TESTAMENT

MARSHA A. ELLIS SMITH

When I took my first course in archaeology as a seminary student, I did so because it was a required course in my degree program. The only day/hour available with the teacher recommended to me was Wednesday/Friday at 3:00. Nothing was more unappealing than the thought of any class—let alone an archaeology class—that had to be endured from three to four on a Friday afternoon. However, when the semester ended, I had decided to continue in archaeology through my master's and Ph.D. degrees. Every Friday afternoon at 3:50 I had wished we had just a few more minutes to hear a little more from our professor before class was dismissed. He had made the land of the Bible—with its people, places, customs, history—come alive to me as they never had before. Archaeology is an exciting and valuable area of study. However, it is a science and a very thorough and technologically advanced one. The dullness sometimes associated with it is the same kind of dullness that surrounds the tediousness of a long and detailed scientific experiment which not only has to be meticulously completed, but also meticulously reported. Once the data has been researched and tabulated, and the information interpreted, its results become exciting even to the nonscientist.

The methodology of archaeological research is a detailed study itself.[1] A location (or archaeological site) must be chosen based upon surface evidence indicating that more could be uncovered through excavation. The site must then be mapped out into large squares to be dug by volunteers using small, handheld picks. Every item found must be marked as to its exact location and a map drawn of each square as it is unearthed inch by inch. Each artifact and pottery piece is analyzed in several different ways, and attempts are made to match the broken pieces together to reconstruct the objects. Modern technological advances and computerization have added much to the dating methods and analytical procedures used in archaeological study today. Archaeology in the twentieth century is in every sense a scientific endeavor.

The raw materials of archaeology have remained relatively constant throughout the millennia. Human remains, pottery, stone objects and metal objects (including implements of war and agriculture), sculpture, inscriptions, coins, structural remains, animal bones, plant remains, and manuscripts—anything left behind by those who have occupied a site—provide the raw data for archaeological study. Just as in a modern-day mystery or criminal investigation much is learned by examining the scene of the crime, so too in an archaeological excavation a vast amount of information about the inhabitants of a site can be learned through examining what they left behind.

Two cautions must be urged regarding the outcome of archaeological research. First, be wary of someone's certainty as to an exact location of what is otherwise an unconfirmed site. This is particularly important in viewing "tourist" sites in the biblical lands. Some sites purported to be undisputed locations for specific events in Christ's life or in the lives of His apostles are not verified by archaeological evidence.[2] This is not to say that it is impossible that these sites are valid, only that some uncertainty may surround them. Other sites are accepted as indisputable by a wide variety of scholars.[3] Care should be taken to differentiate between the two.

Second, archaeology's purpose is not to prove or validate your faith. Just as you should not base your Christian faith on the belief in a particu-

---

1. For a more detailed study of archaeological methodology and the methods of technical analysis, see *HBH*, 69.

2. Sites such as the exact location of Jesus' birth and His baptism, the tree in Jericho into which Zaccheus climbed, and the window from which Paul was lowered by rope in Damascus. Some of these are determined more by tradition than archaeological evidence.

3. Sites such as the location of Herod's temple in Jerusalem, the Pool of Siloam, the "bema" (judgment seat) in the city of Corinth.

lar scientific worldview, neither should you base it on a particular archaeological interpretation. Interpretations can and do change based on new data, and new data may be unearthed at any time. Base your faith on the Bible and allow archaeology to provide background and historical data to illuminate the Scriptures in a new way. While archaeology is a valuable tool in Bible study, it is not the foundation for faith.

Archaeology's relationship to biblical studies can be a lengthy subject and can be approached in a variety of formats. For the purpose of this article, contributions of archaeology to New Testament studies will be grouped into four categories: (1) manuscripts; (2) inscriptions, coins, and tombs; (3) Herod the Great's building activity;[4] and (4) major NT cities.[5]

MANUSCRIPTS

Many groups of manuscripts significant to NT studies have been discovered in the past two centuries.[6] The Codex Sinaiticus[7] and Codex Vaticanus,[8] the Oxyrhynchus Papyri,[9] the Chester Beatty papyri,[10] the Bodmer Papyri,[11] the John Rylands papyri[12] (containing verses from John 18 dating from about A.D. 125—the oldest fragment of any NT book), the Dead Sea Scrolls, the Nag Hammadi texts, and many other papyrus and parchment manuscripts in both scroll and codex (book) form contribute much to both textual and background study of the NT. A discussion of two of these will demonstrate the significance of these texts.

---

4. For a thorough discussion of Herod's building activity, see John McRay, *Archaeology and the New Testament* (Grand Rapids: Baker, 1991), 91–149; for detailed information on Herod's temple mount in Jerusalem, see the four articles by Kathleen and Leen Ritmeyer, *BAR* (November, December, 1989): 23–53.

5. Articles on most of the cities of the NT can be found listed alphabetically by name in *ZPEB*, *HolBD*, and *NIDBA*. Discussions of their archaeological significance also can be found listed alphabetically by name of city in the indexes of McRay, Unger, and others in the "For Further Reading" section at the end of this article.

6. For more information on the contributions and value of manuscripts to biblical studies, see McRay, 360–65.

7. See *ZPEB* 1:901;McRay, 352–53.

8. See *ZPEB* 1:901–2.

9. See *NIDBA*, 348; *ZPEB* 4:556–57; McRay, 354–55; *BWDBA*, 428–32.

10. *NIDBA*, 127–28; *ZPEB* 1:791–92; McRay, 356–57.

11. Jack Finegan, *The Archaeology of the New Testament*, rev. ed. (Princeton, N.J.: Princeton University Press, 1992), 381–82; McRay, 360; *NIDBA*, 103; *ZPEB* 1:632–34.

12. See McRay, 355–56.

THE NAG HAMMADI TEXTS

The Nag Hammadi texts were discovered in 1945 near ancient Chenoboskion and modern Nag Hammadi (about thirty miles north of Luxor on the Nile River) in Egypt.[13] Included in this discovery are thirteen papyrus codices dating from the mid-fourth century written in Coptic (a form of ancient Egyptian). Over fifty different works are represented in these codices, which are translations of Greek originals probably dating from the first century A.D. They vary in size from about 5 1/2 by 9 3/4 inches to 6 by 11 1/2 inches; most were found bound in leather. Perhaps the best known of the texts is *The Gospel of Thomas* (not to be confused with the apocryphal book of the same title) which consists of 112 to 118 "sayings" of Jesus. While the contents of the codices show a wide variety of subject matter, all share one major ingredient—an apparent and strong Gnostic influence. (Gnosticism was a heresy which began during NT times, with its greatest development occurring after the end of the first century.)

The importance of the Nag Hammadi discovery to biblical studies should not be underestimated even though it was overshadowed by the discovery the next year of the Dead Sea Scrolls. Until the appearance of the Nag Hammadi papyri, the only texts from which information could be gleaned on the beliefs of Gnosticism were secondary sources such as the writings of Ireneaus and other early church fathers. No primary sources were known to exist. Gnosticism was a significant belief system in the life of the early church. The discovery of the papyri at Nag Hammadi made possible a better understanding of Gnosticism and the struggles faced by the early church. The Nag Hammadi texts also provide benefit in the area of NT textual studies particularly in dealing with those books which may have addressed some early Gnostic ideas (such as Paul's letter to the Colossians).

DEAD SEA SCROLLS

In 1947, a bedouin boy who was tending his sheep in the Judean wilderness tossed a stone into a cave on the face of one of the sandstone cliffs and heard the sound of pottery breaking. He had unknowingly made one of the greatest discoveries of biblical scholarship in the twentieth century—the Dead Sea Scrolls.[14] Inside that cave was an ancient jar containing a scroll placed there by a member of the Qumran community prior to

---

13. See *BWDBA*, 402–10; *IBD* 1:262–63; *NIDBA*, 327; *HolBD*, 1001–2; McRay, 357–58.

14. See *NIDBA*, 154–57; *ZPEB* 1:53–68; *BWDBA*, 184–92; Seigfried H. Horn, *Biblical Archaeology: A Generation of Discovery* (Washington, D.C.: Biblical Archaeology Society, 1985), 141–57; *HolBD*, 346–47. For more detailed treatments of the subject, see Thurman L. Coss, *Secrets from the Caves: A Layman's Guide to the Dead Sea Scrolls* (Nashville: Abingdon, 1963); Charles F. Pfeiffer, *The Dead Sea Scrolls and*

A.D. 70. Upon a careful search of the surrounding area, scrolls were found in ten more caves, for a total of 40,000 fragments of some 800 ancient manuscripts. Of these 800, 170 are of OT books, all of which are represented except the Book of Esther. The extrabiblical documents found are of three groups: commentaries on OT books, Jewish writings of the interbiblical and NT times, and writings related specifically to the life of the community at Qumran. Scrolls were found in the Hebrew, Aramaic, and Greek languages, and in both parchment and papyrus. (Two scrolls made of copper also were found.) Only scrolls were discovered, no codices (book form as we know it).

While the Qumran community was in existence from about 130 B.C. to about A.D. 70, some of the scrolls themselves date back to 200 B.C. The Essenes, or inhabitants of the Qumran community, were a Jewish sect who showed their devotion to God by copying and studying Scripture. When the seige of their area by the Roman army seemed imminent, the Essenes hid their sacred scrolls in caves in the hills which surrounded their home. It is there they remained until their discovery in this century.

The importance of the Dead Sea Scrolls to biblical studies can be stated as both textual and cultural, the former dealing more with OT study and the latter with NT study. Before the discovery of the Dead Sea Scrolls, the earliest extant OT Hebrew manuscript dated to the ninth century A.D. Some of the OT Hebrew scrolls from the Dead Sea discovery date 1,000 years earlier—from 200–100 B.C. The significance of these dates increases with the realization that these scrolls are probably copies made by the Essenes of originals from an even earlier date, which gives weight to the argument for an early date for the actual writing of the OT. The cultural importance of the scrolls finds basis in the contents of the extrabiblical Dead Sea texts which show the theological and cultural atmosphere of the Jewish world at the time of Jesus Christ. Another benefit to NT studies is the additional text material containing verbal phrases which would be contemporary with the writings of the NT.[15]

---

the Bible (New York: Weathervane Books with Baker Book House, 1969); F. F. Bruce, *Second Thoughts on the Dead Sea Scrolls*, rev. and enl. ed. (Grand Rapids: Eerdmans, 1964); Millar Burrows, *The Dead Sea Scrolls* (New York: The Viking Press, 1955).

15. Work is ongoing on the translation and interpretation of the Dead Sea Scrolls, and periodically a news story will break regarding some aspect of the process. However, much of their value to NT studies already has been discovered. Most of what remains is of importance in biblical textual studies. To say that there is still much to be discovered relating to the origin of Christianity is a statement not based on present factual data, but on a biased interpretation of the currently available data. (For a discussion of the relationship of Qumran to the beginnings of Christianity, see Bruce, 136–53.)

INSCRIPTIONS, COINS, AND TOMBS

INSCRIPTIONS

Inscriptions are words or letters carved on a surface, usually of stone or metal.[16] They are of great significance if the writing can be used to date a location or an event, or if it includes the name of a historical figure. Several inscriptions have been discovered which are of specific value to NT studies.

The Pilate Inscription. In 1961 an Italian archaeologist, Antonio Frova, discovered an inscription at Caesarea Maritima on a stone slab which at the time of the discovery was being used as a section of steps leading into the Caesarea theater.[17] The inscription in Latin contained four lines, three of which are partially readable. Roughly translated they are as follows:

Tiberium

Pontius Pilate

Prefect of Judea

The inscribed stone was probably used originally in the foundation for a Tiberium (a temple for the worship of the emperor Tiberius) and then reused later in the discovered location. This inscription clarifies the title of Pontius Pilate as "prefect" at least during a time in his rulership. Tacitus and Josephus later referred to him as "procurator." The NT calls him "governor" (Matt. 27:2), a term which incorporates both titles. This inscription is the only archaeological evidence of both Pilate's name and this title.

Vespasian-Titus Inscription. This inscription was discovered on a limestone column south of the temple mount in Jerusalem by archaeologist Benjamin Mazar in 1970.[18] It contains the names of both the emperor Vespasian and the emperor Titus. Both of these emperors were of significance to the history of Jerusalem: Vespasian began the conquest of Palestine and, after he became emperor, was succeeded in that task by his son Titus, who conquered Jerusalem in A.D. 70.

Politarch. Many inscriptions have been found in Thessalonica and other locations (Berea and Amphipolis) which include the term "politarch."[19]

---

16. For more information on inscriptions, see Jerry Vardaman, *Archaeology and the Living Word* (Nashville: Broadman Press, 1965), 89–96.

17. See Finegan, 138–39; McRay, 203–4; *BWDBA*, 455–58; and Vardaman, 89–90.

18. See McRay, 197–98, and photo on p. 199; *NIDBA*, 468.

19. See McRay, 295; Merrill F. Unger, 228–29; and *IBD* 3:1557 (which includes a photo of the Greek inscription found in a Roman arch at Thessalonica which names six of that city's politarchs).

Prior to their discoveries, Luke was considered by some scholars to be questionable in his use of the term "politarch" to describe the officials in Thessalonica before whom Paul was called to testify (Acts 17:6).

The Erastus Inscription. On a slab of limestone which was a part of the pavement near the theater in Corinth,[20] a Latin inscription was found which translates, "Erastus, in return for the aedileship, laid the pavement at his own expense."[21] In Romans 16:23 Paul (writing from Corinth) mentioned an Erastus and identified him as a city official. It is possible this is the same person.

Lysanias. An inscription found at Abila dating from the time of Tiberius mentions "Lysanias the Tetrarch."[22] This discovery offers extrabiblical data in support of Luke's mention of a Lysanias who ruled in Syria and Palestine (Luke 3:1).

COINS

Coins are important to archaeological research particularly as a way of dating finds and sites.[23] Although this is true for both Old and New Testament sites, it is especially so for NT locations. Both the date of production and the current ruler were usually inscribed on the coins. Coins of various metals—gold, silver, copper, and bronze—have been found dating from NT times, with the most abundant being bronze. This is probably due to their small value which resulted in a lack of concern on the part of their owners when they were dropped or otherwise lost.[24]

Capernaum. Ten thousand coins have been found beneath the stone pavement of the Byzantine synagogue at Capernaum. They were used as gravel in the structure's mortar. (The first-century synagogue remains have been discovered underneath this later limestone synagogue.) The location of the various segments of this cache of coins assisted the archaeologists in the dating of the various sections of the synagogue.[25]

Caesarea Philippi. Coins have been discovered which give the name and title of the city of Caesarea Philippi. Other coins have been found which

---

20. See *NIDBA*, 138; *BWDBA*, 174; Unger, 247; and McRay, 331–32 (including a photo on p. 331 and a full discussion of the subject).

21. *BWDBA*, 174.

22. See Unger, 3; and Vardaman, 89–90.

23. For more information on coins, see A. Reifenberg, *Israel's History in Coins: From the Maccabees to the Roman Cnquest* (London: East and West Library, 1953); *NIDBA*, 134–35; *ZPEB* 1:902–11 (with excellent color plates 1–71 starting after page 896); *IBD* 2:1018–23.

24. McRay, 33.

25. Ibid., 162–64.

depict various aspects of the Caesarea Philippi site—a temple built by Herod Philip, the sacred cave where the god Pan was probably worshiped, and the god Pan himself leaning against a tree and playing his flute.[26]

New Testament Coins. Three coins mentioned in the Greek NT have been identified with reasonable assurance.[27]

1. The "tribute penny" (Matt. 22:17–21; Mark 12:13–17; Luke 20:20–26). The Greek word for the coin shown to Jesus in these passages is "denarius," a small silver coin which carried the image of the Caesar on one side. Its value was equal to one day's wages for an average worker in Palestine.

2. The "thirty pieces of silver" (Matt. 26:14–15). This amount was probably thirty silver shekels. Originally a shekel was a measure of weight equaling approximately two-fifths of an ounce. It later developed into a silver coin of about the same weight.

3. The "widow's mite" (Mark 12:41–44; Luke 21:1–4). The passage in question reads (in NIV): "two very small copper coins, worth only a fraction of a penny." The first words translate the Greek *"lepta"* which is the smallest Greek copper coin, the second translates the Greek word *"quadrans"* which is the smallest Roman copper coin. Knowing the minute monetary value of these coins gives even greater meaning to the message of the parable.

TOMBS

Tombs and graves have provided much of archaeological value through their contents: human remains, artifacts, and inscriptions.[28] One such valuable find was discovered in 1968 in a rock-cut Jewish tomb at Giv'at ha-Mivtar in Jerusalem. The human remains were of a young man and, based on the pottery at the site, probably date from about A.D. 7 to 66. His name was Yohohanan (which was inscribed on his coffin) and he was about 5 feet 6 inches tall. An iron nail pinning his heels together (with his right foot on top of his left foot) was still in place when the tomb was discovered. His legs had been bent at the knees and both legs were broken. The significance of this find is in the condition of these human remains

---

26. Ibid., 13.

27. For more information on the coins in Scripture, see *HolBD*, 274–75; *IBD* 2:1022–23; and Vardaman, 96–98.

28. For more information on tombs and graves, see Finegan, 292–338; *HolBD*, 577.

which shows the excruciating pain experienced by one who had been crucified in this manner.[29]

HEROD'S BUILDING ACTIVITY

Herod the Great ruled in Judea from 37 to 4 B.C. and was the first of the Herodian rulers.[30] He is the Herod of Matthew 2 and Luke 1:5 who, after hearing from the magi of the birth of a king of the Jews, ordered the slaughter of all male children two years of age and under who lived in and around the area of Bethlehem. He also influenced NT times in another realm—building activity. Like other monarchs of enormous ego (Ramses in Egypt, the Caesars of Rome, and even Solomon in Hebrew history), he undertook massive building projects in order to leave behind his "mark" on the land. His most impressive project was his rebuilding of the temple in Jerusalem, which continued throughout most of his reign, finally being completed in A.D. 64 (just six years before it was destroyed by the Romans in A.D. 70). Other cities benefited from his work—Caesarea Maritima, New Testament Jericho, Sebaste (Old Testament Samaria, which he rebuilt in honor of the emperor), and two others which, while they do not have direct significance on NT study, should be discussed—Masada and Herodium.

Although Herod the Great was not responsible for the initial fortification of the rocky mesa known as Masada, he did make magnificent additions to it. Masada rises 820 feet above the low-lying area on the western shore of the Dead Sea. It is a very strong fortification in its natural state and with the additions made by Herod became almost impenetrable. Herod's enhancements were not only to further fortify the already strong fortress; he also built a three-tiered palace, an elaborate water system which included enormous reservoirs and a large bathhouse, and large storerooms. Masada's name became etched into history when in A.D. 73 a group of over nine hundred Jewish zealots (men, women, and children) occupied the stronghold and withstood the onslaught of the Roman army for several months. When it became apparent that Roman conquest was imminent, the Jewish group chose suicide rather than Roman enslavement. Much has been written about this incident, beginning with the Jewish historian Josephus.[31]

Herodium was a fortress built by Herod the Great about four miles southeast of Bethlehem. He fortified the cone-shaped hill as one of his

---

29. *IBD* 6:343–44; McRay, 204–6; Horn, 63.
30. See chart on the Herodian dynasty in *HBBCMR*, 85.
31. See *ZPEB* 4:112–14; *NIDBA*, 302–3.

fortress/palaces and when he died was buried there (although his tomb has not yet been discovered). It was an imposing stronghold with four large, round towers and high walls on all sides. Herodium was later used like Masada by Jewish resisters to hold out against the Roman army until A.D. 72 when its conquest was accomplished. It may have been used even later as a fortress by the unsuccessful Bar Kochba revolutionaries of the second century.[32]

CITIES OF THE NEW TESTAMENT

CITIES IN JESUS' LIFE

Jerusalem. NT Jerusalem often is referred to as Herodian Jerusalem and rightly so.[33] Herod the Great was responsible for most of the building additions to the city from the time of the conquest of Palestine by Pompey in 63 B.C. until the redesigning of the city into Aelia Capitolina by Hadrian in A.D. 135.

Herod's greatest accomplishment in the city of Jerusalem was the rebuilding of the temple and the expanding of the entire temple mount area.[34] Israeli archaeologist Benjamin Mazar began excavation of the site in 1968 with work continuing there since.

Much has been revealed about the construction of the temple mount itself. Before Herod could build the platform to support the buildings, he had to first construct a terrace around the hill and fill it with rubble. The expansion completed by Herod incorporated an area the size of five football fields from north to south and three football fields from east to west.[35]

---

32. See *NIDBA*, 236; *HolBD*, 641; and Donald J. Wiseman and Edwin Yamauchi, *Archaeology and the Bible: An Introductory Study* (Grand Rapids: Baker, 1980), 74.

33. For an artist's reconstruction of the plan of the city of Jerusalem during the time of Christ, see *HBBCMR*, 158–59. See also *HolBD*, 765–73; *NIDBA*, 261–65; and Wiseman and Yamauchi, 68–71, 81–86. For more information on the extensive excavations done at Jerusalem, see John Wilkinson, *The Jerusalem Jesus Knew: An Archaeological Guide to the Gospels* (Nashville: Thomas Nelson, 1978); W. Harold Mare, *The Archaeology of the Jerusalem Area* (Grand Rapids: Baker, 1987); Yigael Yadin, ed., *Jerusalem Revealed: Archaeology in the Holy City 1968–1974* (New Haven, Conn. and London: Yale University Press and the Israel Exploration Society, 1976).

34. For reconstructions of Herod's temple, see *HBBCMR*, 153–55. For detailed discussion of Herod's temple, see Kathleen Ritmeyer, "Herod's Temple in East Anglia" *BAR* (September/October, 1993): 62–67, 90; and additional articles listed in footnote 28.

35. See Kathleen and Leen Ritmeyer, "Reconstructing Herod's Temple Mount in Jerusalem," *BAR* (November/December, 1989): 23–27.

The entire mount was enclosed with magnificent walls and porches including the grand royal stoa (a grand hall—the largest structure on the temple mount) along the southern wall. Monumental stairways leading up to the double and triple gates on the southern wall were uncovered. Robinson's Arch which was early thought to be a bridge between the temple and the upper city of Jerusalem was discovered instead to be the support for a stairway leading up from a main north-south paved street to the temple area. The magnificence of the entire Herodian structure will not be rivaled.

Herod also constructed a lavish palace in Jerusalem and a citadel area which included three great towers named Hippicus, Phasael, and Mariamne.

Other structures in Jerusalem hold great significance for NT studies. The Church of the Holy Sepulchre is built over the traditional site of Calvary and the tomb of Christ. Excavations show that this area lay outside the city walls of Jerusalem during the NT time. Other excavations done at the site also seem to support its authenticity. The other possible site of the crucifixion was promoted by a General Gordon, thus receiving the name Gordon's Calvary. It is in close proximity to the Garden Tomb, which is the alternative tomb site. Neither set of locations have been certainly identified as the site of the crucifixion and burial of Christ.[36]

The traditional locations of the Pool of Bethesda and the Pool of Siloam, both important in the Gospel accounts of Jesus ministry in Jerusalem, are accepted as authentic sites.

Bethlehem. Bethlehem, five miles southwest of Jerusalem, is known from Scripture to be the birthplace of Jesus.[37] The Church of the Nativity is built over the traditional site of the manger. However, archaeology cannot offer any assistance in this determination. The tradition supporting the site does date back to the second century, and as early as 325 Constantine built a church over some of the caves in the city. After that church was destroyed, the emperor Justinian built a church there in the sixth century, which is the origin of the Church of the Nativity.

Nazareth. Nazareth is located about halfway between the Sea of Galilee and the Mediterranean Sea in the lower Galilee area.[38] The only site with

---

36. For a discussion in support of the Church of the Holy Sepulchre, see Andre Parrot, *Golgotha and the Church of the Holy Sepulchre*, trans. Edwin Hudson, *Studies in Biblical Archaeology*, no. 6 (London: SCM Press Limited, 1957). For a discussion in support of Gordon's Calvary and the Garden Tomb, see L. T. Pearson, *Where Is Calvary?*, 3d ed. (Brighton, Sussex: The Bible Through an Eastern Window, 1960).

37. *HolBD*, 171–72; *NIDBA*, 99–100.

38. See *NIDBA*, 329–30; *HolBD*, 1010–11.

archaeological authenticity is the well built over the only good fresh water spring in the city. The well is referred to as "Mary's Well."

The Catholic Church of the Annunciation is built over where tradition says Mary and Joseph lived in Nazareth. When the most recent church was built (the oldest remains of the Church of the Annunciation date back to the fifth century A.D.), the area beneath the church foundation was excavated. Archaeological evidence of an early (fourth century) church built on the plan of a synagogue was discovered in that excavation.

Bethany. Located on the eastern slope of the Mount of Olives approximately two miles southeast of Jerusalem, Bethany was the site of the raising of Lazarus from the grave. The traditional site of Lazarus' tomb was first mentioned and a church first built over it in the fourth century A.D.[39]

Capernaum. The site identified as Capernaum is Kefar Nahum (Village of Nahum) located on the northwestern shore of the Dead Sea.[40] It has been excavated intermittently since 1856 with probably the most significant find being a third- to fourth-century synagogue constructed of white limestone. When excavations continued underneath the synagogue, foundations were found for a synagogue dating from the first century A.D. This earlier synagogue is probably the synagogue where Jesus preached (Mark 1:21) and probably the one which was built by the centurion (Luke 7:1–5).[41]

The other location that has been identified at Capernaum is the possible site of Peter's home. It was excavated as an octagonal fifth-century church.[42] But underneath the church was a structure from the first century A.D. which appeared to have been a home, or house. A significant amount of Christian graffiti was found among the ruins. In fact, throughout the excavation, many Christian and Jewish symbols have been found—including the ark of the covenant.

Jericho. New Testament Jericho (Tulul Abu el-Alaig) is located at the lower end of the Wadi Qelt about one mile south of the site of OT Jericho (Tell es-Sultan). Most of the NT city was built by Herod the Great—a magnificent winter palace,[43] a bath complex, a theater, sunken gardens,

---

39. Wiseman and Yamauchi, 82.

40. See *HolBD*, 230–32; and John C. H. Laughlin, "Capernaum: From Jesus' Time and After," *BAR* (September/October, 1993): 54–61, 90.

41. For more information on this synagogue and others, see Hershel Shanks and Benjamin Mazar, *Recent Archaeology in the Land of Israel* (Washington, D.C.: Biblical Archaeology Society [Jerusalem: Israel Exploration Society], 1985), 89–96.

42. For information on ancient churches in Israel, see Shanks and Mazar, 97–107; and Yoram Tsafrir, "Ancient Churches in the Holy Land," *BAR* (September/October, 1993): 26–39 (including a wonderful description and sketches of Peter's house in Capernaum on p. 29).

43. For an artist's reconstruction of Herod's winter palace, see *HBBCMR*, 156.

and an amphitheater. Several aqueducts were a part of the elaborate water system built by Herod to furnish water for the city.

Sepphoris. Sepphoris is located about three miles northwest of Nazareth.[44] It was excavated for a short time in 1931, and recent excavations began there in 1983 which are still ongoing.

Sepphoris, while it is not specifically mentioned in Scripture, was an important town in the time period covered by the NT. Herod Antipas literally rebuilt the city after it was given to him along with the rest of Galilee upon the death of Herod the Great. Given Sepphoris' close proximity to Nazareth, and the fact that Joseph was a carpenter in Nazareth, the strong possibility exists that Joseph and Jesus would have been involved in some of the building projects begun by Herod Antipas in Sepphoris. Therefore, much interest surrounds the ongoing excavations.

The finds include a Roman villa, a Roman theater which was probably originally built by Herod Antipas, a ritual bath, and a large group of underground cisterns or chambers whose purpose is still a question. A beautiful mosaic floor panel was discovered in good condition dating from the third or fourth century A.D. Much still lies underneath the ground level waiting (the excavators hope) with the answers to many questions concerning the relationship of Sepphoris to Jesus and the NT.

Caesarea Philippi. Caesarea Philippi, located southwest of Mount Hermon and about thirty miles inland from the Mediterranean Sea, has yet to be fully excavated. Building stones, coins, and other surface debris attest to much archaeological information present underneath the soil. The ancient city was dedicated to the worship of the god Pan which is depicted on coins found in the area.[45] The city was amply supplied with fresh water from the spring Banias, one of the sources of the River Jordan, which still provides a lush resort area. Archaeological work is still ongoing.

THE CITIES OF PAUL AND THE EARLY CHURCH

Tarsus. The ruins of the NT city of Tarsus, Paul's hometown, lie underneath the modern-day city.[46] Several Roman remains have been discovered through excavation for the construction of a new building. The OT city area has been more thoroughly examined.

---

44. See McRay, 175–78; and Richard A. Batey, *Jesus & the Forgotten City: New Light on Sepphoris and the Urban World of Jesus* (Grand Rapids: Baker, 1991).

45. See Caesarea Philippi under the section "Coins" earlier in this article.

46. George L. Kelm, "Tarsus: 'No Mean City,'" *Best of the Illustrator: The Journeys of Paul* (Nashville: The Sunday School Board of the Southern Baptist Convention, 1990), 2–8.

Antioch of Syria. Antioch of Syria (modern Antakya, Turkey) was the home base for Paul's missionary journeys and the first place where the name Christian was used to refer to a follower of Christ.[47] It is located at the southeastern edge of Turkey on the Orontes River just a few miles inland from the Mediterranean Sea. (This city is not to be confused with Antioch of Pisidia which is located in the south central area of mainland Turkey between ancient Galatia and Phrygia. Only a few structures remain from Pisidian Antioch.) Like Tarsus, ancient Antioch of Syria was a thriving city. However, also like Tarsus, its modern counterpart is heavily inhabited; therefore, excavation has been held to a minimum. A large silver cup was found in 1916 which has been named the "Chalice of Antioch" and was thought by some to be the Holy Grail used at the Last Supper.[48] No other important finds have surfaced to this time.

Ephesus. Ephesus is one of the most archaeologically revealed cities of the first-century world.[49] The ancient city was located on the western coast of Turkey between the Maeander River on the south and the Hermus River on the north. The city has been inhabited since several thousand years before the birth of Christ and has been an important cultural, religious, political, and commercial center for most of its existence. It is important to NT studies in two areas: It is prominent in the ministry of Paul—he both visited in the city of Ephesus and wrote a letter to the church in Ephesus, and it is one of the seven churches of the Revelation of John.

The important archaeological finds include the following: the Temple of Artemis (or Diana) which was one of the seven wonders of the ancient world;[50] the Great Theater which would seat 25,000 people; a beautiful marble-paved road leading to the harbor; the harbor baths and gymnasium complex; a wonderful library dating from the second century A.D.—the Library of Celsus—which had its marble facade restored by archaeologists in the 1980s; the Greek agora with shops and public buildings; wealthy Roman villas; temples to the Emperors Hadrian and Domitian and a temple to the Egyptian god Serapis; a brothel (and what has been interpreted as an advertisement for the brothel carved into the marble of

---

47. See Robert O. Coleman, "Antioch of Syria," *Best of the Illustrator,* 16–19.

48. *NIDBA,* 29–30.

49. For more information and photos on the extensive excavations at Ephesus and the importance of the city, see Henry E. Turlington, "Ephesus," *Best of the Illustrator,* 58–65; Steven Friesen, "Ephesus: Key to a Vision in Revelation," *BAR* (May/June, 1993): 24–37; *HolBD,* 424–29.

50. For an artist's reconstruction of the Temple of Artemis, see *HBBCMR,* 163.

the Arcadian Way street); and many more buildings and monuments from the NT through the Byzantine eras.

Corinth. Corinth is located in Greece on the eastern edge of the Corinthian Isthmus, which was bordered on the east by the Saronic Gulf and on the west by the Gulf of Corinth.[51] Its history dates back probably to the New Stone Age, and by the time of the NT it was a flourishing city known for its pleasure-seeking atmosphere.

The foundational archaeological remains of Corinth date primarily from the rebuilding of the city in 46 B.C. by Julius Caesar. (The city had been destroyed by the Romans in 146 B.C. and was in ruins for the next century.) Important remains include the following: the Lechaion Road— a wide paved road with raised sidewalks leading from the marketplace, or agora, to the port of Lechaion; a great bath and public latrine; the agora and the propylaea, or gateway, into the agora; the Fountain of Peirene, comprised of four reservoirs and marbled floors; the Senate House, or Roman administrative office; Greek shops; an odeion, or music hall; six small temples; a theater in which was found the "Erastus inscription;"[52] the Sanctuary of Asklepios and the Fountain of Lerna (hospital facilities); a Greek race course; the ruins of the Temple of Apollo, of which only seven of the original thirty-eight columns remain; and at the center of the agora the "bema" or "judgment seat" before which Paul would have defended himself and his faith to the Roman governor Gallio (Acts 18:12–17). Looming in the background of the ruins is the massive Acrocorinth (mountain) on which stood the Temple of Aphrodite (from the earlier city destroyed in 146 B.C.). The cult of Aphrodite worship was responsible for much of the immorality of the city, and, although the temple itself was gone by Paul's day, the cult was still a strong influence in the city.

Caesarea Maritima. Caesarea, sometimes called Caesarea Maritima (by the sea) to distinguish it from Caesarea Philippi, is located on the Mediterranean Sea a little over twenty miles south of Mount Carmel.[53] The building of Caesarea became one of Herod the Great's greatest building projects, dedicated by him to Caesar, as is evidenced by its name. Herod constructed a magnificent harbor with monumental statues placed at the entrance, a grand theater still in use today, and an elaborate water system

---

51. Robert J. Dean, "Corinth," *Best of the Illustrator,* 50–52; *HolBD,* 298–301; *NIDBA,* 137–38.

52. See Erastus Inscription under the section "Inscriptions" earlier in this chapter.

53. See James F. Strange, "Caesarea," *Best of the Illustrator,* 79–84; *HolBD,* 218–19; *HBH,* 72–73; and for an artist's reconstruction of the city, see *HBBCMR,* 149.

utilizing aqueducts to carry the water into the city from a source several miles away. Excavations began at Caesarea in 1959 by an Italian expedition and have continued intermittently since that time. The "Pilate Inscription" was discovered during the first series of excavations in the work on the theater.[54] Archaeological field work is ongoing at the site—both above ground and under water in the area of the harbor.

Athens. The history of the city of Athens begins in the New Stone Age, but the height of its prominence came in the fifth century B.C. under the rule of Pericles.[55] It was he who built much of what is still partially visible today on the Acropolis of the city. Excavations over a number of years have uncovered many of the buildings and monuments of Athens, and work is continually ongoing. The glory of the Acropolis is, of course, the Parthenon built as a temple for the worship of the goddess Athena. It is this temple and the other structures of the Acropolis which would have been in Paul's view as he addressed the "Areopagus" in Acts 17:15–34. Although some disagreement exists as to the exact location of his address, many scholars think it occurred on the small, marble hill called Areopagus located to the northwest of the Acropolis.

Pergamum. Pergamum has been excavated more completely than any other of the seven churches of Revelation (with the exception of the city of Ephesus which is also significant in the life and ministry of Paul).[56] Archaeological expeditions have continued intermittently since they began in 1878. Among the finds are the Altar of Zeus (thought by some to be the throne of Satan from Rev. 2:13); the famous library of Pergamum (where parchment began); the Aesklepion dedicated to the god of healing; several temples to various pagan deities; a theater; and a gymnasium complex.

Sardis. Sardis, in Asia Minor and one of the seven churches of Revelation, has been excavated for many seasons beginning in 1910, but still has much to be uncovered.[57] The temple of Artemis, a gymnasium complex, and baths have been excavated, while other structures (the theater, major public buildings, and a stadium) still need excavation. Hundreds of coins, sculptures, and inscriptions have been found. Perhaps the most important

---

54. See Pilate Inscription under the section "Inscriptions" earlier in this article.

55. See William H. Stephens, "Athens in Paul's Day," *Best of the Illustrator,* 28–35 (which includes an excellent illustrated map of the city on p. 32); *NIDBA,* 80.

56. See Edwin Yamauchi, *New Testament Cities in Western Asia Minor: Light from Archaeology on Cities of Paul and the Seven Churches of Revelation* (Grand Rapids: Baker, 1980), 30–49; *HBH,* 76; *NIDBA,* 358.

57. See *HBH,* 76; Yamauchi, 63–76; *NIDBA,* 399–400.

find at Sardis involves the Jewish synagogue and the many Jewish inscriptions, indicating a strong Jewish community in the city.

Other Cities. The histories of many other cities of the NT have been revealed through archaeology. Philippi's temples, theater, agora, and the important east-west road—the Via Egnatia—have been excavated.[58] Rome, where Paul was probably imprisoned and killed, is rich in archaeological heritage from the NT time period and earlier.[59] Thessalonica has yielded among other finds the "politarch" inscription.[60] At Thyatira many inscriptions have been found attesting to the presence of trade guilds in the city, showing the importance of the business life of the hometown of Lydia, the seller of purple.[61] Several sites on the island of Cyprus have been excavated, including the ancient cities of Paphos and Salamis, both of which were visited by Paul on his first missionary journey.[62]

Some cities of importance to the NT have had little or no archaeological exploration.[63] Some of these include Philadelphia, Smyrna, and Laodicea from the Book of Revelation, and Colossae, Lystra, Derbe, Iconium, and Perga from the ministry of Paul.

Biblical archaeology has an essential role in the study of the NT. It enables us to step into the culture of the original recipients of the gospel message. We have the responsibility in studying the biblical material to use all the knowledge given to us by our Lord to better understand His message to us. That is an awesome responsibility, but it is that responsibility for which we will be held accountable.

FOR FURTHER READING

BIBLE REFERENCE BOOKS

(which would include articles on archaeology or archaeological information within entries on specific cities, artifacts, topics, etc.)

---

58. See Edmon L. Rowell, Jr., "Philippi of Macedonia: Beachhead in Europe," *Best of the Illustrator,* 45–49; *NIDBA,* 361–62; *HBH,* 76–77; *HolBD,* 1105–6.

59. See William H. Stephens, "Rome: The Eternal City," *Best of the Illustrator,* 85–90.

60. See Politarch under the section "Inscriptions" earlier in this article. See also A. O. Collins, "Thessalonica," *Best of the Illustrator,* 40–44; *NIDBA,* 449.

61. See Yamauchi, 51–54; *NIDBA,* 450.

62. See *NIDBA,* 143–44; *ZPEB* 1:1051–54.

63. Sometimes this is due to a modern-day city located on top of the ruins of an ancient city. When such is the case, only when the area to be excavated lies outside the boundary of endangerment to a modern building, or when construction excavation is required, do the authorities allow archaeological excavation.

The Biblical World: A Dictionary of Biblical Archaeology. Edited by Charles F.
 Pfeiffer. Grand Rapids: Baker, 1966.
The Holman Bible Dictionary. Edited by Trent C. Butler. Nashville: Holman
 Bible Publishers, 1991.
The Holman Bible Handbook. Edited by David S. Dockery. Nashville: Hol-
 man Bible Publishers, 1992.
The Holman Book of Biblical Charts, Maps, and Reconstructions. Edited by
 Marsha A. Ellis Smith. Nashville: Broadman & Holman Publish-
 ers, 1993.
The Illustrated Bible Dictionary, 3 vols. Wheaton: InterVarsity Press and
 Tyndale House, 1980.
The New International Dictionary of Biblical Archaeology. Edited by E. M.
 Blaiklock and R. K. Harrison. Grand Rapids: Zondervan, 1983.
The Zondervan Pictorial Encyclopedia of the Bible. 5 vols. Edited by Merrill C.
 Tenney. Grand Rapids: Zondervan, 1975.

BOOKS

Baez-Camargo, Gonzalo. *Archaeological Commentary on the Bible.* Garden
 City, N.Y.: Doubleday & Company, 1984.
Blaiklock, E. M. *The Archaeology of the NT.* Grand Rapids: Zondervan,
 1974.
Finegan, Jack. *The Archaeology of the NT.* Rev. ed. Princeton, N.J.: Prince-
 ton University Press, 1992.
Horn, Seigfried H. *Biblical Archaeology: A Generation of Discovery.* Washing-
 ton, D.C.: Biblical Archaeology Society, 1985.
McRay, John. *Archaeology and the NT.* Grand Rapids: Baker, 1991.
Mitchell, Michael J. *Best of the Illustrator: The Journeys of Paul.* Nashville: The
 Sunday School Board of the Southern Baptist Convention, 1990.
Shanks, Hershel, and Benjamin Mazar. *Recent Archaeology in the Land of Is-
 rael.* Washington, D.C.: Biblical Archaeology Society (Jerusalem:
 Israel Exploration Society), 1985.
Thompson, J. A. *The Bible and Archaeology.* 3d ed., fully revised. Grand Rap-
 ids: Eerdmans, 1982.
Unger, Merrill F. *Archaeology and the NT.* Grand Rapids: Zondervan, 1962.
Vardaman, Jerry. *Archaeology and the Living Word.* Nashville: Broadman
 Press, 1965.
Wiseman, Donald J., and Edwin Yamauchi. *Archaeology and the Bible: An In-
 troductory Study.* Grand Rapids: Zondervan, 1979.
Yamauchi, Edwin M. *NT Cities in Western Asia Minor: Light from Archaeol-
 ogy on Cities of Paul and the Seven Churches of Revelation.* Grand Rap-
 ids: Baker, 1980.

PERIODICALS

Biblical Archaeology Review. Washington, D.C.: The Biblical Archaeology
    Society.
The Biblical Illustrator. Nashville: The Sunday School Board of the South-
    ern Baptist Convention.

XVIII

Canon of the New Testament

Linda L. Belleville

In the twenty-seven books of the NT we have a body of literature that has claimed the respect and obedience of the believer as no other documents in the history of the church ever have. Christians today accept the thirty-nine books of the OT as Scripture because they comprise the Hebrew Bible that Jesus and the apostles acknowledged and treated as authoritative. But how is it that the documents of the New Testament came to be viewed by the church as possessing an equal authority? And how did the church come to select these twenty-seven from the larger pool of Christian literature in existence in the early centuries of the Christian era?

There is no historical evidence that any one individual, church, or ecumenical council determined in one fell swoop the limits of the NT canon. All the indications point, instead, to a long, gradual process that by no means ever entailed the consensus of the entire Christian church. Indeed, even today the official lectionary followed by the Syrian Orthodox Church is taken from only twenty-two of the twenty-seven NT writings. The lack of any conciliar decree establishing a list of authoritative books for the church at large quite naturally leads one to ask exactly how the NT as a normative collection of books came into being, who collected them, and what criteria were used in the sifting process. Although the history of the church is silent regarding the explicit details, there are enough isolated comments in the literature of the first five centuries to establish a general picture of what the process of canonization involved.

THE TERM "CANON"

"Canon" (*kanōn*) in Hellenistic Greek denoted a "rod" or "bar" that kept a thing straight or tested for straightness and so came to be used metaphorically for a "rule" or "standard" by which something was measured.[1] In the NT the term is found a mere four times, exclusively in the Pauline letters. Paul uses it in Galatians 6:16 of a standard by which Christian conduct is measured and again in 2 Corinthians 10:13–16 of a set geographical area or apportioned sphere of ministry.[2]

During the second century the word came to mean the "rule" or "essentials" of the faith to which Christian life and teaching were to conform ("rule of faith"; Latin *regula fidei*). Alongside this usage, "canon" in the singular started to be applied to such fixed reference points as a list of people or things and a table of numbers,[3] while in the plural it began to be used from the fourth century on of council decrees and resolutions.[4]

From the common notions of a rule of faith and a standard list, it is easy to see how in the fourth century *kanōn* came to be applied to a list of books whose content was viewed as authoritative for matters of faith and practice. Athanasius, bishop of Alexandria (ca. A.D. 353), who states that the *Shepherd of Hermas* "does not belong to the canon," is the first church father to use the word in this sense,[5] while the Synod of Laodicea (ca. 363) is the first church council to employ the term to distinguish "canonical"

---

1. H. G. Liddell, R. Scott, and H. S. Jones, *A Greek-English Lexicon*, s.v. "*kanōn*."

2. See J. P. Louw and E. A. Nida, *Greek-English Lexicon of the NT*, 80.2, "*kanōn*"; and W. Bauer, W. F. Arndt, F. W. Gingrich, F. Danker, *A Greek-English Lexicon of the New Testament and Other Early Christian Literature*, rev. ed., s.v. "*kanōn*." Cf. *1 Clement* 7, where it is used of the standard of conduct "that has been handed down to us" and *1 Clement* 41, where *kanōn* refers to the sphere of service allotted to each office-bearer in the community ("the appointed rule of his service").

3. See, for example, *PLond*. 24.126, where *kanonion* is used of a list of persons liable to the poll tax and Plutarch, *De Solone* 27, where *kanones* are timetables to fix historical events.

4. See the examples in G. W. H. Lampe, *A Patristic Greek Lexicon* (Oxford: Oxford University Press, 1961), s.v.

5. See, for example, *De Decretis* 18.3.

from "uncanonical" books.[6] The actual phrase "canon of the NT" does not appear until about A.D. 400 in Macarius Magnes' *Apocriticus* 4.10.

"THE SCRIPTURES" IN THE FIRST CENTURY A.D.

The idea of a "canon" or collection of authoritative writings was not a new one for the early Christians, who possessed in the Hebrew Bible a body of literature considered normative before any of the NT documents assumed written form. Jesus' behavior toward, teaching about, and personal use of the Old Testament reinforced its normative value. We find references in the Gospels to His attending the feasts of Unleavened Bread and Tabernacles (John 2:23; 4:45;7:2, 14; 12:12)—feasts required by OT law of every circumcised male (e.g., Deut. 16). His practice was that of a faithful synagogue attender and temple supporter. The Gospel writers record that it was Jesus' custom to go about Galilee teaching in the synagogues (e.g., Matt. 4:23) and that it was His habit to attend the temple services (e.g., Luke 21:1ff.) as well as to pay the temple tax in line with OT stipulations (e.g.,

Matt. 17:24ff; Ex. 30:11–16). Moreover, Jesus cites the OT as that which commands obedience ("as it is written").[7] This is especially clear in the temptation narrative, where Deuteronomy 6:13, 16 and 8:3 are quoted as prescriptive for His own conduct (Mark 1:12–13, Matt. 4:1–11, Luke 4:1–13). Indeed, Jesus supports the validity of the OT not only for Himself but also for the would-be disciple. For it is the disciple that obeys the OT commandments who alone will be called "great" in the kingdom of heaven, while it is the one that breaks the OT Law who will be called "least" (Matt. 5:19–20).

The normative value of the OT is reflected as well in the early church's beliefs and practices. It is the OT that provides the authoritative basis for replacing Judas (Acts 1:16–20), for validating the gospel message (Acts 17:11), and for including the Gentiles on equal footing with the Jews (Acts 15:14–19). That the NT writers accepted the OT as the word of God is clear from the frequency with which they use it to support their arguments. In line with Jesus' practice, the OT is referred to as "the Scriptures" (*hai graphai*) and quotations are prefaced by the phrase, "it is written" (*gegraptai*).[8] Paul, for example, uses the OT to support such

---

6. *Canon* 59: "Let no private psalms or any uncanonical books be read in church but only the canonical ones of the New and Old Testament."

7. See, for example, Mark 7:6; 9:12–13; 11:17, and parallels.

8. See, for instance, Matt. 2:5; Luke 2:23; John 12:14; Rom. 1:17; 1 Cor. 1:31; 2 Cor. 8:15; Gal. 3:10; Heb. 10:7; and 1 Pet. 1:16.

wide-ranging arguments as the financial support of the gospel minister (1 Cor. 9:9–10), the need for liberal giving (2 Cor. 8:15; 9:9), vengeance being the sole prerogative of God (Rom. 12:19–20), and the universal pervasiveness of sin (Rom. 3:10ff.). Peter bases the need for holy conduct on OT command (1 Pet. 1:16) and argues from the OT that the people of God are the locus of God's presence and not the temple (1 Pet. 2:6ff.).

The respect and obedience with which the NT authors view the OT arises from a conviction regarding its "God-breathed" character (2 Tim. 3:16a; cf. 2 Pet. 1:20–21), which makes it profitable for "teaching, rebuking, correcting, and training in righteousness" (2 Tim. 3:16b).

CANONICAL DEVELOPMENT IN THE FIRST CENTURY A.D.

Signs of expanding the church's body of authoritative literature to include Jesus' words and the apostolic teachings are already evident in the decades following Jesus' death, resurrection, and ascension. Jesus Himself paved the way for this development by placing His words not merely above scribal interpretation (Matt. 5:33–37, 43–48) but on a par with OT law itself (Matt. 5:21–26, 27–30, 38–42)[9]—a move that was reinforced by the crowd, which on more than one occasion observed that Jesus taught with an authority the scribes lacked (Matt. 7:29; Mark 1:22; cf. Luke 4:32).

---

9. It is commonly argued that with the phrase "you have heard that it was said but I say" Jesus is interacting with oral tradition and not the Law itself. This is in fact the case in 5:34ff. ("Do not swear by heaven, by earth, toward Jerusalem, or by your head") and 5:43ff. ("Love your neighbor and hate your enemy"), where Jesus cites scribal interpretation of OT law. But this phrase also introduces OT law itself, as is apparent from vv. 21ff. ("Do not murder"), vv. 27–30 ("Do not commit adultery"), and vv. 38–42 ("An eye for an eye and a tooth for a tooth"). It is not, however, that Jesus is setting aside the OT Law. In 5:17 He states that He has not come to *katalysai*—a word that means to "dismantle" as one would a tent—but to *plērōsai*, which as a point of contrast must mean to "assemble" or "build up." In each case, what Jesus demands is a higher standard than mere adherence to the letter of the Law. This is clear in Matt. 5:22 where Jesus affirms the criminal law in view but goes beyond to say that state of mind ("anger") and gross verbal assault (*raca, mōre*), and not merely physical abuse ("murder"), render one legally culpable.

A similar heightening of the Law is evident in Jesus' handling of the legal principle of equal recompense ("eye for an eye"), where the disciples are challenged to structure their communities in the case of civil offenses according to a standard higher than that of strict retribution. Four concrete examples are provided where the believer is called to go beyond what the law normally requires (e.g., to voluntarily endure gross personal insult [Matt. 5:39], to pay twice the penalty [v. 40], to carry a Roman soldier's luggage twice the miles required [v. 41], and to loan without interest [v. 42]).

The early church, in turn, gave authoritative status to the words of Jesus by quoting His teaching side by side with the OT Scriptures to support key points of argumentation. A command of Jesus, for instance, is used to argue for the permanence of the marital bond (1 Cor. 7:10–11), to justify financial remuneration of those who preach the gospel (1 Cor. 9:14), and to correct discrimination on the basis of wealth or status at the Lord's Supper (1 Cor. 11:17ff.).[10] It is also by virtue of a word of Jesus that the temporal advantage of the dead over the living on Christ's return is asserted (1 Thess. 4:15) and that "elder" as a salaried position is claimed (1 Tim. 5:17–18).

The normative importance of Jesus' words is evident as well in the care the early church took to preserve and transmit His teaching. Luke makes reference to those who drew up accounts based on reliable eyewitness transmission of Jesus' life and teaching (*kathōs paredosan hēmin*, Luke 1:1–2). The apostolic task, in particular, is defined in terms of the faithful transmission (*paredōka*) of tradition (*tas paradoseis*, 1 Cor. 11:2; 2 Thess. 2:15a; 2 Pet. 2:21)—a process that took both an oral and a written form (2 Thess. 2:15b). Paul, for instance, reminds his converts of his role of faithful transmitter (1 Cor. 15:3; cf. 1 Cor. 11:2, 23) and is concerned that his converts find those who, in turn, could be reliable transmitters (2 Tim. 2:2). Indeed, some churches are praised for "holding to the traditions" just as they were "passed on" to them (1 Cor. 11:2; cf. Rom. 6:17), while others are commanded to do so (Phil. 4:9; 2 Thess. 2:15; 3:6). That some abused their role of faithful transmitter of tradition is evident from Peter's warning about false teachers who turned their backs "on the sacred commandment that was passed on to them" (2 Pet. 2:21).[11]

THE SHIFT TO WRITTEN RECORDS

JESUS' TEACHING

The shift from oral to written records of Jesus' words is commonly thought to have been motivated by the passing of eyewitnesses, which began in earnest in the A.D. sixties and seventies. But the perceived need for orderly, written accounts of Jesus' life and teaching is already evident

---

10. In all three passages it was a command of *ho kurios*. Paul normally distinguishes between Christ, for which he uses the articular *ho kurios*, and Yahweh, for which he uses the anarthrous *kurios*. See Maximilian Zerwick, *Biblical Greek* (Rome: Pontifical Biblical Institute, 1963), no. 169.

11. The importance of the role of transmitter explains the pains taken by the NT writers to distinguish when they were drawing on tradition (e.g., "not I but the Lord," 1 Cor. 7:10; 9:14; 11:23ff.; 1 Thess. 4:15) and when they were not (e.g., "judge for yourselves," 1 Cor. 10:15; cf. 1 Cor. 7:12, 25, 40; 2 Cor. 8:10). For this reason Paul says with confidence that he passed on to his churches exactly what he "received from the Lord" (1 Cor. 11:23).

in the period prior to our recorded Gospels, as the prologue to Luke's Gospel attests (1:1–2). Papias, bishop of Hierapolis at the turn of the century, reflects this shift when he states that "Matthew compiled the Sayings in the Aramaic language and each one interpreted them as best they could." "Mark," as well, "having become the interpreter of Peter wrote down accurately everything that he remembered . . . taking care not to omit anything he heard nor to set down any false statement therein."[12]

The existence of an even earlier account of Jesus' words is thought to be traceable in the verbatim similarities between Matthew and Luke—a source commonly referred to today as *Q*. The impetus to collect the sayings of Jesus continued into the second century, as evidenced in works like the Nag Hammadi tractate, *The Gospel of Thomas* (a collection of sayings, prophecies, proverbs, and parables)[13] and the four fragments of an early and previously unknown Gospel, catalogued in the British Museum as *Egerton Papyrus 2*.[14]

PAUL'S LETTERS

It is easy to see why the early church came to esteem and take steps to preserve the teaching of Jesus. But was this also the case with the teaching of the apostles? There are a number of early indications that Paul's writings came to be valued alongside Jesus' teachings. This is somewhat surprising given the ad hoc and problem-oriented nature of the Pauline letter. Nonetheless, Paul himself attached importance to his writings that extended beyond the needs of a particular local church. He instructed, for example, the churches at Colossae and Laodicea to exchange letters for public reading (Col. 4:16). There are also a number of indications that Paul intended the letter to the Ephesians to circulate among a number of churches in Asia Minor. The words "in Ephesus" are missing from several early, important manuscripts (P46, ℵ, B, 1739)[15] as well as being absent from Origen's text (ca. 254) and Basil's manuscripts (ca. 379). The lack of the usual Pauline personal references combined with the letter's inclusion in Marcion's canon as "the letter to the Laodiceans" has led many to think that copies of this letter were sent to various churches in the Lycus Valley

---

12. Found in Eusebius, *H.E.* 3.39.

13. See, for example, *Gospel of Thomas* 2, 2, 75: "Jesus said, 'Many are standing at the door but it is the solitary who will enter the bridal chamber.'"

14. See, for instance, the following excerpt from Fragment 1: "Jesus spoke this word,'Do not think that I have come to be your accuser before my Father; the one to accuse you is Moses on whom you have set your hopes.'"

15. It is thought that the ancestor of manuscript 1739 was written by a scribe toward the close of the fourth century. For discussion, see Bruce Metzger, *The Text of the New Testament*, 2d ed. (Oxford: Oxford University Press, 1968), 65.

with the name of the church appropriately added. The probability of this is strengthened by the presence of the letter to the Galatians, which was clearly meant to circulate among a number of churches, as the salutation "to the churches of Galatia" indicates (Gal. 1:2).

The value the church placed on Paul's writings can be seen in the early efforts made at collecting his letters. Second Peter 3:15–16, which makes mention of Paul's "letters," is the earliest reference to an existing collection. The language of "as do the other Scriptures" points to the already perceived authoritative character of this collection. Clement of Rome's references to 1 Corinthians (*Clem.* 47) and Polycarp of Smyrna's mention of Philippians (*Phil.* 3) suggest that by the late first to early second centuries A.D. Paul's letters were circulating beyond the geographical areas in which they originated. The fact that both refer their readers to these letters for their perusal shows they were readily accessible as well. By the time of Ignatius, bishop of Antioch around A.D. 110, some kind of Pauline corpus is in view[16] and by Marcion's day (ca. 140) the collecting process is virtually complete.[17]

THE PUSH TO CANONIZE

By the middle of the second century A.D. not only were the four Gospels and the Pauline letters circulated and read in the churches, but a much larger group of documents than is found today in our NT canon were in use as well. Five writings were especially popular: The *Epistle of Barnabas*, thought to have been written by the individual Luke makes mention of a number of times in Acts, was a favorite letter, particularly in the Eastern churches. The *Shepherd of Hermas*, an apocalypse composed in Rome toward the mid-second century, was accepted by such early church fathers as Irenaeus (*Adv.Haer.* 4.20.2), Clement of Alexandria (*Strom.* 1.17.29), and Tertullian (*DeOrat.* 16). *1 Clement's* popularity—a letter written about A.D. 95 to the church of Corinth by the bishop of Rome—is evident in Eusebius' comment that "in many churches this letter was read

---

16. Parallel phraseology strongly suggests that Ignatius was intimately acquainted with at least five of Paul's letters: Romans, 1 Corinthians, Galatians, Ephesians, and Colossians.

17. Except for Galatians, which is placed first in terms of importance, Marcion appears to have arranged Paul's letters in order of length: Galatians, Corinthians, Romans, Thessalonians, Ephesians (called "Laodiceans"), Colossians, Philippians, and Philemon. While the absence of the Pastoral Letters is odd, their lack is not due to unfamiliarity. Polycarp forty years earlier possessed a collection of Paul's letters that included at least two of the Pastorals, as the citations from 1 Tim. 2:1; 4:15, 6:7, 10; 2 Tim. 2:12; 4:10 in his letter to the Philippians indicate.

aloud to the assembled worshipers in early days as it is in our own" (*H.E.* 3.16). The *Apocalypse of Peter* appears in one of the earliest canonical lists, the Muratorian Canon, but with the qualification that "some do not want it to be read in church" (lines 71–72). The *Didache*, or *Teaching of the Twelve Apostles*, commonly thought to have been written in the latter part of the first century A.D. to address questions regarding ethics and polity, is said by Eusebius to be rejected by some but included "among the recognized books" by others (*H.E.* 3.25).[18]

While works such as these were valued and widely used in the early centuries, others, like our canonical James, Hebrews, 2 Peter, 2—3 John, and Revelation, were disputed in certain quarters of the church during this same time period. Yet by A.D. 367 Athanasius in his *Thirty-Ninth Easter Letter* can speak of our twenty-seven canonical books as "the books of the NT" and state that "in these alone the teaching of godliness is proclaimed." What led to the acceptance of some writings and rejection of other writings in the second and third centuries? And what criteria were used to distinguish between canonical and uncanonical books?

It is interesting to observe that the initial attempt to draw up a NT "canon" did not occur in the context of orthodox. In fact, it appears that the church was first prompted to consider the question of canonical status by the activity of heterodox thinking and the growing influence of Gnosticism in the mid-second century. Marcion, a wealthy shipowner from Sinope in Pontus who around A.D. 140 was excommunicated from the church at Rome for his heretical beliefs, is responsible for one of the earliest (if not the earliest) attempts at drawing up a list of canonical writings. The basis for his rejection of a particular writing was simply whether it espoused the "eye for an eye" ethic and retributive divine justice that for Marcion typified Judaism. His application of this negative criterion led to the repudiation of the entire OT and all Christian writings that spoke of a God of justice (the God of the Jews) as opposed to a God of grace (the Father of Jesus). The end result was a canon of authoritative writings that

---

18. One could also add to the list two gospels dating from the second and third centuries that surfaced as favorites principally in the writings of certain Eastern church fathers like Clement of Alexandria, Origen, and Cyril of Jerusalem. The *Gospel of the Hebrews* is preserved for us only through the quotations of the church fathers. From the title it can be inferred that it served the needs primarily of Aramaic-speaking Jewish Christians in Palestine and Syria. The *Gospel of the Egyptians*, which was accepted as canonical in Egypt, is extant only in fragmentary form. From the quotations of the church fathers it is evident that the purpose of this writing was to advance the teachings of those movements espousing an extreme form of asceticism.

amounted to the Gospel of Luke and ten of Paul's letters—but even these writings were appropriately edited to suit his particular beliefs.

Marcion's canonizing efforts stimulated a flurry of activity especially in the Western church, which for the first time was pushed to define what constituted its authoritative writings in a more exact way than it had felt necessary to do until that point. It is during this period of close scrutiny that we can gain an insight into the process of canonization as well as an understanding of how our twenty-seven NT books came to be viewed as exclusively normative for the church's faith and practice.

CRITERIA FOR DETERMINING CANONICITY

While a fair amount of dialoguing went on in the second and third centuries concerning the limits of the canon, it is important to note there was a nucleus of writings that were universally recognized and which became the "rule of faith" against which all other writings were tested. This central nucleus included those books that embodied the apostolic faith and could be traced to an apostle or close companion.

The significance of apostolicity as a criterion of canonicity can be seen in the number of post-apostolic writings that sought to gain acceptance through apostolic association. Two of the apocalypses composed during this period are attributed to apostles (Peter, Paul). Three of the Gospels are said to be authored by apostles (Peter, Thomas, Philip). Then, too, there are the *Acts of John, Peter, Paul, Andrew,* and *Thomas.* So important was apostolicity that it determined to a great extent what was read and not read in many churches in the second century. It explains, for instance, why doubts about the letter to the Hebrews that did not exist prior to this point suddenly appeared during this period and accounts for the acceptance of the Gospels of Mark and Luke, whose writings early on were associated with the ministries of Peter and Paul.[19] The need to demonstrate apostolic connection is also reflected in the attempt of second-century Gnostics to associate their writings with an apostolic source. Valentinus, for example, linked his writings to Paul through a Pauline disciple named Theudas, while Basilides and his followers claimed Matthias and Glaukias, a supposed companion of Peter, as sources of their special teachings.[20]

---

19. See, for example, Irenaeus *Adv.Haer.* 3.1.1: "Matthew issued a written Gospel among the Hebrews in their own dialect. . . . Mark, the disciple and interpreter of Peter, handed down to us in writing what had been preached by Peter. Luke, the companion of Paul, also recorded in a book the gospel preached by him. Afterwards, John, the disciple of the Lord . . . published a Gospel during his residence at Ephesus in Asia."

20. A follower of Valentinus offered inquirers "the apostolic tradition which we received in a succession regulated (*kanonisai*) by the teaching of the Savior" (Epiphanius, *Panarion* 33).

Other canonical "measuring sticks" emerged as well during this period. One such criterion was early dating. As the church became farther and farther removed from the eyewitnesses of the first century, it became natural to value those writings that were demonstrably closest to the time of Jesus' earthly ministry. The importance of early dating can be seen in the Muratorian Canon's exclusion of the *Shepherd of Hermas* from its list because "it was written very recently in our times in the city of Rome" (lines 73–74).

Acceptance and rejection of canonical status was also based on distinguishing those writings that had been "handed down" and those that had not. For example, Serapion, bishop of Antioch around A.D. 200, in writing to the church of Rhossus in Cilicia against "the so-called Gospel of Peter," stated that "we receive Peter and all the apostles as we receive Christ, but the writings falsely attributed to them we are experienced enough to reject, knowing that nothing of the sort has been handed down to us."[21]

An additional test for canonical inclusion was intrinsic soundness, which became an important criterion for excluding writings that embodied Gnostic teachings. Serapion, for instance, recognized only those writings and passages that "accorded with the authentic teaching of the Savior" (Eusebius, *H.E.* 6.12). Even Ignatius' letters, which some considered inspired by some, were eventually excluded as inferior in their grasp of the Christian gospel. Ignatius himself recognized the secondary character of his letters when in writing to the Romans he said: "I do not order you as did Peter and Paul, for they were apostles" (4:3).

DEVELOPMENT OF A NEW TESTAMENT CANON

THE FOUR GOSPELS

Prior to A.D. 180, canonically accepted writings circulated in two groupings, the "gospels" and the "apostles"—much as the OT writings were divided by Jesus and His contemporaries into the "Law" and the "Prophets" (e.g., Matt. 5:17). The church from its very beginnings devoted itself to the "teaching of the apostles" (Acts 2:42). Yet this cate-

---

21. Quoted by Eusebius in *H.E.* 6.12.2. Even Clement of Alexandria, though he personally valued and quoted the *Gospel According to the Hebrews*, in the final analysis excluded this work from the church's canonical list, because continuous acceptance and usage could not be demonstrated. Cf. Irenaeus, who states that he referred opponents like Valentinus to "the tradition which originates from the apostles and which is preserved by means of the successions of presbyters in the churches" (*Adv.Haer.* 3.2.2).

gory of writings is contested in terms of its limits even in the church today, while acceptance of a fourfold gospel was virtually unchallenged by the early part of the third century. How did the church come to settle on four Gospels from among the larger group of contenders? Even more curious is how the church came to accept four as opposed to three, two or even one authoritative Gospel, especially since there is evidence that a single Gospel dominated various ecclesiastical centers and geographical regions.

Initially, authority resided in the gospel message itself rather than in written records. The value that some early fathers placed on the oral over the written word can be seen in Papias' statement that he "did not imagine things written in books" would help him as much as "the utterances of a living and abiding voice" (Eusebius, *H.E.* 3.39.1ff). Yet by the mid-second century, Justin Martyr had set the Gospels, which he called "the memoirs of the apostles," alongside the writings of the prophets and said both groups of writings were to be publicly read in the church (*Apol.* 1.67.3–5). The shift from an authoritative message to an authoritative record, however, was by no means an invariably smooth one. The difficulty some had in accepting the authority of a written account of the gospel is reflected in the assertion of Ignatius' opponents that if they did not find it in the *archeia* (the OT Scriptures) they did not believe it in the *euangelion* (the "gospel record", *Phld.* 8.2).[22]

It is commonly thought today that written Gospels arose in response to the needs of churches in a particular geographical area. This is suggested not only by the theological distinctives of each Gospel writer but also by the fact that only one Gospel was widely known and used in a particular geographical location. Matthew's Gospel, for example, appears to have been broadly read in Palestine, while John's seems to have been primarily used in Asia Minor. Nonetheless, the currency of a four-Gospel collection is already apparent in the Muratorian Canon[23] and is taken as a matter of course in the Western church by the end of the second century.[24]

How did the shift from a parochial, localized use of one Gospel to an acceptance of four Gospels occur? Some, like Tatian (ca. A.D. 160), attempted to deal with a multiplicity of four Gospels by producing a single

---

22. Ignatius was also criticized for using "it is written" with reference to the recorded Gospels (*Phld.* 8.2).

23. Lines 2–8 of the Muratorian Canon read: ". . . at which nevertheless he was present and so he placed [them in his narrative]. The third book of the gospel is that according to Luke. . . . The fourth of the gospels is that of John [one] of the disciples."

24. See, for example, Irenaeus, *Adv.Haer.* 3.11.9: "All who represent the aspects of the Gospel as being either more or fewer than four are vain, unlearned, and audacious."

harmonization (the *Diatessaron*), which was popular in the Syrian church until the fifth century but was never accepted by the church as a whole. Most, however, were able to make this move by thinking in terms of not four Gospels but *the* gospel with four records. So strictly speaking in the understanding of the post-apostolic church, there were not four Gospels but one fourfold gospel—the gospel according to Matthew, Mark, Luke, and John. This is reflected in the Muratorian Canon's statement that "though various elements may be taught in the individual books of the Gospels, nevertheless this makes no difference to the faith of believers, since by the one sovereign Spirit all things have been declared in all [the Gospels]" (lines 16–20). In this way the tension between the need for a single gospel message and the actual presence of multiple gospel documents became manageable.

And what about the process by which these four Gospels were accepted over against the larger number of gospels current in the second century? The argumentation of the post-apostolic fathers for the normative and exclusive authority of these four Gospels rested primarily on apostolic association, the presence of early and authentic material, the late date of rival gospels, and connection with a well-established community. The importance of especially apostolic association and community connection can be seen in Irenaeus' appeal to the fact that Matthew was written for the Hebrews in their own dialect, Mark passed along what had been preached by Peter, Luke recorded the gospel that Paul preached, and John wrote his Gospel during his residence at Ephesus (*Adv.Haer.* 3.1.1).

The fact that Irenaeus had to defend the exclusive authority of these four, by appealing to the "four zones of the world," "the four principal winds," "the four-faced cherubim," and "the four principal covenants given to the human race" indicates that even as late as A.D. 180 this was by no means a universally settled question (*Adv.Haer.* 3.11.8).[25] Nonetheless, Tatian's matter-of-fact choice of just these four for his gospel harmonization at a time when many gospels were competing for attention suggests that Matthew, Mark, Luke, and John were well established and recognized above the competitors.

THE APOSTLES

The second grouping in which canonically accepted writings circulated in the second and third centuries A.D. was called "the apostles." The question that comes to mind in looking at this grouping is how the church came to accept as universally authoritative writings that for the

---

25. For example, Clement of Alexandria, who recognized a fourfold gospel, still valued and cited the *Gospel of the Hebrews* and the *Gospel of the Egyptians*.

most part were written to address particular needs in specific church contexts. Even more intriguing is why some of these writings were preserved and others were not. Paul, for example, makes reference to four letters that he wrote to the church at Corinth, yet copies of only two of these four letters are in existence today.[26] Mention is also made of a letter written to the Laodicean church, but we possess no extant copy of this missive (Col. 4:16).

Those writings that could be unquestionably linked with the apostolic tradition ("the teaching of the apostles") were the first to be recognized in the post-apostolic period. For this reason, Paul's letters were almost immediately used and valued by the church. Yet the extent of the Pauline corpus is not so easily defined. The first evidence of an authoritative collection is Marcion's canon, which included in descending order of length all of Paul's letters, except the Pastoral Letters. Even here, though, it is difficult to be precise since letters to the same community are, for the most part, grouped together, giving the order: Galatians (placed first in terms of importance), Corinthians, Romans, Thessalonians, Ephesians (called "Laodiceans"), Colossians, Philippians, and Philemon.[27] The omission of 1–2 Timothy and Titus is understandable as these letters are addressed to individuals rather than to the church per se and so were slower to be widely received and used.[28]

The fact that Paul wrote to seven churches was used by some as an argument for the catholicity of his writings— the number seven symbolizing universality or completeness in Greco-Roman culture. In the Muratorian Canon, for instance, it is argued that in writing "by name to only seven churches" Paul recognizes "that there is one Church spread

---

26. These four letters are commonly referred to as the "Previous Letter" (1 Cor. 5:9), 1 Corinthians, the "Severe Letter" (2 Cor. 1:23—2:4), and 2 Corinthians.

27. Compare p[46] (ca. A.D. 200), one of the earliest papyrus codices of the Pauline epistles: Romans, Hebrews, 1—2 Corinthians, Ephesians, Galatians, Philippians, Colossians, and 1 Thessalonians. It is sometimes argued that the absense of the Pastoral Letters clearly points to their pseudonymous character. What is commonly overlooked, however, is the similar absense of Philemon (which no one claims to be non-Pauline) Rom. 1:1—5:16 (at the head of the manuscript) and 2 Thessalonians (at the end of the manuscript), suggestive of either damage to the manuscript and/or the scribe running out of room. The increasing closeness of the lines and script toward the end of the manuscript points to the latter as a plausible explanation.

28. Philemon is most likely included because it is addressed to the church as well as to an individual (1:1). Additionally, the prominence of the OT Law, especially in 1 Tim. 1, may have rendered all of the Pastoral Letters suspect in Marcion's eyes. For further discussion, see Tertullian's *Against Marcion*, 5.21.

Marcion's single work, *Antitheses*, is not extant. The contents of his canon must therefore be deduced from patristic writings of the day.

throughout the whole extent of the earth."[29] It is also on this basis that the no longer extant epistles to the Laodiceans and the Alexandrians are labeled as Pauline forgeries.[30]

Relevance to the church at large also became an important criterion of canonicity in the post-apostolic period. For example, Philemon, Titus, and 1–2 Timothy are grouped separately in the Muratorian Canon and accepted as canonical by virtue of their universal relevance for the regulation of ecclesiastical discipline in the wider church.[31] In fact, the push to demonstrate catholicity may be behind the absence in Romans 1:7, 15 of "in Rome" in some Western manuscripts and versions (G, it^g) and in certain Greek and Latin manuscripts of Origen—the omission being an attempt to provide a "catholicized" version of the letter.

The acceptance and use of our thirteen Pauline letters in such diverse geographical locations as Rome (Muratorian Canon), Carthage (Tertullian), France (Irenaeus), and Alexandria (Clement) point to the broadly perceived canonical status of Paul's letters by the early part of the third century. What about the other writings of "the apostles"? Somewhat surprisingly, Revelation was one of the most widely used and accepted apostolic writings in the second century. In the West, Justin Martyr is the first to make direct reference to it (*Dial* 81),[32] Irenaeus quotes extensively from it, and by the early part of the third century Tertullian states that he knows of none besides Marcion who did not accept it. In the East, the value and esteem with which Revelation was received is reflected in its wide usage. Melito, bishop of Sardis (ca .190), for instance, devotes a commentary to it and Clement of Alexandria as well as Theophilus, (bishop of Antioch ca. 185), use and quote from it. One of the most interesting statements regarding the catholicity of Revelation is found in the Muratorian Canon, which states that Paul, following the example of his predecessor John in

---

29. Lines 48–57 of the Muratorian Canon read: "Paul himself writes by name to only seven churches . . . for it is clearly recognizable that there is one Church spread throughout the whole extent of the earth."

30. Lines 63–66 of the Canon read: "There is also current [an epistle] to the Laodiceans [and] another to the Alexandrians, [both] forged in Paul's name to [further] the heresy of Marcion." It is generally thought that the Laodicean letter found in the Peshitta Syriac version, which is a patchwork of genuine Pauline phrases, is different from the Marcionite epistle mentioned in the Muratorian Canon.

31. Lines 60–62 read: "Paul also wrote out of affection and love one to Philemon, one to Titus and two to Timothy; and these are held sacred in the esteem of the catholic church for the regulation of ecclesiastical discipline."

32. Apart from the Gospels, the only other book of the New Testament that Justin mentions by name is Revelation.

writing to "seven" churches, shows that he is speaking to all churches (lines 48–59).

The Acts of the Apostles, although part of a two-volume Lucan work, had a history of its own in terms of canonical acceptance. It was cited in the second and third centuries by both Western (e.g., Justin Martyr, Irenaeus, Tertullian) and Eastern (e.g., Clement) church fathers. The Muratorian Canon refers to it as "the acts of all the apostles" and states that Luke "compiled the individual events that took place in his presence as he plainly shows by omitting the martyrdom of Peter as well as the departure of Paul from the city [of Rome]" (lines 34–38). As with the Gospel the authority of Acts is based on Luke's association with the apostle Paul (e.g., Irenaeus).

Hebrews had a more checkered history. It was known and quoted in the Roman church earlier than anywhere else (e.g., *1 Clement* 17.1) but fell into disuse in the second century. Irenaeus cites minimally from it and it receives no mention in the Muratorian Canon. Tertullian, however, speculates on the authorship of the letter and cited extensively from Hebrews 6:1–6 (*Modesty* 20). Hebrews, on the whole, was better received in the East. Clement of Alexandria, for example, quotes from it and the early manuscript P46 includes it among the Pauline letters.[33]

Of the so-called "catholic epistles" (James, 1—2 Peter, 1—3 John, and Jude), only 1 Peter and 1—2 John were frequently quoted in the second and third centuries—but then Jude, 2—3 John and 2 Peter are little quoted today. All are known, however, by the latter part of the first century—especially 1 Peter, which Polycarp cites extensively. Although James and 1—2 Peter are not mentioned in the Muratorian Canon, Jude is recognized as well as "two of the epistles bearing the name of John, which are counted in the catholic church" (lines 68–69).[34]

THE DEBATES

The virtual acceptance and use in the first two centuries A.D. of all twenty-seven of our NT books is followed in the third and fourth centuries by a period of intense debate regarding the "apostles" portion of the canon as well as some of the commonly valued writings like the *Apocalypse*

---

33. The Muratorian Canon does refer to a letter to the Alexandrians, which some have thought to be an oblique reference to Hebrews. But it is classified as a writing that promotes the heresy of Marcion, which does not square with the contents of our canonical letter.

34. It has been widely debated whether "two of the epistles bearing the name of John" refers to 1—2 John or to 2—3 John. Reference to 1 John early on in the Canon suggests 2—3 John.

of Peter and the *Shepherd of Hermas.* Yet it was these very debates that led to an increasingly more precise definition of what constituted a "canonical" writing and to a clearer determination of the limits of the canon.

The canonical fluidity of this period is reflected in the sixth-century codex Claromontanus and in the fourth-century codex Sinaiticus. Codex Claromontanus is instructive in that it contains a fourth-century list of NT writings that lacks three of Paul's letters (Philippians, 1–2 Thessalonians)[35] and Hebrews, but includes the *Epistle of Barnabas*, the *Shepherd of Hermas*, the *Acts of Paul*, and the *Apocalypse of Peter*. Codex Sinaiticus is informative as well. While including all that is found in our NT canon, it also contains the *Epistle of Barnabas* and the *Shepherd of Hermas*. Even so, the value of such manuscripts in determining what constituted canonically accepted writings is limited in that such lists include without discrimination books that were considered authoritative in the church at large as well as those that were thought to be merely profitable for private use.[36] It also is to be noted that where such writings are included, they are put at the end of the list, suggestive of a distinction in value and authority.

The Muratorian Canon (ca. 200) is more helpful in understanding the kinds of distinctions that were increasingly brought to bear on the canonical question during this period. A distinction, for instance, is made between those books that were authorized for public consumption (e.g., Jude and 1–2 John) and those recommended only for private reading (e.g., *Apocalypse of Peter*, the *Shepherd of Hermas*): "We receive only the apocalypses of John and Peter, though some of us are not willing that the latter be read in church" (lines 71–72).[37] A further distinction is drawn between writings concurrent with the apostolic period and those that postdate the apostles: "But Hermas wrote the Shepherd very recently in our times in the city of Rome . . . and therefore ought indeed to be read, but not publicly to the people in church either among the prophets nor among the apostles, for it is after [their] time" (lines 73–80).

The debates and disputes in the third and fourth centuries regarding the limits of the canon were to a great extent impacted by the rise of millinarian movements like Montanism, which had its beginnings in the second half of the second century, and by imperial persecution. Montanism, with its emphasis on the ongoing gift of inspiration and prophesy, pushed

---

35. Metzger, *Text* 230 suggests that the scribe's eye may have jumped from Eph-es*ious* to Hebra*ious*, thereby omitting Philippians through 2 Thessalonians.

36. See, for example, Clement of Alexandria who distinguishes writings that were considered "useful" but not in general use (*Strom.* 3.13.93).

37. Compare Clement of Alexandria who quotes from the Gospels of the Egyptians and the Hebrews, but acknowledges that they were not in use in his church (*Strom.* 2.9.45; 3.13.93).

the church to consider once and for all which writings would serve as the definitive yardstick for the church's faith and practice. In order to under-cut the theology and practice of such sectarian groups, the church responded by not only rejecting the "inspired" writings of the Montanists but also questioning the authority of long-accepted writings on which Montanists based their beliefs. Revelation was especially subject in certain quarters to severe criticism. Some, like Gaius, a respected third-century presbyter, rejected it because the Montanists used it to support their dis-tinctive claims. Others, like Dionysius, bishop of Alexandria (ca. 250), had difficulty accepting Revelation due to its use by millennialists to defend their expectation of a 1,000-year earthly reign of Christ.[38] The Johannine writings, with their references to the "anointing" activity and "filling" of the promised Spirit, were also the object of debate. Hebrews fared much the same. Its use by Montanists to support a post-baptismal retention of sins made it suspicious in the minds of some. The fact that the West rejected Pauline authorship while the East argued for it served as well to challenge its continuing canonical acceptance.

Imperial persecution also impacted discussion regarding canonical lim-its. This was in large part due to the imperial edict that went into effect during the reign of Diocletian (ca. 303), which called for the burning of all copies of the biblical and liturgical books, the destruction of church build-ings, and the banning of all meetings for Christian worship. This imperial action compelled the church to consider which writings held such author-ity that they were willing to be tortured and killed for them.

Two major third- and fourth-century Eastern church fathers figure prominently in these discussions: Origen, theologian and biblical scholar (ca. 203–54), and Eusebius, bishop of Caesarea (ca. 315–40). Origen is important because through his extensive travels he became acquainted not only with the debates but also with what was and was not generally consid-ered to be authoritative in the wider church.[39] With respect to the Gos-pels, Origen gives as "undeniably authentic in the church of God" only Matthew, Mark, Luke, and John (*Homily on Luke* 1). In terms of the "epis-tles of the apostles," he states that Peter "left us one acknowledged epistle, possibly two—though this is doubtful." John "left us a single gospel, the Revelation, and an epistle of a very few lines and possibly two more—though their authenticity is denied by some." James is referred to as "the epistle that is in circulation," suggesting some question regarding its authenticity (*Commentary on John* 19.61), while Jude is "an epistle of but

---

38. The efforts of fathers like Hippolytus, bishop of Rome around A.D. 220, served to reinstate Revelation in the West by the beginning of the fourth century.

39. See Eusebius, *H.E.* 6.25.

few lines yet filled with the healthful words of heavenly grace" (*Homily on Matthew* 10.17). Origen's acceptance of Hebrews is particularly noteworthy because despite the acknowledgment that "who wrote the epistle is known to God alone," it is nonetheless received as "wonderful and equal in every way to the apostle Paul's accepted writings" (*H.E.* 6.25).

Eusebius with his wide exposure to the thinking and practices of the church in his day also significantly contributes to our understanding of this period of controversy. It is first with Eusebius that a twofold classification of "accepted" writings (*homolegoumena* or those writings whose authority and authenticity are recognized by all the churches) and "disputed" writings (*antilegomena*) emerged. Among the "disputed" writings Eusebius distinguishes (1) those which were generally accepted, (2) those that all the churches rejected as spurious, and (3) those that were labeled as heretical.

In terms of the "recognized books," Eusebius lists "the holy quartet of the gospels, followed by the Acts of the Apostles, then Paul's epistles, 1 John, and 1 Peter."[40] To these "may be added, if it is thought proper, the Apocalypse of John," but Eusebius acknowledges that there are those who would not include Revelation among the recognized books. Those he lists as disputed yet enjoying wide reception and usage are the epistles of James, Jude, 2 Peter, and 2—3 John. Among the spurious books are the *Epistle of Barnabas*, the *Shepherd of Hermas*, the *Acts of Paul*, the *Apocalypse of Peter*, the *Teachings of the Apostles*, and the *Gospel of the Hebrews*. The third category of "disputed" writings, which Eusebius designates as "those which the heretics put forward under the name of the apostles," includes such writings as the Gospels of Peter, Thomas, and Matthias, and the Acts of Andrew and John (*H.E.* 3.25).

The commentary that accompanies Eusebius' list of "heretical writings" is instructive in showing the criteria the churches were using in the fourth century to differentiate canonical from uncanonical writings. It is said of the "heretical" category of writings that their character and style are far removed from apostolic usage, the thought and purport of their contents are completely out of harmony with true orthodoxy, and none of the ecclesiastical writers ever thought it right to refer to these writings. "For these reasons," Eusebius states, "they ought not even to be reckoned among the disputed books but are to be cast aside as impious and beyond the pale" (*H.E.* 3.25).

---

40. Hebrews is missing from Eusebius' list of "recognized" and "disputed" books, probably because it is included among the Pauline letters, which are not listed separately or enumerated.

GROWING CONSENSUS

In the early part of the fourth century the question of canonical versus non-canonical writings was very much a matter of debate in the wider church. Yet, by the end of the century Athanasius, bishop of Alexandria, refers to our twenty-seven NT books as "divinely inspired Scripture concerning which we have been fully persuaded . . . in which alone the doctrine of godliness is proclaimed" (*Easter Letter* 39.3). What accounts for this consolidation of opinion within the space of a few decades? And how is it that no less and no more than these twenty-seven books were accepted?

The emergence of an ecclesiastical consensus was primarily the result of a series of councils that tackled the question of canon in the context of a wider discussion of theological and church-related issues. In view of the Trinitarian and christological controversies of the fourth and fifth centuries and the push to define orthodoxy, it was quite natural for the church to want to establish a list of orthodox writings that would provide the scriptural basis from which doctrine could be drawn. It is important to recognize, however, that these councils did not create *ex nihilo* a canon of writings but merely acknowledged those writings that were already recognized by the churches in attendance.

The first council of canonical significance in the East was the Synod of Laodicea which met in A.D. 363 to consider a range of issues from the relationship of Christians to pagans, Jews, and heretics to the matter of worship practices in the churches. The deliberations resulted in a number of decrees (called "canons"), the last two of which (canons 59–60) deal with matters of Scripture. The importance of *Canon 59* can be seen in its separation of canonical from uncanonical books to form a "New Testament": "Let no private psalms nor any uncanonical books be read in church but only the canonical ones of the New and Old Testament." The general character of this decree led in a subsequent edition to a sixtieth canon that clarified in list form what books were judged "canonical." This list corresponds book for book to our present canon with the exception of Revelation and the qualification that 1—3 John and 1—2 Peter are *una sola*, implying a preference in some churches for only 1 John and 1 Peter.[41]

---

41. The consensus reflected in the Laodicean Canon is especially noteworthy given that three years earlier the Cheltenham Canon, which is thought to have originated in North Africa, included only twenty-four writings in its list (excluding Hebrews, James, and Jude). The number twenty-four was based on the twenty-four elders of Rev. 4:10: "As it is said in the Apocalypse of John, 'I saw twenty-four elders presenting their crowns before the throne,' so our fathers approved that these books are canonical and that the people of old have said this."

Four years later Athanasius, in an attempt to regularize usage in the Egyptian churches under his jurisdiction, issued his *Thirty-ninth Easter Letter* in which he listed as "alone canonical" in order and number the twenty-seven books found in our NT canon today. Athanasius' Easter Letter is significant in a number of other ways. It is the first time that all twenty-seven books are listed in such a definitive way: "In these alone is proclaimed the doctrine of godliness." Moreover, Revelation is unequivocally recognized, which is especially noteworthy given its general rejection in the East a century earlier. It is also the first time that a canonical list concludes with an admonition that "nothing be added to nor anything taken away from these." In addition, the role of other commonly received writings, like the *Teaching of the Twelve* and the *Shepherd of Hermas*, set forth with clarity: "Other books besides these are not included in the Canon but can be read by those who newly join us and who wish for instruction in the word of godliness."

Yet, despite conciliar efforts, universal recognition of the limits of the NT canon remained elusive in the East. Gregory of Nazianzus, a contemporary of Athanasius, drew up a canonical list that differed from Athanasius' in omitting Revelation and concluding with the comment: "If there are any besides these, it is not among the genuine books." Amphilochius, bishop of Iconium, while acknowledging the list of twenty-seven, nonetheless remarks that some say 2 Peter, 2—3 John, and Jude should not be received and that most claimed Revelation to be spurious. The list of twenty-two books in the Peshitta (A.D. 411–35) reflects the state of affairs in the Syrian church in the fourth and fifth century. Indeed, to this day the canon and the official lectionary of the Syrian Orthodox Church lack 2 Peter, Jude, 2—3 John, and Revelation.

By contrast, ecclesiastical agreement regarding canonical limits seems to have progressed much more smoothly in the West. There were two fourth-century councils whose deliberations resulted in the promulgation of canonical lists that match our twenty-seven books: The Synod of Hippo which met at Hippo Regius in A.D. 393 and the Synod at Carthage in A.D. 397. The concluding statement of the Carthaginean canon sums up the character of fourth century Western conciliar deliberations: "Let this be sent to our brother and fellow-bishop, Boniface,and to the other bishops of those parts that they may confirm this canon, for these are the things that we have received from our fathers to be read in church."[42]

---

42. It is to be noted that Hebrews is not included among the Pauline letters in either canonical list. By the time of Jerome, however, it is labeled as Pauline, which although inaccurate nonetheless guaranteed through apostolic association its acceptance in the Western churches.

Two Western church fathers played an important role in these conciliar discussions: Jerome (ca. 380), biblical scholar and translator, and Augustine (ca. 395), bishop of Hippo Regius in Northern Africa. Jerome recognized as canonical our exact twenty-seven NT books. The significance of this cannot be overstated, for it is Jerome's translation of the Scriptures that became the chief Latin version in the West and, so, the generally accepted canon of OT and NT writings. From comments scattered throughout Jerome's writings we gain a glimpse of both the debate as well as the emerging consensus in the West. Jude, he says, was rejected by many because of its appeal to the apocryphal *Book of Enoch*, yet by age and use it had "gained authority and is to be reckoned among the holy scriptures" (*De Vir.Ill.* 4). Disputes regarding the difference in style between 1—2 Peter are resolved by appealing to Peter having used two different amanuenses (*Epist.* 120). As to Hebrews and Revelation, "we receive both," Jerome states, "not following the habit of today but rather the authority of ancient writers, who quote each . . . as canonical and churchly" (*Epist.* 129). Although these twenty-seven alone are recognized as "canonical and churchly," Jerome nonetheless stresses the "value" and "usefulness" of books like the *Epistle of Barnabas* and the *Shepherd of Hermas* for the edification of the church (*De Vir.Ill.* 6–10).

With Augustine, whose influence was even greater than that of Jerome, we bring the debate in the West on the question of the New Testament canon to a conclusion. For it was Augustine's argument for "no more and no less than" our twenty-seven NT books that carried the day at three crucial Western councils held in northern Africa from A.D. 393–419 (cf *De Doct. Chr.* 2). Indeed, with the definitive words that prefaced the canonical list of twenty-seven books promulgated by the A.D. 419 Synod at Carthage, three decades of intense discussion and debate regarding the limits of the NT canon came to a close in the West: "Besides these canonical Scriptures, nothing shall be read in the church under the name of the divine scriptures." Even here, though, it is important to note that the canon of the New Testament arrived at through these Western conciliar meetings was a recognition of what had been generally accepted in the church over several generations rather than something new imposed on the church from without.

FOR FURTHER READING

Aland, Kurt. *The Problem of the New Testament Canon*. London: A. R. Mowbray & Co., 1962.

*Bruce, F. F. *The Canon of Scripture*. Downers Grove, Ill.: InterVarsity, 1988.

Campenhausen, H. F. von. *The Formation of the Christian Bible*. Philadelphia: Fortress Press, 1972.

Eusebius. *The History of the Church From Christ to Constantine*. Translated by G. A. Williamson. Minneapolis: Augsburg, 1965.

Farmer, William R. and Denis M. Farkasfalvy. *The Formation of the New Testament Canon*. New York: Paulist Press, 1983.

*Gamble, H. Y. *The New Testament Canon: Its Making and Meaning*. Philadelphia: Fortress Press, 1985.

Grant, R. M. *The Formation of the New Testament*. New York: Harper & Row, 1965.

Hennecke, Edgar and Wilhelm Schneemelcher, eds. *New Testament Apocrypha*. Translated and edited by R. McL.Wilson. 2 vols. Philadelphia: Westminster Press, 1964.

McDonald, Lee M. *The Formation of the Christian Biblical Canon*. Nashville, Tenn.: Abingdon Press, 1988.

Meade, D. G. *Pseudonymity and Canon: An Investigation into the Relationship of Authorship and Authority in Jewish and Earliest Christian Tradition*. Grand Rapids: Eerdmans, 1986.

*Metzger, B. M. *The Canon of the New Testament: Its Origin, Development, and Significance*. Oxford: Clarendon, 1987.

Moore, E. C. *The New Testament in the Christian Church*. New York: Macmillan, 1904.

*Moule, C. F. D. "How the NT Came into Being." In *Understanding the New Testament*, edited by O. Jessie Lace. Cambridge: Cambridge University Press, 1965.

Westcott, B. F. *A General Survey of the History of the Canon of the New Testament*. 3d ed. London: Macmillan, 1870.

* = Recommended as the most readable

XIX

TEXTUAL CRITICISM OF THE NEW TESTAMENT

DAVID ALAN BLACK

The famous Greek scholar A. T. Robertson once called the Greek New Testament "the Torchbearer of Light and Progress for the world."[1] If this is true, then any light we can shed *on* the text of the NT ought to help us gain light *from* it.

The purpose of NT textual criticism is to recover the original text of the NT from the available evidence. Two factors make NT textual criticism a necessity. The first is that none of the original NT manuscripts have survived. No one can say why this is so. Perhaps if an original manuscript had survived, it would have been exploited as a religious relic.[2] The second reason textual criticism is necessary is that there are numerous mistakes in the copies of the NT that have survived. Examples of such errors will be examined later in this chapter.

---

1. A. T. Robertson, *The Minister and His Greek New Testament* (New York: George H. Doran Co., 1923), 116.
2. The originals were undoubtedly worn out after repeated reading, both private and public.

In learning to resolve textual problems in the Greek NT, several factors should be kept in mind. First, the overwhelming majority of variants between manuscripts are of relatively minor importance. These generally involve such matters as spelling or word order, which hardly affect translation or exegesis.[3]

Second, significant variants number around two thousand. The majority of these variants are carefully discussed in Bruce M. Metzger's *A Textual Commentary on the Greek New Testament*—an indispensable resource for NT students. Some variants are more important than others, of course, but most do affect translation and exegesis in some way.[4]

Third, NT textual critics remain divided over the criteria to be used in the selection of the most likely original reading. These criteria fall broadly into two classes. One class emphasizes external evidence—the age, quality, grouping, and distribution of the MSS. The other class emphasizes internal evidence—the habits of scribes (copyists) and/or the peculiarities, both stylistic and doctrinal, of the author. The ambiguity of these text-critical criteria makes NT textual criticism an art as much as a science, and conclusions regarding any particular variant reading are very often the result of a tenuous balance of criteria for or against it.

Finally, resolving textual problems in the Greek NT obviously presupposes a basic understanding of NT Greek. One need not be an expert in reading the Greek NT, but an elementary understanding of Greek grammar and vocabulary is still required for effective NT textual criticism.[5]

TYPES OF TEXTUAL ERRORS

Textual criticism deals with various kinds of errors found in the existing Greek MSS. The two basic categories of errors are *accidental* errors and *intentional* errors. Accidental errors often resulted from the text being read aloud as scribes relied on their hearing to record it. Romans 5:1 contains a classic example of an error of hearing. Here the slight distinction between long and short vowels in Greek produces a difference in meaning between "we have peace with God"* (following the indicative *echōmen*) and "let us

---

3. Analogous instances of variations in English would include "center/centre" and "labor/labour."

4. An example is John 3:13. Some manuscripts read "the Son of Man who is in heaven," while others omit the clause "who is in heaven." This is a significant variant because it has an important bearing on Christology.

5. For a user-friendly introduction to Greek grammar, see the author's *Learn to Read New Testament Greek* (Nashville: Broadman, 1993).

* Unless otherwise noted, Scripture quotations in this chapter are from the NIV.

have peace with God" (following the subjunctive *echōmen*). Other types of accidental errors include those stemming from misunderstanding or forgetfulness. The result would be changes in word order, the substitution of synonyms, and the unintentional harmonization of similar passages.

Scribes also made intentional errors. These "corrections" were no doubt made in good faith under the impression that a linguistic or theological error had crept into the text. These "improvements" include changes to correct an apparent error of fact (see Mark 1:2, where "Isaiah the prophet" becomes "the prophets"), harmonizations of parallel passages (compare the Matthean and Lukan versions of the Lord's Prayer; Matt. 6:9–13 and Luke 11:2–4), and doctrinal corrections (see Rom. 8:1, where the words "who walk not according to the flesh but according to the Spirit" are omitted in some MSS).

SOURCES OF EVIDENCE FOR TEXTUAL CRITICISM

The NT textual critic uses three kinds of materials in determining the original text: Greek MSS, ancient versions, and citations by early church fathers.[6] It should be noted that, in comparison with other ancient documents, the NT materials are embarrassingly rich. There are almost 5,000 MSS of part or all of the Greek NT, 8,000 MSS in Latin, and 1,000 additional MSS in other ancient versions. Extensive portions of the NT were copied within three centuries after the NT books were written. Indeed, the materials for recovering the original text of the NT are so vast that their study is a somewhat complicated task. Even in the Book of Revelation, the most poorly attested writing in the NT, more than 300 Greek MSS have been preserved.

GREEK MSS

The Greek MSS have traditionally been divided into four groups: papyri, uncials, minuscules, and lectionaries.

Papyri. The earliest NT MSS are written on papyrus. Since papyrus was a very fragile writing material, few of the early copies of the NT have survived except in the dry sands of Egypt. Papyrus MSS are designated by the letter *p* with a superscript numeral and range in date from ca. A.D. 125 (p^{52}, containing John 18:31–34, 37–38) to the early eighth century (p^{41}, p^{61}). Most papyri MSS of the NT date from the third and fourth centu-

---

6. I.e., authoritative writers and teachers of the early centuries.

ries. Fragments or large sections of approximately eighty-eight papyri are known. Every NT book is attested by at least one papyrus MS.[7]

Uncials. By the fourth century, parchment made from animal skins began to replace papyrus as the primary writing material. These early parchment MSS are called uncials, a term referring to the style of the Greek letters used in writing, which are similar to modern capital letters. Uncial MSS date from the fourth to the tenth centuries and are designated in two ways: by capital letters and by Arabic numerals with a zero prefixed. Approximately 274 uncials are known today. The most significant of these MSS include *Codex Sinaiticus* (Aleph, 01, 4th century), *Codex Alexandrinus* (A, 02, fourth century), *Codex Vaticanus* (B, 03, fourth century), *Codex Ephraemi Rescriptus* (C, 04, fourth century), and *Codex Bezae* (D, 05, late fifth century). Most uncial MSS contain large sections of the NT, such as the Gospels or the Pauline letters.[8]

Minuscule. In the ninth century, a style of writing developed out of the cursive or "running" hand that had been used for private writing. This new style was called minuscule, and it had the great advantage of allowing more rapid writing than the uncial style. By the end of the tenth century, the minuscule style of writing had virtually replaced the uncial. Minuscule MSS are designated by Arabic numerals, and approximately 2,500 of these are known today. The more significant minuscule MSS include Codex 1 (twelfth century), Codex 13 (thirteenth century), and Codex 33 (ninth century). The earlier minuscule MSS tend to be more carefully copied than the later ones and to have little or no ornamentation. Being comparatively late in date, few minuscule MSS have a text that is significant for determining the original reading. The vast majority of NT Greek MSS are minuscules.

Lectionaries. The Greek lectionaries are MSS that contain NT passages, not in regular sequence, but as weekly lessons for reading in the church at appointed times. There are about two thousand known lectionary MSS of the NT. They are designated either by the letter *l* or by the abbreviation *Lect.* The text of most lectionaries is quite similar to that found in the majority of minuscules. Many of the lectionary MSS date from the tenth century and later.

The original books of the NT were probably written on papyrus scrolls. However, because of the need to find specific passages quickly, the

---

7. Notable groups of papyri include the Chester Beatty papyri from the third century (p[45], p[46], p[47]) and the Bodmer collection, ranging in date from the late second to the seventh century (p[66], p[72], p[73], p[74], p[75]).

8. *Codex Sinaiticus* has the distinction of being the earliest surviving complete copy of the Greek NT.

scroll form was soon replaced by the codex, or leaf form. All extant MSS of the Greek NT are codices, although recently some scholars have tried without success to identify certain Greek fragments of scrolls discovered in Qumran with portions of the NT. The codex form allowed Christians to include several documents in a single book, and eventually copies of the entire NT were produced.

ANCIENT VERSIONS

During the second century, the Greek NT began to be translated into other languages. The most significant of these early versions for NT textual criticism are the Latin, Syriac, and Coptic.

The Latin versions include the Old Latin, stemming from North Africa, and the Latin Vulgate, a revision of the Old Latin made by Jerome in A.D. 386. The Syriac versions include the Old Syriac, preserved in two MSS, and the Palestinian Syriac, dated to the fifth century. The Coptic includes several dialects, including Sahidic, spoken in Upper (southern) Egypt, and Bohairic, spoken in Lower (northern) Egypt. Other versions of the NT include the Armenian, Georgian, Eghiopic, Gothic, and Arabic translations.

The importance of these ancient versions for NT textual criticism is somewhat limited. None of the original MSS of the versions are extant, and therefore existing MSS must be subjected to textual criticism to determine the original text as nearly as possible. In addition, some versions cannot reflect what the Greek might have read in certain types of variants. The Latin, for example, lacks the definite article, and the Syriac cannot distinguish between the aorist and perfect tenses. The great benefit of versional evidence is that it can show a particular reading was known in the place and time of the version's origin.[9]

CITATIONS FROM THE CHURCH FATHERS

Citations in the writings of the early church fathers furnish an additional basis for evaluating variants in the NT. Most of the ancient Christian writers wrote either in Greek or Latin. Their citations of the NT can establish how the text appeared in particular places and during particular periods in church history. As in the case of the versions, however, caution must be exercised when using patristic citations. It is often difficult to tell whether a scriptural text is being quoted directly or only being alluded to, and scribes would sometimes alter the texts of the fathers when copying them.

---

9. For example, a reading supported by the Old Latin would have been known in the West from at least the beginning of the second century.

THE HISTORY AND METHODS
OF TEXTUAL CRITICISM

To understand the various modern approaches to NT textual criticism, a sketch of the history of the subject is useful.

In the first three centuries after the Greek NT was written, the text of the NT developed rather freely. Scribes made copies from existing copies, and soon MSS assumed the textual peculiarities of other MSS. For example, in the Lord's Prayer (Matt. 6:13) some MSS contained the words "For yours is the kingdom and the power and the glory forever. Amen," while other MSS did not. In some MSS of Matthew 5:22 Jesus condemns the person who is angry "without a cause" (NKJV), while in other MSS the prohibition is total. Did Paul address the letter we call Ephesians to those living "in Ephesus" (some MSS lack these words in Eph. 1:1)? MSS containing certain readings soon arose in various locales, giving rise to the creation of MS families or "text types." Eventually, however, the NT writings were given canonical status, and scribes had less freedom to change the text. It is likely that most variants arose before the end of the second century.

By the seventh century, the use of Greek had all but disappeared, except in the Byzantine Empire. By the time of the printing press, the type of text used by the Greek Orthodox Church was the dominant form of the Greek text.

The first Greek NT was printed in Spain in 1514, but was not issued until 1522. It was part of a polyglot Bible edited by Cardinal Ximenes of Toledo.[10] Meanwhile, Erasmus of Rotterdam was preparing an edition of the Greek NT under the patronage of the Swiss printer Froben. Erasmus' NT was printed in Basel in 1516 after only six months of preparation. He based his text on a handful of late Byzantine MSS available to him, and he had to supply missing portions of the Book of Revelation. The same basic text was later published by Robert Estienne (Stephanus), Theodore Beza, and the Elzevir brothers. The preface to the 1633 edition contained the famous words: "Textum ergo habes, nunc ab omnibus receptum"—"You have therefore the text now received by all." From this statement arose the designation *Textus Receptus* (TR)—i.e., the received text. This text underlies the *King James Version* of 1611 and was the main Greek text until the publication the *English Revised Version* in 1881.[11]

---

10. The term *polyglot* means multilanguage.

11. The *Textus Receptus* and the Byzantine text are not exactly the same thing; the TR differs from the Byzantine text type in more than 1800 instances.

Building on the work of such scholars as Griesbach and Lachmann, B. F. Westcott and F. J. A. Hort inaugurated a new era in NT textual criticism with the publication in 1881 of their *New Testament in the Original Greek*. This edition of the Greek NT was accompanied by a volume carefully explaining the principles upon which they based their work. The Westcott and Hort text was based on MSS that differed considerably from those used by Erasmus. Westcott and Hort argued that the Byzantine text (which they called the Syrian text) was an edited text and that its readings are generally inferior to those found in the Alexandrian MSS. Since 1881, the majority of English translations of the NT—including the *Revised Standard Version*, the *New English Bible*, the *New International Version*, and the *New American Standard Bible*—have used a text that is much closer to the one published by Westcott and Hort than that issued by Erasmus. The main exception to this is the *New King James Version*.[12]

In the twentieth century, the NT in Greek has been edited by both Protestant and Roman Catholic scholars. The most widely used forms of the text are the Nestle-Aland *Novum Testamentum Graece* (26th ed.) and the United Bible Societies' *Greek New Testament* (4th ed.). A small number of scholars, arguing that the text underlying the *King James Version* is closest to the originals, have edited *The Greek New Testament According to the Majority Text* (1982). The many differences between the various witnesses to the text can be seen in notes provided in translations, such as "Other ancient authorities read . . ." or "Some manuscripts have . . . " Indeed, one of the great strengths of the *Revised Standard Version*, the *New Revised Standard Version*, and the *New American Standard Bible* is the number of variants cited in notes.

PRINCIPLES FOR ESTABLISHING THE ORIGINAL READING

As we have seen, textual criticism has developed certain principles for establishing the original reading based on both external and internal criteria. These principles cannot be unthinkingly applied, nor do all apply in each instance of textual variation. Nevertheless, familiarity with the basic

---

12. Major differences between the TR and a modern critical text include the omission or addition of substantial passages (Mark 16:9–20; John 7:53—8:11), the omission or addition of shorter passages (Matt. 6:13; Luke 9:56; Rom. 16:24), the substitution of a word (or words) for another (1 Tim. 3:16; Rev. 22:14), and the omission or addition of a single word or group of words (Matt. 6:4, 6; 1 Cor. 11:24; 1 John 3:1).

principles will increase one's ability to resolve a textual problem encountered in reading or exegesis.

EXTERNAL EVIDENCE

External evidence seeks to determine which reading is supported by the most reliable witnesses (Greek MSS, versions, and patristic citations). Most of these witnesses can be loosely grouped into one of three basic families or "text types" according to variant readings that occur in them.

Alexandrian Text. The Alexandrian text,[13] represented by the majority of papyri, several early uncial MSS (Aleph, B, C), the Coptic versions, and important Alexandrian fathers, is considered by most scholars to be the best text type. It is characterized by readings that are shorter and more difficult, and sometimes by refined grammatical corrections. Some scholars, however, have questioned the readings of the Alexandrian text type, especially where it stands alone. Moreover, the tendency among some scholars (mostly German) to regard this text type as a new "standard text" has not been well received in certain quarters.[14]

Western Text. The so-called Western text is represented by the uncial D (fifth century), the Old Latin, the Old Syriac, and a few other witnesses. It is characterized by harmonistic tendencies and additions. For example, the Western text of Acts is about 8 percent longer than the Alexandrian text of the same book. Scholars continue to debate both the origin and the value of the Western text, and most are hesitant to accept readings that contain only Western support.

Byzantine Text. The Byzantine text, represented by the vast majority of minuscule MSS and most of the later church fathers, is generally considered the least valuable text type. Its readings are often described as smooth and unobjectionable, and difficult readings appear to have been alleviated. A number of scholars, however, continue to champion the Byzantine text as the text closest to the originals, and even those scholars who prefer the Alexandrian text would be reluctant to reject a distinctively Byzantine reading automatically (though this is perhaps more lip service than a reality).

At one time scholars felt there was a fourth text type—the Caesarean. Today, however, there is little consensus as to the existence of this family of witnesses. Often the so-called Caesarean witnesses are subsumed under the Alexandrian text type.

---

13. So named because of its apparent emergence in and around Alexandria, Egypt.

14. In practical terms, this means that at any given point even the oldest MSS may be wrong.

The principles of external evidence include the following: (1) Prefer the reading attested by the oldest manuscripts. Of course, it is always possible that a later MS may preserve an early reading. It is the date of the *reading*, and not of the *MS*, that is important.[15] (2) Prefer the reading supported in widely separated geographical areas. A geographically widespread reading is more likely to be original than a reading preserved in only one locale. (3) Prefer the reading supported by the greatest number of text types. A consensus of witnesses—MSS, versions, and fathers—is necessary before it can be said a text type supports a particular reading. And it is the reading of the text type that is vital, not the reading preserved in only one or two witnesses from a text type.

INTERNAL EVIDENCE

The basic principle of internal evidence is that the reading from which the other readings could most easily have arisen is probably original. This principle has several corollaries: (1) The shorter reading is preferred, since scribes most often added to the text rather than omitted words.[16] (2) The more difficult reading is preferred, since scribes usually altered a difficult text to make it easier than vice versa. (3) The reading that best fits the author's style and diction is preferred. (4) The reading that best fits the context is preferred. (5) A reading that disagrees with a parallel passage is more likely to be original than a reading that harmonizes the parallels.

MODERN APPROACHES TO NT TEXTUAL CRITICISM

Of course, not all scholars consider the above principles equally valid or applicable to NT textual criticisms. Today, NT scholars use four approaches to textual criticism. These approaches may be called radical eclecticism, reasoned eclecticism, reasoned conservatism, and radical conservatism. The term *eclectic* means that the scholar tends to view each textual variant on its own merits instead of following one MS or group of MSS. The term *conservatism* here refers to a generally high view of the Byzantine text type and/or the Textus Receptus.

---

15. For example, MS 1739 (tenth century) preserves a text closely related to p[46] (ca. 200).

16. This principle must be used cautiously, since scribes sometimes omitted material accidentally or intentionally.

RADICAL ECLECTICISM

Radical eclecticism holds to what may be called a purely eclectic text. It prefers a text based solely on internal evidence. Adherents of this view argue that since the history of the NT text is untraceable, none of the text types carry any weight. Hence the reading of *any* MS may be original, since no MS or group of MSS is considered "best." This view, held primarily by a minority of British scholars, has been criticized for ignoring the value and importance of the external evidence, particularly the Greek witnesses.

REASONED ECLECTICISM

Reasoned eclecticism holds that the text of the NT is to be based on both internal and external evidence, without a preference for any particular MS or text type. In practice, however, this approach often represents a predilection for MSS of the Alexandrian text type. This preference is based largely on Westcott and Hort's theory that the Byzantine text is a conflation of the Alexandrian and Western text types, and that the superiority of the Alexandrian text over the Western text can be shown through internal evidence. Both the United Bible Societies' *Greek New Testament* and the Nestle-Aland *Novum Testamentum Graece* were produced by scholars who practiced reasoned eclecticism. This approach has been criticized for producing a new "Textus Receptus"—a canonized form of the NT text.

REASONED CONSERVATISM

What might be called reasoned conservatism holds that each of the main text types is equally early and independent, including the Byzantine text. Like reasoned eclecticism, reasoned conservatism sees both internal and external evidence as useful. However, unlike reasoned eclecticism, which tends to follow the Alexandrian text type, reasoned conservatism insists that no single text type can be preferred over all the others, and instead emphasizes the geographical distribution of the text types. Internal evidence plays an important, though confirmatory, role. This approach has been criticized for restoring the Byzantine text to a place of usefulness despite what most scholars feel is considerable evidence to the contrary.

RADICAL CONSERVATISM

Finally, the approach that may be called radical conservatism holds that the Byzantine, or majority, text represents the original text of the NT most accurately. Scholars who hold to this view prefer the reading of the majority of MSS. This approach has been severely criticized for being too mechanical and for ignoring the fact that MSS must be weighed and not just counted.

These four approaches to NT textual criticism may be summarized as follows:

1. Radical Eclecticism

   a. The text is based on internal evidence alone.

   b. No MS or group of MSS is to be preferred.

   c. The result is an "eclectic" text.

2. Reasoned Eclecticism

   a. The text is based on both internal and external evidence.

   b. The reading of the "best" MSS are generally preferred.

   c. The result is a "critical" text.

3. Reasoned Conservatism

   a. The text is based on both internal and external evidence.

   b. The reading of the majority of text types is preferred.

   c. The result is a "widespread" text.

4. Radical Conservatism

   a. The text is based on external evidence alone.

   b. The reading of the majority of MSS is preferred.

   c. The result is a "majority" text.

The study of NT textual criticism goes on, and much work remains to be done before reaching anything approaching a consensus view. Settling the question of the Byzantine text type seems essential before making progress. The relative weight to be given to internal and external evidence is another critical issue. In view of the absence today of a definitive history of the NT text, it is perhaps best to keep considerations of both internal and external in balance. In the end, NT textual criticism will always remain as much an art as it is a science.

HOW TO READ A TEXTUAL APPARATUS

Being able to read a textual apparatus is necessary for any work in NT textual criticism. Here we discuss both the United Bible Societies' *Greek New Testament* and the Nestle-Aland *Novum Testamentum Graece*. Of course, neither of these texts covers all of the MSS, versions, and fathers.

Instead, *representatives* of larger groups of witnesses are given. This is the best that a handy edition of the Greek NT can do.

THE UNITED BIBLE SOCIETIES' GREEK NEW TESTAMENT

The apparatus provided in this text is fairly simple to read. It is separated from the main text by a solid black line that runs across the entire page. Each set of notes is numbered, beginning with "1." This is followed by a boldfaced numeral that corresponds with the verse number in the text where the variant under discussion is found. The verse number is then followed by a bracket containing the letters A, B, C, or D. These letters indicate the relative certainty of the editors as to the reading printed in the text. ("A" indicates virtual certainty, "B" only some degree of doubt, "C" a considerable degree of doubt, and "D" a very high degree of doubt.) Following immediately is the reading that was adopted by the committee and printed in the text. The manuscript support that follows is listed in the following order: papyrus MSS, uncials, minuscules, lectionaries, versions, and fathers. Then comes the reading(s) rejected by the editors, preceded by a pair of vertical lines. For the symbols used in the apparatus, consult the introduction.

THE NESTLE-ALAND NOVUM TESTAMENTUM GRAECE

This apparatus is more compact than that found in the Bible Societies' NT and contains many more variants (the ratio is about 5 to1). The coverage of MSS is also less full, and usually only those readings not adopted in the text are cited. It uses symbols for the four major types of variants in the NT: additions, omissions, substitutions, and transpositions. A list of these symbols appears in the introduction. Since generally there are several variants listed for each verse, a black dot sets off additional variants in the same verse. Scholars and serious students prefer the Nestle-Aland edition of the Greek NT because it affords a glimpse at more variants and because the reader can easily identify the types of variants involved simply by noting the symbols used in the text.

EXAMPLES OF NT TEXTUAL CRITICISM

One of the best ways of learning about textual criticism is by working through a number of examples. The three variants discussed here are those the author has studied in detail.

MATTHEW 5:22

Our first exemplar comes from Matthew 5:22.[17] The internal evidence allows two possibilities. First, one could argue that the word *eikē* was added to Jesus' statement. This is the argument of Metzger, speaking for the committee that edited the United Bible Societies' *Greek New Testament* (p. 13): "Although the reading with *eikē* is widespread from the second century onwards, it is much more likely that the word was added by copyists in order to soften the rigor of the precept, than omitted as unnecessary." In other words, a scribe thought Jesus was being too rigid and so inserted the word to soften the statement.

However, the internal evidence may be understood in a different way. While it is true that Jesus' usual method of teaching was expressed in absolute and categorical terms, He sometimes laid down important qualifications in His teachings. In the same chapter of Matthew, Jesus states that His followers are blessed when people utter evil against them "falsely" (5:11). Here the verbal persecution is limited to what is produced "by lying" about the character of the disciples. Neither Jesus nor Peter (1 Pet. 3:13–17) was under the delusion that Christian suffering was always for doing good. Hence, it is possible that the shorter reading (minus the word *eikē*) in 5:22 is an erroneous "improvement" of the text intended to make *all* anger reprehensible. A scribe may have expunged the word *eikē* from his copy because he thought it was liable to be understood in a sense too indulgent to anger. Consequently, the internal evidence, as is so often the case, seems inconclusive.

Looking now at the external evidence, we see the shorter text has impressive support, mostly Alexandrian (p[67], Aleph, B, Vulgate). It competes, however, with a reading that is equally early and yet more widespread in its attestation. Behind the reading *eikē* are MSS of the Western, Byzantine, and Alexandrian text types, while the omission of *eikē* is supported almost exclusively by witnesses representing one locality (Egypt). Here the question of the relative weight to be given to the Byzantine text comes into play, as does the question of the relative merit of the Alexandrian text type. In this case external criteria seem to argue that the more widespread reading *eikē* has a slight edge over its more limited alternative.

---

17. See D. A. Black, "Jesus on Anger: The Text of Matthew 5:22a Revisited," *NovT* 30 (1988): 1–8.

JOHN 3:13

Another interesting problem involving textual variation occurs in John 3:13.[18] The NIV renders the verse as follows: "No one has ever gone into heaven except the one who came from heaven—the Son of Man." The margin indicates that some MSS add "who is in heaven" after the words "the Son of Man." This is an important variant, and it has significance for NT Christology. Did Jesus claim to be in heaven while talking to Nicodemus?

The external evidence may be summarized as follows:

1. The omission of "who is in heaven" is supported by a relatively small number of witnesses. This minority, however, comprises MSS generally considered to be of the highest quality: the fourth-century uncials Sinaiticus (Aleph) and Vaticanus (B). On the other hand, this reading is supported by a single text type, the Alexandrian.

2. The inclusion of "who is in heaven" is supported by nearly all the uncial and minuscule MSS of the NT extant in this portion of John, as well as by nearly every ancient version. The longer reading is also supported by the great majority of the earliest patristic witnesses, including the Alexandrian father Origen. In short, the reading "who is in heaven" was accepted as genuine over a wide geographical area, encompassing most of the then ancient world: Rome and the West, Greece, Syria and Palestine, and even Alexandria itself (where its omission also was known).

On the basis of external evidence, then, it appears the longer reading is to be preferred. But what about the internal evidence? Let us examine some of the criteria introduced earlier in this chapter.

Prefer the More Difficult Reading. Preference for the longer reading established on the basis of external evidence finds strong internal support from this principle, since the longer reading is obviously the more difficult one. It has Christ saying He was at that moment present both in heaven and on earth while talking with Nicodemus. The awkwardness of this saying explains the omission of the words "who is in heaven," as well as the origin of the two other minor variants in this verse: "who was in heaven," and "who is from heaven."

Prefer the Shorter Reading. Because scribes were more prone to add words than to omit them, the shorter reading is generally preferred. This fact, coupled with the assumed quality of the external evidence, was no

---

18. See Black, "The Text of John 3:13," *GTJ* 6 (1985): 49–66.

doubt crucial in the decision by the editors of the United Bible Societies' *Greek New Testament* to relegate the words "who is in heaven" to the apparatus. However, this principle states that the shorter reading is to be preferred *unless* the scribe either accidentally omitted material or else intentionally omitted material on stylistic, grammatical, or doctrinal grounds. Therefore, although the longer reading may indeed reflect later christological development, it is also possible the words were found objectionable or superfluous and omitted on that basis. In view of this possibility, the longer reading deserves serious consideration even on the basis of this principle of textual criticism.

Prefer the Verbally Dissident Reading. Some scholars have argued that the words "who is in heaven" were added on the model of John 1:18: "No one has ever seen God, but God the One and Only, who is at the Father's side, has made him known." However, the statement in 1:18 is neither directly parallel with 3:13 nor does it belong to the same historical context as the discourse in John 3. It seems this "parallel" is not a true parallel at all.

Prefer the Reading that Best Accounts for the Others. Had the readings "who was in heaven" or "who is from heaven" been original, there is no reason why a scribe would have altered the text. If however, the longer text is original, one can easily understand the other variants as attempts to modify or, in the case of the shorter text, to remove altogether a difficult expression.

There now remains the matter of what the author was more likely to have written. In this regard one must take into account (1) a reading's harmony with the author's teaching elsewhere and (2) a reading's harmony with the author's style and vocabulary.

The Author's Theology. It is true that the longer reading represents a high Christology. Did John share such a view? The answer is plain: the Johannine Jesus is not only the preexistent Word (1:1) and the post-resurrection exalted Christ (20:28), but also the Revealer who remained "with God" while present on earth (1:1, 14). John's Jesus did not cease to be what He was before the incarnation, for the flesh assumed by the Word was the "tabernacle" in which God was pleased to dwell (1:14). Thus, the words "who is in heaven" fit perfectly into the pattern of Johannine Christology.

The Author's Style. A general knowledge of an author's style often will help determine whether a particular variant reading is in harmony with the rest of the author's writings. A check of a Greek concordance reveals the clause "who is in heaven" faithfully reflects characteristics of Johannine style, grammar, and vocabulary. Six of the eleven occurrences of the participle "who is" with a prepositional phrase appear in the Fourth Gospel (1:18; 3:31; 6:47; 8:47; 12:17; 18:37). Elsewhere, the construction appears only in Matthew 12:30; Luke 11:23; Romans 9:5; 2 Corinthians 11:31; and Ephesians 2:4. It appears this usage is not only Johannine but almost exclusively so in the NT. Hence, there is no linguistic evidence why John could not have written these words, and, indeed, he is given over to the repetition of such a construction.

In summary, although much can be said for certain arguments in favor of the shorter reading in John 3:13, the inclusion of the disputed words appears to be the best solution since it is supported by significant external and internal evidence and since it retains a great deal of John's original use of the term "Son of Man." Therefore, this witness to Christ's deity, on our reading of the evidence, is not a mere dogma handed down by the church but is a witness deriving from Jesus Himself, from His own teaching about Himself, and verified by John the apostle. His record is that the Son of Man, who has come down from heaven, speaks truthfully about heavenly realities as a man speaks about his own home, for the incarnation did not—indeed could not—denude heaven of the Son's presence.

EPHESIANS 1:1

A final example of a textual problem comes from Ephesians 1:1.[19] Are the words "in Ephesus" original or not? Here again the external evidence seems to favor the inclusion of the disputed words—the reading is both early and widespread. Why, then, would anyone want to omit the words? One possibility is that a scribe excised the words to make the letter a universal writing, intended for the church at large rather than for a specific congregation. Recent scholarship has shown that the early church struggled with the peculiarity of the Pauline Epistles. The issue was, How can we read a letter as applicable to our situation when that letter was originally written for and sent to another church? The easiest way to resolve this problem was to omit any reference to a place name in the prescript. The same phenomenon can be seen in Romans 1:7, 15, where the words "in Rome" are omitted in some MSS. Later, when the Pauline Letters came to be regarded as Scripture to be read and used by all, this somewhat mechanical way of resolving the problem disappeared.

These are but three examples out of many instances of textual variation in the Greek NT. You will encounter many more in your reading and study. The field of NT textual criticism is a demanding one, but it is not an impossible one, even for beginners. If you will consult the "For Further Reading" section listed below and begin working through one of the standard introductions to the field, you will be off to a good start.

---

19. See Black, "The Peculiarities of Ephesians and the Ephesian Address," *GTJ* 2 (1981): 59–73.

DEALING WITH TEXTUAL PROBLEMS IN PREACHING

A final matter concerns the rather delicate issue of how to deal with variant readings from the pulpit. Anyone who preaches from the NT regularly will need to know something about textual criticism. Just as importantly, preachers need to proceed with caution when discussing textual problems in public. The Byzantine text served as the basis for the *King James Version*, but almost every other translation uses a more modern, critical text. Differences between versions could become an issue in one's pulpit ministry.

Often there will be no need to discuss textual variants when preaching. When the issue cannot be avoided, however, keep the discussion brief, remembering that most laypeople have no knowledge of Greek. Help them to see that most variants are insignificant, and no doctrine of Scripture rests on a disputed passage. Discuss only those variants that are relevant to the teaching text. Always consult Metzger's *Textual Commentary* and other commentaries. And finally, whatever the textual problem, do not be afraid to tackle it on your own—the reward will be the discovery of the actual words of the New Testament!

FOR FURTHER READING

Aland, Kurt and Barbara, *The Text of the New Testament*. 2d ed. Translated by Erroll F. Rhodes. Grand Rapids: Eerdmans, 1989.

Black, David Alan. "Jesus on Anger: The Text of Matthew 5:22a Revisited." *NovT* 30 (1988): 1–8.

———. *New Testament Textual Criticism: A Concise Introduction*. Grand Rapids: Baker, 1994.

———. "The Peculiarities of Ephesians and the Ephesian Address." *GTJ* 2 (1981): 59–73.

———, ed. *Scribes and Scripture: New Testament Essays in Honor of J. Harold Greenlee*. Winona Lake: Eisenbrauns, 1992.

———. "The Text of John 3:13." *GTJ* 6 (1985): 49–66.

Comfort, Philip W. *Early Manuscripts and Modern Translations of the New Testament*. Wheaton: Tyndale, 1990.

Epp, Eldon J. "Textual Criticism." In *The New Testament and Its Modern Interpreters*. Edited by E. J. Epp and G. W. MacRae. Atlanta: Scholars, 1989.

Fee, Gordon D. "The Textual Criticism of the New Testament." In EBC, vol. 1. Edited by F. E. Gaebelein. Grand Rapids: Zondervan, 1979.

Finegan, Jack. *Encountering New Testament Manuscripts.* Grand Rapids: Eerdmans, 1974.

Greenlee, J. Harold, *Introduction to New Testament Textual Criticism.* Grand Rapids: Eerdmans, 1964.

———. *Scribes, Scrolls, and Scripture.* Grand Rapids: Eerdmans, 1985.

Hodges, Zane C. and Farstad, A. L. eds. *The Greek New Testament According to the Majority Text.* Nashville: Nelson, 1982.

Holmes, Michael W. "Textual Criticism." In *New Testament Criticism and Interpretation.* Edited by D. A. Black and D. S. Dockery. Grand Rapids: Zondervan, 1991.

Metzger, Bruce M. *The Early Versions of the New Testament.* Oxford: Clarendon, 1977.

———. *A Textual Commentary on the Greek New Testament.* New York: United Bible Societies, 1971.

———. *The Text of the New Testament.* 3d. ed. New York: Oxford, 1992.

Streeter, B. H. *The Four Gospels.* London: Macmillan, 1924.

Sturz, Harry A. *The Byzantine Text-type and New Testament Textual Criticism.* Nashville: Nelson, 1984.

Westcott, B. F. and Hort, F. J. A. *The New Testament in the Original Greek,* [ii] *Introduction* [and] *Appendix.* Cambridge: Macmillan, 1881.

413

XX

HISTORICAL CRITICISM
OF THE NEW TESTAMENT

CRAIG L. BLOMBERG

A Christian, relatively young in the faith, was reading her New Testament for the first time from start to finish. She had completed the Gospel of Matthew and was now rereading many of the same episodes from the life of Christ in Mark's Gospel. She got to the account of Jesus walking on the water and recalled how puzzled she had been by it when reading Matthew's version. Trying to determine how it might apply to her life, she had noticed that Peter temporarily had been able to imitate his Lord by walking on the waves. She thought perhaps Matthew 14:31 was the key and that the point of the story was the power of faith. But she also had been impressed by v. 33. Since she doubted she could ever defy the power of gravity, no matter how strong her faith, she wondered if perhaps the message of the miracle really centered on worshiping Jesus as Son of God. But now Mark's account seemed flatly to contradict Matthew. Mark 14:52 was saying nothing about worship or belief but rather that the disciples did not understand and had hardened hearts! How was a person to make sense of all of this?

This young woman's perplexity reflects the regular experience of many believers, old and young, as they read parts of the New Testament, and particularly the historical books, the Gospels and Acts. One of the keys to solving these riddles is to understand and appropriate the insights of historical criticism.

THE MEANING OF HISTORICAL CRITICISM

The term "historical criticism" may mean several things. For some, it is synonymous with historical background—understanding the political, religious and cultural events and institutions of the time and place of the writing of a given book of Scripture. But these items are treated elsewhere in this volume. For others, historical criticism involves the determination of the author, date, audience, and purposes of a given biblical work. For still others, historical criticism refers to the historical-critical method. This method, developed toward the end of the nineteenth century, particularly by the German philosopher Ernst Troeltsch, put forward three criteria for analyzing biblical history: criticism, analogy, and correlation. The principle of criticism adopted a strategy of "methodical doubt," of being inherently suspicious of the historical accuracy of any narrative unless strong corroborative evidence could be put forward. It also emphasized that all judgments as to whether certain things happened were based on degrees of probability. Absolute certainty in such matters was unobtainable. The principle of analogy required that the past resemble the present. The principle of correlation stressed a closed continuum of cause and effect in the universe.

These last two principles effectively ruled out a theistic worldview and a transcendent God who could intervene in the affairs of this world. These principles thus undermined the credibility of miracles and the supernatural. Not surprisingly, many Christians have resisted this understanding of the historical-critical method and have even offered convincing refutations of it, although it has remained a staple in scholarly research outside of evangelical circles. But although many, and perhaps most, writers who today speak of historical criticism refer to something like what Troeltsch advocated: a fourth sense in which one may use the expression. In this usage, historical criticism is viewed as the opposite of literary criticism. In fact, there is a growing debate among scholars today about which of these two approaches should be primary and even if both are simultaneously legitimate. This volume assumes they are and treats them consecutively in separate chapters.

By historical criticism as opposed to literary criticism, we mean the study or analysis of the historical development of a given text as opposed to an ahistorical analysis of the text in its final form. ("Criticism" does not necessarily mean to criticize.) In other words, historical criticism as

415

described in the rest of this chapter refers to a study of the particular sources, both written and oral, which a writer used; of the ways, if any, in which those sources were modified prior to the writing of the text as we know it; and of the processes of selection, abbreviation, and expansion, which the apostolic writers as editors utilized to shape their material into the specific twenty-seven books which form the complete New Testament (NT) canon. Literary criticism, on the other hand, raises questions about the genre, plot, theme, motifs, or character development of the finished products, largely apart from the historical processes which led to their formation. More avant-garde literary critics also apply techniques such as structuralism, reader-response criticism, and deconstruction, which look for meaning, respectively, in the text, in the interaction between text and reader, and almost wholly in the reader's mind, apart from historical constraints.

THREE CATEGORIES
OF HISTORICAL CRITICISM

For our purposes historical criticism may be subdivided into three categories: source criticism, form criticism, and redaction criticism. These tools do not presuppose any particular view of biblical inspiration but they need not conflict with such beliefs. Historical criticism is not an alternative approach to believing that God inspired the biblical writers; rather, it suggests the most probable ways in which those writers, under the superintendence of the Holy Spirit (2 Pet. 1:21), went about their work. Luke 1:1–4 makes it clear that at least one NT writer self-consciously utilized these three methods: "Many have undertaken to draw up an account of the things that have been fulfilled among us" (written sources), "just as they were handed down to us by those who from the first were eyewitnesses and servants of the word" (a period of oral transmission of the Jesus' words and deeds). "Therefore, since I myself have carefully investigated everything from the beginning, it seemed good also to me to write an orderly account for you, most excellent Theophilus, so that you may know the certainty of the things you have been taught"* (Luke's purposeful selection of these sources and traditions to produce his Gospel). The similarities among the four Gospels make it likely that Matthew, Mark, and John shared these techniques. Luke's somewhat parallel preface to Acts (1:1–2) suggests he probably followed similar procedures there. Source, form, and redaction (editorial) criticism, as these three stages of historical criticism

---

* Unless otherwise noted, Scripture quotations in this chapter are from the NIV.

have come to be called, prove less prominent in the study of the epistles and Revelation, but they may at times be applied with profit there as well. We will look at each of these three methods in turn.

SOURCE CRITICISM

Source criticism attempts to establish the written or oral sources which a given biblical writer may have used in compiling his work. Because of the clear interrelationship of the Gospels, particularly the first three Synoptic Gospels (so-called because a synopsis or "together-look" at their parallels quickly demonstrates their similarities outweigh their differences), source criticism has focused most of its attention here. The early church, often citing the testimony of Papias (as quoted in Eusebius, *H.E.* 3.39.16) and St. Augustine, frequently assumed the Gospels were written in the order in which they now appear in the canon and each successive author knew and utilized the Gospels written by his predecessors. At the beginning of the rise of modern biblical criticism in the late eighteenth century, an influential view was that of J. J. Griesbach, who believed Mark was the latest of the three Synoptics, abridging and combining Matthew and Luke. From the nineteenth century on, the hypothesis that has dominated scholarly circles makes the Book of Mark the earliest, with Matthew and Luke both dependent on it. The classic expression of this view came in 1924 by B. H. Streeter, who defended the "four document hypothesis." For Streeter, Matthew and Luke not only borrowed from Mark but also from a lost "sayings source," called Q (from the German word for "source," *Quelle*), accounting for the material they have in common but not found in Mark. Additionally, Matthew and Luke each relied on sources unique to their respective Gospels, designated M and L.[1]

In the last thirty years, a vocal minority of scholars spearheaded by William R. Farmer have tried to revive the "Griesbach hypothesis." [2] But for the most part, their arguments have not convinced most scholars. Others have more profitably explored ways of harmonizing the ancient church tradition with the consensus of modern scholarship, so that Matthew may be given credit for producing some previous draft of his Gospel (perhaps even Q) in Hebrew or Aramaic. The Greek Matthew then becomes a thorough revision of this document incorporating later elements from Mark as well.[3] But a variety of reasons convince most that "Markan priority" (Mark being written first) best accounts for the largest amount of the

---

1. B. H. Streeter, *The Four Gospels: A Study of Origins* (London: Macmillan, 1924).
2. See esp. his *The Synoptic Problem* (New York: Macmillan, 1964).
3. Cf. Craig L. Blomberg, *Matthew* in NAC (Nashville: Broadman, 1992).

data. Some of the most important of these are (1) Mark's detail often seems more vivid than in Matthew and Luke. (2) His grammar is often the roughest, having been smoothed out by later writers. (3) Potentially embarrassing details about the life of Jesus are toned down in the later Gospels. (4) Mark is the shortest Gospel and almost all of his material is duplicated in Matthew or Luke; if he had not written first, there would have been little point in his having written at all. (5) Matthew and Luke rarely deviate in the same way at the same time in sequence or wording from Mark. (6) There is no other good explanation of Mark's "omission" of all the so-called Q material. (7) The types of changes Matthew and Luke would have made if they followed Mark fall into demonstrable patterns; the same is not true on assumptions which do not place Mark first.

The Q-hypothesis has not garnered as widespread acclaim as Markan priority but it remains the favorite of a fair consensus of scholars. It seems less likely that Matthew or Luke directly depended on each other for material they share not found in Mark, because Matthew's wording often seems closer to Jesus' Aramaic speech, while Luke's arrangement of materials often seems closer to the original context. But the amount of verbatim parallelism between Matthew and Luke is also less than the amount either parallels Mark, so it may be that Q is more than one source or some combination of written and oral sources. The M and L hypotheses are even more tentative and viewed by many simply as conventional designations for material unique to these Gospels, without presupposing much about its form, if any, prior to its appearance in the Gospels.

Source criticism of John and Acts rests on far shakier grounds than source criticism of the Synoptics. A majority today favors the independence of John from the Synoptics, though on those occasions where they do overlap (e.g., the feeding of the five hundred, the walking on the water, and the passion narrative) some kind of dependence may be postulated. Theories about hypothetical sources accounting for the miracles or "signs" in John and, to a lesser extent, for the Fourth Gospel's extended discourses or sermons of Jesus also have proved popular. Others have postulated two, three, and even five stages of editing for the Gospel of John. In Acts, attention has focused primarily on the sections in which Luke lapses into first-person plural narrative ("we" did such-and-such). Suggestions have ranged from seeing these sections as part of Luke's own diary to viewing them as complete fabrications following a fictional genre of "travel narrative." The problem with John and Acts is that both final forms demonstrate too much homogeneity of style to make theories about sources very plausible apart from hard data of parallel accounts with which one might compare them. It is no doubt probable that both works employed sources but not likely that we will recover them with any degree of verifiability.

When one turns to the Epistles and Revelation, source criticism becomes even more tentative. Still, it may prove valuable in places. Various creeds (confessions, hymns) often have been isolated in the Epistles, when one encounters tightly packed, poetically structured catalogs of key christological affirmations. Doubtless the most well-known is Philippians 2:6–11. Analyzed in several ways, most helpful is that which arranges these verses into two stanzas (vv. 6–8, 9–11), each with three strophes of three lines each, with each line having approximately three accented syllables in Greek. Such a division also fits the major conceptual breaks of the passage (Christ's incarnation [pre-existence, condescension, suffering] followed by His exaltation [restoration, authority, confession]) and allows us to notice the one line which does not fit into this pattern: "even death on a cross" (v. 8d). It may well be that Paul took over a well-known confession or hymn in the early church and added a line to it, which would have thus stood out. When one realizes that in 1 Corinthians 2:2 Paul identifies the crucifixion as the center of his proclamation, this hypothesis becomes all the more probable. The extent of Christ's willingness to suffer for humanity thus becomes the most emphasized part of these six verses.[4]

Source criticism of the Epistles also may be applied to explain the relationship between 2 Peter and Jude. Most of the Epistle of Jude reappears in the middle (chap. 2) of 2 Peter. Most scholars believe Jude was written first and 2 Peter borrowed and adapted much of Jude's material. Again, no good explanation appears for why Jude would have been written at all if 2 Peter came first. Scholars who believe some of the Epistles attributed to Paul were written by later Christians who at times imitated Paul's style and contents are inclined to apply source criticism, for example, to determine how the allegedly pseudonymous writer of Ephesians used and adapted the genuinely Pauline Epistle to the Colossians. Or they may discuss how the writer of the Pastoral Epistles (1 and 2 Tim. and Titus) incorporated fragments of Paul's authentic memoirs into correspondence for a Christian audience a generation after Paul's life.

Most of the value of source criticism is indirect. By itself, it rarely yields any results for exegesis or interpretation. But, as in the example of Philippians 2:6–11, determining what part of a passage comes from a source and what part was added by a biblical writer may help us determine where the emphasis in the passage lies. Understanding the major emphases of the Synoptic Gospels relies heavily on this process, which actually combines

---

4. This analysis of Philippians 2:6–11 finds its original impetus in Ernst Lohmeyer, *Kyrios Jesus: Eine Untersuchung zu Phil. 2,5–11* (Heidelberg: Winter, 1928).

source criticism with redaction criticism (see the section "Redaction Criticism" below). Determining the order of composition of two or more writings also has direct bearing on the determination of the date or historical circumstances of those books. If Luke used Mark, Mark must have been written before Luke. But many readers of Luke-Acts, struggling to account for Acts' abrupt ending, have assumed Luke wrote Acts immediately after the last events he narrated (ca. A.D. 62). This means the Gospel of Luke preceded Acts and that Mark wrote even earlier, perhaps in the late fifties. Other Bible students find compelling evidence for dating Mark in the late sixties as Christians in Rome were suffering under Nero's persecution; they thus push Luke-Acts at at least into the seventies after Rome's conquest of Jerusalem. These decisions *can* affect interpretation of specific passages. For example, if Luke wrote Luke 21:20 after A.D. 70, he probably intended it as a comment on the events of that year and as an editorial explanation of what Jesus meant by His more cryptic references to "the abomination that causes desolation," as Mark's parallel phrases it (Mark 13:14). In sum, source criticism, not all that exciting in its own right for most students, becomes an indispensable foundation for form and redaction criticism, which have more direct bearing on interpretation.

FORM CRITICISM

New Testament form criticism came into its own in the 1920s through 1940s. Three German scholars pioneered the method: K. L. Schmidt, Martin Dibelius, and Rudolf Bultmann.[5] Form critics moved beyond source critics to study the period of oral tradition in which stories about what Jesus did and said circulated and took on stereotyped form. Depending on when the earliest Gospel (usually agreed by form critics to be Mark) was dated, this period might have lasted from twenty to forty years. Form critics assumed the various accounts of Jesus' words and deeds were passed on in relatively small, isolated units, and these units were reshaped, abbreviated, and embellished as they were told and retold.

Often form critics believed the most common tendency of the oral tradition was what Bultmann called "the law of increasing distinctness"[6]— short forms became longer and more detailed, names were given to name-

---

5. K. L. Schmidt, *Der Rahmen der Geschichte Jesu* (1919; reprint, Darmstadt: Wissenschaftliche Buchgesellschaft, 1969); Martin Dibelius, *From Tradition to Gospel* (Cambridge: James Clarke, 1934 [German orig. 1919]); Rudolf Bultmann, *The History of the Synoptic Tradition* (Oxford: Blackwell, 1963 [German orig. 1921])

6. Rudolf Bultmann, "The New Approach to the Synoptic Problem," in *Existence and Faith*, ed. Schubert M. Ogden (New York: Meridian, 1960 [German orig. 1926]), 41–42.

less characters, legendary embellishments filled in gaps in the stories, and so on. It was usually assumed details were changed to make sense in a more Hellenistic, less Jewish world and narratives were reworded to explain or remove distinctively Semitic features. "Laws" established from the analysis of other oral folklore from antiquity[7] were perceived to be operative in the Gospel tradition as well—for example, the laws of "end-stress" (the end of a passage is its climax), of economy of staging (seldom do more than two or three characters gain central focus in a given passage), and of grouping together like forms (a series of parables would have been told together; so, too, a series of miracle stories).

With these kinds of presuppositions, form critics developed a threefold agenda. First, they sought to classify all the Gospel materials according to form. Common forms included parables, pronouncement or conflict stories, proverbs, discourses, "I-sayings," sentences of holy law, miracle stories, and various passages which were often labeled legends or myths (not always meaning that they were historically untrustworthy). Second, form critics tried to establish a *sitz im leben* ("life-situation") in the early church which would have most likely generated interest in preserving and using a given form. Parables likely formed part of popular storytelling, conflict stories would have proved invaluable in the Christian-Jewish polemic of the latter half of the first century, and miracle stories no doubt provided good ammunition in witnessing to Gentiles who commonly believed in "divine men" or deified heroes. Third, form critics attempted to determine how a given form or passage had been modified by the tradition as it was passed along orally.

First Objective. Strictly speaking, the first form-critical objective lies more in the domain of literary criticism than of historical criticism. Determining form functions on the micro-level of a narrative the way determining genre functions on the macro-level. Important interpretive principles adhere to distinct forms. One cannot interpret a parable in exactly the same way as a proverb or historical account. Here is perhaps the most significant legacy of form criticism but also the one which has the least to do with historical criticism.

Second Objective. Objectives two and three remain in the historical arena. But here form critics stand on shakier ground. The principle of determining a *sitz im leben* in the early church is well-intentioned, but often the data prove simply too sparse for us to know in what contexts a given form would have most likely been used. The laws of oral folklore

---

7. See esp. Axel Olrik, "Epic Laws of Folk Narrative," in *The Study of Folklore*, ed. Alan Dundes (Englewood Cliffs, N.J.: Prentice-Hall, 1965 [German orig. 1909]), 129–41.

prove helpful in certain instances—climaxes usually do come at the ends of narratives—but in other cases rest on faulty assumptions. Most notably, it has been shown in more recent years that a principle of "decreasing distinctness" or abbreviation of detailed narratives was actually more common than any of the alleged laws of increasing distinctness.[8] What is more, it has become clear that the most relevant analogies of the transmission of oral tradition in ancient cultures emphasize memorization and preservation of historically accurate information, albeit within certain flexible parameters, much more so than the first form critics recognized.[9]

Third Objective. Objective three has most left its mark, however, in the practice of what is often termed "tradition history" or "tradition criticism." Here "criteria of authenticity" are utilized to determine to what extent the wording of a given passage in the Gospels reflects what Jesus actually did and said. The three most common of these are the criteria of dissimilarity, multiple attestation, and coherence. Most tradition critics have adopted Troeltsch's principle of methodical doubt and assumed that a given part of the Gospels is inauthentic unless sufficient reason can be shown for accepting it as authentic. This approach reverses the normal procedure of ancient historians in which one usually assumes the testimony of history-writers to be reliable unless specific reasons emerge to believe otherwise.[10]

The criterion of dissimilarity allows one to accept a passage as authentic (i.e., an event really happened or certain words were really spoken) if it noticeably diverges both from prevailing patterns of first-century Judaism and from common tendencies of the early church. Unfortunately, all that the use of this criterion accomplishes is to determine what was distinctive about Jesus' behavior and teaching. By definition, that which He held in common with other Jews of His day or areas in which the church adequately imitated or obeyed Him would not pass this criterion of authenticity.

The criterion of multiple attestation places more weight on sayings or narratives which occur in more than one Gospel, in more than one Gospel

---

8. Leslie R. Keylock, "Bultmann's Law of Increasing Distinctness," in *Current Issues in Biblical and Patristic Interpretation*, ed. Gerald F. Hawthorne (Grand Rapids: Eerdmans,1975), 193–210.

9. See esp. Birger Gerhardsson, *Memory and Manuscript* (Lund: Gleerup, 1961); Albert B. Lord, "The Gospels as Oral Traditional Literature," in *The Relationships Among the Gospels*, ed. William O. Walker, Jr. (San Antonio: Trinity University, 1978), 33–91; Rainer Riesner, *Jesus als Lehrer* (Tübingen: Mohr, 1981).

10. Cf. further Stewart C. Goetz and C. L. Blomberg, "The Burden of Proof," *JSNT* 11 (1981): 39–63.

source (Mark, Q, M, L), or in more than one form. This criterion more closely approximates to what other ancient historians do, but unless the burden of proof is shifted to the skeptic, singly attested material may be unnecessarily excluded. The criterion of coherence accepts as authentic that which is consistent with material authenticated by one of the two previous criteria. This criterion is valid but highly subjective. One reader will perceive a contradiction where another sees a possibility for harmonization.

Not surprisingly, form criticism when used as a historical tool (as opposed to a literary tool) has yielded largely negative results concerning the historicity of the Gospels. Bultmann and Dibelius believed that only a small percentage of the material in the Gospels remained legitimate data for reconstructing a life of Christ or understanding the historical Jesus. An organization of several dozen of the most radical scholars in North America today, known as the Jesus Seminar, reflects the heritage of this brand of form criticism. Using these and other criteria of authenticity, the seminar has produced a four-color-coded edition of the Gospels—red letters for words and events which almost certainly happened as recorded; pink for those which may have happened but on which there is less certainty; gray for those which probably didn't happen as claimed; and black for those which almost certainly did not happen. The vast majority of the Gospel of John is black, and red letters account for only a small percentage of material even in the Synoptic Gospels. Interestingly, the parables come through less scathed than any other portion of Jesus' words and deeds.[11]

Clearly the average Christian reader of the NT has no time for this brand of radical form criticism, and rightly so. It is based on unfounded methodological skepticism and inadequate criteria. On the other hand, a comparison of parallel accounts of the same events as described by different Gospel writers makes it clear that the accounts of Jesus' life did develop over time. One cannot speak of modern degrees of precision in historical reporting when analyzing ancient documents. In languages and cultures that knew nothing of quotation marks and lacked the recording devices which today enable preservation of massive amounts of exact detail about current events, it was considered entirely acceptable to paraphrase, abridge, interpret, rearrange, and combine historical materials together in ways which often seem too "free and loose" to modern readers. Still, the ancients also had constraints. An oft-debated quotation from the Greek historian Thucydides seems to allow historians to invent speeches for his-

---

11. Robert W. Funk, Bernard B. Scott, James R. Butts, *The Parables of Jesus: Red Letter Edition* (Sonoma, Calif.: Polebridge, 1988). This volume illustrates the format of the Seminar's subsequent work as well.

torical characters whose discourses they had not personally heard while at the same time requiring that those invented discourses remain true to what was known of the speaker's views and character and cast in a form appropriate to the context of the speech (1.22.1).[12]

A sober and cautious appropriation of form criticism can therefore remain valuable in accounting for the differences among Gospel parallels without resorting to charges of contradiction. For example, when Matthew describes the two-day incident of the withered fig tree (Matt. 21:18–22; cf. Mark 11:12–14, 20–25), without inserting the intervening temple cleansing, he is likely following the way the oral tradition would have retold these stories. Whatever the actual chronology, it would have been natural to tell the two parts to the one story together and to omit mention of the intervening day. Matthew allows for a day's interval between Matthew 21:19–20, even if he does not call attention to it. He frequently chooses to group his material together topically rather than chronologically and common historiographical convention of the day, and he must be evaluated by the standards of his day and not ours.

As with source criticism, form criticism is best known in NT for its applications to the Gospels, and particularly to the Synoptics. But numerous forms have been isolated in the other NT writings as well. Thucydides' comments, noted above, are often brought to bear on the question of the historicity of the speeches in Acts. Epistolary creeds or confessions can be analyzed according to their literary form and tradition. The use of "midrash" (a Hebrew word for commentary), referring to various forms of OT quotations or allusions and their elaboration in various NT texts, has received considerable attention. Acts 20, 2 Timothy, and 2 Peter all seem to contain "farewell discourses." Elements of "diatribe" (hypothetical questions posed by an imaginary objector followed by their answer) can be discerned throughout Romans (cf. Jas. 2:14–26). Col. 3:18—4:1, Eph. 5:22—6:9, and 1 Pet. 2:13—3:7) all present *Haustafeln* ("domestic codes")—principles for submission and leadership in conventional social hierarchies such as government, marriage, slavery, and child-raising.

Each of these and many other forms find parallels in extra-biblical Jewish and/or Greco-Roman literature. Comparing them can help us understand what biblical writers shared with their surrounding cultures and how they were distinct. For example, the most striking difference between the three domestic codes listed above and their Jewish or pagan counterparts is the amount and nature of instruction given to the authority figure in

---

12. For a "both/and" interpretation of these remarks, see Stanley E. Porter, "Thucydides 1.22.1 and Speeches in Acts: Is There a Thucydidean View?" *NovT* 32 (1990): 121–42.

each relationship—not to take advantage of those under them but actually to defer to their subordinates for the good of the latter. Whatever we decide about the difficult question of whether hierarchical relationships remain normative for all time, we dare not neglect the way Christianity most distinctively modified this literary form—stressing the reciprocal responsibilities of husbands, fathers, and masters.

Most students can become convinced that form criticism offers more immediate benefits for the novice interpreter (despite the common pitfalls into which its more radical practitioners have landed) than does source criticism, however necessary the latter is as a foundation for the former. But when so much of form criticism's use as a historical tool called into question the NT's trustworthiness, it is scarcely surprising that a backlash should ensue. Beginning in the 1950s, several of Bultmann's students, most notably Ernst Käsemann, called for a "new quest for the historical Jesus" which would adopt less-skeptical criteria than classic form criticism.[13] The result was the rise of modern redaction criticism, still the most significant and influential of the three major schools of historical criticism surveyed here. It is to this final critical development which we now turn.

REDACTION CRITICISM

As with form criticism, three influential German scholars are usually credited with giving the initial impetus of redaction criticism major momentum: Günther Bornkamm for Matthew, Marxsen for Mark, and Hans Conzelmann for Luke.[14]

Each of these scholars analyzed the Gospels from the standpoint or conviction that the evangelists were not mere scissors-and-paste compilers of tradition but self-conscious editors, imposing their own distinct theological stamps onto their accounts of the life of Jesus, by means of what they included, excluded, or modified from the written sources and oral traditions they had inherited. As with form criticism, many radical practitioners of redaction criticism have so emphasized the differences among the Gospels and the divergent theologies which emerge so as to deny any possibility of widespread historical trustworthiness or harmonization of apparent contradictions. In response, a few very conservative scholars have

---

13. Ernst Käsemann, "The Problem of the Historical Jesus," in *Essays on New Testament Themes* (London: SCM, 1964 [German orig. 1954]), 15–47.

14. Günther Bornkamm, Gerhard Barth, and Hans-Joachim Held, *Tradition and Interpretation in Matthew* (London: SCM, 1963); Willi Marxsen, *Mark the Evangelist* (Nashville: Abingdon, 1969); Hans Conzelmann, *The Theology of St. Luke* (New York: Harper & Row, 1960).

called the entire method of redaction criticism into question. But when applied in a balanced fashion, without presupposing the unreliability of the biblical text, redaction criticism can be perhaps the most powerful of the three main branches of historical criticism.

Thinking Horizontally. A helpful way of subdividing the task of the redaction critic is to speak of "thinking horizontally" and "thinking vertically."[15] The expression "thinking horizontally" utilizes the imagery of a student perusing a Gospel synopsis or harmony, in which parallel accounts of the same events in different Gospels are laid out in parallel columns. This enables the reader to scan horizontally across the page to see the ways each evangelist narrated any given story and thus to observe the similarities and differences. A major tenet of redaction criticism is that wherever one Gospel differs from its sources, it most likely does so deliberately and often for theological reasons. Thus, when Matthew adds to his account of John the Baptist's initial encounter with Jesus described in Matthew 3:14–15, in which Jesus insists John baptize Him despite his reluctance to do so (a dialogue not found in Mark or Luke or John), he probably does so because it fits a major theme which he emphasizes throughout his Gospel—Jesus as the fulfillment of all of God's word and will.

Unfortunately, many redaction critics borrow form and tradition criticism's criterion of multiple attestation and assume that what one evangelist has added to his sources must be of his own fabrication. This, of course, is patently false. The first evangelist probably had access to numerous sources and traditions not reflected in any other Gospel (cf. John's hyperbolic comment in John 21:25), and if the author of this Gospel was indeed the apostle Matthew, he would have had his own memory on which to rely as well.

More conservative scholars have often focused so much on issues of historical trustworthiness and harmonization they have lost sight of the distinctives of each Gospel. On the one hand, it is a valuable exercise to show how all of the details in the various Gospels might fit together without contradiction. On the other hand, God did not choose to inspire a harmony of the Gospels. He gave us four different versions of the life of Christ apparently for good reason. The most likely reason is that each emphasizes different aspects of Jesus' words and works for different audiences with different needs. To the extent we can recover those emphases we will be able to interpret and apply the Gospels more in keeping with their original intention.

---

15. Gordon D. Fee and Douglas Stuart, *How to Read the Bible for All Its Worth* (Grand Rapids: Zondervan, 1982), 110–16.

Thinking Vertically. The second aspect of redaction criticism may be termed "thinking vertically." Here we imagine putting all of the columns in a synopsis for one particular Gospel end to end creating one long vertical column, much like one might unroll a scroll from top to bottom. In other words, thinking vertically has to do with understanding the outline or progression of thought an individual evangelist used in putting his Gospel together.

Theological emphases emerge not only from a comparison of the distinctives of one Gospel but also from seeing themes recur repeatedly over the course of an entire Gospel, no matter of how often they may occur elsewhere. One also discovers how commonly the Gospels have arranged material in topical rather than chronological sequence. Matthew 8—9, for example, groups together ten miracle stories, not all of which happened in the order Matthew presents them, as a comparison with their parallels in Mark and Luke demonstrates. When one analyzes these stories more closely, one can discern probable motives for Matthew's arrangement. Matthew 8:1–17, for example, seems to group together three miracles in which Jesus heals people whom orthodox Jews would have labeled ritually unclean—a leper, a Gentile centurion, and a woman. Matthew seems to go out of his way to make this point—describing how Jesus deliberately touched the leper, risking the charge of defiling Himself (v. 3) and how He lavishly praised the faith of the centurion above all those in Israel (vv. 10–12—also largely a unique inclusion in Matthew's version). Matthew, and again only he, concludes this section with a quotation from the OT (Isa. 53:4), which he believes was fulfilled in Christ (v. 17).[16]

Interestingly, a major debate in Christian circles today centers on whether Matthew was teaching here that there is physical healing in the atonement. That is to say, by applying one of Isaiah's suffering servant passages to Jesus' miracle-working ministry, it seems as if Matthew believed Jesus died not only to bring spiritual salvation for His followers but also to make physical healing available in this life. But if our understanding of Matthew's theological purposes in grouping the healings of 8:1–17 together is accurate, he may not be focusing on the physical healings nearly so much as on ritual cleanliness.[17] Much as Jesus would later make more explicit (Mark 7:19) and as Peter would have to relearn through an unusual experience (Acts 10:1—11:18), God in Jesus was doing away with all the ritual laws which declared certain kinds of persons unclean based on bodily disease, ethnicity, or gender. Redaction criticism enables us to

---

16. Cf. further Blomberg, *Matthew*, 136–45.

17. Cf. esp. Daniel Patte, *The Gospel According to Matthew: A Structural Commentary* (Philadelphia: Fortress, 1987), 117.

see the real issue at stake in the text and not be distracted by modern questions which, however well intentioned, are not those the passage was primarily designed to address.

A summary of thinking horizontally and vertically about the four Gospels leads to numerous patterns or theological emphasés dear to each evangelist. Mark views Jesus as the Christ and Son of God (1:1; 8:29; 15:39), emphasizes His role as suffering servant (10:45; 14:24; 15:34), stresses the failure and misunderstanding of the disciples (4:40; 6:42; 16:8), focuses on imminent eschatology (9:1; 13:5–37), and distinctively characterizes the Christian message as "good news" or gospel (1:1,15; 8:35).

Matthew views Jesus as a teacher, possibly like Moses (chaps. 5—7, 10, 13, 18, 23—25), as the Son of David (1:1; 9:27; 20:30), and perhaps as Wisdom incarnate (11:19; 25–30; 12:42). He emphasizes the chronological and theological priority of offering the gospel to the Jews (10:5–6; 15:24) but equally stresses the Great Commission to go to all the world (28:18–20), especially following widespread rejection in Israel of that gospel. At times he seems to present a more positive picture of the disciples' faith (13:51; 14:33; 16:16–19), his is the only Gospel to specifically use the word "church" (16:18; 18:17 [2 times]), and he often presents some of the harshest polemic in the Gospels against the Jewish leaders who opposed Jesus (esp. chap. 23).

Luke stresses Jesus' humanity, His teaching in parables (particularly in chaps. 10—18), and His compassion for the outcasts of society, most notably Samaritans (10:25–37; 17:11–19), Gentiles (13:29; 14:23), tax collectors (18:9–14; 19:1–10), women (7:36—8:3; 10:38–42), and the poor (6:20; 16:19–31). His favorite title for Jesus is "Savior" or one who brings "salvation" (2:11, 30; 3:6). He emphasizes the role of prayer (6:12; 11:1–13; 18:1–8) and the Holy Spirit (4:1, 18; 10:21) in the life of Jesus.

John is the only evangelist to call Jesus Lamb of God (1:29, 36) or Word (logos; 1:1, 14) and to equate Jesus directly with God (1:1; 10:30; 20:28). Only John includes Jesus' seven "I am" sayings (the bread of life—6:35; the light of the world—8:12 and 9:5; the good shepherd—10:11; the resurrection and the life—11:25; the way and the truth and the life—14:6; the true vine—15:1; and the "I am" which is the very divine name of God the Father—8:58). More so than in any of the Synoptics, John emphasizes a type of "realized eschatology," i.e., eternal life or death as beginning now in this world (3:16–21; 10:10), miracles as "signs" or pointers to who Jesus is (2:11; 4:54; 20:31), the eternal security of the believer (6:39; 10:29), the death of Christ as exaltation or glorification (12:32; 17:1–5), and the role of the Holy Spirit as "Paraclete"—comforter, advocate, helper (14:15–21; 15:26–27; 16:5–15). Obviously, being alert to these major themes in each

Gospel enables the reader of any particular account of an episode from Jesus' life to be more sensitive to the emphases Matthew, Mark, Luke, or John wished to highlight.

Apart from the smaller parallels between 2 Peter and Jude and perhaps between Ephesians and Colossians, no other part of the NT offers comparative material to allow the redaction critic to think horizontally. But every book may be analyzed vertically. Serious attempts to understand the overall outline of a NT book and to place each of the constituent parts within the whole remains an underemphasized responsibility of every serious reader of Scripture. For example, much as with the debate about healing in the atonement, readers of Acts 8 often bring important but extraneous questions to the text. Why did the Holy Spirit not come when the Samaritans first believed? Was Simon ever truly saved and, if so, did he lose his salvation? Is Philip's baptism of the Ethiopian eunuch a paradigm for believer's baptism by immersion? Does it mean that such baptism should occur as quickly as possible after profession of faith? All of these are legitimate questions and some may even be answerable from the text of Acts 8. But none is likely what Luke most hoped we would think about as we read his work. Rather this chapter appears in that portion of Luke's overall outline (Acts 1:8) in which the Gospel is moving out of exclusively Jewish circles.

When one understands Luke's overall flow of thought, it becomes clear the most striking thing about Philip's encounter with the Samaritans and with the eunuch is that those considered outcast by faithful Israelites are being accepted into God's kingdom on equal terms with everyone else. Proper contemporary application of this chapter should ask who our social outcasts are and whether our ministry is focusing on reaching those people and, when they come to faith, not treating them as second-class citizens of the kingdom.

This vertical use of redaction criticism rests on the border between historical and literary criticism. It shares with literary criticism a concern for the finished form of the text, but (unlike most literary criticism) shares with historical criticism a concern for the theological emphases of the biblical author in light of his original situation and the historical forces which brought him to write as he did. Some prefer to separate this aspect of redaction criticism and call it composition criticism. We may disagree on exactly how to label it, but it remains a crucial task for every Bible reader.

OTHER METHODS

Social-Scientific Analysis. Other recent developments in the scholarly study of the Bible similarly sit on the border between historical and literary criticism. One of the burgeoning fields of biblical study is social-scientific analysis. Passages of Scripture are being analyzed from a wide variety of psychological, sociological, and anthropological perspectives.[18] In some instances, historical concerns come more to the fore. An understanding of the sociological setting of Mark 3:31–35 reveals just how radical were Jesus' pronouncements about His disciples being His true family.

Much more so than in contemporary Western culture, family kinship ties were stronger than any other human relationships; violation of expected loyalties was a grievous social offense. Or consider the domestic codes of Ephesians, Colossians and 1 Peter. Today we ask children, "What do you want to be when you grow up?" We assume their choices are almost unlimited. In the first-century Mediterranean world, few people asked this question; such choices were either restricted or nonexistent. One's place in life usually was determined by one's gender, socioeconomic class, place of residence, and the occupation of one's parents. Parents then taught their children to ask, "How can I best live out my lot in life in a way which is noble, honorable, and ethical?" At least one of the reasons why Paul and Peter commanded submission to authorities is that virtually every other Jew or pagan of the day recognized such submission as a crucial cultural mandate. It simply would not do for Christians to be perceived as less moral than pagans in this arena. But what of our culture in which such submission is often perceived as a morally repulsive feature of Christianity? If submission is to remain normative at all for believers today, it will at the very least have to take on different forms.

In other cases, social-scientific analysis does not so much attempt to recover neglected aspects of historical background as to impose modern theories of human behavior on ancient texts to interpret them in new ways. Jungian psychology, theories of cognitive dissonance, Marxist economics, and feminism are just four of the more prominent "grids" through which NT texts have been read. Jesus may then be seen as a prototype of the healer in our modern therapeutic age, of the church leader whose prophecies about the end time fail to come true, an original socialist, or a supporter of women's liberation. Here, often, the concerns of the interpreter focus on the finished form of the text, read through new spectacles based on modern sets of presuppositions. Strictly speaking, such interpretations do not fall under the purview of historical criticism, and they remain only as valid as the theories or presuppositions which inform them.

---

18. See esp. Bruce Malina, *The New Testament World: Insights from Cultural Anthropology* (Atlanta: John Knox, 1981); and, for a survey and critique of the literature, see Derek Tidball, *The Social Context of the New Testament* (Grand Rapids: Zondervan, 1984).

Canon Criticism. Canon criticism is a second recent method which shares elements of historical and literary criticism. Whereas social-scientific analysis almost always has some elements of historical criticism, even when subordinated to modern concerns, canon criticism at first glance seems to focus entirely on the finished (or canonical) form of the text. It developed precisely because its practitioners (most notably Brevard Childs and James Sanders)[19] found traditional historical criticism sterile and inadequate for meaningful proclamation of the Gospel in the contemporary world. But canon criticism overlaps with historical criticism both by presupposing the results of more traditional source, form, and redaction criticism and by trying to go beyond them to understand the historical forces at work during the years and centuries in which the various biblical books were coming to be recognized as uniquely authoritative and hence canonical.

So whereas traditional historical criticism insists on asking what Luke meant in Acts for Theophilus and other readers in the mid-first century, canon criticism also asks how Acts functioned for the church of the first several centuries of its history after it had been separated from Luke by John and followed by the corpus of Pauline Epistles. Acts thus becomes a bridge from the Gospels to Paul in ways which Luke most likely never conceived but which remain important for the church's self-understanding.

How do all of these sometimes daunting and esoteric tools for biblical study help our average Christian reader struggling to understand Matthew's and Mark's accounts of Jesus' walking on the water? To begin with, she should realize that Mark most likely wrote his account first. His unique emphasis (Mark 6:52) was probably inserted deliberately, to fit a key theme which he wished to stress. Any good NT survey, introduction, or commentary will include a list of these key themes. There she will notice that the failures and misunderstandings of the disciples are a prominent motif for Mark, probably to give encouragement to his Christian readers that their failures are not unique and can be overcome, just as the apostles went on to powerful ministries in the life of the early church.

When she returns to Matthew, our reader should be open to exploring ways of harmonizing Matthew with Mark. Is it possible for a follower of Jesus to worship Him and yet still not understand all he should? Absolutely (cf. Mark 9:24)! This should be of great encouragement to the ordinary Bible reader. But she should go on to notice the other unique aspects of Matthew's account as well. Most notably, only Matthew includes the

---

19. Brevard Childs, *The New Testament as Canon: An Introduction* (Philadelphia: Fortress, 1985); James Sanders, *From Sacred Story to Sacred Text* (Philadelphia: Fortress, 1987).

episode of Peter's aborted attempt to walk on the water (14:28–31). This also fits a recurring pattern. Peter appears more frequently and more prominently in Matthew, often starting from a position of leadership or initiative only to wind up making a fool of himself (cf. esp. 16:16–23). So Matthew in his own way makes much the same point as Mark, but probably also warns us against overly exalting any of the apostles and particularly Peter (as, for example, in certain forms of traditional Roman Catholicism).

Study tools which introduce our Bible reader to form criticism will help her learn one more thing. Jesus' miracle stories, particularly in Matthew, are christologically centered. That is to say they are intended to drive us to our knees to accept and worship Jesus as the Son of God (just as in 14:33). They are not primarily focused on what God can do for us. So the Christian eager to apply this miracle to her life should not worry whether God would ever make it possible for her to walk across a nearby lake rather than around it! Theoretically, God could choose to do so; realistically, He is not likely to do it. Peter's adventures notwithstanding, the point of this passage remains focused on Christ's extraordinary powers, which confirm that He is God's Son who is ushering in the New Testament age and demanding exclusive allegiance on the part of those who would follow Him.

The Bible reader in the midst of her devotions will probably want to pause at this point to ask forgiveness for areas of her life in which she has let her Lord down and to pray for strength to serve Jesus more fully in the tasks at hand for the coming day. Historical criticism (source, form, and redaction) can indeed affect a person's devotional life. These tools deserve widespread application in the church so that we do not impose our own interpretations on the sacred text but rather obey God's command to "correctly handle the word of truth" (2 Tim. 2:15).

FOR FURTHER READING

Black, David A. and Dockery, David S., eds. *New Testament Criticism and Interpretation*. Grand Rapids: Zondervan, 1991.

France, R. T. *Matthew: Evangelist and Teacher*. Grand Rapids: Zondervan, 1989.

Guthrie, Donald. *New Testament Introduction*. 3d ed. Downers Grove, Ill.: InterVarsity, 1990.

Krentz, Edgar. *The Historical-Critical Method*. Philadelphia: Fortress, 1975.

Marshall, I. Howard, ed. *New Testament Interpretation*. Grand Rapids: Eerdmans, 1977.

Marshall, I. Howard. *Luke: Historian and Theologian*. 2d ed. Grand Rapids:

Zondervan, 1989.

Martin, Ralph P. *Mark: Evangelist and Theologian.* Grand Rapids: Zondervan, 1972.

McKnight, Edgar V. *What Is Form Criticism?* Philadelphia: Fortress, 1969.

McKnight, Scot. *Interpreting the Synoptic Gospels.* Grand Rapids: Baker, 1988.

Perrin, Norman. *What Is Redaction Criticism?* Philadelphia: Fortress, 1969.

Smalley, Stephen S. *John: Evangelist and Interpreter.* Exeter, England: Paternoster, 1978.

Stein, Robert H. *The Synoptic Problem: An Introduction.* Grand Rapids: Baker, 1987.

XXI

LITERARY CRITICISM OF THE NEW TESTAMENT

RICHARD R. MELICK, JR.

In the late 1960s, a major shift in biblical studies occurred. Concerned with the relative fruitlessness of previous critical analyses, some biblical scholars called for a new way of approaching the Bible. Source, form, and redaction criticisms left many with the cold feeling that the text had been destroyed by constant cutting, pasting, and reanalysis. Was the Bible ever intended to be so treated?

Many observed that the Bible had remained a powerful book for people of faith, regardless of the historical factors that brought it about. Religious people through the centuries found meaning from the pages of Scripture apart from the historical questions of critical studies. Perhaps it would be better to approach the Bible from literary perspectives. This meant determining appropriate criteria for categorizing Scripture. Further, it meant interpreting Scripture in light of these categories.

These scholars left traditional critical methods for many reasons. Some were disenchanted with the findings of critical scholars. Too often they concluded with their prior assumptions. Others simply sought to approach literature holistically rather than piecemeal. Still others developed new approaches to biblical literature strictly from their literary studies. For various reasons, therefore, many scholars called for new methods in biblical study.

THE CATEGORIES OF LITERARY CRITICISM

Literary criticism brought different approaches. Much like denominations in ecclesiastical circles, these approaches have functioned in mutually exclusive ways until the present. For that reason, literary criticism cannot be considered a unified discipline.

Literary criticism developed into three major divisions. One stream focuses on the response of the reader. Many of those who accept it think of the literature as capable of many different meanings, depending on the outlook of the reader. Depending on the philosophies of Heidegger, Dilthy, Gadamer, Wittgenstein, and Riccour, these scholars point to the subjective nature of literature. The text creates a world of its own, becoming public domain. From that perspective, the text cannot be regulated by such matters as the author's intended meaning or traditional exegetical methods. These approaches present a serious challenge to biblical studies, but few biblical scholars adopt their principles. In actuality, taking these methods to their logical conclusion actually defeats Bible study, since they undermine the whole process which governs it.[1] The primary questions of interpretation deal with the nature of the reader, not the inherent meaning of the text.

Two other divisions of literary criticism take the biblical text more seriously. They are rhetorical criticism and structuralism. In this, literary criticism differs from historical criticism. Historical criticism sought to understand the prehistory of the text. Its adherents examined how the texts came into being, what traditions lay behind them, and how the various Christian communities affirmed these texts in their stages of development. On the other hand, literary criticism approaches these aspects from a different perspective. It seeks to understand the text as it stands.

Literary criticism focuses on three dimensions of inquiry. It asks questions related to the author and the author's intended meaning. It analyzes the text and appropriate exegetical concerns and seeks to understand the

---

1. For example, a true "reader-response" hermeneutic claims that the meaning of a text is what the reader sees in it. Meaning is personal, and neither the text nor other readers can influence that personal meaning. If that approach is accepted, there is no reason for studying the text or commentaries on it. For further analysis of some problems related to this approach, see Richard R. Melick, Jr. "Contemporary Hermeneutics and Authority" in *Authority and Interpretation: A Baptist Perspective* (Grand Rapids: Baker, 1987), 93–126.

nature of the original readers. These concerns force the interpreter to deal with the context of writer and readers and the specific occasion which prompted the writing. For its adherents, literary criticism offers the interpreter a more comprehensive and accurate understanding of these matters than other methods.

GENRE CONSIDERATIONS

By far the most helpful aspect of literary criticism is its focus on genre. In some senses, genre criticism transcends particular approaches to the text. Genre studies attempt to locate and analyze particular works according to their literary type. This assumes a proper analysis of the literature gives understanding as to the meaning of the text.

Genre deals with the form of literature. Simply stated, a genre is "a group of texts that bear one or more traits in common with each other."[2] This means the literature has similar characteristics. Basically, literature uses two primary forms of writing: prose and poetry. While genre may incorporate these forms, it includes other categories as well. Both poetry and prose may include different genre, or, conversely, the genre may at times include poetry or prose. This is true, for example, in apocalyptic literature, which sometimes uses poetic forms to express its distinctive message.

Scholars differ on the genre found in the New Testament. Basically, four genre occur[3]—history, gospel, epistle, and apocalyptic. Each has unique characteristics which set it apart from the others, and proper interpretation demands a sensitivity to these characteristics.

History is a distinct type of writing. In the NT, only Acts conforms to the first-century style of recording history. Even here, some have questioned whether Acts is written in the style of secular historians. Indeed, if history as genre requires an uncommitted objectivity, nothing in the NT qualifies. For that matter, secular literature has its own bias as well. Scholars now realize the impossibility of writing without some perspective which guides the selection and presentation of events.

The application of historical texts to other contexts poses the most difficult problem for biblical scholars. What portion of the text is normative? That is, what portion of historical writing is prescriptive? History is nor-

---

2. Tremper Longman, III, *Literary Approaches to Biblical Interpretation*, vol. 3, *Foundations of Contemporary Interpretation* (Grand Rapids: Academie Books, 1987), 76.

3. An extremely helpful, popular presentation of the issues of genre is Gordon D. Fee and Douglas Stuart, *How to Read the Bible for All Its Worth: A Guide to Understanding the Bible* (Grand Rapids: Academie Books, 1982).

mally descriptive, describing events of the past. It becomes prescriptive only if the writer provides some clue as to why and how it should be taken otherwise. When these clues appear, history teaches an appropriate course of action or challenges to a proper understanding of reality.

The second type of genre is gospel. Again, scholars debate the literary characteristics. In the past, many scholars often considered the Gospels as history. Although most modern scholars deny that parallel, some have revived it. They claim that especially Luke and Acts conforms to a Hellenistic pattern of historical writing.[4] Others view the Gospels as biography, claiming that they conform to a pattern of Greek biography,[5] and other suggestions also occur.[6] Now, however, a host of scholars deny the Gospels are either history or biography. They have determined that they fit into an entirely new genre, that of "story." The Gospels clearly show the characteristics of stories. They have introductions, plots, and conclusions. These stories, however, clearly witness to Jesus Christ. This classification does not deny their historical nature. Nor does it deny their biographical interests, since the writers recorded actual events from the life of Jesus. This classification claims more, however. The Gospels combine biographical and historical materials into a strong witness to Jesus.

As literary constructions, the Gospels contain specific forms and conventions, sometimes called subgenres, used by the writers to accomplish their tasks. These include the categories of pronouncement stories, proverbs, parables, poetry, hymns, midrashim, and miracle stories.[7]

Gospel genre calls for specific hermeneutical methods. Although most of the events may be handled like historical material, another step is needed. The interpreter must determine how a particular story or event calls people to consider Jesus as the Christ.

The third genre is epistolary. The Epistles are letters. In recent years, scholars have devoted considerable attention to the matter of epistolary genre. In the past, many scholars spoke of two types of epistles: formal and

---

4. See David Aune, *The New Testament in Its Literary Environment* (Philadelphia: Westminster, 1989). He argues that the Synoptic Gospels actually do conform to Greek biography, and that Luke is close to Greco-Roman history.

5. In addition to David Aune, see Charles Talbert, "Literary Patterns, Theological Themes, and the Genre of Luke-Acts" in SBLMS 20 (Missoula, Mont.: Society of Biblical Literature and Scholars Press, 1974).

6. For example, Elizabeth Haight suggests they should be considered as romance genre, although her ideas have borne little following to this point. See also her *Essays on the Greek Romances* (Port Washington, N.Y.: Kennikat, 1943).

7. A helpful survey of these issues is found in W. Randolph Tate, *Biblical Interpretation: An Integrated Approach* (Peabody, Miss.: Hendrickson Publishers, Inc., 1991), 115–21.

informal. Formal epistles were prethought and perhaps even partially pre-composed. They reflected a more formal situation the writer addressed, or they demonstrated a more "literary" structure. Informal epistles were more friendly. Either they were composed spontaneously, or they reflected a more conversational tone. Some scholars distinguished these by calling the formal "epistles" and the informal "letters." Now, however, the epistolary questions are more complex. With the refinement of literary studies, scholars have identified more specific types of epistles, and they attempt to classify them more precisely. Much of this comes from rhetorical criticism, as will be described later. Probably it is safe to say most NT scholars identify the letters as falling between purely occasional letters and formal theological treatises.[8]

As with the Gospels, the Epistles contain many subcategories. These include vice and virtue lists, domestic tables (family rules), wisdom sayings, confessions, hymns, diatribes, and midrashic exegesis. Each contributes distinctively to the nature of the argument.

The hermeneutical questions for the Epistles involve their basic characteristic. At the most basic level, Epistles may be viewed as "answers" to "questions." The questions may have been formulated and presented to the author, such as in 1 Corinthians.[9] The questions may also have been prompted by the situations faced by the churches, and they may never have been presented to the writer.[10] Basically, the Epistles are only partial explanations of any subject. Further, the Epistles contain teachings which are shaped by specific contexts. Both of these concerns guide the interpreter.

Finally, the genre of the NT includes apocalyptic. Apocalyptic literature also differs from other materials in the NT. It most nearly resembles prophetic literature, yet it seems that its message comes through mediums other than the prophecy found elsewhere in Scripture. Apocalyptic literature characterized Jewish and Christian circles for approximately five hundred years. First-century readers knew how to handle it, and they were comfortable with it. Although some of the interpretive keys are now lost,

---

8. For more information on the nature of biblical letters, see William G. Doty, *Letters in Primitive Christianity* (Philadelphia: Fortress, 1973).

9. See 1 Corinthians, which gives evidence of this in two ways. First, there was a group sent from the church which brought reports and questions from the church. Second, the formula "now concerning," which occurs regularly from chaps. 7—16, gives evidence that Paul had an agenda in mind.

10. A clear example of this is Colossians, where Paul had a theological agenda in mind but had never met the church personally.

enough apocalyptic material exists to provide knowledge of its characteristics.

Literary criticism contributed the refinements in these areas of analysis. In a sense, all literary criticism deals with the question of genre. It inquires as to the best way to understand specific biblical texts. It correctly assumes that through proper analysis comes more accurate interpretation.[11]

RHETORICAL CRITICISM

One branch of literary critics compared the biblical materials to the Greco-Roman orators. They observed the writers of the Bible had similar interests, similar goals of persuasion, and similar techniques. They began to look for specific literary devices that gave clues to the composition of the passage. If these devices could be found, they would unlock the interpretation of the text.

Rhetorical criticism functioned in two dimensions. (1) Its proponents claimed it helped focus on the writing as a whole, rather than on its individual parts. Such knowledge emphasized the progress (movement) of the text, so the reader knew exactly "where" a particular passage occurred in the logical flow of the book. This location helped identify how that section functioned in relation to the whole text. (2) Rhetorical critics claimed proper analysis of the text provided better knowledge of the provenance of a writing. With proper classification of literature came proper understanding of the circumstances that promoted it. Particularly, they believed the discipline reveals the emotional attitude of the writer, as well as what he hoped to achieve through the material. Thus, rhetorical criticism flourished. The founding of the movement is credited to James Muilenburg; perhaps the most influential early scholar was George Kennedy.

The approach better suits the Epistles than the Gospels and Acts. Consistent with that, it was applied to Epistles like Galatians, Philemon, Philippians, and Thessalonians. It has application, however, to the Gospels, and some have begun to apply it there.

HISTORY OF THE DISCIPLINE

Scholars agree that the modern emphasis on rhetorical criticism began in 1968. In a presidential address before the Society of Biblical Literature,

---

11. One of the most helpful books on this subject of genre which also takes into account the other literary critical methods and focuses them on preaching is Sidney Greidanus, *The Modern Preacher and the Ancient Text: Interpreting and Preaching Biblical Literature* (Grand Rapids: Eerdmans, 1988). Although the title focuses on preaching, the book is a helpful guide for interpreting in general.

Muilenburg called for scholars of the Bible to "go beyond form criticism."[12] Specifically, he was interested in the OT and Hebrew literary composition. He wanted to find "the structural patterns that are employed for the fashioning of a literary unit, whether in poetry or in prose," and to discern "the many and various devices by which the predications are formulated and ordered into a unified whole." He described this "as rhetoric and the methodology as rhetorical criticism."[13] Of course, throughout history scholars had interacted with rhetorical approaches,[14] but the modern revival came because of the bankruptcy of form critical approaches.

In actuality, rhetorical critics do not necessarily oppose other critical approaches. Some claim to see values in other methods. They objected to the fact that a piecemeal dissecting of the text failed to take account of the "wholeness" of the document. Critical methods employed until that time traced the prehistory of the text. They had little value in explaining the impact the whole text had on its readers. Kennedy stated the role of the discipline as follows:

> Rhetorical criticism takes the text as we have it, whether the work of a single author or the product of editing, and looks at it from the point of view of the author's or editor's intent, the unified results, and how it would be perceived by an audience of near contemporaries.[15]

Most scholars see the discipline as complementary. It is "a valuable *additional* methodology, largely untapped, for understanding biblical material."[16]

THE PURPOSE OF RHETORICAL CRITICISM

Rhetorical criticism attempts to understand the text as a whole. It focuses on the point the author made and the response of the reader. Specifically, the goal is to understand two important aspects of biblical study: Why did the author write this text, and how did he put it together?

---

12. Quoted in George A. Kennedy, *New Testament Interpretation Through Rhetorical Criticism* (Chapel Hill: The University of North Carolina Press, 1984), 3.

13. James Muilenburg, "Form Criticism and Beyond," *JBL* 88 (1969): 18.

14. John Kirby represents many who have observed this, "Rhetorical criticism has its origins in the classical canon conceptualized and formulated by the principal rhetoricians of Greek and Roman antiquity. . . . This method sprang from roots in the ancient world. It has a universality that transcends its own cultural boundaries, as well as an extraordinary practicality." *NTS* 34 (1988): 197.

15. Kennedy, *New Testament*, 4.

16. Joanna Dewey, "Markan Public Debate: Literary Technique, Concentric Structure, and Theology in Mark 2:1—3:6" in SBLDS 48 (Chico, Calif.: Scholars, 1980), 7.

Obviously this relates to issues of biblical introduction. It assumes that the literature has a purpose and that the document itself (and sometimes *by itself*) reveals that purpose. It further assumes a given author had access to rhetorical devices that enabled him to address a situation powerfully. In other words, the author arranged his material as he did to make the best impact on his readers.

Some assumptions underlie this approach. (1) A rhetorical study assumes the author *consciously* employed literary devices. Since orators were common in the Greco-Roman world, it seems likely the writer employed such an honored form of persuasion. On the other hand, one might ask: Is this too much to expect of the writers of Scripture who, in some cases, appear to be untrained in classical disciplines? Further, is this consistent with a concept of the inspiration of the Scriptures which the church has affirmed throughout the centuries? (2) Rhetorical criticism assumes the writings were basically formal. If the writers utilized common rhetorical devices, they obviously thought about what they wanted to write and how they wanted to express it.[17] It is indicative of the discipline that Epistles which have been understood traditionally as informal were among the earliest objects of rhetorical criticism. These included Philippians, Galatians, 1 Thessalonians, and Philemon. (3) The discipline assumes the readers were comfortable with a more formal address from the writer. According to this approach, a friendly letter from and to friends seems impossible. The critic assumes the writer employed various persuasive techniques.[18]

Ultimately, rhetorical criticism hopes to reveal the historical situation. The style and tone of written persuasion reveals the atmosphere that existed between the writer and his readers. It also clarifies the seriousness of the situation and the response the writer desired. Other aspects of biblical study contribute to this understanding, but rhetorical critics believe that the flavor of the writing helps most.[19]

---

17. The time factor could be deceptive, however, since a good orator could speak about any subject "on the spur of the moment" and persuade a crowd of anything he or she wanted.

18. This becomes especially problematic in the case of the Corinthian correspondence. Paul clearly stated there that he refused to employ the wisdom of this world, lest their faith should stand on human reason rather than the Holy Spirit's power (1 Cor. 2:1–4). Some object to pressing this statement. They claim such statements were, in themselves, forms of oratory. They were intended to persuade.

19. Several elements contribute to the historical situation, and all critics understand that. For example, one of the early scholars working in this field defined the historical situation as "a complex of persons, events, objects, and relations presenting an actual or potential exigence which can be completely or partially removed if discourse, introduced into the situation, can so constrain human decision or action as to bring about the significant modification of the exigence." Lloyd F. Bitzer, "The Rhetorical Situation," *Philosophy and Rhetoric* 1 (1968): 6.

THE PROCESS OF RHETORICAL CRITICISM

Doing rhetorical criticism involves two major investigations. First, the interpreter must identify the rhetorical unit. Following that, the interpreter must determine the structure of the text and what type of rhetoric it is. Both of these require quite complex forms of analysis.[20]

Discovering the Rhetorical Unit. This task includes both the larger unit—the entire piece of literature—and the smaller units which comprise it. Every complete literary unit has an introduction, body, and conclusion. These may occur on a broad, comprehensive scale, or they may occur in isolated portions of a writing. If the unit is a piece of larger work, clear reasons are needed to identify the particular smaller units.

Generally, rhetorical units have clear literary boundaries. Most of these involve word repetition. The most common "boundary marker" is *inclusio*, called "inclusion" in English. Inclusion is a literary device by which a writer reveals the limits of his discussion of a particular subject. Most often, inclusion occurs with a word or phrase. When the writer first employs the phrase, the discussion begins. At the conclusion of the discussion, the writer uses the phrase again, thus indicating in a summary fashion the discussion has ended. Of course, the word or phrase may be essential to the content of the unit and therefore may be repeated many times within the inclusion.

Sometimes grammatical markers form the inclusion. For example, probably the most common form of inclusion is the chiasm. A chiasm is a discussion of two parts of a subject arranged in an A B B A order. That means the first part of the subject occurs in the first and fourth positions, normally designated as A and A'. The second portion of the discussion occurs in the second and third positions, normally designated as B and B'. The inclusion occurs with the more significant material, the first and fourth positions.[21] When the chiasm concludes, the reader understands that the particular literary unit also concludes. For example, Moises Silva employed this technique in his commentary on Philippians. He used it to

---

20. Two very helpful writings provide insight into the method of doing rhetorical criticism. See Kennedy, *New Testament*, 33–38 and Duane F. Watson, *Invention, Arrangement, and Style: Rhetorical Criticism of Jude and 2 Peter* (Atlanta: Scholars, 1988), 8–28.

21. Chiasms can be quite complex. They may include more than two elements set in parallel. Further, they may have an "odd" single subject in the middle of the sets of parallels. In these cases, the central aspect of the subject receives emphasis. Otherwise, the "outside" members receive the stress.

demonstrate the unity of 1:27—4:3.[22] Vernon Robbins used it to mark off the introduction of Mark's Gospel.[23]

Other common lexical devices help the reader isolate literary units. Another common device is the repetition of words in an anaphoric manner. This means the author repeats a word or phrase frequently enough that a pattern occurs. The Beatitudes of Matthew 5 repeat the word "blessed." Hebrews 11 repeats the word "by faith" (one word in Greek) to form a pattern.[24]

Sound devices also form inclusions and mark literary divisions. Sometimes a writer employs words or phrases that sounded "poetical" for purposes of memory recall. This may well occur in Mark 2:1–12.[25]

A final example of these devices is rhetorical questions. Frequently in the NT the writer asks such questions. They introduce a subject to be addressed, and when the address concludes, the writer asks another question. This device occurs in Romans 5—8 in particular.

Not everyone agrees on the specific rhetorical devices a writer might employ. Sometimes almost diametrically opposite conclusions occur. Perhaps this happens because the science is in its infancy. Perhaps there will never be a consensus. Nevertheless, these methods help in text analysis, particularly in isolating a rhetorical unit.

Analyzing the Kind of Literature. The second step involves analysis of the rhetorical unit. Here the interpreter considers three major categories of rhetoric: invention, arrangement, and style.[26]

Invention refers to the "proofs" and "refutations" of a speech or writing.[27] When a writer addressed a reading audience, he first considered the kinds of proofs he would use. The selecting process came to be known as "inventions."

---

22. Moises Silva, "Philippians" in *WEC* (Chicago: Moody, 1988), 16–17. Similarly, David Allen Black argues for five examples of inclusion in Philippians. See D. A. Black, "The Authorship of Philippians 2:6–11: Some Literary-Critical Observations," *CTR* 2 (1988): 283.

23. Vernon K. Robbins, "Mark 1:14–20: An Interpretation at the Intersection of Jewish and Graeco-Roman Traditions," *NTS* 28 (1982): 224.

24. For this latter, see Michael R. Cosby, *The Rhetorical Composition and Function of Hebrews 11 in Light of Example Lists in Antiquity* (Macon, Ga.: Mercer Press, 1988), 41.

25. This suggestion comes from Dewey, "Markan Public Debate," 74–75.

26. See Edward P. J. Corbett, *Classical Rhetoric for the Modern Student*, 2d ed. (New York: Oxford University Press, 1971), 33–38.

27. Invention comes from the Latin *inventio*, which means "discovery." In that sense, the interpreter hopes to discover the orator's message by the proofs he employs.

"Arrangement" (Lat. *dispositio;* Gr. *taxis*) concerns the organization of the material. The Greek orators divided their speeches into four main parts. The exordium occurred first. It consisted of an introduction to the entire writing. The exordium set the direction of the relationships and prepared for the main elements of the literature. The rhetoricians then moved to the narratio. This was the statement of the case. It set the direction for the literary proofs that would follow. Third came the probatio, which included the body of the speech or writing. Finally, each speech ended with the peroratio. This was the conclusion.[28]

These occurred regularly, so any literary piece could be analyzed this way. If the NT documents parallel the Greek orations, the rhetorical critic will find these elements in each NT book. As will be noted later, the forms may vary, but the structural elements remain.

In addition to invention and arrangement, each orator considered style. This meant he would consciously determine the type of approach to an audience. Many ancient Greeks, such as Aristotle, pointed to two different kinds of persuasive techniques. Some persuasions were "artless"; that is, they occurred "outside" rhetoric. They included such things as laws, witnesses, contracts, and oaths. On the other hand, a rhetorician had at his disposal many "artful" ways of persuasion. These were appeals to action which demonstrated the orator's ability. It made rhetoric powerful.[29]

These "artful" devices corresponded to different aspects of persons. Some arguments appealed to the rational faculties. These sometimes related to logos, the "reasoning" capability of the human mind. Other arguments appealed to the emotions. These were known as pathos arguments. They intended to move someone by touching the feelings. Finally, the ethos involved morality. They called people to action based on ethical or moral principles.

The type of argumentation—the style—helps to determine the nature of the discussion. It further anticipates the type of response desired by the speaker or writer. Ancient orators learned various devices they could use in each of these areas to persuade their hearers of appropriate action.

All of this analysis provides the interpreter with the data to determine the rhetorical situation. The discourse is like an answer to a question; the rhetorical situation is the question. Applying that analogy to the NT, the

---

28. According to Corbett, the Latin rhetoricians included six parts of a discourse: (1) the introduction; (2) the statement of the case; (3) the steps in the argument; (4) the proof of the case; (5) the refutation of opposing argument; and (6) the conclusion. See Corbett, *Classical Rhetoric,* 37–38.

29. Ibid., 33–34.

piece of literature is the answer to a question that surfaces only by considering the rhetorical context.

At this point, it is helpful to note the kinds of rhetoric used by the Greeks. First, they had deliberative oratory. In general use, this was what an orator used to persuade someone of his or her opinion or way of going about something. It occurred commonly, because most of the "everyday" debates involved such decisions. For example, political discussions were deliberative, as were things that had to do with public affairs.

In addition to deliberative orations, the ancient Greeks had judicial oratory. This was the language of the courtroom. Particularly suited to defending or condemning specific actions, it could be used for anyone wishing to accuse or justify himself or someone else. Because of the highly developed legal system of the Greco-Roman world, this style developed into a fine art.

Finally, there were epideictic orations. This was the language of praise and honor, as well as blame and dishonor. Orators used these techniques when they wanted to inspire an audience. It was the oratory of festivals as well.

NT scholars debate which NT writings contain these various types of rhetoric. Their assumption is if a writing fits into one of these styles, it helps the interpreter understand the situation of the readers and the intent of the writer. Of course, there is a circular element here, since the style depends on the literary characteristics, and the literary characteristics are derived from the style of writing.

APPLYING RHETORICAL CRITICISM TO THE NEW TESTAMENT

Many biblical scholars answered the 1968 call of Muilenburg to engage in rhetorical criticism. A little over a decade later, biblical commentaries began to appear.[30] In addition, in the decade of the 1980s many wrote articles examining the literary features of biblical books,[31] and the rhetorical arguments provided ammunition for solving critical questions of

---

30. Among the first were two by Hans Dieter Betz. *Galatians: A Commentary on Paul's Letter to the Churches in Galatia* (Philadelphia: Fortress, 1979) and *2 Corinthians 8 and 9: A Commentary on Two Administrative Letters of the Apostle Paul* (Philadelphia: Fortress, 1985). See also Robert Jewett, *The Thessalonian Correspondence: Pauline Rhetoric and Millenarian Piety* (Philadelphia: Fortress, 1986) and Watson, *Invention, Arrangement, and Style*.

31. Such as Robert G. Hall, "The Rhetorical Outline for Galatians: A Reconsideration," *JBL* 106 (June 1987): 277–87; Robert Jewett, "Following the Argument of Romans," *WordWorld* 6 (fall 1986): 382–89; J. G.van der Watt, "Colossians 1:3–12 Considered as an Exordium," *JTSoA* 57 (December 1986): 32–42. Many others could be added to this list.

introduction.[32] At least one series is dedicated to helping scholars and lay-people appreciate the impact of rhetorical studies.[33]

Rhetorical criticism does not promise an entirely positive picture for biblical interpretation, however. Two questions haunt biblical scholars. Are the NT writings really as rhetorical as many have concluded? Further, is there any unanimity of conviction regarding the specific conclusions of rhetorical critics?

A COMPARATIVE PRESENTATION OF FIVE RHETORICAL ANALYSES ON THE BOOK OF ROMANS*

BOOK OF ROMANS	(1) QUINTIL-IAN	(2) JEWETT	(3) WUELLNER	(4) KENNEDY	(5) ALETTI (VOUGA)
EXORDIUM	1:1–12	1:1–12	1:1–15	1:8–15	1:1–17
NARRATIO	1:13–15	1:13–15		1:18—2:16	1:18—3:20
PROPOSI-TIO		1:16–17		1:16–17	3:21–31
PARTITIO					
PROBATIO	1:18—15:13	1:18—15:13	1:18—15:13	2:17—11:36	4:1—11:36
REFUTATIO				12:1—15:33	12:1—15:13
DIGRESSIO					
PERORATIO	15:14—16:27	15:14—16:27	15:14—16:23	15:14–33	15:14–33
SPECIES?	NON JUD.	DELIB	EPIDEI.	EPIDEI.	JUD.

---

32. See Black, "Authorship of Philippians," 269–89; Thomas L. Brodie, "Toward Unraveling the Rhetorical Imitation of Sources in Acts: 2 Kings as One Component of Acts 8:9–40," *Bib* 67 (1986): 41–67; Elizabeth Schussler Fiorenza, "Rhetorical Situation and Historical Reconstruction in 1 Corinthians," *NTS* 33 (1987): 386–403; and Duane F. Watson, "A Rhetorical Analysis of Philippians and Its Implications for the Unity Question," *NovT* 30 (January 1988): 57–88.

33. Charles H. Talbert, *A Literary and Theological Commentary on 1 and 2 Corinthians* (New York: Crossroads, 1989).

* Source: Columns (1) and (2) are taken from Robert Jewett, "Following the Argument of Romans." *WordWorld* 6 (1986):382–83, (3) adapted from Wilhelm Wuellner, "Paul's Rhetoric of Argumentation in Romans: An Alternative to the Donfried-Karris Debate over Romans." In *The Romans Debate*, ed. Karl P. Donfried (Peabody, Mass.: Hendrickson, 1991; reprint ed., Minneapolis, Minn.: Augsburg, 1977), 130–46, (4) adapted from George A. Kennedy, *NT Interpretation through Rhetorical Criticism* (Chapel Hill, N.C.: University of North Carolina, 1984), 152–56, and (5) adapted from Jean-Noël Aletti, "La présence d'un modèle rhétorique en Romains." *Bib* 71 (1990): 5–7.

Note: The species are abbreviated Jud. for Judicial, Delib. for Deliberative, and Epidei. for Epideictic. This species identification is supposed to be the major difference and benefit over an analysis of the parts of a letter.

The last question may pose the most difficulties. For example, a comparison of five recent approaches to the Epistle to the Romans reveals a broad spectrum of conclusions about the discourse. Romans provides a particularly good illustration of the problem, because scholars agree more on its basic genre than they do on most other NT books. The table below presents the reader with an overview of how rhetorical analysis has been applied to NT studies.[34]

Rhetorical criticism has occupied the minds and energies of an increasing number of scholars in the last twenty-five years. No doubt it will remain for years to come. It brings the promise of helpful analytical insights. It particularly helps the interpreter see the whole of a discourse, and it provides the tools for analysis of the structure of the parts. Nevertheless, interpreters should move slowly into this study, particularly if it is the only perspective taken of the text. As with other approaches, there is need for the wisdom of the community of scholars.

STRUCTURALISM

From another perspective, scholars analyzed the structure of the text. The leading contributors in biblical studies were Daniel Patte, Edgar McKnight, Eugene Nida, J. P. Louw, and Robert Longacre. Some, such as Patte and McKnight, moved in more philosophical directions with the discipline. Others, such as Nida, Louw, and Longacre, approached the subject as professional linguists who had deep interests in the practical use of the Bible. They ultimately hoped to facilitate Bible translation. From their study of many languages, they refined tools of analysis and applied them to the biblical texts.

Discourse analysis, one aspect of structuralism, basically observes the patterns of discourse. It analyzes the way people talk and what they mean by what they say. Meaning comes from the deep structure of language, found in what lies beyond normal semantic and grammatical categories. New approaches to syntax developed, and the discipline took a language of its own. It is particularly helpful in gospel-like narratives, but the initial investigation of books came from the Epistles.

---

34. The following chart comes from a seminar paper analysis of rhetorical criticism done by doctoral student Archie England entitled "A Brief Survey of Greco-Roman Rhetoric and Its Influence upon the Pauline Corpus of the New Testament," prepared for Dr. Richard Melick, (November 21, 1991), 36.

HISTORY OF THE DISCIPLINE

Structuralism is, in part, a reaction to a traditional approach to analyzing texts. It came out of the linguistic schools of France, Russia, and the United States and applied linguistic theory to biblical documents. In actuality, structuralism is a broad movement encompassing many disciplines. It includes linguistics, anthropology, law, philosophy, and sociology.[35] Structuralism is difficult to define. The term describes more a movement than a specific form of exegesis. Those who apply the basic principles often differ with each other, so there seems to be no clear result to the study.[36] Structuralism, therefore, implies more of a statement regarding a perspective of reality than an organized system or method.

Before the twentieth century, most grammarians operated on what now may be called a traditional approach. The first grammatical studies came from the fifth century B.C. in Greece. They represented a clear philosophy about language and corresponded to a consistent philosophical view of reality. The Greek philosophers "debated whether language was governed by 'nature' or 'convention.' "[37] If a grammatical or lexical form was "natural," it came from some universal or even eternal principle. If it were conventional, it came from the construct of the writer only. "To lay bare the origin of a word and thereby its 'true' meaning was to reveal one of the truths of 'nature.' "[38] Etymologies and emphasis on the individual words dominated grammar.

In the twentieth century, several challenged this attitude toward language. Particularly, Ferdinand de Saussure, a Swiss scholar, turned his attention to another perspective. He published his *Cours de linguistique generale*[39] in the first quarter of this century and spawned a host of linguistic interest. Saussure is considered by most to be the founder of modern linguistics. He was followed by Noam Chomsky and others who accepted his basic formulation of linguistic meaning.

THE PURPOSE OF STRUCTURALISM

Structuralism attempts to understand meaning by observing the deeper levels of thought expressed by language. Saussure articulated three major premises which determined the future of linguistic studies. First, he dis-

---

35. Longman, *Literary Approaches*, 27.

36. Vern S. Poythress, "Structuralism and Biblical Studies," *JETS* 21 (September 1978): 221.

37. John Lyons, *Introduction to Theoretical Linguistics* (Cambridge: Cambridge University Press, 1969), 4.

38. Ibid.

39. Ferdinand de Saussure, *Cours de linguistique generale* (Paris: Payot, 1922).

tinguished between *langue* and *parole*. *Langue* refers to a system of organized sounds which communicate effectively. It is a person's ability to
speak a given language. *Parole* refers to the specific use of a language in
making sentences. It occurs when one speaks. This meant the system must
be separated from a person's speaking within that system.

Saussure also distinguished between structural and functional features
of language. For him, languages function differently at times from what
one would expect by a cursory evaluation of their systems. This means
language must be considered functionally, since a writer or speaker may
actually *mean* something different from what he or she expresses. For Saussure, words must be analyzed according to the signified and the signifier.
The particular word employed is the signifier. Determining the meaning
of that word, however, requires some knowledge of how the signifier was
used. The meaning given the word is what the writer signified. In actuality, there may be little or no correlation between the two. In modern
English, for example, the word "bad" may signify something to some
readers, e.g., that one should avoid what is described by it. On the other
hand, the speaker might use the word in a positive sense. He or she might
be actually complimenting someone by the term ("He is a bad ball player,"
meaning he is great!). Thus what is signified has no actual relationship to
the signifier, the word chosen. Only a knowledge of American idiom dis-
closes what the speaker meant.

A third distinction of Sassure's work left a lasting impression. He distinguished between the syntagmatic and paradigmatic relationships of words. A
paradigmatic view of word relationships studies each word according to the
"slot" it occupies in a sentence. Any given word may be related to other
words in a paradigmatic relationship. That means a word is defined largely
by its relationship to words which are *not* used in the sentence. For example,
in the phrase "a brown dog," "dog" is defined by its relationship to other
animal forms, such as "cat" or "sheep." In a sense, meaning comes from what
is imported into the text by a preconceived understanding of the meaning of
words. In a syntagmatic relationship, the reader sees the whole statement of
which a word is a part. The entire context shapes the understanding so no
word has meaning apart from the other words used in connection with it.
This would be expanded beyond the words to the sentences and paragraphs,
so the basic unit for understanding would become the paragraph.

Other linguists added to and modified these ideas. Most notably, Noam
Chomsky, Leonard Bloomfield, Edward Sapir, Benjamin Lee Whorf, and
I. A. Richards contributed to this field of linguistics. The most significant,
however, was Noam Chomsky. Among the many contributions he made,
the most significant for biblical studies was the concept of "deep structure." Chomsky identified deep structure as "the underlying abstract

structure that determines its semantic interpretation."[40] In contrast to deep structure, the interpreter first confronts "surface structure." Chomsky called surface structure the "superficial organization of units which determines the phonetic interpretation and which relates to the physical form of the actual utterance."[41]

Chomsky's work meant that what appeared on the surface did not express the intent of the writer. The author's meaning occurs in the deep structure. The words chosen to express the meaning only function to provide that meaning. Chomsky developed a system of rules to allow an interpreter to get to the deep structure, or the meaning. He called these rules "transformational systems" which allowed one to see how the deep structure became the surface form.[42] Chomsky developed two sets of rules for analyzing literature: the transforms (which allow the interpreter to bring deep meaning to the surface) and the base structure rules (which are employed at the deepest level). These principles formed the basis of Chomsky's system, now called transformational-generative grammar.

Among others, Eugene Nida applied these principles to biblical interpretation. He identified five basic steps in analyzing the deep structure. (1) Identify the basic structural elements of each word. (2) Make explicit any implicit structural elements which are needed to clarify these elements. (3) Determine the basic kernels (elements) which are necessary in making a structurally complete sentence. (4) Group the kernels into related sets. (5) State these relationships in a form which will facilitate understanding and translation.[43] From this perspective, interpretation has three elements: determining the base meaning; determining the transforms employed to bring it to the surface; and determining the best meaning of the combination of "deep" and "surface" structures.

Structuralist exegesis contains at least three common elements. First, the whole of a statement is explained by examining the relationships of its parts. Structuralists sense that the whole will be greater than any individual part. Second, the significant part of communication lies below the surface of the literature. The interpreter, therefore, seeks to analyze meaning beyond what may be seen on the surface. Third, synchronic analysis pre-

---

40. Noam Chomsky, *Cartesian Linguistics: A Chapter in the History of Rationalist Thought* (New York: Harper & Row, 1966), 59.

41. Ibid., 59.

42. bid., 35.

43. Eugene A. Nida and Charles R. Taber, *The Theory and Practice of Translation* (Leiden: E. J. Brill, 1974), 51.

dominates over diachronic. Synchronic analysis involves examining a word, phrase, or sentence in light of the contemporary setting, rather than taking a historical view through time (diachronic).[44]

All of this helps demonstrate the purpose of structural criticism. Structuralists seek to understand the message by analyzing the deeper forms of the text. Assuming that the surface is purely functional, they hope to uncover a real meaning by working beyond the text. In this, structuralists have moved in many different directions. Some assume the author has no meaning intended by the deep structure. For them, the structure *is* the meaning. Others assume this knowledge of linguistic reality provides the necessary tools for understanding and interpreting. They employ the various methods to arrive at the author's intent.

THE PROCESS OF STRUCTURALISM

Structuralism approaches the text in various ways, depending on the particular nuance of the structural system. Some apply the basic methods in a philosophical sense. For example, the principles of Heidegger and Dilthey may be interpreted as conducive to structuralist thought. Indeed, the interaction between reader and writer has led to a "reader-response" hermeneutic which points out the structure of the language (text) and the meaning of the author (or, more likely, the reader's understanding of the text).[45] Like the other methods, one of the frustrations is the fact that differing conclusions have been reached by scholars who apply the same methods to specific biblical texts.[46]

Others apply structuralism in more textually oriented ways. For example, Eugene Nida's work attempts to help translate the text by understanding the author's meaning in the deep structure. Similarly, Robert Longacre and Kenneth Pike developed theories of discourse analysis which applied the functional nature of language and deep structure mod-

---

44. Poythress, "Structuralism and Biblical Studies," 222–23.

45. For example, Edgar V. McKnight has written extensively in the more philosophical vein. See *Meaning in Texts: The Historical Shaping of a Narrative Hermeneutic* (Philadelphia: Fortress, 1978); *Postmodern Use of the Bible: The Emergence of Reader-Oriented Criticism* (Nashville: Abingdon, 1988); and *The Bible and the Reader: An Introduction to Literary Criticism* (Philadelphia: Fortress, 1985). A helpful evaluation of this aspect of McKnight's work may be found in David M. McAlpin, "Epistemological Presuppositions of Selected Contemporary Structural Exegetes: A Theological Evaluation," Doctor of Theology diss., Mid-America Baptist Theological Seminary, 1990.

46. For example, see the different opinion regarding the structure and interpretation of the parable of the good Samaritan in Semeia, 1974.

els in exegesis of texts.[47] These have been applied to various texts and entire books of the NT. The results differ from traditional exegetical approaches but have many fruitful possibilities for analysis.[48]

Structuralism offers many positive helps for the exegesis of texts. It provides tools for understanding language and its functions. Further, it recognizes the dynamics of language and the contexts of people who use it. The distinctions between function and form, and syntagmatic versus paradigmatic approaches are especially helpful.

Negatively, however, some of this type of exegesis is prone to "faddism." In its more philosophical aspects, it depreciates the biblical text and, certainly, the author's intent. Nevertheless, the desire to expose deeper meaning is positive, as long as this quest is undertaken with a seriousness appropriate to understanding an ancient author's mind. That, after all, is the task of biblical exegesis.

CONTRIBUTIONS OF LITERARY CRITICISM

Literary criticism offers some positive contributions to biblical studies. Some values are in the focus of literary criticism. It takes the literary piece as a whole, rather than attempting an analysis of the individual parts. Further, it accepts the value of the document as it stands, rather than seeking to find how the individual parts came about or had meaning on their own. This means literary critics approach the document because it had value as a whole. Each document is approached in light of the contribution it makes theologically or practically. This, therefore, more naturally opens the door to theological investigation.

Literary criticism also makes a contribution in its basic quest for understanding events surrounding the production of a document. Its procedures provide another approach to understanding the author, his situation, his approach to the church, and what he desired to achieve by his writing. Correctly, literary critics assume that, if they understand the nature of the document, they will understand better the function of the document.

---

47. See Robert Longacre, *The Grammar of Discourse* (New York: Plenum Press, 1983) and *An Anatomy of Speech Notions* (Lisse: de Ridder, 1976). He also has written extensively on the subject in other monographs and in the linguistic journal OPTAT: Occasional Papers in Translation and Textlinguistics. Kenneth Pike has contributed in his book *Language in Relation to a Unified Theory of the Structure of Human Behavior*, 2d ed., vol. 24 of *Janua Linguarum: Studia Memoriae Nicolai van Wijk Dedicata*, ed. C. H. van Schooneveld (The Hague: Mouton, 1967).

48. Most of these applications have been in publications of OPTAT.

Third, literary criticism contributes uniquely to biblical studies in providing tools for analysis of the structure of a document. Here the parallels to other first-century literature provide helpful insight. The NT writers were products of their time in the way they constructed their materials. A sensitivity to such parallels, therefore, helps sharpen the analytical tools of biblical scholars.

Some cautions are in order, however. Perhaps the most basic relates to the quest for understanding genre. Has the interpreter indeed found the correct parallel for the specific document? The application of these criteria and characteristics is crucial. Misunderstanding the function of the document could lead to serious misjudgments in applying the Scriptures.

Another caution relates to the focus on structure and function instead of meaning. The assumption that all language is functional contains some dangers. Sometimes language imports meaning into a context. Subtly, the search for structure and functional approaches to the text could cause the exegete to miss important truths that arise from understanding the whole of Scripture. Canon criticism has justly pointed out such a likelihood and offered some corrections for this eventuality.

FOR FURTHER READING

Black, David Allen. "The Authorship of Philippians 2:6–11: Some Literary Critical Observations." In *CTR* 2 (spring 1988).

Cosby, Michael R. *The Rhetorical Composition and Function of Hebrews 11 in Light of Example Lists in Antiquity.* Macon, Ga.: Mercer Press, 1988.

Greidanus, Sidney. *The Modern Preacher and the Ancient Text: Interpreting and Preaching Biblical Literature.* Grand Rapids: Eerdmans, 1988.

Longacre, Robert. *The Grammar of Discourse.* (New York: Plenum Press, 1983).

Longman, Tremper, III. *Literary Approaches to Biblical Interpretation.* Vol. 3 of *Foundations of Contemporary Interpretation.* Grand Rapids: Academie Books, 1987.

McKnight, Edgar V. *The Bible and the Reader: An Introduction to Literary Criticism.* Philadelphia: Fortress, 1985.

Melick, Richard R., Jr. "Contemporary Hermeneutics and Authority." In *Authority and Interpretation: A Baptist Perspective.* Grand Rapids: Baker, 1987.

Silva, Moises, *Philippians.* In *Wycliffe Exegetical Commentary.* Chicago: Moody, 1988.

XXII

HISTORY AND CHRONOLOGY OF THE NEW TESTAMENT

HAROLD W. HOEHNER

PERSIAN RULE 539–331 B.C.

PERIOD OF PERSIAN STRENGTH 539–423 B.C.

In 539 B.C. Cyrus II of Persia defeated the Babylonians and allowed the dispersed nations, including the Jews, to return to their homeland (2 Chron. 36:21–23; Ezra 1; 6:3–5).[1] The Jews returned under Zerubbabel in 538/37 B.C. They set up the altar in October 537 B.C. and laid the foundation of the temple in May/April 536 B.C. (Ezra 2—6).

In 530 B.C., Cyrus was succeeded by his son, Cambyses II. To prevent usurpation of the Persian throne during his planned invasion of Egypt, Cambyses II secretly killed his brother Smeredis. During the war, a coup was nonetheless carried out by Psuedo-Smeredis (Gaumata). When Cambyses II learned of this at Hamath during his victorious return from Egypt, he committed suicide.

---

1. *ANET*, 316.

Cambyses II's general, Darius I, overthrew Pseudo-Semerdis immediately. In two years (521-520), he had won nineteen battles against nine vassal kings who had revolted against Persia. Darius I created an efficient central government in which satraps governed the provinces' civil affairs and military chiefs were responsible directly to him. He established a postal system with 111 stations from Susa to Sardis and Ephesus. Royal couriers traversed this 1,677-mile route in one week by horse relays. Caravans required three months.

The work on the Jewish temple had slowed during Cyrus II's reign and ceased under Cambyses II (Ezra 4:24). Haggai may have interpreted Darius' many battles throughout the Persian Empire as the time of the shaking of the nations when Messiah was to arrive (Hag. 2:6–7, 21–22). During Haggai's series of four messages (August to December 520 B.C.), Zechariah began his ministry (October/November 520 B.C.). They both encouraged the renewal of the temple's construction so Messiah could come.

The Greeks had renewed their resistance against Persian rule under Darius. After his son, Xerxes, ascended to the throne in 486 B.C., plans for an invasion of Greece were made. In the third year of his reign (483 B.C.), Xerxes revealed his plans to his governmental and military leaders at the banquet described in Esther 1:1–3, 19.

Xerxes began attacking Greece three years later during May/June but on 27/28 September 480 B.C., he was defeated at Salamis. He returned to Persia where he married Esther in December 479 or January 478 B.C. (Esth. 2:16). Because she and Mordecai prevented Haman from exterminating the Jews, the Feast of Purim was inaugurated 9/10 March 473 B.C.

Chronology of the Restoration Period			
538–515	483	457	444
Zerubbabel Ezra 1—6	Esther Book of Esther	Ezra Ezra 7—10	Nehemiah Book of Nehemiah

The strong government Darius had left to Xerxes had weakened until the entire empire was troubled when Xerxes was replaced by his son, Artaxerxes I, in 465 B.C. During Artaxerxes' reign, many Jews returned under Ezra from March to July 457 B.C. (Ezra 7—10). Nehemiah came to rebuild the walls of Jerusalem in March/April of 444 B.C. (Neh. 1—6) and remained in Jerusalem until 433/32 B.C. (Neh. 13:6), when he returned to Persia. He returned to Judah sometime before Artaxerxes I's death in 423 B.C. (Neh. 13:6–31).

PERIOD OF PERSIAN DECLINE 423–331 B.C.

Artaxerxes' son, Darius II (423–404) supported the Spartans financially, helping them defeat Athens in the Pelponnesian War (431–404). As Persian forces reoccupied Lydia in 413 B.C., Darius gained strength in the West.

After a massive revolt in Egypt, the Egyptians destroyed the Jewish temple at Elephantine in 410 B.C. because of popular sentiment against animal sacrifices. The Elephantine Jews reported the destruction and need for assistance to the Persian governor Bagoas and to the high priest Johanan (or Jonathan) in Jerusalem during Darius II's reign (Neh. 12:11, 22–23). After a second petition addressed to Bagoas alone to rebuild the temple of Yaho in the fortress of Elephantine, permission was granted.[2] In 419 B.C. Darius II ordered Arsanes, satrap of Egypt, to allow the Jews to celebrate the Feast of Unleavened Bread in the Jewish garrison.[3]

Darius II was succeeded by one of his sons, Artaxerxes II (404–358). Although he crushed his brother Cyrus' rebellion (401 B.C.) and repelled the Spartans' intervention in Asia Minor (386 B.C.), he lost Egypt in 402/1 B.C. Artaxerxes II occupied Jerusalem, defiled the temple, imposed a heavy fine, and persecuted the people for several years. The Samaritans were more willing to submit to the ruler of the day and escaped persecution.

After Artaxerxes III (358–338) succeeded his father, he killed off all his relatives. His failure to drive Egypt back in 351 B.C. caused a general revolt in Palestine. In 345 B.C. he marched against Sidon, and in 343 B.C. reconquered Egypt with the help of Mentor of Rhodes. In 338 B.C. Artaxerxes III was poisoned by his minister Bagoas ("eunuch kingmaker") who placed Arses, son of Artaxerxes III, on the throne. Within two years Arses attempted to poison Bagoas but Bagoas first killed him and all his children. Bagoas appointed to the throne Darius III, Artaxerxes III's cousin (336–330). When Darius became powerful, Bagoas attempted to poison him also, but Darius forced the eunuch to drink the fatal cup himself. Shortly after the accession of Darius III, the Persians were threatened by Philip of Macedon's preparation to destroy the Persian Empire. Much to

---

2. Ibid., 492.
3. Ibid., 491.

Darius' relief, Philip was murdered in 336 B.C. by his bodyguard Pausanius.

Hellenistic Rule 331–143 B.C.

Alexander the Great 356–323 B.C.

Philip's son Alexander III, the Great, was only twenty years old when he took the throne. From the age of thirteen he had been taught by Aristotle and was convinced of the supremacy of Greek culture. Consequently, his dream was to continue his father's conquest of the world in order to Hellenize it. In 334 B.C. he crossed the Hellespont with about 40,000 men and soundly defeated the Persian army of 20,000 men at the foot of Mount Ida by the Grannicus River. This opened Asia Minor to Alexander, and about a year later he was at Issus. There, Darius, with his 400,000 infantry and 100,000 cavalry, was defeated in November 333 B.C. Leaving behind his mother, wife, two daughters, and a son, Darius fled to the East to consolidate his power.

Although this opened the East to Alexander, he adhered to his original plan of occupying Phoenicia, Palestine, and Egypt. Alexander moved south and defeated the Phoenician cities, taking Tyre after a seven-month battle (from January to August 332 B.C.). Palestine fell to him when he conquered Gaza after a two-month siege (from September to October 332 B.C.). It is at this juncture, according to Josephus,[4] that Alexander went to Jerusalem and offered sacrifices to God in the temple under the direction of the high priest Jaddua. Alexander was told, based on the Book of Daniel, that he was the one predicted to destroy the Persian Empire (cf. Dan. 8:5–7, 20–21). He accepted this interpretation and, being favorably disposed, he allowed the Jews in Palestine, Babylonia, and Media to live according to their ancestral laws and to be exempt from tribute every sabbatical year. Although the historicity of this account has been disputed among scholars, there is no reason to doubt that the relationship between Alexander and the Jews was amicable.

Alexander then proceeded to Egypt, which yielded to him with no trouble, and he spent the winter there (332/31 B.C.). In the spring he began his trek northward and, after a great battle, defeated Darius at Guagamela in October 331 B.C. After this decisive battle, Darius fled with his Bactrian cavalry and Greek mercenaries to Ecbatana. Alexander proceeded to occupy the Persian capitals (Babylon, Susa, Persepolis, Ecbatana). In July 330 B.C., when Alexander was approaching Bactra, Darius

---

4. Josephus, *Antiquities* 11.8.4–5, 326–39; cf. also *BT: Yoma 69a*.

was killed by the Bactrian Bessus. Alexander gave him a royal funeral at Persepolis.

Alexander was free to assume the title *king of Asia*. He made a conquest of Bactria and Sogdiana from 330 to 327 B.C. The Indian expedition extended his eastern frontiers to the Hyphasis and Lower Indus (327–325 B.C.). Only thirty-two years and eight months old, Alexander died a world conqueror 23 June 323 B.C. Alexander's dissemination of the Greek language and culture prepared the way for the gospel.

PTOLEMAIC RULE 323–198 B.C.

Division of the Empire 323–301 B.C. When Alexander was upon his deathbed, his generals asked who was to be his successor. He replied that his empire was "to go to the best man."[5] Just before he died, he gave his ring to Perdiccas, one of Philip's generals. The generals met to decide what was to be done. Having been away from home eleven years, the foot soldiers desired to have Alexander's half-sane brother Arrhidaeus. The cavalry preferred the unborn son of Alexander's Bactrian wife Roxane. A compromise was reached by having both Arrhidaeus, whose name was changed to Philip, and Roxane's son rule with Perdiccas as regent. The empire then was divided into more than twenty satrapies.

Perdiccas wanted to become the central figure of the empire, and the satraps regarded him with suspicion. When Alexander's body was brought from Babylon on the way to Macedonia, Ptolemy met the retinue in Syria, seized the body, and took it to Egypt for burial, directly challenging Perdiccas' authority. Perdiccas attacked Egypt but was killed by his generals (321 B.C.), among whom was Seleucus. Antipater was not elected regent, there was a new distribution of the satrapies, and Antigonus was appointed general of the royal army. In 320 B.C., feeling temporarily safe from Babylonian attack, Ptolemy claimed Syrian Palestine as part of Egypt. When Antipater died in 318 B.C., Antigonus, having demonstrated his military skill, was devoted to reuniting Alexander's empire under himself. He began to be assertive and remove generals opposed to him.

Seleucus, not powerful enough to defend himself against Antigonus' demands, fled to warn Ptolemy in 316 B.C. They, with Lysimachus and Cassander, formed an alliance against Antigonus. When Antigonus was in the region of Syria in 315 B.C., Ptolemy claimed that Syria and Palestine were his and that Babylonia belonged to Seleucus. Antigonus invaded Syria and Palestine, occupying all the country down to Gaza. In 312 B.C. Ptolemy and Seleucus attacked Gaza and defeated Demetrius, the son of

---

5. Arrian 7.26.3; Diodorus 18.1.4.

Antigonus. This decisive battle allowed Seleucus to recover Babylonia and by 311 B.C. be acknowledged as its ruler. This was the commencement of the Seleucid dynasty on which much of intertestamental chronology is based. A peace treaty was signed in 311 B.C. by Cassander, Ptolemy, Lysimachus, and Antigonus whereby Ptolemy lost control over Syria and Palestine, and Antigonus gained control of Asia. Antigonus in 310–309 B.C. attempted to gain control of Babylonia but was unable to subdue Seleucus. Antigonus fortified himself in Syria and controlled Palestine.

Ptolemy, Seleucus, Lysimachus, and Cassander made an agreement in 303 B.C. that Ptolemy would receive Coele-Syria Palestine upon Antigonus's defeat. However, Ptolemy did not take part in the decisive battle at Ipsus, Phrygia, at which Antigonus was killed (301 B.C.). Seleucus was about to take the area, but Ptolemy forestalled by taking possession of Lower Syria (south of Lebannon and Damascus), Palestine, and Phoenicia south of the Eleutherus River. This action was the bone of contention between the Seleucidian and Ptolemaic houses for decades. The empire was divided into four areas: Egypt and Palestine up to Sidon went to Ptolemy, Phrygia to the Indus (including Syria north of Sidon) to Seleucus, Thrace and Bithynia to Lysimachus, and Macedonia to Cassander. Palestine changed hands six times in twenty-two years (323–301 B.C.). In interpreting Daniel 11:4, one might identify clearly the rulers between 312 and 301 B.C. as the four who would succeed Alexander (cf. 7:6; 8: 8, 22).

Domination of the Ptolemies 301–198 B.C. Under Ptolemaic control, Judea remained under the leadership of the high priest as in the days of Ezra and Nehemiah. The high priest paid the annual tax out of his own resources, not from the temple's. Relatively unmolested Judea was treated as a sacerdotal province that remained the property of the deity under the high priest's leadership.

There was relative peace in the land under the reign of Ptolemy I. Although Seleucus felt Palestine should have been his, he did not contest it since he realized that Ptolemy had helped him when he fled from Babylon in 316 B.C. However, the years 282–281 B.C. marked a turning point in the relationship between their houses. In 282 B.C. Ptolemy I died and was succeeded by Ptolemy II Philadelphus. In 281 B.C. Seleucus conquered Phrygia, crossed the Hellespont, and marched into Europe. He aimed to possess all of Alexander's empire outside Egypt and Palestine. Soon after crossing the Hellespont, he was assassinated and was succeeded by his son Antiochus I Soter who had been coruler since 293/92 B.C.

In the ensuing confusion Antigonus Gonatas (son of Demetrius, grandson of Antigonus I) gained control of Macedonia. A threefold division resulted that lasted until the Roman invasion. The three superpowers—

the first two of which are more important for this study—were the house of Seleucus over Babylon, Upper Syria, and Asia Minor; the house of Ptolemy over Egypt and Coele-Syria (Lower Syria); and the house of Antigonus over Europe.

Antiochus I and Ptolemy II did not have the same relationship as their fathers had: There were four Syrian Wars between them for the domination of Coele-Syria. In 202 B.C. Antiochus III made a pact with Philip V of Macedon for a division of Egypt between them. In 201 B.C. he invaded Palestine and after great difficulty captured Gaza. Having secured Palestine, Antiochus III invaded the dominions of Attalus, king of Pergamos (who was pro-Roman against Philip V), in the winter of 199/98 B.C.

The Egyptian general, Scopas, hearing of Antiochus' absence from Palestine, invaded the city and recovered the lost territories. Antiochus returned and decisively defeated Ptolemy V at Panias which later became known as Caesarea Philippi (Dan 11:14–16). Antiochus released prisoners; allowed worship to be conducted according to the Jewish laws; allowed the completion and maintenance of the temple; permanently exempted from taxes the council of elders, priests, and scribes at the temple; and exempted the citizens of Jerusalem from taxes for the first three years, after which he exempted them from a third of their taxes. The Battle of Panias in 198 B.C. marked a turning point in Jewish history because from this time until Roman control (63 B.C.) the Jews remained connected with the Seleucid dynasty. Under the Ptolemies, the Jews were treated with considerable tolerance, but after only a brief period of tranquility under the Seleucid rule, the Jews experienced fierce persecution.

SELEUCID RULE 198–143 B.C.

Seleucid Control 198–167 B.C. One reason for the Jews' tranquility immediately after the Seleucid takeover was that the Seleucids were concentrating their efforts in the West. Rome had defeated Hannibal at Zama (near Carthage) in 202 B.C. and then the Macedonian monarchy in 197 B.C. In light of the new threat, the Seleucid king Antiochus III discontinued his war with Egypt. His treaty required Ptolemy V Epiphanes to marry Cleopatra, Antiochus III's daughter. Antiochus expected this marriage to result in his grandson being the next pro-Seleucid king of Egypt (Dan. 11:17). Antiochus III invaded Thrace in 196 B.C. and Greece (which the Romans had evacuated) in 194 B.C. The Romans retaliated and defeated him at Thermopylae in 191 B.C. and at Magnesia in Asia Minor in 190 B.C. In the peace treaty signed at Apamea in 189 B.C., Antiochus agreed to give up Asia Minor north and west of the Tarsus Mountains, reduce much of his military force, and pay a heavy indemnity over a twelve-year period. He had to leave twenty hostages in Rome until the indemnity was paid, one of whom was his third son Antiochus IV Epiphanes (Dan. 11:18–19; 1 Macc. 1:10; 8:6–8).

Antiochus III was succeeded by his second son Seleucus IV Philopator in 187 B.C. To pay the heavy indemnity to Rome, he unsuccessfully attempted to rob the temple via his chief minister Heliodorus (2 Macc. 3:7; cf. Dan. 11:20). In 175 B.C. Heliodorus, in attempting to seize the throne, assassinated Seleucus IV, but was ousted by Antiochus IV Epiphanes. Antiochus had just been released from Rome as a hostage, went to Syria and with the help of Eumenes II, king of Pergamon, made himself king.

Since Antiochus' newly acquired kingdom lacked political and financial stability, he attempted to unify it by a vigorous Hellenization program. He thought religion could be one of the unifying factors, so he encouraged the people to worship him in the form of the Olympian Zeus (Dan. 11:21–24). His title *Theos Epiphanes* ("the manifest god") was modified with one Greek letter by his enemies to *Epimanes* ("madman" or "insane").

Soon after Antiochus' accession he was called upon to settle a dispute between the pro-Ptolemaic high priest Onias III and Onias' pro-Seleucid brother Jason (a Greek name which he preferred to the Hebrew name *Joshua/Jesus*). The high priest formerly belonged to the house of Onias, but it became an appointment made by the Syrian king. In 174 B.C. Jason secured the high priesthood by offering a larger payment of money to Antiochus and by pledging his wholehearted support in the Hellenization of the Jerusalemites (1 Macc. 1:10–15; 2 Macc. 4:7–17). In 171 B.C. Jason's one-time friend Menelaus offered Antiochus three hundred more talents than Jason for the position of high priest, also promising a vigorous Hellenization program. Antiochus gladly accepted Menelaus's higher bid, for it would help financially. Since Menelaus was a Benjaminite and outside the Aaronic line (2 Macc. 4:23; 3:4), Antiochus thought his appointment would break the unifying force of the Jews' religion. It also would allow the Seleucids to select the high priests at will.

The next year (170 B.C.) the amateur regents Eulaeus and Lenueus advised their minor king Ptolemy VI Philometor to avenge Panias and recover Coele-Syria. Antiochus learned of their plans, invaded Egypt with a large army in 170/169 B.C. and defeated Ptolemy VI. He proclaimed himself king of Egypt and allowed a rivalry to exist by making Ptolemy VI Philometor king of Memphis and his brother Ptolemy VIII Euergetes king of Alexandria (Dan. 11:25–27). It was rumored that Antiochus was killed in Egypt. When Menelaus plundered the temple, the Jews, led by Jason, revolted and forced Menelaus to take refuge in the Acra. Unwisely, Jason massacred many innocent people. Consequently, he was driven out of the city and forced to take refuge again in Transjordan (2 Macc. 4:39—5:10).

Upon returning from Egypt, Antiochus interpreted the rebellion to have been against him and subdued Jerusalem. With Menelaus, Antiochus desecrated and plundered the temple of its treasures, leaving the city under one of his commanders, Philip, a Phrygian (1 Macc. 1:20–29; 2 Macc. 5:18–22).

Antiochus' second campaign in Egypt came in 168 B.C. His rival nephews ruling Memphis and Alexandria united against him (winter of 169/68). Antiochus conquered parts of Egypt in the spring of 168 B.C. He subdued Memphis and was near Alexandria when the Roman representative Popillius Laenas (whom Antiochus had known in Rome) handed him an ultimatum from the senate to evacuate Egypt at once (Dan. 11:28–30).[6] Antiochus wanted time for consideration, but the Roman legate arrogantly drew with his walking stick a circle in the sand around Antiochus and demanded an answer before he stepped outside the circle. Having learned Rome's might as a hostage for fourteen years, he quickly retreated. With bitterness he returned to Palestine (Dan. 11:30), determined to make it a buffer state between himself and the Romans.

Maccabean Revolt 167–143 B.C.

Antiochus' Vengeance 167–166 B.C. Considering himself Zeus Epiphanes, Antiochus ordered a cultic Hellenization in Palestine. In 167 B.C. he determined to exterminate the Jewish religion. He forbade their ancestral laws, the observance of the Sabbath, customary festivals, traditional sacrifices, and circumcision of children. He ordered the destruction of copies of the Torah. Idolatrous altars were set up, and the Jews were commanded to offer unclean sacrifices and to eat swine's flesh (2 Macc. 6:18). Anyone who disobeyed any one of these orders was sentenced to death. On 25 Chislev (16 December 167 B.C.) the climactic, contemptuous deed was the offering of swine's flesh on the altar of Zeus which was erected on the altar of burnt offering, making the temple of Jerusalem the place of worship of the Olympian Zeus (Dan. 11:31–32; 1 Macc. 1:41–64; 2 Macc. 6:1–11). On the twenty-fifth of each month sacrifices were dedicated to Antiochus in commemoration of his birthday. He intended to consolidate his empire around the Hellenic culture and religion, but he was unaware of the Jews' loyalty to their God. His actions sparked the Maccabean Revolt.

Mattathias 166 B.C. Every village in Palestine was ordered to set up a heathen altar, and imperial delegates made sure the citizens offered heathen sacrifices. In the village of Modein (seventeen miles northwest of

---

6. Cf. Polybius 29.2.1–4; 27.1–8; Livy 45.12.1–6; Diodorus 31.2; Velleius Paterculus 1.10.1–2; Appian, *The Syrian Wars* 66; Justinus, *Epitome* 24.3.

Jerusalem) an aged priest named Mattathias refused to offer a heathen sacrifice when ordered by Antiochus IV's agent. When another Jew volunteered to offer the sacrifice, Mattathias killed him. He also killed the imperial delegate. He then tore down the altar and proclaimed, "Let everyone who is zealous for the law and supports the covenant come out with me" (1 Macc. 2:15–27; Dan. 11:32–35). Mattathias, his five sons (John, Simon, Judas, Eleazar, and Jonathan), and many followers fled to the mountains.

The Hasidim, a religious group within Judaism with a great passion for the law of God, joined Mattathias in his struggle against Hellenization. Mattathias' forces waged war against the Jews who complied with Antiochus, tore down heathen altars, circumcised children who had been left uncircumcised, and exhorted Jews everywhere to follow in their crusade. During this struggle Mattathias died (166 B.C.), leaving the struggle in the hands of his third son Judas, with whom a new era of fighting commenced (1 Macc. 2:42–70).

Judas Maccabeus 166–160 B.C. Mattathias' selection of Judas was the right choice, for he was the terror of his enemies and the pride of his nation. Under him the Maccabean struggle went from guerrilla warfare to well-planned battles. In his first year of leadership he won more volunteers to fight for freedom when he defeated the Syrian governors, Apollonius and Seron (1 Macc. 3:10–26). Due to troubles in the East, Antiochus ordered Lysias, regent of the western part of the empire, to make an end of the rebellion and to destroy the Jewish race (1 Macc. 3:32–36). But Judas decisively defeated the Syrians at Emmaus (1 Macc. 4:1–27). In 164 B.C. Lysias attacked Jerusalem from the south but was completely defeated at Beth-zur and withdrew to Antioch (1 Macc. 4:28–35).

Having regained the entire country, Judas moved to restore Jewish worship in the temple. He marched on Jerusalem and occupied all of it except the Acra. This left him free to restore the temple. He selected priests who had remained faithful, destroyed the altar of the Olympian Zeus, and rebuilt and refurbished the temple. On 25 Chislev (14 December 164 B.C.), exactly three years after its desecration, the temple was rededicated and the daily sacrifices commenced (1 Macc. 4:36–59; 2 Macc. 10:1–8). This marked the commencement of Hanukkah (Feast of Dedication or Lights). Immediately after this, Judas fortified the Jerusalem walls and the city of Beth-zur on the border of Idumea. The victories of Judas resulted in making Judah reasonably secure. All the Jews of Palestine, after several campaigns, were independent from Antiochus' rule.

Next, the Maccabees sought to break Syrian control of the Acra in Jerusalem. Their domination was a constant reminder that Antiochus' decree forbidding the practice of the Jewish religion had not been withdrawn. In the spring or summer of 163 B.C. Judas laid siege to it. Some Syrian soldiers and Hellenistic Jews escaped and went to Antioch for help (1 Macc. 6:18–27). Antiochus IV had died insane in Tabae/Gabae, Persia (spring/summer of 163 B.C.), and been succeeded by his nine-year-old son Antiochus V Eupator whom Lysias crowned king (1 Macc. 6:5–17). Immediately Lysias and the boy-king went south where they defeated Judas at Beth-zechariah (southwest of Jerusalem). Eleazar, the second youngest of Judas' brothers, was killed while attempting to kill a war elephant. Lysias laid siege to Jerusalem (1 Macc. 6:28–54). Judas was in desperate straits because of a food shortage due to it being a sabbatical year. Lysias heard that Philip (a friend of Antiochus IV who had been promised the guardianship of Antiochus V) was marching from Persia to Syria to claim the kingdom for himself. Lysias became anxious to make a peace treaty with Judas and guaranteed him religious toleration, although he tore down the walls of Jerusalem (1 Macc. 6:55–63). The Jews again were under Syrian rule, but they at least had obtained religious toleration.

To counteract this toleration of Judaism, the Syrian government strengthened the Hellenistic elements among the Jews. Lysias, it seems, appointed the high priest Alcimus (Hebrew *Jakim*, or *Jehoakim*) who, while idealogically a Hellenist, was of Aaronic descent (cf. 1 Macc. 7:14; 2 Macc. 14:3–7). This was unacceptable to Judas. Meanwhile in Syria, Demetrius I Soter, nephew of Antiochus IV and cousin of Antiochus V, escaped from Rome (where he had been a hostage when Antiochus IV was released), killed both Lysias and Antiochus V, and assumed the throne. He confirmed Alcimus as high priest (162 B.C.) and sent him to Jerusalem with an army led by his general Baccahides. The Hasidim accepted Alcimus as high priest probably because of his Aaronic descent and the Syrians' guarantee to tolerate their worship. The Hasidims at first split from Judas' ranks but quickly returned to him when Alcimus slew sixty of them (1 Macc. 7:15–20). Alcimus asked Demetrius for more military help against Judas and his followers, the Hasideans (2 Macc. 14:6). Demetrius sent Nicanor, but he was defeated and killed at Adasa (four miles north of Jerusalem) on 13 Adar (9 March 161 B.C.), which the Jews celebrate annually as Nicanor's Day. Nicanor's army was wiped out at Gazara (twenty miles west of Adasa). Alcimus fled to Syria (1 Macc. 7:26–50). Judas sent for help from Rome, but before any help could come, Demetrius sent Bacchides with Alcimus to avenge Nicanor's death. Because of the might of the Syrian army, many deserted Judas, and in the Battle of Elasa (ten to twelve miles north of Jerusalem) Judas was slain (160 B.C.).

Jonathan 160–143 B.C. Judas' death was a great blow to the Hasideans' morale. The Hellenists were temporarily in control while Jonathan and his followers were in the wilderness of Tekoa, carrying on guerrilla warfare. Bacchides fortified Jerusalem and the Judean cities against possible Maccabean attacks. In May of 159 B.C. Alcimus died, and no successor was chosen. Bacchides left his command in Judah and returned to Antioch. In 157 B.C. Bacchides returned to Jerusalem at the request of the Hellenists but was defeated at Beth-basi (six miles south of Jerusalem), made a peace treaty with Jonathan, and returned to Antioch.

This weakened the Hellenists' position. Jonathan made Michmash (nine miles north of Jerusalem) his headquarters where he judged the people, punishing the Hellenizers (1 Macc. 9:23–27). During the next five years Jonathan's power increased. In 152 B.C. Jonathan was further helped by Syria's internal power struggles. Alexander Balas, who claimed to be the son of Antiochus Epiphanes, challenged Demetrius I. Both vied for Jonathan's support. Fortunately, Jonathan sided with Alexander Balas, for in 150 B.C. Alexander won a battle in which Demetrius was slain. Alexander made Jonathan a general, governor, high priest of Judah, and one of his chief friends (1 Macc. 10:22–66). This was a strange alliance: a professed son of Antiochus Epiphanes in league with a Maccabean!

New troubles came in Syria. Demetrius' son, Demetrius II Nicator, challenged Alexander Balas in 147 B.C. and finally defeated him in 145 B.C. Since Demetrius II was sixteen years old and inexperienced, Jonathan took the opportunity to attack the Acra in Jerusalem where the Hellenistic Jews were still in control. Although Jonathan failed to overtake the Acra, Demetrius II later confirmed him as high priest and granted his request for three districts in southern Samaria.

In 143 B.C. Demetrius II's army rebelled, and Diodotus Tryphon (a general under Alexander Balas) claimed the Syrian throne for Alexander Balas' son, Antiochus VI. Jonathan sided with Tryphon, who made Jonathan head of civil and religious agencies while his brother Simon was made head of the military. However, Tryphon, fearful of Jonathan's success, killed him. Jonathan was buried at Modein (1 Macc. 10:67—13:30).

Jonathan had become both the political and the religious leader, merging the offices of Judea's sole ruler and high priest, ousting the Hellenists. The Maccabean dream had come true: The Israelites were an independent nation. A new phase of the Maccabean rule emerged. Although the term *Hasmonean* was originally the Maccabees' family name, it became assoicated with the high priestly house after this consolidation of power.

HASMONEAN RULE 143–63 B.C.

SIMON 143–135 B.C.

Simon, the second-oldest son of Mattathias, succeeded his younger brother Jonathan. There was a great upheaval in Syria because Tryphon killed Antiochus VI and reigned in his stead (1 Macc. 13:31–32) as a rival to Demetrius. Because of the dastardly act of Tryphon against Jonathan, Simon naturally attached himself to Demetrius II on the condition of Judea's complete independence. Since Demetrius no longer controlled the southern parts of the Syrian Empire, he extended Simon complete exemption from past and future taxation (142 B.C.). This meant that the yoke of the Gentiles over Israel had been removed for the first time since the Babylonian captivity, and Judea's political independence meant they could write their own documents and treaties (1 Macc. 13:33–42).

Because of Tryphon's threat, Simon seized the fortress of Gazara (Gezer, between Jerusalem and Joppa), expelling Gentiles, replacing them with Jews, and appointing his son John Hyrcanus as governor (1 Macc. 13:43–48, 53; 16:1, 21). Shortly thereafter, Simon captured the Acra in Jerusalem which had been in the control of the Hellenizers for more than forty years, serving as a reminder of Syrian control. With the last vestige of Syrian control overthrown, the Acra was purified on the 23 Ziv (3 June 141 B.C., 1 Macc. 13:49–52). Simon made a peace treaty with Rome and Sparta, guaranteeing Jewish worship.

In commemoration of this achievement, on 13 September 140 B.C. the Jews conferred upon Simon the position of political leader and high priest until there should arise a faithful prophet (1 Macc. 14:25–49, esp. v. 41). The high priesthood formerly belonged to the house of Onias, but ended in 174 B.C. Thus, both the political and priestly powers were vested in the Hasmonean line.

Antiochus VII Sidetes enlisted Simon's cooperation in 139 B.C. and they defeated Tryphon together. Antiochus then sent his general Cendebeus to conquer Palestine, but he was defeated by Simon's two sons, Judas and John Hyrcanus (1 Macc. 15:1–14, 25—16:10).

In 135 B.C. Antiochus' son-in-law, Ptolemy, killed Simon and Judas at a banquet near Jericho. Ptolemy also sent men to capture John Hyrcanus, a military leader at Gazara. Being forewarned, Hyrcanus captured his would-be assasins and killed them. He went to Jerusalem and was well received (1 Macc. 16:11–23).

HYRCANUS I 135–104 B.C.

John Hyrcanus succeeded his father as high priest and ruler of the people. In the first year of his reign Antiochus VII reasserted his claim over Judea, seized Joppa and Gazara, ravaged the land, and besieged Jerusalem. With food supplies dwindling, Hyrcanus asked for a seven-day truce to celebrate the Feast of Tabernacles. Antiochus not only complied but also sent gifts for their celebration, indicating Antiochus' willingness to negotiate a peace settlement. The result was that the Syrians could not establish a garrison in Jerusalem, but the Jews had to hand over their arms; pay heavy tribute for the return of Joppa and other cities bordering on Judea; give hostages, one of which was Hyrcanus' brother; and destroy the walls of Jerusalem. The independence gained by Jonathan and Simon was destroyed in one single blow.

However, in 130 B.C. Antiochus became involved in a campaign against the Parthians which resulted in his death the following year. Demetrius II, released by the Parthians, again gained control of Syria (129-125), but troubles within Syria prevented him from bothering Hyrcanus. When Hyrcanus renewed his alliance with Rome, the Romans confirmed his independence and warned Syria against any intervention in Hyrcanus' territory. Hyrcanus took advantage of the situation and extended his borders in three directions: to the east by conquering Medeba in Transjordan; to the north by capturing Shechem and Mount Gerizim and destroying the Samaritan temple (128 B.C.); and to the south by overtaking the Idumean cities of Adora and Marisa forcing upon the Idumeans either circumcision or emigration. In 109 B.C. Hyrcanus and his sons conquered Samaria which enabled him to occupy the Esdraelon Valley all the way to Mount Carmel. Hyrcanus' independence was further demonstrated with the minting of coins bearing his own name which no other Jewish king had ever done (110/109).

During the reign of Hyrcanus I, the Pharisees and the Sadducees first came into prominence. Although the origins of the two parties are obscure, they were well established by Hyrcanus I's reign. With Hyrcanus' successes there came a rift between him and the Pharisees. The Pharisees, descendants of the Hasidim, were indifferent to the political successes of the Hasmoneans and critical of the high priesthood's Hellenization and secularization. They questioned whether Hyrcanus should be high priest. However, the Sadducees, a party of mostly aristocratic priests, opposed the Pharisees and sided with Hyrcanus.

After thirty-one years of rule, Hyrcanus I died peacefully, leaving five sons (104 B.C.). Hyrcanus desired that his wife would head the civil government while his oldest son Aristobulus I would be the high priest.

ARISTOBULUS I 104–103 B.C.

Unpleased with his father's division of power, Aristobulus imprisoned his mother, who died of starvation, and imprisoned all of his brothers except Antigonus who shared in his rule until Aristobulus had him killed. Aristobulus's rule lasted only a year, but that was long enough for him to conquer Galilee, whose inhabitants he compelled to be circumcised. Aristobulus died of a severe illness.

ALEXANDER JANNEUS 103–76 B.C.

Upon the death of Aristobulus, his widow Salome Alexandra released his three surviving brothers from prison. She appointed Alexander Janneus king and high priest, subsequently marrying him. He endeavored to follow in the footsteps of his father and brother in territorial expansion. He captured the coastal Greek cities from Carmel to Gaza (except Ascalon), compelling the Jewish law upon the inhabitants. He was so successful in his conquests in Transjordan and to the south that the size of his kingdom was equal to David's and Solomon's.

However, there were real conflicts within his domain. Janneus was a drunkard and loved war. The Pharisees saw that the Hasmoneans and Sadducees were deviating more from Jewish ideals. At a Feast of Tabernacles celebration Janneus poured the water libation over his feet instead of on the altar as prescribed by the Pharisaic ritual. The people, enraged, shouted and pelted him with lemons. Janneus ordered his mercenary troops to attack, and 6,000 Jews were massacred.

In 94 B.C. Janneus attacked Obedas, the king of the Arabs, but suffered a severe defeat, barely escaping with his life. Upon his return to Jerusalem the people turned against him, and with the help of foreign mercenaries Alexander Janneus fought six years against his people, slaying no less than 50,000 Jews. The Pharisees called upon the Seleucid Demetrius III Eukairos to help them in 88 B.C. Thus, the descendants of the Hassadim asked the descendants of Antiochus Epiphanes to aid them in their fight against the descendants of the Maccabees! Wars create strange allies. Janneus was defeated at Shechem and fled to the mountains. However, six thousand Jews, realizing their national existence was threatened, sided with Janneus because they felt it the lesser of two evils to side with him in a free Jewish state than to be annexed to the Syrian Empire. But when Janneus reestablished himself, he forced Demetrius to withdraw, and he ordered eight hundred Pharisees to be crucified, seeing their wives and children killed while he feasted and caroused with his concubines. Because of these atrocities eight thousand Jews fled the country.

Upheavals in the Seleucid Empire affected Janneus. The Nabateans were becoming strong and opposed a Seleucid rule. Around 85 B.C. the Nabatean king Aretas invaded Judea. Janneus retreated to Adida (twenty miles northwest of Jerusalem), but Aretas withdrew after coming to terms with Janneus. From 83 to 80 B.C. Aretas was successful in his campaign in the East, conquering Pella, Dium, Gerasa, Gaulana, Seleucia, and Gamala. He was ill the last three years of his life (79–76) due to over-drinking.

ALEXANDRA 76–67 B.C.

Upon his deathbed, Janneus appointed his wife Salome Alexandra as his successor. She selected their eldest son Hyrcanus II as the high priest. Janneus advised Alexandra to make peace with the Pharisees since they controlled the masses. She followed his advice, reviving the Pharisaic influence. This switch was not difficult since her brother Simeon Ben Shetah was the Pharisees' leader. This move was vehemently opposed by her younger son Aristobulus who sided with the Sadducees. With Alexandra's permission, the Sadducees were allowed to leave Jerusalem and take control of several fortresses in various areas of the land. Her reign was marked with peace both at home and abroad. Hyrcanus complained to Alexandra of Aristobulus' military strength, but she died (67 B.C.) before anything could be done.

ARISTOBULUS II 67–63 B.C.

Hyrcanus II assumed the position of king and high priest but Aristobulus declared war on him. With many soldiers deserting, Hyrcanus fled to Jerusalem's citadel (later known as Antonia's Fortress). After three months, Hyrcanus was forced to relinquish his positions as king and high priest to Aristobulus and to retire from public life.

Hyrcanus was willing to accept this, but other plans were made for him by Idumean Antipater II (whose father had been appointed governor of Idumea by Janneus and whose son was Herod the Great). Antipater could not be high priest, but he knew that Hyrcanus was a weak, idle man whom he could control. Antipater convinced Hyrcanus he had been deprived of his hereditary rights by his younger brother and persuaded him to flee to Aretas, king of Arabia, with a view to recovering his rightful place as king and high priest of Israel. Aretas was willing to help on the condition that Hyrcanus would give him the twelve cities of Moab taken by Janneus. Hyrcanus agreed, and Aretas attacked Aristobulus, who retreated to the temple mount at the time of Passover of 65 B.C. Many people sided with Hyrcanus.

Meanwhile, the Roman army under Pompey was moving through Asia Minor and was approaching Palestine. After some delay and signs of rebellion by Aristobulus, Pompey sided with Hyrcanus. Pompey made war against Aristobulus, killing 12,000 Jews and besieging the Jerusalem temple for three months (autumn of 63 B.C.). Pompey entered the temple mount and the Holy of Holies but did not disturb it. In fact, on the following day he gave orders for cleansing it and resuming sacrifices. Hyrcanus was reinstated as high priest, and Aristobulus, his two daughters, and two sons, Alexander and Antigonus, were taken to Rome as prisoners of war. Alexander escaped. In the triumphal parade in 61 B.C. Aristobulus was made to walk before Pompey's chariot.

Thus ended the seventy-nine years (142–63) of the Jewish nation's independence as well as the Hasmonean house. Hyrcanus, the next high priest, was merely a vassal of the Roman Empire.

ROMAN RULE THROUGH THE FIRST CENTURY 63 B.C.–A.D.100

BEFORE CHRIST 63–4 B.C.

Hyrcanus II 63–40 B.C. Although Hyrcanus II was reappointed high priest, Antipater II was the power behind the throne who was responsible for Hyrcanus' honor. Antipater proved himself useful to the Romans in government and in their operation against the Hasmoneans. Gabinius defeated Alexander, Aristobulus' son, for the second time (55 B.C.), and in Jerusalem he reorganized the government according to Antipater's wishes.

Antipater married Cypros, of an illustrious Arabian family, by whom he had four sons—Phasael, Herod, Joseph, Pheroras—and a daughter, Salome.

Hyrcanus and Antipater attached themselves to Julius Caesar when he defeated Pompey in Egypt (48 B.C.). Caesar made Antipater a Roman citizen with an exemption from taxes and appointed him procurator of Judea. Caesar reconfirmed Hyrcanus' high priesthood and gave him the title of Ethnarch of the Jews. Antipater then suppressed disorder in the country and appealed to the restless Judean population to be loyal to Hyrcanus. However, the real ruler was Antipater, who appointed his son Phasael as governor of Jerusalem and his second son Herod as governor of Galilee (47 B.C.). Herod was successful in ridding Galilee of bandits.

After Cassius, Brutus, and their followers murdered Caesar (15 March 44 B.C.), Cassius controlled Syria. Needing to raise certain taxes required by Cassius, Antipater selected Herod, Phasael, and Malichus for the job. Herod was successful in this, and Cassius appointed him governor of

Coele-Syria. Since the Herods were gaining strength, Malichus, whose life Antipater had previously saved, bribed the butler to poison Antipater. Herod then killed Malichus.

Herod, an Idumean, became betrothed to Mariamne, the granddaughter of Hyrcanus II. She was the daughter of Aristobulus' son, Alexander, and thus a niece to Antigonus, the rival of Herod. This marriage strengthened Herod's position immensely, for he became the natural regent when the aging Hyrcanus would pass away.

When Antony defeated Cassius in 42 B.C., the Jewish leaders accused Herod and Phasael of usurping power, leaving Hyrcanus with only titular honors. Herod's defense nullified these charges. Since Hyrcanus was there, Antony asked him who would be the best qualified ruler, and Hyrcanus chose Herod and Phasael. Antony appointed them as tetrarchs of Judea.

The Parthians soon appeared in Syria (40 B.C.). They joined Antigonus in the effort to remove Hyrcanus. After several skirmishes, the Parthians asked for peace. Phasael and Hyrcanus went to Galilee to meet the Parthian king while Herod remained in Jerusalem, suspicious of the proposal. The Parthians treacherously put Phasael and Hyrcanus in chains. Herod moved to Masada and then Petra with Mariamne, his close relatives, and his troops.

Antigonus 40–37 B.C. Antigonus was made king. To prevent the possibility of his uncle Hyrcanus being restored to the high priesthood, Antigonus mutilated him. Phasael died either of suicide or poisoning, and Hyrcanus was taken to Parthia.

Herod went to Rome where Antony, Octavius Caesar, and the senate designated him king of Judea.[7] In late 40 or early 39 B.C. Herod returned to Palestine and, with the help of Antony's legate Sossius, recaptured Galilee. He married his betrothed Mariamne, the niece of Antigonus. Jerusalem fell in the summer of 37 B.C. At Herod's request, the Romans beheaded Antigonus. Herod, therefore, ceased to be merely the nominee for king for now he became king de facto.

Herod the Great 37–4 B.C.

Consolidation 37–25 B.C. Herod had to contend with four powerful adversaries: the people (led by the Pharisees), the ruling class, the Hasmonean family, and Cleopatra.

The first adversary was the people led by the Pharisees. The Pharisees did not like Herod as their king because he was an Idumean, a half-Jew, and a friend of the Romans.

---

7. Josephus *Antiquities* 14.14.6, 381–85; *BJ* 1.14.4, 282–85; cf. also Strabo 16.2.46; Appian, *The Civil Wars* 5.75; Tacitus, *Histories* 5.9.

The second adversary was the aristocracy. They had supported Antigonus. Herod executed forty-five of the wealthiest and most prominent Jews, confiscating their properties to replenish his coffers.

The third adversary was the Hasmonean family. Herod needed a high priest to replace Hyrcanus whom Antigonus had mutilated. He wanted to replace the Hasmonean priesthood with an insignificant priest from the Aaronic line. He chose Ananel (Hananeel), a priest of the Babylonian Diaspora. Herod's mother-in-law Alexandra was insulted by this. She pressured Herod through Cleopatra and her own daughter Mariamne to set aside Ananel (which was unlawful because the high priesthood was held for life) and to make her seventeen-year-old son Aristobulus high priest. Because of Aristobulus' growing popularity Herod had him drowned in a swiming pool. Alexandra never believed the official report that the drowning was accidental and devoted her life to revenge. She had Cleopatra persuade Antony to summon Herod for an account of such actions. Herod persuaded Antony to clear him of the charges. When Herod returned, he put Alexandra in chains and under guard.

The fourth adversary was Cleopatra. In 34 B.C. she convinced Antony to give her the whole of Phoenicia, the coast of Philistia south of the Eleutherus River (with the exception of the free cities of Tyre and Sidon), a portion of Arabia, and the district of Jericho. Jericho, with its palm trees and balsams, was the most fertile area of Herod's kingdom.

In 32 B.C. civil war broke out between Antony and Octavius. Antony was defeated by Octavius in the Battle of Actium (2 September 31 B.C.). This was a blow to Herod. Since Hyrcanus II was his only possible rival, he charged Hyrcanus of plotting with the king of the Nabateans and subsequently killed him.

With political skill, Herod met Octavius at Rhodes and convinced him he was the only legitimate ruler of Judea (spring of 30 B.C.). Octavius confirmed Herod's royal rank. Octavius gained control of Egypt when he defeated Antony, who with Cleopatra committed suicide (August 30 B.C.). Herod went to Egypt to congratulate Octavius and to secure a great reward for himself. Octavius conferred upon him the title of king and gave back to him not only Jericho, but also Gadara, Hippos, Samaria, Gaza, Anthedon, Joppa, and Straton's Tower (which later became Caesarea). Thus, Herod secured much territory for himself.

Herod's domestic affairs were far from peaceful. Having been suspicious of Mariamne's loyalty, he finally had her executed (29 B.C.). Herod never sanely accepted Mariamne's death. He fell ill and, because his recovery was doubtful, Alexandra began to scheme to secure the throne. He had her executed in 28 B.C. A similar fate befell his brother-in-law Costobarus, governor of Idumea, who was suspected of Hasmonean loyalties.

Herod killed Costobarus and his followers who remained loyal to Antigonus (25 B.C.). Herod could console himself with the fact that all the male relatives of Hyrcanus were dead.

Prosperity 25–14 B.C. Herod introduced the quinquennial games in honor of Caesar and constructed theaters, amphitheaters, and race courses. Around 24 B.C., Herod built for himself a royal palace. He also built or rebuilt many fortresses and Gentile temples, including Straton's Tower which was renamed Caesarea. Of course, his greatest building was the temple in Jerusalem which was begun around 20 B.C. Josephus considered it the most noble of his achievements.[8] Rabbinic literature states: "He who has not seen the Temple of Herod has never seen a beautiful building."[9] The rabbis considered it his "atonement for having slain so many sages of Israel."[10]

Herod also took great interest in Greek culture, surrounding himself with men accomplished in Greek literature and art. The highest offices of state were entrusted to Greek rhetoricians, one of whom, Nicolas of Damascus, was Herod's instructor in philosophy, rhetoric, and history. He was Herod's advisor and figured much in the government both before and after Herod's death.

In 22 B.C. Herod sent his two sons by Mariamne I, Alexander and Aristobulus, to Rome for their education. At this time Augustus gave him the territories of Trachonitis, Batanea, and Auranitis. These areas had been occupied by nomad robber tribes with whom the neighboring tetrarch Zenodorus had made common cause. Herod, undoubtedly, was considered an important friend to Rome for he kept that section of the Roman Empire well under control.

Augustus came to Syria in 20 B.C. and bestowed upon Herod the territory of Zenodorus that lay between Trachonitis and Galilee (containing Ulatha and Panias). The procurators of Syria had to get Herod's consent for all their actions. Augustus also granted Perea to Herod's brother Pheroras. Because of these gracious bestowments of Augustus, Herod erected a beautiful temple for Augustus in the territory of Zenodorus, near the place called Panias. At the same time Herod remitted only a third of the taxes under the pretext of crop failure, when actually it was to gain goodwill among his subjects who were displeased with his emphasis on Graeco-Roman culture and religion. This was effective for the most part.

Domestic troubles 14–4 B.C. Herod was now nearly seventy years old, and his sickness grew worse. As news spread that he had an incurable dis-

---

8. Josephus, *Antiquities* 15.11.1, 380.

9. *BT: Baba Bathra* 4a.

10. Midrash: Num. 14:8.

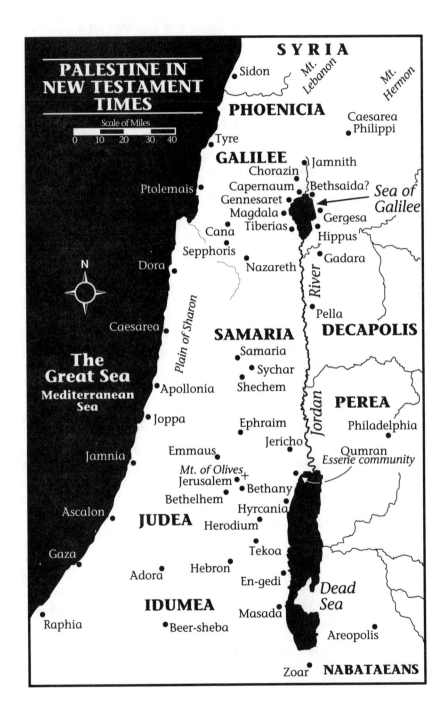

ease, two rabbis stirred up the people to tear down the offensive eagle from the temple gate. Herod had the principal leaders burned alive. Herod received permission from Rome to execute his son Antipater.

Herod made out his sixth will by nominating Archelaus, the older son of his fourth wife Malthace, as king. Malthace's other son Herod Antipas was named tetrarch of Galilee and Perea. Herod Philip, son of Cleopatra of Jerusalem (Herod's fifth wife), was named tetrarch of Gaulanitis, Trachonitis, Batanea, and Panias. Five days later Herod died in Jericho (spring of 4 B.C.). A pompous funeral procession accompanied his body one mile from Jericho to Herodion, where he was buried.

DURING THE NEW TESTAMENT PERIOD 4 B.C.–A.D. 100

After the death of Herod the Great, the kingdom was divided among his three sons. Archelaus was made ethnarch with the promise of being made king if he ruled well. His territories were Samaria and Judea (including Idumea). He was not a good ruler (Matt. 2:22) and was removed after ten years (4 B.C.–A.D. 6). After him, his domain was ruled by a series of prefects, the most notable of whom was Pontius Pilate who ruled when Jesus was ministering (A.D. 26–36/37).

Herod Philip was made tetrarch of Iturea, Gaulanitis, Trachonitis, Batanea, and Auranitis (4 B.C.–A.D. 34). He was a good ruler; it was in his territory at Caesarea Philippi that Peter confessed that Jesus is the Christ (Matt. 16:13–20; Mark 8:27–30; Luke 9:18–22). After his death, his domain was given to Syria and then to Herod Agrippa I in A.D. 37.

Herod Antipas was made tetrarch to govern Galilee and Perea, the territories of John the Baptist's and Jesus' ministries (4 B.C.–A.D. 39). He was a good ruler although he did behead John the Baptist (Matt 14:3-12; Mark 6:17-29; Luke 3:19-20) and tried Christ (Luke 23:6-12). After his death, his domain was given to Herod Agrippa I.

For establishing a New Testament chronology, there are two certain fixed points. Luke 3:1 marks the commencement of John the Baptist's ministry as the fifteenth year of Tiberius which would be in A.D. 29. Luke gives another concrete date in Acts 12:23 mentioning the death of Herod Agrippa I which was in A.D. 44.

Two other points mentioned by Luke, though somewhat more difficult to pin down precisely, are in Acts 18:1–2, 12: Claudius's edict to expel the Jews from Rome which probably was in A.D. 49 and the proconsulship of Gallio in Achaia which most likely was from the summer of 51 to the summer of 52.

The far more difficult dates to pinpoint precisely are the procurator-ships of Felix and Festus mentioned in Acts 23:24, 26; 24:27; 25:1, 13, 24; 26:30–32. It seems that Felix was procurator from the latter part of A.D. 52 to the late summer of 59 and Festus from the late summer of 59 to the winter of 61/62. These dates are determined by various data from secular and biblical sources.

Jesus' Life and Ministry 4 B.C.–A.D. 33

Birth of Jesus. Matthew 2:1 and Luke 1:5 indicate Herod the Great was living when Jesus was born. Hence, Jesus must have been born before Herod's death (spring of 4 B.C.). More specifically, Jesus must have been born after the census of Quirinius (Luke 2:1–5). Though difficult to pinpoint, the census probably was sometime between 6 and 4 B.C. Some think Jesus' birth must have been around 6 B.C. because Herod killed children up to two years of age (Matt. 2:16). However, a full two years need not have elapsed because Herod might have killed children up to two years of age to be certain Jesus was included. Given Herod's paranoia concerning a successor, this would not have been unusual.

Herod and the magi might have thought that Jesus had been born when the magi first saw the star in the East, possibly a year or two before they talked with Herod. It has been proposed that the magi came to Bethlehem because of a series of three unusual and significant astronomical events: first, a triple conjunction of Saturn and Jupiter in the constellation Pisces in 7 B.C. (which occurs every 900 years); second, massing of Saturn, Jupiter, and Mars in Pisces in 6 February B.C. (which occurs every 800 years and less frequently in Pisces); and third, a comet appeared in the constellation Capricornus in the spring of 5 B.C. This comet appeared in the East (Matt. 2:2) and reappeared in Bethlehem (2:9).[11] (It is not unusual for a comet to reappear.) Although the traditional date of Christ's birth has been 25 December (or 6 January in the Eastern Church), it could have been any time between the spring of 5 B.C. and the winter of 5/4 B.C.

Ministry of Jesus. There is no specific historical reference point for determining exactly *when* Jesus' ministry occurred. Luke stated specifically that John the Baptist began to minister in the fifteenth year of Tiberius (Luke 3:1–3) which was A.D. 29. If John's ministry began in early A.D. 29 and Jesus' ministry began sometime between the summer of 29 and the Passover of 30, Jesus would have been around thirty-two or

---

11. Colin J. Humphreys, "The Star—A Comet in 5 B.C.—and the Date of the Birth of Christ," *The Quarterly Journal of the Royal Astronomical Society* 32 (December 1991): 389–407; idem, "The Star of Bethlehem, a Comet in 5 B.C. and the Date of Christ's Birth," *TynBul* 43.1 (May 1992): 31–56.

thirty-three years old. This would fit nicely with Luke's statement that Jesus was *about* thirty years of age (Luke 3:23). Furthermore, at the first Passover of Jesus' ministry (John 2:13) when He mentioned He could destroy and raise the temple in three days, the Jews asked how He could do this to a building that had stood for forty-six years (John 2:20). If the temple edifice (not its precincts) was started in 20/19 B.C. and was completed in 18/17 B.C., then the forty-six years of its standing would have been in A.D. 29/30. Thus, the Passover of A.D. 30 fits well as the first Passover of Jesus' public ministry which would have started four to nine months previously.

Facts relating to the *length* of Jesus' ministry are gathered primarily from John. John mentioned three Passovers (John 2:13; 6:4; 11:55). However, there must have been an additional year of His ministry between the Passovers of John 2:13 and 6:4. After the Passover in Judea of John 2:13, the Synoptic Gospels mention the disciples plucking grain in Galilee (Matt. 12:1; Mark 2:23; Luke 6:1). The Passover of John 2:13 occurred shortly after His baptism and the locale of His ministry was Judea; the plucking of the grain occurred a considerable time after Jesus' baptism and the locale of His ministry was Galilee. The Passover of 6:4 is around the time Jesus fed the five thousand, the only miracle mentioned in all four Gospels. Therefore, the plucking of the grain would fit well around the Passover between those of John 2:13 and 6:4.

There are two other time notes in John that would indicate there was an additional year between these two Passovers. First, after the Passover of John 2:13, Jesus ministered in Judea and then went to Samaria where He mentioned there were four months until harvest (John 4:35), which would mean the following January/February. Although some would make this proverbial, it seems best to take this as a literal chronological reference. The second time note is in John 5:1 where there is mention of another feast. Some would make it another Passover, although it is more likely the Feast of Tabernacles. Thus, these two time notes substantiate that there was another Passover between those of John 2:13 and 6:4. This would mean a total of four Passovers during Jesus' public ministry; hence, His ministry would have been 3 1/2 to 3 3/4 years in length.

Regarding the date of Christ's death, two issues need to be discussed. The first issue is the *year* of Christ's death. The discussion above concluded that Jesus began His ministry in the summer or fall of A.D. 29 and it lasted for 3 1/2 or 3 3/4 years, which would place His death at the Passover of A.D. 33. This fits well astronomically and politically. Astronomically the two most viable dates are A.D. 30 and 33 and the latter date fits better.

Politically, the A.D. 33 date makes more sense. Pilate at first was pictured in the writings of Josephus and Philo as a ruthless, greedy, and inflexible ruler. This view is reinforced by the record of his slaughtering Galileans at the time of sacrifice mentioned in Luke 13:1. However, when Jesus was tried, Pilate attempted to release Him. Under the pressure of the religious leaders, he gave in. This is quite a different character from that of his earlier days. This mellowness can be explained. Pilate was appointed by the anti-Semitic Sejanus, the prefect of the Praetorian Guard, who was virtually in control of the Roman government. When Sejanus was deposed and executed on 18 October A.D. 31, his appointees, including Pilate, no longer had an ally in the Roman government. Sometime in A.D. 32 his neighbor, Herod Antipas, reported to Tiberius the trouble Pilate had caused in Jerusalem and forced Pilate to back down. Shortly thereafter, Jesus was brought to Pilate by the religious leaders, and they mentioned that Jesus ministered in Judea and Galilee. When Pilate heard this he sent Jesus to Herod Antipas, the ruler of Galilee and Perea, so he would not make another wrong judgment that could be reported to Rome. Herod Antipas also wanted to disassociate himself from Sejanus, so he made no judgment on Jesus and returned Him to Pilate. From the day of the trial onward, Pilate and Herod Antipas were friends (Luke 23:12). Therefore, the A.D. 33 date fits historically, because if the crucifixion were in A.D. 30, Luke's statement would have been inaccurate.

The second issue is the *day* of the week of Christ's crucifixion. Although there have been proposals for the crucifixion to have occurred on either Wednesday or Thursday, most think it occurred on Friday. The Gospels name the day of preparation (Friday), the day before the Sabbath, as the day when Christ was crucified (Matt. 27:62; 28:1; Mark 15:42; Luke 23:54, 56; John 19:31, 42). All the Gospels describe Jesus' meal with His disciples on the evening before His death; the Synoptics are clear that this was a Passover meal (Matt. 26:2, 17–19; Mark 14:12–16; Luke 22:1, 7–8, 13, 15). The difficulty is to reconcile the Synoptics' portrayal of Jesus having partaken of the Passover with His disciples and John's statement that the Jews on the next morning did not want to enter the Praetorium and be defiled before eating the Passover (John 18:28). If Jesus and His disciples had eaten the Passover, how could the Jews on the next day say they had *not* eaten the Passover? There has been much debate over this problem, but there is strong evidence of different ways the Jewish day was reckoned by different Jewish groups. Thus, the Passover was celebrated on two different days: Thursday and Friday. The passion week can be outlined as follows:

Day	Event	Scripture
Saturday	Arrived at Bethany	John 12:1
Sunday	Crowd came to see Jesus	John 12:9–11
Monday	Triumphal entry	Matt. 21:1–9; Mark 11:1–10; Luke 19:28–44
Tuesday	Cursed fig tree	Matt. 21:18–19; Mark 11:12–14
Wednesday	Cleansed temple	Matt. 21:12–13; Mark 11:15–17; Luke19:45–46
	Fig tree withered	Matt. 21:20–22; Mark 11:20–26
	Temple controversy	Matt. 21:23—23:39; Mark 11:27—12:44; Luke 20:1—21:4
	Olivet Discourse	Matt. 24:1–25:46; Mark 13:1–37; Luke 21:5–36
Thursday	Last Supper	Matt. 26:20–30; Mark 14:17–26; Luke 22:14–30
	Betrayed and arrested	Matt. 26:47–56; Mark 14:43–52; Luke 22:47–53; John 18:2–12
	Tried by Annas and Caiaphas	Matt. 26:57–75; Mark 14:53–72; Luke 22:54–65; John 18:13–27
Friday	Tried by Sanhedrin	Matt. 27:1; Mark 15:1; Luke 22:66
	Tried by Pilate, Herod, Pilate	Matt. 27:2–30; Mark 15:2–19; Luke 23:1–25; John 18:28—19:16
	Crucified and buried	Matt. 27:31–60; Mark 15:20–46; Luke 23:26–54; John 19:16–42
Saturday	Dead in tomb	
Sunday	Resurrected	Matt. 28:1–15; Mark 16:1–8; Luke 24:1–35

In conclusion, Jesus was crucified on Friday, 3 April A.D. 33. Jesus' ministry is summarized in the following table:

Time	Event
Summer 5–winter 5/4 B.C.	Jesus' birth
March/April 4 B.C.	Herod the Great's death
Passover, 29 April A.D. 9	Jesus at the temple at age twelve
A.D. 29	Commencement of John the Baptist's ministry
Summer/autumn A.D. 29	Commencement of Jesus' ministry
7 April 30	First Passover of Jesus' ministry (John 2:13)
25 April 31	Second Passover of Jesus' ministry
21–28 October 31	Feast of Tabernacles (John 5:1)
13/14 April 32	Third Passover of Jesus' ministry (John 6:4)
10–17 September 32	Feast of Tabernacles (John 7:2, 10)
18 December 32	Feast of Dedication (John 10:22-39)
Friday, 3 April 33	Death
Sunday, 5 April 33	Resurrection
Thursday, 14 May 33	Ascension (Acts 1)
Sunday, 24 May 33	Day of Pentecost (Acts 2)

Apostolic Ministry A.D. 33–100

Peter and James A.D. 33–64. In the early part of the Book of Acts Peter played a prominent role. The ministry of Peter and the other apostles mentioned in the first eight chapters of Acts took place in the two years between A.D. 33 and 35.

In the persecution of Herod Agrippa I in A.D. 44, James, the brother of John, was killed and Peter was imprisoned (Acts 12:2–3). It was in that same year that Agrippa I died (Acts 12:20–23).[12] James, the brother of the Lord, was an important leader in the early church (Acts 15:13; Gal. 1:19; 2:9; 1 Cor. 15:7). Josephus spoke of his death as having occurred in the period of anarchy after the death of Festus (winter 61/62) and before the arrival of his successor Albinus (summer 62).[13] Hence, James was killed in the spring of 62. Peter played a prominent part in the Jerusalem council in A.D. 49 (Acts 15).

It is most likely that Peter went to Rome toward the end of his life. It seems that Peter was not in Rome before A.D 62 or after 66, since he was not mentioned by Paul in Romans, one of the Prison Epistles, or 2 Timothy, nor by Luke when he narrated Paul's imprisonment in Acts 28:14–30. It is probable that Peter was in Rome when Paul was not there. Thus, Peter may have come to Rome around A.D. 62, being martyred in the Neronian persecution following the fire in the summer of 64.

Paul's ministry A.D. 35–68. Paul's conversion date is based primarily on two passages of Scripture. First, Galatians 1:17–18 states that he went from Damascus to Jerusalem three years after his conversion (cf. Acts 9:25–26). When Paul left Damascus Aretas IV was in power and since he reigned from A.D. 37–39, Paul's conversion must have been sometime between 34 and 36.

The second passage, Galatians 2:1, states that Paul again went to Jerusalem fourteen years later. This probably refers to the famine visit he made with Barnabas described in Acts 11—12 which can be dated from A.D. 47 to 49. It is likely that the fourteen years are to be reckoned from his conversion rather than after the time of his first visit to Jerusalem, so his conversion would have been sometime between 33 and 35. These two references overlap in 34 to 35; therefore, the best date for Paul's conversion would be in the summer of A.D. 35.

Paul returned to Jerusalem the summer of 37 (Acts 9:26–29; Gal. 1:18–20). Paul went to Tarsus and Syria–Cilicia in the fall of 37 (Acts 9:30; Gal. 1:21) and then to Antioch around 41 (Acts 11:19–24). Paul visited Jerusalem during the time of famine, probably the fall of 47 (Acts 11:30; Gal. 2:1–10), and returned to Antioch between the fall of 47 to the spring of 48 (Acts 12:25—13:1).

---

12. Cf. Josephus, *Antiquities* 19.8.2, 343–53.

13. Josephus, *Antiquities* 20.9.1, 197–203.

Paul made three missionary journeys. The first missionary journey (Acts 13—14) would have been from the spring of 48 to the fall of 49. Upon his return to Antioch, he wrote the Epistle to the Galatians and went to the council meeting in Jerusalem in the fall of 49 (Acts 15).

After wintering in Antioch (Acts 15:33–35), Paul started on his second missionary journey (Acts 15:36—18:22) which would have been from the spring of 50 to the fall of 52. On this missionary journey he entered Europe, stayed in Corinth eighteen months (Acts 18:11), and was tried before the proconsul Gallio, who ruled in Achaia probably from the summer of 51 to the summer of 52. In Corinth Paul met Priscilla and Aquila who were Jewish Christians forced out of Rome under the edict of Claudius probably in 49 or 50. While in Corinth Paul wrote 1 and 2 Thessalonians in the summer of 51.

The third missionary journey (Acts 18:23—21:16) was from the spring of 53 to the spring of 57. Paul stayed in Ephesus nearly three years (Acts 19:8, 10; 20:31), from the summer of 53 until May of 56, writing 1 Corinthians in the spring of 56. When he left Ephesus, he went to Macedonia and Greece for three months (Acts 20:3). While in Macedonia he wrote 2 Corinthians in the fall of 56. In Corinth (Rom. 16:23) he wrote Romans in the winter of 56/57. From Corinth Paul retraced his steps through Europe and then returned to Jerusalem by Pentecost of 57 (Acts 20:16).

While in Jerusalem he was arrested and taken to Caesarea for a trial before Felix, who was probably procurator from the latter part of 52 to the summer of 59. Felix heard Paul (Acts 24), and Paul remained in the Caesarean prison for two years at the end of which time Felix was succeeded by Festus (Acts 24:27). Both Festus and Herod Agrippa II heard Paul in Caesarea in the late summer of 59 (Acts 25:7–12; 26:1–32). Paul was in prison in Caesarea from June of 57 until August of 59. He left Caesarea in August of 59 and arrived in Rome in February of 60 (Acts 27:1—28:29), remaining in prison there two years (Acts 28:30), from February 60 to March of 62. While in prison, he wrote the Prison Epistles: Ephesians in the fall of 60, Colossians and Philemon in the fall of 61, and Philippians in the spring of 62.

The Book of Acts does not record Paul's travels after the Roman imprisonment. From Paul's stated intentions, his travel notes in the Pastoral Epistles, and early church history one can attempt to reconstruct his itinerary. After his release from the Roman prison in the spring of 62, it seems probable that he traveled east, possibly to Ephesus and Colossae first (spring to fall 62). Later, in Macedonia (fall 62 and winter 62/63) he wrote 1 Timothy (1:3), afterwards returning to Asia Minor (spring 63 to spring 64). After Asia Minor, Paul may have gone to Spain (spring 64 to spring 66, Rom. 15:24, 28). After Spain, it is possible that Paul, with Titus, returned to the East, leaving Titus in Crete (early summer 66). Paul then returned to Asia Minor (summer to fall 66, 2 Tim. 4:13–14) where he wrote Titus (1:5). Paul went to Nicopolis for the winter of 66/67 (Titus 3:12). It seems that Paul went to Macedonia and Greece (spring to fall 67, 2 Tim. 4:20) and was possibly arrested when Nero was in Greece in the fall of 67. It is probable that Paul was again imprisoned in Rome (2 Tim. 1:8; 2:9) where he wrote 2 Timothy (fall of 67). Paul's death may have occurred in the spring of 68.

A chronology of the apostolic ministries prior to the destruction of Jerusalem is summarized in the table beginning on the following page .

AFTER THE NEW TESTAMENT PERIOD A.D. 66–100

Destruction of Jerusalem A.D. 66–70. The fall of Jerusalem was predicted by Christ (Matt. 24:15; Mark 13:14; Luke 21:20), and the first phase of the fulfillment was accomplished in A.D. 70. Because of the persecution, many Christians fled to Pella, east of the Sea of Galilee.[14]

In A.D. 66 the Jewish war began when the greedy procurator Florus raided the temple treasury, which was regarded as sacrilege by the Jews. Eleaszar, captain of the temple, convinced the priests to discontinue offering daily sacrifices for the emperor's welfare. This was a sign of open rebellion against the Romans. The Zealots seized Masada and then under Menahem, a descendent of Judas Maccabeus, marched on Jerusalem. At the same time there was a slaughter of the Jews in Caesarea that only strengthened the Jewish resolve against Rome.

When Vespasian arrived in the spring of 67 he was able to subdue Galilee, Perea, western Judea, and Idumea. At the time he was ready to beseige Jerusalem, news came of Nero's death (9 June 68) and civil war followed. Vespasian suspended fighting for a year to see how things in Rome would be resolved. He resumed fighting in June 69 and quickly controlled all of Palestine except Jerusalem, Herodion, Masada, and Machaerus. Vespasian was proclaimed emperor on 1 July 69. As he left for Rome, he entrusted to his son Titus the crushing of the Jewish revolt.

Titus began his siege of Jerusalem in April 70 and by August, the recently completed temple of Herod was burned and the upper city was captured a few weeks later. The other three strongholds fell, Masada being the last. Its defenders committed mass suicide in April or May 73. Titus and his father Vespasian held the triumphal march in Rome (A.D. 71).

---

14. Eusebius, *Ecclesiastical History* 3.5.2–3.

Time	Event
Friday, 3 April 33	Crucifixion
Sunday, 24 May 33	Pentecost (Acts 2)
summer 33	Peter's second sermon, Peter first brought before the Sanhedrin (Acts 3:1—4:31)
33–34	Death of Ananias and Sapphira (Acts 4:32—5:11)
34–35	Peter again brought before Sanhedrin (Acts 5:12–42)
late 34–early 35	The Seven selected (Acts 6:1–7)
April 35	Stephen martyred (Acts 6:8—7:60)
summer 35	Paul's conversion (Acts 9:1–7)
summer 35–summer 37	Paul in Damascus and Arabia (Acts 9:8–25; Gal. 1:16–17)
summer 37	Paul in Jerusalem, first visit (Acts 9:26–29; Gal. 1:18–20)
autumn 37	Paul went to Tarsus and Syria–Cilicia area (Acts 9:30; Gal. 1:21)
40–41	Peter ministers to Gentiles (Acts 10:1—11:18)
41	Barnabas sent to Antioch (Acts 11:19–24)
spring 43	Paul went to Antioch (Acts 11:25–26)
spring 44	Agabus predicts a famine (Acts 11:27–28)
spring 44	Agrippa's persecution, James martyred (Acts 12:1–23)
autumn 47	Relief visit, Paul's second visit to Jerusalem (Acts 11:30; Gal. 2:1–10)
autumn 47–spring 48	Paul in Antioch (Acts 12:25—13:1)
April 48– September 49	Paul's first missionary journey (Acts 13—14)
autumn 49	Peter at Antioch (Gal. 2:11–16)

Time	Event
autumn 49	Galatians written from Antioch
autumn 49	Jerusalem council, Paul's third visit to Jerusalem (Acts 15)
winter 49/50	Paul in Antioch (Acts 15:33–35)
April 50– September 52	Paul's second missionary journey (Acts 15:36—18:22)
early summer 51	1 Thessalonians written (from Corinth)
summer 51	2 Thessalonians written (from Corinth)
winter 52/53	Paul's stay at Antioch
spring 53–May 57	Paul's third missionary journey (Acts 18:23—21:16)
early spring 56	1 Corinthians written (from Ephesus)
September/ October 56	2 Corinthians written (from Macedonia)
winter 56/57	Romans written (from Corinth)
eve of Pentecost, 25 May 57	Jerusalem, Paul's fifth visit
28 May 57	Meeting with James (Acts 21:13–23)
29 May –9 June 57	Paul's arrest and trial before Felix (Acts 21:26—24:22)
February 60– March 62	Paul's first Roman imprisonment (Acts 28:30)
autumn 60	Ephesians written
autumn 61	Colossians and Philemon written
early spring 62	Philippians written
spring 62	James, Lord's brother, martyred
spring–autumn 62	Paul in Ephesus and Colossae
62	Peter went to Rome

Time	Event
summer 62–winter 62/63	Paul in Macedonia (1 Tim. 1:3)
autumn 62	1 Timothy written
spring 63–spring 64	Paul in Asia Minor
spring 64–spring 66	Paul in Spain (Rom. 15:24, 28)
summer 64	Christians persecuted, Peter martyred
early summer 66	Paul in Crete
summer–autumn 66	Paul in Asia Minor (Titus 1:5)
summer 66	Titus written
winter 66/67	Paul in Nicopolis (Titus 3:12)
spring–autumn 67	Paul in Macedonia and Greece (2 Tim. 4:13, 20)
autumn 67	Paul arrested and brought to Rome (2 Tim. 1:8; 2:9)
autumn 67	2 Timothy written
spring 68	Paul's death
2 September 70	Destruction of Jerusalem

Spread of Christianity A.D. 70–100. Some have surmised that because of the destruction of Jerusalem, John the apostle fled to Asia Minor, possibly to Ephesus. Part of his time was spent on the Island of Patmos (Rev. 1:9) and, although there is no certainty regarding the time of his death, traditionally it has been held to have occurred in A.D. 100.

Knowledge of the early church after the destruction of Jerusalem is sporadic. John mentions the seven churches in Asia Minor (Rev. 2—3). Several letters by Ignatius (who lived 35–107/8), bishop of Antioch, attest to the survival of these churches. He wrote that the church of Ephesus was renowned throughout the world and that the Smyraneans were acquainted with the church in Antioch.

Emperor Domition (81–96) renewed the emphasis on a national religion of polytheism and emperor-worship. Due to the fall of the Jewish state, the Christians came into focus as the worshipers of an invisible deity; thus, they were suspected of conspiracy and atheism. Although there is mention in the Roman historians regarding empire-wide persecution of the Christians in the first century, undoubtedly the social and religious climate of the empire made it difficult for the Christians. In some localities they were brought to trial.

Domition's successors, Nerva (96–98) and Trajan (97–117) seemed to carry out the same policies regarding religion. Trajan's letter to Pliny the Younger gives evidence of tolerence. Trajan, in fact, instructed Pliny the Younger not to go out of his way to look for the Christians. Trajan was not too concerned as long as they did not undermine the state. Though there may have been outbursts of persecutions in some locales, the church under Trajan fared well. Pliny the Younger mentioned the recession of paganism and the advancement of Christianity in the cities and villages of Asia Minor.

From the fearful disciples of Jesus (Acts 2), the Christians spread throughout the Roman Empire to the notice of the emperors. This spread cannot be accounted for by the disciples' courage alone. The message of the cross wedded with the power of the Holy Spirit brought thousands into a personal interaction with the living God in the person of Jesus Christ.

FOR FURTHER READING

Barrett, Charles Kingsley. *The New Testament Background: Selected Documents with Introductions.* New York: Harper & Row, 1957.

Bruce, F. F. *New Testament History.* Garden City, N.Y.: Doubleday, 1969.

Charlesworth, James H., ed. *The Old Testament Pseudepigraha.* 2 vols. Garden City, N.Y.: Doubleday, 1983–85.

Grant, Michael. *Herod the Great.* New York: American Heritage Press, 1971.

———. *Jesus: An Historian's Review of the Gospels.* New York: Scribner's, 1977.

Hengel, Martin. *Judaism and Hellenism: Studies in Their Encounter in Palestine during the Early Hellenistic Period.* 2 vols. Translated by John Bowden. Philadelphia: Fortress, 1974.

———. *The Zealots: Investigations into the Jewish Freedom Movement in the Period from Herod I until A.D. 70.* Translated by David Smith. Edinburgh: T. & T. Clark, 1989.

Hoehner, Harold W. *Chronological Aspects of the Life of Christ.* Grand Rapids: Zondervan, 1977.

———. *Herod Antipas.* SNTSMS, no. 17. Cambridge: University Press, 1972. Reprint, Grand Rapids: Zondervan, 1980.

Jeremias, Joachim. *Jerusalem in the Time of Jesus.* Translated by F. H. Cave and C. H. Cave. Philadelphia: Fortress, 1969.

Jewett, Robert. *A Chronology of Paul's Life*. Philadelphia: Fortress, 1979.

Josephus. Loeb Classical Library. 1926–65.

LaSor, William Sanford. *The Dead Sea Scrolls and the New Testament*. Grand Rapids: Eerdmans, 1972.

Niswonger, Richard L. *New Testament History*. Grand Rapids: Zondervan, 1988.

Neusner, Jacob. *The Rabbinic Traditions about the Pharisees Before 70*. 3 vols. Leiden: E. J. Brill, 1971.

Philo. Loeb Classical Library.1929–53.

Reicke, Bo. *The New Testament Era*. Translated by David E. Green. Philadelphia: Fortress, 1968.

Safrai, S. and M. Stern, eds. *The Jewish People in the First Century*. CRINT. 2 vols. Philadelphia: Fortress, 1974–76.

Schürer, Emil. *The History of the Jewish People in the Age of Jesus Christ*. 4 vols. Revised and translated by Geza Vermes, Fergus Millar, and Matthew Black. Edinburgh: T. & T. Clark, 1973–87.

Sherwin-White, A. N. *Roman Society and Law in the New Testament*. Oxford: Clarendon Press, 1963.

Smallwood, Mary. *The Jews under Roman Rule*. Leiden: E. J. Brill, 1970.

Vermes, Geza. *The Dead Sea Scrolls: Qumran in Perspective*. Philadelphia: Fortress, 1981.

XXIII

CULTURAL BACKGROUND OF THE NEW TESTAMENT

MARK A. SEIFRID

INTRODUCTION

"Culture" may be understood as the shared ideas, values, practices, and assumptions which regulate and protect the collective life of a group or society.[1] It demarcates the boundaries among groups, defining "insiders" and "outsiders." Culture is a "map of the world" of social relations, by which obligation and expectation, privilege and respect, honor and shame may be assigned. Often the individual is not aware of the influence of culture upon his or her behavior. For those who "know the terrain," there is little need to refer to the "map."

A discussion of the cultural background of the New Testament writings involves only one dimension of the larger task of describing their social setting and function. As we have noted, culture involves moral codes of which one might be more or less conscious. Other important factors shape the life of groups and influence the values which they adopt. In recent

---

1. See Bruce J. Malina, *Christian Origins and Cultural Anthropology: Practical Models for Biblical Interpretation* (Atlanta: John Knox, 1986).

decades, biblical scholars have increasingly recognized that the issues with which first-century believers were concerned, and the manner in which they responded to their culture, emerged not only from their faith, but also from their particular situations in society. As a result there is presently considerable interest in discovering what the "world" of the person on the street in Capernaum, Jerusalem, or Rome in the first century was like. What would the practices of Jesus and His band of followers have meant to a villager in Galilee? What features did the movement which surrounded Jesus share with other groups, and in what ways did it differ? How many of the earliest believers were rich and how many were poor? How would membership in a community of Christians influence the status of a resident of one of the larger cities, such as Corinth? These and other matters having to do with daily life bear an obvious relevance for understanding the cultural setting of the New Testament.

Long before the current renewal of interest in the description of society and culture, it was apparent there were a number of cultural settings represented in the NT. Jesus and those who followed Him reflected a different social dynamic from the communities of believers which sprang up in Jerusalem and elsewhere in Palestine after His resurrection. These in turn were unlike the churches which Paul and others planted across the Mediterranean world outside Palestine, in which Gentile Christians came to predominate. Within a very brief period of time, Christians and their communities developed distinctive ways of living and of dealing with one another which gave them a subculture of their own.

In the following survey we will highlight some of the social and economic conditions prevailing in the first century which were important to its culture. We then will consider some cultural elements of the "world" of Jesus and His followers. Finally, we will give attention to aspects of urban Greco-Roman society which had a major influence upon the nascent Christian community as it spread and developed its own institutions.

RURAL AND URBAN SOCIETY IN THE FIRST CENTURY

THE BEGINNING OF SOCIETIES

The Greco-Roman cities scattered across the Mediterranean world had a fundamental influence on social, economic, and cultural forms in the first century. These cities did not arise spontaneously. They represented the ambitions of the rulers who established them and who, by them, hoped to increase their own wealth, power, and influence. Since the time of the conquests of Alexander the Great (334–323 B.C.) and his successors, Greek cities had been planted across the eastern Mediterranean. A number of them at first were military outposts, designed to ensure peace and the regular collection of tribute. Others were planted for the purpose of maintaining stability and increasing income from taxes gathered through the urban economy. Settlers were introduced to a region, given a village and extensive lands surrounding it, and provided a Greek constitution by which to govern themselves. The ruler founding the city would construct the required public works.

This practice had several effects. The transplanted inhabitants and citizens of the city would have considerable loyalty to their ruling benefactor and (in the period with which we are concerned) to Rome, helping to secure control of the area. As an example, one may point to the city of Sepphoris, not far from Nazareth where Jesus grew up in Galilee. It had been destroyed at the time of Herod's death but was reestablished as a city by Antipas, Herod's son. Decades later, during the Jewish revolt, its inhabitants remained loyal to Rome.[2] Another result of the establishment of cities was that the agricultural potential of the land allocated to them was developed and exploited as a source of revenue. They became centers of trade from which taxes could be extracted. The cities also had a direct impact on social life. Through them, local cultures across a wide area, including Jewish Palestine, were "Hellenized." That is to say, they were brought under the influence of Greek language, education, and social forms.

ECONOMY

The economic conditions in the cities were considerably better than those in the country. Although there was nothing comparable to the broad middle class of modern Western society, there were people of moderate means in the cities, prosperous tradespeople and merchants, such as Lydia, the "dealer in purple cloth," whom we meet in the Book of Acts (17:4). Even in Palestine there were those of intermediate standing, such as Zebedee, the father of James and John, who employed day laborers for his fishing enterprise (Mark 1:20). Yet this group of middle economic status was dependent on the cities in and around Palestine for the trade from which their income was generated. Their number was decidedly smaller than in urban society, a fact reflected in the sharp contrast between rich and poor in the Gospel narratives and in Jesus' parables, particularly those reported by Luke.[3] There was very little middle ground in rural Palestine.

---

2. Josephus, *Life* 140.

3. See the parable of the rich fool, Luke 12:13–21; the parable of the rich man and Lazarus, Luke 16:19–31.

SOCIAL STATUS

The absence of a sizeable middle class with social mobility in first-century Greco-Roman society undoubtedly contributed to the general consciousness of traditional roles and status. Much of the population of the Mediterranean world was located in rural areas like that of Palestine, where community life was especially close-knit and interdependent, a setting transparently present in the Gospel accounts of Jesus' ministry.[4] This rural culture allowed relatively little room for the self-determination of the individual. One's identity and place in society was to a considerable extent determined by group expectations, as may be illustrated from Jesus' own experience: "Isn't this the carpenter? Isn't this Mary's son and the brother of James, Joseph, Judas, and Simon?"* (Mark 6:3). There were greater opportunities for social advancement in an urban environment than the backwaters of the provinces, but even here a large area of one's life was prescribed by whether one was male or female, slave or free, of aristocratic or common birth. One might properly carry out one's role and receive appropriate honor, or fail to do so and bear the corresponding shame.

GEOGRAPHICAL CONDITIONS

The difficult nature of rural existence was due in part to the fact that in the first-century Mediterranean world, the ownership of the best land was concentrated in the hands of an affluent urban aristocracy. Although much of the land was in agricultural use, farming was not easy in all areas. The susceptibility of Palestine to drought is attested in the NT. The reader of the Gospels is familiar with the image of a dry climate and stony soil in Jesus' parable of the sower (Mark 4:3–9). Luke records a famine during the reign of the Emperor Claudius, probably the one which hit Judea in about A.D. 46–48.[5] There were more fertile areas: lower Galilee and especially the wide Esdraelon plain and sections of the Jordan valley.[6] Such productive lands, however, frequently became the property of the powerful.

From the accounts of the Jewish historian Josephus, we learn of the reapportionment of desirable territories and large estates to allies and

---

4. See Ramsay MacMullen, *Roman Social Relations 50 B.C. to A.D. 200* (New Haven: Yale University Press, 1976).

5. Acts 11:27–30; cf. Josephus, *Antiquities* 20.101.

6. See Sean Freyne, *Galilee from Alexander the Great to Hadrian 323 B.C.E. to 135 C.E.: A Study in Second Temple Judaism* (Wilmington: Del.: Michael Glazier, 1980), 101–53.

* Unless otherwise stated, Scripture quotations in this chapter are from the NIV.

members of the Herodian family.[7] A number of Jesus' parables presuppose such a situation. We find, for example, tenant farmers working a vineyard on behalf of an absentee landlord (Mark 12:1–2). Likewise, there are wealthy landowners with servants and day laborers who are entirely dependent on them for their livelihood (Matt. 13:24–30; 20:1–16; 24:45–51). Stewards and managers of large households appear (Matt. 24:45–51; Luke 16:1–8). One should not push this evidence too far. There are indications in both Josephus' writings and the Gospels that there also were small familial land holdings in Palestine.[8] But the feudal arrangement was extensive, and no one in rural Palestine was exempt from the heavy pressure of tax and tribute.

GOVERNMENT

One significant aspect of the prominent role which the city played as an institution in the first century was the power of local authorities in matters of governance. Rome did not centralize or impose uniformity of jurisdiction to the extent the laws of modern nation-states do. So long as external expectations were met (especially those of tribute), the rights of Roman citizens guarded, and the peace maintained, considerable room was given to local customs and the personal discretion of those in authority.[9] We find evidence of this situation regularly in the NT. Jesus' parable of the widow who persisted in her request until she received justice from an unwilling village magistrate makes sense only under such conditions (Luke 18:1–8). The proconsul Gallio in Corinth not only had the right to decide what matters he would adjudicate, but his attitude toward the complaint of the Jews against Paul ("See to it yourselves!") reflects the wide area of self-jurisdiction given to associations in the city.[10]

JESUS AND HIS FOLLOWERS IN FIRST-CENTURY PALESTINE

The culmination of Jesus' earthly mission in His arrest and execution was a violent manifestation of the cultural conflict at work in first-century Palestine. Roman rule in Palestine inevitably created tension between

---

7. *Antiquities* 15.292–98.

8. See Josephus, *Antiquities* 18.272–274 where in protest the spring planting is delayed, and the parable of the two sons, Matthew 21:28–32.

9. See John E. Stambaugh and David L. Balch, *The New Testament in Its Social Environment* (Philadelphia: Westminster, 1986), 32–34.

10. Acts 18:15. Note his indifference to the beating Sosthenes received, Acts 18:17.

those who in some way benefited from the new order and those who regarded it as a threat to the religious and economic life of the Jewish people. Ultimately, the greed and brutality of the Roman procurators moved the general population to the riots from which the revolt of A.D. 66 emerged. During the period of Jesus' ministry, the forces which sought to maintain the status quo maintained the upper hand. They came to see Jesus as a threat and reacted accordingly.

HEROD THE GREAT

The temporary stability of first-century Palestine was in considerable measure due to relief from the reign of Herod the Great (37–4 B.C.). During his rule, Herod had sought to secure his power by establishing himself as a noteworthy benefactor of Greco-Roman culture and a loyal client of Rome. In the non-Jewish districts of his realm, he reconstructed and established a number of new cities in honor of his patron Augustus, most notably Caesarea and Sebaste. These were Hellenistic cities with the full complement of public buildings: aqueducts, baths, fountains, stoas, theaters, amphitheaters, hippodromes, and temples for emperor worship. Even within Jewish Palestine the edifices of Greek culture were erected. A theater and an amphitheater in which athletic and gladitorial contests took place were constructed for Jerusalem itself. Added to these endeavors were the generous gifts Herod donated to distant cities such as Rhodes and Syrian Antioch.[11] At the periphery of his realm, he built a number of temples to Caesar, such as the one at Panias, the city which Herod's son Philip reestablished as Caesarea Philippi. Above all other projects in its splendor was Herod's elaborate reconstruction of the temple in Jerusalem, by which the disciples of Jesus were later overawed (Mark 13:1).

Through a combination of political skill and brutality, Herod managed to suppress all effective dissent to his purposes. The measures which he took at some points of his career made life in his kingdom very much like that in a modern police state. Meetings of citizens were prohibited; even walking together was not allowed. People were arrested, sometimes secretly, and imprisoned or put to death. Herod paid agents to spy on gatherings. He required an oath of loyalty from the entire population. At the same time, he knew the limits of the people's tolerance: He balanced the religiously unacceptable construction of the temple to Augustus in Panias with the remission of one-third of that year's tax requirement.[12]

Herod's imposition of Hellenistic culture upon Jewish Palestine met resistance only when it transgressed the religious sensibilities of his sub-

---

11. See Josephus, *War* 1.422–428.
12. Josephus, *Antiquities* 15.364–365.

jects. Greek language and thought had penetrated Jewish society in Palestine long before Herod's reign. Already in the second century B.C., upper echelons of Jewish society had come under the influence of Greek culture. Probably some of the elite instigated the aggressive program of forced, mass Hellenization under Antiochus Epiphanes, which prompted the revolt of conservative Jews under the leadership of the Maccabees.[13] The dynasty of Jewish Hasmonean rulers, which came into being as a result of Jewish independence itself, became increasingly drawn toward Greek institutions. One indication of this is the bilingual coinage (Hebrew and Greek) which appeared under the Hasmonean Alexander Janneus (103–76 B.C.) and again under Antigonus (40–37 B.C.).

Later evidence of papyri, inscriptions, and coinage confirms that knowledge of the Greek language was widespread in first-century Palestine, particularly in Jerusalem and the Hellenistic cities. Many Jews would have had a basic knowledge of the Greek language through the necessity of trade. It may be that Jesus Himself, growing up in Nazareth as a carpenter's son, became acquainted with Greek through contact with the city of Sepphoris, not more than four miles from Nazareth. Galilee, where much of Jesus' mission took place, was surrounded by Greek-speaking cities. Two of Jesus' disciples from Galilee had Greek names: Philip and Andrew. Greek-speaking Jews throughout the Mediterranean world flocked to Jerusalem during the Jewish feasts, and a considerable number emigrated there. Herod's various efforts to bring Hellenistic culture and education into his kingdom exposed the upper strata of Palestinian Jewish society directly to Greek institutions.

Difficulties arose between Herod and his subjects because he gave massive expenditures to pagan projects and openly transgressed the restrictions of the law in Palestine itself. The gladitorial contests were a source of dissent among the populace, particularly the trophies bearing human images awarded to the victors. Despite Herod's decision to yield to the objections of the people in this matter, an abortive assassination attempt resulted from the resentment he had created.[14] Even the temple in Jerusalem became the source of trouble. During an illness near the end of Herod's life, a pair of noted scholars of the law inspired a band of youth to make a daring attempt to remove the large golden eagle Herod had placed over the gate of the temple, because it violated the Law's prohibitions against images of living creatures.[15]

---

13. See Martin Hengel, *Judaism and Hellenism: Studies in Their Encounter in Palestine during the Early Hellenistic Period*, trans. John Bowden (Philadelphia: Fortress, 1981), 267–309.

14. Josephus, *Antiquities* 15.267–291.

15. Josephus, *Antiquities* 17.149–163.

Herod's death and the subsequent imposition of direct Roman rule over Judea after the deposition of his son Archelaus in A.D. 6 left a certain vacuum of power which was critical to the developments which followed, including the temporary calm in Palestine. The aristocracy, particularly the high priestly families, enjoyed enhanced privilege and authority over internal affairs. Formerly, Herod deposed high priests at will. Now the high priests and the Sadducean party, to which their allies among the lay aristocracy belonged, in effect ruled Judea, balanced only by the influence of the Pharisees.

THE PRIESTLY CLASS

The leading role which the priestly aristocracy assumed intensified the contradictions already inherent to their position. The Jewish people owed the chief priests traditional honors, tithes, and taxes, as the proper temple functionaries. Yet the same group mediated the rule of Rome to the populace as Herod once had done and shared in economic benefits derived from maintaining order. They had a temple police force under their authority, which they sometimes used for oppressive ends. A later tradition in the Talmud reflects this abuse of power:

> Woe is me because of the house of Ishmael the son of Phabi. Woe is me because of their fists. For they are high priests, and their sons are treasurers, and their sons-in-law are Temple overseers, and their servants beat the people with clubs.[16]

When the social unrest under Roman rule later penetrated Jerusalem, the high priestly families became the primary targets of assassinations and kidnappings.[17]

The strategy of the ruling priestly class in the period covered by the Gospels and Acts was to strengthen their traditional cultural claims to honor, while quieting potential outbreaks of violence which would have brought a response from Rome. In their perception, Jesus represented a threat to their status and to the stability of society. His challenge to their authority in Jerusalem provoked them to action against Him, although His popularity among the people forced them to take Him by stealth (Mark 11:12—12:12; 14:1–2; cf. John 11:45–50). Their later response to the apostolic proclamation of Jesus in Jerusalem was similar (Acts 5:27–28). It is noteworthy that Luke recorded their unhappiness over the mes-

---

16. b. Pesah. 57a. The translation is by Richard Horsley and James S. Hanson, *Bandits, Prophets, and Messiahs: Popular Movements in the Time of Jesus* (Minneapolis: Winston Press, 1985), 42. Cf. Josephus, *Antiquities* 20.181.

17. Josephus, *Antiquities* 20.208–210.

sage of the resurrection (Acts 4:1–2). The Sadducean rejection of this belief had its political side: The aristocracy feared such a hope might incite resistance to Rome, just as it had fueled the Maccabean revolt.

Herod's death also brought changes for a number of those of middling rank, professional interpreters of the law of Moses, scribes, and teachers. Like the aristocracy, most of those who guided the civil and religious life of the nation had an interest in preserving their role in the new arrangement. Many, but not all, legal experts were Pharisees who sought to encourage quiet obedience to the law under Roman rule. Herod's descendants were generally less ambitious than he had been in attempting to further Greek culture in Palestine. Without Herod's program of cultural imperialism, the Pharisees had a renewed hope of defining and promulgating faithfulness to the traditions of the law under the circumstances they believed God had allowed to come upon the nation. Josephus reported that although they were relatively few in number, they enjoyed considerable influence among the common people, a claim supported by their prominence in the Gospel narratives.[18]

JESUS' CONFLICT WITH THE PHARISEES

The Gospels indicate it was with Pharisees that Jesus first and most frequently came into conflict. His message and His claim to authority threatened the Pharisaic cause of gaining adherence to Jewish traditions in a setting in which the constant threat of Hellenizing influences was present. The narratives of the Gospels indicate that His treatment of the Sabbath was a source of irritation to them, especially His healings. His behavior seemed to violate what was to them a fundamental symbol of allegiance to the Law. Likewise, His freedom of contact with those who were lax in their observance of the law or marked by defiling associations—the customs agents and sinners—transgressed the boundaries of acceptable conduct. Jesus' practices threatened to undo what the Pharisees sought to inculcate.

The generally passive response of the Pharisees to Roman rule was not shared by all of their contemporaries. In the period following Herod's death various uprisings took place led by figures who made claims to prophetic or messianic status. Josephus reports that at the time that Archelaus was deposed as ethnarch of Judea (A.D. 6), a fresh impetus was given to resistance to Roman rule by a certain Judas of Gamala (elsewhere named "the Galilean") and a Pharisee named Saddok. These two gained adherents to the teaching that "God alone is leader and master" and that any form of submission to Roman rule, especially the payment of tribute, was

---

18. Josephus, *Antiquities* 18.12–17

contrary to the law.[19] Traditionally this movement has been associated with the "Zealots," a name which Josephus applied to a faction of the revolutionaries in Jerusalem during the war with Rome. Although the connection between the followers of Judas and the later Zealots has been questioned, it appears likely while various other revolutionary groups arose, Judas' group and its religious views played a significant role in the bringing about the revolt against Rome in A.D. 66.[20]

The Gospels and Acts provide indications that during the period of Jesus' ministry there was already considerable sympathy for the sort of teaching Judas the Galilean offered. Luke reported the Pharisee Gamaliel's knowledge of Judas and another revolutionary named Theudas (Acts 5:37). John's Gospel indicates that at the feeding of the five thousand the crowd determined to take Jesus and to make Him king (John 6:15). In Jerusalem, Jesus' adversaries attempted to force Him into an unpopular answer on the question of paying taxes to Caesar (Mark 12:13–17). One of Jesus' followers named Simon had been a member of a Zealot group (Mark 3:18; cf. Luke 6:15).

Jesus' message had aspects in common with most of the groups of His day, yet it presented a challenge to all of them. Like John the Baptist before Him, He proclaimed the kingdom of God was near and called for repentance in preparation for its coming (Mark 1:15). His announcement of the kingdom embodied traditional Jewish hopes and values, and to this extent stood in continuity with the culture of His day. The nature of His proclamation was unique, however. Unlike the Baptist, Jesus claimed the kingdom was present already in His person and ministry, even though it was still to be consummated in the future (e.g., Luke 11:20). As the Son of Man, He bore divine authority (Mark 2:10). The means by which Jesus asserted this unique status went beyond the normal channels by which authority was legitimated in His culture. His leadership was based on the particular appeal of His person and actions as a "charismatic" authority.[21] John the Baptist fulfilled certain cultural expectations of a reforming prophet or messianic figure through his withdrawal to the wilderness and

---

19. Ibid., 18.23.

20. See Martin Hengel, *The Zealots: Investigations into the Jewish Freedom Movement in the Period from Herod I until A.D. 70*, trans. David Smith. (Edinburgh: T. & T. Clark, 1989). This reconstruction has been challenged. See especially Richard Horsley, "The Zealots: Their Origin, Relationships and Importance in the Jewish Revolt," *NovT* 28 (1986): 159–92.

21. See Hengel, *The Charismatic Leader and His Followers*, trans. James Greig (New York: Crossroad, 1981), who uses the categories of the sociologist Max Weber.

ascetic lifestyle (Mark 1:6; cf. 2 Kings 1:8). Jesus did not distance Himself from society in this manner. Instead, He acted in a way that broke with conventional categories.

Jesus' intentional rejection of common messianic expectations is perhaps the most noteworthy feature of His activity. In part, Jesus' behavior was based upon His commitment to faith in God, who would vindicate Him at the proper time (Mark 8:31–38). Yet as we noted above, for many in the culture of first-century Palestine, "Messiah" translated into the notion of a revolutionary leader who would by force establish a just theocracy for Israel. In refusing to allow the immediate announcement by His disciples that He was "Messiah," Jesus set aside these political overtones. In the Gospels, Jesus made openly messianic statements in public only upon His approach to Jerusalem at the final Passover of His ministry. Even then He avoided association with the "zealot" conceptions which even His disciples shared.[22]

In other ways, too, Jesus acted contrary to the values of the revolutionaries of His society. He did not regard all those who were well-off or who profited from association with Rome as His enemies. He accepted support from various wealthy individuals, including some of the Herodian aristocracy (Luke 8:1–3; 22:7–13). He freely associated with those who served as customs agents of Rome, including the notoriously rich Zacchaeus (Luke 19:1–10). One of them came to be numbered among the twelve.[23]

The call to discipleship which Jesus issued during the course of His ministry also was an expression of charismatic leadership, which broke normal cultural boundaries. As Martin Hengel has shown, Jesus' demand for allegiance differed in important ways from other religious or philosophical teachers of his day.[24] When one of His disciples requested permission to attend to the customary duties of burial for a deceased father, Jesus responded, "Follow me, and let the dead bury their own dead" (Matt. 8:22). The Gospels indicate that Jesus' summons to discipleship required a number of those whom He called to suspend their occupations and familial relations (Mark 1:14–20; 10:28–31). Rabbinic teachers of a later period did not require the setting aside of such customary duties as Jesus did. Wandering Hellenistic philosophers inculcated pursuit of the

---

22. Recall, for example, Jesus' famous response to the question of paying the census tax to Rome, Mark 12:13–17.

23. Matthew 9:9–13. For Jesus, the primary issue concerning possessions was their proper and just use in light of the coming kingdom of God. See Hengel, *Property and Riches in the Early Church: Aspects of a Social History of Early Christianity*, trans. John Bowden (Philadelphia: Fortress Press, 1974).

24. Hengel, *The Charismatic Leader and His Followers.*

truth, but not the personal encounter with the will of God contained in Jesus' call. One did not attach oneself to Jesus the Teacher, but rather certain individuals were called to discipleship.[25] The activist prophets, messiahs, and Zealot figures sought the following of the masses, not the small band of committed followers whom Jesus called personally.

Spontaneous healings and exorcisms, by their very nature as extraordinary acts, represented a challenge to the structure of religious authority. Later rabbinic materials seem to have assimilated traditions about wonder-workers only by transforming them into conventional teachers.[26] Jesus' healings commended Him to many as an agent of God and often led to His being acclaimed as a prophet. But even healings and exorcisms could be rejected as illegitimate by those who came to regard Jesus as a threat. In these instances, Jesus' deeds were characterized as being outside the accepted norms, and hence dangerous and evil: "He casts out demons by the ruler of the demons" (Mark 3:22, NASB).

Jesus intentionally departed from social conventions in performing healings on a number of occasions. Cultures like that of first-century Jewish Palestine, which draw sharp distinctions between themselves and outsiders, tended to regulate tightly the body and its interaction with the world. Acts such as touching, in which the boundary around the body is penetrated, were allowed only under certain conditions.[27] Jesus' readiness to come in contact with lepers and people known for sinful behavior signaled His claim to stand above such standards. Mark's Gospel reports two incidents in which Jesus "defiled" individuals by His use of His saliva in healing them (7:31–37; 8:22–26). These acts were most likely intended to communicate not only to those whom He healed, but to Jesus' disciples. Either they had to regard fellowship with Jesus as polluting or as holy, separating them for the purposes of the kingdom.

Jesus set His band of followers apart from society in other ways. By virtue of their association with Him, Jesus' disciples were allowed to transgress usual cultural norms such as picking grain on the Sabbath and eating without prior ceremonial washing (Mark 2:23–38; 7:1–4). This sort of religious freedom expressed concretely what Jesus taught when using

---

25. See *EDNT,* s.v. "didaskolos."

26. W. S. Green, "Palestinian Holy Men: Charismatic Leadership and Rabbinic Tradition," in *ANRW* 2.19.2, ed. H. Temporini and W. Haase (Berlin: de Gruyter, 1979), 619–47.

27. See Mary Douglas, *Natural Symbols: Explorations in Cosmology* (New York: Pantheon, 1982); *Purity and Danger: An Analysis of Concepts of Pollution and Taboo* (London: Routledge and Kegan Paul, 1978), 29–57; David Smith, "Jesus and the Pharisees in Socio-Anthropological Perspective," *TJ* 6 (1985): 151–56.

other symbols such as the selection of twelve apostles (like the tribes of Israel) and the institution of the Lord's Supper in remembrance of Him. His disciples constituted the beginning of the true people of God prepared for the last days. They were to live with the new, higher code of ethics taught in the Sermon on the Mount, as the community which represented the coming kingdom of God on earth.

As a result of the apostolic proclamation, a community of believers was gathered in Jerusalem, Judea, and the remainder of Palestine. These "followers of the Way," as this self-designation suggests, existed as a relatively small sect, alongside the larger religious body of Judaism (Acts 9:2; 19:9; 22:4; 24:14, 22). It was only with the spread of faith in Christ to Gentiles and the growth of churches in the cities of the Greco-Roman world that Christians came to be seen as an independent social entity.

CHRISTIANITY IN THE FIRST-CENTURY GRECO-ROMAN CITIES

CENTRAL IMPORTANCE OF ROME

As important as the city was to the social world of the first century, life and thought extended far beyond its walls. There was an awareness, not merely at the level of the philosophers, but in the street, of the link between local concerns and the larger world. The most direct and perceptible unifying force in this period was, of course, Rome. The prosperity and well-being of each city depended on good relations with this "center." From the Roman side, efficient administration and the effective projection of military power created an infrastructure which became proverbial. Cities and villages were linked to one another by the roads which led to Rome. The danger of robbers and bandits was considerably reduced by the presence of military outposts along important routes. The sea lanes were likewise substantially cleared of piracy.[28]

The freedom and frequency of travel during the first century is immediately apparent in the NT writings. In the Book of Acts, one reads not only of the extensive travels of Paul and his companions, but also of the movements of ordinary people. Luke introduced us to a certain Aquila, a native of Pontus (in Asia Minor), and his wife Priscilla. These two, having been expelled from Rome by Claudius with other Jews, took up residence as tentmakers in Corinth where they met Paul (Acts 18:2). At the end of Paul's ministry there, the pair accompanied him to Ephesus (Acts 18:18–19). Later, when Paul wrote to Rome, he greeted the same pair, who had

---

28. See *HDB*, s.v. "travel in the New Testament." See also Acts 18:2.

apparently returned there (Rom. 16:3–4). It is likely, in fact, Christianity was spread to Rome by individuals such as these. It reached the center of the empire long before Paul did.

The early congregations of believers were aware of being related to one another through the missionaries who planted and nurtured the churches. Those who were recognized as apostles commissioned by Christ bore special authority, but there were numerous others sent by churches for various tasks.[29] The exigencies of travel required churches, like other associations in the ancient world, to provide hospitality and support for traveling Christian ministers.[30] This practice was obviously susceptible to abuse. The letters of 2 and 3 John were intended to deal with problems arising from this practice.[31] One way in which churches attempted to ensure only the proper messengers were received and given assistance was through letters of commendation. Paul's letter to Rome includes such an endorsement of Phoebe, who delivered the letter (Rom. 16:1–2). Elsewhere, Paul regularly commended his associates who carried letters to his churches (e.g., Phil. 2:25–30).

The use of written communication by the earliest Christians went far beyond the authorization of delegates, despite the fact that letters frequently served that purpose. Most of the NT writings, especially the letters, were composed in order to bridge the distance between a Christian leader and a congregation or congregations for which he had responsibility. The addressees, to the extent they accepted these writings, acknowledged the legitimacy of the apostles, prophets, or teachers who exhorted and taught them. Most importantly, in numerous instances this is expressed in the idea that the Gospel had created a new "nation" which was to be united in belief and practice (e.g. 1 Cor. 1:2; Eph. 4:1–6; 1 Pet. 2:9–11).

EDUCATION

Early Christian instruction took place within the context of the schooling which was available in the Greco-Roman cities.[32] Primary education which was available for children between the ages of seven and fourteen was usually provided either by an association of citizens or by the city

29. For example, the "apostles of the churches" accompanying Paul in his collection for Jerusalem, 2 Corinthians 8:23.

30. See Paul's expectation of support from Corinth (1 Cor. 16:5–6) and from Rome (Rom. 15:24).

31. See Abraham Malherbe, *Social Aspects of Early Christianity* (Philadelphia: Fortress, 1983).

32. On this topic, see *ISBE,* s.v. "education."

administration. It consisted of the familiar "reading, writing and arithmetic," with heavy emphasis on rote memorization. Paul may have learned the proverbial statements of Greek authors attributed to him in Acts and which occasionally appear in his letters in this way.[33] Secondary education consisted in grammar and familiarization with the poets, especially Homer, for which parents hired a tutor to instruct their children. Frequently, young men between the ages of fifteen and seventeen spent a year or two at a *gymnasium*, where instruction was supplemented with athletics and military training. Higher education was limited primarily to rhetoric or philosophy. Most chose the former, as preparation for a public career.

Many of the first generation of believers in Christ were Jewish. They brought with them the educational ideals with which they had been imbued as children and young adults. Josephus pointed to the pride which Jews took in the instruction of their children.[34] Education was essential to maintaining their cultural identity in the Hellenistic world. The family itself took responsibility for their training, a commitment which early Christians also assumed (Eph. 6:4). In considerable measure, this practice may be traced to the desire to pass on traditional morals and religious values not shared by the larger society. The Roman upper classes embraced similar ideals.[35]

As might be expected, the attainment of higher education, especially in rhetoric, was a mark of status. Unless one was a citizen of one of the few cities with a school of rhetoric, this level of study was available only to those who had sufficient means. Among the NT writers, only Luke and the author of Hebrews display the elevated style which indicates a rhetorical education. Paul certainly did not enjoy this advantage and openly said so (2 Cor. 11:6). His opponents at Corinth apparently did, making use of it to win the allegiance of this status-conscious congregation (2 Cor. 10:10; 11:6).

ECONOMIC AND SOCIAL LIFE

Most of the congregations of the earliest Christians in the cities seem to have been economically and socially diverse. Many were handworkers and tradespeople, working in occupations such as the one Paul took up, a leatherworker and tentmaker.[36] Such believers of modest means assisted

---

33. Acts 17:28 (Aratus, Phenomena); 1 Cor. 15:33 (Menander, Thais).

34. Josephus, *Against Apion* 1.60, 2.204; *Antiquities* 4.211.

35. See Stanley F. Bonner, *Education in Ancient Rome* (Berkeley: University of California Press, 1977), 10–33.

36. Ronald Hock, *The Social Context of Paul's Ministry: Tentmaking and Apostleship* (Philadelphia: Fortress, 1980).

in the collection of a gift for Jerusalem by setting aside what they could on a weekly basis (1 Cor. 16:2). Some believers were among the urban poor, for whom slavery might mean economic improvement (1 Cor. 16:2). Nevertheless, others were of relatively high standing. The lawsuits in Corinth suggest that part of the congregation had some wealth (1 Cor. 6:1–11). Gaius owned a house large enough for the entire Corinthian church to meet in, an instance which probably reflects the practice in many cities of meeting in the houses of the wealthier members (Rom. 16:23). The rented housing which the average believer could afford was generally extremely small, insufficient for such a gathering. Phoebe, from the nearby city of Cenchrea, had been a patron to Paul and others, supporting them from her means (Rom. 16:1–2). A very few, such as Erastus, the "director of public works" in Corinth, may have risen as high as the local aristocracy.[37]

Status was asserted and maintained through benefactions from the superior and corresponding obligation by the inferior party.[38] The slave who was manumitted, for example, remained a client without legal rights of the former master who became the patron and legal guardian of the freedman or freedwoman. "Friendship" was initiated by the greater in a favor to the lesser, who was expected to conform to the wishes of the former. Paul's financial independence and his refusal to enter into a client relation with members of the church in Corinth became a major element of his conflict with this congregation.[39] He also found it necessary to combat the tendency of the Corinthian congregation to import social distinctions into the life of the church. Wealthy members of the church engaged in conspicuous consumption in the face of poorer fellow believers at the meal in which the Lord's Supper was celebrated (1 Cor. 11:17–34). Urban associations were usually far more socially segregated than the church. In an unthinking manner, the rich Corinthian believers had allowed their practice to violate the message of the cross.

The local persecution of believers in Christ was no doubt in many instances precipitated by the perception they had violated conditions of "friendship" or clientalism. Their refusal to participate in offerings to the patron gods of their cities and their trade guilds was perceived as an expression of enmity toward their neighbors, whose well-being it jeopar-

---

37. Romans 16:23. See Gerd Theissen, *The Social Setting of Pauline Christianity: Essays on Corinth*, ed. and trans. John H. Schütz (Philadelphia: Fortress, 1982), 75–83.

38. See E. A. Judge, "Cultural Conformity and Innovation in Paul: Some Clues from Contemporary Documents," *TynBul* 35 (1984): 3–24.

39. See Peter Marshall, *Enmity in Corinth: Social Conventions in Paul's Relations with the Corinthians* (Tubingen: J.C.B. Mohr [Paul Siebeck], 1987), esp. 1–69.

dized. There was pressure, therefore, to conform to these demands. In some instances the believing community was tempted to return to simple Judaism, which was tolerated as a religious association and given legal rights in many cities.[40]

Like the larger society, the Greco-Roman household was hierarchical. The familiar NT codes of household duties of wives and husbands, children and parents, masters and slaves, reflect this ordering, which had deep cultural roots (Eph. 5:21—6:9; Col. 3:18—4:1; 1 Pet. 2:18—3:7). From at least the time of Aristotle, this patriarchal structure served as the dominant pattern in Mediterranean society.[41]

The manner in which it influenced public life varied according to time, place, and circumstance.[42] Women in Macedonia and Asia Minor participated to a great extent in community affairs, including political life. Roman society was more restrictive, but even here the matrons of the patrician households could exert considerable influence.

The situation was even more varied in the case of slavery. Individuals came into slavery by various paths: military conquests, being sold or selling oneself for debts, or by being born as a slave.[43] Slaves assumed varying tasks, from simple chores, through participation in the tasks of a family business, to administration and supervision of a large household, including other slaves. As demeaning as slavery could be, generally it was not the worst situation possible in an urban setting. One was at least assured of the provision of one's daily needs. That was not the case for the urban poor. For those few slaves from aristocratic households, especially the *familia Caesaris*, manumission was accompanied by considerable upward mobility. Other slaves, too, who knew or had learned a business, sometimes could accumulate considerable wealth as freedmen and freedwomen.[44]

The early Christian teaching found in the NT did not advocate the overthrow of the patriarchal structure of the household or the broader hierarchical structure of society. Instead, it sought to teach believers, whatever their position in the world, to live in light of the coming kingdom of God which would bring the present system to an end. In an unprecedented manner in the NT household codes, those of superior "rank"—husbands, fathers, and masters—have their rights restricted and

---

40. This situation lies behind the letter to the Hebrews.

41. See Aristotle, *Politics* 1.5.1–12.

42. See Ben Witherington III, *Women in the Earliest Churches*, SNTSMS 59 (Cambridge: Cambridge University Press, 1988).

43. On this topic, see *ISBE*, s.v. "slavery. II. in the NT."

44. See Dale B. Martin, *Slavery as Salvation: The Metaphor of Slavery in Pauline Christianity* (New Haven: Yale University Press, 1990), 1–49.

are enjoined to show love, kindness, and respect toward the other (Eph. 5:21—6:9; Col. 3:18—4:1; 1 Pet. 2:18—3:7).

In another way, the relations between individuals were set in a new constellation through common membership in the community of faith. Associations were a central feature of urban social life. They were sometimes formed for community tasks, such as the support of *gymnasia*. There were a host of professional and trade associations. There were burial societies (which also served purely social functions) and religious associations (including not only the Jewish synagogues, but other foreign cults). The church took its place among all these. Within its fellowship, women and men, slaves and masters, Gentiles and Jews were not only called into unity in Christ but placed in new social relations with one another through the call to mutual edification. It was only natural that questions should arise regarding the relationship between traditional social roles and those of the new creation in which the community of believers participated. Consensus on such matters was necessary not only for unity within the church, but for apologetic purposes. Foreign cults which generally offered expanded roles to women and slaves were regarded with suspicion as undermining the stability of the household.[45]

From the very start, the congregations of Gentile believers engaged in practices which distinguished them from the rest of society and gave them internal cohesion and organization. New converts marked their entrance into the faith and the community of believers through baptism (e.g., Acts 2:41; 18:12–13). The earliest Christians gathered regularly on the first day of the week for worship, prayer, edification, and the celebration of a common meal in remembrance of Jesus' death and resurrection (Acts 20:7; 1 Cor. 16:2). They expressed their kinship and mutual love through the exchange of a "holy kiss" (Rom. 16:16). Those appointed to ministry within the congregations entered into their tasks through the laying on of hands by the leaders (Acts 13:3; 1 Tim. 4:14; 2 Tim. 1:6). Criteria were developed to determine who was qualified for offices such as elder, deacon, or widow (e.g., 1 Tim. 3:1–13; 5:3–16).

As noted above, instruction was an important element of the life of the early Christian communities. New converts were assimilated into the group not only by their profession of faith and baptism, but by catechesis, that is, introduction to basic teaching about Christ and faith in Him (e.g., Heb. 5:12—6:1). Learning did not end there. The gatherings of believers were marked not only by worship and prayer, but by instruction (e.g., Acts 2:42;15:35;1 Cor. 14:26). "Teachers" assumed a prominent role in the

---

45. See David L. Balch, *Let Wives Be Submissive: The Domestic Code in I Peter,* SBLMS 26 (Chico, Calif.: Scholars, 1981).

churches (Jas. 3:1). The content of their instruction seems to have consisted primarily in Christian interpretation of the Jewish Scriptures, the transmission and exposition of the words and deeds of Jesus, and ethical standards. The letters of Paul and others came to be exchanged between churches as well, so that epistolary literature was subsumed into the body of materials used in teaching (2 Pet. 3:16).

As this survey indicates, the relation of the earliest Christians to their culture was marked not only by assimilation, but distancing. Perhaps the best overall characterization of the attitudes the New Testament writers took toward first-century culture is found in E. A. Judge's assessment of the earliest Christian relation to government and society: "Whether socially acquiescent, socially defiant, or socially militant, it is from belief that the end of all things is realized in Christ's resurrection to power, and from the expectation of the inauguration of the kingdom, that their attitudes are defended."[46]

FOR FURTHER READING

Cohen, Shaye J. D. *From the Maccabees to the Mishnah.* Library of Early Christianity. Philadelphia: Westminster, 1987.

Elliott, John H. *What Is Social-Scientific Criticism?* Minneapolis: Fortress, 1993.

Ferguson, Everett. *Backgrounds of Early Christianity.* Grand Rapids: Eerdmans, 1993.

Hengel, Martin. *Jews, Greeks, and Barbarians: Aspects of the Hellenization of Judaism in the Pre-Christian Period.* Translated by John Bowden. Philadelphia: Fortress, 1980.

Hengel, Martin with Christoph Markschies. *The "Hellenization" of Judaea in the First Century After Christ.* Philadelphia: Trinity Press International, 1989.

Hengel, Martin. *Property and Riches in the Early Church: Aspects of a Social History of Early Christianity.* Translated by John Bowden. Philadelphia: Fortress, 1974.

Holmberg, Bengt. *Sociology and the New Testament: An Appraisal.* Minneapolis: Fortress, 1990.

Jeremias, Joachim. *Jerusalem in the Time of Jesus: An Investigation into Economic and Social Conditions during the New Testament Period.* Translated by F. H. and C. H. Cave. London: SCM, 1969.

Judge, E. A. *The Social Pattern of the Christian Groups in the First Century.*

---

46. E. A. Judge, *The Social Pattern of the Christian Groups in the First Century* (London: Tyndale, 1960), 75.

London: Tyndale, 1960.

MacMullen, Ramsay. *Roman Social Relations 50 B.C. to A.D. 200.* New Haven: Yale University Press, 1976.

Malherbe, Abraham. *Social Aspects of Early Christianity.* Philadelphia: Fortress, 1983.

Malina, Bruce. *The New Testament World: Insights from Cultural Anthropology.* Rev. ed. Atlanta: John Knox, 1993.

Meeks, Wayne. *The First Urban Christians: The Social World of the Apostle Paul.* New Haven: Yale University Press, 1983.

Safrai, S. and Stern M., eds. *The Jewish People in the First Century: Historical Geography, Political History, Social, Cultural and Religious Life and Institutions.* Compendia Rerum Iudaicarum ad Novum Testamentum. Section 1, 2 vols. Philadelphia: Fortress, 1974–76.

Saldarini, Anthony J. *Pharisees, Scribes and Sadducees in Palestinian Society.* Wilmington, Del.: Michael Glazier, 1988.

Schürer, Emil. *The History of the Jewish People in the Age of Jesus Christ.* 3 vols. Revised and edited by Geza Vermes, Fergus Millar and Matthew Black. Edinburgh: T. & T. Clark, 1973–87.

Sherwin-White, A. N. *Roman Society and Roman Law in the New Testament.* Oxford: Clarendon, 1963.

Stambaugh, John E. and David L. Balch. *The New Testament in Its Social Environment.* Library of Early Christianity. Philadelphia: Westminster, 1986.

XXIV

Religious Background of the New Testament

Chris Church

The disparate peoples of the Mediterranean had been exchanging religious ideas since before the Greek colonization of coastal Asia Minor in the 800s B.C. The rate of exchange increased with Alexander's conquest, his successors' struggle to consolidate power, and Rome's seizure of power. By the first century, a common Greek language, cities with ethnically mixed populations, a "worldwide" economy in the Mediterranean, Roman military roads, and a sea free of pirates all aided the trading of religious ideas. Foreign-born slaves, merchants, and soldiers carried their gods to distant lands. Though the religious sentiment of the majority remained conservative, that is, individuals generally worshiped their ancestral god(s), the mixing of ethnic groups in the cities exposed the majority to alien religions to some degree or other.

First-Century Judaism

Judaism was already a world religion in the first century, spread throughout the cities of the Mediterranean world by Jewish slaves, mercenaries, and merchants. Judaism flourished in part because of its loyalty to core beliefs and institutions and its adaptability to the varied needs of the Diaspora and of various interest groups in Palestine.

THE VARIETY OF FIRST-CENTURY JUDAISM

Once it was fashionable to speak of a first-century "normative Judaism." Now some even speak of first-century "Judaisms." Though it showed great variety in its expression, first-century Judaism was one faith, and as Meeks has observed, much of its variety could be met in an individual Jew. Paul, for example, was a Hellenistic Jew who wrote Greek and used the Septuagint (LXX); he was an apocalyptic Jew who anticipated the end of the present evil age and warned the children of light to distinguish themselves from the children of darkness; he was a Jewish mystic caught up into the third heaven to see the indescribable; he was a Pharisee with regard to the law.[1] That a Jew like Paul transcended these modern categories warns against an easy compartmentalization of Judaism. Though individual Jews like Paul could exhibit complex sets of beliefs and behaviors that defy ready classification, even first-century writers such as Josephus or the author of Acts knew there were differences between a Sadducee and a Pharisee or tensions between Greek-speaking and Aramaic-speaking Jews in Palestine. This discussion addresses some of the facets contributing to first-century Judaism's variety and vitality.

Sadducees. The Sadducees were priestly aristocrats and theological conservatives. These guardians of the temple were concerned primarily with cultic matters, such as the legitimate descent and ritual purity of priests or the proper procedure for sacrifices. In their view the Torah, the five books of Moses, literally interpreted, gave adequate instructions for operation of the temple cultus, the central acts of Jewish faith; no other Scripture was needed. Since they rejected later Hebrew Scripture, the Prophets and Writings, the Sadducees dismissed belief in the resurrection or in hierarchies of angels drawn from these. The Sadducees in principle rejected the Pharisees' oral law, preferring their own traditions where the Torah was silent or sketchy on rules for a given rite. In practice, the Sadducees submitted to much of the Pharisaic tradition, for to cross the Pharisees was to awaken the wrath of the common people. The Sadducees controlled the majority of seats on the Sanhedrin, the seventy-member supreme court, where they generally pursued a course of accommodation to Roman rule. Again, they sometimes felt compelled to bow to the will of the court's influential Pharisaic minority.

---

1. Wayne A. Meeks, *The First Urban Christians: The Social World of the Apostle Paul* (New Haven: Yale University Press, 1983), 33.

Chief Priests. Before the destruction of Jerusalem in A.D. 70, the high priest was the dominant figure in Jewish religious life. His responsibilities included praying for the daily meal offering and for the bull sacrificed on the Day of Atonement. He officiated on the Day of Atonement, on the three pilgrim festivals (Passover, Pentecost, and Tabernacles), and over the red heifer ceremony. The high priest also presided over the Sanhedrin. The chief priests included "retired" high priests; the temple captain, who oversaw day-to-day temple operations; the directors of the 24 weekly and 156 daily courses or shifts of priests; seven overseers; and three treasurers. The Jerusalem-based captain, overseers, and treasurers were often drawn from the high priest's immediate family.

Pharisees. Primarily a lay movement, the Pharisees sought by means of the oral law, "the traditions of the fathers," to apply the Torah to all of life, even in new situations remote from those in which the Law was first formulated. Pharisees were not a monolithic group but were theologically progressive compared to the Sadducees and Essenes. Some such as Shammai were more strict; others such as Hillel were more flexible in their interpretations. They accepted the whole of the OT as Scripture: Law, Prophets, and Writings. Pharisees greatly stressed their tradition of interpretation. The NT picture is accurate in stressing their particular concern with matters of tithing, Sabbath observance, agricultural law, and ritual purity. Pharisees applied the strictest purity rules, which the Old Testament meant only for those priests eating the temple offerings, to all members of their associations (haburot).

Scribes. The scribes were ordained scholars. Their job was to pass on the traditional interpretations of the Torah and to meet new situations by turning over the Torah. The Pharisees were devoted to living out the teaching of the scribes.

Essenes. The NT writers do not mention the Essenes. Their primary community was located near the shores of the Dead Sea. They lived a monastic life, sharing their property in common and stressing very strict observance of the Law. Like the Pharisees, they accepted the larger canon of Hebrew Scripture. Like the Samaritans, they rejected the Jerusalem temple cult, though for different reasons. They apparently began as a group of priests protesting the Hasmonean's acceptance of the Jewish high priesthood. (Though priests, the Hasmoneans were not descendants of Zadok and thus not qualified to be high priests.) Like the early Christians, they saw events of their own day foreshadowed in the ancient prophecies. Their intense and highly developed expectation of the end involved the prophet, a priestly Messiah as a final interpreter of the Law, and a royal Messiah, who would lead in the final conflict between the sons of light and the sons of darkness. The Romans destroyed their community during the Jewish revolt of A.D. 66–73.

Zealots. The zealots were spiritual heirs of the Maccabees' war-inspired, God-helps-those-who-help-themselves piety. They took it upon themselves to rid the Holy Land of pagan influences by assassination and by revolt.

Am-ha-ares. The am-ha-ares, or people of the land, were Palestine's common folk. They lacked the training or resources to keep the myriad oral laws of the Pharisees, who regarded the am-ha-ares as hopeless sinners. But these folk welcomed Jesus.

Samaritans. The Samaritans were the descendants of the old Northern Kingdom and the pagans the Assyrians settled in their conquered territory. Like the Sadducees, the Samaritans accepted the Torah, the books of Moses, as their Scripture, though in revised form. Like the Essenes, they expected a prophet equal to Moses. Again, like the Essenes—but for different reasons—the Samaritans rejected worship at the Jerusalem temple. After the Babylonian exile, the returning Jews rejected the Samaritans' aid in rebuilding the temple (Ezra 4:1–3). About two centuries later, the Samaritans, sponsored by Alexander the Great, built their own temple on Mount Gerizim. In 128 B.C. the Jewish priest-king, John Hyrcanus, destroyed the Gerizim temple when he incorporated Samaria into his territory. During the first century, ancient Samaria was a pagan city. The native Samaritans occupied nearby Shechem.

The Diaspora. The Diaspora, meaning "scattering," refers to those Jews living outside the promised land. Meeks estimated there were five to six million Diaspora Jews in the first century, normally organized as distinct communities within their host cities and governed by their own laws and institutions.[2] Meeks also noted "a substantial Jewish population in virtually every town of any size in the lands bordering on the Mediterranean. Estimates run from 10 to 15 percent of the total population of a city—in the case of Alexandria, perhaps higher."[3]

The Romans generally supported the freedom of Diaspora Jews to worship and settle internal matters according to their ancestral laws. For example, in 49 B.C. Lucius Antonius, a Roman magistrate with financial and judicial oversight of Asia, confirmed that the Jews of Sardis traditionally had their own association, governed themselves by their own ancestral

---

2. Ibid., 13 and 34.

3. Ibid., 34. According to Philo, the Kerateion, Alexandria's Jewish district, made up two fifths of the city (Flacc. 55). The Jews inhabited the Transtiberinum district in Rome.

laws, and had their own place (perhaps their synagogue) in which they decided their internal affairs and controversies (Josephus Ant., 14:259-61).

THE UNITY OF FIRST-CENTURY JUDAISM

The varieties of first-century Judaism were bound by unifying ideas and institutions. Chief among the unifying ideas were monotheism, with its attendant rejection of idolatry; the Torah, or books of Moses as God's revealed Word; and the covenants, which marked the Jews as God's chosen people. Rooted in these ideas were shared habits, such as Sabbath-keeping, circumcision, and observance of food laws. Unifying institutions included the synagogue, the temple, and the Jewish family.

The Synagogue. The synagogue was the institution most familiar to first-century Jews worldwide. Many a Diaspora Jew might travel to worship at the Jerusalem temple but once in his lifetime. Throughout the Mediterranean world and Mesopotamia, Jews attended the synagogue each Sabbath.

The synagogue met many needs, as translations of its varied Hebrew names suggest: house of prayer, house of study, house of assembly. Worship place, study, court, community center—all were roles of the synagogue.

Unlike the temple, the synagogue was lay-led. Any community with ten Jewish men (a minyan, a religious quorum) was responsible for a synagogue. No priest was needed. Any man might be called upon to lead the prayers, read from the Scriptures, or offer a sermon. If a priest were present, he was invited to offer the priestly benediction. In the first century, it seems men, women, and children attended with no segregation in seating.

The shofar, or ram's horn, called the synagogue service to order. The congregation recited the Shema, beginning "Hear, O Israel: The Lord our God is one Lord,"[4] and in the first century, the Decalogue or Ten Commandments. Following this recitation, someone led the congregation in praying the benedictions. Eventually the wording of the Eighteen Benedictions was set, but in the first century the one leading prayer was free to improvise shorter or longer blessings in similar style.

Scripture reading was the central feature of synagogue worship. In the first century the sacred scrolls were probably kept in a portable chest or in a wall niche. The assistant, the hazzan, invited two men to read and presented them with the proper scroll(s). Scripture reading and prayer were done standing. There were generally two readings, one from the Law (Torah) and one from the Prophets (Haptorah). Throughout much of the Diaspora these readings were in Greek. Where the reading was in

---

4. The Shema eventually consisted of Deut. 6:4–9; 11:13–21; and Num. 15:37–41.

Hebrew, a targum, or Aramaic paraphrase of the Scripture text, was offered. On feast days when the readings were longer, more men were called on to read. On these days especially, the service included singing of hymns. The invited speaker sat to deliver his sermon. Sermons were offered on the Sabbaths, as well as Mondays and Thursdays. Sermons typically made generous use of Scriptures, sometimes tying the Torah and Haptorah readings together ingeniously. If a priest was available, his benediction closed the service.

The Temple. One might say that first-century Jews were a people divided by a common institution, the temple. Pharisees and Sadducees fought over the proper form of its rituals, including such issues as the water libation at the Feast of Tabernacles, a rite not even mentioned in Scripture. The Pharisees argued that the water should be poured on the altar; the Sadducees said it should be poured at its foot. The Essenes rejected the temple's high priesthood of non-Zadokite, political appointees. The zealots viewed its aristocratic priests as Roman collaborators. The Samaritans rejected the Jerusalem temple altogether in favor of their own holy site.

The temple was a massive complex with a circumference of first 3,400, then 5,000 feet. (For comparison, the agora, or market square of Roman Corinth had a circumference of only 1,800 feet.) Begun by Herod in about 20 B.C., its construction continued over eighty years until Albinus' term as procurator (A.D. 62–64).

From the golden gate on the east, worshipers entered the Court of the Gentiles. For a time during Jesus' ministry this area doubled as a bazaar, where animals could be purchased for sacrifice and money exchanged. The Soreg, a latticed partition about four and a half feet high, separated the inner courts from the Court of the Gentiles. Archaeologists have uncovered two inscriptions warning Gentiles that they crossed this partition at the risk of their own lives. Paul was falsely accused of bringing Gentiles within the Soreg and thus profaning the temple (Acts 21:28).

Jewish worshipers entered the court of the women from the east, probably through the beautiful gate. Chambers for temple supplies (wood and oil) or for those with needs for special sacrifices (lepers and Nazirites) occupied the four corners of this court. At the court's west end, fifteen semicircular stairs rose to the east, or Nicanor gate, which was of Corinthian bronze, more highly prized than gold. (All other temple gates were gilded.) Levites performed music on the steps before this gate.

The east gate opened into the narrow court of Israel, where only Jewish males could enter. A latticed partition a foot and a half high separated this court from that of the priests. The position and names of the courts suggest the relative status of the worshipers; Jewish women had a mixed status, superior to Gentiles, inferior to male Jews, who alone are designated Israel.

The court of priests held areas for tethering, slaughtering, and skinning sacrificial animals, as well as the altar for burnt offerings and the great basin. At Passover when immense numbers of lambs were slain, this court resembled a great slaughterhouse. To the west lay the temple itself. The marble facade of the sanctuary measured 165 feet by 165 feet. According to Josephus, it was gilded as was the temple porch. Two pillars of reddish marble stood beside the entrance. A great gold vine, representing Israel, separated the porch from the Holy Place. Gold tendrils to be added to the vine were a common offering.

This temple, like many others, had two interior rooms separated by a veil. The holy place contained the incense altar, the table for the bread of the Presence, and the great menorah, said to contain between 150 and 176 pounds of gold. Here priests burned incense twice daily at the times of the morning and evening sacrifices.

Beyond the veil lay the most holy place, where only the high priest could enter and then but once a year on the Day of Atonement. In the first century this room lay empty, perhaps with a raised floor to mark the spot where the lost ark of the covenant had stood.

The Family. The Jewish home was where faith was lived out each day. Here children were taught the rudiments of faith. Here the Shema, Israel's central confession of faith, and in the first century, the Decalogue were recited on rising from sleep and, on going to bed. Here grace was said before and after meals. Here the mezuzah on the doorpost, a small box containing Scriptures, marked the home as a Jewish household. Here the Jews kept the multitude of purity laws. Here the pious showed their faith in their day-to-day dress, wearing tassels on their cloaks (zizith) and small Scripture boxes on their arms and foreheads (phylacteries, tefillin). In these and other ways, first-century Jews witnessed to their faith in the God of Israel.

GRECO-ROMAN PAGANISM: THE VITALITY OF PAGANISM

The paganism that confronted early Christianity in the eastern Mediterranean was robust and pervasive, not impotent and quarantined into few of life's units. The Book of Acts pictures pagans zealous for, and economically dependent on, their ancestral cults. For example, at Ephesus a theater crowd of perhaps 24,000 cheered for two hours, "Great is Artemis of the Ephesians!" (Acts 19:29, 34).* At Philippi a charge of advocating

---

* Unless otherwise stated, Scripture quotations in this chapter are from the *NKJV.*

religious customs not lawful for "'Romans to adopt or observe'" (16:21) caused Paul and Silas to be beaten with rods and imprisoned. True, both disturbances were rooted in economics, but in the economics of soothsaying (16:16, 19) and idol manufacture (19:24–27).

Likewise, Acts pictures pagans ready to see their gods interrupt their day-to-day routines. Awed by a healing, a crowd at Lystra hailed Barnabas and Paul as Zeus and Hermes and prepared to acknowledge this "epiphany" with a sacrifice of oxen (14:11–13). Convinced by shipwreck and snakebite, natives of Malta dubbed Paul a murderer hunted and bagged by the Maltese equivalent of the goddess Dike (Justice): "Though he escaped from the sea, Justice has not allowed him to live" (28:4, NIV). Challenged by Paul's continuing health, the Maltese "changed their minds and said he was a god" (28:6, NIV). Amazed by his "magic," Samaritans hailed a sorcerer named Simon as "the power of God that is called Great" (8:10). Familiar with apotheosized mortals, a self-seeking crowd from Tyre and Sidon exaggerated Herod Agrippa's oratory—"The voice of a god, not of man!" (12:22, NIV). It seems the gods were everywhere, at least for pagans in Acts.

Acts also pictures the high visibility and potential attraction of paganism in Greco-Roman cities. Athens was "full of idols" (17:16) and altars, including a catchall in case some god had been missed (17:23). Ephesus had its world-renowned temple to Artemis (19:27, 35). Even backwater Lystra had its temple to Zeus (14:13). The Jerusalem Council's instructions to Gentile believers to avoid "'things polluted by idols'" and "'what has been sacrificed to idols'" presupposed the prominence of idols and pagan cult meals throughout the cities Paul and Barnabas evangelized (15:20, 29; cf. 21:25). Paul's similar warnings to the Corinthians (1 Cor. 8:1–13) assume an audience "so accustomed to idols" and their feasts (1 Cor. 8:7) and perhaps reluctant to forfeit these rare opportunities for socializing, eating meat, and drinking wine (1 Cor. 8:10, 13; 10:14—11:1; cf. Rom. 14:1—15:1). The charges against the churches at Pergamum and Thyatira (Rev. 2:14, 20) also reflect early Christians' familiarity with and participation in pagan rites.

Paganism was no straw man to early Christian eyes. Paul took idolatry as the real force driving all manner of moral decline (Rom. 1:18–32; esp. 1:23, 25).[5] His converts had been "enslaved to beings that by nature are not gods" but had now "turned to God from idols" (Gal. 4:8; 1 Thess. 1:9). This bondage remained tight and harsh for those without Christ.

---

5. The NT often links idolatry and immorality: "What pagans choose to do" is to live "in debauchery, lust, drunkenness, orgies, carousing, and detestable idolatry" (1 Pet. 4:3, NIV). "The immoral of this world" include idolaters (1 Cor. 5:10).

Even dread plagues could not convince hardened pagans to "give up worshiping demons and idols of gold and silver and bronze and stone and wood, which cannot see or hear or walk" (Rev. 9:20). To recognize paganism's force, bondage, and pervasiveness is to hear the urgency of 1 John's closing appeal: "Keep yourselves from idols" (5:21).

THE VARIETY OF PAGANISM

In writing social history, Meeks observed, "it will not do" to describe the early Christian environment "in terms of vague generalities. . . . Rather, to the limit that our sources and our abilities permit, we must try to discern the textures of life in particular times and particular places."[6] Given these limits, what shape did paganism take in some cities of Paul's mission? And what shape in those seven cities in John's Asian sphere?

Antioch (Psidian). By A.D. 50 Antioch boasted an Imperial sanctuary in the Roman style—a podium temple with a semicircular portico. Antioch's coins featured Men, the native moon and fertility god. Like Asclepius, who appears in relief in Men's Antioch sanctuary, Men was a god of healing. Men is sometimes equated with Attis, the consort of the Great Mother Cybele.

Antioch (Syrian). Zeus was worshiped under various names. Astarte, goddess of fertility, love, and war, was popular in Antioch as throughout Syria. She was often equated with the Greek Aphrodite (Venus) or Egyptian Isis. The OT knows Astarte as Ashtoreth. Nemesis (Divine Wrath) was worshiped. City coins show Antioch's Orontes River personified, swimming at Tyche's feet.[7] Tyche (Good Fortune) served as protector of the city. Other coins picture Augustus as high priest of his own cult. Other "classical" gods and goddesses honored by Antioch's temples or shrines included Ares (war god), Asclepius (god of healing), Athena, Calliope (muse of epic poetry), Demeter (earth goddess), Dionyss, Hecate (fertility goddess), Herakles (Greek hero), Hermes (messenger of the gods), Io (river goddess), Jupiter Capitolinus (the Roman sky god, one of the three principle Roman dieties), Kronos (father of Zeus, perhaps once a fertility god), Minos (king of Crete, after death one of three judges in Hades), the Muses (personifications of the arts), and Nemesis (Divine Wrath).

Mosaics from the time of Trajan (98–117) feature the Greek fertility god Dionysus.[8] The Isis mystery was also active.

---

6. Meeks, *Urban Christians*, 2.

7. According to Pliny the Elder, Tyche "is alone invoked and praised throughout the world, in all places, at all hours, and through the voices of all men" (*Nat. Hist.* 2:22).

8. For a fuller treatment of Dionysus, see the later sections on Athens and Pergamum.

Athens. Athens bears the name of its patron goddess, Athena, and its Parthenon honored her as the virgin goddess. Nearby, a second temple, the Erechtheum, honored Athena's triumph over Poseidon for mastery of Attica. There, every fourth year during the great Panathenaia, Athena's wooden statue was presented a new robe. The yearly Panathenaia offered competitions in athletics, torch races, and recitations of Homer. As judged from inscriptions, only Zeus and Apollo were more popular than Athena in the Greek-speaking areas of the empire.[9]

Athens hosted in late March the great Dionysia, a five-day dramatic and musical competition honoring Dionysus. "Next to Asclepius, Dionysus was most widely accepted among all Greek gods in the Hellenistic period."[10] On the first day, the god's image was carried from his temple to the 14,000-seat theater to oversee the plays.[11] For three mornings, a playwright presented three tragedies and a satyr play. For five afternoons, the play was a comedy. The best plays won prizes. Men's and boys' choruses also competed in singing dithyrambs in honor of Dionysus.

Dionysus was not always worshiped in so civilized a manner. Followers of this god of animal life wore fawn skins or wove snakes in their hair. Followers paraded as part-human, part-animal characters: seileni (part-horse), satyrs and Pans (part-goat). Followers carried fertility symbols, such as a phallus or a thyrsus, a cone-topped wand wound with ivy. As god of wine Dionysus (Bacchus) was worshiped in Bacchanalia, or drinking parties. By drinking wine, the Bacchanals took into themselves the god of wine and with him his power of rejuvenation.

His orgiastic feast was held in midwinter. Female followers (maenads, meaning "mad ones") danced wildly, until dizzy. In a mad frenzy, they killed game and consumed raw meat. Those caught in such frenzied worship were held to be more than mortal. Since their wild behavior was seen as a return to primitive nature's freedom and a foretaste of the afterlife's revel, the ecstatic experiences were believed to leave them with miraculous powers of healing and prophecy.

---

9. Ramsay MacMullen, *Paganism in the Roman Empire* (New Haven: Yale University Press, 1981), 7.

10. Helmut Koester, *History, Culture, and Religion of the Hellenistic Age* (Philadelphia: Fortress, 1982), 181.

11. Perhaps even the terms tragedy and comedy are tied to Dionysus' worship. Tragedy means "goat song" or "song [at the sacrifice] of a goat." Dionysus is sometimes represented as a goat. Comedy means "song for a group revel." Frenzied celebration was one form of Dionysus' worship.

The myth underlying the Eleusinian mysteries explained the changing seasons.[12] The Hellenistic fascination with this myth was likely not in Demeter's power over the seasons but in Persephone's power over death and freedom from Hades. Initiation offered hope for life even in Hades. The two-staged initiation was open to any Greek-speaker, male or female, citizen or noncitizen, slave or free. The lesser mysteries honored Persephone in midwinter. Wreathed initiates (mystai) paraded with myrtle branches, and a woman representing Demeter offered seeds as gifts to Persephone. The week-long greater mysteries began in late summer. On the second day, mystai bathed in the sea with suckling pigs they would later sacrifice for their purification. The fifth day, celebrants processioned from Athens, arriving at Eleusis by torchlight on the sixth night. Wheat for a thousand men was sacrificed to Demeter on the final day. Initiation into the greater mysteries took place that night inside a great hall that could hold 10,000. The rite involved dramatization of the myth, explanations, and the viewing of sacred objects. Only full initiates viewed the sacred objects, perhaps an ear of grain, a shaft of light, or a phallus.

Caesarea Maritima. Judea's Roman capital reflected Roman religious interests. Statues of Augustus and Roma guarded the entrance to Caesarea's harbor. Herod's temple to Augustus and Roma with its colossal statue ominated the port city. Caesarea, like many sites that garrisoned Roman troops, had its Mithraeum, or temple to Mithra. Mithraeums were generally underground, for a cave was where Mithra, representing day, killed the primeval bull, representing night. This all-male mystery cult is known for its feasts—most Mithreaums were found littered with animal bones—and frightening rituals, such as mock murders and the taurobolium. In the latter rite, a bull slaughtered above the mystics bathed them in its blood, representing all creative, life-giving fluids. In addition, a statue of Artemis in Ephesian style points to her worship at Caesarea in a form assimilated to the Great Mother of Asia Minor.

Corinth. Roman Corinth had the expected temples to the major Greek gods. A large temple of Aphrodite, goddess of love, overlooked the city from the Acrocorinth 1,500 feet above the agora. A smaller shrine stood at the southwest end of the agora; another was at Cenchreae, Corinth's eastern port. Aphrodite was also a favorite with makers of terra-cotta images. Her image appears on city coins.

---

12. The underworld god, Hades, stole Persephone (Kore) to be his bride. The grieving of Persephone's mother, the vegetation goddess Demeter, brought famine. Each year afterward, Hades allowed Persephone to return to the upper world for nine months, during which Demeter gave the earth fertility. For three months while Persephone was back in Hades, fertility ceased.

At the city's center stood the archaic temple of Apollo (or perhaps Athena), built in the sixth century B.C.E. and restored in first century A.D. A second shrine to Apollo, the Peribolos (sacred enclosure), stood on the east side of the Lechaeum road. Apollo was god of sunlight, prophecy, music, poetry, and medicine.

The temple of Asclepius, the god of healing, stood just north of the city. The facilities included an open exercise area, a fountain house for therapeutic bathing, three banquet rooms for eleven diners, and an abaton, or sleeping facility. Asclepius was believed to appear to the faithful in dreams and declare them healed. Those thankful for cures brought terracotta offerings shaped like their afflicted body parts. Excavators have uncovered a thirty-foot-tall heap of such parts.

The temple of Athena the Bridler, commemorating Athena's aid in bridling Pegasus, stood near the archaic temple of Apollo, unless that structure is in fact Athena's shrine. A bronze statue of Athena stood in the center of the agora. Athena also appeared on the city's coins.

An extant relief of Dionysus, patron of the theater, animal life, and wine, perhaps decorated the Pantheon. A theater and an odeum (for musical presentations) stood northwest of the city.

A fountain honoring Poseidon stood on the southwest side of the agora. The fountain featured the sea god with Aphrodite and dolphins. Nine miles east of Corinth, the biannual Isthmian games honored Poseidon. Competitions included athletics, music, drama, and oratory. Poseidon's temple at Isthmia held a statue three times life size.

Other Greek gods worshiped at Corinth included Demeter, who had temples on the Acrocorinth and at Isthmia; and Heracles, Hermes, and Tyche, who were honored with small shrines on the southwest side of the agora. The large temple southwest of the agora was likely the Pantheon, a temple to all the gods. Extant reliefs depicting Demeter, Zeus, Kore (Persephone), Athena, Ge (Earth), and Dionysus likely adorned this temple.

In addition to native Greek cults, Corinth boasted a massive temple to the Roman imperial cult. Built during Claudius' reign, it measured approximately 425 feet by 295 feet.

Eastern mysteries were also well established. Isis and her consort Serapis had two shrines each on the Acrocorinth. Isis also had a shrine at the southwest end of the harbor in Cenchreae. Serapis likely had a shrine in a room on the southeast side of the agora. Isis' devotees engaged in daily worship. In the morning, a singer opened her temple, which was purified with water. A priest burned incense and sprinkled the faithful with water. The priest clothed Isis' statue and presented it with food. In addition, the goddess was entertained with dancing and music and was offered sacrifice and prayer. In the afternoon her temple was open for meditation. In the evening the goddess was disrobed and the temple closed. Her annual festival began in late October with Isis' mourning Osirus/Serapis. The fourth day commemorated her joy at finding her consort. Initiation rites were similar to those at Eleusis. Priests kept strict purity rules, bathing repeatedly, shaving their entire bodies every three days, and abstaining from certain foods.

Ephesus. The Ephesian Artemis was a many-breasted fertility goddess. Her temple, the Artemision, was one of the Seven Wonders of the World. Five times larger than Athens' Parthenon, it measured 361 feet by 180.5 feet and utilized 127 pillars 60 feet tall. The largest all-marble structure in the Hellenistic world, it was once staffed by a thousand female servants. Its horseshoe-shaped altar measured 105 feet by 72 feet. Nearby was a sacred woods with rare trees and perhaps a deer park. (Artemis is often depicted with stags.) In the first century the shrine suffered some neglect. Staff had to be reduced and repairs put off.[13] At such a time, Paul's verbal assault on the gods would truly smart (Acts 19:26–27).

At the Artemisia, her yearly festival, armed youths escorted Artemis' statue from her temple to the theater. Enthroned before 24,500 spectators, the goddess "watched" music, drama, acrobats or dancers, and athletics.

Magic played a part in Ephesian religious life. The "Ephesian scripts," strange inscriptions on the crown, girdle, and feet of Artemis' cult statue, reputedly held great powers. Acts 19:19 mentions Ephesian magical texts valued at 50,000 drachmas.

Laodicea. Zeus was the city's chief deity. The temple of Men Carus, a Phrygian deity, lay between Laodicea and Caura. A school of medicine and healing sanctuary were connected with that shrine.

Lystra. Inscriptions support worship of Zeus and Hermes in Lystra's vicinity. Zeus headed the Greek Pantheon, and Hermes was god of speech, as well as having other responsibilities. Teuates, the chief Celtic deity, perhaps stands behind Hermes; he is often equated with Mercury in the West.[14]

Miletus. Apollo, the primary deity, was worshiped in the Delphinion overlooking the harbor. That temple bore the name of the god's most famous oracle, that at Delphi, and highlighted Apollo's role as god of prophecy. A temple to Athena lay south of the theater. The city also boasted shrines to Asclepius and to the imperial cult. A mosaic floor featured Orpheus with his lyre and Eros, perhaps representing Dionysus, hunting animals. The Orphic mystery sought to free the immortal soul from bodily taint.[15] This was

---

13. MacMullen, *Paganism*, 107.

14. Ibid., 5.

15. In the underlying myth, Zeus had formed humankind from the ashes of the Titans who had eaten Dionysus. Humans thus had two natures—a Titanic mortality and a Dionysian immortality.

achieved either through three periods of reincarnation or, better yet, through proper rites in this life and the next. The rites included consumption of raw flesh, to free the Dionysus within, and covering the body with mud and pitch. Orphics were buried with gold tablets exhorting them not to drink from the "well of forgetting" but from the "well of remembering," so that they might live as heroes and gods Orphism was ascetic, stressing the overcoming of bodily passion.

Paphos. The temple of Aphrodite at Paphos was the major shrine on Cyprus. Titus consulted the oracle there en route to Jerusalem (Tacitus, *Hist* 2.4).

Pergamum. Athena Polins, patron of Pergamum, had her temple above the theater. The healing god, Asclepius, was perhaps the primary deity. His Asclepion was a major shrine, enlarged in Augustus' time, and his image appears on city coins. The great altar to Zeus (perhaps the "Satan's throne" of Rev. 2:13) was the largest altar in the Greco-Roman world. Its pediment measured 119 feet by 112 feet at its base. Stairs rose in front of, then between, two side wings. The top step was thirty feet across. Other Greek gods honored with temples include Aphrodite, Demeter, Hera (Zeus' consort), the Magna Mater (the Great Mother, a fertility goddess), and Nike (goddess of victory). Altars to Asclepius, Helios (the sun god), Heracles, Hermes, and Zeus stood within Demeter's sanctuary as testimony to the inclusiveness of paganism.

Pergamum was the first city in Asia Minor to erect a temple to the Roman ruler cult (to Augustus in 29 B.C.). This temple appeared on the city's coins.

The city had cultic hall for Dionysus' worship near the theater. The "oriental" deities Isis and Serapis also were worshiped. Serapis' shrine held a statue of seated Serapis thirty-five feet tall.

Philadelphia. Dionysus was worshiped in this city set amidst vast vineyards.

Philippi. The Capitoline Triad of Jupiter (Zeus), Juno (Hera), and Minerva (Athena) are found in inscriptions from Philippi as would be expected in a Roman colony.[16] Dionysian and Cybelene mysteries were practiced. The temple to Bacchus (Dionysus) included inscriptions to Liber Pater (Dionysus), Liber (Roman god of wine and fertility), Libera (Liber's consort identified with the Greek Kore, or Persephone), and Hercules. Acts 16:16–18 notes that in Philippi Paul exorcised a pneuma Pythona, or spirit of divination connected with the god Apollo and his sanctuary at Delphi. Greek inscriptions (first-century Philippians preferred Latin) point to the

---

16. Other deities mentioned include the Italian deity Vertumnus, Souregethes Myndrytus, and Etepaucus. (See MacMullen, *Paganism*, 1).

popularity of Egyptian mysteries among the Greek population. No Philippian inscription mentions the more "oriental" deities, Mithra, Sabazius, or Jupiter Doichenus.[17]

Sardis. The temple to Artemis (or perhaps Cybele) was the fourth-largest Ionic temple known.

Smyrna. Cybele, the native fertility goddess, was Smyrna's patron. Nemesis was also quite popular, and Zeus had a temple as well. The mysteries were well established. Smyrna was the first city in Asia Minor to build a temple to Roma (195 B.C.). In A.D. 23, Smyrna competed with ten Asian cities and won the honor of building a temple to the genius of Tiberius, to his mother, Livia, and to the Roman Senate—an important step toward emperor worship in Roman Asia.

Thessalonica. At least as early as the second and third centuries A.D., Cabiros (an Asian fertility god) was a primary civic deity. Zeus "the highest," Aphrodite, Apollo, the Dioskouri, Herakles, and Nemesis were also worshiped. City coins from the last third of the first century B.C. designated the emperor Augustus as "god," and he was served by priests as "son of god," that is, the apotheosized Julius Casear. The Serapis cult was popular in the city.

Thyatira. Artemis was worshiped as in most of Asia. Athena appears supervising metal workers on city coins. On others, Apollo Tyrimnaeos appears on horseback, bearing a battle axe. On still others, Helios appears.

THE UNITY OF PAGANISM

Having acknowledged something of the variety of paganism, something must be said, even if cautiously, about Greco-Roman paganism as a unity confronting Judaism and Christianity. The mass of pagans were polytheists. Business, government, home life, theater, athletics, all were under the care of various gods, who in turn were honored in all these settings. Pagan deities were seen to promote worship of many gods: The gods appeared together in pantheons and artwork; Demeter shared her Pergamum temple precinct with others' altars. For pagans it was not enough to worship a god, as Jews and Christians did. The mass of pagans viewed monotheists as little better than atheists.

Paganism was syncretistic, fusing different beliefs and practices. Throughout the Mediterranean, local gods were identified with similar Greek or Latin deities or prominent Eastern deities such as Cybele or Isis. In an extreme form, the many gods were viewed as various aspects of or names for the one god. Even a philosophically minded pagan "monotheist," however, thought no ill of honoring the god under any of his or her

---

17. Ibid., 141, n. 2.

varied names and rites. Paganism was basically tolerant; Judaism and Christianity, basically exclusive.

FOR FURTHER READING

Aune, D. E. "Greco-Roman Religion." *Dictionary of Paul and His Letters.* Downers Grove, Ill.: InterVarsity, 1993.

Bruce, F. F. *New Testament History.* Garden City, N.Y.: Doubleday-Galilee, 1980.

Jeremias, Joachim. *Jerusalem in the Time of Jesus: An Investigation into Economic and Social Conditions During the New Testament Period.* Philadelphia: Fortress, 1975.

Koester, Helmut. *History, Culture, and Religion of the Hellenistic Age.* Philadelphia: Fortress, 1982.

MacMullen, Ramsay. *Paganism in the Roman Empire.* New Haven: Yale University Press, 1981.

Meeks, Wayne A. *The First Urban Christians: The Social World of the Apostle Paul.* New Haven: Yale University Press, 1983.

Safrai, S. and M. Stern. *The Jewish People in the First Century: Historical Geography, Political History, Social, Cultural and Religious Life and Institutions.* Vol. 2. Philadelphia: Fortress, 1976.

Sandmel, Samuel. *Judaism and Christian Beginnings.* New York: Oxford University Press, 1978.

Stephens, William H. *The New Testament World in Pictures.* Nashville: Broadman, 1987.

XXV

POLITICAL BACKGROUND OF THE NEW TESTAMENT

JOHN B. POLHILL

The one constant factor in the political setting of the New Testament writings is the presence of Rome. It is there from first to last. Jesus was born in the time of Augustus. The scarlet harlot of Revelation, seated on her seven hills, was surely imperial Rome. But Rome is not the whole story. A key to Rome's own political success was its tolerance of a great deal of local self-government throughout its vast empire. The political backdrop of the NT is thus a whole amalgam of political situations—self-governing Hellenistic cities, client kingdoms, the Jewish theocracy. The latter occupies a major portion of the NT setting, and it is necessary to consider it in some detail. The following treatment is thus divided into two main parts, focusing first on the overall political power which lay in the hands of Rome and then considering the special case of the Jews under the Romans.

THE ROMAN EMPIRE

THE EMPEROR

The NT is set within the period of Roman history which is generally denoted the early principate, the days of the first emperors. Before Augustus, Rome had been ruled through a republican form of government with a senate as its main governing body. The senate had proved increasingly ineffective in maintaining the burgeoning overseas conquests of Rome, and with Octavian's defeat of Antony at the battle of Actium (31 B.C.) the fate of the old republican government was sealed.

Octavian had sixty legions under his command, and the senate confirmed him as *princeps*, "first" in command. They delegated to him all the powers of the former main officials of Rome—the power of the proconsuls to command the military, and the power of the tribunes to convene the popular assembly and the senate itself. In subsequent years his powers were increased. He became the *pontifex maximus*, the head priest of the state religion. He was given powers to make war and peace and to negotiate treaties. He appointed all the officials for the provinces in which troops were located. In short, he had the powers of a king. No longer Octavian, he was "Augustus," meaning "the revered one."

The senate was not disbanded, but now served primarily as an advisory council to the emperor. Though it continued to have many administrative responsibilities, the real power lay with the *princeps*. The one significant power that still lay with the senate was the confirmation of new emperors, although even this was usually determined by pervious emperors in their wills or, in a later period, by the choice of the military.

The NT is surprisingly restrained in its reference to the Roman emperors. Luke mentions Augustus (31 B.C.–A.D. 14) being emperor at the time of Jesus birth (2:1) and Tiberius (A.D. 14–37) at the beginning of His public ministry (3:1). Claudius (A.D. 41–54) is mentioned for expelling Jews from Rome (Acts 18:2). These are the only references to emperors by name, and all of these are found in Luke's writings, perhaps because of all the NT writers he had the most concern for setting Christian history within the framework of world history. There are other less direct references to the emperors, however. The emperor whom the Jews declared to be their "only king" at Jesus' trial was Tiberius (John 19:15), and the emperor to whom Paul appealed was Nero (Acts 25:10).[1]

---

1. For a concise history of the Roman emperors during the NT period, see *OCD*, ed. M. Cary, et al. (Oxford: Clarendon Press, 1949), 774–76.

The most significant impact of the Roman emperors on the early Christians was entirely negative. It was the imperial cult of emperor worship. Based on the old oriental concept of the divine origin of kings, this first emerged in Rome in 42 B.C., when the senate voted to include Julius Caesar among the gods of the state. This took place *after* the death of Caesar. The same was true of Augustus and Claudius. After their deaths, the senate declared them gods and erected shrines to them. The primary motive for this seems not be have been religious but to provide unity for the empire, an expression of loyalty and allegiance from the diverse throngs of the far-flung empire. Imperial shrines were set up in major cities of the empire, and subjects were expected to pay their homage.

During their reigns, neither Augustus nor Tiberius allowed himself to be worshiped, but Tiberius' successor Gaius ("Caligula," A.D. 37–41) entertained divine aspirations and had images set up of himself throughout the empire. When he ordered one to be placed in the temple of Jerusalem, a major crisis was averted only through the wise delaying tactics of the Tribune Petronius and the providential death of the emperor. Paul's vivid picture of the "man of lawlessness" taking his set in the temple of God (2 Thess. 2:3) may have evoked for his readers recollections of this recent event.

The first emperor to enforce the cult throughout the empire was Domitian (A.D. 81–96). In his later years, he insisted on being addressed as *dominus et deus* ("Lord and god") and considered refusal to bow before his image as treason. For pagan polytheists this presented no real problem, but for Jews and Christians such worship of a mortal was intolerable. Christians in particular were persecuted for their refusal to participate in the cult. The beginnings of this persecution are already evident in the NT, such as the constant exhortations in 1 Peter to endure persecution (3:12–17). The reference to "Satan's throne" in the letter to the church at Pergamum is likely a reference to the prominent shrine to the emperor which was located there (Rev. 2:13).

PROVINCES

One of the most pervasive evidences of the Roman imperial administration in the NT is the use of official provincial designations. They are found in every part of the NT—from the Judaea of the Gospels to the Asian setting of the seven churches addressed in Revelation. Provinces were the main administrative units for Rome's overseas possessions. They were of two types: senatorial and imperial.

Senatorial provinces had a basically civil government, ruled by a governor of senatorial rank, appointed by the Roman senate and with a term generally limited to one year. These were mostly settled territories which the Romans had acquired during the republican period and where no real threat to the peace existed; hence no Roman legions were stationed in these provinces. In the NT period, senatorial provinces included Sicily, Sardinia, Spain, Pamphylia, Africa, Macedonia, Asia, Bithynia, Achaea, Crete, and Cyprus.

Imperial provinces were those whose governors were appointed by the emperor. They were usually a non-senatorial, equestrian rank, and commanded the legions which were stationed in the province. It is the presence of Roman legions which most characterized the imperial provinces. These were areas which either formed the borders of the empire or where there was reason to fear insurrection. Syria, Gaul, Galatia, and Britain are examples of imperial provinces. From the time of Augustus, it was the policy of emperor to stabilize the empire and engage in no further expansion. Their organization of these military provinces was a key ingredient in that policy.[2]

Not all territory within the Roman sphere was organized into provinces. Italy was not a province. All Italy from just north of Florence to the "boot" of Italy was under the direct jurisdiction of the city of Rome, and its inhabitants were considered its citizens. Overseas there were many small client kingdoms not directly administered by Rome but still very much subject to it. Such was the case with Palestine.

Herod the Great ruled from 40 B.C. to 4 B.C. over all of Palestine—Judaea, Samaria, Galilee, Peraea, Idumea. He was an independent ruler, appointing his own officials, establishing his own laws, determining his own policies. Still, he was very much a Roman subject, a "client king." He was made king in the first place by vote of the Roman senate, and it was likewise only through formal Roman ratification that his last will and testament took effect which divided his territory among three of his sons. To Archelaus went Judaea, Idumea, and Samaria. To Philip went the area north of Galilee, consisting primarily of the Hellenistic cities known as the Decapolis. To Antipas went Galilee and Peraea. Archelaus proved ineffective, and after ten years was removed by the Romans (A.D. 6). Judaea, Samaria, and Idumea were placed under the direct administration of Roman procurators, among whom were Pilate, Felix, and Festus. Some fourteen of these procurators served between A.D. 6 and A.D. 66, when war broke out between the Jews and Rome. Antipas fared somewhat better than Archelaus. He ruled over Galilee for some forty-one years, making Tiberias his capital city, maintaining his own army. Still, he was very much a client king. In the end, the Romans deposed him also (A.D. 37). He is, of

---

2. See also my article on "Roman Provinces" in *HBH*.

course, the "Herod" in the Gospel narratives of Jesus' ministry. Philip is the only one of the three tetrarchs to die a natural death (A.D. 34).

In the meantime, another client Jewish king was in the making. On his death, Philip's territory was granted to Agrippa, a grandson of Herod the Great. Agrippa had grown up in Rome, and it was his boyhood friends who saw to the bequest. In A.D. 37, after deposing Antipas, the Romans added Galilee and Peraea to Agrippa's realm. Finally, in A.D. 41 when Claudius, a longtime friend of Agrippa, became emperor, he added Judaea to Agrippa's territory. Thus, from 41 to his death in 44, Agrippa I ruled over the same territory his grandfather had held. He is the "Herod" of Acts 12, and his untimely death is narrated vividly there.

Agrippa was a pro-Roman client king, as was his son, Agrippa II. The latter never held significant territory, only small claims like Abilene, Trachonitis, and Carsarea Philippi. Perhaps his most significant grant from the Romans was the right to appoint the Jewish high priest. He is the Agrippa before whom Paul appeared (Acts 25—26).

As far as political reality was concerned, the real power always remained in Rome's hands. It was quite openly so, when after the death of Agrippa I all of Palestine, now including Galilee, was placed in the hands of Roman governors. Still, the Herods are significant. Even though strongly pro-Roman puppet kings, they formed part of the political backdrop for the Gospels and Acts. It is not by chance that Jesus' parables often had a king as their primary subject.[3]

COLONIES AND FREE CITIES

There were also political entities within the various provinces which were not subject to direct Roman administration. These were the colonies and so-called "free cities." Colonies were self-governing settlements of Roman citizens in the overseas provinces which were organized in the Roman fashion and followed Roman law but were subject neither to the jurisdiction of the provincial governor nor to the provincial taxes. Utilizing lands which Rome had acquired militarily, the colonies were often used to provide land for military veterans. This seems to have been the case with Philippi. Often colonies were located in strategic areas where troops might be needed.

Two cities which Paul visited on his first missionary journey were located in such a border area and both had colony status—Lystra and Antioch in Pisidia. Corinth was also a Roman colony, having been destroyed in 146 B.C. and rebuilt as a colony by Julius Caesar in 44 B.C. It

---

3. For an excellent treatment of the Herodians, see Werner Forster, *From the Exile to Christ* (Philadelphia: Fortress, 1964), 82–96.

was unusual in that many in its population were local inhabitants who were granted Roman citizenship at the time of the colony's organization. The more common pattern was to bring in a nucleus of citizen military veterans or of citizen proletariat from Italy in need of living space.

Another Roman colony where Paul established work was Troas. Caesarea, which was the seat of the Judaean governor in Jesus' and Paul's day, was made a colony after the Jewish defeat in A.D. 70. Jerusalem itself was made a colony after the second Jewish War (A.D. 135), was given a Roman name Aelia Capitolina, and Jews were banned from entering it.

The scene of Paul's imprisonment in Philippi (Acts 16:19–40) vividly illustrates a typical Roman colony. The magistrates who arrested Paul and Silas were the two typical judicial heads of a colony (the *duoviri iuri dicundo*). The rods with which they were beaten were the fasces of the Roman police force (the *lictors*). Perhaps the most instructive portion in the whole incident was Paul's insistence that the magistrates come *in person* and deliver him from jail (v. 37). He was indeed right that it was against Roman law for citizens to be beaten without a formal sentence, and as a colony Philippi was bound to Roman law. Colonies were far from independent of Rome. They owed their privileged status to Rome, and Rome had equal power to remove it. The illegal treatment of Paul and Silas could have jeopardized that status.[4]

Somewhat below the standing of colonies was that of the free cities. Still, these enjoyed considerable privileges. Based on the old Hellenistic ideal of an independent city-state, these were Greek cities which the Romans formally recognized as "free" and allowed to have a considerable degree of self-government. In theory they were allowed to have and to enforce their own laws and to elect their own magistrates. They were exempt from provincial taxes and permitted to levy their own. Imperial troops were not to be billeted in the city, and the governor had no formal jurisdiction over it. The theory behind this was the Roman policy of allowing as much local government as possible so long as it promoted harmony and presented no threat to the interests of the empire.[5]

Government of free cities was consequently not as uniform as that in the colonies, which followed the organization of Rome itself. Each of the free cities enjoyed its own system of law and civic administration. Many free cities are mentioned in the NT. Among the most prominent are Antioch in Syria, Thessalonica, and Athens. Thessalonica is a good example of

---

4. A. N. Sherwin-White, *Roman Society and Roman Law in the NT* (Oxford: Clarendon, 1963), 71–6.

5. For a thorough treatment of the Greek cities during the Roman period, see A. H. M. Jones, *The Greek City from Alexander to Justinian* (Oxford: Clarendon, 1940).

the administrative diversity in these cities. Luke refers to the magistrates there as "politarchs" (Acts 17:6). This is a unique term not documented for any other locale as a designation for public officials, but it has been found on many inscriptions in Macedonia and is evidently the precise designation used in Thessalonica for its chief magistrates.

Major cities in the Roman provinces not granted "free" status still enjoyed considerable local autonomy. This was the case with Ephesus. Although not a free city in Paul's day, it enjoyed considerable prestige. Its temple was not only the most prominent shine but also the largest bank in all of Asia. It was the seat of the proconsul of the province. It also had considerable self-government, as is evident from Luke's account in Acts 19 of Paul's encounter with the silversmiths of the city.[6]

Luke refers to the crowd in the theater both as the *dēmos* (v. 30) and the *ekklēsia* (v. 32), which are technical terms for the popular assembly of a Greek city. The town clerk (v. 35) quiets the crowd by accusing them of unlawful assembly and reminds them of their courts and proconsuls who settle such things (v. 38).

A typical Greek city government includes several components: the popular assembly, the council, the presiding officer of the council (the town clerk), and the proconsul. Since Ephesus was not a free city, the administration of the city was largely in his hands. If he were a typical Roman governor, he probably preferred the council handle most matters, and the town clerk be the main liaison between him and the council.

During imperial times, the popular assembly had lost its power. It was mainly convened to make acclamations and bestow honors. The real power was in the hands of the council and its officials, so long as the Roman procurator was content with their conduct of affairs. The town clerk was rightly concerned that the unlawful assembly might provoke the procurator to curtail the city's self-governing rights.

ROMAN CITIZENSHIP

In ancient times, Rome maintained that one could be a citizen of only one city. By the first century, this had changed and dual citizenship was recognized. One could, like Paul, be a citizen of a great city like Tarsus and a Roman citizen at the same time. This became all the more essential in consideration of the unity of the empire. The granting of citizenship to large numbers of people throughout the empire ensured their loyalty, particularly when this was coupled with the special privileges citizenship provided. A Roman citizen was subject to Roman law and thus was protected from such things as being beaten without a trial, from cruel pun-

---

6. See further John B. Polhill, *Acts*, NAC (Nashville: Broadman, 1992), 408–414.

ishments like crucifixion, and from unlawful imprisonment, rights which did not belong to an ordinary provincial *(peregrinus)*. Citizens had the right of appeal. Only a Roman citizen could legally marry another Roman citizen. Citizens were exempted from certain taxes. Beyond this, there was the considerable factor of the honor and deference such a status afforded.

There were several ways one could obtain citizenship. The most common means was by birth to two citizens. In the first century, army veterans were regularly given citizenship upon their discharge. The emperor could confer citizenship, either on individuals or on whole communities, as in the establishment of a new colony. The Tribune Lysias may have received his citizenship by imperial conferral (Acts 22:28). The emperor Claudius is known to have granted citizenship rather promiscuously, and Lysias' full name would indicate that Claudius was the source of his (Acts 23:26). Lysias' large sum of investment would not have been a direct payment but the necessary bribes for access to the proper circles. Paul, conversely, obtained his citizen status by birth to Roman citizens (22:28). How his family secured the status is another question. It may be they secured it through one of the most common means of all. Roman law provided that when a Roman citizen freed a slave the slave became a Roman citizen. Paul's ancestors may have been freedmen from among the thousands of Jews whom Pompey took as slaves in 63 B.C.

The question has often been raised as to how one proved citizenship. Military veterans were given small bronze tablets when granted citizenship. Others had their citizenship recorded on small wooden diptychs. These, however, were probably deposited in a safe place and not carried on one's person. Local records of citizenship were scrupulously maintained, and this probably sufficed in an era which was not too transient.

One telling mark of a citizen was one's name. Roman citizens had three names—a *praenomen*, a *nomen*, and *cognomen*, as in Gaius Julius Caesar. The *praenomen* was like our "first name," but was extremely limited, there being only about fifteen of them. The *nomen* was one's tribal name *(gens)* and linked one to family or to the patron through whom citizenship was obtained (as in the case of Lysias' "Claudius"). The most commonly used name was the *cognomen*. Pilate, Lysias, Felix, and probably Paul, are *cognomens*. The NT never gives a full Roman name. Often only one is given (Gallio) or the last two (Sergius Paulus). We know from other sources the full names of both of these: Lucius Junius Gallio, Lucius Sergius Paulus. Non-citizens were forbidden to bear a full Roman name, so one could readily ascertain citizenship status through the name. As in the case of fake citizenship claims, the only insurance against one's using a false name seems to have been the threat of heavy legal penalties.[7]

ROMAN LAW

In republican Rome, laws could only be passed by the citizens of the city in legal assembly. The senate possessed no legislative powers. But resolutions made by the senate, edicts of magistrates, and legal interpretations by jurists formed a considerable body of precedents .

By the time of Augustus, a considerable legal system know as the *ordo* had developed. It covered offenses against persons, society, and the government and applied to all citizens. Offenses not covered by the *ordo* and *all offenses of non-citizens* were designated as cases outside the *ordo (extra ordinem)* and were left to the local magistrate to judge on his own opinion *(cognitio)*. Thus, in the provinces Roman citizens were subject to the *ordo*. All others were subject to the governor's personal judgment, and it was up to his discretion whether to follow local law, to follow the regular Roman *ordo*, or to delegate the judgment to others. In most situations governors would leave matters to local law and local jurisdiction. The exceptions would be crimes involving Roman citizens, who came under the *ordo* and could not be tried by local courts, and crimes which posed a threat to Rome itself.[8]

We have several instances in the NT of trials before Roman governors. The most notable is the trial of Jesus. The main question surrounding it is whether the Jewish Sanhedrin lacked the authority to condemn a person to death, as John 18:31 would indicate. There is no question but that the ultimate judicial authority in an imperial province like Judaea belonged to the governor, who as the emperor's representative was delegated the emperor's own virtually absolute powers. On the other hand, governors usually preferred to delegate responsibility as much as possible to local courts and local laws. The one power they seemed never to delegate was the power over life and death *(ius gladii)*. This seems amply borne out in the trial of Jesus. The Jewish authorities could formulate charges against Him, but only the Roman procurator could pronounce the death sentence.

Chapters 24—26 of Acts vividly illustrate many aspects of Roman trials. Paul was a Roman citizen and so could only be tried by a Roman court. This is why Festus made it plain to Paul that if he were transferred to Jerusalem for trial it would still be before himself as judge (25:9). Roman

---

7. On Roman citizenship, see further A. N. Sherwin-White, *The Roman Citizenship*, 2d edition (Oxford: Clarendon, 1963).

8. Sherwin-White, *Roman Society and Roman Law*, 14–23.

law required that formal accusations be made, as Tertullus did against Paul (24:5–8). On the other hand, Paul made a telling point when he pointed out his actual accusers were not even present in the courtroom (24:19). Roman law required that accusers bring their charges before the defendant face-to-face (25:16). Of course, the most interesting point of law was Paul's appeal to Caesar. This right of appeal *(provocatio)* belonged to every Roman citizen and went back to ancient days when a citizen was guaranteed the right of trial by a jury of fellow citizens. In imperial times the emperor himself replaced the jury as this court of appeal. In actual fact, emperors probably did not hear all cases in person but delegated much of this responsibility.[9]

In Roman law, punishments for Roman citizens usually consisted of fines for minor crimes or exile for more serious ones, usually with confiscation of one's property. John seems to have suffered such a sentence of exile for his Christian faith (Rev. 1:9). The death penalty was rarely given to citizens except when found guilty of treason. The Jews who sought Paul's death thus tried to convince the Roman officials that Paul was guilty on that charge (Acts 24:5). The customary manner of execution for citizens was decapitation, though most opted to commit suicide instead. For non-citizens, there were more cruel methods, such as burning, being thrown to beasts, or crucifixion.

THE ROMAN ARMY

Imperial provinces like Judaea, Syria, and Galatia were characterized by the presence of Roman troops. The basic unit of the military was the legion, consisting of approximately six thousand personnel. During the time of Augustus, the number of active legions in the empire varied from eighteen to twenty-five. There were two types of soldiers, the nobility and the career military.

Nobility held the high-ranking posts. Legions were commanded by imperial legates, who were usually the governors of the provinces in which they were stationed. Under these were six tribunes for each legion. The tribunes comprised the personal staff of the legate and often served as his board of consultation *(concilium)* in civil as well as military matters. For a noble who wanted to climb the ladder in the imperial civil service, the usual course of service *(cursus honorum)* was to begin as a military tribune, then serve a minor civil service post, then rise to the position of legate of a legion, and from there to a higher civil service post, such as that of consul.

---

9. C. Hemer, *The Book of Acts in the Setting of Hellenistic History* (Tubingen: Mohr/ Siebeck, 1989), 130–31; Sherwin-White, *Roman Society and Roman Law*, 57–70.

The top rung on the ladder was to serve as a proconsular legate in a senatorial province.

Career soldiers were the backbone of the army. The basic unit was a squad of eight men known as a *contubernium*. These shared a common mess, a common tent, and a common pack animal. Often they were divided into groups of four for such responsibilities as sentry duty for the four watches of the night. It was probably such a squad of four who guarded Peter in his cell (Acts 12:6). Ten *contubernia* comprised the basic fighting unit, a *centuria*, whose officer was known as a centurion. One often meets centurions in the Gospels and Acts, such as Cornelius (Acts 10) and Julius (Acts 27). The centurion of Capernaum (Matt. 8:5) was most likely in Herod Antipas' army. There would have been no Roman troops in Herod's realm, and there is every evidence the Herods followed the Roman pattern in organizing their armies.

Completing the organizational sketch of the Roman army is the cohort. There were ten cohorts to a legion. The remaining members of a legion were the auxiliary personnel—clerics, medics, and the like—and the cavalry, who were separate from the regular cohorts. There were two types of legions. Regular legions in the republican period and early principate were composed solely of Roman citizens with nobility as high-ranking officers and plebians as regular troops. In the provinces there were auxiliary legions consisting of troops drawn from the native populace and mercenaries. Most of the troops in Palestine were auxiliary. From the time of Claudius it became a regular practice to grant Roman citizenship to auxiliary legionnaires on their discharge from the army. No legions were stationed in Italy. The only forces there were the Praetorian Guard, an elite force consisting of nine cohorts in the time of Augustus.

Rome took good care of its military. A foot soldier received only 225 denarii a year during the time of Augustus, but the fringe benefits were excellent—a grant of 3,000 denarii and often land in a colony upon retirement. The salary of a centurion was considerably better—3,750 denarii a year. This is perhaps reflected in Cornelius' considerable substance. He had a private house and servants (Acts 10:7). A centurion so fortunate as to become the top-ranking centurion of a legion (called *primus pilus*) received a salary of 15,000 denarii and was generally granted equestrian status on discharge, which qualified him for offices available only to the nobility, such as tribune and provincial praefect. Lysias may have risen through the ranks in such a manner.

The military were a powerful political force in the Roman world. The Roman provincial governors were primarily the commanders of the armies. The armies secured their power. In the later NT period, in the aftermath of Nero's catastrophic rule, the armies became the main factor in the choice of new emperors. The military also were a significant factor in the spread of early Christianity. Military personnel generally appear in a favorable light in the NT, especially the centurions. Many were undoubtedly attracted to the new faith, and their mobility likely had much to do with the rapid spread of the gospel throughout the Roman world.[10]

TAXATION

Under the Roman imperial regimen, provincials were subject to a diversity of taxes. Some of these were levied by Rome itself. The most universal was the poll tax on every adult, including women and slaves. Poll taxes were used for financing the affairs of the province. For purposes of collection, regular censuses were made throughout the empire. The one conducted by Quirinius in the time of Augustus (Luke 2:1) provoked considerable resentment from the Jews. Judas the Galilean organized a resistance movement, arguing that the taxes, which had to be paid in Roman coinage that bore Caesar's image, were an affront to the sovereignty of God (Acts 5:37). His group developed into the highly nationalistic Zealot party which continually resisted Rome and played a decisive role in the Jewish War with Rome of A.D. 66–70. It was this zealot opposition to the poll tax with which the Pharisees confronted Jesus (Mark 12:13–17). When they showed Him a denarius, a Roman coin bearing Caesar's image, He pointed out the inconsistency of their question. If they enjoyed the use of Caesar's financial system, using the imperial coinage, how could they object to rendering the Romans their due?

The Romans also levied a land tax which was paid directly into the imperial treasury and administered by the senate. In the provinces, the Roman officials seldom engaged in direct collection of the taxes themselves. The usual procedures were to levy a set amount on a city and leave collection to the local government or to farm out collection rights to the highest bidder. These practices led to considerable abuse and gave tax collectors like Zacchaeus a reputation for dishonesty (Luke 19:1–10). The land and poll taxes were not the whole story. There were numerous other taxes: sales taxes, inheritance taxes, a tax on the manumission of slaves, taxes on animals used in sacrifices, taxes on the transport of goods, harbor fees, and an extensive system of customs duties.

For the provinces, these Romans levies do not give the entire picture. Cities levied their own taxes. These were seldom direct taxes but usually took the form of rents for such things as the stalls in a marketplace, *ad*

---

10. James L. Jones, "The Roman Army," in *The Catacombs and the Colosseum: The Roman Empire as the Setting of Primitive Christianity*, ed. S. Benko and J. J. O'Rourke (Valley Forge, Pa.: Judson Press, 1971), 187–217.

valorem taxes on the sale of goods, and duties for imports and exports into and out of the city. Even these were often insufficient to maintain the public works, and civic officials were called upon to make considerable personal bequests. This led to a system in which local officials were mainly drawn from the wealthy nobility. Their titles were often mainly honorary and their chief role was to serve as patrons of the city. Paul's friends among the "Asiarchs" of Ephesus probably belonged to this class of city patrons (Acts 19:31).

Judaea was particularly inflicted with excessive taxation. The Herodian puppet kings had unlimited rights of taxation and imposed a heavy burden on the people for their extensive building projects, many of which were solely to curry favor with the Romans. Herod the Great, for example, financed building projects in such faraway places as Rhodes, Laodicea, Tyre, Athens, Sparta, and Antioch. Jews also had to pay the annual temple tax of one-half shekel per year, which was the obligation of every male Jew age twenty or older in the empire. It was due in the month of Adar (February–March) and was used to defray the costs of the daily sacrifices. In the usual account of the shekel in the mouth of a fish, Jesus was concerned with the payment of this tax for himself and Peter (Matt. 17:24). After the Roman defeat of the Jews in A.D. 70, the emperor Vespasian continued this levy on the Jews of the empire, no longer to support the Jewish temple, which was in ruins, but now a pagan temple to Jupiter built on its former site.[11]

BENEFITS UNDER ROME

One wonders how the Romans succeeded in unifying such a vast empire and securing the allegiance of its diverse peoples. Of course, there was some unrest, notably among the Jews, but for the most part in the provinces there was an acceptance of the Roman presence, even considerable enthusiasm and competition for its favors. A key ingredient to the Roman success was surely the general peace and order it provided, the famous *pax Romana*. Nowhere is this more evident than in Paul's missionary travels. A century earlier, such journeying would have been impossible because of pervasive activity of bandits on land and piracy on the seas. But the Roman legions had cleared the highlands of their robbers and the seas of the pirates, and Paul could travel in relative peace.[12]

Commerce could flourish as never before. The extensive Roman road system provided relative ease of land travel. All roads literally did lead to Rome. The Romans built an extensive series of roads throughout the

---

11. William White, Jr., "Finances," in *The Catacombs and the Colosseum*, 218–36.
12. Sherwin-White, *Roman Society and Roman Law*, 121.

empire which interconnected with one another and with sea routes, and all eventually led to the center of Rome. Every Roman road had mile markers which indicated the distances to a central marker which stood in the heart of the Roman forum. The first century was a major period of road-building for Rome. The primary purpose of the roads was for the rapid deployment of troops, and Roman legions often provided the labor for their construction. Paul often travelled these roads, such as the Via Egnatia between Philippi and Thessalonica, the Via Augusta between Antioch and Lystra, the Via Appia to Rome (Acts 28:15).[13] Equally important to commerce were the benefits which Rome provided for sea travel. Rome had cleared the Mediterranean of piracy. This was done primarily to protect its own fleets. Rome never had much of a navy, but it did have an extensive system of grain ships which saw to the distribution of grain throughout the empire. The Roman government itself regulated the production and distribution of this basic staple. The ready availability of grain was a key to maintaining stability. Egypt was a major grain-producing area, and Roman grain ships often plied between Alexandria and the Italian ports. The ships which carried Paul to Italy may well have been involved in the Roman grain distribution (cf. Acts 27:38; 28:11).

Another benefit of the Roman presence was the provision of a standard for monetary exchange. In pre-Roman times, commerce must have been utterly chaotic. Each Greek city state had its own coinage, each small kingdom likewise. The Gospels themselves witness to this confusion. All sorts of terms appear. Some are Greek coins—*lepta* (Mark 12:42), *drachmai* (Luke 15:8). Others are Roman—*assaria* (Luke 12:6), *quadrans* (Mark 12:42), *denarius* (Matt. 20:2ff.). The references to the *didrachma* and *stater* of Matt. 17:24–27, though Greek coinage terms, refer to the temple tax which had to be paid in *shekels* of the Tyrian standard. It is likely that Judas' thirty pieces of silver consisted of these Tyrian shekels (Matt. 26:15). Since the temple currency was solely this *skekel* standard, one can readily understand the presence of money-changers in the temple area (John 2:14). By far the most common monetary term in the NT, however, is the *denarius*, the standard Roman silver coin, which was about the size of our dime (Matt. 18:28, 20:2ff., 22:19 pars.; Mark 6:37, 14:5 par.; Luke 10:35; John 6:7, 12:5; Rev. 6:6). This predominance of the Roman coinage in the NT is itself a witness to the extent that Roman coinage was providing a monetary standard throughout the empire.[14]

---

13. *OCD*, s.v. "roads."

14. On Roman coinage, see David R. Sear, *Roman Coins and Their Values* (London: Seaby Publications, 1988), 8–14.

THE JEWS UNDER THE ROMANS

As has been shown, Rome's policy was to allow as much local governance as possible. The Jews were no exception to this rule. In actual fact, the Romans seem to have granted them special rights that were truly exceptional within the empire.

SPECIAL PRIVILEGES

Because of their religious convictions, the Romans granted the Jews a number of special exemptions and privileges. Perhaps the most notable was exemption from participation in the imperial cult. Every resident of the empire was expected to express loyalty to the emperor by participation in the cult. The Romans, however, honored the Jewish objection to rendering homage to any but God. The Jews in return expressed their loyalty in other, non-objectionable ways, such as offering prayers and sacrifices in the temple for the well-being of the Emperor. The Romans likewise honored the Jewish scruples against graven images and banned them from Jerusalem. They even left the Roman standards with their golden eagle outside the walls of the holy city. Caligula, it is true, went against precedent in endeavoring to install his own image in the temple, but the Roman tribune resisted his order, and Caligula's successor Claudius was quick to reaffirm the ban.

Other special privileges allowed Jews to live consistently with their religious law. They were exempted from appearance in court on sabbaths, and when the local dole of food stuffs fell on a sabbath, an alternative day was set aside for the Jews to collect theirs. In many instances the Jews were exempted from military service. When they did serve, they were granted special rights. Jewish soldiers, for instance, were organized into special Jewish cohorts which were not required to march on sabbaths. Jews could substitute their own oaths for the pagan oaths in law courts. And, most important of all, Jews were guaranteed the right to assemble for worship on the sabbath. When Greek cities attempted to deny the Jews this right, the Romans imposed severe penalties on the cities.

The Romans also permitted the Jews to levy the temple tax and to collect it throughout the empire. They provided protection for the caravans of Diaspora Jews who transported the monies to Jerusalem. Anyone caught stealing this money was stripped of all rights of refuge and was sent to Jerusalem for trial by the Jews.

It was Diaspora Jews who benefited the most from the Roman privileges. They were settled in large numbers in every part of the empire. In Egypt, for instance, there were a million Jews in the time of Tiberius out of a total population of seven and a half million. In the same period, there were fifty to sixty thousand Jews in Rome out of a total population of eight hundred thousand. All told, there were some six to seven million Jews in the Diaspora in the early principate. Diaspora Jewish communities were given a virtual "free city" status within the cities in which they resided. In addition to all the privileges outlined above, they were allowed to live in their own communities and to be subject to their own laws. Even Jews who were Roman citizens were allowed to live under Jewish rather than Roman law.

The general practice seems to have been to allow Diaspora communities to live by Jewish law insofar as it did not conflict with Roman law or involve non-Jews. In the latter instance, the matter would have to be considered in the local Gentile courts. Diaspora Jewish communities were organized around synagogues. They had their own financial and administrative organization and had their own judicial system, which could consider suits between Jews, draw up contracts, perform marriages, and even inflict penalties for religious infractions. Paul's reference to receiving on five occasions the thirty-nine stripes is probably indicative of such Diaspora synagogue discipline (2 Cor. 11:24).

Diaspora synagogues really constituted little Jewish communities. They had their own schools and their own archives and libraries. Some even had their shops, baths, hospitals, and cemeteries. The Romans permitted the Jews to own land, and sometimes the holdings were extensive. The Synagogues were civic centers. Community meetings of Jews were held there; Jewish professional associations met there. In some Diaspora cites, where the Jewish community was numerous, the Jews carried considerable political clout. Sometimes they came into serious conflict with the Gentile population. Bloody confrontations arose, for instance, in Caesarea, Alexandria and Antioch, all of which had extensive Jewish communities. Often in such instances the Jews would send formal delegations to Rome to appeal for imperial intercession on their behalf. They often met with success. Josephus mentions many imperial edicts assuring Jewish rights in such varied locales as Sidon, Ephesus, Sardis, Ionia, Alexandria, and Rome itself.

Many Jews became Roman citizens. In Rome itself there were citizen Jews, many no doubt descending from freedmen of the more than four thousand slaves Pompey brought to the city in 63 B.C. Sometimes the entire Jewish community in a city or province was granted citizenship by imperial decree. Such was the case with Alexandria, Syrian Antioch, Tiberias, Lybia and Cyrene. It is also quite likely that many of the aristocracy of Jerusalem were granted citizenship. Some Jews even rose to high rank in Roman official circles. Tiberious Julius Alexander, an Alexandrian Jew, served as procurator of Judaea from A.D. 46–48. There is even evidence that by the later principate there were Jews among the senators of Rome.[15]

THE JEWS IN PALESTINE

The Jews in Palestine in many ways parallel the Diaspora communities as far as their political status is concerned. The privileges which Rome extended to the Jews pertained everywhere; so that what was true of the Diaspora communities was equally true in Palestine. The land of the Gospels was by no means a strictly Jewish territory in the first century. Centuries of foreign domination by Babylonians, Persians, Greeks, and Romans had left a genuine cultural, racial, and political diversity. There were many cities which, though subject to Jewish dominion under the Hasmoneans and Herods, had mainly Gentile populations. After A.D. 44 these were no longer subject to the Jews. Such, for example, were the cities east of the Jordan river designated as the Decapolis. These included Damascus, Gardara, Scythopolis, Pella, and Gerasa. These were first settled as colonies by the Seleucids, had a predominantly Gentile population, and were thoroughly Hellenistic both in architecture and in culture. Herod the Great was a builder of cities. Several of these were established as miliary colonies for settlement of his veterans, who were mainly Gentile mercenaries. Among them were Hesbon east of the Jordan and Gaba on the slopes of Mt. Carmel. The most notable of Herod's colonies was Sebaste, the old city of Samaria first built by Alexander the Great and settled with Macedonians. Herod rebuilt it in grand Hellenistic style and settle six thousand veterans there. There were cities even within the borders of Judaea with large non-Jewish populations, like Antipatris, another of Herod's building projects. Caesarea's population was about equally divided between Jews and Gentiles. It was the residence for the governor of Judaea. In Galilee, Herod Antipas rebuilt Sepphoris in Hellenistic style and constructed a new capital at Tiberias, which he organized on the pattern of a Greek city. In short, the cities of Palestine were something of a mixed bag. Each major city had a large degree of local autonomy. Samaria had more Gentiles than Samaritans. Galilee had a significant Gentile population, and even in Judaea there was a significant non-Jewish population.

The Romans divided the country into toparchies, consisting of a capital city and its surrounding lands and villages. There were eleven toparchies for Judaea, including those organized around Jerusalem, Lydda, Pella, and

---

15. For further treatment of Diaspora Judaism, see Jean Juster, *Les Juifs dans l'Empire Romain: Leur Condition Juridique, Economique, et Sociale*, 2 vols. (New York: Burt Franklin, 1914).

Jericho. In Galilee Sepphoris and Tiberias were head cities of toparchies. The Romans probably followed this arrangement for revenue purposes. Probably also the head cities served as the judicial center where the governor would hear legal matters as he made his rounds of the province.[16]

As we have seen the Romans granted the Jews self-governing rights, particularly in matters of religion. This pertained to Palestine as well as to the Diaspora. Jewish government was a theocratic government. Religious law and civil law were not distinguished. Hence, the main courts were the religious courts. The Roman authorities decided cases involving non-Jews and cases between non-Jews and Jews. Matters involving Jews fell to the jurisdiction of the Jewish courts. During the period of the Herods, the kings usually assumed all civil jurisdiction and restricted the religious courts to religious matters, but under the procurators the Jewish courts had both civil and religious jurisdiction. The main legal body was the Sanhedrin, and there were a number of local Sanhedrins throughout Palestine. The Sanhedrin in Jerusalem was the local Sanhedrin for that city, but it also served as the "Great Sanhedrin" for all Judaea, the supreme court of the land. The local Sanhedrins would refer difficult cases to the Jerusalem Sanhedrin as the high court of the land. The Jerusalem Sanhedrin does not seem to have had jurisdiction beyond Judaea, however, though its prestige and opinion were probably of great influence among Jews everywhere.

The Jerusalem Sanhedrin was not only the supreme judicial authority for Judaea, it also had extensive administrative and governmental responsibilities. For example, all matters involving boundaries in Judaea were delegated to the Sanhedrin. It maintained a police force to keep order in the temple area. It managed the finances for the province. It alone could declare war. It appointed the High Priest. In many ways, the Sanhedrin during the Roman period could be likened to the city council of a Greek city, or even to the Roman senate. It was conservative, wealthy, hereditary, and loyal to the emperor. It consisted of seventy-one members, seventy "elders" and the High Priest as the "ruling elder." The center of its power resided in the Sadducean element on the council, the old high-priestly families and the landed aristocracy. From the time of Queen Alexandra, there had been Pharisees on the Sanhedrin, but they were in the minority. The Pharisees were more religiously than politically oriented, and the Sadducees totally controlled the appointments to the important adminis-

---

16. On the Hellenistic Jewish cities during the Roman period, see E. Schürer, *The History of the Jewish People in the Age of Jesus Christ,* revised English version by Geza Vermes, Fergus Millar and Matthew Black, vol. II (Edinburgh: T. and T. Clark, 1979), 85–183.

trative positions. Among these were the various Temple offices, such as the captain of the Temple guard and the various officers who managed the large Temple treasury.

The High Priest was chosen from these aristocratic Sadducean circles. He was the single most powerful political figure among the Jews. In addition to his religious duties, he was the main Jewish leader with whom the Roman governors related, the primary liaison between the Jews and the Romans. Because of this political role, during the procuratorial period the Roman governors appointed new high priests almost at will. The Herodian kings did likewise. Neither honored the biblical standard that a high priest should have a lifetime appointment. In the one-hundred-year period between Herod the Great's accession and the outbreak of the Jewish War (37 B.C.–A.D. 66), the Herods and the procurators appointed some twenty-seven high priests—an average tenure of less than four years. The High Priest, like the client kings, was a political pawn, always subject to the Roman will.[17]

The High Priest Caiaphas spoke for all the Sadducees when he advised that it was better for one man to die than that the whole nation suffer (John 11:50). This was their political agenda: accommodation to the Roman rule, preservation of the *status quo*, toleration of nothing that might make the Romans nervous. They themselves had prospered under the Romans. They wanted nothing to threaten that. So, it was with their group, the high priestly circles, that Judas made his pact (Matt. 26:14ff. pars.). *They* were the ones who arrested the apostles and sought to put them to death (Acts 5:17, 33). *They* joined in plots to ambush Paul (Acts 23:14f., 25:2ff.). *They* used their influence with the governors to bring capital charges against him (Acts 24:1ff.). It is a consistent picture. They were politically the most powerful people among the Jews. They held the key offices. They controlled the court. They were concerned about the Christian popularity with the people, concerned about the possibility of rebellion and Roman reprisals. Unfortunately, they were out of touch with their people. Unable to check either the growing resentment of their people toward the Romans or the rising tide of the zealot movement, war finally broke out against the Romans in A.D. 66. In 70, Jerusalem fell. The Sadducean policy of accommodation had failed. No longer of any political significance—and that is actually the *only* significance they had ever had—they ceased to be. The tragedy of Judaea did not reach the Diaspora. Diaspora Jews continued to live in their communities throughout the empire, still enjoying the benefits Rome had granted them.

---

17. On the high priestly circle, see J. Jeremias, *Jerusalem in the Time of Jesus*, 3d revised edition (Philadelphia: Fortress, 1969), 175–82.

The political world of the NT was a Roman world. The remarkable unity Rome was able to accomplish in the Mediterranean world provided the matrix for the rapid dispersion of the Christian gospel with its vision of that ultimate unity where there is "neither Jew nor Greek, neither slave nor free, neither male nor female; for you are all one in Christ Jesus" (Gal. 3:28).

FOR FURTHER READING

Benko, Stephen and John J. O'Rourke, eds. *The Catacombs and the Colosseum: The Roman Empire as the Setting of Primitive Christianity.* Valley Forge, PA: Judson Press, 1971.

Forster, Werner. *From the Exile to Christ.* Trans. Gordon E. Harris. Philadelphia: Fortress, 1964.

Hengel, Martin. *Jews, Greeks and Barbarians: Aspects of the Hellenization of Judaism in the Pre-Christian Period.* Trans. John Bowden. Philadelphia: Fortress, 1980.

Jeremias, Joachim. *Jerusalem in the Time of Jesus.* Trans. F. H. and C. H. Cave from 3rd German ed. Philadelphia: Fortress, 1969.

Jones, A.H.M. *The Greek City from Alexander to Justinian.* Oxford: Clarendon Press, 1940.

Juster, Jean. *Les Juifs dans l'Empire Romain: Leur Condition Juridique, Economique, et Sociale.* Burt Franklin Research and Source Works Series, 79. 2 Vols. New York: Burt Franklin, 1914.

MacMullen, Ramsay. *Enemies of the Roman Order.* Cambridge: University Press, 1966.

_____. *Paganism in the Roman Empire.* New Haven: Yale University Press, 1981.

Rostovtzeff, Mikhail. *Social and Economic History of the Roman Empire.* 2d rev. ed. 2 vols. New York: Oxford University Press, 1957.

Schürer, Emil. *The History of the Jewish People in the Age of Jesus Christ.* Revised English version by Geza Vermes, Fergus Millar and Matthew Black. 4 vols. Edinburgh: T. and T. Clark, 1986.

Sherwin-White, A. N. *The Roman Citizenship.* 2d edition. Oxford: Clarendon Press, 1973.

_____. *Roman Society and Roman Law in the NT.* Oxford: Clarendon Press, 1963.

Tcherikover, Victor A. *Hellenistic Civilization and the Jews.* Philadelphia: Jewish Publication Society of America, 1.

XXVI

BIBLICAL THEOLOGY
OF THE NEW TESTAMENT

BRUCE CORLEY

The New Testament, a book of twenty-seven Greek documents written in the first Christian century, is the Word of God revealed through Jesus Christ; it stands alongside the Old Testament as a primary witness to the person and work of the Son of God (Heb. 1:2; Rom. 3:21). The phrase "new testament" or "covenant" echoes the OT promise of a new covenant written in the heart by the indwelling Spirit (Jer. 31:31–34; Joel 2:28–32). The inaugural for this covenant was at Calvary, for Jesus described His death as "the new covenant in my blood, which is poured out for you" (Luke 22:20; Mark 14:24; 1 Cor. 11:25).* From the viewpoint of faith in the crucified Lord, the message of the former era can be called the "old covenant" (2 Cor. 3:6, 14; Heb. 8:13). This distinction has been affirmed from the second century onward in the title New Testament given to the collected writings that declare the message of the new covenant in Jesus Christ.[1]

---

1. Eusebius, *Ecclesiastical History* 4.26.13; 5.16.3.

* Unless otherwise stated, Scripture quotations in this chapter are from the NIV.

Though diverse in many particulars, the NT is bound together by a common faith—a unity of personal trust and reasoned belief. Such unity finds expression in the biblical confession of one hope, one Lord, one faith, one baptism, and one God and Father of all (Eph. 4:5–6). Where similar faith statements occur, we can distinguish the experience of trust in God from the concept of what is believed about God, but these two aspects of faith cannot be separated.[2]

Whereas the subjective element of faith, an act of believing or personal trust, prevails in NT references (474 occurrences of the noun and verb), the objective content of faith, the message believed, is also significant. The faith can be preached as truth (Gal. 1:23; 2:5), heard as a message (Acts 6:7; Rom. 10:17; 1 Thess. 2:13; Heb. 4:2), taught with certainty (Luke 1:4; Col. 2:7; Rom. 16:17), and entrusted as a pattern of sound words to the faithful (2 Tim. 1:14; 1 Thess. 2:4). Here "faith" refers to a body of truth handed down by apostolic eyewitnesses, believed by the church, and promoted as a safeguard against false teaching (cf. 2 Pet. 1:1; 1 Tim. 1:2, 4; 2:7; 3:9; 4:1, 6; Titus 1:1, 4; 3:5). Indeed, the "faith that was once for all entrusted to the saints" (Jude 3) was what the church fought for.

Early Christians like Theophilus felt the need for an "orderly account" of what they had believed in order that they might know the "certainty" of the matters they had been taught (Luke 1:3–4). In another setting the disturbance of a young church by false prophecy would call forth a written corrective from its founding apostle (2 Thess. 2:2). Whether Gospel, historical narrative (Acts), letter, or apocalypse (Revelation), the writings produced in the apostolic circle were documents of the common faith addressed to various situations. The very richness of the biblical and historical data, seen in matters of literary form, origin, aim, and contents of the writings, suggests a thoroughgoing theological enterprise from the beginning, first lived out and reflected upon in the various dimensions of the church's life and then preserved as a sacred literature.[3] Thus, the "unity in the faith" (Eph. 4:13) must not be reduced to a simplistic uniformity, because biblical faith has been revealed in and

---

2. On the phrase "faith of the New Testament," W. T. Conner observed that "we mean by it both the act or attitude of faith and also the content of faith—the act of believing and the fact or truth believed. . . . These two aspects of New Testament faith are vitally and inseparably linked together" (*The Faith of the New Testament* [Nashville: Broadman, 1940], 13). Cf. A. Schlatter, *Der Glaube im Neuen Testament*, 5th ed. (Stuttgart: Calwer, 1963), 348.

3. R. B. Sloan, "Unity in Diversity: A Clue to the Emergence of the New Testament as Sacred Literature," *New Testament Criticism & Interpretation*, ed. D. A. Black and D. S. Dockery (Grand Rapids: Zondervan, 1991), 439–42.

through profound variety. The Lord chose many witnesses—they must all be heard (Acts 13:31). NT theology is an explication of this fundamental premise.[4]

APPROACHING NEW TESTAMENT THEOLOGY

Constructing a theology, however, that treats adequately both the inner unity and the manifold witness of the NT has proved to be a daunting task. Basic questions concerning the nature and purpose of NT theology continue to be debated after more than two centuries of scholarly inquiry; the contemporary period in particular has been preoccupied with the issues of why and how a NT theology should be written.

Even a recent attempt to propose a synthesis of Pauline theology— a rather modest task by comparison, featuring only one biblical author's thought—has been encumbered by a definition of "just what is and is not meant by 'theology.'"[5] Are we to derive a coherent, logical, and necessary system of ideas from Paul, or will it be adequate to analyze his thought world in descriptive fashion and call this "Pauline theology"? When the rest of the NT witnesses are considered alongside Paul, the complexity of the answer increases dramatically. Is each piece of the NT part of a theological tapestry that beckons us to give a holistic account of all the writings, or only of the major witnesses—Jesus, Paul, and John—or should each writing stand alone in order to present its "theology" without distortion (e.g., "the theology of James")?

We can restate the choices as an ambiguous tension in the phrase "theology of the NT": the preposition "of" can mean both a theology *contained in* the NT and a theology *derived from* the NT. The former emphasis assigns NT theology a descriptive, historical aim to analyze the past meaning of the text in its full variety ("what it meant"); while the latter is a constructive, theological aim to appropriate the present meaning of the

---

4. Cf. D. Wenham, "Appendix: Unity and Diversity in the New Testament," in G. E. Ladd, *The Theology of the New Testament*, rev. ed., ed. D. A. Hagner (Grand Rapids: Eerdmans, 1993), 684-719.

5. An observation made to the SBL Pauline Theology Group in 1986 by J. P. Sampley, "From Text to Thought World: The Route to Paul's Ways," *Pauline Theology, Volume I: Thessalonians, Philippians, Galatians, Philemon*, ed. J. M. Bassler (Minneapolis: Fortress, 1991), 4 n. 4; cf. the aftermath in the methodology and synthesis sections of vol. 1 and now *Pauline Theology, Volume II: 1 & 2 Corinthians*, ed. D. M. Hay (Minneapolis: Augsburg Fortress, 1993).

text for contemporary faith ("what it means").[6] Both emphases have their roots in the beginnings of NT theology as a separate discipline of study. A brief review of the historical development of the discipline will clarify the difference between the two emphases and the importance of keeping them in balance.

THE RISE OF THE DISCIPLINE

The first NT theology was published at the beginning of the nineteenth century, a four-volume work by the Altdorf theologian, Georg Lorenz Bauer, titled *Biblical Theology of the NT* (1800–1802).[7] Bauer's work marked the separation of what had been known as "biblical theology" into Old and New Testament disciplines. In Bauer's opinion, the previous generation of research had failed to produce a "pure biblical theology" that answered the decisive question, "What have Jesus and the apostles taught as essential truths of religion valid for all people and times?"[8] He thus used a doctrinal grid of Christology, theology, and anthropology to examine each section of the NT, moving historically from the Synoptic Gospels to Paul's letters. Bauer's attempt to write a "pure biblical theology" was the first serious application of a distinction made by Johann Philipp Gabler, a faculty colleague whose inaugural address, when he assumed his professorship of theology at Altdorf (March 30, 1787), became in many ways "the program for all that was accomplished since then on the subject."[9]

Gabler's address, "An Oration on the Proper Distinction between Biblical and Dogmatic Theology and the Specific Objectives of Each," proved epoch-making because it defined for the first time the modern conception

---

6. The terminology harks back to the now classic essay by K. Stendahl, "Biblical Theology, Contemporary," *IDB* (1962): 1.418–32. For background, see G. Ebeling, "The Meaning of 'Biblical Theology'," *Word and Faith* (London: SCM, 1963), 79–97; and H. Boers, *What Is New Testament Theology? The Rise of Criticism and the Problem of a Theology of the New Testament* (Philadelphia: Fortress, 1979), 9–22; current responses are summarized by B. S. Childs, *Biblical Theology of the Old and New Testaments: Theological Reflection on the Christian Bible* (Minneapolis: Fortress, 1993), 3–26.

7. G. L. Bauer, *Biblische Theologie des Neuen Testaments*, 4 vols. (Leipzig: Weygand, 1800–1802).

8. Ibid., 1.vi. See the descriptions of Bauer's work by W. Baird, *History of New Testament Research, Volume 1: From Deism to Tübingen* (Minneapolis: Augsburg Fortress, 1992), 188–94; and O. Merk, *Biblische Theologie des Neuen Testaments in ihrer Anfangszeit* in MTS 9 (Marburg: Elwert, 1972), 178–89.

9. Boers, *What Is New Testament Theology?*, 25.

of biblical theology as a historical discipline.[10] The task of the biblical theologian, Gabler argued, was first to collect, arrange, and sift the religious ideas of the Bible and only then to mediate them as a basis for dogmatics. He contrasted biblical theology, "of historical origin, conveying what the holy writers felt about divine matters," with dogmatic theology, "of didactic origin, teaching what each theologian philosophises rationally about divine things." The first step was to classify the biblical writings according to OT and NT periods, individual authors, and styles of writing; only then could "a careful and sober comparison of the various parts" be made with the help of "universal notions" to reveal where the separate authors agree and differ. This analysis would produce a "true biblical theology," broad in scope and historically accurate. A final step in Gabler's proposal narrowed his aim even more: Those ideas that are universally true and divine must be separated, as wheat from chaff, from the temporal and merely human. This distilled historical product represented for Gabler a "pure biblical theology": "For only from these methods can those certain and undoubted universal ideas be singled out, those ideas which alone are useful in dogmatic theology."[11]

Gabler's last step rests squarely on the Enlightenment assumption that timeless, universal truths are measured solely by human reason. A "pure" extract produced from the Bible by this criterion featured rationalizing explanations of biblical stories, skepticism toward miracles, and a restriction of inspiration to certain portions of Scripture. More than Gabler or Bauer ever recognized, their method was a philosophical offspring of its time and by the middle of the nineteenth century was judged to be more indebted to rationalism than history. What lasted was the principle embodied in Gabler's first step: a purely historical investigation of the NT.

The earlier "biblical" theologies of seventeenth-century Orthodoxy and Pietism were actually collections of "proof texts" (called *dicta probantia*). They were arranged under OT and NT headings to support doctrines with corresponding statements from Scripture (the earliest known work of this kind is Wolfgang Jacob Christmann, *Teutsche biblische Theologie* [*German Biblical Theology*], 1629). According to this procedure, the use of the Scripture was restricted to the aims and categories of Protestant

---

10. For the original Latin text, see "Oratio de iusto discrimine theologiae biblicae et dogmaticae regundisque recte utriusque finibus," *Kleinere theologische Schriften*, ed. T. A. Gabler and J. G. Gabler, 2 vols. (Ulm: Stettin, 1831), 2.179–98. An English translation is provided by J. Sandys-Wunsch and L. Eldredge, "J. P. Gabler and the Distinction between Bibical and Dogmatic Theology: Translation, Commentary, and Discussion of His Originality," *SJT* 33 (1980): 133–58.

11. Ibid., 137, 139, 141, 143.

dogmatics, and the biblical witnesses were heard without regard to their distinctive context and purpose. The reappearance of medieval scholasticism in Lutheran dogmatics heightened fears that "true biblical theology" espoused by the reformers had been lost. Philipp Jacob Spener, the leading voice of evangelical Pietism, had lamented in 1675 that "the scholastic theology which Luther had thrown out the front door had been introduced again by others through the back door."[12] The call for an openness to the Bible on its own terms signaled a widespread disaffection with dogmatism and prepared the way for Gabler, Bauer, and others to follow. The historical method, "what the Bible meant," was in place to stay.

MAJOR LINES OF DEVELOPMENT

The ascendancy of historical thinking early in the nineteenth century fueled a series of developmental changes in NT theology that carried through the mid-twentieth century. First, the theology of the NT was separated from Old Testament theology, its anterior counterpart, and was organized according to the historical development of concepts in the NT. Based on a proposed chronology and grouping of the writings, a very popular format was to present the "doctrinal concepts" (*Lehrbegriffe*) of each group in order, beginning with Jesus, on to Paul, then to John and Hebrews, and end with the later NT documents. Many published theologies followed this pattern.[13]

Second, where awareness of the gap between the time and circumstances of the NT world and that of the modern world was keenly felt, the discipline shifted in a historicist direction. This type of NT theology showed no concern for the revelatory claims of the biblical texts and refused to treat them as more than information about the religious past. That the aim and scope of NT theology should be reduced in this fashion to a history of early Christianity, unfettered by normative theological interests, was rigorously argued in a seminal essay by William Wrede (1897).[14] Wrede's program was carried out in the researches of the history-of-religions school.

---

12. P. J. Spener, "Pia Desideria," *Pietism* in Christian Classics, ed. G. T. Halbrooks, trans. T. G. Tappert (Nashville: Broadman, 1981), 211.

13. G. F. Hasel, *New Testament Theology: Basic Issues in the Current Debate* (Grand Rapids: Eerdmans, 1978), 28–53.

14. W. Wrede, "The Task and Methods of 'New Testament Theology,'" *The Nature of New Testament Theology: The Contribution of William Wrede and Adolf Schlatter* in SBT 2/25, ed. and trans. R. Morgan (Naperville, Ill.: Allenson, 1973), 68–116.

Third, those who opposed the historicist line of reasoning arose on several fronts. Some, like the conservative Theodor Zahn (1838–1933), inclined more or less toward a biblicist viewpoint: The givenness of biblical revelation demanded that the historical and exegetical data of NT theology were determinative for, if not identical with, contemporary theological convictions. From the other side, Adolf von Harnack (1851–1930) led the attempt of liberalism to maintain only a historical residue of NT theology as the "essence of Christianity." A "domesticated" version of the historical Jesus was made the groundwork for an ethical message[15]—the fatherhood of God and the brotherhood of man. In the wings waited another response that has occupied much of the present century; the primacy of "what it means" reentered with the dialectical theology of Rudolf Bultmann and Karl Barth. The NT was to be interpreted so that, as Barth memorably put it, "a distinction between yesterday and today becomes impossible."[16]

We can trace the separate lines of development through major NT theologies written from four perspectives: (1) purely historical, (2) existential, (3) historical positive, and (4) salvation historical.

The Purely Historical Line. The most influential exponent of the historicist principle was Ferdinand Christian Baur (1792–1860), whose *Lectures on New Testament Theology* were published posthumously in 1864.[17] Baur had pioneered "tendency criticism" (*Tendenzkritik*) in the 1840s, a developmental historical method that read the entire NT in terms of a Pauline-Petrine antithesis. This dialectic, the cornerstone of the Tübingen school formed by Baur's devotees, was the criterion by which NT documents and concepts were dated and grouped; e.g., the Acts of the Apostles "tended" toward synthesis and hence had to be a late, second-century writing.[18] Although Baur described his work as "purely historical science," it leaned

---

15. Stephen Neill observes: "The danger for the liberal lies always in his tendency to domesticate Jesus Christ, to make him out to be less dangerous than he really is, to rob him of his mystery, and to offer solutions of the Gospel problems which are no real solutions" (S. Neill and T. Wright, *The Interpretation of the New Testament 1861–1986*, 2d ed. [Oxford: Oxford University Press, 1988], 146).

16. K. Barth, *The Epistle to the Romans*, trans. E. C. Hoskyns (New York: Oxford University Press, 1933), 7.

17. F. C. Baur, *Vorlesungen über neutestamentliche Theologie*, ed. F. F. Baur (Leipzig: Fues, l864).

18. For evaluation of Baur's method, see H. Harris, *The Tübingen School: A Historical and Theological Investigation of the School of F. C. Baur* (reprint ed.; Grand Rapids: Baker, 1990); R. Morgan, "F. C. Baur's Lectures on New Testament Theology," *ExpTim* 88 (1977): 202–6; and W. Baird, *History of New Testament Research* , 258–78.

heavily on Hegelian idealism; thus, the demise of Hegel's philosophy also undercut Baur's conclusions. This line, however, culminated in the influential textbook by Heinrich Julius Holtzmann (1897; 2d ed., 1911) and continued through the history-of-religions school down to the present day.[19]

The Existential Line. While in agreement with the history-of-religions school, particularly the development of Christology traced in Wilhelm Bousset's *Kyrios Christos* (1913), Rudolf Bultmann moved beyond historical analysis to apply the NT word as an address to modern man. His crowning achievement, *Theology of the New Testament* (1948), "has been the most influential of all modern studies, whether it is seen positively as a stimulus to new insights or negatively as a goad to provoke creative reactions."[20] The NT message (or *kerygma*) for Bultmann was a call to authentic faith, leading the believer "to develop out of his faith an understanding of God, the world, and man in his own concrete situation." Because the "understanding which is inherent in faith itself" is determined by NT proclamation, the theological task, Bultmann argued, is to make clear the relationship between the kerygma and self-understanding.[21]

Of decisive importance for Bultmann's program is the separation of history from theology. He accepted as fact that the Gospels report little reliable information about Jesus; hence, the historical Jesus is a presupposition of NT theology, not a part of it. On this view, theology arose as a response to the apostolic kerygma, principally represented by Paul and John, and focused on the Christ of faith with no interest in what actually happened. There are serious defects at every step. This is bad history, but even worse, theology has been reduced to anthropology. When all is said, the Bultmannian approach offers the Word who became word not flesh and shifts the subject matter of NT theology to the human condition.[22]

---

19. See ABD, s.v. "theology (NT)." Heikki Räisänen has revived the view of Baur and Wrede that NT theology has the aim of historical information about early Christian thought without regard to church, canon, or proclamation (*Beyond New Testament Theology: A Story and a Programme* [Philadelphia: Trinity Press International, 1990], 120–21).

20. I. H. Marshall, *Jesus the Saviour: Studies in New Testament Theology* (Downers Grove, Ill.: InterVarsity, 1990), 24. NT theology following the lead of Bultmann includes writings of G. Bornkamm, H. Conzelmann, E. Käsemann, and E. Fuchs.

21. R. Bultmann, *Theology of the New Testament*, trans. K. Grobel, 2 vols. (New York: Scribner's, 1952, 1955), 2.237–39, 251.

22. See L. Goppelt, *Theology of the New Testament*, trans. J. Alsup, 2 vols. (Grand Rapids: Eerdmans, 1981–82), 1.264–67; and J. R. Donahue, "The Changing Shape of New Testament Theology," *HBT* 11 (1989): 4–6.

The Historical Positive Line. This approach set forth the counter proposal to the purely historical line from Baur to Bultmann: (1) the historicity of the biblical traditions are to be viewed in "positive" fashion, and (2) the foundations of NT theology must be safeguarded through historical apologetic. Standing at the head of this line is the famous Cambridge triumvirate of Joseph Barber Lightfoot (1828–1889), Brooke Foss Westcott (1825–1901), and Fenton John Anthony Hort (1828–1892), although none of them produced a full-fledged theology.[23] A series of textbooks produced for the German scene were forerunners of the widely used theologies of Ethelbert Stauffer (1941), Werner Georg Kümmel (1969), and Joachim Jeremias (1971).[24] These three volumes stand together as a solid front against the Bultmann school in the common assumption that the NT faith has its basis in the historical Jesus, especially in the context of first-century Judaism.

The Salvation Historical Line. A movement closely aligned to the previous one has its roots in the "salvation history" (*Heilsgeschichte*) emphasis of the Erlangen school, led by the distinguished scholars Johann Tobias Beck (1804–1878) and Johann Christian Konrad von Hofmann (1810–1877). Biblical theology seen from this perspective interprets the revelation of the acts of God in saving history that fulfill the divine purpose to redeem humanity through Christ. So history is viewed with the eyes of faith. It is this point that was championed by Adolf Schlatter (1852–1938) and thus ties him closely to the salvation history line. According to Schlatter, the NT "utterly repudiates the thesis that revelation and history cannot be united, and this at the same time destroys the view that historical research is a denial of revelation." The words and events recorded by the NT are based on faith convictions and must be studied from that point of view: "As soon as the historian sets aside or brackets the question of faith, he is making his concern with the New Testament and his presentation of it into a radical and total polemic against it."[25]

---

23. See Neill and Wright, *Interpretation of the New Testament*, 35–64.

24. The theologies of B. Weiss (1868) and P. Feine (1910), which both went through several editions, belong in the group with E. Stauffer, *New Testament Theology*, trans. J. Marsh (London: SCM, 1955); W. G. Kümmel, *The Theology of the New Testament According to Its Major Witnesses: Jesus—Paul—John*, trans. J. E. Steely (Nashville: Abingdon, 1973); and J. Jeremias, *New Testament Theology, Volume 1: The Proclamation of Jesus*, trans. J. Bowden (London: SCM, 1971).

25. A. Schlatter, "The Theology of the New Testament and Dogmatics," *The Nature of New Testament Theology: The Contribution of William Wrede and Adolf Schlatter* in SBT 2/25, ed. and trans. R. Morgan (Naperville, Ill.: Allenson, 1973) 122, 152.

Schlatter's two-volume theology, which appeared in a second edition with the titles *The History of the Christ* (1923) and *The Theology of the Apostles* (1922), has its successors in the more recent works of Oscar Cullmann (1967), George Eldon Ladd (1974), and Leonhard Goppelt (1975–76). The latter's theology is in many ways the most satisfying expositon of the salvation historical line. Goppelt regards the NT as a faith interpretation of God's self-revelation in history; as such, it "wishes to attest to a fulfillment event coming from the God of the Old Testament and having Jesus at its center."[26] Both the historical positive and salvation historical lines, with varying emphases, attempt to expound "what the Bible means" without taking a flight from history.

CONSTRUCTING A NEW TESTAMENT THEOLOGY

We are now ready to ask what we have learned from the history of research that will aid us in putting together the aims and methods for constructing a NT theology. The most satisfactory model is one that maintains a careful balance between "what the Bible meant" and "what it means" and at both levels shows the interplay of unity and variety.

CRITERIA FOR A MODEL

The last two centuries have demonstrated that the step from using historical methods to defining the aims of NT theology in exclusively historical terms set it at odds with many students of the Bible, for whom historical and literary approaches were important only because they served theological aims. Robert Morgan rightly points out "that literary methods can serve historical aims, and historical methods can serve literary aims, or both may serve religious and theological aims."[27] In order to sort out these issues, the following criteria for a constructive model may be suggested:

1. History is the arena of God's activity. Rigid application of "the historical-critical method" drives a wedge between faith and history if historical judgments are made solely on the basis of "analogy"—with previous human experience—and "correlation"—with an unbroken continuum of

---

26. Goppelt, *Theology of the New Testament*, 1.281. Cf. O. Cullmann, *Salvation in History*, trans. S. G. Sowers (New York: Harper & Row, 1967); G. E. Ladd, *A Theology of the New Testament* (Grand Rapids: Eedmans 1974; rev. ed., 1993). Schlatter's volumes have not been translated (*Die Geschichte des Christus* and *Die Theologie der Apostel*, 2d ed. [Stuttgart: Calwer, 1923, 1922]).

27. Morgan with J. Barton, *Biblical Interpretation* in Oxford Bible Series (Oxford: Oxford University Press, 1988), 171.

cause and effect. This by definition rules out the possibility of the supernatural, namely, that God can act in history.[28] The increasing protest against the legacy of historicism is a plea for openness to transcendence and a correction of method. In the words of Wolfhart Pannenberg, "as long as historiography does not begin dogmatically with a narrow concept of reality according to which 'dead men do not rise,' it is not clear why historiography should not in principle be able to speak about Jesus' resurrection" as the best explanation of the appearances and the empty tomb.[29]

2. The OT is a primary witness for NT theology. A focus upon God and history brings the relationship of the two testaments to the forefront of theological discussion. The NT writers began with their experience of Jesus Christ from whom they received a new understanding of the OT, then "on the basis of this transformed Old Testament, the New Testament writers interpreted the theological significance of Jesus Christ to the Christian church by means of the Old."[30] The essential vocabulary and conceptual framework for the New is drawn from the Old, functioning both as an authoritative guide to an enriched understanding of Christ and also as a dutiful servant bearing witness to Him. A primary task of NT theology is to describe the elements of continuity and discontinuity with the Scriptures of Israel which testify to the one God, the father of the Lord Jesus Christ.[31]

3. The story of Jesus Christ the Redeemer sent from God who fulfills the promises of salvation is the authoritative center of the church's witness. Current literary approaches utilize the narrative category of "story" as an index to the biblical worldview whose plot and themes are structured by a revealed story. This insight has been explored in a helpful fashion by N. T. Wright

---

28. See the critique of Ernst Troeltsch's formulation (1898) by Goppelt, *Theology of the New Testament*, 1.260; and cf. Kümmel, *Theology of the New Testament*, 60.

29. W. Pannenberg, *Jesus—God and Man*, trans. L. L. Wilkins and D. A. Priebe (Philadelphia: Westminster, 1968), 109; cf. B. F. Meyer, *The Aims of Jesus* (London: SCM, 1979), 54; and P. Stuhlmacher, *Historical Criticism and Theological Interpretation of Scripture*, trans. R. A. Harrisville (Philadelphia: Fortress, 1977), 89–90.

30. Childs, *Biblical Theology of the Old and New Testaments*, 93.

31. P. Stuhlmacher, *Biblische Theologie des Neuen Testaments*, 2 vols. (Göttingen: Vandenhoeck & Ruprecht, 1992, 1994), 1.8. For the entire topic, see D. L. Baker, *Two Testaments, One Bible: A Study of the Theological Relationship Between the Old & New Testaments*, rev. ed. (Downers Grove, Ill.: InterVarsity, 1991); E. E. Ellis, *The Old Testament in Early Christianity: Canon and Interpretation in the Light of Modern Research* in WUNT 54 (Tübingen: Mohr, 1991); and D. A. Carson and H. G. M. Williamson, eds., *It Is Written: Scripture Citing Scripture, Essays in Honour of Barnabas Lindars* (Cambridge: Cambridge University Press, 1988).

in *The New Testament and the People of God* .[32] He proposes a model of the biblical story encompassing both testaments in a five-act play: (1) creation, (2) fall; (3) Israel; (4) Jesus; (5) the church and the writing of the NT then form the first scene in the fifth act with other scenes to follow. The followers of Jesus, according to Wright, are actors chosen for the coming scenes and, having immersed themselves in the drama of the previous acts, will carry the story to its fitting conclusion. This model takes seriously the salvation history of the OT in the context of Judaism, appeals to the entire canon as witness, and provides an important literary, narrative criterion for establishing the theological norm of the NT.

PART ONE: FOUNDATIONAL CONVICTIONS

We take as a foundation for a constructive model of NT theology a threefold presupposition: (1) God, sending His Son, acted in the history of Israel; (2) the OT Scriptures testify to this saving act; and (3) the story of Jesus Christ and His people is the center of a manifold witness. This foundation integrates a set of faith convictions that everywhere underlie the writings of the NT. Convictions, by this definition, need not be expressed in every point of argument and in a given setting may be shaped by a contextual warrant. Thus, foundational convictions point to a coherent, integrated set of beliefs that may be expressed in concrete, contingent forms of application.[33] Faith and praxis in apostolic Christianity reflect this distinction: "For no one can lay any foundation other than the one already laid, which is Jesus Christ" (1 Cor. 3:11). What we will construe as part 1 of a NT theology now follows in three categories: (1) the gospel of God; (2) the triumph of God; and (3) the people of God.

The Gospel of God. For the first generation of believers, the "gospel of God" (Rom. 1:1) was the spoken message of God's power to save by means of the death and resurrection of Christ. Before any writings of the NT appeared, the gospel was personally experienced in the power of the Holy Spirit, being received by faith in response to preaching (1 Thess. 1:5–6). To believe in more than one gospel was a contradiction in terms (Gal. 1:7); the noun "gospel" (Gk. *euangelion*) occurs seventy-five times in the NT,

---

32. This is the first volume of an ambitious five-volume NT theology: *Christian Origins and the Question of God, Volume 1: The New Testament and the People of God* (Minneapolis: Fortress, 1992), 140–41.

33. Cf. the discussions in Hay, *Pauline Theology, Volume II* , passim; J. C. Beker, *The Triumph of God: The Essence of Paul's Thought*, trans. L. T. Stuckenbruck (Minneapolis: Fortress, 1990), 15–19; R. P. Martin, "New Testament Theology: Impasse and Exit—The Issues," *ExpTim* 91 (1980): 267–69; and G. R. Osborne, "New Testament Theology," *Evangelical Dictionary of Theology*, ed. W. A. Elwell (Grand Rapids: Baker, 1984), 769–73.

never in the plural form and always with reference to the proclaimed word.

With antecedents in the OT announcement of the coming victory of God (Isa. 40:9; 52:7; 61:1–2; Pss. 40:9; 68:11), Jesus saw His kingdom message and mission in terms of the promised one whom God would send (Luke 4:18–21; 7:22; Matt. 11:5). The long-expected herald had ushered in the promised era: "The time is fulfilled, and the kingdom of God is at hand; repent and believe in the gospel" (Mark 1:14–15, NASB). The messianic deliverance accomplished in the death and resurrection of Jesus extends also to His future coming; thus the kingdom of God in both its present and future aspects is inseparably linked to the person of Christ. Jesus embodied the kingdom in His own person (Matt. 12:28; 19:29; Mark 10:29; Luke 17:20–21; 18:29); a remarkable shift happened during the earthly ministry—the kingdom messenger had become the message.[34] Thus, the apostles speak more about the king than they do the kingdom; to enter the kingdom of God one must have a faith relationship to the king, confessing Jesus as Lord (Acts 2:33–36; 17:6–7; Mark 11:3; 12:36; 1 Cor. 16:22).

This gospel had a stable, core content (Gk. *kērygma* , "proclamation" or "message," cf. 1 Cor. 1:21) that was received from the Lord by the apostles and passed on to converts (Acts 1:3; Gal. 1:12; 1 Cor. 15:3). One can even speak of "the gospel" without further qualification because the term was so well established, as Paul does in one-half of his uses of the word (twenty-three times, e.g., "our gospel came to you," 1 Thess. 1:5). The data for the core content derives primarily from two apostolic sources: (1) creedal formulas and summaries found in the letters (Rom. 1:1–6; 3:21–26; 10:9–10; 1 Cor. 11:23–25; 15:3–5; Phil. 2:6–11; Col. 1:15–20; 1 Thess. 1:5–10; 1 Tim. 3:16; Heb. 5:7–10; 1 Pet. 2:22–25), and (2) speeches in the Book of Acts (2:14–39; 3:12–26; 4:8–12; 5:29–32; 7:2–53; 10:34–43; 13:16–41; 14:15–17; 15:7–11; 17:22–31; 22:3–21; 23:1–6; 24:10–21; 26:2–23).

Furthermore, a formal kerygmatic pattern with six constant elements has been isolated in no less than nineteen of the NT writings. It is usually introduced by a statement indicating what follows is the gospel or a word about (1) God who (2) sent or raised (3) Jesus; (4) a faith response (5) to God (6) brings salvation.[35] This tacit narrative framework or "story of Jesus" has been detected in the NT (Matt. 10:40–41; Mark 9:37; Luke 1:68–75; John

---

34. See D. Guthrie, *New Testament Theology* (Downers Grove, Ill.: InterVarsity, 1981), 412-15; and P. Stuhlmacher, *Biblische Theologie des Neuen Testaments* , 1.71–72.

35. E. E. Lemcio, "The Unifying Kerygma of the New Testament (I and II)," *JSNT* 33 (1988): 3–17 and *JSNT* 38 (1990): 3–11.

5:24; Acts 5:30–32; 13:30–32, 37–39, 43; Rom. 10:8–9; 2 Cor. 5:19–20; Gal. 4:4–7; Eph. 2:4–10; Phil. 2:5–11; Col. 2:12–13; 1 Thess. 1:5–10; 1 Tim. 3:15–16; 4:9–10; 2 Tim. 2:9–11; Titus 3:4–8; Heb. 13:20–21; 1 Pet. 1:18–21, 25; 1 John 4:7–10; and Rev. 12:1–11, 17). These texts are strikingly theocentric—the gospel is God's activity through Jesus Christ. While explicit details are often lacking, this foundational story is narrated in allusive fashion, especially in the shared themes of Jesus, Paul, and John.[36]

The Triumph of God. In the earliest NT writings, Jesus is ascribed divine honors, sharing a rank alongside God the Father in blessing the world: grace and peace from God the Father and the Lord Jesus Christ (1 Thess. 1:1; Gal. 1:3). His exalted status presupposes a hinge event that shaped early Christian thought about Jesus—the resurrection.[37] In the sermon at Pentecost, Peter announced that God raised Jesus to life and exalted him to the right hand of power and blessing: "God has made this Jesus, whom you crucified, both Lord and Christ" (Acts 2:32–33, 36). The death and resurrection of Jesus signaled more than a transaction for human sin; it was a cosmic event that opened up the future for the entire created order. The apocalyptic dimensions of God's triumph in Christ point to the ultimate manifestation of life in the age to come: Christ "gave himself for our sins to rescue us from the present evil age, according to the will of our God and Father" (Gal. 1:4). The apocalyptic perspective can be summarized in the following points:

1. Prophecy. The Scriptures of Israel have been fulfilled in Jesus the Messiah, who will reign on the throne of David.

2. Mission. Anointed by the Holy Spirit and attested by signs and wonders, Jesus lived in obedience to the Father's will.

3. Crucifixion. As the Son of God, Jesus died on the cross to free mankind from the bondage of sin.

---

36. For the coherence of the gospel substructure in Jesus, Paul, and John, see Marshall, *Jesus the Saviour,* 36–53; R. B. Hays, "Crucified with Christ: A Synthesis of the Theology of 1 and 2 Thessalonians, Philemon, Philippians, and Galatians," *Pauline Theology, Volume I,* ed. J. M. Bassler, 232–34; Wright, *The New Testament and the People of God,* 407; and B. Witherington, "Christology," *Dictionary of Paul and His Letters,* ed. G. F. Hawthorne and R. P. Martin (Downers Grove, Ill.: InterVarsity, 1993),103–5.

37. "What possessed them to transfer to Jesus of Nazareth titles and activities which belonged to God alone? Nothing but the assurance that God himself had set them a precedent by so highly exalting Jesus" (F. F. Bruce, *Jesus: Lord & Savior* in *The Jesus Library,* ed. M. Green [Downers Grove, Ill.: InterVarsity, 1986], 204, cf. 126).

4. Resurrection. On the third day, Jesus was raised from the dead, having triumphed over death.

5. Ascension. Declaring Him as Lord, God exalted Jesus to the right hand, whence He will come again to judge the world.

6. Invitation. All who call on the name of the Lord will be saved, receiving the gift of the Holy Spirit and life of the age to come.

The OT prophets had announced the "new thing" that God would do in the last days with the revelation of the kingdom of God and the redemption of His people (Isa. 43:18–19; cf. 2:2–4; 65:17; Dan. 10:14; Hos. 3:4–5; Amos 5:18–27). During the NT era, Jewish apocalyptic literature had fully developed this conception of history as a dualism of two ages, this age and the age to come: "The Most High has made not one age but two" (4 Ezra 7:50; 8:1; 1 Enoch 71:15). This present evil age, dominated by sin and the satanic adversary of God (1QM 18:1; 1QS 4:18–29; T. Dan. 5:10–11; T. Mos. 8; Sib. Or. 5:33–34; 2 Enoch 29:4), was destined for a catastrophic end. The messianic deliverer would appear in glory after a time of suffering and tribulation, execute judgment, and usher in the age to come. Often the texts refer to "woes" or "birthpangs" accompanying a temporary messianic kingdom (1 Enoch 91:1–10; 93:12–17; 4 Ezra 7:26–44, 113; 12:32–34; 2 Baruch 29:3—30:1; 40:1–4; 72:2—74:3) to be followed by the resurrection of the dead in the eternal kingdom.[38]

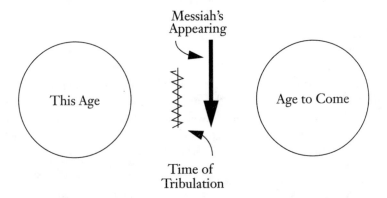

Messiah's
Appearing

This Age

Age to Come

Time of
Tribulation

---

38. For the worldview of Jewish apocalyptic, see D. E. Aune, "Apocalypticism," *Dictionary of Paul and His Letters*, 27–30; Ellis, *The Old Testament in Early Christianity*, 101–5; and Wright, *The New Testament and the People of God*, 280–338.

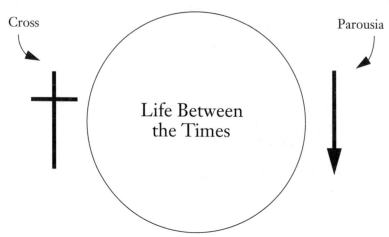

A distinctively new element is found in the message of Jesus; the king-dom age expected as coming was now present. Jesus' authoritative words, no less than His mighty works, were signs that the kingdom had invaded history and that the domain of evil was tottering (Mark 1:22, 27; 3:23–27; Matt. 12:25–29; Luke 11:17–22). Jesus said, "But if I cast out demons by the Spirit of God, then the kingdom of God has come upon you" (Matt. 12:28, NASB). Jesus' miracles and parables manifested the presence of the kingdom and signified Him as its Spirit-empowered agent.[39] The dead already hear the voice of God's Son and live (John 5:25); the judgment of this world has taken place (John 3:18; 12:31); whoever believes in the Son now has eternal life—the life of the age to come (John 3:36).

As participants with Christ in His death, burial, resurrection, and exal-tation (Rom. 6:3–7; Col. 2:12, 30; 3:1–5; Eph. 2:5–6), believers have expe-rienced the "powers of the age to come" (Heb. 6:5, NASB), but they continue to live temporally in this age. Thus, Christian existence is con-stantly subject to the tension between the "already" and the "not yet," between the claims of the new creation in Christ and the threat of evil in this age (Rom. 12:2; 1 Cor. 1:20; 3:18; 2 Cor. 4:4; 5:17; Eph. 1:21; 2:2; Titus 2:12).[40]

---

39. Ladd, *Theology of the New Testament*, 68–78, esp. 68: "The most distinctive fact in Jesus' proclamation of the Kingdom was its present inbreaking in history in his own person and mission."

40. See *ISBE*, s.v. "age." The classic statement of this tension is O. Cullmann, *Christ and Time: The Primitive Christian Conception of Time and History*, 3d rev. ed., trans. F. V. Filson (London: SCM, 1962).

The struggle of the individual believer is but a microcosm of the overlapping of the ages; those on whom "the fulfillment of the ages has come" (1 Cor. 10:11) engage the conflict of old man and new man, of flesh and the Spirit, of death and life. The interim period of existence between the times, called the "last days" or the "last hour" (Acts 2:17; Rom. 13:12; Heb. 1:2; Jas. 5:3; 1 Pet. 1:5; 1 John 2:18), stretches from the first advent of Christ to His parousia. Only at the Lord's coming and the resurrection day will the triumph be made complete (1 Thess. 4:13–18; 1 Cor. 1:8; 15:50–58; Phil. 3:20).

The People of God. The cross and resurrection of Christ is the twofold sign under which His followers live. By His cross, they have died to this world and share in His sufferings, but by His resurrection, they live to serve in power: "For just as the sufferings of Christ flow over into our lives, so also through Christ our comfort overflows" (2 Cor. 1:5; 4:14; 13:4; Gal. 6:14). Because the dawning of the new age did not abolish the hostile forces of this present age, the messianic woes endured by Christ spill over into His body, the church (Col. 1:24), which suffers with Him and for His name's sake (Rom. 8:17–18; Phil. 1:29; 3:10; 1 Pet. 4:12–16).[41] The "god of this age" stands against the church's witness (2 Cor. 4:4), just as the "rulers of this age" (1 Cor 2:6, 8) through human ignorance crucified the Lord of glory. This fallen order is ruled by principalities and powers who have been vanquished by Christ (Col. 2:15; Eph. 1:20–23) but engage in warfare against the people of God (Eph. 2:2; 6:12; Gal. 4:3, 9; Col. 1:16; 2:8; 1 John 2:18; 4:3; 2 Thess. 2:1–11; Rev. 13:1–10). In the midst of this battle, there is necessary suffering—not only passive resistance to the onslaught of the demonic powers but also, as J. C. Beker puts it, "suffering as a result of active Christian engagement with the world,"[42] wherein the church carries out God's redemptive mission.

Not even the "gates of Hades" will be able to stand against the mission of Christ's church (Matt. 16:18; cf. 1 Cor. 15:25). That Jesus deliberately chose twelve apostles emphasizes the continuity of His followers with the congregation of Israel, not simply a new Israel that supersedes the old, but in fact the true Israel, one that is gathered to the Messiah. The choice of the term "assembly" (Gk. *ekklēsia*, 115 occurrences) for the Messiah's people carries in it the secret of the church's mission: This people is gathered to the Messiah by confession and empowered by Him to be scattered in the earth (Acts 1:6–8). "The chief characteristic of the new people of God

---

41. This point is forcefully made by R. B. Sloan, "Images of the Church in Paul," *The People of God: Essays on the Believers' Church,* ed. P. Basden and D. S. Dockery (Nashville: Broadman, 1991), 163–64.

42. Beker, *The Triumph of God,* 29.

gathered together by Jesus is their awareness of the boundlessness of God's grace."[43] The outpouring of the Holy Spirit, a sign of God's work in the last days (Ezek. 36:26–27; 37:14; Zech. 12:10; Jer. 31:34; Joel 2:28–32), filled the church with power to witness. Each believer was gifted for ministry and made a partaker in the fellowship of the Spirit (Acts 2:4; 1 Cor. 10:17; 12:4–11; 14:6; Gal. 5:22; Eph. 2:18; Heb. 2:11). The Holy Spirit brings the presence of Christ among His people (Rom. 8:9; 2 Cor. 3:16) so that the authority of Christ is with the church to the end of the age (Matt. 28:20). Christ's people are characterized by the ethic of love, whereby the "is-ness" of grace is linked to the "ought-ness" of love through the work of the Spirit (Gal. 5:6, 25; 6:2; Jas. 3:17-18; John 13:34-35; 1 John 4:7).

PART TWO: STRUCTURAL WITNESSES

From the side of human response to the theocentric convictions we have surveyed, there are three respective answers: faith in God's gospel, hope in God's triumph, and love in God's people. Paul, for example, was fond of recalling the dynamics of faith, hope, and love to his readers: "remembering without ceasing your work of faith, and labor of love, and patience of hope" (1 Thess. 1:3, KJV; cf. Rom. 5:1–5; 1 Cor. 13:13). Such themes bear witness to foundational convictions that have been shaped by human responses in concrete life situations. To pursue the idea in the architectural metaphor, a distinction must be made between foundation and superstructure. Paul wrote, "By the grace God has given me, I laid a foundation as an expert builder" (1 Cor. 3:10). What follows upon the foundation of Jesus Christ is the rearing of the superstructure—the work of edifying and consolidating, both the individual convert and the corporate community of faith.[44] This prolonged task produced much of what became the NT and accounts for in large measure the variety of the NT witness.

Rather than competing "theologies" or diverse "proclamations," the concept of witness provides a more adequate vehicle for understanding the distinctive (superstructure) of NT theology. The principle of multiple witness is honored in the NT (Matt. 18:16; John 5:31–32; 2 Cor. 13:1; Heb. 10:28; 1 Tim. 5:19), but the most significant use of witness terminology is in connection with the church as God's witnesses (Luke 24:48; John 15:27;

---

43. Jeremias, *New Testament Theology*, 78.

44. See the judicious comments in the chapter "Building the Superstructure and Consolidating" by C. F. D. Moule, *The Birth of the New Testament*, 3d rev. ed. (New York: Harper & Row, 1982), esp. 177–78. The inadequacy of the approach offered by J. D. G. Dunn is twofold: It finds too much in proposing diverse kerygmata and finds too little in the core identity of the historical Jesus with the risen Lord (*Unity and Diversity in the New Testament: An Inquiry into the Character of Earliest Christianity* [Philadelphia: Westminster, 1977], 29–32).

Acts 1:8; 2:32; 5:32; 10:39, 41).[45] In light of the canonical shaping of the NT, we can sketch a brief outline of three major witnesses to its theological superstructure.

The Witness of Paul and His Circle. Paul's letters, among the earliest writings of the NT, may be grouped under three headings: (1) the travel letters emphasize eschatological hope (1 and 2 Thess.) and the saving power of the cross (Gal., 1 and 2 Cor., Rom.); (2) the *prison letters* (Eph., Col.–Philem., Phil.), the christological basis of the church's life; and (3) the *pastoral letters* (1 and 2 Tim., Titus), safeguarding the household of faith. The Letter to the Hebrews, which shares many Pauline themes, depicts the life of God's people as a pilgrimage of faith, hope, and love.

The Witness of the Evangelists. The Gospel of John stands closest to the Christology of Paul in its majestic presentation of Jesus as the incarnate Word of God (1:1–18). Paul and John then represent the earliest known proclamation of Jesus as the divine Son of God. The Acts of the Apostles take a similar vantage point: The ascended Lord sent the gift of the Spirit to advance the Word of God. In order to anchor the significance of Christ in the realities of history, the Synoptic evangelists—Matthew, Mark, and Luke—provide a complementary witness alongside the church's faith. Out of pastoral and theological concerns, they thus echo the Spirit of God that "acknowledges that Jesus Christ has come in the flesh" (1 John 4:2–3). The rich and full portraits of Jesus we have in the fourfold Gospel were preserved by memorable images in the early church: Matthew the lion, the messianic king of Judah's tribe; Mark the man, the man of sorrows suffering for the many; Luke the bull, the only sacrifice for the sins of all mankind; and John the eagle, the eternal word come down from heaven.[46]

The Witness of the Pillar Apostles. The last third of the New Testament canon enshrines the witness of Peter, James, and John, those regarded as "pillars" of faith in Jewish Christianity (Gal. 2:8–10). Their writings are pastoral admonitions that address issues of the church's conduct in an increasingly hostile society. They testify to an essential apostolic tradition of a Christian "way" of life in the world, not of the world, that kept theology and ethics together. The Letter of James is an exhortation to a faith that works; the letters of 1 and 2 Peter (with its companion tract, Jude) call the church to the hope of salvation in the face of persecution and false teaching; the Letters of 1, 2, and 3 John marshal the tests of truth, faith, and love against the spirit of error; and the Revelation of John trumpets the victory of Christ over the kingdoms of this world.

---

45. A. A. Trites, "Witness," *Dictionary of Jesus and the Gospels*, ed. J. B. Green and S. McKnight (Downers Grove, Ill.: InterVarsity, 1992), 877.
46. See Augustine, *The Harmony of the Evangelists*.

FOR FURTHER READING

Boers, Hendrikus. *What Is New Testament Theology?: The Rise of Criticism and the Problem of a Theology of the New Testament.* Guides to Biblical Scholarship: New Testament Series. Philadelphia: Fortress, 1979.

Childs, Brevard S. *Biblical Theology of the Old and New Testaments: Theological Reflection on the Christian Bible.* Minneapolis: Augsburg Fortress, 1993.

Dunn, James D. G. *Unity and Diversity in the New Testament.* Philadelphia:Westminster, 1977.

Goppelt, Leonhard. *Theology of the New Testament.* 2 vols. Translated by John Alsup. Grand Rapids: Eerdmans, 1981–82.

Guthrie, Donald. *New Testament Theology.* Downers Grove, Ill.: InterVarsity, 1981.

Hasel, Gerhard F. *New Testament Theology: Basic Issues in the Current Debate.* Grand Rapids: Eerdmans, 1978.

Ladd, George Eldon. *A Theology of the New Testament.* Rev. ed. Edited by Donald A. Hagner, with chapters by R. T. France and David Wenham. Grand Rapids: Eerdmans, 1993.

Morgan, Robert. *The Nature of New Testament Theology: The Contribution of William Wrede and Adolf Schlatter.* Studies in Biblical Theology. Second Series 25. Naperville, Ill.: Allenson, 1973.

Morris, Leon. *New Testament Theology.* Grand Rapids: Zondervan, 1986.

Moule, C. F. D. *The Birth of the New Testament,* 3d rev. ed. New York: Harper & Row, 1982.

Neill, Stephen and Tom Wright. *The Interpretation of the New Testament 1861–1986.* 2d ed. Oxford: Oxford University Press, 1988.

Wright, N. T. *Christian Origins and the Question of God. Volume 1: The New Testament and the People of God.* Minneapolis: Augsburg Fortress, 1992.

XXVII

CANONICAL THEOLOGY
OF THE NEW TESTAMENT

ROBERT B. SLOAN

The importance of apostolic origin and connection to the apostolic generation for settling theological disputes and establishing religious and ecclesiastical authority in the earliest generations of the Christian faith must not be underestimated. The use, for example, of succession lists of bishops[1] in the earliest Christian centuries bears testimony to the efforts of orthodoxy to establish its claims over divergent movements (such as Marcionitism and Gnosticism) by means of an appeal to apostolic tradition.

It is widely and rightly argued that apostolic authorship and/or historical connection to Jesus, the apostles, or the eyewitness generation was also a major factor in the attribution of canonical status to most, if not all, NT

---

1. See the unpublished dissertation by Robert Lee Williams, "Bishop Lists—Episcopal Authority in Ecclesiastical Polemics," Ph.D Dissertation, University of Chicago, 1982; Robert M. Grant, *Eusebius as Church Historian* (Oxford: Clarendon, 1980), 45–59; and Hans von Campenhausen, *Ecclesiastical Authority and Spiritual Power in the Church of the First Three Centuries*, trans. J. A. Baker (Stanford, Calif.: Stanford University Press, 1969), 149–77.

documents. Even in cases where authorship is now unknown (e.g., Heb.) or greatly disputed (e.g., 2 Pet.), canonicity originally may have been aided by, if not largely owing to, an early perception or historical tradition of apostolic authorship. To be sure, what was thought to be of apostolic origin in the first three centuries of Christian history and what many scholars today regard as pseudonymous literature are not identical judgments.[2] In any case, the importance of apostolic authorship and/or an eyewitness connection is seen in the fact that pseudonymity occurred and was certainly regarded as literary fraud in at least some circles of early Christianity.[3] That is, pseudonymity was objectionable not merely on simple moral grounds (i.e., that one should not deceive), but largely because of the virtually given connection between true apostolic origin and religious authority—matters of grave moral and theological importance indeed.

Still, without downplaying the role of historical "connectivity" for the acquisition of canonical status, it is also important to realize that other factors blended into the providential mix which produced our NT canon, not the least of which were the practices of the early churches. These practices included the actual habits and traditions of use of the documents in worship, and the theological quality and/or outlook of a book. Without examining here the importance of tradition or "historical habits" of use as a factor in canonicity, it is worth remembering that each book had a significant history of use long before it was ever placed on anything like an authoritative list, or canon, of books acceptable for use in Christian worship. Thus, it is salutary to note that canonical status did not make the NT books authoritative; rather, it was their growing authority, as evidenced and reinforced by their ongoing tradition of use in the churches, which made them canonical.

A factor in canonicity which we will study here, however—one that is commonly overlooked in such studies—is the theological dimension of the canonical process. It is the conviction of this essay that something like a canonical theology of the NT can be critically and analytically isolated from the individual documents. However, the theology we will attempt to

---

2. For a helpful discussion of pseudonymity in the New Testament see Conrad Gempf, "Pseudonymity and the New Testament," *Them* 17:2 (1992): 8–10; David G. Meade, *Pseudonymity and Canon: An Investigation into the Relationship of Authorship and Authority in Jewish and Earliest Christian Tradition* (Grand Rapids: Eerdmans, 1986); Donald Guthrie, *New Testament Introduction* (Downers Grove, Ill.: Intervarsity, 1990); and Bruce M. Metzger, "Literary Forgeries and Canonical Pseudepigrapha," *JBL* 91 (1972): 3–24.

3. See the often cited account in Tertullian, *De Baptismo* 17, where an elder of Asia was censured for his attempt to compose an "Acts" in the name of Paul.

isolate is not a synthetically abstracted set of propositions which represent a kind of theological "lowest common denominator." Rather, there was a core of theological convictions, historically and literarily recoverable through the NT, which actually preceded the NT documents. These convictions were held together as a preached (or otherwise reproduced) corpus of beliefs and also contributed conceptually to the emergence and character of the NT. Thus, if that set of assumptions is correct, it may well be that certain theological criteria were just as influential as historical connectivity to Jesus and the apostles in determining the ongoing use of certain early Christian documents in the churches and, ultimately, their canonical status. Indeed, it may be that the existence of a truly theological criterion (even if unconsciously applied) explains better than mere historical accident the apparent fact that not even all apostolic writings were preserved (note 1 Cor. 5:9; 2 Cor. 2:3–4, 9; 7:8, 12) much less used sufficiently to warrant canonical status.[4]

Certainly theological criteria for evaluating various theological claims existed in the earliest communities of faith (note 1 Cor. 12:3; 14:29; 1 John 4:1–3). Furthermore, such normative criteria seem to have been largely christological in nature. Thus, while many NT books—because they were written to Christians—focus upon ecclesiological[5] issues, it may

---

4. It is important to note that theological criteria were important alongside what I have called "historical connectivity" claims (appeals to apostleship and/or Jerusalem connections) already within the primitive Christian era. In fact, it may be that, when the two criteria compete (though usually they are blended), the theological criterion, at least within the first century (and especially for Paul), took precedence. Note that *theological* criteria were appealed to by Paul even against his *own* apostolic status (Gal. 1:6–8) and presumably against any other human appeal, *including* apparently—see Gal. 2:1–9!—an apostolic one. See also 2 Cor. 11:4–5, 13–15, 22, where apostolic appeals and appeals to Jewish (and Jerusalem?) connectivity were rejected by Paul in favor of the gospel. See also 2 Cor. 2:17—3:18; Gal. 1:11–20. Possibly 1 Cor. 15:11* has the effect (note the "whether it was I or they") of subordinating apostolic status to the message commonly preached by the eyewitnesses; see also 1 Cor. 1:18–20; 3:4–11, 21–23; 4:1. Possibly, too, the church's memory in Matt. 16:13–24 of Jesus' harsh words to Peter (16:23)—directly after the highly personal affirmation given to the leading apostle's heavenly insight and confession—would have encouraged the first-century church's will to give theological criteria the upper hand in ecclesiastical disputes, if theological criteria and apostolic status (and/or historical connectivity) were implicitly set against one another.

5. Richard B. Hays, *Echoes of Scripture in the Letters of Paul* (New Haven: Yale University Press, 1989).

* Unless otherwise stated, Scripture quotations in this chapter are from the RSV.

be that the theological criteria applied in the earliest churches for settling various disputes were based upon the largely christological and evangelistic *preaching* that formed the basis of those early communities. If that is so, then the preaching of the highly christological gospel that historically initiated those first communities of faith continued to influence strongly the ongoing foundational theological parameters that shaped the developing practices, traditions, and literature of the churches.

As part of the literature of the early churches, the NT documents themselves give every evidence of having been influenced by the form and content of early Christian preaching. We will now consider the potential unity of the NT documents—documents which clearly reflect a rich literary and theological variety. We will seek to recover the foundational convictions that lay "behind" these variously and situationally targeted books, thus also striving to recover the major theological themes (i.e., the "canonical theology")[6] which not only influenced the creation of individual books, but also contributed significantly to the emergence of the NT as a collection of acceptable and authoritative Christian works.

UNITY AMID DIVERSITY: THE SEARCH FOR A THEOLOGICAL CRITERION

The New Testament may be known and studied in terms of both its unity and its diversity. While professional NT scholarship typically busies itself with details of literary and theological diversity, the ordinary Christian worshiper more likely thinks of the NT in terms of its unity as a sacred book pertaining to religious faith and practice. But just as the unity of the NT should be neither ignored nor preemptively ruled out by NT scholarship, so ought not the rich diversity of the NT be overlooked by anyone. We have, for example, many different kinds of literature in the NT. There are Gospels, history, hymns, prayers, confessions, letters, sermons, wisdom, and of course a very stirring piece of apocalyptic at the end. Indeed, the diversity of the NT goes deeper than the types of literature. It is also reflected in the messages of those various books. In the Gospels we read of Jesus, the great miracle worker, preacher, and teacher. In the Acts of the Apostles we hear of the work of the Spirit in the life of the early church. In the Epistles we find pastoral exhortations regarding both theological and behavioral problems in the early churches. And in the

---

6. For a brief but helpful recent discussion and bibliography of the discipline of biblical theology and/or canonical theology (where the entire biblical canon is under discussion) see Charles H. H. Scobie, "New Directions in Biblical Theology," *Them* 17:2 (1992): 4–7.

Revelation we read, in words of strange and wondrous imagery, of a rider on a white horse, a conquering Lord who will appear and rescue His beleaguered people. The more one pursues issues related to the variety of thought and expression in the NT, the more the question of coherence thrusts itself upon us. Therefore, without overlooking—indeed, rather presuming—the multiformity of the NT in terms of both style and content, the burden of this study relates more to the unity of the NT, and, more specifically, to the role that the forces of coherence may have played in the emergence of the NT canon.

What, then, if it exists at all, is the unity of the NT? What is its "center"? What holds these books together? Or, to put it another way, why should we have bothered to bind these twenty-seven—in many ways very different—books with one cover? What, for example, do the rather Jewish-sounding Epistle to the Hebrews (in which Jesus is a high priest after the order of Melchizedek) and the rather Gentile-sounding Gospel of Mark (in which a Roman soldier declares, "truly this was the Son of God") have to do with one another?

In spite of the obvious literary and theological variety in the NT, the NT *is* dominated by a center—the message of the crucified and risen Lord Jesus. The first four books of the NT, for example, which could just as easily have been called "biographies," were not called biographies; they were called "Gospels."[7] And they were called Gospels precisely because they are devoted primarily to the gospel: that is, the message of the crucified and risen Lord. It is the gospel, the story of that fateful week in Jerusalem, when Christ was crucified and raised, that dominates each Gospel. Turning from the Gospels to Acts, we may similarly note a kind of gospel centrality, for Acts is more than the history of the early church: It is a theological history of the progress of the gospel to the uttermost parts of the earth. In the same vein, the Epistles, which represent pastoral exhortations regarding doctrine and behavior in the early church, have as their fundamental pattern and basis for exhortation the fact of Christ's death and resurrection for us. Since, for example, Christ has conquered sin and death, we must lay aside our evil practices (e.g., 1 Cor. 5:7–8; 15:20–58; Col. 2:8—3:17; Heb. 12:1—13:17; 1 Pet. 4:1–6). Since Christ has been raised from the dead, we too must walk in newness of life (Rom. 6:4; cf. 1 Pet. 3:13–22). Since Christ in His death and resurrection has fulfilled

---

7. Though this is not to deny that Greek *bios* literature may provide the closest literary analogy, for purposes of genre comparison. For reading and understanding our Gospels, see Charles Talbert, *What Is a Gospel?* (Philadelphia: Fortress, 1977). For a more nuanced view, see David E. Aune, *The New Testament in Its Literary Environment* (Philadelphia: Westminster, 1987), especially 17–76.

the ancient scriptural promises of salvation for Israel and the nations, thereby ushering in a new aeon of life and peace, Jew and Gentile may now live together in a *koinonia* of God's Spirit (Rom. 14:1—15:13; Eph. 2:11—3:15). Similarly, in the Revelation, we soon discover that it is no strange and unknown figure who appears to John on the Isle of Patmos and later rides forth to rescue a suffering people. Indeed, both the mysterious son of man (1:13) and the rider on the white horse (19:11–16) are none other than the risen Lord Himself, who, because He was slain, is worthy to receive all glory, dominion, power, and majesty (5:9–14).

Thus, with all the rich variety of expression in the NT, the message of the crucified and risen Lord stands as a kind of coherent center, a theological core, of early Christian literature. The books of the NT, as diverse literary expressions, were each intended to meet the specific needs of specific people in light of the grand and glorious center, the news that God had acted decisively to save His people through the crucified and resurrected Jesus. If this is so, however, this gospel unity is more than an interesting historical fact about the NT, and it is certainly not an artificially deduced synthesis of a collection of ancient, diverse books. Rather, it reflects what may have been the heart and theological criterion of a (perhaps unconscious) way of living and thinking in normative, early Christian experience. Indeed, this common core of connection is very similar to the theological pattern of the earliest Christian preaching. It is thus the earliest Christian preaching that perhaps best accounts for the common core of belief reflected in the various NT documents.

Seen in this way, the problem of unity and diversity offers a significant clue to the reconstruction of at least some of the historical processes which led to the emergence of the NT as sacred literature. Indeed, the theological core of the NT constituted a theological canon—a kind of conceptual organizing principle—which explains the placement of the individual books of the NT into a single collection of sacred literature. Or, to put it the other way around, the proper starting point for any discussion of the theological and literary diversity of the NT is the historical fact of its unity in the form of a canon: i.e., an established list of authoritative books that are suitable for use by the churches. What, however, were the forces which produced this collection and thus, in some sense, presupposed and/or drew upon some level of coherence among the individual books?

HISTORICAL PARAMETERS

We will start with two relatively fixed points. The first is the beginning of the Christian movement, or the church, sometime around the advent of the fourth decade of the first century A.D. The other is the *Easter Letter* of Athanasius, bishop of Alexandria, written in A.D. 367. The rise of the church may no doubt be attributed to the stupendous events that occurred in connection with the life of Jesus of Nazareth. A charismatic preacher, miracle worker, friend of sinners, and innovative interpreter of the Jewish law, Jesus was put to death at the instigation of the Jewish authorities during the procuratorship of Pontius Pilate. A series of dramatic resurrection appearances that began three days later, coupled with the fact of the empty tomb, convinced His disillusioned followers that He had been raised by God to absolute life. This fact, coupled with the profound religious experiences of the following Pentecost, propelled the new movement into the Roman world. Using what Christians now call the "Old Testament" as their Scriptures, these followers of the risen Lord formed churches, engaged in worship and benevolence, and, through the impetus of persecution and their sense of divinely ordained mission began to spread the message of the crucified and risen Lord throughout the Mediterranean world.

Some three centuries later, by the time of Athanasius, it could be written down—and was in fact (rather casually) in his *Easter Letter* of A.D. 367—that there were certain books (the twenty-seven which we now call the New Testament) acceptable for reading in worship. How we got from a movement that had only the OT as its Scriptures to one that widely accepted a second collection of twenty-seven books as an addition to its Scriptures is another way of approaching our central question: What were the theological forces which led toward and made possible the unified collection of sacred books we call the New Testament canon?

THE RISE OF INDIVIDUAL BOOKS FROM APOSTOLIC TRADITION

In tracing the processes which led to the rise of given books of the NT, it is essential to understand that the early church had a theology before it had a NT. This point is rather obvious to those of us who spend our lives studying the origins of Christianity, but it is a point worth considering. Confessionally and doctrinally, of course, it is the other way around. We are accustomed to speaking of theology as a derivative of the NT; but it was not always the case that Christians had a NT. Assuming for the sake of argument that 1 Thessalonians, written about A.D. 50 or 51, represents the earliest of our twenty-seven NT documents, and assuming Jesus died no later than the year A.D. 33, we are confronted with a period of nearly two decades in which early Christians prayed, preached, sang, worshiped, evangelized, and experienced the presence of the risen Lord in their midst without having even one document of what we call the New Testament. Of course, even by the year A.D. 50, we are still decades away from a situation in which the books of the NT have in any significant way been copied, exchanged, circulated, and thus generally used in the major Christian congregations. Nonetheless, from the very beginning, the earliest Christians had a theology. The Book of Acts specifically suggests that from Pentecost on there were certain things preached and believed by the leaders of early Christianity, convictions which set the Christian movement apart theologically from its Jewish and/or Hellenistic culture. Indeed, there is a substantial enough pattern (see next page) in the entire collection of sermons in Acts to suggest to us that the early preachers shared a fairly consistent core of proclamation and belief.[8]

Not only do the early sermons attest to a common core—designated here as "apostolic theology"—of early Christian belief, but literary analysis of other portions of the NT has revealed that embedded within the documents are portions of early Christian hymns, confessions, and other traditional material that reflect the theology and beliefs of the earliest generation of Christian evangelists and teachers. For example, most NT scholars assume—based upon literary analysis of the passage—that Philippians 2:6–11 represents a hymn commonly sung by early Christians.[9] The same conclusion can be drawn concerning 1 Timothy 3:16 and 2 Timothy 2:11–13, where we find, in rhythmic Greek, passages specifically introduced as common confessional material. Apart from the very interesting fact that these statements suggest that the highest Christology in the NT is in fact the earliest, and thus give the lie to evolutionary models of christological development,[10] for current purposes these examples confirm the earlier point: namely, that there is a very consistent pattern of theology and belief reflected in the NT that dates from the earliest period of Christian experience and is therefore prior to the NT documents themselves.[11]

---

8. See Bo Reicke, *Glaube und Leben der Urgemeinde* (Zürich: Zwingli, 1957), 39, where he refers to the speeches in Acts as representing that which is theologically "characteristic" of the early church. See also F. F. Bruce, *The Acts of the Apostles* (1951; reprint, Grand Rapids, Mich.: Eerdmans, 1986), 18–21.

9. See Ralph Martin, *Carmen Christi: Philippians 2:5–11 in Recent Interpretation and in the Setting of Early Christian Worship* (Cambridge: University Press, 1967).

10. Cf. C. F. D. Moule, *The Origin of Christology* (New York: Cambridge University Press, 1977), 1–10.

11. This is not to deny the diversity, both literary and theological, alluded to earlier.

Thus, though one finds variations of detail, analysis of the sermons in Acts as well as the confessional material throughout the NT suggests that early Christian teachers were convinced of several things.[12] They believed (1) that in connection with the events surrounding the person of Jesus, God had been acting in fulfillment of the ancient Jewish Scriptures; (2) that the crucifixion of Jesus had been ordained by God and was moreover a mighty act of conquest and deliverance for His people, as confirmed by God's vindication of Jesus in the resurrection; (3) that this same crucified and risen Jesus had been exalted to a heavenly throne at the right hand of God and was thus installed as both Messiah and Lord, the supreme Agent and Executor of the kingdom of God; (4) that Jesus had poured out the Spirit of God upon His people and was thus Himself present in their midst as the living Lord; (5) that this same Jesus would again be manifested to the world to vindicate His people and judge all the earth, and (6) that to participate in the saving work of God through Christ and thus to be included among the people of God, one must turn from sin and believe on the risen Christ as Messiah and Lord, confessing Him through baptism in His name.

If it is asked where these early Christian leaders got their theology, the simple answer is their theology reflects their own Jewish heritage on the one hand, and their encounter with the life, teachings, and exaltation of Christ on the other. Wherever they obtained it, however much it continued to develop, and however diverse it was in nuance and detail from one teacher/preacher to the next, a core of apostolic theology was nonetheless there from the beginning of the church and served as both historical predecessor of and intellectual substructure for the NT books. We will now consider emergence of these books in the context of varied historical situations.

THE CORRESPONDENCE LITERATURE

We usually divide the NT into two parts: the narrative/historical material and the correspondence material.[13] The narrative/historical material covers the four Gospels and Acts; the correspondence literature, the rest of the NT. As to why the correspondence literature is written, the simple answer is that the given author could not be present to deliver his remarks

---

12. Similar to C. H. Dodd, *The Apostolic Preaching and Its Developments* (London: Hodder and Stoughton, 1944), 17.

13. Cf. W. G. Kümmel, *Introduction to the New Testament*, trans. A. J. Mattill, Jr. (Nashville: Abingdon, 1966), 9–11. Kümmel does not include the Apocalypse with the correspondence literature, though it clearly has certain epistolary features.

in person.[14] The geographical expansion of Christianity had made the use of writing materials inevitable. The "epistle" was—most scholars agree—essentially a substitute for the apostolic presence.[15]

But that doesn't answer the question entirely. There were also circumstances in the life settings of both the recipients and the authors of the correspondence literature that called forth a given document. At Corinth, for example, we see that problems and questions related to division within the community, church discipline, lawsuits, sexual immorality, meat offered to idols, women praying and prophesying without their heads covered, drunkenness and quarreling at the Lord's table, the resurrection of the dead, and a proposed offering for Christians in Jerusalem all contributed to the writing of what we now call 1 Corinthians. So it was for most of the correspondence literature. Questions and problems of a theological nature (sometimes of a very practical nature) and concerns related to worship, heresy, church leadership, persecution, and the return of the Lord were factors contributing to the historical causes for given pieces of literature. Everything from a thank-you note for a gift of money (Phil.) to a highly symbolic answer to the question, "How long, O Lord, must we wait?" (Rev.), could be cited as reasons for writing.

The point being developed here is really twofold. On the one hand, it is true to say the NT literature is not a "systematic theology." That is, it does not represent a meticulous, systematic laying out of early Christian doctrine by topical arrangement. The literature was called forth by specific needs in either the life of the writer or the lives of the recipients, or in both. It is what we call "occasional literature," written to meet specific needs, for specific people, at a specific time in history. On the other hand, however, when we say that the NT writers did not write a systematic theology, we do not mean that they are not systematic thinkers. From the very earliest days of the church there was something I prefer to call "apostolic theology." There was a core of theological belief which,

---

14. Romans, which is best understood as a kind of advance letter (cf. also 2 Cor. 10—13), is thus not strictly a substitute for the apostolic presence—i.e., it is its designed forerunner. My colleague, Mikeal Parsons, also suggests to me that Philemon likewise accomplishes things in apostolic absence that could not be done with apostolic presence. With these qualifiers, however, I think the general point about the apostolic letters serving as a substitute for the apostolic presence still stands.

15. See Robert W. Funk, "The Apostolic *Parousia*: Form and Significance," in *Christian History and Interpretation: Studies Presented to John Knox*, ed. W. R. Farmer, C. F. D. Moule, and R. R. Niebuhr (Cambridge: University Press, 1967), 249–68. See also IDBSup, s.v. "letter."

when confronted with specific problems and needs, was able to adapt itself in response. At least one of the literary fruits of that theological, pastoral adaptation of the early theology to specific needs is the correspondence literature of the NT.

THE NARRATIVE/HISTORICAL LITERATURE

The situation with regard to the narrative/historical material is somewhat different, though not completely unrelated. The Gospels and Acts are not as obviously pastoral, or hortatory, as the Epistles, but the teachings of Jesus and the apostles, as well as the example of their lives, certainly served a teaching function for early Christians, a fact which no doubt contributed to both the emergence and shape of the Gospels. The story of Jesus had an inherent value for those who confessed Him as Lord. Accounts of His life, words, death, and resurrection were no doubt repeated to eager audiences countless times by those who had either seen and heard the Lord, or else knew those who had.[16] Eventually, factors such as the geographical spread of the gospel, the desire to preserve as accurately as possible the testimony of the apostles, the need to instruct new converts even in the absence of eyewitnesses, and conflict with alien religious forces led to the production of what we now call "Gospels."

The Gospels were something of a theological narrative of the essential (especially gospel) elements of the history of Jesus. That is, the story of Jesus was important as the background and basis of the apostolic preaching.[17] Indeed, the opening line of the Gospel of Mark describes the forthcoming literary production as "the beginning of the gospel of Jesus Christ." Thus, according to its expressed intention, what follows in Mark is the historical genesis (the beginning) of the apostolic message about Jesus Christ.[18] The Gospel of Luke likewise has its roots in the apostolic preaching, as seen from Luke's reference to the sources of his literary product as being those who were "eyewitnesses and ministers of the word" (1:2), where "word" is a common Lukan expression for the preached gospel (Acts 8:4; 14:25; 16:6; 17:11). Though probably not

---

16. A "problems"-oriented way of discussing the occasionality of a given piece should not be allowed to overwhelm the significance of other historical factors, e.g., sheer curiosity, devotion, etc. See T. W. Manson, *Studies in the Gospels and Epistles*, ed. Matthew Black (Philadelphia: Westminster, 1962), 3–12.

17. Dodd, *Apostolic Preaching*, 30–31, 36–56.

18. Bo Reicke, *The Roots of the Synoptic Gospels* (Philadelphia: Fortress, 1986), 152.

originally conceived as correspondence to be sent from one place to another,[19] the Gospels reflect the felt need in some early Christian communities to have an account of the words and deeds of Jesus—particularly the events of the last days leading up to and including His death and resurrection. Thus, Gospel accounts of the teachings of Jesus, coupled with the events of His ministry, suffering and resurrection, likewise reflect the "apostolic theology" of early Christianity, especially regarding its historical roots in the person and history of Jesus. Therefore, though the Gospels were no doubt written a number of decades after the lifetime of Jesus, it was the continued apostolic *preaching* of the death and resurrection of Jesus which gave decisive shape to the Gospels as we now have them, a reality attested by the fact that the central themes of early Christian preaching and teaching were also emphasized in the Gospels. It is no secret to anyone who has looked at the Gospels that the focus is on the last eight days of Jesus' life, the period from Palm Sunday to Easter Sunday. His life and teachings prior to that were, of course, important for early Christians and certainly received significant, though differing, amounts of emphasis in our four Gospels. But it is no accident that the Gospels were given (very early in Christian history) titles (the Gospel According to Matthew, the Gospel According to Mark, etc.) which reflect the assumption of a singular Christian message (the gospel)[20] with its focus upon certain central events, namely the death and resurrection of Jesus for our salvation.[21]

As for Acts, its reason for being was also related to the gospel as the oral message of early apostolic preaching. If the "former treatise" (1:1) related, the historical basis of the gospel, Acts, as its sequel,[22] is the subsequent history of the progress of the apostolic preaching. In other words, it is an account of the spread of the gospel from its Jewish beginnings in Jerusalem to its acceptance by Gentiles in "the uttermost parts of the earth" (1:8). Luke's Gospel represents the historical basis of the "word"; Acts, its

---

19. This fact is perhaps, at least initially, the best suggestion as to why the Gospel authors do not state their names, in addition to the fact that they probably do not think of themselves as authors. See the discussion of these and related issues in Martin Hengel, *Studies in the Gospel of Mark* (Philadelphia: Fortress, 1985), 64–84.

20. Again, note the word "gospel" in each title functions as a reference to the gospel as *message*, not a literary genre.

21. See below for further discussion regarding the titles to the Gospels.

22. Mikeal C. Parsons, "The Unity of the Lukan Writings: Rethinking the *Opinio Communis*," in *With Steadfast Purpose: Essays on Acts in Honor of Henry Jackson Flanders, Jr.*, ed. Naymond H. Keathley (Waco: Baylor University Press, 1990).

historical progress;[23] but for both works, the "word," i.e., the preached gospel, is the confessional given behind each literary historical product.

In summary, the great diversity of historical settings and circumstances standing behind the books of the NT accounts for its rather obvious theological variety; but underlying the evident theological and historical variety reflected in the NT, there is also a profound unity. The unity lies not in our ability to derive a classical, systematic theology from the NT. Rather, the unity of the NT is seen in the proclaimed theology—recovered by various historical, exegetical, and other critical means—that lies behind the NT. Thus, it could be argued the NT as literature is the product of NT theology, where the latter expression suggests the earliest, theological sense of the phrase "NT." We, of course, from our later vantage point, must use the NT as the basis of NT theology. But we must always remember that behind these documents were Christian preachers and thinkers who had a consistent core of faith and belief. A proper NT theology seeks these central convictions.

THE COEXISTENCE OF NEW TESTAMENT LITERATURE AND APOSTOLIC TRADITION

THE PRIMACY OF CHRISTIAN ORAL TRADITION

What we have called the "apostolic theology" is also called the "tradition of Christ" (cf. Col. 2:6, 8) or simply "tradition" (1 Cor. 11:2; 2 Thess. 2:15; 3:6; cf. Rom. 6:17; 1 Cor. 11:23; 15:1, 3; Gal. 1:9, 12; Phil. 4:9; 1 Tim. 1:18; 2 Tim. 2:2; Jude 3) in the NT period. The word "tradition" usually has negative connotations for us, but in the NT literature "tradition" may be either positive or negative. Certainly Jesus loudly criticized the tradition of the Pharisees because He believed they had thereby subverted the clear intent of the Scriptures (Matt. 15:1–8). Paul, too, warned the Colossians against the "traditions of men" (2:8). On the other hand, the gospel also is referred to as "tradition" (1 Cor. 15:1, 3; Gal. 1:9, 12), and it is this word which in fact still captures for us the character of much that happened in the earliest decades of the first century A.D.

Jesus appeared on the Jewish scene as a miracle worker and teacher of rather dramatic, if not provocative, presence. Though the reasons for His break with the religio-political leaders of Judaism were no doubt many, surely in tracing the cause of His eventual death at their hands one must begin with an account of His "halakah," that is, His, to them, utterly unac-

---

23. Cf. W. C. van Unnik, "The 'Book of Acts' the Confirmation of the Gospel," *NovT* 4 (1960): 26–59.

ceptable interpretations of Jewish Scripture, law, and tradition. His teaching tradition, moreover, was dramatically reinforced by His lifestyle. Jesus was on a collision course with the religious authorities because of His outspoken criticism of the rabbinic traditions of scriptural exegesis (Matt. 5:17–48; Mark 7:1–13), His mockery of the Pharisees for their ritual observances done in the absence of "the weightier matters of the law" (Matt. 23:23), His numerous run-ins with religious authorities regarding Sabbath keeping, as well as His extremely disconcerting words about the status (and future) of the temple in Judaism (Matt. 2:16; John. 2:19; cf. Matt. 26:61). To be sure, His willingness to accept the ritually impure into the kingdom of God, His belittling of Pharisaical fastidiousness, His non-ascetical view of life, and His willingness to eat and drink with sinners made Him extremely popular with the crowds, but only served to deepen the religious establishment's resentment and fear of Him. The Galilean rabbi had to be suppressed.

It must be noticed that nowhere did Jesus seem to have disagreed with the religious authorities on questions of inspiration, text, or canon. No doubt He was accused of rejecting Moses and the Scriptures, but such accusations were commonly made of those whose interpretations of Scripture were being rejected. Besides, Jesus seems to have countered such accusations with His own declarations of faithfulness to the Law and the Prophets (Matt. 5:17–20). Of course, He criticized the religious establishment for their traditions which, He argued, functionally supplanted the Scriptures (Matt. 15:1–12), but the arguments of each were nonetheless essentially arguments regarding matters of interpretation—the authority, tradition, and/or law of Jesus on the one hand[24] versus the authority and traditions of the elders (Matt. 15:2; Mark 7:3) on the other. Jesus Himself could often be heard asking the teachers of the Law, no doubt with irony, if not sarcasm, "Have you not read . . . ?" (Matt. 12:3; 21:42; 22:31; Mark 2:25). Ultimately, His tradition, His teaching, His torah was too radical, too different, and too threatening to their perceptions of Jewish

---

24. It does not seem historically inappropriate to refer to Jesus' teachings with the word "law" given (a) the nature and contextual force of His teachings as reported in the Matthean Sermon on the Mount, where not only do the introductory warnings (5:17–20) propose the words of Jesus as the fulfillment of the Law and the Prophets and as constituting a righteousness that is "greater" than that of the scribes and Pharisees but, more specifically, the "but I say to you" references are rhetorically juxtaposed to the commonly received interpretations of the Mosaic Law (5:21, 27, 33, 43); and (b) the repeated uses of the term "law" in James (1:25; 2:8–12; 4:11–12; 5:7–9) with at least some connection to the teachings of Jesus (cf. Matt. 7:1–2). See Robert B. Sloan, "The Christology of James," *CTR* 1:1 (1986): 22–29.

identity—to say nothing of the political threat it posed for them regarding their status in Jewish/Roman society—to go unchallenged.

With regard to a distinctive "tradition," the same was true of the followers of Jesus. The "tradition of Jesus" (meaning *both* the interpretive tradition handed down by Him and the apostolic interpretation of Him),[25] which received its decisive illumination in His death and resurrection, stands as the point of division between primitive Christianity and Judaism. Of course, Christianity was first regarded as a sectarian movement *within* Judaism, but its theological claims soon tested the limits of official Judaism's patience. Christian views became marginally tolerable, if at all. But even Jewish sanctions against Christianity reflect the latter's identity as an internal threat to the traditional faith of Judaism and force us to ask historically for the causes of the burgeoning split, at least some of which must have been the too radical, apparently anti-torah nature of the new "teaching" (Acts 4:18; 5:28, 40; cf. 6:13–14). The new sectarian movement experienced the arrest and flogging of some of its teachers (Acts 4—5) and even the death of one of its most dynamic—indeed, incitative—preachers (Acts 6—8). Among other things, including political developments which converged around the year A.D. 37,[26] the death of Stephen was certainly brought on as well by his theological challenge to the traditional role and ongoing authority of the law and the temple cultus in Jewish life (Acts 6:10–14; 7:46–50). It was a challenge which Stephen, according to Luke, provocatively and theologically tied to the betrayal and death of Jesus at the hands of the Jewish leaders (Acts 7:51–53).

The story of Philip's encounter with the Ethiopian eunuch (Acts 8:26–39) likewise illustrates this conflict of traditions between established first-century Judaism on the one hand and emergent (though still within Judaism) Christianity on the other.[27] The Ethiopian court official had been to Jerusalem to worship. He had surely heard the conflicting assertions of the historically brash and exegetically novel traditions of the followers of the

---

25. The apostolically interpreted gospel events (*about* Jesus) of the cross and resurrection cannot finally be separated from the Jesus traditions initiated by Him, e.g., Jas. 1:18, 25; 2:8–12; 4:11–12; 5:7–9, where gospel as "the word of truth" is called, or at least related to, the "law," the "law of liberty," the "royal law," etc., which are in turn to some extent related to the teachings of Jesus. Sloan, ibid.; cf. Brevard S. Childs, *The New Testament as Canon: An Introduction* (Philadelphia: Fortress, 1984), 67–69, where Childs argues that (there is canonical significance in the fact that) in Matthew "the time of Jesus and the time of the church have been fused."

26. Bo Reicke, *The New Testament Era*, trans. David E. Green (Philadelphia: Fortress, 1968), 190–91.

27. See F. F. Bruce, *Tradition Old and New* (Grand Rapids: Zondervan, 1970), 74–86, for a helpful elaboration of this issue, especially the relationship between competing interpretive traditions which claim a common body of sacred text.

crucified Nazarene over against the established orthodoxies of the more traditional scribes and Pharisees. When Philip first met the Ethiopian, the latter was already reading what was no doubt, by that time, a much-disputed text in Jerusalem—the text of Isaiah 53 regarding the humble servant of Yahweh whose life "is removed from the earth" (v. 8). In Jerusalem the argument must have raged between Christians and Jews regarding the identity of the speaker. Did the prophet speak of himself (as no doubt many Jews had begun to argue), or did his enigmatic words refer to someone else (as no doubt the Christians had insisted)? There was no question as to which side of the debate Philip would take. Invited to join the Ethiopian in his chariot, Philip gave the text a decidedly Christocentric interpretation. Luke tells us that, "beginning from this Scripture he preached Jesus to him" (Acts 8:35, NASB).

Thus, in the earliest years, the conflict between church and synagogue did not center upon the authority, text, or canon of Scripture. Of course, the widespread Christian use of the Septuagint, the Greek Old Testament, led to Jewish reticence about the LXX in later years and eventually brought about its displacement for Jews by the Greek version of Aquila. Indeed, Jewish efforts at fixing the Hebrew Scriptures and canon toward the end of the first century A.D. may likewise be attributed in part to the emergence of Christianity and the co-opting by Christians of the LXX, which had previously enjoyed rather significant popularity among most Jews.[28] But that debate over the authentic text and/or translation of the (OT) Scriptures was for later generations. In the earliest days, Christians and Jews did not argue over the authority, text, or canon of Scripture. It was the interpretation of Scripture which divided them. Early Christians, believing that the resurrection of Jesus had vindicated Him before His detractors (He is Lord of all), as a matter of course accepted as authoritative the "tradition of Jesus"—that is, His understanding of the mysteries, ways, and laws of God as revealed in Holy Scripture. The word of Jesus was authoritative. It was a law/Torah/tradition which included His teachings, the events of His life, and the culminating expression/vindication of His interpretation(s) of Scripture and His messianic mission in His death and resurrection.[29] Early Christian tradition, therefore, had the gospel events at its heart, which of necessity also involved the Christian understanding of the ancient Scrip-

---

28. See S. Jellicoe, *The Septuagint and Modern Study* (Ann Arbor: Eisenbrauns, 1978), 74–77.

29. See note 25 above.

tures—an interpretive perspective which in its central features was no doubt learned from Jesus.[30]

Therefore, with regard to religious authority, it seems the earliest formative/normative center of the Christian movement lay in the apostolic theology, a largely oral tradition of preaching and teaching. But the apostolic message did not stand alone as a merely conceptual/doctrinal authority unto itself. Rather, it was the early consensus interpretation—seen against the backdrop of the Jewish Scriptures[31]—of certain historical events that were believed to be divine acts of salvation. That is, the apostolic tradition had its historical roots in the life of Jesus, was proclaimed and preserved by a body of eyewitnesses and bearers of the tradition, and was both interpretively shaped by early Christian teachers in the spiritual experience of the church (cf. Eph. 2:19—3:11) and continually reapplied to new situations of life encountered by the earliest believers.

While we may assume, therefore, that the letters of the NT were not thought of as "Scripture" by the original authors or readers of those documents, they were nonetheless literary applications of apostolic tradition and thus were both certainly perceived and intended from the beginning as authoritative pieces of communication. In this regard, it may be noted that apostolicity was nearly always a significant feature of the correspondence literature. The letters, then, are a kind of literary crystallization of the apostolic tradition at a given point in time, in response to a given situation. The correspondence literature is, therefore, in occasional form, a specialized case or subset of the primitive tradition. Again, though the letters were certainly not thought of as Scripture either by the original authors or recipients, they were certainly intended—and no doubt regarded—as possessing religious authority. With the exception of Hebrews, all the correspondence literature of the NT had the name of a noteworthy apostle attached to it. In fact, even Hebrews, with its somewhat checkered canonical career, may well owe, in part, its inclusion in the

---

30. "It is individual minds that originate. Whose was the originating mind here? . . . [T]he New Testament itself avers that it was Jesus Christ Himself who first directed the minds of His followers to certain parts of the scriptures as those in which they might find illumination upon the meaning of His mission and destiny. . . . To account for the beginning of this most original and fruitful process of rethinking the Old Testament we found need to postulate a creative mind. The Gospels offer us one. Are we compelled to reject the offer?" C. H. Dodd, *According to the Scriptures* (New York: Charles Scribner's, 1953), 110.

31. The significance of the Scriptures for understanding the theology of Jesus and/or early Christianity would be difficult to overestimate. For an impressive illustration of this fact as well as an excellent treatment of intertextuality in Paul, see Hays, *Echoes of Scripture*.

canon to its (in some early circles) presumed Pauline authorship. To be sure, the book does show some connection with the Pauline circle of theology.

Much the same can be said for the narrative literature. However different the situations may have been that called forth the narrative literature, especially the Gospels, they represent in narrative form the historical basis of early Christian tradition and thus surely reproduce much of the early Christian teaching and/or catechesis. As such, the Gospels, like the Epistles, were an "occasional" literary subset of the broader, authoritative, and oral apostolic tradition.

THE DECLINE OF THE ORAL TRADITION

The next stage in the transition from tradition to Scripture may be seen in the passing of time and the natural consequences thereof. The spread of the gospel into areas that were geographically remote from its origins; the loss of first generation, apostolic presence and apostolic memory; as well as the fact that writing by its nature tends to displace memory,[32] are all factors that led to the eventual decline of the authoritative oral traditions and their being superseded by the written apostolic tradition. A brief look at Ignatius of Antioch and Papias of Hierapolis will serve to illustrate, and somewhat demonstrate, the transition from oral to written tradition with respect to the increased investment in the latter of religious authority.[33]

Ignatius, the bishop of Antioch, whose death may be dated in either A.D. 108 or 116,[34] seems clearly on the one hand to have known much of the NT literature (especially Matthew, Johannine traditions, and the letters of Paul), but on the other hand to have preferred the living prophetic voice (Phld. VI.1; VIII.2; IX.2; Smyrn. V.1; VII.2). Certainly Ignatius never referred to any of the NT materials as "Scripture," nor did he associate what appear to us to be NT literary traditions[35] with the traditional

---

32. Regarding the relationship between orality and written materials, see Walter J. Ong, *Orality and Literacy* (London: Methuen, 1982).

33. Dependence on the magisterial work of Reicke will be evident to those familiar with it; see Reicke, *Roots of the Synoptic Gospels*, 45–47, 155–74.

34. The A.D. 116 date is to be preferred. See Glanville Downey, *A History of Antioch in Syria* (Princeton: University Press, 1961), 292ff.

35. This cautious way of referring to Ignatius' *apparent* use of NT materials is necessary because we may not often be certain that what looks to us in Ignatius to be a NT *literary* citation, allusion, or echo may not in fact have come to Ignatius in the form of an *oral* tradition. See Christian Maurer, *Ignatius von Antiochien und das Johannesevangelium* (Zürich: Zwingli, 1949).

categories and/or formulas suggestive of the use of Scripture. Papias, fragments of whose work are preserved for us only by Eusebius, was bishop of Hierapolis and a contemporary of Ignatius, though he (Papias) outlived him some fifteen to twenty years. Papias clearly stated his preference for the "living voice" of tradition (EH III.39.4), but it is not clear that such a preference had to do with oral sayings of Jesus over against their written form, as some have interpreted the purpose of his no longer extant five-volume work on the *Explanation of the Sayings of the Lord* (*logiōn kuriakōn exēgēsis*). Papias' preference may have been more a general statement about historical method with respect to his examination of the origins and meaning of certain written "reports" (*logia*), i.e., our Gospels. That is, Papias, in his investigation of the historical background of the Gospels, preferred, as a matter of historical caution, the voice of those "elders" who were in a historical line with the Lord and/or the disciples of the Lord as opposed to either "wordy" or secondary written sources. However, whatever view one takes of the purpose of Papias' work, whether it was to recover unrecorded sayings of Jesus or to comment upon the meaning and origin of certain already existent texts (our Gospels), we may conclude that by about A.D. 120, there was not much oral material, not already included in the Gospels, left to be found. The year A.D. 120 is a convenient and reliable approximation of the final decline of the oral tradition and the emerging dominance of the written traditions for other reasons as well. In this connection, the use of the word "gospel" also provides an illuminating window into that historical transition.

The evidence is strong that rather generally in second-century papyri the four canonical Gospels were called, "The Gospel According to Matthew," "The Gospel According to Mark," and so on. It is evident that the use of the word "gospel" had a kind of collective, or unifying, function in these titles. That is, the word "gospel" was a reference to the basic Christian message. Its use in the second-century titles of our Gospels implies the individual quality of each book as a version of that preached message otherwise known as the "gospel." In other words, we have "Matthew's Version of the Gospel" or "Mark's Version of the Gospel"; or we could speak of "The Message that We Preach According to the Testimony of Luke" or " . . . John." Similar conclusions may be drawn for the word "gospel" as employed in the NT itself, where the noun is found seventy-seven times and is *always* used in a collective/unitary sense to refer to a preached, oral message. Thus, the collective notion of the word "gospel," as reflected in the NT documents, is still in use at the time of the application of the titles in the second century.[36]

---

36. Irenaeus, *Adversus Haereses* 5.33.3–4.

The Apostolic Fathers, a general designation for referring to the earliest post-biblical literature up to about the year A.D. 120, likewise continued this unitary, or collective, sense of the word "gospel." In the *Didache*, the *Epistle of Barnabas*, and Ignatius, where the noun "gospel" is used, it is found only in the collective sense of the good news preached by Jesus and the early church. In fact, it is this pattern in the Apostolic Fathers that convinces many scholars that the traditional titles of our four Gospels must have been given sometime not much later than the beginning of the second century, i.e., around A.D. 100. By the middle of the second century, however, the situation had changed. Justin Martyr, who died about A.D. 165, clearly used the word "gospel" to refer to a book (see *Apology* I.66.3 and *Dialogue* 100.1). Similarly, Irenaeus, about A.D. 180, referred to the "four Gospels" (*Against Heresies* III.1.1). Therefore, in the first part of the second century (up to about A.D. 120), the word "gospel" still seems exclusively to have referred to a message, and as such would seem to bear witness to the continued existence, as late as the first or second decade of the second century, of a living Christian tradition. This living tradition co-existed with some important and no doubt influential written expressions of that tradition (various NT documents), but was not yet completely displaced by those literary products.

But the memory of the apostolic voice was soon to fade. (Indeed, as stated earlier, the mere fact that apostolic tradition had been written down likely contributed to the beginning of the process of the decline of the oral tradition.) By A.D. 150, the authoritative apostolic writings had become indispensable. The Gospels, at least, were being read in worship alongside the writings of the prophets (Justin, *Apology*, I.67) and could be appealed to with the religiously pregnant phrase, "it is written" (Justin, *Dialogue*, 100.1). Eventually, the apostolic literature (various NT documents) became, among other things, the final link to the older, eyewitness generation. With such indispensability also doubtlessly came increased religious stature.

By the time of Irenaeus (ca. A.D. 180), the Gospels were sacred books and were referred to as "Scripture" (*Against Heresies*, I.1.3; III.1.1). The same was said of the letters of Paul (*Against Heresies* I.3.4). Indeed, if anything, for Irenaeus, the "living voice" is secondary, if not suspect, having been claimed by Gnostics as their authoritative key (*Against Heresies* III.2.1).

THE LITERARY TRADITIONS AS SCRIPTURE

The transition from written, authoritative apostolic tradition to Scripture is the final stage in a process that extended from A.D. 33 until the middle of the second century. Though the description of the apostolic writings as "Scripture" was not inevitable, it was not unnatural once the writings themselves, grouped in various collected bodies,[37] in the absence of apostolic memory, and with the continued loss of connection between church and synagogue, continued to be read alongside OT Scripture in the churches and became indispensable as the last link to the apostolic generation.

Some movement in that last step toward the label "Scripture" may also have come with the increased threat of the various Gnostic movements in the second century. It is interesting to note in this connection that, as far as we know, the first commentary on a portion of the NT can be dated to the middle of the second century. Though his work is known to us only in fragmentary fashion through the work of Origen, the Gnostic teacher Heracleon, who flourished from A.D. 145 to 180, is known to have written a commentary on the Gospel of John. Whether it was the emergence of written commentaries on NT books that encouraged the final shift in nomenclature (i.e., the use of the term "Scripture" with reference to NT books) or whether it was the kind of disputed interpretation and analysis of the apostolic literature that was already going on orally before the production of written commentaries, cannot be decided with certainty. It seems, however, that the rise of groups such as the various Gnostic communities, which incorporated Christian language and confession into their alien metaphysical and mythological structures, must certainly have contributed to the emergent status of the various NT writings as "Scripture."[38]

Of course, the Gnostic connection and its mutual interpenetration with Judaism preceded the Christian era. Indeed, Gnostic authors no doubt

---

37. Irenaeus, *Adversus Haereses* 5.33.3–4.

38. Though not sufficient to explain the use of the term "Scripture" with regard to various NT documents, the fact of their collection seems to have been historically integral to the emergent process of their being so described. The religious value of the apostolic witness in terms of both personal authority and theological normativity—both a function of historical connection to Jesus—had been immediately accorded various individual documents and led no doubt to their repeated use and preservation. But the label "Scripture" seems historically to have been connected to *bodies* of sacred literature. The evidence seems to suggest that one document, unless it were presumed to be part of and/or inextricably linked to a larger collection of literature, would not be called "Scripture." Religious authority and value seem historically to have preceded canonicity, but the label "Scripture" seems to have required the process of collecting (which itself required the "collectibility" of the individual documents) as a necessary antecedent to its use. As suggested earlier, the preservation and ongoing use of individual documents may be explained in terms of their intrinsic historical and theological worth. Their *collection* (i.e., being grouped together in bodies or anthologies—great or small—of literature) seems to imply historical and theological commonalities among the documents. Once collected, however, fresh possibilities emerged, not the least of which was the functional (and increasingly favorable) comparison of the new apostolic literature with the ancient (Jewish) Scriptures.

commented upon OT Scripture before they did upon the authoritative apostolic literature. But a Gnostic commentary on an apostolic document may well have created a new religious (ecclesiastical and theological) crisis. For when Ignatius was confronted by docetic teachers who appealed to written records, presumably OT, he could appeal to the authoritative apostolic tradition, i.e., the traditional core of belief which included the birth of Jesus and His suffering and resurrection. What, however, was to be done when it was no longer the OT Scriptures which were misinterpreted, but the apostolic traditions themselves—that is, the very materials that had originally served as the hermeneutical/interpretive guidelines for understanding OT Scripture—which were now misinterpreted?[39] One solution was to develop and/or employ theological summaries—themselves apparently comprised of traditional confessional material—as the hermeneutical keys to the apostolic literature.

The dying out of apostolic memory and oral tradition, and the emergent status of the written (and collected) apostolic traditions as indispensable, made inevitable the onset of debate over what we now call the New Testament materials. As long as the apostolic traditions were oral, they were certainly authoritative, but were themselves not so much the object of scrutiny as they were the authoritative witness to other highly scrutinized matters: either the interpretation of OT Scripture or historical events and words pertaining to Jesus and the apostles. But written materials themselves not only soon displace oral material, but themselves become the object of interpretive analysis. It is interesting to note that in this same time, about the middle of the second century, there emerged a series of labels and categories to refer to the correct interpretation of the apostolic tradition itself. Irenaeus and Tertullian refer to such things variously as "the rule of faith" (regula fidei),[40] "the truth" (alētheias/veritatis),[41] or "the canon/rule of truth" (kanon tēs alētheias/regula

---

39. The role of Marcion has been reevaluated by several scholars in *The Second Century: A Journal of Early Christian Studies* 6 (fall 1987–88): Gerhard May, "Marcion in Contemporary Views: Results and Open Questions," 129–51; Han J. W. Drijvers, "Marcionism in Syria: Principles, Problems, Polemics," 153–72; R. Joseph Hoffmann, "How Then Know This Troublous Teacher? Further Reflections on Marcion and His Church," 173–91. See also David Salter Williams, "Reconsidering Marcion's Gospel," *JBL* 108 (1989): 477–96.

40. If the Gospel of John, as was certainly the case by the mid-second century, was part of a collected body of literature, the threat to one document may well have been felt as a threat to all and thus to the larger historical and theological traditions standing behind them.

41. Tertullian, *De Praescriptione Haereticorum* 13; *De Virginibus Velandis* 1.3; *Adversus Praxean* 2:1–2.

veritatis).[42] These labels do not refer so much to any given confession per se but to interpretive material that, while sounding very much like creedal material, had not yet been formalized as a creed. To be sure, the sociological function of the "rule of faith" was not unlike that of later, more formalized creeds; i.e., it served as an interpretive guideline to distinguish acceptable from unacceptable theology and thus to reveal those who are truly within the church and those who are heretics. But, more specifically, for Irenaeus the "rule of faith" served as the standard for judging whether or not one had correctly interpreted Scripture, especially the apostolic Scriptures, which were themselves now the object of both focus and abuse (*Against Heresies*, I.8.1; 9.1; 9.4). Indeed, it may be that the rise of a more formalized language and theological vocabulary of "inspiration" as applied to the apostolic (NT) documents was itself not only a natural outgrowth of the long-existent function of those texts, but also a response to the interpretive abuse of them by those outside the theological parameters of the *regula fidei*. The connection between the rule of faith and the interpretation of Scripture was still being evidenced by the beginning of the third century when Origen declared himself at liberty to interpret the Scriptures in his own "higher," "spiritual" senses, so long as he did not deny the ground floor of belief, that is, the rule of faith.[43]

In summary, the transition in religious status for the various NT writings—from authoritative literary tradition to Scripture—took place for several reasons. First, it could happen because the once oral, but always authoritative, apostolic tradition became reflected in written (albeit "occasional") form. Second, a complex of factors relating to the geographical expansion of Christianity, the collection and grouping of the materials, a growing distance between church and synagogue, and the loss of apostolic presence and memory led to the increased functional status of the written materials over the oral traditions. Third, as the collected materials themselves became indispensable within the life (especially the worship) of the church, they began de facto to function on a par with OT Scripture and in that setting may have first received the appellation of "Scripture." Finally, once the written materials became themselves no longer the interpretive key to the (OT) Scriptures, but the object of reflection and analysis, it was not unnatural to see the written traditions given the authoritative title "Scripture." What had already begun to function as Scripture had to be defended as Scripture.[44]

---

42. Irenaeus, *Adversus Haereses* 1.10.1; 3.2.1; 3.24.2; 4.26.2.

43. Irenaeus, *Adversus Haereses* 1.9.4; 3.2.1.

44. *De Principiis*, 1.Praef.2.

FROM SCRIPTURE TO CANON

The path toward Athanasius and his *Easter Letter* of A.D. 367 was thus set by virtually the middle or end of the second century. Of course, a great deal of sorting and sifting still was to be done. The arduous task of preserving, copying, collecting, excluding, and sharing the apostolic materials was still in its infancy, but the use of the label "Scripture" to refer to portions of what we now call the New Testament came into practice. Issues related to the number, order, and textual shape of the NT materials were still in various stages of transition. The core, however, was already established. Athanasius no more created the canon than modern-day politicians create opinion—he rather reflected the emerging consensus. His letter was only one result of a long process that had gone on at much lower levels in the life and related experiences—not of "the" church, but—of hundreds of communities of faith scattered about the Mediterranean world.

The core of what eventually came to be the list of authoritative books was functionally set probably no later than the earliest decades of the second century. Many scholars have argued that Marcion was the driving force behind the creation of an orthodox canon of Scripture. But Marcion probably played no more a part, and possibly less, than the Gnostic and other heretical movements of the second century played in forcing the more traditional churches to establish as clearly as possible their historical links with Jesus and the apostles.[45] The four Gospels and the traditional

---

45. The author is aware of the many attempts to use 1 Tim. 5:18 and 2 Pet. 3:15–16 as evidence that within the NT some portions refer to other portions as Scripture; see, e.g., Wayne Grudem, "Scripture's Self-Attestation and the Problem of Formulating a Doctrine of Scripture," in *Scripture and Truth*, ed. D. A. Carson and John D. Woodbridge (Grand Rapids: Zondervan, 1983), 46, 48; but the issues involved in each case are manifold and not easily resolved. In the case of 1 Tim. 5:18, the allusion to the saying contained in Luke 10:7 need not assume Luke's Gospel as the literary source for the saying. In any case, however, the allusion could represent, taking the *kai* as epexegetic, the standard Christian *interpretation* (learned from Jesus) of Deut. 25:4, so that the reference to "Scripture" in 1 Tim. 5:18 is a reference to Deut. 25:4 and not Luke 10:7 (cf. the apparently epexegetic *kai* in 2 Thess. 1:8 which likewise precedes, as an introduction, the Christian interpretation of an OT allusion). In the case of 2 Pet. 3:15–16, the reference to "the rest of the Scriptures," an expression which seemingly includes the letters of Paul, may, but need not, be so understood. See Charles Bigg, *Epistles of St. Jude and St. Peter* (Edinburgh: T. & T. Clark, 1902), 301f.; see also Robert Sloan, "Evangelicals and the Authority of the Bible: A Response to David Wells," in *Evangelical Affirmations*, ed. Kenneth S. Kantzer and Carl F. H. Henry (Grand Rapids: Zondervan, 1990).

Pauline corpus already were being collected by the beginning of the second century, a phenomenon itself which certainly facilitated their eventual perception as Scripture.[46] The very fact that the Gospels were given titles suggests that they were being used and/or bound together. There are signs in the NT itself that at least some of the Pauline letters were being collected, perhaps even within his lifetime, and circulated among various churches (Gal. 1:1; Eph. 1:1; Col. 4:16; cf. 2 Tim. 4:13 and 2 Pet. 3:15–16).[47] Certainly the beginning of the second century is not too early to assume some sort of collection of most of what we call the traditional Pauline letters. The rest of the NT books had greater or lesser degrees of success in finding acceptance, with 2 Peter, Hebrews, and James having perhaps the greatest difficulties.[48] But even these books were ultimately, if not originally, associated with the names of leading apostles and therefore were being used widely in the second century.

To be sure, materials that are not now a part of our NT were also used in the churches. The *Shepherd of Hermas*, *First Clement*, and the *Didache*, for example, were widely read and appreciated in the second century.[49] Ultimately, however, a number of criteria coalesced to leave us with the twenty-seven documents that comprise our current list. The three factors of apostolic theology, apostolic connection (which was the guarantee of apostolic tradition), and use in the churches were perhaps the three major, mutually interrelated criteria that finally led to the various lists of authoritative books (that began to circulate from the middle to late second century[50]) and ultimately to the list referred to by Athanasius in A.D. 367.

The canonical process was precisely that—a process. The books of the NT did not become authoritative because they were canonical. Rather, they became canonical because they already were authoritative. That is, because these books contain the apostolic theology,[51] represented a link to the generation of Jesus and the apostles, and because the sheer experience

46. See note 39 above.

47. See note 38 above.

48. Of course, with 2 Peter, a lot depends on the date of the document. While I do not think Paul's letters are referred to in 3:15–16 as "Scripture" (see note 45 above), it is nonetheless evident that at least some of Paul's letters were being collected, and presumably accorded some kind of authoritative status, by the time of 2 Peter's composition.

49. See Theodor Zahn, *Grundriss der Geschichte des Neutestamentlichen Kanons*, 2d corr. ed. (Leipzig: A. Deichert, 1904), 14–35. See also Kurt Aland, *The Problem of the New Testament Canon* (Oxford: A. R. Mowbray, 1962), 8–13.

50. Zahn, *Grundriss*, 22–27.

51. F. W. Grosheide, ed., *Some Early Lists of the Books of the New Testament* (Leiden: E. J. Brill, 1948).

of repeated use in the churches caused people to affirm the value of these books as media for the voice of God, they were regarded first as authoritative, then as Scripture, and finally as canonical (exclusively acceptable for use in worship as Scripture).

CONCLUDING OBSERVATIONS

This study began by alluding to the importance of this topic for Christian thinking and confession today. I propose to conclude my remarks by returning to that arena and therefore offer the following three observations.

First, I am convinced that the discussion in some circles over the authority of the original manuscripts, though well-intended, is theologically shortsighted. Certainly, there is a meaningful sense in which one can speak of original manuscripts and their inspiration. That is, if we have a document now, then sometime, at some place, someone must have put pen to paper and, with the use of some combination of sources and literary creativity, produced something we could legitimately call an "original" in relationship to the given document in our possession. But such statements often imply too severe a stricture upon the fuller canonical *process*, which Christians traditionally have also regarded as the work of God.

To speak of the authority of the NT is to refer not only to the nature of the given texts, but to say something about a *collection* of texts, and thus as well to imply something about the limits of that collection. But the acknowledged authority of the individual documents (an authority both perceived and intended even from their inception) and/or various sub-collections of those documents was a phenomenon that historically preceded the final shaking out of the limits of that collection, i.e., the historical emergence of consensus regarding the canon. Which means that, in probably every case it was not an original manuscript that was first called "Scripture" and/or later deemed canonical by Christians of the second, third, and fourth centuries; rather, it was no doubt copies of the originals, handed down for decades, if not a couple of centuries, that were first regarded as Scripture.

We must not pre-emptively cut God out of the longer historical process of canonization, which, ironically, is precisely what people do who limit theological authority to the original manuscripts. The limits of the canon are just as important religiously and theologically as the inspiration and authority of the individual literary parts. Put another way, in the case of Scripture, divine authority is not only tied to production of "original" texts, but also to canonicity, where the latter term relates to the historically worked out delimitation of what in fact could, and could not, be regarded as Scripture, and thus authoritative. Though the authority of the individual books preceded their canonicity, it was ultimately the latter that, at least in the act of excluding certain documents, pronounced limits upon the extent and nature of their collective authority. Thus, we should confess the authority of the canonical Scriptures. Such a confession does not obviate the text-critical task; indeed, it makes it all the more significant, for such a confession places us squarely within the tradition of our earliest Christian forebears who confessed the inspiration and authority of their non-original, but historically received, texts. However we deal with and critically analyze our received texts,[52] it is still the "received as canonical"—and not a by now hopelessly irretrievable original—text that we confess to be true and faithful. It is the Scriptures we read in church which, when rightly interpreted, tell us the truth about God, ourselves, the world, and salvation.

Second, speaking of "right interpretation," if anything is to be learned from the study of canon, it is the importance of interpretation. Early Christians did not regard themselves as Christian simply because they possessed an authoritative text. No doubt they were glad to have their sacred collection of books (initially only what we now call the Old Testament), as indeed we should be to have ours. Most Christians are unashamed to confess their commitment to the authority of the Bible. But we must not assume that, having declared our commitment to the authority of Scripture, we have thereby made ourselves fully, or even adequately, Christian. In the history of Christendom, virtually every branch, limb, and twig of the visible church has pronounced upon its commitment to the authority of the Scriptures. Such commitments are commonly attested among the ranks of Baptists, Lutherans, Roman Catholics, Methodists, and Jehovah's Witnesses. But surely none would disagree to the proposition that there are significant theological differences among, say, Baptists, Jehovah's Witnesses, and Roman Catholics. One sometimes hears a kind of ecumenically pious maxim which suggests that as long as you believe in the authority of the Bible, it does not matter how you interpret it. I disagree. Interpretive decisions about biblical texts and their meaning for life and faith are inescapable and thus in practice no less important than the

---

52. To summarize: I am suggesting that the apostolic theology not only gave the individual books an intrinsic confessional and theological value but also served as a cohesive force—a canonical theology—which tended to draw the books together into intellectually and historically associated collections. The task of analysis/interpretation is never done, beginning with the texts we receive and extending through all the processes of reading, exegesis, and synthesis which culminate in the proclamation of the Word.

value we place upon the very use of the Bible at all for Christian life and faith. Thus, while it seems to me possible to make the parameters of faith and fellowship either too broad or too narrow, in every case it must be understood that interpretive parameters *are* being employed, however much we continue to work toward enunciation and clarification of those parameters. What is at stake in such matters is not whether we use theological parameters for the articulation of faith, but the appropriation of historically and theologically *legitimate* parameters. If the Scriptures themselves are to provide any relevant clues in these matters, it would seem that what has herein been called the "apostolic theology" is historically and theologically the proper place to start. Put another way, good theology must not only confess biblical authority, but it must have a biblical "shape." This writer believes in the authority of the Bible *as correctly interpreted* and thus not necessarily in every interpretation of those who loudly proclaim its authority. We must do our best to seek the center of the NT, to research its own internal parameters of interpretation, and, under the guidance of God's Spirit, to live our lives together as faithful witnesses to its truths.

Third, the canon still has a valuable role to play in both Christian confession and scholarly research. Its value for Christian confession will certainly continue—if for no other reason—by the sheer dint of tradition. But more than that, a list of authoritative books has value not only for confession but also for historical research, by virtue of the fact that the canon stands as a literary witness to a theological unity. Put another way, the fact is that we have a canon. For some set of reasons, at least one of which must be, it seems to me, theological, these books have been bound together. It is just as important for the historian/theologian as it is for the believer to understand the conceptual unity that underlies this collection of diverse literature. There is a unity underlying this diversity. However, the unity lies not so much on the literary level as it does on a historical/ theological level. That is, when we focus our attention both as worshipers and as scholars upon this particular collection of literature, we must remember that we are not purely literary critics. There are people, situations, and living ideas that lie behind and underneath these texts. Indeed, the problem of the canon for both theology and confession is that the distinctives of the various books tend to be flattened out when what was originally an isolated literary piece is transplanted to a new setting: i.e., a literary *collection*.

The various problems and specific historical needs that brought each individual piece into being can easily be obscured when the individual books are studied only in the light of one another. When either academic research or ecclesiastical confession becomes focused upon these documents only as collected documents, and ignores the history, the people, and the particularities, i.e., the social and political environments in which the documents emerged, it becomes stultified. For confession, the pre-empted result can be interpretive schemas which may have a certain intra-canonical coherence but are in fact misrepresentations of the texts due to anachronisms and/or other failures at the point of historically responsible reading. For research, a kind of scholasticism can emerge that never truly discovers new models of understanding—though it may develop new labels for old methods—and ultimately must fail because, often under the guise of "literary" analysis, it ignores the complexities of life behind the texts.

On the other hand, while the tendency of literary collections to over-whelm the historical distinctives of the individual pieces must be respected, it ought to be neither exaggerated nor feared. The academic tendency to eliminate the canon for the sake of recovering the historical particularity of each individual piece also brings an immeasurable loss, one that is both confessional and historical in significance. The fact that individual works could be put into a unified collection tells us not only something about the historical forces which drove toward coherency, but also something about the individual pieces themselves and the way in which they were historically understood. Moreover, the unified religious, historical, and theological experiences and convictions that gave rise to the individual literary pieces themselves were probably like those which also preserved and collected the individual works. History, theology, and canon are inextricably linked. The existence of this literature in a collection is a historical fact, and we are obligated to understand why such diverse texts should have been bound together. Certainly, one of those reasons is the core of apostolic theology and tradition that existed from the earliest days of Christianity, a core which had its own historical beginnings—the history, teachings, suffering, and resurrection of Jesus.

The study of the NT canon as a canon of sacred Scripture brings us back precisely to the very beginnings, not only of Christian history, but also of Christian confession. We are brought back to the historical person of Jesus Christ. He is the theological canon both within and behind the NT canon. As a devoted student of (OT) Scripture Himself, He is the adhesive binding of this new collection of sacred books. The crucified, risen, and exalted Lord is both the originating influence and the reflective object of the theology that eventually gave rise to the NT literature itself. In this, as in other matters, He must forever stand at the center.

FOR FURTHER READING

Bruce, F. F. *The Canon of Scripture*. Downers Grove, Ill.: InterVarsity, 1988.

———. *Tradition Old and New*. Grand Rapids: Zondervan, 1970.

Dunn, James D. G. *Unity and Diversity in the New Testament*. Philadelphia: Westminster, 1977.

Goppelt, Leonhard. *Theology of the New Testament*. 2 vols. Translated by John Alsup. Grand Rapids: Eerdmans, 1981–82.

Meade, David G. *Pseudonymity and Canon*. Grand Rapids: Eerdmans, 1987.

Morris, Leon. *New Testament Theology*. Grand Rapids: Academie/Zondervan, 1986.

Moule, C. F. D. *The Birth of the New Testament*, 3d rev. ed. San Francisco: Harper & Row, 1982.

IDB. s.v. "Biblical Theology."

Scripture
Index

Name
Index